MARRIAGE
FAMILY
97/98

Twenty-Third Edition

Editor

Kathleen R. Gilbert
Indiana University

Kathleen Gilbert is an associate professor in the Department of Applied Health Science at Indiana University. She received her B.A. in Sociology and her M.S. in Marriage and Family Relations from Northern Illinois University. Her Ph.D. in Family Studies is from Purdue University. Dr. Gilbert's primary areas of interest are loss and grief in a family context, trauma and the family, family process, and minority families. She has published several books and articles in these areas.

A Library of Information from the Public Press
Dushkin/McGraw·Hill
Sluice Dock, Guilford, Connecticut 06437

Visit us on the Internet—http://www.dushkin.com

The Annual Editions Series

ANNUAL EDITIONS is a series of over 65 volumes designed to provide the reader with convenient, low-cost access to a wide range of current, carefully selected articles from some of the most important magazines, newspapers, and journals published today. ANNUAL EDITIONS are updated on an annual basis through a continuous monitoring of over 300 periodical sources. All ANNUAL EDITIONS have a number of features that are designed to make them particularly useful, including topic guides, annotated tables of contents, unit overviews, and indexes. For the teacher using ANNUAL EDITIONS in the classroom, an Instructor's Resource Guide with test questions is available for each volume.

VOLUMES AVAILABLE

Abnormal Psychology
Adolescent Psychology
Africa
Aging
American Foreign Policy
American Government
American History, Pre-Civil War
American History, Post-Civil War
American Public Policy
Anthropology
Archaeology
Biopsychology
Business Ethics
Child Growth and Development
China
Comparative Politics
Computers in Education
Computers in Society
Criminal Justice
Criminology
Developing World
Deviant Behavior
Drugs, Society, and Behavior
Dying, Death, and Bereavement

Early Childhood Education
Economics
Educating Exceptional Children
Education
Educational Psychology
Environment
Geography
Global Issues
Health
Human Development
Human Resources
Human Sexuality
India and South Asia
International Business
Japan and the Pacific Rim
Latin America
Life Management
Macroeconomics
Management
Marketing
Marriage and Family
Mass Media
Microeconomics

Middle East and the
 Islamic World
Multicultural Education
Nutrition
Personal Growth and Behavior
Physical Anthropology
Psychology
Public Administration
Race and Ethnic Relations
Russia, the Eurasian Republics,
 and Central/Eastern Europe
Social Problems
Social Psychology
Sociology
State and Local Government
Urban Society
Western Civilization,
 Pre-Reformation
Western Civilization,
 Post-Reformation
Western Europe
World History, Pre-Modern
World History, Modern
World Politics

Cataloging in Publication Data
Main entry under title: Annual Editions: Marriage and Family. 1997/98.
   1. Family—United States—Periodicals. 2. Marriage—United States—Periodicals. I.
Gilbert, Kathleen, *comp.* II. Title: Marriage and Family.
ISBN 0-697-37311-8   301.42'05   74-84596

Twenty-Third Edition

Cover image © 1996 PhotoDisc, Inc.

Printed in the United States of America

Printed on Recycled Paper

Editors/Advisory Board

Members of the Advisory Board are instrumental in the final selection of articles for each edition of ANNUAL EDITIONS. Their review of articles for content, level, currentness, and appropriateness provides critical direction to the editor and staff. We think that you will find their careful consideration well reflected in this volume.

EDITOR

Kathleen R. Gilbert
Indiana University

ADVISORY BOARD

Staff

Ian A. Nielsen, Publisher

To the Reader

In publishing ANNUAL EDITIONS we recognize the enormous role played by the magazines, newspapers, and journals of the *public press* in providing current, first-rate educational information in a broad spectrum of interest areas. Many of these articles are appropriate for students, researchers, and professionals seeking accurate, current material to help bridge the gap between principles and theories and the real world. These articles, however, become more useful for study when those of lasting value are carefully *collected, organized, indexed,* and *reproduced* in a *low-cost format,* which provides easy and permanent access when the material is needed. That is the role played by ANNUAL EDITIONS. Under the direction of each volume's *academic editor,* who is an expert in the subject area, and with the guidance of an *Advisory Board,* each year we seek to provide in each ANNUAL EDITION a current, well-balanced, carefully selected collection of the best of the public press for your study and enjoyment. We think that you will find this volume useful, and we hope that you will take a moment to let us know what you think.

The purpose of *Annual Editions: Marriage and Family 97/98* is to bring to the reader the latest thoughts and trends in our understanding of the family, to identify current concerns as well as problems and possible solutions, and to present alternative views of family process. The intent of this anthology is to explore intimate relationships as they are played out in marriage and family and, in doing this, to reflect the family's changing face.

The articles in this volume are taken from professional publications, semiprofessional journals, and popular lay publications aimed at both special populations and a general readership. The selections are carefully reviewed for their currency and accuracy. In some cases, contrasting viewpoints are presented. In others, articles are paired in such a way as to personalize the more impersonal scholarly information. In the current edition, a number of new articles have been added to reflect reviewers' comments. As the reader, you will note the tremendous range in tone and focus of these articles, from first-person accounts to reports of scientific discoveries as well as philosophical and theoretical writings. Some are more practical and applications-oriented, while others are more conceptual and research-oriented.

This anthology is organized to cover many of the important aspects of marriage and family. The first unit looks at varied perspectives on the family. The second unit examines the beginning steps of relationship building as individuals go through the process of exploring and establishing connections. In the third unit, means of finding and maintaining a relationship balance are examined. Unit four is concerned with crises and ways in which these can act as challenges and opportunities for families and their members. Finally, unit five takes an affirming view as it looks at families, now and into the future.

Instructors can use *Annual Editions: Marriage and Family 97/98* as a primary text for introductory marriage and family classes, particularly when they tie the content of the readings to basic information on marriage and family. This book can also be used as a supplement to update or emphasize certain aspects of standard marriage and family textbooks. Because of the provocative nature of many of the essays in this anthology, it works well as a basis for class discussion about various aspects of marriage and family relationships.

I would like to thank everyone involved in the development of this volume. My appreciation goes to those who sent in *article rating forms* and comments on the previous edition as well as those who suggested articles to consider for inclusion in this edition. Finally, to all of the students in my Marriage and Family Interactions class who have contributed critiques of articles, I would like to say thanks.

Anyone interested in providing input for future editions of *Annual Editions: Marriage and Family* should complete and return the postage-paid *article rating form* at the end of this book. Your suggestions are much appreciated and contribute to the continuing high quality of this anthology.

Kathleen R. Gilbert
Editor

Contents

The concepts in bold italics are developed in the article. For further expansion please refer to the Topic Guide and the Index.

The concepts in bold italics are developed in the article. For further expansion please refer to the Topic Guide and the Index.

UNIT 3

Finding a Balance: Maintaining Relationships

Fourteen articles consider the complex issues related to keeping a relationship going. From marriage to parent/child relationships to sibling relationships, relationship maintenance requires thought and commitment from members.

The concepts in bold italics are developed in the article. For further expansion please refer to the Topic Guide and the Index.

UNIT 4

Crises— Challenges and Opportunities

A wide variety of crises, normative and catastrophic, are detailed in fourteen articles. Ranging from broad cultural factors impacting on families to the intimate crises of infidelity and divorce, these articles provide accounts of devastation and hope.

The concepts in bold italics are developed in the article. For further expansion please refer to the Topic Guide and the Index.

Topic Guide

This topic guide suggests how the selections in this book relate to topics of traditional concern to students and professionals involved with the study of marriage and family. It is useful for locating articles that relate to each other for reading and research. The guide is arranged alphabetically according to topic. Articles may, of course, treat topics that do not appear in the topic guide. In turn, entries in the topic guide do not necessarily constitute a comprehensive listing of all the contents of each selection.

TOPIC AREA	TREATED IN	TOPIC AREA	TREATED IN
Abuse	34. After He Hits Her 36. Helping Children Cope with Violence	Divorce	1. New Crusade for the Old Family 20. What's Happening to American Marriage? 38. Beyond Betrayal 42. Should This Marriage Be Saved? 43. Politics of Divorce 44. Lessons from Stepfamilies
Adolescence	10. Choosing Mates—the American Way 18. Adolescent Childbearing 37. Resilience in Development		
Adoption	19. Lifelong Impact of Adoption	Finances	2. Family: Home Sweet Home 17. What a Baby *Really* Costs 24. Receipts from a Marriage
Aging	24. Receipts from a Marriage 46. Caregiving 48. Trace Your Family Tree		
		Gender Roles	8. Why Don't We Act Like the Opposite Sex? 10. Choosing Mates—the American Way 14. Men, Sex, and Parenthood in an Overpopulating World 15. Staying Power 16. Albanian 'Virgins' Wear the Pants in Their Families 21. Peer Marriage 22. Who Needs Love! 23. For Better or Worse 25. Saving Relationships 30. Effective Fathers 31. Fathers Strongly Influenced by Culture 34. After He Hits Her 40. Myth of the Miserable Working Woman 41. Look Who's Talking about Work and Family 45. Myths and Misconceptions of the Stepmother Identity
Bereavement	19. Lifelong Impact of Adoption 47. Hard Lessons		
Children and Child Care	2. Family: Home Sweet Home 6. Love: The Immutable Longing for Contact 17. What a Baby *Really* Costs 18. Adolescent Childbearing 19. Lifelong Impact of Adoption 21. Peer Marriage 26. Vanishing Dreams of America's Young Families 27. Nation (Still) at Risk? 30. Effective Fathers 35. Behind Closed Doors 37. Resilience in Development 45. Myths and Misconceptions of the Stepmother Identity		
Communication	6. Love: The Immutable Longing for Contact 8. Why Don't We Act Like the Opposite Sex? 12. Back Off! 15. Staying Power 21. Peer Marriage 25. Saving Relationships 30. Effective Fathers 44. Lessons from Stepfamilies 47. Hard Lessons 49. Happy Families: Who Says They All Have to Be Alike?	Health Concerns	13. Choosing a Contraceptive 14. Men, Sex, and Parenthood in an Overpopulating World 41. Look Who's Talking about Work and Family 46. Caregiving 47. Hard Lessons 48. Trace Your Family Tree
		Infidelity	38. Beyond Betrayal 39. Sex in America
		Intimacy/Romantic Love	6. Love: The ImmutableLonging for Contact 7. What Makes Love Last? 10. Choosing Mates—the American Way 11. Mating Game 12. Back Off! 21. Peer Marriage 22. Who Needs Love! 23. For Better or Worse? 38. Beyond Betrayal 39. Sex in America
Dating/Mate Selection	6. Love: The ImmutableLonging for Contact 7. What Makes Love Last? 9. Studies Put Genetic Twist on Theories about Sex and Love 10. Choosing Mates—the American Way 11. Mating Game		

TOPIC AREA	TREATED IN	TOPIC AREA	TREATED IN
Marriage	7. What Makes Love Last? 8. Why Don't We Act Like the Opposite Sex? 10. Choosing Mates—the American Way 20. What's Happening to American Marriage? 21. Peer Marriage 22. Who Needs Love! 23. For Better or Worse? 24. Receipts from a Marriage 30. Effective Fathers 38. Beyond Betrayal 40. Myth of the Miserable Working Woman 41. Look Who's Talking about Work and Family 42. Should This Marriage Be Saved? 44. Lessons from Stepfamilies	**Resilience**	5. African American Families 37. Resilience in Development 44. Lessons from Stepfamilies 49. Happy Families: Who Says They All Have to Be Alike? 50. Rewriting Life Stories
		Sex/Sexuality	9. Studies Put Genetic Twist on Theories about Sex and Love 11. Mating Game 13. Choosing a Contraceptive 14. Men, Sex, and Parenthood in an Overpopulating World 18. Adolescent Childbearing 20. What's Happening to American Marriage? 21. Peer Marriage 23. For Better or Worse? 25. Saving Relationships 38. Beyond Betrayal 39. Sex in America
Parents/Parenting	6. Love: The Immutable Longing for Contact 17. What a Baby *Really* Costs 18. Adolescent Childbearing 21. Peer Marriage 24. Receipts from a Marriage 26. Vanishing Dreams of America's Young Families 27. Nation (Still) at Risk? 28. Myth of AWOL Parents 29. Family Affair 30. Effective Fathers 31. Fathers Strongly Influenced by Culture 42. Should This Marriage Be Saved? 43. Politics of Divorce 44. Lessons from Stepfamilies 45. Myths and Misconceptions of the Stepmother Identity 49. Happy Families: Who Says They All Have to Be Alike?		
		Siblings	32. Siblings and Development 33. Secret World of Siblings
		Single Parent Homes	2. Family: Home Sweet Home 43. Politics of Divorce 49. Happy Families: Who Says They All Have to Be Alike?
		Values	2. Family: Home Sweet Home 3. The Way We Weren't 4. Family under Siege by Its "Friends" 10. Choosing Mates—the American Way 14. Men, Sex, and Parenthood in an Overpopulating World 16. Albanian 'Virgins' Wear the Pants in Their Families 20. What's Happening to American Marriage? 21. Peer Marriage 22. Who Needs Love! 23. For Better or Worse? 28. Myth of AWOL Parents 42. Should This Marriage Be Saved? 43. Politics of Divorce 47. Hard Lessons 49. Happy Families: Who Says They All Have to Be Alike? 51. Rituals for Our Times
Poverty	1. New Crusade for the Old Family 18. Adolescent Childbearing 26. Vanishing Dreams of America's Young Families 37. Resilience in Development 43. Politics of Divorce		
Pregnancy/ Childbirth	14. Men, Sex, and Parenthood in an Overpopulating World 17. What a Baby *Really* Costs 18. Adolescent Childbearing		
Remarriage	20. What's Happening to American Marriage? 44. Lessons from Stepfamilies 45. Myths and Misconceptions of the Stepmother Identity	**Work and Family**	21. Peer Marriage 27. Nation (Still) at Risk? 40. Myth of the Miserable Working Woman 41. Look Who's Talking about Work and Family

Varied Perspectives on the Family

Our image of what family is and what it should be is a powerful combination of personal experience, family forms we see, and attitudes we hold. Once formed, this image informs decision making and interpersonal interaction throughout our lives. It has far-reaching impacts: On an intimate level, it influences individual and family development as well as relationships both within the family and without. On a broader level, it affects social policy and programming.

In many ways, this image can be positive. It can act to clarify our thinking and facilitate interaction with like-minded individuals. It can also be negative, as it can narrow our thinking and limit our ability to see other ways of carrying out the functions of family as having value. Their very differentness makes them "bad." In this case, interaction with others can be impeded because of contrasting views.

This unit is intended to meet several goals with regard to perspectives on the family: (1) to sensitize the reader to sources of beliefs about the "shoulds" of the family: what the family should be and the ways in which family roles should be carried out, (2) to show how different views of the family can influence attitudes toward community responsibility and family policy, and (3) to show how views that dominate one's culture can influence awareness of ways of structuring family life.

First, "The New Crusade for the Old Family," addresses our understanding of the reality of "family breakdown," particularly as this term is understood and researched. The positive and negative impacts of government policies, intended to help strengthen families, are documented in "The Family: Home Sweet Home." The accuracy of our memories of "the good old days" is discussed by historian Stephanie Coontz in "The Way We Weren't: The Myth and Reality of the 'Traditional' Family." "The Family under Siege by Its 'Friends'" chronicles the sometimes damaging effects of well-intentioned efforts. The final reading in this unit, "African American Families: A Legacy of Vulnerability and Resilience," debunks the stereotype of African American families as uniformly dysfunctional, pre

Looking Ahead: Challenge Questions

If you had the power to propose a government program to support today's families, what would it be? What image do you have of families that would take advantage of that program?

Discuss why you are—or are not—hopeful for the future of children and families.

How would you go about expanding your ideas of what is acceptable in terms of family relationships and family roles? How far do you think you should go in this?

In what ways can we be responsive to the needs of members of society while also encouraging responsibility?

Several of the readings suggest that many of our ideas about families, past and present, are based on myth and stereotype. If this is true, how do we overcome it?

UNIT 1

THE FAMILY

The New Crusade for the Old Family

Arlene Skolnick and Stacey Rosencrantz

Arlene Skolnick, a research psychologist at the Institute of Human Development at the University of California (Berkeley), is the author of Embattled Paradise: The American Family in an Age of Uncertainty. *Stacey Rosencrantz is a graduate student in Stanford University's psychology department.*

What is the root cause in America of poverty, crime, drug abuse, gang warfare, urban decay, and failing schools? According to op-ed pundits, Sunday talking heads, radio call-in shows, and politicians in both parties, the answer is the growing number of children being raised by single parents, especially by mothers who never married in the first place. Restore family values and the two-parent family, and America's social problems will be substantially solved.

By the close of the 1992 presidential campaign, the war over family values seemed to fade. Dan Quayle's attack on Murphy Brown's single motherhood stirred more ridicule on late night talk shows than moral panic. The public clearly preferred Bill Clinton's focus on the economy and his more inclusive version of the family theme: "family values" means "valuing families," no matter what their form—traditional, extended, two-parent, one-parent.

Yet Clinton's victory was quickly followed by a new bipartisan crusade to restore the two-parent family by discouraging divorce as well as out-of-wedlock childbearing. The conservative right has for years equated

family values with the traditional image of the nuclear family. The new crusade drew people from across the spectrum—Democrats as well as Republicans, conservatives, liberals, and communitarians. Eventually, even President Clinton joined in, remarking that he had reread Quayle's speech and "found a lot of good things in it."

While the new family restorationists do not agree on a program for reducing the number of single-parent families, they generally use a language of moral failure and cultural decline to account for family change. Many want to revive the stigma that used to surround divorce and single motherhood. To change the cultural climate, they call for government and media campaigns like those that have discouraged smoking and drinking. They propose to make divorce harder or slower or even, as the late Christopher Lasch proposed, to outlaw divorce by parents with minor children. And some have also advocated restricting welfare benefits for unmarried mothers or eliminating benefits entirely for mothers who have an additional out-of-wedlock child.

Focusing attention on the needs and problems of families raising children could be enormously positive. But the current crusade draws on the family values scripts of the 1980s, posing the issue in a divisive way (are you against the two-parent family?) and painting critics into an anti-family corner. Restricting legal channels for divorce, cutting off welfare to unmarried mothers, and restoring the old censorious

Reprinted with permission from *The American Prospect*, Summer 1994, pp. 59-65. © 1994 by New Prospect, Inc.

> *Despite these strong claims of scientific backing, the research literature is far more complicated than the family restorationists have let on.*

attitudes toward single parenthood may harm many children and deepen the very social ills we are trying to remedy.

There's nothing new in blaming social problems on "the breakdown of the family" or in making the "fallen woman" and her bastard child into objects of scorn and pity. Throughout our history, public policies made divorce difficult to obtain and penalized unwed parents and often their children. In the 1960s and 1970s, however, public opinion turned more tolerant and legal systems throughout the West became unwilling to brand some children as "illegitimate" and deprive them of rights due others. Now we are being told that this new tolerance was a mistake.

Most Americans, even those most committed to greater equality between women and men, are deeply uneasy about recent family changes and worried about crime and violence. The new case for the old family owes much of its persuasive power to the authority of social science. "The evidence is in," declares Barbara Dafoe Whitehead, author of a much-discussed article, "Dan Quayle Was Right," which appeared in the April 1993 *Atlantic Monthly*. Divorce and single-parent families, Whitehead argues, are damaging both children and the social fabric. Another family restorationist, Karl Zinsmeister, a fellow at the American Enterprise Institute, refers to "a mountain of evidence" showing that children of divorce end up intellectually, physically, and emotionally scarred for life.

Despite these strong claims of scientific backing, the research literature is far more complicated than the family restorationists have let on. Whitehead says, "The debate about family structure is not simply about the social-scientific evidence. It is also a debate over deeply held and often conflicting values." Unfortunately, the family restorationists' values have colored their reading of the evidence.

Few would deny that the divorce of one's parents is a painful experience and that children blessed with two "good enough" parents generally have an easier time growing up than others. Raising a child from infancy to successful adulthood can be a daunting task even for two people. But to decide what policies would improve children's lives, we need to answer a number of prior questions:

■ Are children who grow up in a one-parent home markedly worse off than those who live with both parents?

■ If such children are so disadvantaged, is the source of their problems family structure or some other factor that may have existed earlier or be associated with it?

■ How effectively can public policies promote a particular form of family and discourage others? Will policies intended to stigmatize and reduce or prevent divorce or single parenthood cause unintended harm to children's well-being? Would positive measures to help single-parent families or reduce the stress that accompanies marital disruption be of more benefit to children?

Finally, is there a direct link, as so many believe, between family structure and what a *Newsweek* writer calls a "nauseating buffet" of social pathologies, especially crime, violence, and drugs? In his Murphy Brown speech, given in the wake of the Los Angeles riots, Quayle argued that it wasn't poverty but a "poverty of values" that had led to family breakdown, which in turn caused the violence. The one sentence about Murphy Brown in the speech—borrowed incidentally from an op-ed by Whitehead—overshadowed the rest of the message. Charles Murray was more successful at linking family values with the fear of crime. In a *Wall Street Journal* article, he warned that because of rising white illegitimacy rates, a "coming white underclass" was going to engulf the rest of society in the kind of anarchy found in the inner cities. But what is the evidence for this incendiary claim? And why do countries with similar trends in family structure not suffer from the social deterioration that plagues us?

The family restorationists do not provide clear answers to these questions. And the answers found in the research literature do not support their extreme statements about the consequences of family structure or some of the drastic policies they propose to change it.

Of course, it's always possible to raise methodological questions about a line of research or to interpret findings in more ways than one. The perfect study, like the perfect crime, is an elusive goal. But some of the family restorationists seem to misunderstand the social science enterprise in ways that seriously undermine their conclusions. For example, they trumpet findings about correlations between family structure and poverty, or lower academic achievement, or behavior problems, as proof of their arguments. Doing so, however, ignores the principle taught in elementary statistics that correlation does not prove causation.

For example, suppose we find that increased ice cream consumption is correlated with increases in drownings. The cause, of course, has nothing to do with ice cream but everything to do with the weather: people swim more and eat more ice cream in the summer. Similarly, single parenthood may be correlated with many problems affecting children, but the causes may lie elsewhere—for example, in economic and emotional problems affecting parents that lead to difficulties raising children and greater chances of divorce. Making it hard for such parents to divorce may no more improve the children's lives than banning ice cream would reduce drowning. Also, causation can and often does go in two directions. Poor women are more likely to have out-of-wedlock babies—this is one of the oldest correlates of poverty—but raising the child may impede them from escaping poverty. In short, finding a correlation between two variables is only a starting point for further analysis.

The social science research itself is also plagued by methodological problems. Most available studies of divorce, for example, are based on well-educated white families; some are based on families who have sought clinical help or become embroiled in legal conflict. Such families may hardly be representative. Comparing one study with one another is notoriously difficult because they use different measures to assess children of different ages after differing periods have elapsed since the divorce. Some studies, such as Judith Wallerstein's widely cited work on the harm of divorce reported in the 1989 book *Second Chances* by Wallerstein and Sandra Blakeslee, use no comparison groups at all.

Others compare divorced families with intact families—both happy and unhappy—when a more appropriate comparison would be with couples that are unhappily married.

In addition, the family restorationists and some researchers lump together children of divorce and children whose parents never married. Yet never-married mothers are generally younger, poorer, and less educated than divorced mothers. And by some measures children living with never-married mothers are worse off than those living in divorced families.

The restorationists paint a far darker and more simplistic picture of the impact of divorce on children than does the research literature. Researchers agree that around the time their parents separate almost all children go through a period of distress. Within two or three years, most have recovered. The great majority of children of divorce do not appear to be impaired in their development. While some children do suffer lasting harm, the family restorationists exaggerate the extent and prevalence of long-term effects. For example, they may state that children of divorce face twice or three times the psychological risk of children in intact families. But the doubling of a risk may mean an increase from 2 to 4 percent, 10 to 20 percent, or from 30 to 60 percent. The effects of divorce tend to be in the smaller range.

In fact, a meta-analysis of divorce findings published in 1991 in the *Psychological Bulletin* reported very small differences between children from divorced and intact families in such measures of well-being as school achievement, psychological adjustment, self concept, and relations with parents and peers. (A "meta-analysis" combines data from separate studies into larger samples to make the findings more reliable.) Further, the more methodologically sophisticated studies—that is, those that controlled for other variables such as as income and parental conflict—reported the smallest differences.

In general, researchers who interview or observe children of divorce report more findings of distress than those who use data from large sample surveys. Yet even in the clinical studies the majority of children develop normally. One point that researchers agree on is that children vary greatly in response to divorce, depending on their circumstances, age, and psychological traits and temperament.

Where differences between children of divorce and those in stable two-parent families show up, they may be due, not to the divorce itself, but to circumstances before, during, and after the legal undoing of the marital bond. Most researchers now view divorce not as a single event but as an unfolding process. The child will usually endure parental conflict, estrangement, and emotional upset, separation from one parent, and economic deprivation. Often divorce means moving away from home, neighborhood, and school. Particular children may go through more or fewer such jolts than others.

Researchers have known for some time that children from intact homes with high conflict between the parents often have similar or even worse problems than children of divorced parents. Recent studies in this country as well as in Australia and Sweden confirm that marital discord between the parents is a major influence on chidren's well-being, whether or not a divorce occurs.

Some of the family restorationists recognize that children in high-conflict families might be better off if their parents divorced than if they stayed together. They want to discourage or limit divorce by parents who are simply bored or unfulfilled. But how should we draw the line between unfulfilling and conflict-ridden marriages? And who should do the drawing?

High-conflict marriages are not necessarily violent or even dramatically quarrelsome like the couple in Edward Albee's *Who's Afraid of Virginia Woolf?*. One major recent study operationally defined a high-conflict family as one in which a spouse said the marriage was "not too happy" or the couple had arguments about five out of nine topics, including money, sex, chores, and in-laws. A number of recent studies do show that even moderate levels of marital dissatisfaction can have a detrimental effect on the quality of parenting.

The most critical factor in a child's well-being in any form of family is a close, nurturant relationship with at least one parent. For most children of divorce, this means the mother. Her ability to function as parent is in turn influenced by her physical and psychological well-being. Depression, anger, or stress can make a mother irritable, inconsistent, and in general less able to cope with her children and their problems, whether or not marital difficulties lead to divorce.

Until recently, the typical study of children of divorce began after the separation took place. However, two important studies—one directed by Jack Block and another by Andrew Cherlin—examined data on children long before their parents divorced. These studies found that child problems usually attributed to the divorce could be seen months and even years earlier. Usually, these results are assumed to reflect the impact of family conflict on children. But in a recent book analyzing divorce trends around world, William J. Goode offers another possibility:

> ... the research not only shows that many of the so-called effects of divorce were present before the marriage, but suggests an even more radical hypothesis: in at least a sizeable number of families the problems that children generate may create parental conflict and thereby increase the likelihood of divorce.

The problems of never-married single mothers and their children set off some of today's hottest buttons—sex, gender, race, and welfare. Dan Quayle's attack on Murphy Brown confused the issue. It is true that more single, educated, middle-class women are having children. The rate nearly tripled in the last decade among women in professional or managerial occupations. But despite this increase, only 8 percent of professional-status women are never-married, Murphy Brown mothers. Out-of-wedlock births continue to be far more prevalent among the less educated, the poor, and racial minorities.

Most people take the correlation between single parenthood and poverty as proof of a causal relation between the two. But the story is more complex. In his book *America's Children*, Donald Hernandez of the Census Bureau shows that if we take into account the income of fathers in divorced and unwed families, the increase in single mothers since 1959 probably accounts for only 2 to 4 percentage points of today's childhood poverty rates. As Kristen Luker has pointed out in these pages ("Dubious Conceptions: The Controversy Over Teen Pregnancy," *TAP*, No. 5, Spring 1991), the assumption that early childbearing causes poverty and school dropouts is backward; these conditions are as much cause as effect.

Elijah Anderson, Linda Burton, William Julius Wilson, and other urban sociologists have shown the causal connections linking economic conditions and racial stigma with out-of-wedlock births and the prevalence of single-mother families in the inner cities. Cut off from the rest of society, with little or no hope of stable, family-supporting jobs, young men prove their manhood through an "oppositional culture" based on machismo and sexual prowess. Young women, with little hope of either a husband or economic independence, drift into early sexual relationships, pregnancy, and childbirth.

Middle-class families have also been shaken by economic change. The family restorationists, however, have little to say about the impact of economic forces on families. In her *Atlantic* article, Whitehead mentions—almost as an afterthought—that the loss of good jobs has deprived high school graduates across the country as well as inner-city young people of the ability to support families. "Improving job opportunities for young men," she writes, "would enhance their ability and presumably their willingness to form lasting marriages." Yet these considerations do not affect the main thrust of her arguments supporting Quayle's contention that the poor suffer from a "poverty of values."

There is no shortage of evidence on the impact of economic hardship on families. The studies of ghetto problems have their counterparts in a spate of recent books about other groups.* Much quantitative research reinforces these analyses. As Glen Elder and others have found, using data

---

* John E. Schwarz and Thomas J. Volgy's *The Forgotten Americans* portrays the fast growing population of working poor, people who "play by the rules" but remain below the poverty line. Lillian Rubin's *Families on the Fault Line* documents the impact on working-class families of the decline of well-paying manufacturing jobs. Katherine Newman's ethnographic studies, *Falling from Grace* and *Declining Fortunes*, document the effects of downward mobility in middle-class families.

from the Great Depression to the 1980s, economic conditions such as unemployment are linked to children's problems through their parent's emotional states. Economic stress often leads to depression and demoralization, which in turn lead to marital conflict and such problems in child-raising as harsh discipline, angry outbursts, and rejection. Child abuse and neglect as well as alcoholism and drug use increase with economic stress.

New research has confirmed earlier findings that poverty and inadequate income are major threats to children's well-being and development. Poverty has a deep impact because it affects not only the parent's psychological functioning but is linked to poor health and nutrition in parents and children, impaired readiness for education, bad housing, the stress of dangerous neighborhoods, and poor schools as well as the stigma of being poor. One recent study comparing black and white children across income levels found that family income and poverty were powerful determinants of children's cognitive development and behavior, controlling for other differences such as family structure and maternal schooling.

Child poverty in the United States, as the family restorationists point out, is higher than it was two decades ago among whites as well as blacks. It is also much higher in the United States than in other Western countries. But it is not an unalterable fact of nature that children born to single mothers have to grow up in poverty. Whereas our policies express disapproval of the parents, the policies of other Western countries support the well-being of the children.

The family structure debate raises larger questions about the changes in family, gender, and sexuality in the past three decades—what to think about them, what language to use in talking about them. The language of moral decay will not suffice. Many of the nation's churches and synagogues are rethinking ancient habits and codes to accommodate new conceptions of women's equality and new versions of morality and responsibility in an age of sexual relationships outside of marriage and between partners of the same gender.

The nation as a whole is long overdue for a serious discussion of the upheaval in

American family life since the 1960s and how to mitigate its social and personal costs, especially to children. The point of reference should not be the lost family of a mythical past conjured up by our nostalgic yearnings but the more realistic vision offered by the rich body of historical scholarship since the 1970s. From the beginning, American families have been diverse, on-the-go, buffeted by social and economic change. The gap between family values and actual behavior has always been wide.

Such a discussion should also reflect an awareness that the family trends we have experienced over the past three decades are not unique. Every other Western country has experienced similar changes in women's roles and family structure. The trends are rooted in the development of the advanced industrial societies. As Andrew Cherlin puts it, "We can no more keep wives at home or slash the divorce rate than we can shut down our cities and send everyone back to the farm."

However, our response to family change has been unique. No other country has experienced anything like the cultural warfare that has made the family one of the most explosive issues in American society. Most other countries, including our cultural sibling Canada, have adapted pragmatically to change and developed policies in support of working parents, single-parent families, and all families raising children. Teenagers in these countries have fewer abortions and out-of-wedlock births, not becase they have less sex, but because sex education and contraceptives are widely available.

Sooner or later, we are going to have to let go of the fantasy that we can restore the family of the 1950s. Given the cultural shocks of the past three decades and the quiet depression we have endured since the mid-1970s, it's little wonder that we have been enveloped by a haze of nostalgia. Yet the family patterns of the 1950s Americans now take as the stand-ard for judging family normality were actually a deviation from long-term trends. Since the nineteenth century, the age at marriage, divorce rate, and women's labor force participation had been rising. In the 1950s however, the age of marriage declined, the divorce rate leveled off, the proportion of the population married reached a new high, and the American birth rate approached that of India. After the 1950s, the long-term historical trends resumed.

Most of us would not want to reverse all the trends that have helped to transform family life—declining mortality rates, rising educational levels for both men and women, reliable contraception, and greater opportunities for women. Barring a major cataclysm, the changes in family life are now too deeply woven into American lives to be reversed by "just say no" campaigns or even by the kinds of changes in divorce and welfare laws that the restorationists propose.

The task is to buffer children and families from the effects of these trends. Arguing for systematic economic reform in *Mother Jones*, John Judis writes that between the new economic realities and the kinds of broad measures needed to address them, there is "a yawning gulf of politics and ideology into which even the most well-meaning and intelligently conceived policy can tumble." A similar gulf lies between the new realities of American family life and the policies needed to address them.

Yet the potential for ameliorative reform may be greater than it now appears. As E.J. Dionne has pointed out, the debate is more polarized than the public. The 1992 Democratic convention showed how an inclusive pro-family message could be articulated and combined with proposals for economic and social reform. Such a message, recognizing both the diversity of family life and the continuing importance of family, appealed to a broad cross-section of Americans. It continues to make more sense and offer more hope than the punitive and coercive prescriptions of the family restorationists.

THE FAMILY

Home sweet home

In many American inner cities, the two-parent family has all but vanished. Elsewhere in America, divorce is up and single-parenthood is rising fast. Europe is not far behind. What, if anything, should governments do?

TO EUROPEAN ears, America's "family values" debate can sound shrill, even surreal. It is taken as a sign that the citizens of the new world remain considerably less sophisticated, and more moralistic, than those of the old. But Europe would do well to listen. In many American neighbourhoods, the family has collapsed: among households with children in poor inner cities, fewer than one in ten has a father in residence. If there are lessons from this awful experience, they are worth learning.

Many argue that the plight of the inner cities reflects a wider social malaise. America and Europe alike are witnessing profound changes in the structure of the family—increases in divorce and in births outside marriage. Great economic and social forces, combined with policy itself partly shaped by those forces, have weakened the link between parenthood and partnership. Compared with 30 years ago, it is easier for women to raise children without men, and for men to escape the burdens of fatherhood.

The weakening of that link has hurt children. Multi-generational studies in Sweden, Britain and America all seem to show that, compared with their peers of the same economic class, children in lone-parent families do less well in school, get in trouble more often and have more emotional and health problems. They are also more likely to become single parents themselves.

Demands for government to arrest the decline of the family are mounting. If governments were to heed these calls, what could they do?

Solo Swedes and German groupings

Governments act in ways that, intentionally or otherwise, affect the family: in this sense, every country has a "family policy". In Britain and America, these policies are a mess. To see how they might be changed, it is helpful to look at systems elsewhere. In Europe, the most distinctive approaches are those of Sweden and Germany. These start from very different assumptions about what such policy should be, but each acts upon a relatively coherent philosophy. Both manage to do moderately well by their children.

Sweden defines itself as a nation of individuals; its policy reflects that outlook. There is no married-couple's allowance, no tax deduction for children, no way to file jointly for income tax. Benefits are also assessed on an individual basis.

This treatment dates from reforms in the early 1970s. Sweden had a labour shortage and wanted to encourage married women into the job market. High marginal tax rates on joint filings, however, took an enormous bite out of a second income. By taxing both incomes independently, a major disincentive to work was removed; and as tax rates increased, two incomes became the norm. As a considered national policy to get women into work, it worked. Sweden has a higher proportion of working women than any other country. Everyone is expected to have a job. Mothers with young children generally work part-time.

Swedes are not particularly religious, and with such an individualised tax structure it is no surprise that many couples do not bother to marry. About half the babies in Sweden are born to unwed mothers, though very few are born to young girls. And thoug 19 out of 20 babies will go home to a father, many will not grow up with one. Half of Swedish marriages end in divorce, and unmarried parents split up three times as often as married ones. The result is that the number of lone-parent families as a proportion of all families with children has increased steadily, to 18% in 1991.

The children in those families will not necessarily be in material need, though they do tend to be slightly worse off. Generous benefits mean that if one parent leaves, the other parent and children do not slip into poverty. Child support enforcement is ferocious. In 1990, only 6.8% of Swedish children lived in families with less than half the average income. Though there are no premiums for children in the Swedish tax code, there are numerous state-supported goodies for them—parental leave, subsidised day care, leave to care for sick children, and so on. This may be why Swedish women have more children than their European sisters. It is the only OECD country in which the birth rate has increased since 1970.

Germany, by contrast, is a nation of families. People are legally required to help elderly parents and hard-up family members. There are tax allowances for dependants and a high level of child benefit. A minimum subsistence level for children is exempt from taxation.

Marriage is rewarded in the tax code. A parent who stays at home to care for a child can keep many of the perks of her job. And it is, normally, hers not his; the old idea of a woman's world dominated by "*Kinder, Küche, Kirche*"—children, kitchen and church—still persists, albeit to a diminishing extent. A full-time parent keeps her pension rights, and cannot be dismissed from her job for three years. When fathers fail to pay up, the state covers the child-support payment and enforces collection.

It is hardly surprising, given its dramatically different policies, that compared to Sweden Germany has: fewer births to unmarried mothers; a higher rate of marriage; a divorce rate a third lower; a smaller percentage of children being raised in one-parent families; and a smaller percentage of women in the workforce. The gaps between the two countries are shrinking, though. Taxes and benefits have an effect on behaviour, but not a decisive one. If government policy were the only factor in such decisions, Sweden would never see a wedding.

Not back to basics

British family policy combines aspects of the Swedish and the German approaches without the coherence of either. The Tory government has preached "back to basics", an alliterative nostrum not that far in feeling from Germany's three Ks. At the same time, its tax policies have been anything but encouraging to families with children, particularly those in which the father works and the mother stays at home. Since the late 1960s, Britain has steadily moved towards a tax system that treats adults as individuals, not as part of a family unit.

Critics say that these changes have made policy hostile to nuclear families. They have a point. Single adult occupiers pay 25% less local council tax than a married or co-habiting couple, and those with children may be given higher priority for public housing. Taxes have increased more steeply for the married. In 1964 a married couple with two children making the national average paid 9% of its income in tax; now it pays 22%, a faster rise than for single people or childless couples. The married-couple's tax allowance is probably doomed.

According to Patricia Morgan of London's Institute of Economic Affairs, a lone parent may end up with more income after tax than a working father with the same number of children and a dependent wife—even though in the latter case there is an additional adult in the house. Although Ms Morgan's conclusions have been hotly contested, there is little argument that, at lower levels of income, marriage becomes uneconomic. Parents with little money do better on benefit if they live apart than if they live together; boyfriends vanish when social workers come calling. As the Labour-affiliated Institute for Public Policy Research put it in a 1994 study, young mothers may be making a realistic assessment of the available options when they choose not to marry.

This realistic assessment lies behind the most dramatic change in patterns of marriage and parenting. While most British children live with their two natural, married parents, 20% of households with children now contain only one parent. The majority of these single parents are divorced, but an increasing proportion never married, and many became mothers when very young (though the birth rate among teenagers has recently levelled off). One in three British births is out of wedlock. Half those children start life with no father at home; the others run an increased risk of losing him—unmarried fathers are more likely to walk out than married ones.

Almost three-quarters of those households depend on state income support, comprising the largest single group on benefit. Child benefit, itself less generous than the child tax allowance/family allowance it replaced in the mid-1970s, has been allowed to erode. In 1992 one in three British children lived in a poor household, three times the rate of 1979. More than half those poor children live in single-parent housholds.

America first

In America families are valued tremendously—so much so that most people will

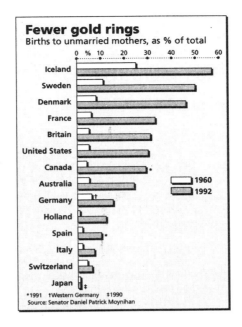

Fewer gold rings
Births to unmarried mothers, as % of total

Iceland
Sweden
Denmark
France
Britain
United States
Canada
Australia
Germany
Holland
Spain
Italy
Switzerland
Japan

☐ 1960 ▧ 1992

*1991 †Western Germany ‡1990
Source: Senator Daniel Patrick Moynihan

have at least two of them. Americans are religious, but have one of the highest divorce rates in the world. They are ambivalent about abortions but have a lot of them. Government has worked hard to make public policy as contradictory as private choices.

There is a marriage penalty at the middle to upper end of the income-tax schedule: married couples pay more tax than two single people with the same income. Under other conditions there is a marriage bonus. Divorce is easy. Three out of ten American children will sleep in a different home from their father tonight. Among black children, the rate is six out of ten.

Child benefits are low—the government spends four times as much on the elderly as on children, although old people are much better off. Lone parents are six times more likely to be poor than married couples. Benefits designed to alleviate that poverty have put the family under further strain. Until quite recently, women could not get income support if there was a man in the

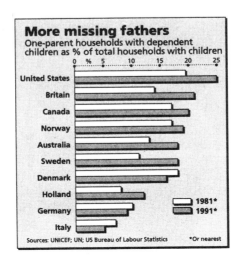

More missing fathers
One-parent households with dependent children as % of total households with children

United States
Britain
Canada
Norway
Australia
Sweden
Denmark
Holland
Germany
Italy

☐ 1981* ▧ 1991*

Sources: UNICEF; UN; US Bureau of Labour Statistics   *Or nearest

house. The welfare cheque, with its attendant medical benefits and food stamps, became considerably more valuable to have than a low-wage husband and father.

With the breakdown of marriages has come a breakdown in the idea of marriage as a precursor to family life. Half a million teenagers have babies every year; very few of them go home to their father. More than half the 5m women on welfare started as teenage mothers. Their daughters often follow in their mothers' footsteps; their sons often follow in their fathers'.

When did you last see your father?

The only common thread to America's chaotic policies is that they are intended to allow adults freedom. That goal is now being questioned. There is widespread agreement that the design of America's modest safety net has helped to destabilise the family. Republican redesigns on offer include time limits and no increase in benefits for additional children; Democrats are talking about work requirements and group homes for teenaged mothers. Few, however, are talking about family policies that affect the middle class, such as state laws on divorce or the erosion of the dependants' allowance.

The problem with the American and British approach is not that benefits are too generous; they are stingy. The fundamental mistake is that fathers have been airbrushed out of the picture. Although there cannot be lone mothers without a roughly equivalent number of fathers lurking somewhere, the latter are mostly ignored.

Throughout the world, the lack of fathers is a key factor in the impoverishment of children. In Britain, almost half the single-parent families have incomes of £100 ($155) a week or less, compared with only 5% of couples with children. This is not simply because the poor are more likely to become single parents. As the Rowntree Foundation, a British research organisation, notes: "Poverty is more obviously one of the consequences of breakdown than a cause." The result of divorce or abandonment is often two poor households rather than a single struggling one. Children bear the brunt: when money is tight, studies show, parental discipline gets harsher and more arbitrary.

A father is not just a cash cow. Daniel Patrick Moynihan, a Democratic senator who has taken these problems seriously for 30 years, says that a community without fathers "asks for and gets chaos." As an American, he has been able to see that chaos for some time, but it is now visible elsewhere. There are neighbourhoods in Britain where more than two-thirds of homes with children lack fathers; some of Paris's wilder *banlieues* are not that different.

Humans have long childhoods in order to learn; they are very sensitive to the environment in which they grow up. In most societies, quite possibly throughout the evolution of the species, that environment has contained men—and, in particular, a man who is their mother's partner. If the environment is not like that but society tries to act as if it is, it should be no surprise that the child is affected in all sorts of ways. For boys, the absence of men can induce what sociologist Elijah Anderson calls "hypermasculinity," characterised by casual, even predatory, sex and violence. Fatherless girls, like their brothers, tend to do less well in school and have greater difficulty in making the transition to adulthood; they are much more likely than girls who grew up with a father to be young and unmarried when they first get pregnant.

Asserting the value of fathers is not to say that lone mothers are rotten; it is to recognise that their children tend to have more of the kinds of social, economic and academic difficulties that a generous society would seek to spare them. But if that idea moves society to prefer faithful fatherhood, it will face two big problems: divorce and low pay.

At all levels of income, divorce destroys fatherhood. When men do not live under the same roof as their children, they find it more difficult to maintain a relationship. Researchers from Exeter, in Britain, found in a 1994 study that more than half the children of divorce did not see the non-custodial parent—almost always the father—on a regular basis. A quarter did not even know where he lived. Studies from other countries confirm that Britain's divorced fathers are not unique in their isolation from their children. Never-married fathers are even more remote. Stepfathers and boyfriends are, as a

group, a poor substitute. They tend to offer less emotional and financial commitment than resident fathers. They are many times more likely to abuse the children with whom they live.

Low incomes may also discourage men from living with any family they have fathered. In the 1992-93 British Social Attitudes survey, men without an academic qualification were far more likely than those better educated to think that the husband's role was to earn money, and the wife's to stay at home. Unfortunately, many less-educated men cannot find work that pays enough to allow them to play this role. This is particularly true in Britain and America, less so in Sweden and Germany, where wage differentials are narrower.

In America, the earnings for black male high-school dropouts fell by half, in real terms, in the period 1973-89. Roughly a third of all American men aged between 25 and 34 earn too little to lift a family of four out of poverty. American research has found that men's willingness to live as part of a family rises as their income does. When women get used to the idea that the state is a better breadwinner, they come to devalue fatherhood. "How do you get a bloke to make a go of it with his girlfriend if the wage he can get is no more than welfare?" asks Frank Field, a Labour MP who chairs the House of Commons Select Committee on Social Security.

The Swedish response has been to nationalise the family. This may deal with the economic side of the problem. It is little help on the psychological front. And it is expensive. Britain and America, with their

low tolerance for high taxes, are unlikely to choose the Swedish road. Nor are they likely to favour the heavy-handed approach that Germans accept. It should be possible, however, for these countries to build a consensus around three principles: first, that tax-and-benefit policies should not discriminate against the family; second, that fathers should be obliged to face up to their parental responsibilities; and third, that the working poor should be given every opportunity to achieve financial self-reliance.

Proposed British legislation to make the welfare of children the first priority in divorce is a step in the right direction. Looking at ways to boost the take-home pay of working parents makes sense, as does getting lone mothers into work, something which Sweden does excellently, and which helps break down the belief that men must either be sole earner or nothing. Rules that are hostile to fathers staying with their families should be scrapped.

Even if all this were done, the effects might be disappointingly limited: far larger forces are at work. But incentives do matter. Sweden's marriage rate more than doubled in 1989 as couples married in order to take advantage of a one-off pension reform. Since people do respond to the tax-and-benefit structure, a systematic attempt to stop that response being socially destructive is not unreasonable. It is difficult for democratic government to create incentives so strong that they greatly change the behaviour of lots of people. But, as the effect of too many bad incentives in Britain and America has made clear, it is not impossible.

The Way We Weren't

The Myth and Reality of the "Traditional" Family

Families face serious problems today, but proposals to solve them by reviving "traditional" family forms and values miss two points. First, no single traditional family existed to which we could return, and none of the many varieties of families in our past has had any magic formula for protecting its members from the vicissitudes of socioeconomic change, the inequities of class, race, and gender, or the consequences of interpersonal conflict. Violence, child abuse, poverty, and the unequal distribution of resources to women and children have occurred in every period and every type of family.

Stephanie Coontz

Second, the strengths that we also find in many families of the past were rooted in different social, cultural, and economic circumstances from those that prevail today. Attempts to reproduce any type of family outside of its original socioeconomic context are doomed to fail.

Colonial Families

American families always have been diverse, and the male breadwinner-female homemaker, nuclear ideal that most people associate with "the" traditional family has predominated for only a small portion of our history. In colonial America, several types of families coexisted or competed. Native American kinship systems subordinated the nuclear family to a much larger network of marital alliances and kin obligations, ensuring that no single family was forced to go it alone. Wealthy settler families from Europe, by contrast, formed independent households that pulled in labor from poorer neighbors and relatives, building their extended family solidarities on the backs of truncated families among indentured servants, slaves, and the poor. Even wealthy families, though, often were disrupted by death; a majority of colonial Americans probably spent some time in a step-family. Meanwhile, African Americans, denied the legal protection of marriage and parenthood, built extensive kinship networks and obligations through fictive kin ties, ritual co-parenting or godparenting, adoption of orphans, and complex naming patterns designed to preserve family links across space and time.

The dominant family values of colonial days left no room for sentimentalizing childhood. Colonial mothers, for example, spent far less time doing child care than do modern working women, typically delegating this task to servants or older siblings. Among white families, patriarchal authority was so absolute that disobedience by wife or child was seen as a small form of treason, theoretically punishable by death, and family relations were based on power, not love.

The Nineteenth-Century Family

With the emergence of a wage-labor system and a national market in the first third of the nineteenth century, white middle-class families became less patriarchal and more child-centered. The ideal of the male breadwinner and the nurturing mother now appeared. But the emergence of domesticity for middle-class women and children depended on its absence among the immigrant, working class, and African American women or children who worked as servants, grew the cotton, or toiled in the textile mills to free middle-class wives from the chores that had occupied their time previously.

Even in the minority of nineteenth-century families who could afford domesticity, though, emotional arrangements were quite different from nostalgic images of "traditional" families. Rigid insistence on separate spheres for men and women made male-female relations extremely stilted, so that women commonly turned to other women, not their husbands, for their most intimate relations. The idea that all of one's passionate feelings should go toward a member of the opposite sex was a twentieth-century invention — closely associated with the emergence of a mass consumer society and promulgated by the very film industry that "traditionalists" now blame for undermining such values.

Early Twentieth-Century Families

Throughout the nineteenth century, at least as much divergence and disruption in the experi-ence of family life existed as does today, even though divorce and unwed motherhood were less common. Indeed, couples who marry today have a better chance of celebrating a fortieth wedding anniversary than at any previous time in history. The life cycles of nineteenth-century youth (in job entry, completion of schooling, age at marriage, and establishment of separate residence) were far more diverse than they became in the early twentieth-century. At the turn of the century a higher proportion of people remained single for their entire lives than at any period since. Not until the 1920s did a bare majority of children come to live in a male breadwinner-female homemaker family, and even at the height of this family form in the 1950s, only 60 percent of American children spent their entire childhoods in such a family.

years as unhealthy. From this family we get the idea that women are sexual, that youth is attractive, and that marriage should be the center of our emotional fulfillment.

Even aside from its lack of relevance to the lives of most immigrants, Mexican Americans, African Americans, rural families, and the urban poor, big contradictions existed between image and reality in the middle-class family ideal of the early twentieth century. This is the period when many Americans first accepted the idea that the family should be sacred from outside intervention; yet the development of the private, self-sufficient family depended on state intervention in the economy, government regulation of parent-child relations, and state-directed destruction of class and community institutions that hindered the development of family privacy.

Not until the 1920s did a bare majority of children come to live in a male breadwinner-female homemaker family . . . .

From about 1900 to the 1920s, the growth of mass production and emergence of a public policy aimed at establishing a family wage led to new ideas about family self-sufficiency, especially in the white middle class and a privileged sector of the working class. The resulting families lost their organic connection to intermediary units in society such as local shops, neighborhood work cultures and churches, ethnic associations, and mutual-aid organizations.

As families related more directly to the state, the market, and the mass media, they also developed a new cult of privacy, along with heightened expectations about the family's role in fostering individual fulfillment. New family values stressed the early independence of children and the romantic coupling of husband and wife, repudiating the intense same-sex ties and mother-infant bonding of earlier

Acceptance of a youth and leisure culture sanctioned early marriage and raised expectations about the quality of married life, but also introduced new tensions between the generations and new conflicts between husband and wife over what were adequate levels of financial and emotional support.

The nineteenth-century middle-class ideal of the family as a refuge from the world of work was surprisingly modest compared with emerging twentieth-century demands that the family provide a whole alternative world of satisfaction and intimacy to that of work and neighborhood. Where a family succeeded in doing so, people might find pleasures in the home never before imagined. But the new ideals also increased the possibilities for failure: America has had the highest divorce rate in the world since the turn of the century.

In the 1920s, these contradictions created a sense of foreboding about "the future of the family" that was every bit as widespread and intense as today's. Social scientists and popular commentators of the time hearkened back to the "good old days," bemoaning the sexual revolution, the fragility of nuclear family ties, the cult of youthful romance, the decline of respect for grandparents, and the threat of the "New Woman." But such criticism was sidetracked by the stock-market crash, the Great Depression of the 1930s, and the advent of World War II.

Domestic violence escalated during the Depression, while murder rates were as high in the 1930s as in the 1980s. Divorce rates fell, but desertion increased and fertility plummeted. The war stimulated a marriage boom, but by the late 1940s one in every three marriages was ending in divorce.

The 1950s Family

At the end of the 1940s, after the hardships of the Depression and war, many Americans revived the nuclear family ideals that had so disturbed commentators during the 1920s. The unprecedented postwar prosperity allowed young families to achieve consumer satisfactions and socioeconomic mobility that would have been inconceivable in earlier days. The 1950s family that resulted from these economic and cultural trends, however, was hardly "traditional." Indeed it is best seen as a historical aberration. For the first time in 100 years, divorce rates dropped, fertility soared, the gap between men's and women's job and educational prospects widened (making middle-class women more dependent on marriage), and the age of marriage fell—to the point that teenage birth rates were almost double what they are today.

Admirers of these very *nontraditional* 1950s family forms and values point out that household arrangements and gender roles were less diverse in the 1950s than today, and marriages more stable. But this was partly because diversity was ruthlessly suppressed and partly because economic and political support systems for socially-sanctioned families were far more generous than they are today. Real wages rose more in any single year of the 1950s than they did in the entire decade of the 1980s; the average thirty-year-old man could buy a median-priced home on 15 to 18 percent of his income. The government funded public investment, home ownership, and job creation at a rate more than triple that of the past two decades, while 40 percent of young men were eligible for veteran's benefits. Forming and maintaining families was far easier than it is today.

Yet the stability of these 1950s families did not guarantee good outcomes for their members. Even though most births occurred within wedlock, almost a third of American children lived in poverty during the 1950s, a higher figure than today. More than 50 percent of black married-couple families were poor. Women were often refused the right to serve on juries, sign contracts, take out credit cards in their own names, or establish legal residence. Wife-battering rates were low, but that was because wife-beating was seldom counted as a crime. Most victims of incest, such as Miss America of 1958, kept the secret of their fathers' abuse until the 1970s or 1980s, when the women's movement became powerful enough to offer them the support denied them in the 1950s.

The Post-1950s Family

In the 1960s, the civil rights, antiwar, and women's liberation movements exposed the racial, eco-

nomic, and sexual injustices that had been papered over by the Ozzie and Harriet images on television. Their activism made older kinds of public and private oppression unacceptable and helped create the incomplete, flawed, but much-needed reforms of the Great Society. Contrary to the big lie of the past decade that such programs caused our current family dilemmas, those antipoverty and social justice reforms helped overcome many of the family problems that prevailed in the 1950s.

In 1964, after fourteen years of unrivaled family stability and economic prosperity, the poverty rate was still 19 percent; in 1969, after five years of civil rights activism, the rebirth of feminism, and the institution of nontraditional if relatively modest government welfare programs, it was down to 12 percent, a low that has not been seen again since the social welfare cutbacks began in the late 1970s. In 1965, 20 percent of American children still lived in poverty; within five years, that had fallen to 15 percent. Infant mortality was cut in half between 1965 and 1980. The gap in nutrition between low-income Americans and other Americans narrowed significantly, as a direct result of food stamp and school lunch programs. In 1963, 20 percent of Americans living below the poverty line had *never* been examined by a physician; by 1970 this was true of only 8 percent of the poor.

Since 1973, however, real wages have been falling for most Americans. Attempts to counter this through tax revolts and spending freezes have led to drastic cutbacks in government investment programs. Corporations also spend far less on research and job creation than they did in the 1950s and 1960s, though the average compensation to executives has soared. The gap between rich and poor, according to the April 17, 1995, *New York Times*, is higher in the United

States than in any other industrial nation.

Family Stress

These inequities are *not* driven by changes in family forms, contrary to ideologues who persist in confusing correlations with causes; but they certainly exacerbate such changes, and they tend to bring out the worst in *all* families. The result has been an accumulation of stresses on families, alongside some important expansions of personal options. Working couples with children try to balance three full-time jobs, as employers and schools cling to policies that assume every employee has a "wife" at home to take care of family matters. Divorce and remarriage have allowed many adults and children to escape from toxic family environments, yet our lack of social support networks and failure to forge new values for sustaining intergenerational obligations have let many children fall through the cracks in the process.

Meanwhile, young people find it harder and harder to form or sustain families. According to an Associated Press report of April 25, 1995, the median income of men aged twenty-five to thirty-four fell by 26 percent between 1972 and 1994, while the proportion of such men with earnings below the poverty level for a family of four more than doubled to 32 percent. The figures are even worse for African American and Latino men. Poor individuals are twice as likely to divorce as more affluent ones, three to four times less likely to marry in the first place, and five to seven times more likely to have a child out of wedlock.

As conservatives insist, there is a moral crisis as well as an economic one in modern America: a pervasive sense of social alienation, new levels of violence, and a decreasing willingness to make sacrifices for others. But romanticizing "traditional" families and gender roles will not produce the changes in job structures, work policies, child care, medical practice, educational preparation, political discourse, and gender inequities that would permit families to develop moral and ethical systems relevant to 1990s realities.

. . . romanticizing "traditional" families and gender roles will not produce the changes . . . that would permit families to develop moral and ethical systems relevant to 1990s realities.

America needs more than a revival of the narrow family obligations of the 1950s, whose (greatly exaggerated) protection for white, middle-class children was achieved only at tremendous cost to the women in those families and to all those who could not or would not aspire to the Ozzie and Harriet ideal. We need a concern for children that goes beyond the question of whether a mother is waiting with cookies when her kids come home from school. We need a moral language that allows us to address something besides people's sexual habits. We need to build values and social institutions that can reconcile people's needs for independence with their equally important rights to dependence, and surely we must reject older solutions that involved balancing these needs on the backs of women. We will not find our answers in nostalgia for a mythical "traditional family."

Stephanie Coontz teaches history and family studies at The Evergreen State College in Olympia, Washington. Her publications include *The Way We Never Were: American Families and the Nostalgia Trap* **and** *The Way We Really Are: Coming to Terms with America's Changing Families* **(both published by Basic Books). She is a recipient of the Washington Governor's Writer's Award and the Dale Richmond Award of the American Academy of Pediatrics.**

The Family under Siege by Its "Friends"

The person who reads the publications or listens to the pronouncements of the Christian Right cannot escape the emphasis on the family and "family values." An undiscerning individual easily might conclude that at last the family has found the friend it has needed in dealing with the crises it faces. That conclusion is not surprising because the Christian Right often leaves the impression that it owns the word "family" along with sole understanding of its problems. It thinks it speaks for God.

Kenneth Chafin

Others who have so much experience and insight to share — people in schools, the behavioral sciences, agencies public and private, and the broader religious community — are dismissed either as "liberal" or "secular humanists." Thus, freed of self-doubt, the Christian Right paints itself as the family's only friend but too often brings shallow analysis and simplistic answers to complex problems.

The concern that makes people vulnerable to superficial answers is fed by their sense of the importance of the family. The family is the "people making" institution in society. Within the family an individual's identity is formed. As children are held, talked to, and passed around to others, they begin to develop first a sense of belonging and later a separate identity. Within the context of the expanded family, a child develops attitudes about self, others, work, play, and possessions, as well as a sense of right and wrong. Students of their history suggest that the roots for moral values in so-

ciety arose from the family. While other influences ultimately affect the person, the first and most powerful influence for developing self-esteem and character is the family. Consequently, everything that undermines the family erodes the whole fabric of society.

A part of people's panic comes from the mistaken notion that the family has changed only recently. This notion makes it easier for them to be led to believe some specific person or force is to be blamed — such as the media or Washington — and that a simple solution can be found. But the family is the oldest of all institutions, having preceded religious institutions, schools, and governments. It has never been static but is always changing, always living with new threats and opportunities.

What casual observers fail to realize is that during the past centuries the family has lost many of its original functions yet has remained family. At one time the family was the place where most work was done, education took place, people

worshiped, and justice was meted out. Now work has been moved to an office or a factory, education has been taken over by schools, the church claims authority in religion, and government attempts to administer justice. So change is not new to the family.

If the Christian Right represented nothing but the ranting of some isolated and irrelevant pulpit it could be ignored, but that is not the case. Its ideas are being preached by pastors of megachurches whose sermons are syndicated on cable television. They are promoted by gurus on the family whose successful radio and television shows have generated huge mailing lists and millions of dollars. Several publishing houses are feeding the public's appetite for printed material. Add to this the host of politicians who have been elected to office while running on the "family values" ticket and are now busy working on "fixing" the family from Washington. The Christian Right's success is not so much tied to its understanding of the problems as to

From *National Forum*, Volume 75, Number 3 (Summer 1995,) pp. 33-35. © 1995 by Kenneth Chafin. *National Forum: The Phi Kappa Phi Journal.* Reprinted by permission of the publishers.

In schools that the Christian Right controls, married female professors are allowed to teach men only after they acknowledge that they are under the authority of their husband and their dean.

its ability to use rhetoric to tap the anxiety that exists about the problems which are affecting the family. This is rhetoric coated with piety — old words but with new meanings. Consequently, it seems necessary to raise a few caution flags.

Bible Families

The makeup of families in society is amazingly diverse, a fact that makes it impossible to sew a "one size fits all" garment in which to dress the family. Yet the Christian Right holds up as a norm the "June and Ward Cleaver" type of the family — an authoritative husband who works outside the home, a submissive wife who is a full-time homemaker, and obedient children. As popular as this myth is, it does not reflect the great diversity of forms of family either in the Bible or in our society.

Moses was reared by a foster parent, the Pharaoh's daughter. Scholars agree that Joseph was much older than Mary, so much of Jesus' life could have been spent in a single-parent family. The apostle Paul's young protégé, Timothy, was the product of an inter-generational family — a loving mother and grandmother. The home Jesus spent much time in during his ministry was made up of three adult siblings living as family — Mary, Martha, and Lazarus. The pivotal leader of the church in Philippi was Lydia, who was head of a large household and a businesswoman. Except for turning away from polygamy, our society reflects the many forms of family first portrayed in the Bible — complex, diverse, and needing insight and understanding.

Family and Gender

The Christian Right undermines the potential for a more mature husband-wife relationship by consistently coming down on the wrong side of the gender issue — suggesting that women are both different and inferior. In schools that the Christian Right controls, married female professors are allowed to teach men only after they acknowledge that they are under the authority of their husband and their dean. Women are not allowed to pastor churches, despite the abundant evidence of their giftedness and sense of calling. And in the home, women are admonished to accept the authority of their husbands, claiming that this "chain of command" is God's plan and that to resist it is a sin.

The authority quoted was the Apostle Paul's word to the believers in Ephesus: "Wives, be in subjection unto your own husband, as unto the Lord" (Ephesians 5:22). However, these biblical literalists attempt to manipulate the scripture to justify their chauvinistic ideas. The verb about submitting was drawn from the previous verse, which states that husbands and wives are to submit themselves *to one another*. Whatever submission means, it is to be reciprocal. The whole context of this much-misused verse suggests that the essential ingredient in a mature healthy relationship is self-giving love, not who the authority is. On the issue of gender, the Christian Right ignores the heart of its own Bible because Paul also wrote that no distinction should be made among races, among classes, or between

genders: "For ye are all one in Christ" (Galatians 3:28).

The Unwed Mother

One of the issues that the Christian Right appears to be addressing is that of the unwed mother. It is interesting that the problem is seldom attached to the father who does not marry the mother or give support for his child. The focus is the same as when the woman was caught in the act of adultery and brought to Jesus to judge. No one asked where the guilty man was. Much of the study that attempts to discover the root cause for unwed mothers is being brushed aside with the cruel suggestion that the only reason the women are having the children is in order to get a check from welfare.

This statement shows a lack of both compassion and understanding. For some it is the reflection of a thinly disguised social and racial hatred. While the government's assistance might be a factor, many other questions should be raised. What part is played by ingrained poverty, poor education, and lack of family planning? What will it take to break the cycle that is reinforced by generations of an inability to find work and the absence of any hope? This problem will require study, shared ideas, hard decisions, and the whole of society working together. It will not be solved by the government refusing to budget for assistance to the children born out of wedlock.

Divorce and the Christian Right

By devoting so much of its energy to issues that attract followers and increase political clout, the Christian Right is missing a wonderful opportunity to address the problems created for both adults and children by the large percentage of

When it is difficult to distinguish the church's agenda on the family from the platform of the Republican Party, the family is in trouble.

marriages that end in divorce. The failure of a marriage has the same effect on everyone involved — spouses, children, friends, and extended families — as a physical death in the family, except that the usual support system is absent. As an angry woman told the members of her support group, "Nobody shows up at the courthouse with a casserole."

But often churches that seek to make everyone welcome are sending different signals to the formerly married. Ministers who refuse to perform weddings for those who have been married before or eliminate them from positions of service leave the impression that they are second-class members. This attitude suggests that the only unforgivable sin is the one that can be checked at the courthouse.

This posture turns its back on those who already feel rejection. A divorce, no matter what kind of a happy face people try to give it, creates pain, guilt, and anger, and it undermines the self-confidence of everyone involved. It makes people feel vulnerable and frightened of re-lationships; they have a desperate need for acceptance, for patience, and for compassion.

This is one crisis in which the church has great potential for helping. It has a word of grace that can be very freeing to those who struggle with guilt. The love and acceptance of a congregation has enormous potential for restoring self-esteem. The church should be able to hold up ideals for marriage without being judgmental and to provide a support system for beginning again. Because religion's first focus on the family was to bless it, the Christian Right needs to help those who have been scarred by the failure of a marriage rather than to ostracize them.

Politicizing the Family

One of the worst things that the Christian Right has done to the family has been to politicize it — to create an unholy alliance between politicians and a part of the church. When it is difficult to distinguish the church's agenda on the family from the platform of the Republi-can Party, the family is in trouble. Too many important related issues that affect the family will fall through the cracks — drugs, alcohol, poverty, and abuse and violence in the home. Public opinion will masquerade as the truth. Politicians and preachers will create empty slogans and gather confused followers who are frightened by the complexity of life and too anxious for easy solutions.

But even with the pressures on the family, the sky is not actually falling. The family is tough, or it would not have managed throughout the centuries. It will survive today's crises. But it can always use more friends who will understand it and help it. Doing so is the only way to truly strengthen our society.

Kenneth Chafin divided a forty-year career between being a professor in two theological seminaries and pastoring two urban congregations. In addition to writing and speaking on the family, he led churches to pioneer in ministries to the family in all its diversity. He lives in Louisville, Kentucky, with his wife Barbara and continues to write and lecture.

African American Families

A Legacy of Vulnerability and Resilience

African Americans, despite a legacy of stigmatizing psychological folklore and an antagonistic environment manifested in centuries of racial discrimination, display an undeniable development of adaptive coping strategies and resilience. Understanding the realities in the lives of contemporary African American families requires an examination of the history of African Americans in the United States.

Beverly Greene

African Americans are one of the oldest and largest groups of persons of color in the United States. The first census in 1790 counted 760,000 African Americans. By 1990, over 30,000,000 were counted. African Americans are descendants of people who belonged to the tribes of the West African coast and were the primary objects of the U.S. slave trade. Many African Americans have Native American and European ancestry as well.

They are perhaps the only ethnic group in the United States whose immigration was wholly involuntary. Entry into the United States was not, as it was for members of white ethnic groups and other groups of persons of color, the result of an effort to better their circumstances or find a more advantageous political climate than their homeland could offer. Instead of bettering their circumstances, their forced departure from the West African coast resulted in pervasive losses. Aside from the loss of life for many, there was a loss of community, the loss of original languages, and the loss of status as human beings for those who survived the Atlantic Passage.

As slaves, literally deprived of all human rights, they were to provide free labor and were bought and sold as any other commodity. Their children were salable commodities as well. In this system, family attachments were routinely ignored as slaves were transported, sold, and regarded as livestock with no regard for their family or important emotional ties. In this context, slave families came to place less emphasis on the role of biological parents because most children were separated from and not raised by them. Rather, children were informally "adopted" and raised by other people in their immediate community in extended rather than nuclear family arrangements. These extended family arrangements are still a prominent feature of contemporary African American families and may be considered a major survival tool.

The struggles of African Americans are often viewed as if they

From *National Forum*, Volume 75, Number 3 (Summer 1995,) pp. 29-32. © 1995 by Beverly Greene. *National Forum: The Phi Kappa Phi Journal.* Reprinted by permission of the publishers.

ended with emancipation. This belief ignores over a century more of legal racial discrimination that led to the civil rights struggles which reached a peak in the 1950s and 1960s. Even in the wake of legislation designed to make racial discrimination illegal, discrimination in more subtle, institutionalized forms still operates to this day in ways that continue to challenge the optimal physical, psychological, and economic well-being of African Americans.

Characteristics of African American Families

Characteristics of contemporary African American families represent an interaction of African cultural derivatives, the need to adapt to a racially antagonistic environment, and the influence of American cultural imperatives. They include extended networks of kinship between family members and persons who are not blood-related in complex networks of obligation and support. African Americans as a group are geographically and socioeconomically diverse. However, they share both cultural origins and the need to manage the anxieties and prejudices of a dominant group that is culturally different and that discriminates against African Americans both actively and passively on the basis of race. In some form, all African Americans must make psychological sense out of their disparaged condition, deflect hostility from the dominant group, and negotiate racial barriers under a wide range of circumstances. If the group is to survive, the members must teach their children to do so as well.

In this regard, African American parents have a special task and a unique stressor that are not shared by their white counterparts.

These consist of the special things they must do to prepare their children to function in an adaptive fashion without internalizing the dominant culture's negative messages about African American people. In *Children of Color*, Allen and Majidi-Ahi note that teaching African American children how to cope with racism represents a socialization issue that exemplifies all that is distinct about the African American experience in America. A major component of this experience entails the task of communicating to African American children the racial realities and dangers of the world, how to correctly identify and

cope with the resulting barriers, and how to seek support for the feelings evoked when confronting these barriers.

Succeeding Against Odds

Despite many historical and contemporary obstacles, African Americans have succeeded against many overwhelming odds in every generation. African American families are an important source of socialization and support for their members and can be an important translator of the dominant culture for African American children. At its best, this system teaches African American children to imitate and function in the dominant culture without believing that its demeaning images of African Americans are true.

Another role of the family is to pass along different kinds of successful coping strategies against racism. One strategy, the heightened sensitivity to the potential for exploitation by white persons, has been referred to by Grier and Cobbs in *Black Rage* as cultural paranoia. While this heightened sensitivity often has been pathologized by the dominant culture, it is a realistic and adaptive way of approaching situations that have frequently been antagonistic. Hopson and Hopson in *Different and Wonderful* suggest that another important coping strategy and a major source of psychological

resilience is reflected in the sharing of African cultural derivatives with children while encouraging them to take pride in their ancestry. In *Long Memory*, Mary Berry and John Blassingame note that each generation of African Americans prepares the next for survival in a society that devalues them by passing along "searing vignettes" about what has preceded them. They view this process as a long collective memory that is in and of itself an instrument of survival.

African American families must do all of these things in addition to providing the normal range of basic necessities that all families must provide for their children. In the context of a racist society, however, African American families' ability to do this may be compromised by the institutional barriers

. . . all African Americans must make psychological sense out of their disparaged condition, deflect hostility from the dominant group, and negotiate racial barriers under a wide range of circumstances.

that providers in the family invariably confront. In these scenarios there may be a drain on the family's emotional and material resources, making the extended family structure an important resource in this regard. Sharing the burden of child care and child rearing helps to ease this burden in many families and can be seen as an example of resilience.

Multiple Mothering

In *Black Families*, Nancy Boyd-Franklin gives one example of this in what she describes as "multiple mothering." "Multiple mothers" refers to grandmothers, aunts, cousins, close friends, or people considered "kin" to a child's mother. They need not be biologically related. These multiple mothers provide

single-parent families, extensive networks of other family members, family friends, neighbors, and others are routinely involved in the caretaking of children. Hence, the unmarried status of the mother does not automatically tell us what the rest of the family structure is like. The single-parent family as a large and diverse group among African Americans is not synonymous with teenaged or underaged mothers. Becoming a parent before one is biologically and emotionally mature, or when it interferes with important developmental tasks of the parent, is certainly not what is recommended. Rather, I suggest that African American family structures be viewed as perhaps having a wider range of flexibility in what is available to its members, reflected

American families. This flexibility in gender roles is explained in part as a derivative of the value of interdependence among group members, typical of Western African precolonial cultures, that is unlike the value of rugged individualism of the West. It is also a function of the need to adapt to racism in the United States in many different ways.

One of the features that distinguished African American women from their white counterparts was their role as workers. Aside from being brought into the country as slaves whose primary function was to work, the status of African American women as slaves superseded their status as women. Hence they were not given the courtesies of femininity that were routinely accorded white women. Conventions of femininity considered many forms of labor that were routine for white males inappropriate for white females. Slavery deprived African American women of this protection, and as such their roles as workers did not differ from those of African American males. Hence at the very outset, rigid gender-role stratification among African Americans was not permitted. Later, because African American men faced significant racial barriers in the workplace and could not fit the idealized image of the Western male provider, women were forced to work to help support the home. Thus, the dominant cultural norm of women remaining in the home. while men worked outside the home was never a practical reality for African American families.

The single-parent family as a large and diverse group among African Americans is not synonymous with teenaged or underaged mothers.

emotional safety valves, sounding boards, and alternative role models to children while often providing their real mothers with important tangible support in the form of child care. These arrangements also emphasize the important role for elder members of the family and the importance of their connection to members of the next generation. It is important to remember this extended family structure when viewing "single-parent families." The fact that African American families may deviate in structure from the White Anglo Saxon Protestant norm does not warrant pathologizing them or presuming that this deviation accounts for family problems.

In what appear to be many

in a wider range of persons, in addition to biological parents, involved in parenting roles.

Gender Role Flexibility

Robert Hill, in *The Strengths of Black Families*, identifies major characteristics of African American families: strong kinship bonds, a strong achievement motivation, a strong religious and spiritual orientation, and a strong work orientation. Hill views these characteristics as strengths that have helped African Americans survive and function under difficult circumstances. He further cites gender-role flexibility as an important and adaptive characteristic of African

This does not mean that there is no sexism within African American families. Tensions are often produced when African American men internalize the dominant culture's value of male domination and female subordination. Working women become the targets of African American male frustration rather than institutional racism. Despite such occurrences, flexibility in gender roles represents another example of an adaptive strategy that has contributed to the survival of African American families.

Summary

African American families have functioned under a legacy of challenges to their survival, beginning with slavery when families were not allowed to exist and when they were continually disrupted by abrupt and permanent separations. Surviving these disruptions, African American families have continued to demonstrate their flexibility and resilience under many adverse circumstances. It is not surprising that many African American families would be in crisis, given the range of routine assaults they face. What is more surprising is that many of these families display a remarkable legacy of adaptive strengths. James Comer, in *Maggie's American Dream*, reminds us that what we learn from survivors will tell us more about the circumvention of problems than will an exclusive focus on victims. African Americans are, if anything, survivors of historical and contemporary circumstances that may increase their vulnerability. However, as survivors they have much to teach us about resilience.

Beverly Greene is a professor of psychology at St. John's University and a clinical psychologist in private practice in New York City. A Fellow of the American Psychological Association and the recipient of national awards for her distinguished professional contributions, she is a coeditor of *Women of Color: Integrating Ethnic and Gender Identities in Psychotherapy*.

Exploring and Establishing Relationships

- Emotions, Relating, and Mating (Articles 6–12)
- Gender and Sexuality in Relationships (Articles 13–16)
- The Next Generation (Articles 17–19)

By and large, humans are social animals and, as such, we seek out meaningful connections with other humans. John Bowlby, Mary Ainsworth, and others have proposed that this drive toward connection is biologically based and is at the core of what it means to be human. However it plays out in childhood and adulthood, the need for connection, to love and be loved, is a powerful force moving us to establish and maintain close relationships.

As we explore various possibilities, we engage in the complex business of relationship building. In this business, many processes simultaneously occur: messages are sent and received; differences are negotiated; assumptions and expectations are or are not met. The ultimate goals are closeness and continuity.

How we feel about others and what we see as essential to these relationships play an important role in our establishing and maintaining relationships. In this unit, we look at factors that underlie the establishment of relationships as well as the beginning stages of relationships.

The first section takes a broad look at factors that influence the building of meaningful relationships and at the beginning stages of adult relationships. The first two essays explore the nature of love itself. "Love: The Immutable Longing for Contact" uses attachment theory as the basis for a depiction of the need for a strong connection as a force pushing people toward meaningful relationships. "What Makes Love Last?" considers different ways in which love is played out in long-term relationships. "Why Don't We Act Like the Opposite Sex?" explores the difficulties faced by couples as they struggle to understand gender differences. "Studies Put Genetic Twist on Theories about Sex and Love" incorporates studies in two seemingly disparate fields, animal behavior and feminism, to explain motivations and drives toward sex and love. A more traditional approach is taken in "Choosing Mates—

the American Way," which traces the history of mate selection, contrasting the qualities considered desirable in the past with those considered to be so today. "The Mating Game" focuses on the physical and sexual components of relationships, which have not changed much over the centuries. "Back Off!" takes what may seem to be a contrary position in suggesting that, just as time together is important for a relationship, so too do individuals need time alone for themselves.

In the second section, two important aspects of adult relationships are explored, gender and sexuality. Particular attention is given to the idea of responsibility to oneself and others in acting out our sexuality. "Choosing a Contraceptive" looks at the strengths and weaknesses of contraceptives available in the United States. Contraception often is seen as a woman's responsibility, both in interpersonal relationships and in social policy. Aaron Sachs, in "Men, Sex, and Parenthood in an Overpopulating World," takes an international perspective as he contends that it is essential to involve men in the decision making for a successful contraception program. The next two selections look at gender in families. The first, "Staying Power: Bridging the Gender Gap in the Confusing '90s," promotes the idea of a less traditional approach to gender roles. The second, "Albanian 'Virgins' Wear the Pants in Their Families," documents the fascinating case of women living as men, socially accepted as such, in a highly conservative culture.

In the final section, building new family relationships is explored. Readers of "What a Baby *Really* Costs" may find themselves amazed at the high cost of having an uncomplicated birth. Next, "Adolescent Childbearing: Whose Problem? What Can We Do?" asks the reader to step back and look at the bigger picture of childbearing. What *are* the implications for society of teens having and

26

raising children? The final reading addresses another way of creating parent-child bonds, adoption. "The Lifelong Impact of Adoption" is a cautionary look at the long-term impacts, particularly those related to a sense of loss, that are found among those who have been touched by adoption.

Looking Ahead: Challenge Questions

What is your definition of love? How do you know you are in love? How do you know you love someone? What does it take for you to believe someone loves you? What can you do when love fades?

What do you look for in a mate? Would you be willing to settle for less? Why or why not?

What are your beliefs about appropriate sexual behavior in intimate relationships? Whose responsibility is contraception? Would you feel comfortable discussing this with your partner? Why or why not?

What are appropriate gender roles? What is appropriate behavior in these roles? What would your response be if you encountered someone behaving in a way you found inappropriate for the role?

Do you see children as a part of your life? Why or why not? Discuss whether or not you would consider adopting. How do children enrich a relationship? What are the drawbacks of having children? If you do have children, how will it affect you and your relationship with your partner?

LOVE

The Immutable Longing for Contact

As the child is connected to the parent, to be connected with another person is the only security we ever have in life. In that sense, we never grow up.

**Susan Johnson, Ed.D.,
with Hara Estroff Marano**

An illusion. An anesthetic. An irrational compulsion. A neurosis. An emotional storm. An immature ideal. These are the descriptions of love that have long populated the psychological literature. Let us not even consider the obvious fact that they are highly judgmental and dismissive. The question I want to pose is, does any one of them, or even all of them together, come close to capturing the extraordinary experience that for most people is an enormous part of the meaning of life—an experience that fosters well-being and growth?

As a marital therapist, my job is to help people experience love, to move from distance and alienation to contact and caring. But in order to help distressed couples change, I realized early on that I needed a model of what a good relationship is. For too long, the choices have been confined to two. There is the psychodynamic, or psychoanalytic, view, which holds that adult relationships are more or less reflections of childhood relationships—replays of old conflicts. And there is the behaviorist view: Love is a rational exchange in which couples make deals based on their needs, and they succeed to the degree that they master the negotiation process. Love is then either a crazy compulsion or, after couples calm down, a kind of rational friendship where partners make good deals.

I can assure you that if I tried to persuade the couples I see in therapy to leave with an understanding of their childhood or a rational friendship, they would not be satisfied. The truth is that these conventional descriptions do not adequately reflect the process of marital distress or the rekindling of love that I observe as a marital therapist. Possessing insights as to why you have certain sore spots or honing negotiation skills seems to somehow miss the mark. Neither addresses the intense emotional responses that consume distressed couples. As I watch couples, I see that raw emotion, hurt, longing, and fear are the most powerful things in the room. Couples seem to have a desperate need to connect emotionally—and a desperate fear of connecting.

'Couples seem to have a desperate need to connect and a desperate fear of connection.'

There are, of course, many elements to a relationship. It is true that echoes of the past are present in relationships, but this focus does not capture enough of what goes on and ignores the power of present interactions. Couples do also make bargains. But the essence of their connection is not a bargain. It is, rather, a bond.

The bond between two people hinges on two things-their accessibility and responsiveness to each other. The notion that the tie between two people is created through accessibility and responsiveness is an outgrowth of attachment theory. First put forth by the late British psychiatrist John Bowlby 30 years ago and later elaborated both by him and psychologist Mary Ainsworth in America, attachment theory is only now gathering significant momentum. It promises to be one of the most significant psychological ideas put forth in the 20th century. As many researchers are now demonstrating, it is certainly the most viable way of making sense of the mother-infant (and father-infant) bond.

VIEWING LOVE THROUGH A LENS

Over the past decade, a number of psychologists, including myself, have begun to see in attachment theory an understanding of adult relationships. In my experience attachment is the best lens for viewing adult love. When viewed through this lens, love relationships do not seem irrational at all; we do not have to pronounce them mysterious or outside our usual way of

Reprinted with permission from *Psychology Today*, March/April 1994, pp. 32-37, 64, 66. © 1994 by Sussex Publishers, Inc.

being. Nor do we have to shrink them to fit the laws of economic exchange. They make perfect—many would say intuitive—sense. And attachment theory goes a long way toward explaining what goes wrong in relationships and what to do about it.

John Bowlby observed that the need for physical closeness between a mother and child serves evolutionary goals; in a dangerous world, a responsive caregiver ensures survival of the infant. Attachment theory states that our primary motivation in life is to be connected with other people—because it is the only security we ever have. Maintaining closeness is a bona fide survival need.

Through the consistent and reliable responsiveness of a close adult, infants, particularly in the second six months of life, begin to trust that the world is a good place and come to believe they have some value in it. The deep sense of security that develops fosters in the infant enough confidence to begin exploring the surrounding world, making excursions into it, and developing relationships with others—though racing back to mom, being held by her, and perhaps even clinging to her whenever feeling threatened. In secure attachment lie the seeds for self-esteem, initiative, and eventual independence. We explore the world from a secure base.

Thanks to Mary Ainsworth, a large and growing body of research supports attachment theory. She devised a procedure to test human attachment. Called the "strange situation," it allows researchers to observe mothers and children during a carefully calibrated process of separation and reunion. Ainsworth found that whenever children feel threatened or can no longer easily reach their attachment figure, they engage in behavior designed to regain proximity—they call, they protest, they seek, they cry, they reach out. Closeness achieved, they do all they can to maintain it: They hug, they coo, they make eye contact, they cling—and, that all-time pleaser, they smile.

Ainsworth noticed that children differ in their attachment security and their patterns of behavior sort into three basic "attachment styles." Most children are securely attached: They show signs of distress when left with a stranger, seek their mother when she returns, hold her for a short time, then go back to exploring and playing. These infants develop attachment security because they have mothers who are sensitive and responsive to their signals.

On the other hand, she found, 40 percent of kids are insecurely attached. Some are anxious/ambivalent. They show lots of distress separating, and on reunion, they approach and reject their mother. Their mothers usually respond inconsistently to them, sometimes unavailable, other times affectionate. So preoccupied are these infants with their caregiver's availability that they never get to explore their world.

The third group of children have an avoidant attachment style. They do not seem distressed during separation, and they don't even acknowledge their mother during reunion. These infants keep their distress well-hidden; though they appear to dismiss relationships entirely, internally they are in a state of physiological arousal. These children are usually reared by caregivers who rebuff their attempts at close bodily contact.

These responses are not arbitrary but universal. Evolution has seen to that because they serve survival needs. Some researchers are busy identifying the neurobiological systems that underlie attachment behavior and mediate the response to attachment threats. They are finding specific patterns of changes in biochemistry and physiology during experimental separation experiences.

Attachment bonds are particularly durable, and once an infant is attached, separation—or the threat of it—is extremely stressful and anxiety-producing. In the absence of attachment danger, children explore the world around them. But if the accessibility of a caregiver is questionable or threatened, the attachment behavior system shifts into high gear. Facing the loss or unreliability of an attachment figure, infants typically are thrust into panic and they mount an angry protest. Eventually, however, the protest dies down and they succumb to a despair that looks like classic depression.

The implications of attachment theory are extraordinary and extend to the deepest corners of our psyche. Attachment impacts the way we process information, how we see the world, and the nature of our social experience. Our attachment experience influences whether we see ourselves as lovable. Research now shows that we carry attachment styles with us into life, where they serve as predispositions to later behavior in love relationships.

We seek close physical proximity to a partner, and rely on their continuing affections and availability, because it is a survival need. What satisfies the need for attachment in adults is what satisfies the need in the young: Eye contact, touching, stroking, and holding a partner deliver the same security and comfort. When threatened, or fearful, or experiencing loss, we turn to our partner for psychological comfort. Or try to.

The core elements of love are the same for children and adults—the need to feel that somebody is emotionally there for you, that you can make contact with another person who will respond to you, particularly if you are in need. The essence of love is a partner responding to a need, not because it's a good deal—but even when it's not. That allows you to sense the world as home rather than as a dangerous place. In this sense, we never grow up.

It is growing clear that the dynamics of attachment are similar across the life span. Implicit in the anger of a couple who are fighting over everything is the protest of the child who is trying to restore the closeness and responsiveness of a parent. In the grief of adults who have lost a partner is the despair of a child who has lost a parent and experiences helplessness and withdrawal.

THE MUSICALITY OF EMOTION

Attachment theory makes sense of a matter that psychology has just begun to puzzle over—how we come to regulate our emotions. We regulate feelings, specifically negative ones—fear, sadness, anger—through the development of affectional bonds with others, and continuing contact with them. Through

After the Fight

Anger and hostility in marital relationships are usually interpreted by a partner as rejection. They are felt as distancing behaviors, and set off attachment alarms; you respond as if your life is threatened. But hostility itself is often an outgrowth of feelings of fear; your partner is perhaps feeling threatened. It is important to recognize that it may be an attempt to bring you back into contact rather than to control you. In one sense, the appropriate response to hostility may be a hug rather than a return of verbal barrage. But we fight for our life when threatened; we defend ourselves with anything that comes to mind.

It's after the fight that you have a real chance to reprocess the events more accurately, to enlarge the experience to include elements that were left out of the argument while you were trying to win. An attachment lens on relationships encourages us to look at aggression in intimate relationships as a common way of dealing with fear. It also implies there's nothing wrong with dependency needs; it gives us permission to have feelings of wanting to be cared for without feeling weak or judging ourselves as "dependent." After the fight, you need to recapitulate the events with the inclusion of these feelings.

After a fight, in non-distressed relationships, the immediate emotionally reactivity dies down. (The problem in distressed relationships is that it never quite dies down.) When it does die down, if you have a secure base in a relationship, then is the time to talk about fears and attachment concerns.

This creates the opportunity for real closeness. As in: "When I heard you saying that you wanted to go away with your friends for a golfing vacation, I just got scared all to hell. You're saying that you don't need to be with me as much as I need to be with you. I get totally terrified if I think I'm hearing that."

If I have a secure base, I'm much more likely to allow myself to access the feeling that I'm afraid. I'm much more likely to tell my partner I'm afraid. Hopefully, my partner will actually help me with that fear. My fear level will be reduced. My partner's response will help me see myself as lovable, and that exchange also then becomes a positive intimacy experience in the history of the relationship.

This kind of sharing is what adult intimacy is all about. You and your partner find each other as human beings who need comfort, contact, and caring.

---

the lens of attachment we also come to understand that the expression of emotion is the primary communication system in relationships; it's how we adjust closeness and distance. Emotion is the music of the interpersonal dance. And when attachment is threatened—when we feel alienated from a partner or worry about our partner's availability—the music either gets turned way up, into the heavy metal of angry protest, or way down, shut off altogether.

'The expression of emotion is the primary communication system in relationships; it's how we adjust to closeness and distance.'

The lens of attachment sharply illuminates the dangerous distortion personified in a popular icon of Western culture: the John Wayne image of the self-contained man, the man who is never dependent and never needs anyone else. Our need for attachment ensures that we become who we are as individuals because of our connection with other people. Our personality evolves in a context of contact with other people; it doesn't simply arise from within. Our attachment needs make dependence on another person an integral part of being human. Self-sufficiency is a lie.

A PLACE FOR VULNERABILITY

The most basic message of attachment theory is that to be valid adults, we do not need to deny that we are also always, until the end of our life, vulnerable children. A good intimate adult relationship is a safe place where two people can experience feelings of vulnerability—being scared, feeling overwhelmed by life, being unsure of who they are. It is the place where we can deal with those things, not deny them, control them, or regulate them, the old John Wayne way. Relatedness is a core aspect of our selves.

Yet Western psychology and psychiatry have often labeled feelings of dependency as pathologic and banished them to childhood. Our mistaken beliefs about dependency and self-sufficiency lead us to define strength as the ability to process inner experience and regulate our emotions all by ourselves. Attachment theory suggests that, not only is that not functional, it is impossible. We are social beings not constituted for such physiological and emotional isolation. For those who attempt it, there are enormous costs. A great deal of literature in health and psychology shows that the cost of social isolation is physical and psychological breakdown. Under such conditions, we simply deteriorate.

There is nothing inherently demeaning or diminishing in allowing someone else to comfort you. We need other people to help us process our emotions and deal with the slings and arrows of being alive—especially the slings and arrows. In fact, the essence of making intimate contact is sharing hurts and vulnerability with someone else. You allow someone into a place where you are not defended. You put contact before self-protection. In marital distress the opposite happens, self-protection comes before contact. If you cannot share, then a part of your being is excluded from the relationship.

The couples I see have taught me that it is almost impossible to be accessible, responsive, emotionally engaged with someone if you are not able to experience and express your own vulnerabilities. If you cannot allow yourself to experience and show your vulnerability, you cannot tell others what you need and explicitly ask others to respond to you. But troubled couples naturally want to hide and protect their vulnerability although that usually precludes any satisfying kind of emotional contact.

Like psychoanalytic theory, attachment theory sees early relationships as formative of personality and relationships later on. But unlike Freudian theory, it sees our view of ourselves and relationship styles as subject to revision as we integrate new experiences. This capacity makes growth possible. The past influences the present, but we are not condemned to repeat it.

The attachment system involves attachment behaviors, emotional responses, and internal representations, or models. In our psyches, we create working models of attachment figures, of ourselves, and of relationships. Built from our experience in the world, these internal working models are at the same time cognitive and affective, and they in turn guide how we organize our experience and how we respond to intimate others.

The reason our behavior in relationships is relatively stable is that, although they are susceptible to revision, we carry these internal working models into new social situations. They write the script by which we navigate the social world. Our internal working models of ourselves, our relationship, and our close ones create expectations of support and nurturance—and become the architects of the disappointments we feel. They are the creators of self-fulfilling prophecies.

But the existence of internal models also explains why you can have very different experiences in two different relationships. Essentially, you meet a new potential partner who brings a different behavioral repertoire. This allows you to engage in a different dance of proximity and distance—she is home to receive your phone calls, he doesn't react with veiled hostility when you call him at the office. Being accessible and responsive, your new partner doesn't ignite your anxiety and launch you into attachment panic. What's more, with a different set of internal working models, your new partner appraises your behavior differently and then offers a different response. From such new experience, a tarnished inner vision of relationships or of your sense of self can then begin to change.

A NEW WAY OF CONTACT

That may be what passionate love really is—we find someone who connects with us and alleviates our attachment fears, which opens up a whole new possibility of acceptance and responsiveness. Love is transforming—not just of the world but of the self. We find a whole new way of contacting another human being, and this emotional engagement opens up new possibilities of becoming ourselves. That is the intoxicating thing about the relationship. It modifies how people experience themselves and how they see other people.

From my point of view, attachment theory also redefines the place of sexual behavior. For the past 40 years, we seem to have come to believe that sex is the essence of love relationships. That is not my experience in working with couples. Sex per sex is often but a small part of adult intimacy. Attachment theory tells us that the basic security in life is contact with other people.

We need to be held, to be emotionally connected. I think that the most basic human experience of relatedness is two people—mother and child, father and child, two adults—seeing and holding each other, providing the safety, security, and feeling of human connectedness that for most, in the end, makes life meaningful. Many people use sex as a way to create or substitute for the sense of connection they are needing. I would guess that many a man or woman has engaged in sex just to meet a need for being held.

So perhaps now the mystery of love is becoming clear. We fall in love when an attachment bond is formed. We stay in love by maintaining the bond. We use our repertoire of emotions to signal the need for comfort through contact, the need for a little distance. We help each other process our inner and outer worlds and experience each other's pain, fear, joy.

What, then, goes wrong in couples? As I see it, healthy, normal attachment needs go unmet and attachment fears begin to take over the relationship.

We know that distressed couples settle into rigid interaction patterns. Perhaps the most distressed pattern is that of the disappointed, angry, blaming wife demanding contact from a man who withdraws. Couples can stay stuck in this for years. We know from the research of John Gottman that this is a sure killer of marriages.

But it is only through the lens of attachment that we come to understand what makes such patterns of behavior so devastating. The answer is, they block emotional engagement; they stand in the way of contact and exacerbate attachment fears. As partners hurl anger and contempt at each other or withdraw, emotional engagement becomes more and more difficult. Patterns of attack-defend or attack-withdraw are highly corrosive to a relationship because they preclude a safe way for a couple to emotionally engage each other and create a secure bond.

What couples are really fighting about is rarely the issue they seem to be fighting about—the chores, the kids. It is always about separateness and connectedness, safety and trust, the risk of letting someone in to see the exposed, vulnerable self.

Marital distress, then, is not a product of personality flaws. Nor is anger in relationships irrational. It is often a natural part of a protest that follows the loss of accessibility and responsiveness to a partner. It is an adaptive reaction—anger motivates people to overcome barriers to reunion. Self-defeating as it may be, anger is an attempt to discourage a partner from further distancing.

A COMPELLING EMOTION

But fear is the most compelling emotion in a distressed relationship. Hostility in a partner is usually a sign that the fear level has gone way up—the partner feels threatened. Attachment fears—of being unlovable, abandoned, rejected—are so tied to survival that they elicit strong fight or flee responses. In protecting ourselves, we often undermine ourselves as a secure base for our partner, who becomes alarmed. Our partner then confirms our fears and becomes the enemy, the betrayer.

Such fear sets off an alarm system. It heightens both the anger of those experiencing anxiety in attachment and the dismissal of emotional needs by those given to avoidance.

A NEW FRAME FOR BEHAVIOR

The lens of attachment puts a whole new frame on our behavior in relationships. The angry, blaming wife who continues to pursue with blame, even though she understands this behavior may drive her husband away, is not acting irrationally. Nor do her actions necessarily reflect a lack of communication skill. She is engaged in a desperate intensification of attachment behaviors—hers is an entreaty for contact. She perceives her husband as inaccessible and emotionally unresponsive: a threat that engages the attachment behavioral system. Of course, the defensiveness and conflict make safe contact increasingly less likely, and the cycle of distress escalates. It keeps going because the person never gets the contact and the reassurance that will bring closure and allow the attachment fears to be dealt with.

In working with couples, my colleague Les Greenberg and I have elaborated a therapy, "Emotionally Focused Couples Therapy," that views marital distress in terms of attachment insecurities. It recognizes that relationship problems are created by how individuals react to, cope with, and disown their own attachment needs and those of their spouse. A major goal of therapy is owning and validating needs for contact and security, helping people to expand their emotional range, rather than shut their feelings down or constantly control them. It is not about ventilating feelings, but about allowing people to immerse themselves more deeply in their experience and process elements of it they usually protect against—the desperation and loneliness behind anger, the fear and helplessness behind silent withdrawal.

The most powerful change agent in a distressed relationship seems to be the expression of the tender, more disarming emotions, such as longing, fear, and sadness. It is the most powerful tool to evoke contact and responsiveness from a significant other. If I help couples create contact, couples can then solve their own problems.

Most couples begin by declaring how incredibly angry they are. They have good reason to be angry. As they come to feel more of their anger, not justify or contain it, they usually begin to explore and experience more of what it is about. The experience starts to include elements they don't usually focus on, which they may even [see] as inappropriate. In fact one reason for feeling so angry is that they feel totally helpless and unlovable, which scares them.

Soon one partner begins talking to the other about what happened one second before lashing out—an incredible sense of helplessness, a voice that comes into the head and said, "I'm not going to feel this way. I refuse to feel so helpless and needy. This is unacceptable." And now the experience has been expanded beyond anger and partners start to contact hidden parts of themselves—in the presence of the other.

This is a new and compelling experience for them that enables one partner to turn to the spouse and confide, "Somehow, some part of me has given up the hope of ever feeling cherished, and instead I've become enraged because I am so sure that you could never really hold me and love me." This kind of dialogue redefines the relationship as one where a person can be vulnerable and confide what is most terrifying about him or herself or the world. And the partner, with the therapist's help, is there both for comfort and as a validating mirror of those experiences of the self.

BUILDING A SECURE BASE

The relationship is then starting to be a secure base where people can be vulnerable, bring out the neediness or other elements of themselves that frighten them, and ask for their attachment needs to be met. In this safe context, the husband or wife doesn't see the partner as weak but as available—not dangerous. I may hear one say: "That's the part I fell in love with." In a sense, the language of love is the language of vulnerability. While Western psychology focuses on the value of self-sufficiency, in our personal lives we struggle to integrate our needs for contact and care into our adult experience.

Attachment theory is an idea whose time has finally come because it allows us to be whole people. It views behavior gone awry as a well-meaning adaptation to past or present experience. And it views the desire for contact as healthy. Secure attachments promote emotional health and buffer us against life's many stresses. Love then becomes the most powerful arena for healing and for growth, and from this secure base, both men and women can go out and explore, even create, the world.

**PSYCHOLOGISTS
AT THE "LOVE LAB"
ARE USING SCIENCE
TO UNCOVER THE
REAL REASON
WHY MARRIAGES
SUCCEED OR FAIL.**

What Makes Love Last?

Alan AtKisson

Alan AtKisson is a writer, songwriter, and consultant living in Seattle, Washington. He and partner, Denise Benitez, recently celebrated their ninth wedding anniversary by hiking in the North Cascades.

My old friends Karen and Bill, married since 1955, recently celebrated another anniversary. "I wore the same nightgown I wore on our wedding night," confessed Karen to me over the phone. "Just as I have every anniversary for thirty-nine years."

"I wore pajamas on our wedding night," offered Bill. "But last night I didn't wear nothin'." They laughed, and even over three thousand miles of telephone wire I felt the strength of their love for one another.

Long-lasting marriages like Bill's and Karen's are becoming increasingly rare. Not only do more than 50 percent of all first marriages in the United States end in divorce (make that 60 percent for repeat attempts), but fewer people are even bothering to tie the slippery knot in the first place. One fourth of Americans eighteen or older—about 41 million people—have never married at all. In 1970, that figure was only one sixth.

But even while millions of couples march down the aisle only to pass through the therapist's office and into divorce court, a quiet revolution is taking place when it comes to understanding how long-term love really works. Inside the laboratories of the Family Formation Project at the University of Washington in Seattle—affectionately dubbed the Love Lab—research psychologists are putting our most cherished relationship theories under the scientific microscope. What they're discovering is that much of what we regard as conventional wisdom is simply wrong.

"Almost none of our theory and practice [in marital therapy] is founded on empirical scientific research," contends the Love Lab's head, John Gottman, an award-winning research psychologist trained both as a therapist and a mathematician. Indeed, it is this lack of solid research, Gottman believes, that contributes to a discouraging statistic: for 50 percent of married couples who enter therapy, divorce is still the end result.

Gottman believes that, although relationship counseling has helped many people, much of it just doesn't work. Not satisfied with warm and fuzzy ideas about how to "get the love you want," Gottman is scouting for numbers, data, *proof*—and he's finding it.

From *New Age Journal,* September/October 1994, pp. 74-79, 146-148. © 1994 by New Age Publishing, Inc. Reprinted by permission.

33

For the past twenty years, in a laboratory equipped with video cameras, EKGs, and an array of custom-designed instruments, Gottman and his colleagues have been intensely observing what happens when couples interact. He watches them talk. He watches them fight. He watches them hash out problems and reaffirm their love. He records facial expressions and self-reported emotions, heart rhythms and blood chemistry. He tests urine, memories, and couples' ability to interpret each other's emotional cues. Then he pours his data, like so many puzzle pieces, into a computer. The resulting picture, he says, is so clear and detailed it's like "a CAT scan of a living relationship." [See "Putting Love to the Test," at right.]

What Gottman and his colleagues have discovered—and summarized for popular audiences in a new book, *Why Marriages Succeed or Fail* (Simon & Schuster)—is mind-boggling in its very simplicity. His conclusion: Couples who stay together are . . . well . . . *nice* to each other more often than not. "[S]atisfied couples," claims Gottman, "maintained a five-to-one ratio of positive to negative moments" in their relationship. Couples heading for divorce, on the other hand, allow that ratio to slip below one-to-one.

If it ended there, Gottman's research

Fighting, whether rare or frequent, is sometimes the healthiest thing a couple can do for their relationship.

might remain just an interesting footnote. But for him and his colleagues, this discovery is just the beginning. In fact, Gottman's novel and methodical approach to marriage research is threatening to turn much of current relationship therapy on its head. He contends that many aspects of wedded life often considered critical to long-term success— how intensely people fight; whether they face conflict or avoid it; how well they solve problems; how compatible they are socially, financially, even sexually

—are less important than people (including therapists) tend to think. In fact, Gottman believes, none of these things matter to a marriage's longevity as much as maintaining that crucial ratio of five to one.

If it's hard to believe that the longevity of your relationship depends primarily on your being five times as nice as you are nasty to each other, some of Gottman's other conclusions may be even more surprising. For example:

❤ Wildly explosive relationships that vacillate between heated arguments and passionate reconciliations can be as happy—and long-lasting—as those that seem

more emotionally stable. They may even be more exciting and intimate.

❤ Emotionally inexpressive marriages, which may seem like repressed volcanoes destined to explode, are actually very successful—so long as the couple maintains that five-to-one ratio in what they do express to each other. In fact, too much emotional catharsis among such couples can "scare the hell out of them," says Gottman.

❤ Couples who start out complaining about each other have some of the most stable marriages over time, while those who don't fight early on are more likely to hit the rocky shoals of divorce.

Putting Love to the Test

How the "Love Lab" researchers decode blood, sweat, and tears.

THE STUDIO APARTMENT IS TINY, BUT IT affords a great view of Seattle's Portage Bay. The ambiance is that of a dorm room tastefully furnished in late-'80s Sears, Roebuck. A cute kitchen table invites you to the window. A Monet print graces one wall. Oh, and three video cameras—suspended from the ceiling like single-eyed bats—follow your every move.

Welcome to the "Love Lab," wherein Professor John Gottman and a revolving crew of students and researchers monitor the emotions, behaviors, and hormones of married couples. Today, lab coordinator Jim Coan—a calm, clear-eyed, pony-tailed young man in Birkenstocks who started out as a student volunteer three years ago—is giving me the tour.

The Love Lab is actually two labs. I have entered through the "Apartment Lab," whose weekly routine Coan describes: A volunteer couple arrives on a Sunday morning, prepared to spend the day being intensely observed (for which they are modestly compensated). Special microphones record every sound they make; videotape captures every subtle gesture. The only true privacy is found in the bathroom, but even there science has a presence: A cooler by the toilet has two

little urine collection bottles, today marked "Bill" and "Jeannie."

At the end of a relaxed day doing whatever they like (and being watched doing it), the couple welcomes a house guest—a psychologist who listens to the story of how they met, fell in love, and began building a life together. This "oral history," which most people greatly enjoy telling, will later be closely scrutinized: Gottman and company have learned that how fondly a couple remembers this story can predict whether they will stay together or divorce.

Then, after a sleep-over on the Lab's hide-a-bed (cameras and microphones off) and a blood sample, a technician takes the pair out for breakfast, gives them their check, and sends them on their way. The videotapes will later be analyzed in voluminous detail. Every affectionate gesture, sarcastic jab, or angry dispute will be recorded and categorized using Gottman's "specific affect" emotional coding system (the lab folks call it SPAFF for short). At the same time, the couple's blood and urine will be sent to another lab and tested for stress hormone levels. Finally, in four years or so (depending on the study), the lab will follow up with the

❤ Fighting, whether rare or frequent, is sometimes the healthiest thing a couple can do for their relationship. In fact, blunt anger, appropriately expressed, "seems to immunize marriages against deterioration."

❤ In happy marriages, there are no discernible gender differences in terms of the quantity and quality of emotional expression. In fact, men in happy marriages are more likely to reveal intimate personal information about themselves than women. (When conflict erupts, however, profound gender differences emerge.)

❤ Men who do housework are likely to have happier marriages, greater physical health, even better sex lives than men who don't. (This piece of news alone could cause a run on aprons.)

❤ Women are made physically sick by a relentlessly unresponsive or emotionally contemptuous husband. Gottman's researchers can even tell just how sick: They can predict the number of infectious diseases women in such marriages will suffer over a four-year period.

❤ How warmly you remember the story of your relationship foretells your chances for staying together. In one study that involved taking oral histories from couples about the unfolding of their relationship, psychologists were able to predict—with an astonishing 94 percent accuracy—which couples would be divorced within three years.

THE THREE VARIETIES OF MARRIAGE

In person, Gottman is a fast-talking, restless intellect, clearly in love with his work. Now in his late forties and seven years into a second marriage (to clinical psychologist Julie Schwartz), he seems very satisfied. Yet, in his book, he sheds

---

couple to see if they're still together—and take another look at the data they gathered to see if a predictable pattern can be discerned.

OTHER COUPLES WHO VISIT THE FAMILY Formation Project, as the "Love Lab" is more formally known, merely pass the pleasant apartment on their way to a less cozy destination: the "Fixed Lab." Here they are seated ("fixed") in plain wooden chairs and hooked up with a dizzying array of instruments—EKG electrodes, finger-pulse detectors, and skin galvanometers ("a fancy word for sweat detectors," says Coan). A thick black spring stretched across their chests registers breathing. Their chair itself is a "jiggleometer," recording every fidget and tremor.

A "facilitator" first interviews the pair about what issues cause conflict in their marriage, then gets them talking about the most contentious ones. Video cameras focus on the couple's faces and chests. Computers track the complex streams of data coming in through the sensors and displays them on a color monitor in a rainbow of blips and graphs.

After fifteen minutes of surprisingly "normal" and often emotional conversa-tion, the couple are stopped by the facilitator, who plays back the videotape for them. While watching, each partner rates his or her own emotional state at every moment during the conversation, using a big black dial with a scale running from "extremely negative" through "neutral" to "extremely positive." Then the pair watch the tape again, this time in an attempt to similarly judge their partner's emotional state (with widely varying levels of success).

Later, students trained by Coan will review the tape using a specially designed dial and the SPAFF coding system, to chart the feelings being displayed. It's eerie to see the range of human emotional expression represented on a high-tech instrument panel: disgust, contempt, belligerence, domination, criticism, anger, tension, tense humor ("very popular, that one," Coan tells me), defensiveness, whining, sadness, stonewalling, interest, validation, affection, humor, joy, and positive or negative surprise (students made Gottman aware of the two different kinds). In the middle is a neutral setting for when couples are merely exchanging information without noticeable emotion.

BACK IN THE APARTMENT LAB, COAN SHOWS me videos of couples who have agreed to be involved with the media. Two young parents from Houston discuss the stress around caring for their new baby, and Coan gives me the play-by-play: "He's being very defensive here" or "See that deep sigh? She's feeling sad now" or "Now that was a nice validation."

Coan says that most people seem to enjoy the lab experience—and even get some benefit from it (though it's not meant to be therapeutic). Amazingly, even with sensors attached to their ears and fingers and chests, the couples seem to forget that they're being watched. They giggle and cry and manage to create a genuine closeness while fixed under a physiological microscope.

"It's a real privilege to work here," Coan says thoughtfully. Even in a short visit, I feel it too. The observation of intimacy, both its joy and its pain, is more than just scientific video voyeurism. It's as though the love these couples are trying so devotedly to share with each other seeps out of the box, a gift to the watchers.

— A. A.

the mantle of guru in the first sentence: "My personal life has not been a trail of great wisdom in understanding relationships," he says. "My expertise is in the scientific observation of couples."

Gottman began developing this expertise some twenty years ago, when a troubled couple who came to him for help didn't respond well to conventional therapy. In frustration, Gottman suggested that they try videotaping the sessions. "Both the couple and I were astonished by the vividness and clarity on the tape of the pattern of criticism, contempt, and defensiveness they repeatedly fell into," he recalls. "It shocked them into working harder . . . [and] it gave me my life's work."

Struck by the power of impartial observation, Gottman became fascinated with research. His goal: to systematically describe the differences between happy and unhappy couples, and from those observations develop a scientific theory capable of predicting marital success. This seemed a daunting task, both because "marriage is so subjective" and because "personality theory, in psychology, has been a failure at predicting anything."

The result of Gottman's passion is a veritable mountain of data: tens of thousands of observations involving thousands of couples, gathered by the Love Lab's researchers and stored in its computer data-bases. The geography of that mountain reveals a surprising pattern: Successful marriages come in not one but three different varieties, largely determined by how a couple handles their inevitable disagreements. Gottman calls these three types of stable marriages *validating*, *volatile*, and *conflict-avoiding*.

Validating couples are what most people (including most therapists) have in mind when they think of a "good marriage." Even when these couples don't agree, they "still let their partner know that they consider his or her opinions and emotions valid." They "compromise often and calmly work out their problems to mutual satisfaction as they arise." And when they fight, they know how to listen, acknowledge their differences, and negotiate agreement without screaming at each other. "These couples," Gottman notes, "look and sound a lot like two psychotherapists engaging in a dialogue."

But where modern therapy often goes wrong, says Gottman, is in assuming that this is the only way a marriage can work—and trying to force all couples

Couples who start out complaining about each other have some of the most stable marriages over time.

into the validating mold. While "viewing this style of marriage as the ideal has simplified the careers of marital therapists," it hasn't necessarily helped their clients, he says, who may fall into the other two types of stable pattern.

Volatile couples, in contrast to validating ones, thrive on unfiltered emotional intensity. Their relationships are full of angry growls and passionate sighs, sudden ruptures and romantic reconcilia-

Men who do house-work are likely to have happier marriages, greater physical health, even better sex lives than men who don't.

tions. They may fight bitterly (and even unfairly), and they may seem destined for divorce to anyone watching them squabble. But Gottman's data indicate that this pessimism is often misplaced: These couples will stay together if "for every nasty swipe, there are five caresses." In fact, "the passion and relish with which they fight seems to fuel their positive interactions even more." Such couples are more romantic and affectionate than most—but they are also more vulnerable to a decay in that all-important five-to-one ratio (and at their worst, to violence). Trying to change the style of their relationship not only isn't necessary, Gottman says, it probably won't work.

Nor will conflict-avoiding couples, the third type of stable marriage, necessarily benefit from an increase in their emotional expression, he says. Gottman likens such unions to "the placid waters of a summer lake," where neither partner wants to make waves. They keep the peace and minimize argument by constantly agreeing to disagree. "In these relationships, solving a problem usually means ignoring the difference, one partner agreeing to act more like the other . . . or most often just letting time take its course." The universal five-to-one ratio must still be present for the couple to stay together, but it gets translated into a

Four Keys to a Happy Relationship

DESPITE ALL HIS SOPHISTICATED ANALYSIS of how relationships work (and don't work), researcher John Gottman's advice to the lovelorn and fight-torn is really quite simple.

LEARN TO CALM DOWN.
This will cut down on the flooding response that makes further communication so difficult. "The most brilliant and philosophically subtle therapy in the world will have no impact on a couple not grounded in their own bodies to hear it," he says. Once couples are calm enough, suggests Gottman, they can work on three other basic "keys" to improving their relationship.

LEARN TO SPEAK AND LISTEN NONDEFENSIVELY.
This is tough, Gottman admits, but defensiveness is a very dangerous response, and it needs to be interrupted. One of the most powerful things you can do—in addition to working toward the ideal of listening with empathy and speaking without blame—is to "reintro-

much smaller number of swipes and caresses (which are also less intensely expressed). This restrained style may seem stifling to some, but the couple themselves can experience it as a peaceful contentment.

Things get more complicated when the marriage is "mixed"—when, say, a volatile person marries someone who prefers to minimize conflict. But Gottman suggests that, even in these cases, "it may be possible to borrow from each marital style and create a viable mixed style." The most difficult hurdle faced by couples with incompatible fighting styles lies in confronting that core difference

---

duce praise and admiration into your relationship." A little appreciation goes a long way toward changing the chemistry between people.

VALIDATE YOUR PARTNER.
Validation involves "putting yourself in your partner's shoes and imagining his or her emotional state." Let your partner know that you understand how he or she feels, and why, even if you don't agree. You can also show validation by acknowledging your partner's point of view, accepting appropriate responsibility, and apologizing when you're clearly wrong. If this still seems too much of a stretch, at least let your partner know that you're *trying* to understand, even if you're finding it hard.

PRACTICE, PRACTICE, PRACTICE.
Gottman calls this "overlearning," doing something so many times that it becomes second nature. The goal is to be able to calm yourself down, communicate nondefensively, and validate your partner automatically—even in the heat of an argument.

---

and negotiating which style (or combination of styles) they will use. If they can't resolve that primary conflict, it may be impossible to tip the overall balance of their relational life in the direction of five-to-one.

The important thing here is to find a compatible fighting style—not to stop fighting altogether. Gottman is convinced that the "one" in that ratio is just as important as the "five": "What may lead to temporary misery in a marriage —disagreement and anger—may be healthy for it in the long run." Negativity acts as the predator in the ecosystem of marriage, says Gottman. It's the lion that feeds on the weakest antelopes and makes the herd stronger. Couples who never disagree at all may start out happier than others, but without some conflict to resolve their differences, their marriages may soon veer toward divorce because their "ecosystem" is out of balance.

THE FOUR HORSEMEN OF THE APOCALYPSE

Even the most stable marriages of any style can fall apart, and Gottman and company have observed an all-too-predictable pattern in their decline and fall. He likens the process to a cascade—a tumble down the rapids—that starts with the arrival of a dangerous quartet of behaviors. So destructive is their effect on marital happiness, in fact, that he calls these behaviors "The Four Horsemen of the Apocalypse."

The first horseman is criticism: "attacking someone's personality or character" rather than making some specific complaint about his or her behavior. The difference between saying, say, "I wish you had taken care of that bill" (a healthy and specific complaint) and "You never get the bills paid on time!" (a generalizing and blaming attack) is very significant to the listener. Criticism often engenders criticism in return and sets the stage for the second horseman: contempt.

"What separates contempt from criticism," explains Gottman, "is the intention to insult and psychologically abuse your partner." Negative thoughts about the other come out in subtle put-downs, hostile jokes, mocking facial expressions, and name-calling ("You are such an idiot

---

around money"). By now the positive qualities that attracted you to this person seem long ago and far away, and instead of trying to build intimacy, you're ushering in the third horseman.

Defensiveness comes on the heels of contempt as a seemingly reasonable response to attack—but it only makes things worse. By denying responsibility, making excuses, whining, tossing back counter-attacks, and other strategies ("How come I'm the one who always pays the bills?!"), you just accelerate your speed down river. Gottman also warns that it's possible to skip straight to the third horseman by being oversensitive about legitimate complaints.

Once stonewalling (the fourth horseman) shows up, things are looking bleak. Stonewallers simply stop communicating, refusing to respond even in self-defense. Of course, all these "horsemen" drop in on couples once in a while. But when a partner habitually shuts down and withdraws, the final rapids of negativity (what Gottman calls the "Distance and Isolation Cascade") can quickly propel the marriage through whirlpools of hopelessness, isolation, and loneliness over the waterfall of divorce. With the arrival of the fourth horseman, one or both partners is thinking negative thoughts about his or her counterpart most of the time, and the couple's minds—as well as their bodies—are in a perpetual state of defensive red alert.

The stress of conflict eventually sends blood pressure, heart rate, and adrenaline into the red zone—a phenomenon Gottman calls *flooding*. "The body of someone who feels flooded," he writes, "is a confused jumble of signals. It may be hard to breathe. . . . Muscles tense up and stay tensed. The heart beats fast, and it may seem to beat harder." Emotionally, the flooded person may feel a range of emotions, from fear to anger to confusion.

The bottom line is that flooding is physically uncomfortable, and stonewalling becomes an attempt to escape that discomfort. When flooding becomes chronic, stonewalling can become chronic, too. Eighty-five percent of the time the stonewaller (among heterosexual couples) is the man. The reason for this gender discrepancy is one of many physiological phenomena that Gottman sees as critical to understanding why mar-

Women are made physically sick by a relentlessly unresponsive or emotionally contemptuous husband. Gottman's researchers can even tell just how sick.

riages go sour, and what people can do to fix them.

Though flooding happens to both men and women, it affects men more quickly, more intensely, and for a longer period of time. "Men tend to have shorter fuses and longer-lasting explosions than women," says Gottman. Numerous observations in the laboratory have shown that it often takes mere criticism to set men off, whereas women require something at least on the level of contempt. The reasons for this are left to speculation. "Probably this difference in wiring had evolutionary survival benefits," Gottman conjectures. An added sensitivity to threats may have kept males alert and ready to repel attacks on their families, he suggests, while women calmed down more quickly so they could soothe the children.

Whatever its origin, this ancient biological difference creates havoc in contemporary male-female relationships, because men are also "more tuned in to the internal physiological environment than women," Gottman reports. (For example, men are better at tapping along with their heartbeat.) Men's bodily sensitivity translates into greater physical discomfort during conflict. In short, arguing hurts. The result: "Men are more likely to withdraw emotionally when their bodies are telling them they're upset." Meanwhile, "when men withdraw, women get upset, and they pursue [the issue]"—which gets men more upset.

Here is where physiology meets sociology. Men, says Gottman, need to rely on physiological cues to know how they're feeling. Women, in contrast, rely on social cues, such as what's happening in the conversation.

In addition, men are trained since early

childhood not to build intimacy with others, while women "are given intense schooling on the subject" from an equally early age. Socially, the genders are almost totally segregated (in terms of their own choices of friendships and playmates) from age seven until early adulthood. Indeed, it would seem that cross-gender relationships are set up to fail. "In fact," Gottman writes, "our upbringing couldn't be a worse training ground for a successful marriage."

Yet the challenge is far from insurmountable, as millions of marriages prove. In fact, Gottman's research reveals that "by and large, in happy marriages there are *no* gender differences in emotional expression!" In these marriages, men are just as likely to share intimate emotions as their partners (indeed they may be more likely to reveal personal information about themselves). However, in unhappy marriages, "all the gender differences we've been talking about

Men's bodily sensitivity translates into greater physical discomfort during conflict. The result: Men are more likely to withdraw emotionally.

emerge"—feeding a vicious cycle that, once established, is hard to break.

Married couples who routinely let the Four Horsemen ransack their living rooms face enormous physical and psychological consequences. Gottman's studies show that chronic flooding and negativity not only make such couples more likely to get sick, they also make it very difficult for couples to change how they relate. When your heart is beating rapidly and your veins are constricting in your arms and legs (another evolutionary stress response), it's hard to think fresh, clear thoughts about how you're communicating. Nor can the brain process new information very well. Instead, a flooded person

relies on "overlearned responses"—old relationship habits that probably just fan the flames.

All this physiological data has enormous implications for relationship therapists as well as their clients. Gottman believes that "most of what you see currently in marital therapy—not all of it, but most of it—is completely misguided."

For example, he thinks it's an exercise in futility when "the therapist says 'Calm down, Bertha. Calm down, Max. Let's take a look at this and analyze it. Let's remember the way we were with our mothers.' Bertha and Max can do it in the office because he's doing it for them. But once they get home, and their heart rates get above 100 beats per minute, whew, forget about it."

Teaching psychological skills such as interpreting nonverbal behavior also misses the mark. "We have evidence that husbands in unhappy marriages are terrible at reading their wives' nonverbal behavior. But they're great at reading other people's nonverbal behavior. In other words, they have the social skills, but they aren't using them." The problem isn't a lack of skill; it's the overwhelming feelings experienced in the cycle of negativity. Chronic flooding short-circuits a couple's basic listening and empathy skills, and it undermines the one thing that can turn back the Four Horsemen: the repair attempt.

HEADING OFF DISASTER

Repair attempts are a kind of "metacommunication"—a way of talking about how you're communicating with each other. "Can we please stay on the subject?" "That was a rude thing to say." "We're not talking about your father!" "I don't think you're listening to me." Such statements, even when delivered in a grouchy or complaining tone, are efforts to interrupt the cycle of criticism, contempt, defensiveness, and stonewalling and to bring the conversation back on track.

"In stable relationships," explains Gottman, "the other person will respond favorably: 'Alright, alright. Finish.' The agreement isn't made very nicely. But it does stop the person. They listen, they accept the repair attempt, and they actually change" the way they're relating.

Repair attempts are "really critical," says Gottman, because "everybody screws up. Everybody gets irritated, defensive, contemptuous. People insult one another," especially their spouses. Repair attempts are a way of saying "we've got to fix this before it slides any deeper into the morass." Even people in bad marriages make repair attempts; the problem is, they get ignored.

Training people to receive repair attempts favorably—even in the middle of a heated argument—is one of the new frontiers in relationship therapy. According to Gottman, "Even when things are going badly, you've got to focus not on the negativity but on the repair attempt. That's what couples do in happy mar-

Even people in bad marriages make repair attempts; the problem is, they get ignored.

riages." He's convinced that such skills can be taught: One colleague has even devised a set of flash cards with a variety of repair attempts on them, ranging from "I know I've been a terrible jerk, but can we take this from the top?" to "I'm really too upset to listen right now." [See Upfront, July/August 1993.] Even in mid-tempest, couples can use the cards to practice giving, and receiving, messages about how they're communicating.

Breaking the Four Horsemen cycle is critical, says Gottman, because "the more time [couples] spend in that negative perceptual state, the more likely they are to start making long-lasting attributions about this marriage as being negative." Such couples begin rewriting the story of how they met, fell in love, made commitments. Warm memories about how "we were so crazy about each other" get replaced with "I was *crazy* to marry him/her." And once the story of the marriage has been infected with negativity, the motivation to work on its repair declines. Divorce becomes much more likely (and predictable—consider that 94 percent accuracy rate in the oral history study).

Of course, not all relationships can, or should, be saved. Some couples are trapped in violent relationships, which "are in a class by themselves." Others may suffer a fundamental difference in their preferred style—validating, volatile, or conflict-avoidant—that leaves them stuck in chronic flooding. With hard work, some of these marriages can be saved; trying to save others, however, may do more harm than good.

In the end, the hope for repairing even a broken marriage is to be found, as usual, in the courage and effort people are willing to invest in their own growth and change. "The hardest thing to do," says Gottman, "is to get back to the fundamentals that really make you happy." Couples who fail to do this allow the Four Horsemen to carry them far from the fundamentals of affection, humor, appreciation, and respect. Couples who succeed cultivate these qualities like gardeners. They also cultivate an affirming story of their lives together, understanding that that is the soil from which everything else grows.

The work may be a continuous challenge, but the harvest, as my long-married friends Bill and Karen would say, is an enormous blessing: the joy in being truly known and loved, and in knowing how to love.

The Lovers' Library

A slew of new books appearing in 1994 address some of the most entrenched problems facing long-term lovers:

■ *Hot Monogamy: Essential Steps to More Passionate, Intimate Lovemaking*, by Patricia Love and Jo Robinson (Dutton, 1994). This is a wonderful guide to enriching your sex life in a host of imaginative ways, and to reducing the shame and anxiety caused by differences in sexual appetite. (Also available as an excellent workshop on cassette from The Sounds True Catalog, 800-333-9185.)

■ *When Opposites Attract: Right Brain/Left Brain Relationships and How to Make Them Work*, by Rebecca Cutter (Dutton, 1994). A very helpful and thorough guide to dealing with the wide range of problems that can stem from fundamental differences in brain wiring.

■ *The Couple's Comfort Book: A Creative Guide for Renewing Passion, Pleasure, and Commitment*, by Jennifer Louden (HarperSanFrancisco, 1994). A highly usable compendium of nurturing and imaginative things to do together, cross-referenced so you can hop around the book and design your own program of relationship rebirth.

Why Don't We Act Like The Opposite Sex?

The new field of sociobiology prompts arguments as to whether different behavior by men and women is inherited or learned.

Anthony Layng

Dr. Layng is professor of anthropology, Elmira (N.Y.) College

Social scientists long have been aware of the distinctive sex roles characteristic of tribal societies around the world, but many are reluctant to conclude that this is anything other than learned behavior. Most American cultural anthropologists have assumed that sex roles are largely arbitrary. This is illustrated by citing examples characteristic of males in one population and females in another—as in the American Southwest, where Navajo weavers are women and Hopi weavers are men.

To suggest that female roles are determined to any significant degree by biological factors invites an implication that the lower social status of women found in most societies also might be attributed to innate differences between the sexes, that "anatomy is destiny." American anthropologists have been influenced by social liberalism to such an extent that any scholarly proponent of biological determinism (racism, sexism, etc.) is likely to be challenged immediately. Their arguments against racism have pointed out that there is no reliable correlation between race and social behavior; people of the same race may have sharply contrasting cultures; and a given population can alter its culture dramatically without, presumably, altering its genes. For instance, the Aztecs and Apache were of the same race, but the former evolved a complex state civilization while the latter remained primitive nomads. The post–World War II Japanese have shown us how much a homogeneous racial population can change its culture in a very short time.

When it comes to sexism—the belief that the distinctive behavior of females and males is influenced significantly by their differing physiology—ethnographic challenges are less convincing. One major difficulty is the fact that there are no societies where men and women act alike. Even where conscious attempts have been made to eliminate behavioral differences between the sexes, distinctions remain. A study of American communes in the 1970s found that none have "come anywhere near succeeding in abolishing sex-role

---

It is far more usual for women to be in favor of the binding relationship of marriage, while men are reluctant to commit themselves.

---

distinctions, although a number . . . have made this their highest ideological priority."

Another reason why cross-cultural comparisons have been relatively inef-

fectual in undermining sexist thinking is that, regardless of the great variability of sex roles from one society to another, there are certain behavior patterns and attitudes that appear to be the same in both traditional and modern societies. For example:

- Women generally prefer older men as mates, while most males prefer younger females.
- In courtship and mating behavior, most men are more sexually aggressive and most women are more coy.
- Males are more inclined to delay marriage.
- Men are more likely to seek a variety of mates.
- Women tend to be more tolerant of adulterous mates.
- Females are more likely to be domestic and nurturing.

In some societies, women prefer men who are considerably older than themselves; in others, the age discrepancy is slight. What is constant is that, on average, the male in each couple is older. Unlike bands of apes, where females are the usual initiators of copulation, "presenting" themselves to males, it is far more common for men to initiate sex, while women are more likely to take a relatively passive role beyond flirtation. Nearly everywhere, shyness or coquettishness is associated strongly with female sexual behavior.

Although some males may have to sell the idea of marriage to their mates, it is far more usual for women to be in the position of favoring such a binding relationship and men to be reluctant to commit themselves. However, males are less reticent about participating in purely sexual relationships, often doing so with more than one partner concurrently. Females seem far more inclined to restrict themselves to one mate, or at least to one at a time. These behavioral differences often are reflected in the "double standard"—the attitude that female infidelity is a far more serious moral breech than male unfaithfulness. Typically, both men and women are more inclined to condemn the adultress. This is not to say that wives do not disapprove strongly of spouses who cheat on them. The point is that a woman far more often will put up with such a husband. Men, on the other hand, are more likely to leave, severely beat, or even kill an unfaithful mate.

Finally, men are far less inclined toward "nesting" and nurturing. It is the women in all societies who are the most domestic and more adept at nursing the sick and comforting those who are troubled. Both sexes generally agree that it is a woman's nature that makes her so well suited to these activities.

If women and men naturally are inclined to view each other in programmed ways regardless of their class or culture and naturally are predisposed to act toward each other in similarly uniform ways, it might seem reasonable to conclude that female human nature is clearly distinct from that of males and that an Equal Rights Amendment goes against nature. As an active proponent of the ERA and an opponent to all sexism, I am troubled by such a conclusion, but unable simply to dismiss it.

In light of such global uniformity in behavior and attitudes, it is difficult to account for these patterns solely in terms of socialization. Cultures differ dramatically from one to another, and religious beliefs, kinship systems, social structures, political traditions, and subsistence systems vary. So why do men in such contrasting societies all behave so aggressively in the pursuit of sex? Why do male hunters, farmers, and warriors tend to show such interest

in seducing new sex partners? Why do Latin American and Asian women put up with adulterous husbands? Why do females in primitive tribes and industrial societies usually prefer older men? Why do peasant women and debutantes tend to want marriage before their male counterparts do? Why are both American and African men relatively disinterested in domestic chores? If it is all a matter of learning, of cultural conditioning, why are there not some societies where most men and women do not conform to these patterns?

Are these traits determined to some extent by the biological peculiarities of the different sexes? If so, it is distressing to consider the social and political implications of such a finding. If human nature (and not only nurture) leads females to behave in a distinctive way, is it therefore not suitable that they be treated in a discriminating fashion? If chasing women only is doing what comes naturally to men, then promiscuous females should have less

---

The reproductive strategy of a female stresses quality of offspring, therefore they are inclined to seek established and mature males as providers and protectors of their children.

---

excuse for their infidelities. Should husbands, even of working wives, be excused from house cleaning and child care? Clearly, one need not be a militant feminist to be made very uncomfortable by such questions.

It is further disturbing to liberals to learn about the findings of sociobiology, a new discipline which suggests some rather startling explanations for behavior traits such as those cited above. According to many sociobiologists, mating practices are the result of an evolutionary process favoring genes that most successfully replicate themselves. This theory states that those

most successful in this regard give rise to behavior and attitudes maximizing reproductive success.

Supposedly, genetically inherited behavior that causes people to have the most offspring eventually results, through natural selection, in such action becoming more and more common. Genes which induce people to behave otherwise, by the same selective process, are weeded out since people who behave this way have fewer children—that is, they do not produce as many carriers of their genes. Over time, as the result of this process, genes which most successfully cause men and women to produce carriers of these genes become more and more prevalent.

The most convincing illustrations of sociobiological explanations have been provided by studies of animal populations. For example, when a male langur monkey takes over a harem from an older male, he proceeds to kill all the infants of nursing mothers in the troop. From the perspective of Darwin's Theory of Evolution (survival of the fittest), this makes no sense at all, for it destroys healthy and fit infants as well as any others. From a sociobiological perspective, however, this wholesale infanticide is a sound reproductive strategy because it ensures that the genes of this newly dominant male soon will be replicated and in maximum numbers. Were he to wait until each female weaned her infant and ceased to lactate—a prerequisite to coming back into heat—it would be that much longer before he could impregnate them. By killing all the infants carrying some other male's genes, he speeds up the process whereby his genes begin to predominate. Also, he does not waste any energy protecting infants not carrying his genes.

The females of any species, goes this theory, are likely to develop very different kinds of reproductive strategies given the fact that they produce fewer offspring than do males. The genes of males, in competition with those of other males, induce behavior that results in the greatest number of offspring. Females, who are not able to produce nearly as many offspring as are males, compete for quality, rather than quantity, behaving so as to ensure that each child produced will be likely to survive and reproduce. In these ways, males and females alike are directed by their genes to see to it that they reproduce them as successfully as possible.

REPRODUCTIVE STRATEGIES

Among human beings, the fact that men prefer younger wives is fully consistent with their desire to have children since young women are highly fertile and the most likely to bear full-term healthy offspring. A young wife may devote her entire reproductive potential to producing children fathered by her husband. Since the reproductive strategy of women stresses *quality* of offspring, they are inclined to seek established and mature men as providers and protectors of their children. Male sexual aggressiveness serves to spread male genes. Female coyness helps to assure a potential mate that pregnancy has not occurred already. Her fidelity helps to convince him to stay around to protect what he therefore can assume to be his own offspring. (The sexual aggressiveness of female apes would be inappropriate in a human population, but not for them since male apes are not providers. Given the human sexual division of labor, men and women are economically dependent on each other; apes are not.)

By delaying marriage, a man is free to impregnate more women who will bear his children (his genes) without obligating him to care for them. A woman seeks marriage to monopolize not a man's sexuality, but, rather, his political and economic resources, to ensure that her children (her genes) will be well provided for. She may worry about her husband's infidelities, but only because this can siphon off resources she wants for her children. He, on the other hand, is far more concerned about sexually monopolizing her. He wants assurance that he is the father of any child she gives birth to; otherwise, he will be providing for those who do not carry his genes. Moreover, if she becomes pregnant by another man, it will be many months

before she can produce a fetus carrying her husband's genes. With or without her husband's faithfulness, she can get pregnant and produce the maximum number of children carrying her genes. Thus, a wife's affair is less tolerable to her husband for, according to the sociobiological perspective, it threatens to diminish the number of offspring he can produce by her.

The domesticity of women and the wanderings of men also are consistent with the differential reproductive strategies each sex has evolved. In stressing the quality of her offspring, since she can have relatively few, a woman provides a comfortable domicile for her children and stays home to nurture them, to better ensure their survivability so they are most likely to mature and further reproduce her genes. Meanwhile, the man is off chasing women, producing as many children as possible and being far less concerned with sticking around to guarantee their welfare. If he were to limit himself sexually to one woman, he greatly would diminish the number of children he potentially could propagate. In short, from a sociobiological perspective, she "succeeds" by being faithful to her husband since this helps to ensure that he will provide for her children; he does so not only by monopolizing her as a producer of his offspring, but by having children with other women as well.

By this point, you probably are thinking of people who exemplify sociobiologically sound traits of lecherous males and the women who put up with them. Certainly, we all are familiar with this behavior. Even though it often runs counter to accepted moral standards, we frequently hear people say, "That's the way men (or women) are." Sociobiologists seem to be offering theoretical confirmation of this folk wisdom.

Is human social behavior influenced by our genes? Whether further research will confirm or refute sociobiological theory as it applies to human behavior, we shall have to wait until far more information is available. No matter what the effect on our behavior, we should keep in mind that learning plays

an important role. Consequently, social policy should not be based on any assumption that biological determinants of human behavior and attitudes are more instrumental than learning, for cultural factors can counteract human genetic predispositions. Our early ancestors were subject to natural selection. Since the time of the Neanderthals, though, human populations have adapted to environmental change almost entirely by altering their learned behavior and attitudes—their culture, not their genes. There are individuals whose behavior conforms to sociobiological generalizations, but, especially among the educated, one finds many contrasting examples—men who do not chase young women, females who are sexually aggressive and/or disinterested in marriage, and couples who choose to have no children at all.

If traditional social inequality between men and women somewhat is perpetuated by genetically determined and sexually specific reproductive strategies, why are contraceptives and abortions so popular in modern society? Even most modern women may seem to conform to sociobiologically correct behavior (being attracted to older men, tolerating unfaithful spouses, accepting primary responsibility for domestic duties, etc.). Since most males still earn more than females do and since society continues to socialize boys and girls quite differently (encouraging girls to play with infant dolls, rewarding boys for being physically aggressive, etc.), the continuation of such behavior may be more a matter of cultural inertia than genetic compulsion.

So, even if inborn factors influence male and female human sexual behavior, the extent to which they do so clearly is limited and subordinate to learning and conditioning. Consequently, we neither need fear intellectually the findings of sociobiologists nor allow them significantly to influence interpersonal behavior and social attitudes regarding gender-specific behavior. If men and women continue to behave differently (and it seems there is no clear trend away from this pattern), we may yet learn just why we do not act like the opposite sex.

Studies Put Genetic Twist on Theories About Sex and Love

New research into human sexuality is being framed not only by the dictates of science, but by feminist hypotheses as well as animal behavioral studies.

Chi Chi Sileo

A woman is far more likely to become pregnant by her extramarital lover than by her husband; sexual fidelity is more important to men than emotional fidelity. These declarations may sound like the sirens of moral decline, but actually they are findings emerging from the study of evolution.

"In the past five years, there has been a flurry of activity" when it comes to understanding human sexuality through the evolutionary perspective, according to Meredith Small, a professor of anthropology at Cornell University and author of the forthcoming book *What's Love Got to Do with It? The Evolution of Human Mating.* "Yes, everybody likes to read and think and talk about sex. But there are two big factors that are really at play here. First, there is much more interest and focus on female behavior, spurred partly by the feminist movement and the sexual revolution. Second, there is a lot of new science coming out, especially in the areas of homosexuality and mate choice."

Patricia Adair Gowaty, an associate professor of biology at the University of Georgia who specializes in avian mating behavior, calls the renewed interest in human sexuality "a paradigm shiftlet." Says Gowaty: "There is certainly a more profound female perspective in evolutionary studies. In the last 10 years, I have seen a dramatic acceleration."

Much of this research centers on animal behavior. In his new and critically acclaimed book, *The Red Queen: Sex and the Evolution of Human Nature,* writer Matt Ridley draws upon detailed observations of apes, topminnows and water fleas, among other familiar and obscure species. Gowaty studies the behavior of the socially monogamous Eastern bluebirds and has found evidence that the females are having what a layman might call extramarital sex. "Twenty percent of their young are being sired by an extrapair mate," she says, "and yet these are birds that have been assumed to be completely monogamous all along. Females are supposed to be sexually passive, but after watching animals, we have to wonder why it took male researchers so long to catch up? It appears that men just can't imagine that female birds or monkeys could be sexually proactive."

Of course, adds Gowaty, who calls herself a Darwinian feminist, "we can't import conclusions across species, but we can import hypotheses." She is careful to draw distinctions between feminist theory and the dictates of science, while noting that the two can be complementary. "The source of a hypothesis can be anything — a gut feeling, a hunch, the logical next step in a formalized series. As a scientist, you develop a testable hypothesis and you set up an experiment, controlled against your own biases, to check it out."

David Buss, professor of psychology at the University of Michigan and author of *The Evolution of Desire,* agrees that the female perspective has been neglected in science, but says that some feminist researchers fail to "acknowledge the profound, fundamental differences between males and females," differences that he says no amount of cultural or societal conditioning can change. Buss notes that although there are some women who have very strong desires for sexual variety — a trait that exists to a high degree in most men — even those women cannot comprehend "the degree to which sex is on a man's mind. A woman who likes a lot of sexual variety might think that she thinks and acts like men do, but in fact she's probably not anywhere close."

Such intellectual scuffling is demonstrated by the already famous "Attractive Stranger" experiment, in which good-looking men and women approach the opposite gender and suggest a dinner date, offer an invitation to the stranger's apartment or make a flat-out proposition. The study has been replicated many times, each with the same results: Men overwhelmingly (in the area of 70 percent or higher) agreed to the sexual invitations—even more often than they agreed to the dinner date—while women overwhelmingly said yes to dinner but no to sex.

To Small, these results reflect less bio-

The Mating Game, or Why Wit Turns Us On

There has been a flurry of new research into human sexuality, much of it influenced to varying degrees by feminist studies. Among the recent offerings:

What's Love Got to Do With It? The Evolution of Human Mating by Meredith Small, anthropologist:

I suggest [that] over our evolutionary history, women have been selected not for monogamy, but to be promiscuous....

Science today tells us the following: Eggs aren't passive participants in the conception game; menstruation may have evolved to keep the bacteria from the sperm of males out of the reproductive tract; women have the potential for serial or multiple orgasms;... and women might have the ability to regulate the passage of sperm in their reproductive tracts....

The composite picture is one of a female who seeks sexual pleasure and has developed biological defenses that protect her from the consequences of an active sex life, a creature designed ... to improve her reproductive success by carefully directing her intimate life.

The Red Queen: Sex and the Evolution of Human Nature by Matt Ridley, journalist:

It is a disquieting thought that our heads contain a neurological version of a peacock's tail — an ornament designed for sexual display whose virtuosity at everything from calculus to sculpture is perhaps just a side effect of the ability to charm. Disquieting and yet not altogether convincing. The sexual selection of the human mind is the most speculative and fragile of the many evolutionary theories....

I began this book by asking why all human beings were so similar and yet so different, suggesting that the answer lay in the unique alchemy of sex.... And I end with one of the strangest of the consequences of sex: that the choosiness of human beings in picking their mates has driven the human mind into a history of frenzied expansion for no other reason except that wit, virtuosity, inventiveness and individuality turn other people on. It is a somewhat less uplifting perspective on the purpose of humanity than the religious one, but it is also rather liberating. Be different.

---

logical urges than cultural conditioning. Women in the study were not necessarily turning down sex. "What this study doesn't consider is that it's simply very dangerous for women to go off with men they don't know," says Small. "I don't think it has to do with not wanting casual sex, but with fear of physical danger" and of social ostracism. Buss brushes aside such notions, claiming his own studies were fully controlled for the fear factor. "We controlled for everything," he says. "You still get the same conclusions."

Despite disagreements, researchers such as Small are bringing original insights to the field of human behavior. Take the matter of war. Earlier theories of aggression held that men waged war for scarce resources like food and land. But Leda Cosmides, a biologist at the University of California at Santa Barbara, and anthropologist Napoleon Chagnon both note that men vie for resources to win women and provide for their offspring. In Chagnon's words, "Why bother to fight for mangango nuts when the only point of having mangango nuts is so that you can have women? Why not fight over women?"

Equally novel is the notion that women, consciously or not, can control their retention of male sperm. Researchers now claim that women retain more sperm when they have orgasms — thus providing a biological incentive for men to be skillful lovers.

In addition, women who have extramarital affairs tend to do so precisely when they're most fertile. The result: Women who fool around are more than twice as likely to be impregnated by their lovers than by their husbands. "That's why male sexual jealousy is so powerful," notes Buss.

Research into sexual behavior naturally includes research on sexual orientation. What intrigues evolutionary scientists is the question of why homosexuality exists and how it has survived natural selection. Increasingly, these scientists are beginning to view human sexual orientation as "fluid," not strictly an "either-or" choice between heterosexuality or homosexuality. In this view, homosexuality is not an isolated evolutionary aberration but part of a continuum of sexual behavior. Says Cornell's Small, "If homosexuality is a variant of the human sexual continuum, then we need not search for a 'why' answer for its appearance.... It doesn't make sense to me to target homosexuality as if it were a disease and then search for a cause."

Anthropologists point to practices in certain cultures as evidence of such a continuum. Small documents a number of these: the American Indian "berdaches," or men who dress as women and are regarded as spiritually gifted, and the Indian "hijras," a group that includes eunuchs, transvestites and

homosexuals. Small also describes tribal rites in parts of Australia and New Guinea where boys take part in obligatory homosexual acts with men, and sometimes with younger boys, as part of their passage into manhood.

Still, many of the commonsense notions that evolution has given us about male and female sexual behavior continue to withstand the test of time—and new science. Buss notes, for instance, that men still seek mates among attractive young women and women still look for powerful, resourceful men. Yet there are twists to even this conventional wisdom. For Ridley, these forces of attraction stem from our earliest hunter-gatherer days. The male's voice, says Ridley, tells him: "Strive to acquire power and use it to lure women who will bear heirs. . . . Women are means to genetic eternity." The female's voice tells her: "Strive to acquire a provider husband who will invest food and care in your children; strive to find a lover who can give those children first-class genes."

According to Brian Gladue, an evolutionary psychologist at the University of Cincinnati: "When you ask, 'why are we the way we are?' the answer is simply — because it works. The ones who know how to eat, fight, have sex and cooperate are the ones who survive — the ones whose offspring, if they inherit those traits, survive. And in evolution, survival of the offspring is the currency, the profit, the bottom line."

Choosing Mates—The American Way

Martin King Whyte

Martin King Whyte is professor of sociology and faculty associate in the Center for Chinese Studies at the University of Michigan. He has published numerous works on family sociology and contemporary Chinese social organization. His is currently involved in a comparative study of mate choice and marital relations in China and the United States. His latest book is Dating, Mating, and Marriage.

As America's divorce rate has been soaring, popular anxieties about marriage have multiplied. Is it still possible to "live happily ever after," and if so, how can this be accomplished? How can you tell whether a partner who leaves you breathless with yearning will, as your spouse, drive you to distraction? Does "living together" prior to marriage provide a realistic assessment of how compatible you and your partner might be as husband and wife? Questions such as these suggest a need to examine our American way of mate choice. How do we go about selecting the person we marry, and is there something wrong with the entire process?

For most twentieth-century Americans choosing a mate is the culmination of a process of dating. Examination of how we go about selecting mates thus requires us to consider the American dating culture. Dating is a curious institution. By definition it is an activity that is supposed to be separate from selecting a spouse. Yet, dating is expected to provide valuable experience that will help in making a "wise" choice of a marital partner. Does this combination work?

How well dating "works" may be considered in a number of senses of this term. Is it easy or difficult to find somebody to go out with? Do dates mostly lead to enjoyable or painful evenings? However, these are not the aspects of dating I wish to consider. The issue here is whether dating works in the sense of providing useful experience that helps pave the way for a successful marriage.

Dating is a relatively new institution. The term, and the various practices associated with it, first emerged around the turn of the century. By the 1920s dating had more or less completely displaced earlier patterns of relations among unmarried Americans. Contrary to popular assumptions, even in colonial times marriages were not arranged in America. Parents were expected to give their approval to their children's nuptial plans, a practice captured in our image of a suitor asking his beloved's father for her hand in marriage. Parental approval, especially among merchants and other prosperous classes, put some constraint on the marriages of the young. For example, through the eighteenth century, children in such families tended to marry in birth order and marriage to cousins was not uncommon. (Both practices had declined sharply by the nineteenth century.) However, parents rarely directly arranged the marriages of their children. America has always exhibited "youth-driven" patterns of courtship. Eligible males and females took the initiative to get to know each other, and the decision to marry was made by them, even if that decision was to some degree contingent on parental approval. (Of course, substantial proportions of later immigrant groups from Southern and Eastern Europe, Asia, and elsewhere brought with them arranged marriage traditions, and contention for control over marriage decisions was often a great source of tension in such families.)

How did young people get to know one another well enough to decide to marry in the era before dating? A set of customs, dominant for the two centuries, preceded the rise of the dating culture. These activities came to be referred to as "calling" and "keeping company." Young people might meet in a variety of ways—through community and church socials, informally in shops or on the street, on boat and train trips, or through introductions from friends or relatives. (America never developed a system of chaperoning young women in public, and foreign observers often commented on the freedom unmarried women had to travel and mix so-

From *Society*, March/April 1992, pp. 71-77.

cially on their own.) Usually young people would go to church fairs, local dances, and other such activities with family, siblings, or friends, rather than paired off with a partner. Most activities would involve a substantial degree of adult and community supervision. Nonetheless, these gatherings did encourage some pairing off and led to hand holding, moonlit walks home, and other romantic exploration.

By late nineteenth century, a formal pattern of "calling" developed among the upper and middle classes.

As relationships developed beyond the platonic level, the suitor would pay visits to the home of the young woman. By the latter part of the nineteenth century, particularly among the middle and upper classes, this activity assumed a formal pattern referred to as "calling." Males would be invited to call on the female at her home, and they were expected to do so only if invited. (A bold male could, however, request an invitation to call.) Invitations might be extended by the mother of a very young woman, but eventually they would come from the young woman herself. Often a woman would designate certain days on which she would receive callers. She might have several suitors at one time, and thus a number of men might be paying such calls. A man might be told that the woman was not at home to receive him, and he would then be expected to leave his calling card. If this happened repeatedly, he was expected to get the message that his visits were no longer welcome.

Initiative and control in regard to calling were in the hands of women (the eligible female and her mother). Although some variety in suitors was possible, even in initial stages the role of calling in examining potential marriage partners was very clear to all involved. The relatively constrained and supervised nature of calling make it certain that enjoyment cannot have been a primary goal of this activity. (During the initial visits the mother was expected to remain present; in later visits she often hovered in an adjacent room.) If dating is defined as recreational and romantic pairing off between a man and a woman, away from parental supervision and without immediate consideration of marriage, then calling was definitely not dating.

The supervised and controlled nature of calling should not, however, lead us to suppose that propriety and chastity were always maintained until marriage. If the relationship had deepened sufficiently, the couple might progress from calling to "keeping company," a

precursor of the twentieth-century custom of "going steady." At this stage, the primary activity would still consist of visits by the suitor to the woman's home. However, now she would only welcome calls from one man, and he would visit her home on a regular basis. Visits late into the evening would increasingly replace afternoon calls. As the relationship became more serious, parents would often leave the couple alone. Nineteenth-century accounts mention parents going off to bed and leaving the young couple on the couch or by the fireplace, there to wrestle with, and not infrequently give in to, sexual temptation.

Even though some women who headed to the altar toward the end of the nineteenth century had lost their virginity prior to marriage, premarital intimacy was less common than during the dating era. (The double standard of the Victorian era made it possible for many more grooms to be non-virgins at marriage than brides. Perhaps 50 percent or more of men had lost their virginity prior to marriage, as opposed to 15 to 20 percent of women, with prostitutes and "fallen women" helping to explain the differential.) What is less often realized is that the formalization of the calling pattern toward the end of the nineteenth century contributed to a decline in premarital sexual intimacy compared to earlier times. America experienced not one but two sexual revolutions—one toward the end of the eighteenth century, at the time of the American Revolution, and the other in the latter part of the twentieth century.

The causes of the first sexual revolution are subject to some debate. An influx of settlers to America who did not share the evangelical puritanism of many early colonists, the expansion of the population into the unsettled (and "unchurched") frontier, the growth of towns, and the individualistic and freedom-loving spirit of the American revolution may have contributed to a retreat from the fairly strict emphasis on premarital chastity of the early colonial period. Historians debate the extent to which the archetypal custom of this first sexual revolution, bundling, (which allowed an unmarried couple to sleep together, although theoretically fully clothed and separated by a "bundling board") was widespread or largely mythical. Whatever the case, other evidence is found in studies of communities, such as those by Daniel Scott Smith and Michael Hindus, which found that the percentage of married couples whose first births were conceived premaritally increased from about 11 percent before 1700 to over 33 percent in the last decades of the eighteenth century.

This first sexual revolution was reversed in the nineteenth century. The reasons for its demise are also not clear. The closing of the frontier, the rise of the middle class, the defensive reactions of that new middle class to new waves of immigrants, the growth of Christian revivalism and reform movements, and the spread of models of propriety from Victorian England (which were in turn influenced by fear of the chaos of the French Revolution)—all these have been suggested as having contributed to a new sexual puritanism in the nineteenth century. According to Smith and Hindus, premarital conceptions decreased once again to about 15 percent of first births between 1841 and 1880.

It was in the latter time period that the customs of calling and keeping company reached their most formal elaboration—calling, in less ritualized forms, can be traced back to the earliest colonial period. Not long after reaching the formal patterns described, calling largely disappeared. In little more than a generation, dating replaced calling as the dominant custom.

Dating involved pairing off of couples in activities not supervised by parents, with pleasure rather than marriage as the primary goal. The rules governing dating were defined by peers rather than by adults. The initiative, and much of the control, shifted from the female to the male. The man asked the woman out, rather than waiting for her invitation to call. The finances and transportation for the date were also his responsibility. The woman was expected to provide, in turn, the pleasure of her company and perhaps some degree of romantic and physical intimacy. By giving or withholding her affection and access to her body, she exercised considerable control over the man and the date as an event. Nonetheless, the absence of parental oversight and the pressure to respond to a man's initiatives placed a woman in a weaker position than she was in the era of calling.

The man might pick up the woman at her home, but parents who tried to dictate whom their daughters dated and what they did on dates generally found such efforts rejected and evaded. Parents of a son might not even know where junior was going or whom he was dating. Dates were conducted mostly in the public arena, and in some cases—such as at sporting events or school dances—adults might be present. But dates often involved activities and venues where no adults were present or where young people predominated—as at private parties or at local dance halls. Or in other cases the presence of adults would have little inhibiting effect, as in the darkened balconies of movie theaters. American youths also developed substantial ingenuity in finding secluded "lovers' lanes" where they could escape the supervision of even peers. (Localities varied in the places used for this purpose and how they were referred to. In locales near bodies of water young people spoke of "watching submarine races;" in the

rural area of upstate New York where I grew up the phrase was "exploring tractor roads.") Community dances and gatherings for all generations and ages practically disappeared in the dating era.

Greater privacy and autonomy of youths promoted romantic and physical experimentation. Not only kissing but petting was increasingly accepted and widespread. Going beyond petting to sexual intercourse, however, involved substantial risks, especially for the female. This was not simply the risk of pregnancy in the pre-pill era. Dating perpetuated the sexual double standard. Men were expected to be the sexual aggressors and to try to achieve as much intimacy as their dates would allow. But women who "went too far" risked harming their reputations and their ability to keep desirable men interested in them for long. Women were expected to set the limits, and they had to walk a careful line between being too unfriendly (and not having males wanting to date them at all) and being too friendly (and being dated for the "wrong reasons").

Rules governing dating were defined by peers rather than adults.

During the initial decades of the dating era, premarital intimacy increased in comparison with the age of calling, but still a majority of women entered marriage as virgins. In a survey in the greater Detroit metropolitan area, I found that of the oldest women interviewed (those who dated and married prior to 1945), about one in four had lost her virginity prior to marriage. (By the 1980s, according to my survey, the figure was closer to 90 percent.) Escape from parental supervision provided by dating weakened, but did not immediately destroy, the restraints on premarital intimacy.

When Americans began dating, they were primarily concerned with enjoyment, rather than with choosing a spouse. Indeed, "playing the field" was the ideal pursued by many. Dates were not suitors or prospects. Seeing different people on successive nights in a hectic round of dating activity earned one popularity among peers. One of the early students and critics of the dating culture, Willard Waller, coined the term "rating and dating complex" to refer to this pattern. After observing dating among students at Pennsylvania State University in the 1930s, Waller charged that concern for impressing friends and gaining status on campus led to superficial thrill-seeking and competition for popularity, and eliminated genuine romance or sincere communication. However, Waller has been accused of both stereotyping and exaggerating the influence of this pattern. Dating was not always so exploitative and superficial as he charged.

Dating was never viewed as an endless stage or an alternative to courtship. Even if dates were initially seen as quite separate from mate selection, they were always viewed as only the first step in a progression that would lead to marriage. By the 1930s, the stage of "going steady" was clearly recognized, entailing a commitment by both partners to date each other exclusively, if only for the moment. A variety of ritual markers emerged to symbolize the increased commitment of this stage and of further steps toward engagement and marriage, such as wearing the partner's high school ring, being lavaliered, and getting pinned.

Growing affluence fueled new industries designed to entertain and fill leisure time.

Going steady was a way-station between casual dating and engagement. Steadies pledged not to date others, and they were likely to become more deeply involved romantically and physically than casual daters. They were not expected explicitly to contemplate marriage, and the majority of women in our Detroit survey had several steady boyfriends before the relationships that led to their marriages. If a couple was of a "suitable age," though, and if the steady relationship lasted more than a few months, the likelihood increased of explicit talk about marriage. Couples would then symbolize their escalated commitment by getting engaged. Dating arose first among middle and upper middle class students in urban areas, and roughly simultaneously at the college and high school levels. The practice then spread to other groups—rural young people, working class youths, to the upper class, and to employed young people. But what triggered the rapid demise of calling and the rise of dating?

One important trend was prolonged school attendance, particularly in public, co-educational high schools and colleges. Schools provided an arena in which females and males could get to know one another informally over many years. Schools also organized athletic, social, and other activities in which adult supervision was minimal. College campuses generally allowed a more total escape from parental supervision than high schools.

Another important influence was growing affluence in America. More and more young people were freed from a need to contribute to the family economy and had more leisure time in which to date. Fewer young people worked under parental supervision, and more

and more fathers worked far from home, leaving mothers as the primary monitors of their children's daily activities. These trends also coincided with a rise in part-time and after-school employment for students, employment that provided pocket money that did not have to be turned over to parents and could be spent on clothing, makeup, movie tickets, and other requirements of the dating culture. Rising affluence also fueled the growth of entire new industries designed to entertain and fill leisure time—movies, popular music recording, ice cream parlors, amusement parks, and so on. Increasingly, young people who wanted to escape from supervision of their parents found a range of venues, many of them catering primarily to youth and to dating activities.

Technology also played a role, and some analysts suggest that one particular invention, the automobile, deserves a lion's share of the credit. Automobiles were not only a means to escape the home and reach a wider range of recreation spots. They also provided a semi-private space with abundant romantic and sexual possibilities. New institutions, such as the drive-in movie theater, arose to take advantage of those possibilities. As decades passed and affluence increased, the borrowed family car was more and more replaced by cars owned by young people, advancing youth autonomy still further.

All this was part of a larger trend: the transformation of America into a mass consumption society. As this happened, people shifted their attention partially from thinking about how to work and earn to pondering how to spend and consume. Marketplace thinking became more and more influential. The image of the individual as *homo economicus* and of modern life typified by the rational application of scientific knowledge to all decisions became pervasive. The new ideological framework undermined previous customs and moral standards and extended to the dating culture.

Dating had several goals. Most obviously and explicitly, dates were expected to lead to pleasure and possibly to romance. It was also important, as Waller and others have observed, in competition for popularity. But a central purpose of dating was to gain valuable learning experience that would be useful later in selecting a spouse. Through dating young people would learn how to relate to the opposite sex. Dating would increase awareness of one's own feelings and understanding of which type of partner was appealing and which not. Through crushes and disappointments, one would learn to judge the character of people. And by dating a variety of partners and by increasingly intimate involvement with some of them, one would learn what sort of person one would be happy with as a marital partner. When it came time to marry one would be in a good position to select "Mr. Right" or "Miss Right." Calling, which limited the possibilities of romantic experimentation, often to only one partner, did not provide an adequate basis for such an informed choice.

What emerged was a "marketplace learning viewpoint." Selecting a spouse is not quite the same as buying a car or breakfast cereal, but the process was seen as analogous. The assumptions involved in shopping around and test driving various cars or buying and tasting Wheaties, Cheerios, and Fruit Loops were transferred to popular thinking about how to select a spouse.

According to this marketplace learning viewpoint, getting married very young and without having acquired much dating experience was risky, in terms of marital happiness. Similarly, marrying your first and only sweetheart was not a good idea. Neither was meeting someone, falling head over heels in love, and marrying, all within the course of a month. While Americans recognized that in some cases such beginnings could lead to good marriages, the rationale of our dating culture was that having had a variety of dating partners and then getting to know one or more serious prospects over a longer period time and on fairly intimate terms were experiences more likely to lead to marital success.

Eventually, this marketplace psychology helped to undermine America's premarital puritanism, and with it the sexual double standard. The way was paved for acceptance of new customs, and particularly for premarital cohabitation. Parents and other moral guardians found it increasingly difficult to argue against the premise that, if sexual enjoyment and compatibility were central to marital happiness, it was important to test that compatibility before marrying. Similarly, if marriage involved not just hearts and flowers, but also dirty laundry and keeping a budget, did it not make sense for a couple to live together prior to marriage to see how they got along on a day-to-day basis? Such arguments on behalf of premarital sex and cohabitation have swept into popular consciousness in the United States, and it is obvious that they are logical corollaries of the marketplace learning viewpoint.

Our dating culture thus is based upon the premise that dating provides valuable experience that will help individuals select mates and achieve happy marriages. But is this premise correct? Does dating really work? What evidence shows that individuals with longer dating experience, dates with more partners, or longer and more intimate acquaintances with the individuals they intend to marry end up with happier marriages?

Surprisingly, social scientists have never systematially addressed this question. Perhaps this is one of those cherished beliefs people would prefer not to examine too closely. When I could find little evidence on the connection between dating and other premarital experiences and marital success in previous studies, I decided to conduct my own inquiry.

Dating was to give valuable experience to help in future mate selection.

My desire to know whether dating experiences affected marriages was the basis for my 1984 survey in the Detroit area. A representative sample of 459 women was interviewed in three counties in the Detroit metropolitan area (a diverse, multi-racial and multi-ethnic area of city and suburbs containing about 4 million people in 1980). The women ranged in ages from 18 to 75, and all had been married at least once. (I was unable to interview their husbands, so unfortunately marriages in this study are viewed only through the eyes of women.) The interviewees had first married over a sixty year span of time, between 1925 and 1984. They were asked to recall a variety of things about their dating and premarital experiences. They were also asked a range of questions about their marital histories and (if currently married) about the positive and negative features of their relations with their husbands. The questionnaire enabled us to test whether premarital experiences of various types were related to marital success, a concept which in turn was measured in several different ways. (Measures of divorce and of both positive and negative qualities in intact marriages were used.)

The conclusions were a surprise. It appears that dating does not work and that the "marketplace learning viewpoint" is misguided. Marrying very young tended to produce unsuccessful marriages. Premarital pregnancy was associated with problems in marriage. However, once the age of marriage is taken into account, none of the other measures—dating variety, length of dating, length of courtship or engagement, or degree of premarital intimacy with the future husband or others—was clearly related to measures of marital success. A few weak tendencies in the results were contrary to predictions drawn from the marketplace learning viewpoint. Women who had dated more partners or who had engaged in premarital sex or cohabited were slightly less likely to have successful marriages. This might be seen as evidence of quite a different logic.

Perhaps there is a "grass is greener" effect. Women who have been led less sheltered and conventional lives prior to marriage may not be as easily satisfied afterward. Several other researchers have found a similar pattern with regard to premarital cohabitation. Individuals who had been living together prior to marriage were significantly less likely to have successful marriages than those who did not.

Individuals who had been living together were less likely to have successful marriages.

In the Detroit survey, these "grass is greener" patterns were not consistent or statistically significant. It was not that women with more dating experience and greater premarital intimacy had less successful marriages; rather, the amount and type of dating experience did not make a clear difference one way or the other.

Women who had married their first sweethearts were just as likely to have enduring and satisfying marriages as women who had married only after considering many alternatives. Similarly, women who had married after only a brief acquaintance were no more (nor less) likely to have a successful marriage than those who knew their husbands-to-be for years. And there was no clear difference between the marriages of women who were virgins at marriage and those who had had a variety of sexual partners and who had lived together with their husbands before the wedding.

Dating obviously does not provide useful learning that promotes marital success. Although our dating culture is based upon an analogy with consumer purchases in the marketplace, it is clear that in real life selecting a spouse is quite different from buying a car or a breakfast cereal. You cannot actively consider several prospects at the same time without getting your neck broken and being deserted by all of them. Even if you find Ms. Right or Mr. Right, you may be told to drop dead. By the time you are ready to marry, this special someone you were involved with earlier may no longer be available, and you may not see anyone on the horizon who comes close to being as desirable. In addition, someone who is well suited at marriage may grow apart from you or find someone else to be with later. Dating experience might facilitate marital success if deciding whom to marry was like deciding what to eat for breakfast (although even in the latter regard tastes change, and toast and black coffee may replace bacon and eggs). But these realms are quite different,

and mate selection looks more like a crap-shoot than a rational choice.

Is there a better way? Traditionalists in some societies would argue that arranged marriages are preferable. However, in addition to the improbability that America's young people will leave this decision to their parents, there is the problem of evidence. The few studies of this topic, including one I have been collaborating on in China, indicate that women who had arranged marriages were less satisfied than women who made the choice themselves. So having Mom and Dad take charge is not the answer. Turning the matter over to computerized matchmaking also does not seem advisable. Despite the growing sophistication of computers, real intelligence seems preferable to artificial intelligence. As the Tin Woodman in *The Wizard of Oz* discovered, to have a brain but no heart is to be missing something important.

Perhaps dating is evolving into new patterns in which premarital experience will contribute to marital success. Critics from Waller onward have claimed that dating promotes artificiality, rather than realistic assessment of compatibility. Some observers suggest that the sort of superficial dating Waller and others wrote about has become less common of late. Dating certainly has changed significantly since the pre-Second World War era. Many of the rigid rules of dating have broken down. The male no longer always takes the initiative; neither does he always pay. The sexual double standard has also weakened substantially, so that increasingly Americans feel that whatever a man can do a woman should be able to do. Some writers even suggest that dating is going out of style, replaced by informal pairing off in larger groups, often without the prearrangement of "asking someone out." Certainly the terminology is changing, with "seeing" and "being with" increasingly preferred to "dating" and "going steady." To many young people the latter terms have the old fashioned ring that "courting" and "suitor" had when I was young.

My daughter and other young adults argue that current styles are more natural and healthier than the dating experienced by my generation and the generation of my parents. Implicit in this argument is the view that, with formal rules and the "rating and dating" complex in decline, it should be possible to use dating (or whatever you call it) to realistically assess compatibility and romantic chemistry. These arguments may seem plausible, but I see no evidence that bears them out. The youngest women we interviewed in the Detroit survey should have experienced these more informal styles of romantic exploration. However, for them dating and premarital intimacy were, if anything, less closely related to marital success than was the case for the older women. The changes in premarital relations do not seem to make experience a better teacher.

While these conclusions are for the most part quite negative, my study leads to two more positive observations. First, marital success is not totally unpredictable. A wide range of features of how couples structure their day-to-day marital relations promote success— sharing in power and decision-making, pooling incomes, enjoying similar leisure time activities, having similar values, having mutual friends and an active social life, and other related qualities. Couples are not "doomed" by their past histories, including their dating histories, and they can increase their mutual happiness through the way they structure their marriages.

Second, there is something else about premarital experience besides dating history that may promote marital success. We have in America not one, but two widely shared, but quite contradictory, theories about how individuals should select a spouse: one based on the marketplace learning viewpoint and another based on love. One viewpoint sees selecting a spouse as a rational process, perhaps even with lists of criteria by which various prospects can be judged. The other, as song writers tell us, is based on the view that love conquers all and that "all you need is love." Love is a matter of the heart (perhaps with some help from the hormonal system) and not the head, and love may blossom unpredictably, on short notice or more gradually. Might it not be the case, then, that those couples who are most deeply in love at the time of their weddings will have the most successful marriages? We have centuries of poetry and novels, as well as love songs, that tell us that this is the case.

In the Detroit study, we did, in fact, ask women how much they had been in love when they first married. And we did find that those who recalled being "head over heels in love" then, had more successful mar-

riages. However, there is a major problem with this finding. Since we were asking our interviewees to recall their feelings prior to their weddings—in many cases weddings that took place years or even decades earlier—it is quite possible and even likely that their answers are biased. Perhaps whether or not their marriage worked out influenced these "love reports" from earlier times, rather than having the level of romantic love then explain marital success later. Without either a time machine or funds to interview couples prior to marriage and then follow them up years later, it is impossible to be sure that more intense feelings of love lead to more successful marriages. Still, the evidence available does not question the wisdom of poets and songwriters when it comes to love. Mate selection may not be a total crap-shoot after all, and even if dating does not work, love perhaps does.

READINGS SUGGESTED BY THE AUTHOR:

Bailey, Beth. *From Front Porch to Back Seat.* Baltimore: Johns Hopkins University Press, 1988.

Burgess, Ernest W. and Paul Wallin. *Engagement and Marriage.* Chicago: Lippincott, 1953.

Modell, John. "Dating Becomes the Way of American Youth," in *Essays on the Family and Historical Change,* Leslie P. Moch and Gary Stark (eds.). College Station, Tex.: Texas A&M University Press, 1983.

Rothman, Ellen K. *Hands and Hearts: A History of Courtship.* New York: Basic Books, 1984.

Smith, Daniel S. and Michael Hindus. "Premarital Pregnancy in America, 1640-1971: An Overview and Interpretation," *Journal of Interdisciplinary History,* 4 (1975), 537-570.

Waller, Willard, "Rating and Dating Complex," *American Sociological Review,* (1937), 2:737-739.

Whyte, Martin King. *Dating, Mating, and Marriage.* New York: Aldine de Gruyter, 1990.

THE
Mating
GAME

The sophisticated sexual strategies of modern men and women are shaped by a powerful Stone Age psychology.

It's a dance as old as the human race. At cocktail lounges and church socials, during office coffee breaks and dinner parties—and most blatantly, perhaps, in the personal ads in newspapers and magazines—men and women perform the elaborate ritual of advertisement and assessment that precedes an essential part of nearly every life: mating. More than 90 percent of the world's people marry at some point in their lives, and it is estimated that a similarly large number of people engage in affairs, liaisons, flings or one-night stands. The who, what, when and where of love, sex and romance are a cultural obsession that is reflected in everything from Shakespeare to soap operas and from Tristram and Isolde to 2 Live Crew, fueling archetypes like the coy ingénue, the rakish cad, the trophy bride, Mrs. Robinson, Casanova and lovers both star-crossed and blessed.

It all may seem very modern, but a new group of researchers argues that love, American style, is in fact part of a universal human behavior with roots stretching back to the dawn of humankind. These scientists contend that, in stark contrast to the old image of brute cavemen dragging their mates by the hair to their dens, our ancient ancestors—men and women alike—engaged in a sophisticated mating dance of sexual intrigue, shrewd strategizing and savvy negotiating that has left its stamp on human psychology. People may live in a thoroughly modern world, these researchers say, but within the human skull is a Stone Age mind that was shaped by the mating concerns of our ancient ancestors and continues to have a profound influence on behavior today. Indeed, this ancient psychological legacy

HOW WE CHOOSE

Women are more concerned about whether mates will invest time and resources in a relationship; men care more about a woman's physical attractiveness, which in ancient times reflected her fertility and health.

influences everything from sexual attraction to infidelity and jealousy—and, as remarkable new research reveals, even extends its reach all the way down to the microscopic level of egg and sperm.

These new researchers call themselves evolutionary psychologists. In a host of recent scientific papers and at a major conference last month at the London School of Economics, they are arguing that the key to understanding modern sexual behavior lies not solely in culture, as some anthropologists contend, nor purely in the genes, as some sociobiologists believe. Rather, they argue, understanding human nature is possible only if scientists begin to understand the evolution of the human mind. Just as humans have evolved

specialized biological organs to deal with the intricacies of sex, they say, the mind, too, has evolved customized mental mechanisms for coping with this most fundamental aspect of human existence.

Gender and mind. When it comes to sexuality and mating, evolutionary psychologists say, men and women often are as different psychologically as they are physically. Scientists have long known that people typically choose mates who closely resemble themselves in terms of weight, height, intelligence and even earlobe length. But a survey of more than 10,000 people in 37 cultures on six continents, conducted by University of Michigan psychologist David Buss, reveals that men consistently value physical attractiveness and youth in a mate more than women do; women, equally as consistently, are more concerned than men with a prospective mate's ambition, status and resources. If such preferences were merely arbitrary products of culture, says Buss, one might expect to find at least one society somewhere where men's and women's mating preferences were reversed; the fact that attitudes are uniform across cultures suggests they are a fundamental part of human psychology.

Evolutionary psychologists think many of these mating preferences evolved in response to the different biological challenges faced by men and women in producing children—the definition of success in evolutionary terms. In a seminal paper, evolutionary biologist Robert Trivers of the University of California at Santa Cruz points out that in most mammals, females invest far more time and energy in reproduction and child rearing than do males. Not only must females go through a long gestation and weaning of their offspring, but childbirth itself is relatively dangerous. Males, on the other hand, potentially can get away with a very small biological investment in a child.

Human infants require the greatest amount of care and nurturing of any animal on Earth, and so over the eons women have evolved a psychology that is particularly concerned with a father's ability to help out with this enormous task—with his clout, protection and access to resources. So powerful is this psychological legacy that nowadays women size up a man's finances even when, as a practical matter, they may not have to. A recent study of the mating preferences of a group of medical students, for instance, found that these women, though anticipating financial success, were nevertheless most interested in men whose earning capacity was equal to or greater than their own.

Healthy genes. For men, on the other hand, reproductive success is ultimately dependent on the fertility of their mates. Thus males have evolved a mind-set that homes in on signs of a woman's health and youth, signs that, in the absence of medical records and birth certificates long ago, were primarily visual. Modern man's sense of feminine beauty—clear skin, bright eyes and youthful appearance—is, in effect, the legacy of eons spent diagnosing the health and fertility of potential mates.

This concern with women's reproductive health also helps explain why men value curvaceous figures. An upcoming paper by Devendra Singh of the University of Texas at Austin reveals that people consistently judge a woman's figure not by whether she is slim or fat but by the ratio of waist to hips. The ideal proportion—the hips roughly a third larger than the waist—reflects a hormonal balance that results in women's preferentially storing fat on their hips as opposed to their waists, a condition that correlates with higher fertility and resistance to disease. Western society's modern-day obsession with being slim has not changed this equation. Singh found, for instance, that while the winning Miss America has become 30 percent thinner over the past several decades, her waist-to-hip ratio has remained close to this ancient ideal.

Women also appreciate a fair face and figure, of course. And what they look for in a male's physique can also be explained as an evolved mentality that links good looks with good genes. A number of studies have shown that both men and women rate as most attractive

More than 90 percent of all people marry and, they typically choose mates who closely resemble themselves, from weight and height, to intelligence and values, to nose breadth and even earlobe length.

faces that are near the average; this is true in societies as diverse as those of Brazil, Russia and several hunting and gathering tribes. The average face tends to be more symmetrical, and, according to psychologist Steven Gangestad and biologist Randy Thornhill, both of the University of New Mexico, this symmetry may reflect a person's genetic resistance to disease.

People have two versions of each of their genes—one from each parent—within every cell. Sometimes the copies are slightly different, though typically each version works just as effectively. The advantage to having two slightly different copies of the same gene, the researchers argue, is that it is harder for a disease to knock out the function of both copies, and this biological redundancy is reflected in the symmetry in people's bodies, including their faces. Further evidence for a psychological mechanism that links attractiveness with health comes from Buss's worldwide study of mating preferences: In those parts of the world where the incidence of parasites and infectious diseases is highest, both men and women place a greater value on attractive mates.

Some feminists reject the notion that women should alter physical appearance to gain advantage in the mating game. But archaeological finds suggest that the "beauty myth" has been very much a part of the human mating psychology since the times of our ancient ancestors—and that it applies equally to men. Some of the very first signs of human artistry are carved body ornaments that date back more than 30,000 years, and findings of worn nubs of ochre suggest that ancient humans may have used the red and black chalklike

substance as makeup. These artifacts probably served as social signs that, like lipstick or a Rolex watch today, advertised a person's physical appearance and status. In one grave dating back some 20,000 years, a male skeleton was found bedecked with a tunic made from thousands of tiny ivory beads—the Stone Age equivalent of an Armani suit.

Far from being immutable, biological mandates, these evolved mating mechanisms in the mind are flexible, culturally influenced aspects of human psychology that are similar to people's tastes for certain kinds of food. The human sweet tooth is a legacy from a time when the only sweet things in the environment were nutritious ripe fruit and honey, says Buss, whose book "The Evolution of Desire" is due out next year. Today, this ancient taste for sweets is susceptible to modern-day temptation by candy bars and such, though people have the free will to refrain from indulging it. Likewise, the mind's mating mechanisms can be strongly swayed by cultural influences such as religious and moral beliefs.

Playing the field. Both men and women display different mating psychologies when they are just playing around as opposed to searching for a lifelong partner, and these mental mechanisms are also a legacy from ancient times. A new survey by Buss and his colleague David Schmitt found that when women are looking for "short term" mates, their preference for attractive men increases substantially. In a study released last month, Doug Kenrick and Gary Groth of Arizona State University found that while men, too, desire attractive mates when they're playing the field, they will actually settle for a lot less.

Men's diminished concern about beauty in short-term mates reflects the fact that throughout human evolution, men have often pursued a dual mating strategy. The most successful strategy for most men was to find a healthy, fertile, long-term mate. But it also didn't hurt to take advantage of any low-risk opportunity to sire as many kin as possible outside the relationship, just to hedge the evolutionary bet. The result is an evolved psychology that allows a man to be sexually excited by a wide variety of women even while committed to a partner. This predilection shows up in studies of men's and women's sexual fantasies today. A study by Don Symons of the University of California at Santa Barbara and Bruce Ellis of the University of Michigan found that while both men and women actively engage in sexual fantasy, men typically have more fantasies about anonymous partners.

Surveys in the United States show

that at least 30 percent of married women have extramarital affairs, suggesting that, like men, women also harbor a drive for short-term mating. But they have different evolutionary reasons for doing so. Throughout human existence, short-term flings have offered women an opportunity to exchange sex for resources. In Buss and Schmitt's study, women value an "extravagant lifestyle" three times more highly when they are searching for a brief affair than when they are seeking a long-term mate. Women who are secure in a relationship with a committed male might still seek out attractive men to secure healthier genes for their offspring. Outside affairs also allow women to shop for better partners.

Sperm warfare. A woman may engage the sexual interest of several men simultaneously in order to foster a microscopic battle known as sperm competition. Sperm can survive in a woman's reproductive tract for nearly a week, note biologists Robin Baker and Mark Bellis of the University of Manchester, and by mating with more than one man within a short period of time, a woman sets the stage for their sperm to com-

─────── JEALOUS PSYCHE ───────

Men are most disturbed by sexual infidelity in their mates, a result of uncertainty about paternity. Women are more disturbed by emotional infidelity, because they risk losing their mate's time and resources.

pete to sire a child—passing this winning trait on to her male offspring as well. In a confidential survey tracking the sexual behavior and menstrual cycles of more than 2,000 women who

said they had steady mates, Baker and Bellis found that while there was no pattern to when women had sex with their steady partners, having sex on the side peaked at the height of the women's monthly fertility cycles.

Since in ancient times a man paid a dear evolutionary price for being cuckolded, the male psychology produces a physiological counterstrategy for dealing with a woman's infidelity. Studying the sexual behavior of a group of couples, Baker and Bellis found that the more time a couple spend apart, the more sperm the man ejaculates upon their sexual reunion—as much as three times higher than average.

This increase in sperm count is unrelated to when the man last ejaculated through nocturnal emission or masturbation, and Baker and Bellis argue that it is a result of a man's evolved psychological mechanism that bolsters his chances in sperm competition in the event that his mate has been unfaithful during their separation. As was no doubt the case in the times of our ancient ancestors, these concerns are not unfounded: Studies of blood typings show that as many as 1 of every 10 babies born to couples in North America is not the offspring of the mother's husband.

Despite men's efforts at sexual subterfuge, women still have the last word on the fate of a man's sperm in her reproductive tract—thanks to the physiological effects of the female orgasm. In a new study, Baker and Bellis reveal that if a woman experiences an orgasm soon after her mate's, the amount of sperm retained in her reproductive tract is far higher than if she has an earlier orgasm or none at all. Apparently a woman's arousal, fueled by her feelings as well as her mate's solicitous attentions, results in an evolutionary payoff for both.

Cads and dads. Whether people pursue committed relationships or one-night stands depends on their perceptions of what kind of mates are in the surrounding sexual environment. Anthropologist Elizabeth Cashdan of the University of Utah surveyed hundreds of men and women on whether they thought the members of their "pool" of potential mates were in general trustworthy, honest and capable of commitment. She also asked them what kinds of tactics they used to attract mates. Cashdan found that the less committed people thought their potential mates would be, the more they themselves pursued short-term mating tactics. For example, if women considered their world to be full of "cads," they tended to dress more provocatively and to be more promiscuous; if they thought that the world was populated

─────── BEAUTY QUEST ───────

the most attractive men and women are in fact those whose faces are most average, a signal that they are near the genetic average of the population and are perhaps more resistant to disease.

by potential "dads"—that is, committed and nurturing men—they tended to emphasize their chastity and fidelity. Similarly, "cads" tended to emphasize their sexuality and "dads" said they relied more on advertising their resources and desire for long-term commitment.

These perceptions of what to expect from the opposite sex may be influenced by the kind of home life an individual knew as a child. Social scientists have long known that children from homes where the father is chronically absent or abusive tend to mature faster physically and to have sexual relations earlier in life. Psychologist Jay Belsky of Pennsylvania State University argues that this behavior is an evolved psychological mechanism, triggered by early childhood experiences, that enables a child to come of age earlier and leave the distressing situation. This psychological mechanism may also lead to a mating strategy that focuses on short-term affairs.

The green monster. Whether in modern or ancient times, infidelities can breed anger and hurt, and new research suggests subtle differences in male and female jealousy with roots in the ancient past. In one study, for example, Buss asked males and females to imagine that their mates were having sex with someone else or that their mates were engaged in a deep emotional commitment with another person. Monitoring his subjects' heart rates, frowning and stress responses, he found that the stereotypical double standard cuts both ways. Men reacted far more strongly than

EVOLVED FANTASIES
Eroticism and gender

For insights into the subtle differences between men's and women's mating psychologies, one need look no further than the local bookstore. On one rack may be magazines featuring scantily clad women in poses of sexual invitation — a testimony to the ancient legacy of a male psychology that is acutely attuned to visual stimulus and easily aroused by the prospect of anonymous sex. Around the corner is likely to be a staple of women's erotic fantasy: romance novels.

Harlequin Enterprises Ltd., the leading publisher in the field, sells more than 200 million books annually and pro-duces about 70 titles a month. Dedicated romance fans may read several books a week. "Our books give women everything," says Harlequin's Kathleen Abels, "a loving relationship, commitment and having sex with someone they care about." Some romance novels contain scenes steamy enough to make a sailor blush, and studies show that women who read romances typically have more sexual fantasies and engage in sexual intercourse more frequently than nonreaders do.

Sexual caricature. Since sexual fantasy frees people of the complications of love and mat-ing in the real world, argue psychologists Bruce Ellis and Don Symons, it is perhaps not surprising that in erotic materials for both men and women, sexual partners are typically caricatures of the consumer's own evolved mating psychology. In male-oriented erotica, for instance, women are depicted as being lust driven, ever willing and unencumbered by the need for emotional attachment. In romance novels, the male lead in the book is typically tender, emotional and consumed by passion for the heroine, thus ensuring his lifelong fidelity and dependence. In other words, say Ellis and Symons, the romance novel is "an erotic, utopian, female counterfantasy" to male erotica.

Of course, most men also enjoy stories of passion and romance, and women can be as easily aroused as men by sexually explicit films. Indeed, several new entertainment ventures, including the magazine *Future Sex* and a video company, Femme Productions, are creating erotic materials using realistic models in more sensual settings in an attempt to appeal to both sexes. Still, the new research into evolutionary psychology suggests that men and women derive subtly different pleasures from sexual fantasy — something that even writing under a ghost name can't hide. According to Abels, a Harlequin romance is occasionally penned by a man using a female pseudonym, but "our avid readers can always tell."

---

women to the idea that their mates were having sex with other men. But women reacted far more strongly to the thought that their mates were developing strong emotional attachments to someone else.

As with our evolved mating preferences, these triggers for jealousy ultimately stem from men's and women's biology, says Buss. A woman, of course, has no doubt that she is the mother of her children. For a man, however, paternity is never more than conjecture, and so men have evolved psychologies with a heightened concern about a mate's sexual infidelity. Since women make the greater biological investment in offspring, their psychologies are more concerned about a mate's reneging on his commitment, and, therefore, they are more attentive to signs that their mates might be attaching themselves emotionally to other women.

Sexual monopoly. The male preoccupation with monopolizing a woman's sexual reproduction has led to the oppression and abuse of women worldwide, including, at its extremes, confinement, domestic violence and ritual mutilation such as clitoridectomy. Yet the new research into the mating game also reveals that throughout human evolution, women have not passively acquiesced to men's sexual wishes. Rath-

DUELING SPERM

*I*f a couple has been apart for some time, the man's sperm count goes up during sex at their reunion — an ancient, evolved strategy against a female's possible infidelities while away.

er, they have long employed a host of behavioral and biological tactics to follow their own sexual agenda — behaviors that have a huge impact on men's behavior as well. As Buss points out, if all women suddenly began preferring to have sex with men who walked on their hands, in a very short time half the human race would be upside down.

With its emphasis on how both men and women are active players in the mating game, evolutionary psychology holds out the promise of helping negotiate a truce of sorts in the battle of the sexes — not by declaring a winner but by pointing out that the essence of the mating game is compromise, not victory. The exhortations of radical feminists, dyed-in-the-wool chauvinists and everyone in between are all spices for a sexual stew that has been on a slow boil for millions of years. It is no accident that consistently, the top two mating preferences in Buss's survey — expressed equally by males and females worldwide — were not great looks, fame, youth, wealth or status, but *kindness* and *intelligence*. In the rough-and-tumble of the human mating game, they are love's greatest allies.

WILLIAM F. ALLMAN

BACK OFF!

We're putting way too many expectations on our closest relationships. It's time to retreat a bit. Consider developing same-sex friendships. Or cultivating a garden. Whatever you do, take a break from the relentless pursuit of intimacy.

Geraldine K. Piorkowski, Ph.D.

You can't miss it. It's the favorite topic of Oprah and all the other talk shows. It's the suds of every soap opera. And I probably don't have to remind you that it's the subject of an extraordinary number of self-help books. Intimate relationships. No matter where we tune or turn, we are bombarded with messages that there is a way to do it right, certainly some way of doing it better—if only we could find it. There are countless books simply on the subject of how to communicate better. Or, if it's not working out, to exit swiftly.

We are overfocused on intimate relationships, and I question whether our current preoccupation with intimacy isn't unnatural, not entirely in keeping with the essential physical and psychological nature of people. The evidence suggests that there is a limit to the amount of closeness people can tolerate and that we need time alone for productivity and creativity. Time alone is necessary to replenish psychological resources and to solidify the boundaries of the self.

All our cultural focus on relationships ultimately has, I believe, a negative impact on us. It causes us to look upon intimate relationships as a solution to all our ills. And that only sets us up for disappointment, contributing to the remarkable 50 percent divorce rate.

Our overfocus on relationships leads us to demand too much of intimacy. We put all our emotional eggs in the one basket of intimate romantic relationships. A romantic partner must be all things to us—lover, friend, companion, playmate, and parent.

We approach intimate relationships with the expectation that this new love will make up for past letdowns in life and love. The expectation that this time around will be better is bound to disappoint, because present-day lovers feel burdened by demands with roots in old relationships.

We expect unconditional love, unfailing nurturance, and protection. There is also the expectation that the new partner will make up for the characteristics we lack in our own personality—for example, that he or she will be an outgoing soul to compensate for our shyness or a goal-oriented person to provide direction in our messy life.

If the personal ads were rewritten to emphasize the emotional expectations we bring to intimacy, they would sound like this. "WANTED: Lively humorous man who could bring joy to my gloomy days and save me from a lifetime of depression." Or, "WANTED: Woman with self-esteem lower than mine. With her, I could feel superior and gain temporary boosts of self-confidence from the comparison."

From my many years as a clinical psychologist, I have come to recognize that intimacy is not an unmitigated good. It is not only difficult to achieve, it is treacherous in some fundamental ways. And it can actually harm people.

The potential for emotional pain and upset is so great in intimate relationships because we are not cloaked in the protective garb of maturity. We are unprotected, exposed, vulnerable to hurt; our defenses are down. We are wide open to pain.

Intuitively recognizing the dangers involved, people normally erect elaborate barriers to shield themselves from closeness. We may act superior, comical, mysterious, or super independent because we fear that intimacy will bring criticism, humiliation, or betrayal—whatever an earlier relationship sensitized us to. We develop expectations based on what has happened in our lives with parents, with friends, with a first love. And we often act in anticipation of these expectations, bringing about the result we most want to avoid.

The closer we get to another person, the greater the risks of intimacy. It's not just that we are more vulnerable and defenseless. We are also more emotionally unstable, childish, and less intelligent than in any other situation. You may be able to run a large company with skill and judgment, but be immature, ultrasensitive, and needy at home. Civilized rules of conduct often get suspended. Intimacy is both unnerving and baffling.

HEALTHY RETREATS

Once our fears are aroused in the context of intimacy, we tend to go about calming them in unproductive ways. We make exces-

 Reprinted with permission from *Psychology Today,* January/February 1995, pp. 50-53. © 1995 by Sussex Publishers, Inc.

sive demands of our partner, for affection, for unconditional regard. The trouble is, when people feel demands are being made of them, they tend to retreat and hide in ways that hurt their partner. They certainly do not listen.

Fears of intimacy typically limit our vulnerability by calling defensive strategies into play. Without a doubt, the defense of choice against the dangers of intimacy is withdrawal. Partners tune out. One may retreat into work. One walks out of the house, slamming the door. Another doesn't call for days. Whatever the way, we spend a great deal of time avoiding intimacy.

After many years of working with all kinds of couples, I have come to believe that human nature dictates that intimate relationships have to be cyclical.

When one partner unilaterally backs off, it tends to be done in a hurtful manner. The other partner feels rejected, uncared about, and unloved. Typically, absolutely nothing gets worked out.

However, avoidance is not necessarily unhealthy. Partners can pursue a time out, where one or both work through their conflict in a solitary way that is ultimately renewing. What usually happens, however, is that when partners avoid each other, they are avoiding open warfare but doing nothing to resolve the underlying conflicts.

Fears of intimacy can actually be pretty healthy, when they're realistic and protective of the self. And they appear even in good relationships. Take the fears of commitment that are apt to surface in couples just before the wedding. If they can get together and talk through their fears, then they will not scare one another or themselves into backing off permanently.

After many years of working with all kinds of couples, I have come to believe that human nature dictates that intimate relationships have to be cyclical. There are limitations to intimacy and I think it is wise to respect the dangers. Periods of closeness have to be balanced with periods of distance. For every two steps forward, we often need to take one step back.

An occasional retreat from intimacy gives individuals time to recharge. It offers time to strengthen your sense of who you are. Think of it as constructive avoidance. We need to take some emphasis off what partners can do for us and put it on what we can do for ourselves and what we can do with other relationships. Developing and strengthening same-sex friendships, even opposite-sex friendships, has its own rewards and aids the couple by reducing the demands and emotional expectations we place on partners.

In our culture, our obsession with romantic love relationships has led us to confuse all emotional bonds with sexual bonds, just as we confuse infatuation with emotional intimacy. As a result, we seem to avoid strong but deeply rewarding emotional attachments with others of our own sex. But having recently lost a dear friend of several decades, I am personally sensitive to the need for emotionally deep, same-sex relationships. They can be shared as a way of strengthening gender identity and enjoying rewarding companionship. We need to put more energy into nonromantic relationships as well as other activities.

One of the best ways of recharging oneself is to take pleasure in learning and spiritual development. And there's a great deal to be said for spending time solving political, educational, or social ills of the world.

Distance and closeness boundaries need to be calibrated and constantly readjusted in every intimate relationship. Such boundaries not only vary with each couple, they change as the relationship progresses. One couple may maintain their emotional connection by spending one evening together a week, while another couple needs daily coming together of some sort. Problems arise in relationships when partners cannot agree on the boundaries. These boundaries must be jointly negotiated or the ongoing conflict will rob the relationship of its vitality.

S.O.S. SIGNALS

When you're feeling agitated or upset that your partner is not spending enough time with you, consider it a signal to step back and sort out internally what is going on. Whether you feel anxiety or anger, the emotional arousal should serve as a cue to back off and think through where the upset is coming from, and to consider whether it is realistic.

That requires at least a modest retreat from a partner. It could be a half hour, or two hours. Or two days—whenever internal clarity comes. In the grip of emotion, it is often difficult to discriminate exactly which emotion it is and what its source is. "What is it I am concerned about? Is this fear realistic considering Patrick's behavior in the present? He's never done this to me before, and he's been demonstrating his trustworthiness all over the place, so what am I afraid of? Is it coming from my early years of neglect with two distant parents who never had time for me? Or from my experiences with Steve, who dumped me two years ago?"

Introspective and self-aware people already spend their time thinking about how they work, their motives, what their feelings mean. Impulsive people will have a harder time with the sorting-out process. The best way to sort things out is to pay attention to the nature of the upset. Exactly what you are upset about suggests what your unmet need is, whether it's for love, understanding, nurturance, protection, or special status. And once you identify the need, you can figure out its antecedents.

The kinds of things we get upset about in intimacy tend to follow certain themes. Basically, we become hurt or resentful because we're getting "too much" or "too little" of something. Too many demands, too much criticism, too much domination. Or the converse, too little affectional, conversational, or sexual attention (which translates into "you don't feel I'm important" or "you don't love me"). Insufficient empathy is usually voiced as "you don't understand me," and too little responsibility translates into failure to take on one's share of household and/or financial tasks. All these complaints require some attention, action, or retreat.

SHIFTING GEARS

It's not enough to identify the source of personal concern. You have to present your concerns in a way your partner can hear. If I say directly to my partner, "I'm afraid you're going to leave me," he has the opportunity to respond, "Darling, that's not true. What gave you that idea?" I get the reassurance I need. But if I toss it out in an argument, in the form of "you don't care about me," then my partner's emotional arousal keeps him from hearing me. And he is likely to back away—just when I need reassurance most.

If people were aware that intimate relationships are by nature characterized by ambivalence, they would understand the need to negotiate occasional retreats. They wouldn't feel so threatened by the times when one partner says, "I have to be by myself because I need to think about my life and where I'm going." Or "I need to be with my friends and spend time playing." If people did more backing off into constructive activities, including time to meditate or to play, intimate relationships would be in much better shape today.

If couples could be direct about what they need, then the need for retreat would not be subject to the misrepresentation that now is rampant. The trouble is, we don't talk to each other that openly and honestly. What happens is, one partner backs off and doesn't call and the partner left behind doesn't know what the withdrawal means. But he or she draws on a personal history that provides room for all sorts of negative interpretations, the most common being "he doesn't care about me."

No matter how hard a partner tries to be all things to us, gratifying all of another's needs is a herculean task—beyond the human calling. Criticism, disappointment, and momentary rejection are intrinsic parts of intimate life; developing a thicker skin can be healthy. And maintaining a life apart from the relationship is necessary. Energy invested in other people and activities provides a welcome balance.

GOOD-ENOUGH INTIMACY

Since our intimate partner will never be perfect, what is reasonable to expect? The late British psychiatrist D. W. Winnicott put forth the idea of "good-enough mothering." He was convinced that mothering could never be perfect because of the mother's own emotional needs. "Good-enough mothering" refers to imperfect, though adequate provision of emotional care that is not damaging to the children.

In a similar vein, I believe there is a level of imperfect intimacy that is good enough to live and grow on. In good-enough intimacy, painful encounters occasionally occur, but they are balanced by the strength and pleasures of the relationship. There are enough positives to balance the negatives. People who do very well in intimate relationships don't have a perfect relationship, but it is good enough.

The standard of good-enough intimacy is essentially subjective, but there are some objective criteria. A relationship must have enough companionship, affection, autonomy, connectedness, and separateness, along with some activities that partners engage in together and that they both enjoy. The relationship meets the needs of both partners reasonably well enough, both feel reasonably good about the relationship. If one person is unhappy in the relationship, then by definition it is not good enough for them.

People looking for good-enough intimacy are bound to be happier than those seeking perfect intimacy. Their expectations are lower and more realistic. Time and time again, those who examine the intricacies of happiness have found the same thing—realistic expectations are among the prime contributors to happiness.

CHOOSING A CONTRACEPTIVE

What's Best for You?

Joseph Anthony

Joseph Anthony is a Contributing Editor at AMERICAN HEALTH.

If you've been frustrated by a lack of contraceptive choices, there's good news: In the last couple of years, several new forms of contraception specifically, the long-lasting, hormone-based products Depo-Provera and Norplant and the female condom have been approved for use in the U.S., which means that we're finally catching up with the rest of the world. Depo-Provera and Norplant have been in use in other countries for years. But much ballyhooed new methods, such as contraceptive "vaccines" and a male birth control pill, are still probably a decade or more away.

Why? Manufacturers worry about boycotts and other protests from the religious right and antiabortion activists. And, says Dr. Michael Policar, vice president for medical affairs at the Planned Parenthood Federation of America, "the threat of litigation has had an incredibly chilling effect on contraceptive development in the last 10 years."

What are in the pipeline are mostly variations on existing themes—a two-capsule Norplant (instead of today's six); re-designed, baggier male condoms that promise greater comfort; intrauterine devices (IUD's) that release hormones; barrier methods that release spermicides, creams or gels with anti-HIV as well as antisperm properties; and perhaps some new inject-ables. There has also been some movement toward making the Pill available over the counter (without a prescription), although the Food and Drug Administration (FDA) is not currently considering any formal proposals to do so.

Here's a rundown on newly available methods of birth control, followed by more-established and better-known alternatives.

THE FEMALE CONDOM: This device looks like a large, floppy tube closed at one end. Marketed by Wisconsin Pharma-cal under the name Reality, the polyurethane barrier (thinner, stronger and a better conductor of heat than latex) was approved by the FDA last May. Like other barrier methods this one can take some time and patience to use correctly. The device has two rings, one around the outer rim and one inside. The inner ring is designed to fit over the cervix, anchored in place behind the pubic bone, like a diaphragm. The outer ring covers the labia and the base of the penis during intercourse. Some women have complained that the condom can rise into the vagina if not sufficiently lubricated; it can also twist around if not inserted properly.

The one-year failure rate with "typical use" is high, esti-mated at 21% to 26%, which means that about one in four women using it may become pregnant over the course of a year. (The pregnancy rate for "perfect use" would be much lower—about 5%.)

DEPO-PROVERA: This injectable prescription contraceptive, first available in New Zealand in 1969 and subsequently used by 30 million women in 90 countries, was finally approved in the U.S. in late 1992. One injection of this synthetic version of the female hormone progesterone every three months blocks ovulation.

The drug, which provides no protection against sexually transmitted diseases (STD's), may cause irregular periods, and women may not regain fertility until six to 12 months after they stop taking it.

Side effects of Depo-Provera are similar to those of other hormonal contraceptives and may include weight gain, head-aches and fatigue. Women usually experience some irregular bleeding or spotting during the first months of use. On the plus side, studies by the World Health Organization have found a link between Depo-Provera use and a reduced risk of cancer of the endometrium (the lining of the uterus).

NORPLANT: This implant of six thin capsules, placed under the skin of a woman's arm, releases the hormone levonor-gestrel, which keeps the body from producing the hormones necessary for ovulation. Norplant is effective for up to five years.

The implant was approved after two decades of testing on more than 50,000 women. More than 900,000 American women have received Norplant since it was introduced in February of 1991 by U.S. distributor Wyeth-Ayerst Laboratories. It's not appropriate for women who have liver disease, blood clots, inflammation of the veins or a history of breast cancer, or for those who are breast-feeding in the first six weeks after delivery. Fertility returns soon after the implant is removed.

The most common side effect of Norplant is irregular menstrual bleeding during the first six months after implantation. Norplant provides no STD protection.

Wyeth-Ayerst Laboratories has been charging $365 for Norplant in the U.S. (With doctor's fees, Norplant generally costs between $500 and $800.) After congressional hearings last year revealed that the drug sells for as little as $23 in other countries, the company announced that the price to public clinics would be lowered in 1995. But company officials won't comment on what the new price will be.

STERILIZATION: Every year more than 600,000 women in the U.S. have their fallopian tubes surgically blocked or severed, thus preventing eggs from reaching the uterus. About 25% of all women at risk of pregnancy (sexually active, heterosexual and fertile) aged 15 to 50 have had this procedure, called a tubal ligation; among such women 35 to 44 the number soars to more than 60%, according to the Alan Guttmacher Institute, a nonprofit group studying contraceptive issues. In addition, each year about half a million American men have vasectomies, in which the tube that carries sperm from the testes is cut and sealed. Vasectomy, which is performed under local anesthesia, carries less surgical risk than tubal ligation, which requires general anesthesia.

Both forms of sterilization are more than 99% effective and virtually permanent. (Though surgical sterilizations can sometimes be reversed—the success rate for such procedures is better for vasectomies than for tubal ligations—but anyone contemplating surgical sterilization is generally advised to consider the operation irreversible.)

ORAL CONTRACEPTIVES: Commonly known as the Pill, oral contraceptives, which suppress ovulation, are the most popular form of birth control for women in the U.S. About 28% of American women at risk of pregnancy between 15 and 44 use oral contraceptives. Fewer than 1% of women using oral contraceptives properly will become pregnant in the course of a year.

Literally hundreds of studies over the past four decades have attempted to analyze the effect of the Pill on women's health. No solid connections between taking the Pill and getting breast cancer have been made. The Pill does appear to increase the risk of blood clots, heart attack and stroke for women over 35 who smoke. The authors of *Contraceptive Technology,* a leading reference manual in the field, characterize the risk for nonsmokers and smokers under 35 as relatively minor.

While the Pill has been linked to circulatory problems in women who have high cholesterol, hypertension or any heart or vascular disease, as well as those who have a family history of heart disease, oral contraceptives also have been associated with several health *benefits.* Some studies indicate that birth control pills can actually reduce a woman's chances of developing ovarian or endometrial cancer, as well as lower her risk of pelvic inflammatory disease. Women taking the Pill also have fewer ovarian cysts and benign breast tumors than other women.

There are more than a dozen side effects attributed to the Pill, including breast tenderness, fluid retention, weight gain and headaches.

BARRIER METHODS: Condoms, diaphragms, cervical caps, sponges and spermicides all operate on the same basic principle: preventing sperm from reaching an egg. Latex condoms have the added benefit of providing the most protection against STD's, although all barrier methods, even spermicides, are thought to provide some protection when used properly.

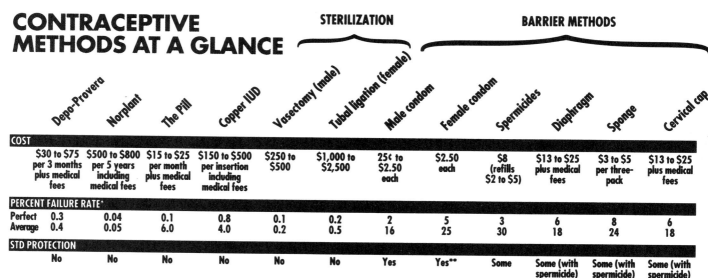

CONTRACEPTIVE METHODS AT A GLANCE

STERILIZATION — BARRIER METHODS

	Depo-Provera	Norplant	The Pill	Copper IUD	Vasectomy (male)	Tubal ligation (female)	Male condom	Female condom	Spermicides	Diaphragm	Sponge	Cervical cap
COST	$30 to $75 per 3 months plus medical fees	$500 to $800 per 5 years including medical fees	$15 to $25 per month plus medical fees	$150 to $500 per insertion including medical fees	$250 to $500	$1,000 to $2,500	25¢ to $2.50 each	$2.50 each	$8 (refills $2 to $5)	$13 to $25 plus medical fees	$3 to $5 per three-pack	$13 to $25 plus medical fees
PERCENT FAILURE RATE*												
Perfect	0.3	0.04	0.1	0.8	0.1	0.2	2	5	3	6	8	6
Average	0.4	0.05	6.0	4.0	0.2	0.5	16	25	30	18	24	18
STD PROTECTION	No	No	No	No	No	No	Yes	Yes**	Some	Some (with spermicide)	Some (with spermicide)	Some (with spermicide)

*Estimated percentage of women who get pregnant unintentionally in the first year of use. "Perfect use" is calculated from pregnancies occurring among couples who use the method correctly each time they have intercourse; "average use" combines perfect use figures with pregnancies occurring among couples who use the method sporadically or incorrectly.

**Although the female condom does provide protection against sexually transmitted diseases (STD's), its manufacturer is required by the Food and Drug Administration to note that for "highly effective protection" against STD's, including AIDS, it is important to use latex condoms for men.

FAILURE RATE DATA: ALAN GUTTMACHER INSTITUTE.

RU-486 and MORNING-AFTER TREATMENTS

Women who fear they may have become pregnant because they experienced condom rupture or otherwise engaged in unprotected intercourse have a little-publicized "morning-after," or postcoital, contraceptive option. Take what Dr. Felicia Stewart, director of research for the Sutter Medical Foundation in Sacramento, Calif., calls emergency contraceptive pills as soon as possible after the unprotected intercourse but no later than 72 hours afterward.

The "emergency pills" are regular birth control pills, but taken in two larger-than-usual doses (the second 12 hours after the first). The number of pills per dose depends on the brand: two Ovral, or four Lo/Ovral, Nordette, Levlen or yellow-colored Triphasil or Tri-Levlen (the yellow versions of both are the strongest formulas). By taking a larger-than-normal dose of birth control pills, you'll disrupt your body's natural hormone patterns, thereby reducing your chances of becoming pregnant by about 75%.

Obviously, the morning-after option shouldn't be looked at as a regular birth control method—it's a one-time emergency measure. And the procedure may not be suitable for women suffering from severe liver disease, blood clots or other circulation problems. Up to half of all women using this approach report short-term nausea or vomiting.

The drug RU-486, which prevents a fertilized egg from implanting itself in the uterine wall, might also find a secondary use as a morning-after contraceptive if it's approved for sale in the U.S. A University of Edinburgh study published in *The New England Journal of Medicine* found that if taken within 72 hours of unprotected sexual intercourse, RU-486 also prevents pregnancy. The women surveyed in the study reported much milder side effects than those taking birth control pills as morning-after measures.

Last year RU-486 manufacturer Roussel-Uclaf announced it would grant U.S. rights to the drug to the nonprofit research organization the Population Council, which would market and test the drug. As of the beginning of this year, however, the final details of the agreement had not been ironed out.

The main side effects of barrier methods are allergies or sensitivity to latex or spermicides. (The sponge is off-limits to women who have had toxic shock syndrome.)

INTRAUTERINE DEVICES (IUD's): IUD's are placed in a woman's uterus, where they prevent pregnancy by interfering with sperm transport and egg fertilization. The Dalkon Shield gave IUD's a terrible name in this country during the 1980s. After more than 10,000 lawsuits over pelvic inflammatory disease linked to the shield, IUD's have fallen out of favor. Fewer than 2% of women in the U.S. currently use them, a fact some experts regard as unfortunate.

"Compare that to around 30% of the women in Finland who choose an IUD," says Dr. Daniel Mishell, chairman of obstetrics and gynecology at the University of Southern California School of Medicine. "The IUD is effective and is one of the least expensive forms of long-term contraception, but it is also one of the least used in the U.S. because of the perception that it is dangerous." Recent studies have shown modern copper IUD's present little, if any risk of pelvic inflammatory disease.

The only IUD's currently sold in the U.S. are the Copper T-380A, which can be used for up to eight years, and the Progestasert, which releases progesterone and can be used for up to one year.

What form of contraception is right for you? People who have new or multiple partners have to be concerned about STD's as well as pregnancy. That means they should use condoms for maximum STD protection. A survey of 678 women receiving Norplant in Texas indicated that about half who had previously used condoms intended to keep doing so at least some of the time. "Until the last few years, nobody even *asked* questions about whether women using a hormonal contraceptive like Norplant would also continue to use barrier methods like condoms," says Margaret Frank, a contraceptive researcher at the University of New Haven in Connecticut and coauthor of the Texas study. People in monogamous, long-term relationships shouldn't have to worry about diseases and may focus instead on effective contraception.

But there's no way of saying that any one choice is "best." "Some women are going to get along really well with a particular method, and that's great," says *Contraceptive Technology* coauthor Dr. Felicia Stewart, director of research for the Sutter Medical Foundation, a managed-care organization in Sacramento, Calif. "If you have a method that is a comfortable fit with your hormonal makeup or your anatomy and your habits, then that method is fine for you. Trying, to say there's one best method is just ridiculous."

Men, Sex, *and* Parenthood *in an* Overpopulating World

Because women bear the primary responsibility for childrearing and family life in every country, they are also presumed to bear the primary responsibility for excess population growth. But family planning is unlikely to succeed—and population is unlikely to stabilize—until men share fully in those responsibilities.

Aaron Sachs

Aaron Sachs is a staff researcher at the Worldwatch Institute.

In almost all mammalian species, the male lives the life of a philanderer. From pandas to pumas, mammalian fathers tend to abandon their mate right after conception, leaving to the mother the entire burden of childrearing. The very classification "mammal" refers to a mother's independent capacity to nurse her babies: it's always the female bear that people see feeding, training, and protecting the cubs.

But human males are different. From the beginning, they have tended to stay with their mates and their children, and today many anthropologists and biologists believe that men's participation in the family played a critical role in the evolution of *homo sapiens'* most distinctive features, especially our capacity for psychosocial development. The children of very few other species, over the millennia, have been lucky enough to receive the attention of two caring adults.

Unfortunately, as human culture continues to evolve, more and more men are breaking with tradition and shirking their childrearing responsibilities. And the world's women and children are bearing the costs of this neglect. According to Judith Bruce, a senior associate at the Population Council in New York, the amount of time contributed by mothers to childcare is commonly seven times greater than that contributed by fathers, and the mothers' share only seems to be increasing. While important social revolutions in the industrialized world have begun to

free women from an imposed dependence on men, some husbands and fathers are using this broadening of women's opportunities as an excuse to contribute less time and money to their families. By 1980, for instance, American men aged 20 to 49 were spending almost 50 percent less time living with their young children than they were in 1960. In less developed countries, even when there is a long tradition of male financial contributions to the family, men often abandon their wives and children because of increasing economic pressures: fewer and fewer are able to succeed as breadwinners. A recent Chilean study of low-income adolescent couples and their first-born children found that, by the children's sixth birthday, 42 percent of the fathers were providing no child support whatsoever.

Male sexual behavior, too, puts a strain on society: besides the indirect stresses caused by men's failure to avoid fathering children they might not be able to support later, their higher fertility levels contribute disproportionately to population growth. Because men stay fertile much longer than women do, and because they tend to be more promiscuous, the average man, by the end of his lifetime, is responsible for more children than the average woman. In the 18th century, a Moroccan emperor had reportedly fathered more than 1,000 children by the time he turned 50. Though childrearing is becoming more expensive and parents are finding themselves with fewer resources to pass on to their children (whether in the form of cash or land), many men have continued to have large families. In some sub-Saharan African countries, the average man wants to have more than 10

Of 333 fathers with eight-year-old children, only 22 percent were still living with their child.

children, in part because large families serve as cultural symbols of a man's virility and wealth. Consequently, under male-dominated social systems that tend not to hold fathers accountable for the well-being of their children, the women of the Third World are increasingly finding themselves doing hard labor for food as well as walking several miles every day for water and fuelwood—all with babies on their backs or at their breasts.

Society has long expected women to take ultimate responsibility for the duties of raising a family. Currently in the United States, fathers head only one of every 40 single-parent households: men just aren't expected to juggle childcare and a job. Single women often end up simply raising their children by themselves, whether or not they have access to resources. In all parts of the world, both women and children would no doubt be better off if women faced fewer barriers to economic independence—and if men fulfilled their familial obligations. According to a recent study in Barbados, of 333 fathers with eight-year-old children, only 22 percent were still living with their child, and the children of the fathers who stayed were doing significantly better in school than all the others. And in the Chilean study, children's diets and nutrition levels tended to be much healthier when their fathers were living at home.

Men's failure to embrace their familial responsibilities begins with a failure to acknowledge that families get started through sex. A growing body of sociological research suggests that a family's eventual size and welfare depend largely on how the father and mother interact in bed—that men who are attentive to their partner's concerns tend later to be attentive to their family's concerns. Unfortunately, many men continue to see sex not as a shared experience but as their prerogative, as simply an opportunity to fulfill their desires. When interviewed by the demographer Alex Chika Ezeh, men in Ghana explained bluntly that their large families reflected, most of all, their desire to assert their culturally sanctioned sexual dominance over their wives. "The woman has no right to choose the number [of children] she prefers," said one man, "since it is you, the man, who decides when to have sex with her."

Over the past decade, then, many advocates for women's and children's welfare have turned to fam-

ily planning as a way of addressing men's irresponsibility. And many family planning organizations, in turn, have recognized a need to supplement their efforts to provide women with safe, appropriate contraception with efforts to educate men. In the mid-1980s, for instance, the poster campaigns of many national-level affiliates of the International Planned Parenthood Association (IPPF) targeted men's sexual attitudes quite explicitly. They attempted to make men empathize with women, to help them understand that, though they themselves do not get pregnant, they do have a role in reproduction.

Family planners reason that if men take full responsibility for their potential to procreate by participating in family planning, then each of the children they do father will be both expected and wanted—and presumably they will father only the number of children for whom they are able to provide. No culture directly encourages men not to care about their families, after all. Emphasizing male responsibility in family planning, therefore, is a key to getting men both to fulfill their broader responsibilities as husbands and fathers and to contribute their fair share to population stabilization.

THE HIGHER FERTILITY OF MEN

Of course, family planning is still, at heart, a women's issue. The development of the birth control pill, the IUD, and safe methods of female sterilization have remained the most important and revolutionary innovations in the history of family planning, because they finally gave a significant number of women control over their own fertility. After all, as Margaret Sanger, America's family planning pioneer of the early 20th century, frequently noted, it is the woman who risks her life in childbirth. Even at the end of the 20th century, maternal mortality rates remain high in the developing world. In Afghanistan and Sierra Leone, for instance, according to the World Health Organization (WHO), one mother dies for every 100 live births—a rate 250 times higher than that of some European countries. And many maternal deaths in developing countries are attributed by WHO to excessive childbearing.

The focus of family planning policies and programs, then, should not be shifted away from women, but rather broadened to include men as well. Though the importance of female methods of birth control seems to lie in their very independence from male influence, and though many women would not be using contraception were it not for private, female-only clinics, the exclusion of men from family planning has also had some negative consequences for women that were not foreseen by many activists. "Putting all the responsibility onto women," says Gill Gordon of IPPF's AIDS prevention unit, "has the effect of marginalizing men and making them *less* likely to behave responsibly." In many places where female birth control methods predominate, the connection between sexuality and reproduction has disappeared in the minds of many men, and they simply haven't had to confront or even consider the very serious reasons women might have for wanting to limit their childbearing. Though giving all women control over their fertility would be a significant accomplishment, it would not insure their well-being, or the well-being of any children they might eventually want to have.

The reality in many developing countries is that if a man's wife resists childbearing, he will often simply withdraw his financial support and marry another woman. Even worse, many men have resorted to violence in order to keep their wives from using contraception. One recent study showed that more than 50 percent of Mexican women using state-sponsored birth control services do so secretly, for fear of being physically abused by their husbands. A woman's ability to regulate her own fertility is often contingent upon her partner's recognition of her right to do so—which means that family planners need to work that much harder to make men empathize with women and understand their own responsibilities.

Changing men's sexual attitudes in a patriarchal world is delicate, time-consuming, expensive work, and the cost-effectiveness of education campaigns aimed at men is always difficult to measure, since progress is inevitably so slow. It would be a mistake, then, to let male-focused policies and programs take away any of the already limited resources currently devoted to women and family planning. But changing men's attitudes about familial decision-making is still crucial, especially since men currently tend to be responsible for more children than do women. All around the developing world, the population pressures caused by high fertility are contributing at least indirectly to problems as varied as wood and water shortages, joblessness, inadequate sanitation, the spread of infectious diseases, and the accumulation of waste—all of which have a direct impact on families. And, if current demographic trends continue, the globe's current population of almost 5.6 billion will probably have risen to about 8.4 billion by 2025. Ninety-five percent of those new babies will be born in the Third World.

Traditionally, population programs and policies have held women responsible for high fertility, at least implicitly. For years, national censuses and surveys did not even consider men's fertility. A country's fertility rate—the target of most programs and policies—is always measured as the average *female* fertility rate, because women are the ones who actu-

MEN HAVE MORE CHILDREN

Average Number of Living Children of Men and Women over 50, Selected Countries in Sub-Saharan Africa.

COUNTRY	MEN	WOMEN	PERCENTAGE BY WHICH MALE RATE IS HIGHER
CAMEROON	8.1	4.8	69
NIGER	6.7	4.9	37
KENYA	9.6	7.9	22
GHANA	8.5	7.4	15

Source: Demographic and Health Surveys

ally have children. Over the last decade, however, as demographers have begun to provide more relevant data, population policies guided solely by analyses of women's fertility have begun to seem less appropriate. Especially in societies where polygyny is common, family planning programs would do better to focus on men, since most of the excess childbearing in such societies can be traced to sexual pairings of older men—who might be able to provide child support for only a few more years—with much younger women. In Kenya, Ghana, and Cameroon, for instance, married men over the age of 50, who might continue to father children until their death, tend to have between eight and 10 living children. Married women at the end of their reproductive years report having five to eight.

THE POLITICS OF CONTRACEPTION

Since so many men in the developing world are so strongly predisposed to reject family planning, and since progress in changing their attitudes is so hard to measure in the short term, Third World development experts have tended to focus their family-planning efforts on couples who are already interested in limiting childbearing. Most development funders like to support programs that aspire to deliver a certain number of contraceptives to a certain number of people and achieve a measurable decline in fertility. And, without question, expanding access to birth control devices is crucial in the struggle both to improve women's and children's health and welfare and to help stabilize the world's burgeoning population. A 1992 study by Population Action International (then called the Population Crisis Committee) found 22 countries in which men and women still have no access, in effect, to birth control information or services. The contraceptive prevalence rate—or percentage of married women of reproductive age (15 to 49) using birth control—has surpassed 50 percent in a few countries in Latin America and Asia, but in sub-Saharan Africa, for example, it averages only 14 percent.

Simply flooding developing nations with contraceptives will go only so far, however. To make a significant contribution to population stabilization on a global scale, family planning programs will have to change people's attitudes, and especially men's attitudes, about the number of children they want to have. Unfortunately, in addition to the broad social and cultural factors that discourage men from participating in family planning, there are several more intimate factors about which men tend to express concern. Some men worry, for instance, that their wives would become promiscuous if provided with the means of preventing pregnancy. More generally, many men fear—probably with good reason—that, whether or not their wives ended up using birth control for extramarital affairs, the simple fact that it would allow them to assert a new form of control over sex and their bodies would probably change **the power dynamics of the marriage. And men often have genuine concerns about the threats to** their partner's health that many contraceptive devices are reputed to pose. Some of their fears—about pelvic inflammatory disease from IUDs, and nausea and headaches from the pill—are valid, while others—that the pill causes arthritis and sterility—are myths perpetuated by failings in information and education systems.

Men usually have even stronger negative feelings about the three birth control methods commonly thought of as male-initiated—withdrawal, the condom, and vasectomy. Withdrawal and the condom represent an unreasonable sacrifice of sexual pleasure to many men. Family planning field workers commonly report that suggestions of condom use are most often greeted with smiles and quickly composed maxims, such as "You can't wash your feet with your socks on," or "That would be like eating a sweet with the wrapper still on it." Vasectomies are even less acceptable in many parts of the developing world, because it seems highly unnatural to many men to have surgery on their sexual organ, or because they don't understand exactly what the operation entails. In the Sudan, 34 percent of male participants in a recent study thought that getting a vasectomy was equivalent to being castrated.

Many of these concerns could be easily overcome, though, since they stem from simple gaps in information or services. Family planning programs that cater to the specific concerns of men, and that offer a wider selection of contraceptive options, with complete explanations of their risks and how they are to be used, could make converts of millions. Already, more men than ever before are at least considering the use of family planning, if only, in many cases, for spacing their children further apart.

In the early 1970s, surveys of men in sub-Saharan Africa showed consistently that more than half fervently disapproved of birth control. In the 1990s, though, outright rejection of contraception is rare even in this region. Approval ratings are still low in some countries, such as Mali, where only 17 percent of men aged 20 to 55 support family planning; but in Burundi, for instance, male approval has soared to 94 percent. In 10 other recent Third World surveys cited in a paper written by Cynthia Green for WHO, countries reported contraceptive approval rates among men of between 56 percent and 96 percent. Of course, a positive survey response hardly guarantees that a man will practice contraception, but it is a first step. Some men have even begun to express a more philosophical attitude about so sensitive an issue as female promiscuity. If a woman "wants to go out," noted a member of a 1989 focus group in Burkina Faso, "whether she takes the pill or not, she can go out." And a young telephone operator in Quito, Ecuador, went so far as to connect family planning with shared parental responsibility: "Even if you have enough money to ensure the children have a good education, they probably suffer from lack of attention if there are too many. And men here never help the women at home—she has to do everything. These kinds of decisions must be taken together by the man and the wife."

JUST FOR MEN

One way for a man to begin sharing the burden of planning and caring for a family is to offer to use a male method of birth control. Unfortunately, though, because contraceptive research has always been guided by the assumption that contraception is woman's work, men's options remain limited. While women theoretically have access to several modern, semi-permanent but fully reversible methods, ranging from the pill and the IUD to Norplant and injectables such as Depo-Provera, research on modern methods for men seems to have stopped at vasectomy. The IPPF's *Medical Bulletin* estimates that "only approximately 8 percent of the world contraceptive budget is spent on the development of male methods." It is true that certain chemical methods just aren't well suited to male physiology: developing a "male pill," for instance, would mean finding a way of blocking the ongoing production of millions of sperm without blocking the production of male hormones, a task much more daunting than chemically blocking the production of one egg every month. "Physically," however, as Elaine Lissner, the director of the Male Contraception Information Project in Santa Cruz, points out, "it's easier to stop millions of sperm than one egg. The sperm all travel through the vas deferens, a small, easily accessed tube, where they can be incapacitated or blocked." In any case, family planning researchers have hardly even begun to develop the potential range of useful contraceptive services for men.

Meanwhile, about one quarter of the world's couples who are currently using contraception rely on male methods. Withdrawal is perhaps the most dubious birth control method, with a failure rate of about 18 percent. But it has a long and notable history. Withdrawal was especially important in the 19th century during Europe's massive demographic transition to replacement-level fertility (when each man and woman have, on average, just two surviving children). The men of the Victorian era, perhaps aided by a pervasive cultural prudery, present the ultimate example of male responsibility, remembering their duty to their family even at the height of passion. Today, withdrawal still provides a free, safe method of birth control for about 15 million couples in the developing world who perhaps have no other options.

Vasectomy remains an important birth control method for men who don't want any more children. Because so many births are accidental, and because sterilization is almost 100 percent successful as a birth control method, the average vasectomy in the developing world is thought to prevent about two births. More reproductive health clinics are expanding their services and offering comprehensive vasectomy programs. PRO-PATER, in Sao

Of 204 published references on the Latin American family, only two discussed the role of fathers.

Paulo, Brazil, has been particularly successful in attracting men, thanks to a carefully planned, high-profile outreach program. Its staffers go to workplaces to talk about family planning with men in settings where they feel at ease. The clinic also runs a series of television advertisements that describe vasectomy as "an act of love" and reassure men that it does not affect sexual functioning—a key strategy with male sterilization. Nick Danforth, men's programs advisor for the Association of Voluntary Surgical Contraception in New York, likes to point out that although vasectomy—increasingly performed without a scalpel—is technically simpler, safer, and quicker than female sterilization, it is still used only a third as often.

Overall, condom use is probably the most significant male method, because it is not only cheap, easy, highly effective, and free of side effects, but it is also the one contraceptive additionally capable of preventing the spread of sexually transmitted diseases (STDs), including AIDS. Unfortunately, the condom's association with disease makes it that much more controversial as a birth control device. Many men and women, especially in regions where STDs have become widespread, take suggestions of condom use as insults: the person making the suggestion is either admitting that he or she might have a disease or expressing the fear that his or her partner might have a disease. In both cases, the implication is that someone has been unfaithful. For this reason, many couples feel uncomfortable about even acquiring condoms. "The condom is not seen as a contraceptive like, for example, the pill," explains a 50-year-old man in Burkina Faso. "It has come with AIDS. . . . If you want a condom, then that means you want to have an affair. So you have to get it via a third person. You cannot go yourself." Obtaining condoms may be even more problematic for women, because of the double standard operating in so many cultures. Men are expected to be discreet if they want to be promiscuous, but women are simply not expected to be promiscuous. Many women, intimidated by such strong stigmatization and by their male-dominated societies, end up risking pregnancy and disease rather than risking their partner's wrath by asking him to use a condom.

As with all male methods, condoms leave the woman in a particularly vulnerable situation: she

MEN *WANT* MORE CHILDREN			
Average Number of Desired Children of Men and Women, Selected Countries in Sub-Saharan Africa.			
COUNTRY	MEN	WOMEN	PERCENTAGE BY WHICH MALE RATE IS HIGHER
CAMEROON	11.2	7.3	53
NIGER	12.6	8.5	48
GHANA	7.6	5.3	43
BURUNDI	5.5	5.5	0
KENYA	4.8	4.8	0

Source: Demographic and Health Surveys

must depend on her partner to use them, and use them correctly. But AIDS is making condoms increasingly important to women's health in the developing world. HIV is passed much more easily from a man to a woman than from a woman to a man, and it has already infected a significant portion of the adult, heterosexual population in Africa and Asia, where prostitution and male promiscuity are common. For now, women have to rely on male condoms for their safety, and while the female condom might give women slightly more control, using it will still probably entail complicated sexual negotiations. It is essential, then, that men acknowledge the sensitivity of the situation and take the lead in encouraging condom use. Perhaps family planners and AIDS activists can join forces to produce education campaigns that will help to inform couples about the specifics of sexually transmitted diseases and their consequences, and help to dissipate sexual tensions by allowing partners to anticipate and understand each other's anxieties.

In the end, a willingness to participate in sexual and familial decisions as a concerned, forthcoming, equal partner is the real key to male responsibility. More than being willing to use a male method of birth control, men have to be willing to listen—to learn how to be sensitive to their partners' health, welfare, and desires. As Mary Daly, a leader of the modern feminist movement, has remarked, true responsibility is defined by an ability to be responsive.

NOT-SO-GREAT EXPECTATIONS

In almost all matters of policy, the family is defined as the mother-child unit: policymakers and program directors forget about gender dynamics, or simply don't expect men to take part. All too often, well-intentioned representatives of industrialized countries simply press packages of pills into the outstretched palms of Third World women, "as if women alone," in the words of the Population Council's Judith Bruce, "could bring about fertility decline, and as if their sexual and parental roles were determined autonomously." The United Nations Educational, Scientific, and Cultural Organization (UNESCO) recently asked a sociologist to do a review of the current literature on the Latin American family. Of the 204 documents she examined, only two mention fatherhood or the situation of men.

In the 1990s, men's family planning and parenting responsibilities need to be explicitly defined. A logical starting point would be prioritizing the goal of establishing paternity and enforcing child support payments—as leaders have in Nigeria, where, according to the new national population policy,

children have a legal claim on their father's time and money. Even in so "advanced" a country as the United States, where most of the so-called "deadbeat dads"—fathers who have abandoned their partner and child to the welfare system—could actually afford to pay child support, only about 18 percent do.

Changes in men's roles will not emerge quickly or with anything resembling ease. In some places, as economies modernize, the direct costs of child-rearing—from medicines and nutritious foods to schooling fees—are increasing, and familial resources are getting tight. Instead of having smaller families, though, many fathers simply shift the financial burden to the mother or the older children. And even when men genuinely want to act more responsibly, they sometimes believe they are unable to because of certain social and economic factors that continue to be neglected by policymakers. Both fathers and mothers, for instance, feel in many cases that children provide them with their only means of achieving economic and social security. And many fathers insist that they would have fewer children if they could be sure that more of them would survive: a study by the World Bank revealed that, on average, the prevention of 10 infant deaths results in one to five fewer births. But fathers in sub-Saharan Africa, where the infant mortality rate has remained as deplorably high as 10 percent—compared to one percent in the industrialized world—feel that they cannot afford to take chances with their fertility. And some fathers are contributing no financial resources to their children simply because they have none to give. Often they are desperately searching for work, perhaps in a far-off city.

YOU REAP WHAT YOU SOW

Still, educational efforts—ideally in tandem with pointed policy initiatives that force men to take up some of the economic burden of raising children—have considerable potential. If more field workers sought out men and provided them with better information, they would surely have more influence over men's family planning decisions. Good strategies for increasing male responsibility range from integrating family planning into community development programs to integrating sex and gender education into primary school systems. A recent IPPF report stated that, in general, field workers have had the most success changing men's attitudes and behavior through peer counseling: when men felt they were being advised by people who really identified with their concerns, whether sexual or financial, they were much more likely to respond favorably to suggestions of taking on more familial responsibility.

2. RELATIONSHIPS: Gender and Sexuality in Relationships

In Colombia, men started turning out in droves at vasectomy clinics modeled after Sao Paulo's PRO-PATER when male clinicians began offering more reproductive health services, including urological exams, infertility treatment, and sexuality counseling. Between 1985 and 1987 the number of vasectomies being performed quadrupled in Bogota and increased tenfold in Medellin.

The National Family Planning Council of Zimbabwe ran an intensive media campaign in 1989 designed specifically to increase men's responsibility in family planning and encourage joint decision making among couples. Male educators gave a series of 80 informational and motivational talks, and an entertaining serial drama about the consequences of irresponsible sexual and familial behavior was broadcast over the radio twice a week for six months, reaching about 40 percent of the country's men. By the end of the campaign, 61 percent of the men who had tuned in to "Akarumwa Nechekuchera"—variously translated as "Man is his own worst enemy" or "You reap what you sow"—reported a change in their attitudes about their families, and 17 percent of the men who had attended at least one talk reported that they actually started using a family planning method. Most importantly, the number of men saying that family planning decisions ought to be made jointly by husband and wife had risen by 40 percent: the council's educational programs were getting men and women to talk.

Some fatalists argue that because of undeniable evolutionary and physiological differences between men and women, men aren't likely ever to take much responsibility as parents: they are no better than all the other mammalian males. But such arguments overlook thousands of years of male contributions to family welfare—from big-game hunting to protection, wage earning, counseling, mentoring, and even nurturing. Men have the potential to participate fully in planning and raising a family. It is only because they have society's implicit permission that some men still limit their participation to the act of sex.

Staying Power

Bridging the Gender Gap in the Confusing '90s

Melinda Blau

Melinda Blau is the author of Families Apart: Ten Keys to Successful Co-Parenting.

Karen Mason*, 40, considers herself lucky. "I have a husband who's a real parent—kissy-huggy with the kids. And three nights a week he cooks dinner so I can be on the swim team."

Yet even this seeming paragon of a modern husband continues to exhibit what she considers to be typically male characteristics. Peter, 40, isn't much of a talker, Karen notes wistfully, and yes, he likes sex whereas she likes romance. And sometimes Karen gets frustrated because her husband just doesn't seem to focus when it comes to the house and children.

When they got married, Karen and Peter were determined not to be bound by traditional gender-role assumptions—that he would bring home the bacon and she would cook it. Peter, a salesman, shared the housework and put in almost equal time with their first child. But then the demands of Peter's work increased, a second child arrived and the couple's time together began to slip away.

Even though Peter is a far cry from

*Couples' names and some identifying details have been changed.

his own father, who wasn't home much or "always had his head in the newspaper," some evenings Peter understands how his dad must have felt. "I like to bury myself in the TV," he admits. "I'm exhausted at night." Karen agrees that Peter "is doing his best" but says she's sometimes saddened by what she perceives as their real gender differences.

Many '90s couples are grappling with new ways of being men and women. At the same time that expectations and demands have changed for both, the popular press suggests the battle of the sexes may never end because men and women are irreconcilably different. Books proclaim that *Men Are From Mars, Women Are From Venus,* and personal accounts highlight the issues on which couples differ: Communication (she wants more talk; he wants more action). Intimacy (she needs to relax to have sex; he needs sex to relax). Division of household labor and child care (she says she does more; he talks about how much he does). Money and careers (she says he doesn't value her job as much as his; he notes that he makes more money).

Yet despite these differences, the fact that men and women can transcend traditional gender roles indicates that many of these distinctions may be more a result of socialization than biology. "Men are not emotionally defective monsters, and women aren't depen-

dent, helpless creatures," says psychologist Susan Johnson at the University of Ottawa in Ontario.

While researchers debate the contributions of nature and nurture to gender differences, family therapists suggest we examine why couples become polarized in the first place. Boston psychologist Kathy McMahon notes that "gender rage," as she calls it, stands for the disappointment couples feel when reality doesn't live up to expectations.

Dr. McMahon offers a typical scenario: Both parents work, and their child gets sick. In a spirit of fairness, they decide to split caretaking, but by the end of the week, they're fighting about who does what around the house. The problem, says McMahon, is that neither has a model for this new behavior—Mom working when a child is sick, Dad staying home—and they can't buck their inner cultural imprinting. When it's time for Mom to go to work, she feels guilty for not living up to her role as mother. And Dad's upset because he's not living up to his role as provider.

Today's couples, say the experts, must acknowledge their unconscious expectations and speak up before gender rage erodes their relationship. "This is not so much about understanding differences," says family therapist Jo-Ann Krestan, "as it is about holding partners equally accountable for the quality of life in a family. Sharing responsibility doesn't mean the husband saying, 'Honey, I'll cook tonight—where's the stove?'"

In essence, men and women usually want the same things from a relationship: closeness, support, respect, fairness, healthy children, a nice home and longevity. But, says California psychologist Lonnie Barbach, co-author of *Going the Distance,* they often differ about how to achieve these things and don't necessarily talk productively with each other about them.

Couples who talk about their needs and feelings fare far better than those who don't. But the longer people stay together, the less time they spend thinking and talking about their relationship, says University of Michigan psychologist Linda Acitelli. Complaining about a spouse's behavior doesn't count. Relationship work, Dr. Acitelli says, is like car maintenance—for safety's sake, you shouldn't wait until the vehicle breaks down.

The process of divvying up both practical *and* emotional responsibilities should be worked out thoughtfully. Some couples allocate chores arbitrarily, according to what has to be done; others earmark assignments based on preference. However it's done, structure—a chart or other means of clarifying who does what—can be helpful.

New York City designer Sara Roark, 41, and her husband, Carl, 42, an architect, drew up a "contract" and even included their four-year-old son, Orin. The major headings represent a bird's-eye view of what it takes to run a house and a family: meals and dishes, laundry, school, shopping, housecleaning, home maintenance, car, mail, finances, medical care, lifestyle decisions and leisure time.

At first the Roarks wanted to keep the assignments objective, but they wound up basing certain responsibilities on each person's skills and availability. "I took over more of the financial things, because it took me less time. My husband is more of a morning person, so he gets Orin ready for school, while I do more of the night things."

To a woman who complains that she's always in charge or that her husband does less than she does, Krestan would say it's her own fault for doing his share. "Sometimes you just have to leave his empty yogurt container on the kitchen counter. Throw it away and you cripple his ability to notice empty yogurt containers in the future."

Indeed, Sara Roark had to redefine "what needs to be done" and to accept the fact that things might not be done the way she'd do them, or when. "It's tough to let go. Sometimes when I come home late, I find that he's given our son crackers and cheese and put him to bed. A lot of women just take over at that point."

Dr. Ron Taffel, a New York City family therapist, concurs: "The biggest complaint I hear from men is, 'She wants me to do it, but when I do, she criticizes me.'" Our society, he explains, puts each member in a no-win situation. "The woman feels responsi-

Arguments over dirty dishes are signs of deeper issues.

ble for how the house looks and how the kids turn out. Society will hold her accountable, so she feels driven to be in charge. And even though the man may want to participate as an equal, he often feels like he has a boss."

Taffel's prescription goes beyond chores: Couples must also reserve time every night for reviewing the day. "One couple began to talk for 15 minutes each night after the kids went to bed about what happened with each other and with their sons. It made them feel more in synch."

While women typically will participate in such sessions, men are generally more resistant. Men tend to focus on what's in front of them, Taffel explains. "When they leave the office, they don't want to talk about work, and when the children finally are in bed, they don't want to talk about them. I try to get them to realize that the more they separate the different aspects of their lives, the more they end up zoning out in front of the TV or walking out on wives who want to talk."

Dave Goodrich, 34, an estate manager in Indianapolis, was happy to share the housework and child care for his two sons. But intimacy was another matter. "When Annie first complained that she was always the one to initiate conversations about our relationship, I was very defensive," he admits. "Guys don't talk about those kinds of things. We had a number of conversations, till

all hours of the night. Now I understand where she's coming from. It's hard sometimes, but I really make an attempt to share the emotional work of our marriage too."

Annie Goodrich, 37, a teacher, realizes that her attitude also made a difference. "In the beginning I would yell and scream, which just pushed him further away. I finally realized that when we had an argument, he needed a cooling-off period before he could talk."

Certainly, it takes perseverance—not

HOW TO CLOSE THE GAP

Get honest before you get angry: Something deeper than dry cleaning is probably bothering you.

Establish systems for sharing chores and child care.

Negotiate the division of labor *and* the division of love.

Don't get locked into your role: Try swapping responsibilities on occasion.

Express your emotional needs and expectations and really listen to your partner.

Review the cultural messages of your childhood to help understand the conflicts inherent in your new roles.

Give each other time to change; don't monitor or criticize.

Accept your differences and applaud each other's strengths.

Protect your intimate time together.

---

the same as nagging—to get some men to talk. More important, it requires the woman to speak honestly about what she needs, not rant about what her spouse is doing wrong. In most relationships, in fact, both partners are usually afraid of intimacy; the fear just looks different on men and women. As Dr. Johnson points out, "To love and to be intimately connected is to be incredibly at risk." A woman may believe she's doing "relationship work" because she starts conversations, but if she doesn't allow herself to be vulnerable and doesn't take responsibility for her own feelings, she may be dodging intimacy by focusing on him. Unexpressed feelings can contaminate a relationship—and obscure the real issues. Arguments over dirty dishes, vacuuming or food shopping or even a partner's infidelity are usually symptoms of deeper problems.

After two children and 14 years of marriage, Dana Berk, 37, finally had to confront why she felt so depressed, so sexually apathetic, so envious of other couples. It had nothing to do with chore wars. "Over the years, without realizing it, Hal and I had both shut down."

Realizing she was attracted to another man was Dana's wake-up call. Rather than act on impulse, she decided to talk to her husband. "It was brutal having to express our bottled-up feelings. I have tremendous gratitude because he was wonderful in terms of being able to face the issues, deal with the pain and support me. We had many talks late into the night. There was anger, but we also cried a lot. I even have a sex drive now, and there's a passion in our relationship that's deeper than we ever had. I think we've really learned how to be there for each other."

Dave and Annie Goodrich learned to be there for each other through a series of crises—beginning with Annie's miscarriage—that made their different styles pale in comparison with their ability to share life's hard knocks. "When we lost the baby, Dave really let go," Annie says. "He knew that we both had to talk about it. When I developed an eating disorder, he was really supportive. Then our youngest was born with a birth defect. Just knowing we can talk about it makes it bearable."

Successful couples constantly and consciously nurture their relationship. "The need to protect intimacy—their time with each other—is central to being together," stresses Taffel, "all the way from having conversations without being interrupted to having weekends together without the kids. When that starts to disappear, it's dangerous; the reservoir dips too low."

Taffel suggests creating rituals. One couple he knows takes a brief walk after dinner. The Roarks try to set aside a portion of every weekend for themselves. The Goodriches try to get away one weekend a month.

Of course, some gender differences will persist: She may not feel as comfortable being away from the kids; he may never be as observant. But such issues don't have to be divisive if you remember to reserve time to be alone together and if you appreciate your common victories instead of bemoaning each other's failings.

"Your partner is probably not going to get it the first time," Dr. Barbach emphasizes. "Acknowledge small changes, even if they're not perfect." Whether your differences are over housework, child care or emotions, she adds, "really value what each of you gives." In some areas, one person probably is more proficient. "If you're better at bringing romance into your relationship, do it."

Last year Karen Mason did just that. On Peter's 40th birthday, she "surprise kidnapped" him for a weekend alone, planning the whole thing meticulously, down to taking his clothes "bit by bit" so she could pack their suitcase. "He was so appreciative," she recalls, "but he admitted that he could never have done it for me. He wouldn't have thought of all the details."

Karen is satisfied, however, because Peter is a loving husband and father who can tolerate that her idea of a great birthday present is to go away *with* the kids. Thus the Masons have reached a workable détente. "As I get older, I realize there are some real differences between men and women," says Karen, "and I'm happier when I accept it."

Albanian 'virgins' wear the pants in their families

Barbara Demick

KNIGHT-RIDDER NEWSPAPERS

LEPUROSH, Albania—Sema Brahimi was 14 when she decided to become a man.

It was a sacrifice dictated by the harsh circumstances in which her family found itself living. Sema's father had died, leaving his widow, four daughters and a baby son to cope on their own. In these pitiless mountains choked with rock and brush, it was unthinkable to run a household without a man in charge. Sema volunteered to take on the job.

She cropped her hair short and donned trousers. She went to work in the fields. She changed her name from Sema to its masculine equivalent, Selman, and her mother and sisters began referring to her with the pronouns "he' and "him."

"I've lived my whole life as a man. I've got the habits of a man. . . . .If anybody has a problem with it, I've got my gun to deal with them," said Selman Brahimi, now 55, with a blustery gesture to the back pocket of her baggy, gray trousers.

Perhaps more remarkable than Brahimi's permutation of gender is that nobody "does" have a problem with it. The men in the village accept Selman as a man among equals. In this deeply conservative culture in which the responsibilities and customs of men and women are sharply delineated, Brahimi's decision to become a man is regarded as part of a centuries-old, noble tradition.

In a 1909 book about Albania, the British travel writer Edith Durham described the tradition of the "Albanian virgins"—women who took an oath never to marry in order to fill a void left by a dearth of males. The folklore of northern Albania and bordering Montenegro is rich with heroic accounts of these vowed virgins who sometimes became fierce warriors or village chieftans.

Until recently, when Albania reopened to outsiders after a half-century of Stalinist communism, it was widely believed that the tradition had died out. Its survival into the modern era can be attributed to the extreme isolation of mountainous villages such as Lepurosh, which are terra incognita even for most Albanians.

The village itself (population 300) has not a single telephone, automobile or house with indoor plumbing. The women wear traditional attire of long skirts, aprons and white head scarves.

The Brahimis live in a sun-bleached stone house overlooking the fields of tobacco, cucumbers, tomatoes and onions from which the family ekes out a hard-scrabble existence.

Selman Brahimi was born in this house in 1940, the youngest of four daughters. The older girls already were married or engaged, their brother still a baby, when their father died. Selman gradually assumed responsibility for tending to the fields and for making the arduous, three-hour trip to the nearest city by mule when it was time to sell crops.

"The idea came as the result of necessity. There was nobody to take care of the men's work," said Selman, recalling her remarkable life as she rolled a cigarette with home-grown tobacco.

"Until I was 18 to 20, I had proposals of marriage. My brother was old enough to work, and my mother said that I should follow the fate of my sisters and get married. But once something is decided, you can't undo it, and I already thought of myself as a man."

As the head of the household, Brahimi took responsibility for selecting a wife for her brother. She wore a suit and tie at his wedding, assuming the role of father of the groom. In keeping with village tradition, she learned to play musical instruments reserved for men, the flutelike *fyell* and a stringed instrument known as the *lahute.*

"I've had to work very hard to earn bread for the family and to be honest and correct in my relations with others," she said. "But, no, I never regret the decision. I've not had a bad life as a man."

Although she has the petite stature of a woman, Brahimi has a wry, masculine smile, displaying gold-capped teeth through a crooked grin. She happily acknowledges that her life is far easier today than before. Her brother, Elez, has four sons—two of whom work abroad, sending money back to the family, and two who work the fields. She now spends much of her time smoking and drinking the brandy known as *raki* with the men of the village.

Selman Brahimi is the first and only vowed virgin in Lepurosh, which is entirely Muslim. The tradition is more common among Albanian Catholics, but villagers do not seem in the least perturbed.

As far as the Albanian government is concerned, Selman is still a woman by the name of Sema. She never has made any effort to legally change her gender; that would have obliged her to serve in the military. But Selman notes that it doesn't matter much, because her special status is recognized under a centuries-old body of law that prevails in the region.

The Kanun of Lek, named for a 15th-century Albanian hero, Lek Dukagjini, is the unofficial bible of northern Albania. Paperback copies can be purchased in kiosks and are found in many homes. The Kanun lays down formal rules of etiquette for family and village life. Women can be beaten or chained if they disobey their husbands, and they have no property or inheritance rights whatsoever.

Under the strictures of Kanun law, the only escape from this dismal fate is to vow virginity and assume the life of a man.

"We have a Kanun that prohibits a lot of things for women, but some of our women are braver and smarter than men and the vow of virginity allowed them to take a man's place," said Palok Lunaj, a 70-year-old expert in Kanun law who lives in Bajza in northern Albania.

It is unclear how many Albanian virgins are still alive—in part because many villages are accessible only on foot and are seldom, if ever, visited by outsiders. Journalists, aid workers and anthropologists have identified at least four such women, but the number is probably much larger.

What a baby *really* costs

Grab that calculator and see what you can expect to spend during your child's first year.

Jessica Rosenthal Benson and Maija Johnson

The average first baby costs his parents approximately $8,000 by the time he celebrates his first birthday, according to the Family Economics Research Group of the U.S. Department of Agriculture (USDA). But your cost may be much more or less than that: Where you live, how many gifts you receive, and how much you can afford, or want, to spend are just a few of the factors involved in the accounting. Plus, what you dub a lifesaver may be considered an unnecessary expenditure by another parent.

One cost that the USDA omits is that of prenatal care and delivery—an average $4,720 for a normal pregnancy and birth, and $7,826 if a cesarean is needed. These numbers, however, don't shed much light on actual regional costs. An uncomplicated pregnancy and birth in New York City might cost $10,000, while in Oregon the cost could be half that amount.

In addition to taking into account regional costs, you should check your health-insurance policy. Traditional fee-for-service plans often do not reimburse obstetrical costs until after the delivery. And under some insurance plans, well-baby care is not covered.

Once they are home with their baby, many new parents are surprised how the cost of indispensable items, such as diapers, adds up, not to mention the cost of incidentals, such as film. And then there are the totally unexpected expenses, such as take-out food. "My husband I were too overwhelmed to go grocery shopping and prepare meals, so we ordered in a lot," says Nancy Brower, of Madison, Wisconsin.

New parents may also face a jump in housing costs. Depending on whether you are decorating a nursery, remodeling, or moving to a bigger home, the cost of making room for a baby can range from under $100 to thousands of dollars.

In compiling these lists, we discovered that calculating costs for the first year is tricky at best. Besides some of the variables already mentioned, manufacturer and store prices vary widely, as does product quality. Nevertheless, you an use the lists, or individual items within them, to get an idea of how much you can expect to spend during your baby's first year of life. And no parent has ever been known to complain that having a child wasn't worth the expense!

From *Parents*, April 1994, pp. 92-94. © 1994 by Jessica Rosenthal Benson and Maija Johnson. Reprinted by permission.

73

Feeding

Breast-feeding:
4 nursing bras, $52–$116
360 disposable bra pads for early months, $40
Breast pump, $26–$165
Lactation consultant, $0–$225
6 waterproof lap pads, $8
6 bibs, $6–$46
total: $132–$600

Bottle-feeding:
8 eight-ounce bottles, $9–$28
4 four-ounce bottles, $4–$14
18 nipples, $21–56
Formula, $616–$956
Bottle and nipple brush, $1–$2
6 waterproof lap pads, $8
6 bibs, $6–$46
total: $665–$1,110

Solids:
24 boxes of infant cereal, $24–$30
432 jars of baby food, $127–$217
156 jars of infant juice, $42–$73
Food grinder, $8
Feeding dish, $2–$9
3 baby spoons, $4–$8
3 training cups, $5–$13
6 large bibs, $15–$51
High chair, $25–$100
Hook-on chair, $28–$35
total: $280–$544

Dressing

Chest of drawers, $200–$350
20 undershirts, $36–$125
6 "onesies" or bodysuits, $19–$36
4 drawstring nightgowns, $20–$28
6 pairs of pajamas, $20–$69
10 stretchies, coveralls, or creepers, $90–$200
2 pairs of overalls, $32–$80
7 jumpsuits, $133–$280
6 tops, $54–$78
4 pairs of pants, $28–$36
2 dresses, $34–$56
4 pairs of booties, $16–$18
8 pairs of socks, $8–$10
1 pair of walking shoes, $25–$32
3 sweaters, $30–$60
3 sunsuits, $30–$63
2 cool-weather hats, $4–$10
1 sunbonnet, $4–$5
1 snowsuit, $48–$60
2 jackets, $64–$120
total: $895–$1,716

Bathing and skin care

Baby bathtub, $10–$20
Baby bath seat, $13–$15
6 washcloths, $4–$9
6 hooded bath towels, $48–$60
2 containers of liquid baby soap, $5
Baby shampoo, $3–$4
Baby lotion, $2
Baby powder or cornstarch, $2–$3
Baby oil, $2–$3
Baby nail clippers, $2
Isopropyl rubbing alcohol, $1
520 cotton balls, $10–$11
Baby brush and comb, $2–$14
total: $104–$149

Diapering

Home-laundered:
4-dozen cloth diapers, $36–$432
Water, utilities, laundry products, $243
Diaper pail, $8–$20
12 diaper pins, $2–$6
18 pairs of waterproof pants, $24–$90
4,160 diaper wipes, $156
Diaper-rash ointment, $3–$4
Changing pad, $9–$30
Changing table, $70–$100
total: $551–$1,081

Diaper service:
Weekly supply of cloth diapers for one year, $552–$803
Diaper pail, $8–$20
12 diaper pins, $2–$6
18 pairs of waterproof pants, $24–$90
4,160 diaper wipes, $156
Diaper-Rash ointment, $3–$4
Changing pad, $9–$30
Changing table, $70–$100
total: $824–$1,209

Disposable diapers:
2,600 diapers for one year, $676–$884
Diaper pail, $8–$20
360 diaper-pail liners, $29
4,160 diaper wipes, $156
Diaper-rash ointment, $3–$4
Changing pad, $9–$30
Changing table, $70–$100
total: $951–$1,223

Outings

Infant car seat, $30–$83
Convertible car seat, $40–$118
Stroller, $20–$200
Soft front carrier, $15–$40
Metal-framed back carrier, $30–$89
Diaper bag, $7–$20
Stroller bag, $8–$9
Travel bassinet, $45
Portable crib, $70–$142
total: $265–$746

Sleeping

Crib, $100–$600
Mattress, $20–$200
2 waterproof mattress covers, $6–$12
2 quilted mattress pads, $4–$16
6 fitted sheets, $54–$80
6 receiving blankets, $24–$48
3 crib blankets, $27–$57
Quilt or comforter, $17–$21
Bumper pads, $23–$30
Dust ruffle, $16–$20
Night-light, $4–$5
Musical mobile, $25–$30
total: $320–$1,119

Playing

Infant seat, $25–$50
Play yard, $47–$120
Baby swing, $24–$110
Toys, $143
total: $239–$423

Child care

One parent cares for child: $0 (does not account for loss of income if this parent has left a full-time job)
Day-care center: $3,326
Family day care: $2,650
At-home sitter: $3,703
Relative: $2,151
Occasional baby-sitter: $448
If these numbers seem particularly low or high to you, keep in mind that they are national averages. Fees vary according to region. For example, fees in the Northeast and West are relatively higher than in the South and Midwest. Centers in the Northeast average $4,534 per year, while centers in the South cost about $2,683.

Health care and safety

Well-baby care, $617
Vitamin and mineral supplements, $80
Thermometer, $2–$10
Liquid acetaminophen, $4–$6
Nasal aspirator, $2
Cool-mist humidifier, $15–$150
Syrup of ipecac, $2–$3
8 pacifiers, $8–$22
Nursery monitor, $29–$49
2 safety gates, $30–$80
Smoke detector (includes battery), $12–$25
Safety gadgets (such as outlet covers and latches), $20–$130
total: $821–$1,174

Nice-to-haves

Cradle, $69–$100
Household help, $3,265–$11,821
35-mm camera, $50–$1,250
14 rolls of film, $52–$62
Film processing, $61–$122
Camcorder, $700–$2,300
22 camcorder tapes, $77–$242
Washing machine, $280–$900
Clothes dryer, $249–$799
Cordless phone, $59–$280
total: $4,862–$17,876

Grand total

From the low end to the high end, here is what your bottom-line expenses—excluding childbirth and child-care costs—could amount to:
total: $3,607–$26,080

Cost Cutters

Gifts and hand-me-downs.
Clothing can be a big expense, but there is good news: You'll probably receive some clothing as gifts—and more as hand-me-downs—which will help cut costs.

Secondhand equipment.
If you are given—or if you buy—a used piece of baby equipment, you must be absolutely sure that it is in good condition and safe for your child to use. For a free safety checklist called *Safe and Sound for Baby,* send a self-addressed, business-size envelope to the Juvenile Products Manufacturers Association, Public Informa-tion, 2 Greentree Centre, Box 955, Marlton, NJ 08053.

Free or at cost.
There are programs that offer car seats, either free or at cost. Your health-insurance carrier or the hospital where you plan to deliver may provide such a service.

Renting.
Breast pumps can be rented. To locate a rental station near you, call Ameda/Egnell, Inc., at 1-800-323-8750; or call Medela at 1-800-TELL-YOU (call collect from Illinois, Alaska, or Hawaii at 815-363-1166).

—J.R.B. and M.J.

Adolescent Childbearing

Whose Problem?
What Can We Do?

Diane Scott-Jones

DIANE SCOTT-JONES is an associate professor in the Department of Psychology, Temple University, Philadelphia.

ATTENTION to the phenomenon of adolescent childbearing typically focuses on its most sensational and titillating aspects. The image of an impoverished 13- or 14-year-old African American or Latino female with more than one baby becomes imprinted in the public mind as the symbol of the problem. Yet the issues surrounding adolescent childbearing are more complex than this stereotypical image suggests. Even the statistics are often presented in a dramatic and misleading fashion.

A careful examination of the data on adolescent childbearing yields the following statistical composite of the typical adolescent mother in the U.S.: she is white and in her late teen years. Childbearing among her peers is not an "epidemic." Indeed, the rate is lower than in the 1950s. However, she is more likely to bear children than are her counterparts in any other industrialized democracy in the world.

Our understanding of adolescent childbearing and our efforts to ameliorate its attendant problems are diminished by unexamined, emotionally charged beliefs regarding race/ethnicity, poverty, gender, and even the transitional nature of adolescence in the course of life. As is often true of issues about which we care deeply, the problem of adolescent childbearing is surrounded by myths that are perpetuated in the mass media and in everyday discussions of concerned and caring individuals. In order

> **Young people in our society become biologically mature at very early ages, putting biological forces at odds with social ones.**

to understand complex problems, we sometimes oversimplify our explanations and proposed solutions. We come to see such problems as limited only to certain groups, and we ignore the broader social contexts — thus allowing normal aspects of human behavior to be defined as problematic. Pregnancy and parenthood are, after all, highly valued in American society. Unlike other problems of adolescence, such as drug abuse or delinquency, pregnancy and parenthood are problematic only because of their early timing in the lifecourse.

As we explore adolescent childbearing and consider what we can do to prevent it, we must keep in mind the enormous changes adolescents experience. The dramatic physical changes of adolescence occur very rapidly; this rate of growth is unsurpassed at any point in life, with the exception of the prenatal period and infancy. To this great change within individuals, we must add the changes in social expectations for adolescents, changes in the structure and

content of formal education for middle and high school students, and the effect of difficult conditions in our society. Then one can imagine how tough the transition into adulthood can be for many adolescents. As a society, we must ask how we can establish more supportive contexts for adolescents' transition to adulthood. It is in that spirit that I ask "whose problem" adolescent childbearing is and what we can do about it.

WHOSE PROBLEM?

As is the case with any social phenomenon, we need to begin our analysis with an accurate and thorough description. Adolescent childbearing is embedded in pervasive societal problems and cannot be understood completely as a problem *within* individual adolescents. Adolescent childbearing affects many segments of society and is not limited to ethnic minority groups. Moreover, the behavior of males is an important factor. Finally, the problems are different for younger and older adolescents.

For the most part, *adolescence* is defined as ages 13 through 19, although some studies have used slightly different age ranges. For example, adolescent fertility is often reported as live births to females 15 to 19 years of age. The reason for this range is that relatively few births occur to females younger than 15. Age differences within the adolescent years are very important for any research or intervention program.

 From *Phi Delta Kappan,* November 1993, pp. K1-K12.

NOT JUST INDIVIDUAL ADOLESCENTS

Sometimes we mistakenly assume that adolescents' problems are *within* the adolescents themselves. Yet adolescents must make the transition from childhood to adulthood in a society that places many obstacles in their paths. For some adolescents, the prospects for adult life look bleak. For many families and communities the recession of the early 1990s might well be called a depression. And in these tough economic times, some individuals have created lucrative businesses from the manufacture and distribution of drugs in the communities that are least able to fight them. Our social climate is infected with racism, sexism, and class bias that we have not overcome despite valiant efforts.

Current social conditions make it generally difficult to become a responsible adult, and developing sexual responsibility is particularly difficult for those making the transition to adulthood. We are plagued with the mysterious and uncontrolled sexually transmitted disease AIDS. In spite of the life-threatening nature of AIDS, the mass media continue to bombard adolescents with sexual stimuli and sexual themes in all genres, from rock videos to product advertisements.[1] At the same time, sexual harassment too frequently invades the workplace. As a result, adolescents have few positive role models for adult sexual behavior and lack clear standards for accepting themselves as sexually mature and sexually responsible individuals.

In addition, two important changes have occurred in the *timing* of adolescence in the life span. First, girls today reach biological maturity at very early ages. The average age of menarche is 12.5 years, and for some girls the first menstrual period occurs as early as age 9. We can contrast this early age with the average for European populations in the 19th century: the average age for the first menstrual period in the mid-19th century was 16.5 to 17 years.[2]

Why does menarche occur so early today? Menarche is triggered by a girl's proportion of body fat. High-calorie diets and a relatively sedentary lifestyle have combined to lower the average age of menarche. The current average age of menarche may be the earliest possible for the human species. Boys are, on average, two years behind girls in attaining reproductive maturity.

But as young people in our society become biologically mature at very early ages, we have not responded by accepting them as adults at earlier ages. Instead, we have done just the opposite. We have delayed the time that adolescents can begin to function as adults.

We now expect girls and boys to complete many more years of education than was true in the past. Advanced education is now needed for adequate employment outside the home. Marriage is often delayed, and many women delay childbearing until they are close to the end of their reproductive years.[3] Thus, at the same time that young girls become biologically ready to have children at very early ages, we as a society expect them to wait until they are much older before they behave as adults. Biological forces and social forces are at odds.

The current trend toward later marriage and childbearing in our society, especially among affluent women, causes us to consider adolescent childbearing quite inappropriate. Yet, in the not too distant past, early childbearing was the norm in our society, just as adolescent childbearing remains the norm throughout most of the world. Biologically, optimal time for childbearing begins in the late adolescent years. In fact, in *Walden Two* B. F. Skinner advocated childbearing in late adolescence. In the United States in the 1950s, many young women in their late teens became pregnant, and the adolescent birthrate was higher than in recent years. For every 1,000 females between 15 and 19 years of age, there were 90 births in 1955, 68 births in 1970, and 51 births in 1986.[4] These facts are surprising to those who think that adolescent childbearing is a recent phenomenon and that it has become an epidemic.

Adolescent childbearing was not widely acknowledged as a problem in the 1950s because pregnant adolescents tended to get married, to remain in stable families, and to live relatively prosperous lives. Even men with little formal education could find good jobs in factories, steel mills, and so on. But those manufacturing jobs are no longer widely available, and young people with the same level of education today are faced with low-paying service jobs, such as those in the fast-food industry. Thus today's economy makes it very difficult for young people to form families as they did in the 1950s. Marriage is made still more unlikely by the current economic recession. Many young fathers are not able to find employment that would allow them to support a family. The situation today is vastly different from that of the 1950s.

The fact that adolescent childbearers tend to be unmarried must be placed in the context of the increase in nonmarital childbearing for older women in our society. A recent Census Bureau report of data from June 1992 indicates that approximately 24% of single adult women had given birth.[5] The greatest increases in the rate of childbearing among single adult women occurred among women who were college-educated, employed, and white. Nonmarital childbearing actually declined slightly for African American women at the same time as it rose sharply, almost doubling, for white women. Although higher percentages of nonmarital childbearing still occur among African American women and women who have not completed high school, these figures indicate that nonmarital childbearing among adult women does not fit stereotypes and cuts across ethnic and socioeconomic lines.

It is in the current social and economic environment that we must try to understand the challenges facing adolescents and the opportunities we can provide them as they move into their adult lives. The current focus on adolescent childbearing as a social problem of enormous magnitude results at least partly from changed societal conditions. Thus we can conclude that adolescent childbearing is a socially constructed problem and not simply the result of individual pathology. In addition to interventions with individuals, social change is necessary to eliminate the problems associated with adolescent childbearing.

NOT JUST AFRICAN AMERICANS AND LATINOS

There is a bias among researchers and the mass media that shifts the focus of adolescent sexual behavior, pregnancy, and childbearing almost exclusively to African Ameri-

> For every 1,000 females between the ages of 15 and 19, there were 90 births in 1955, 68 births in 1970, and 51 births in 1986. These facts are surprising to those who think that adolescent childbearing is a recent phenomenon and that it has become an epidemic.

Adolescent birth rates declined from the 1970s to the 1980s, and the decrease was sharper for African Americans than for whites.

cans and Latinos and ignores the same problems in white adolescents. Rates of sexual activity, pregnancy, and childbearing are higher for African American adolescents than for white adolescents. Yet many problems exist for white adolescents as well. In addition, statistical comparisons of racial and ethnic groups can be misleading, because a disproportionate number of members of ethnic minority groups are poor. Differences attributed to race or ethnicity often stem at least partly from socioeconomic differences. With that caveat, I will briefly review the data on sexual activity, pregnancy, and childbearing. (The comparisons are reported most frequently for African Americans and whites, and data are not as readily available for other American racial and ethnic groups.)

The largest increase in adolescent sexual activity over the past two decades has occurred for white adolescents. Consequently, the difference between African Americans and whites in rates of sexual activity has declined dramatically in the past two decades, almost to a point of convergence. In 1970, 27% of white adolescent females

and 46% of black adolescent females had become sexually active. In 1988, the figures were 51% for white and 59% for black adolescent females.[6] Furthermore, older (18- to 19-year-old) black adolescent females' rate of sexual activity actually declined, from 83% in 1985 to 77% in 1988. The rate of sexual activity for white 18- to 19-year-old females, in contrast, increased from 61% in 1985 to 73% in 1988.

Adolescent females of all racial and ethnic groups are becoming sexually active at earlier ages. In 1988, 25.6% of 15-year-old female adolescents reported having had sexual intercourse, compared to 4.6% in 1970.[7] Once they become sexually active, white adolescent females have sex more frequently and with more partners than do black adolescent females.[8]

The pregnancy rate for 15- to 19-year-old adolescents has been approximately 11% since 1982, which is an increase over the rate of 9.9% in 1974.[9] The overall increase in the pregnancy rate is the result of increases for white adolescents. The pregnancy rates for African American and white adolescents are not close to convergence,

however. In 1985 the adolescent pregnancy rate of 18.6% for African Americans was twice that of the 9.3% rate for white adolescents.[10]

However, white adolescents who become pregnant are more likely than pregnant African American adolescents to be married, and both groups are less likely to be married than were pregnant adolescents in the past. In the 1950s one-third of first births to adolescents were conceived out of wedlock; in the 1980s two-thirds of first births to white adolescents were conceived out of wedlock, and 97% of first births to African American adolescents were conceived out of wedlock. White adolescents who become pregnant are somewhat more likely to have abortions than are their African American counterparts. In 1985, 41% of 17- to 19-year-old pregnant African American adolescents had abortions, compared to 46% of white adolescents in this age group.[11]

Adolescent birthrates declined from the 1970s to the 1980s, and the decrease was sharper for African Americans than for whites. The birthrate for African American adolescents between the ages of 15 and 19 was 12.3% in 1973 and 9.5% in 1983. Corresponding rates for white adolescents were 4.9% in 1973 and 4.4% in 1983.[12] From 1986 to 1988, birthrates for both African American and white adolescents increased but remained below the 1973 rates. The birthrate for African American adolescents remains double that of white adolescents. Although adolescent birthrates are higher for African Americans, two-thirds of adolescent childbearers are white.[13]

The U.S. has the highest adolescent birthrate of all industrialized, democratic nations. Even if only white adolescents are considered, the U.S. rate remains higher than that in all other similar countries.[14] Included in this cross-national comparison were 37 countries selected on the basis of two criteria: a relatively low fertility rate for women overall and a relatively high percapita income. Canada, England (including Wales), France, the Netherlands, and Sweden were chosen for more extensive analyses because of their similarity to the U.S. in cultural heritage and economic growth.

In addition to the higher birthrate, the adolescent pregnancy rate is higher in the U.S. than in any other Western country.[15] In addition, the adolescent abortion rate in the United States in 1983 was the highest of any country for which data were available.[16]

These comparisons with other developed countries strongly suggest that the common stereotypes regarding adolescent sexuality in this country cannot explain our higher adolescent childbearing rate. The U.S. rate is not higher because of African Americans, for the rate remains higher when only white adolescents in the U.S. are considered. In addition, other countries in the cross-national comparisons also include nonwhite minority groups. Moreover, U.S. adolescents do not have a higher rate of sexual activity than adolescents in the comparison countries. Nor does U.S. welfare assistance explain higher rates of pregnancies and births; the comparison countries have more generous welfare provisions.

One important difference, however, is that the comparison countries have a more equitable distribution of income and more extensive benefits in such areas as health and unemployment. A second pronounced difference is that sex education, contraceptives, and abortion services are more widely available in the comparison countries.[17] I should point out that the availability of abortion typically coincided with the availability of contraception in the comparison countries, so that the need for abortion

among adolescents in those countries was minimized. Another important difference is that the comparison countries have a more open and accepting attitude toward sexual activity among young people. The rate of sexual activity among adolescents is not greater in the comparison countries than in the U.S., but apparently adolescents in the comparison countries are more responsible when they become sexually active.

In addition to the notion that adolescent childbearing is almost exclusively a problem of ethnic minorities, another common stereotype is that children born to African American adolescent mothers will themselves become adolescent parents. It is assumed that a cycle of early parenting is repeated generation after generation. How-

---

> **Apparently adolescents in the comparison countries are more responsible when they become sexually active.**

---

ever, the majority of daughters of adolescent mothers delay their first birth beyond the adolescent years. In a 20-year followup of urban African American adolescent mothers, Frank Furstenberg, Judith Levine, and Jeanne Brooks-Gunn found that nearly two-thirds of the daughters had delayed their first birth until they were 19 years of age or older. The three researchers found the same result when they examined data for African Americans in the National Longitudinal Survey of Youth; two-thirds of the daughters of adolescent mothers delayed their first birth until age 19 or older.[18] This research clearly demonstrates that the cycle of adolescent childbearing is not repeated generation after generation in African American families.

NOT JUST FEMALES

The role of males in adolescent childbearing has received too little attention. Adolescent males who become fathers typically are not included in intervention programs for adolescent parents. However, the majority of fathers of babies born to adolescent females are not adolescents; they are men older than 20. This creates a serious problem in understanding early unplanned pregnancies as an *adolescent* issue. The interactions of an adolescent female and a young adult male may involve a compelling power

differential that is not acknowledged in research or in prevention and intervention programs. Thus the sexual encounters of adolescent females may involve some elements of coercion, whether psychological or physical.

Curbing the physical and psychological intimidation of females in schools is also important. The Educational Foundation of the American Association of University Women sponsored a national survey of eighth-through 11th-graders in 1993. The survey found that sexual harassment is widespread in our middle schools and high schools. Although males were also victims of sexual harassment, far more females than males had experienced and were disturbed by sexual harassment. Some females reported being afraid in school because of the sexual harassment they experienced.[19]

Males' attitudes toward females and sexuality are especially important, given that adolescents, when they do use contraception, rely heavily on a male contraceptive method—the condom.[20] Adolescent males, however, tend not to use contraceptives regularly. Estimates of contraceptive nonuse range from approximately one-half to two-thirds of adolescent males in research samples, including a study of black male inner-city junior and senior high school students and the 1988 National Survey of Adolescent Males.[21]

Although adolescent males do not use contraceptives regularly, most indicate that they are willing to share the responsibility for contraceptive use.[22] Joseph Pleck and his colleagues used a perceived costs-benefits model to test the importance of different motivations for condom use and found that adolescent males' belief in male responsibility for pregnancy prevention was related to condom use. However, the personal benefit that would result from preventing pregnancy was not a factor in their decision to use condoms. Other important factors were the perception that their female partners expected them to use condoms, and the perception of personal risk of acquiring AIDS. Perceptions of reduced sexual pleasure and of embarrassment were negatively related to condom use.[23]

Ethnic differences may exist in adolescent males' use of contraceptives, but current research is not consistent on this point. African American adolescents in the 1979 and 1988 national surveys conducted by Pleck and his colleagues reported the highest consistency of condom use, compared to white and Hispanic adolescents. However, in a small sample of 13- to 14-year-olds, of those who used contraception of any kind, Afri-

2. RELATIONSHIPS: The Next Generation

can Americans tended to use withdrawal, which is not effective as a contraceptive, and whites tended to use condoms.[24] Age and the lower rates of sexual activity among younger adolescents may account for the inconsistencies between these studies.

Media warnings delivered by a highly regarded celebrity may have some limited impact on risky sexual behaviors, but adolescents may be influenced even less than young adults. The November 1991 announcement that basketball star Earvin "Magic" Johnson was infected with the human immunodeficiency virus (HIV) appears to have affected some but not all risky sexual behaviors of young patients in a suburban Maryland clinic.[25] The study was ongoing at the time of Johnson's announcement; comparisons were made of those interviewed prior to and after the announcement. The participants were 60% male and 73% African American; 85% had at least a high school diploma. Their average age was 25. No difference was found in reported condom use before and after Johnson's announcement. However, the number of sexual partners reported by participants was significantly lower for those interviewed after the announcement than for those interviewed prior to the announcement. Unfortunately, this reduction took effect for patients aged 25 and older but not for the younger patients (16 to 24 years of age).

YOUNGER AND OLDER ADOLESCENTS

The majority of births to adolescents are to older adolescents. Only 1% to 2% of all births to adolescents are to those younger than 15.[26] Childbearing and related issues are very different for older adolescents than for younger ones. With adolescent mothers who are at least 15 years of age, the medical risks of pregnancy could be normalized with adequate nutrition and adequate prenatal care.[27] Older adolescent childbearers face issues related to the transition to adulthood: completing school, finding employment, and forming stable adult relationships.

Although childbearing occurs less frequently in young adolescents, the potential negative outcomes are great. Adolescents younger than 15 face serious biomedical risks when they become pregnant. In addition, the younger the adolescent female is when she becomes sexually active, the more likely she is to experience little intimacy and some degree of coercion in her relationships. The transition from late childhood to early adolescence is often difficult, and

early sexual relations, pregnancy, and childbearing greatly exacerbate the normal developmental challenges.

> **Although childbearing occurs less frequently in young adolescents, the potential negative outcomes are great.**

WHAT CAN WE DO?

What can we do to help adolescents make good choices about sexual activity, pregnancy, and childbearing? Adolescents need guidance at many decision points. They need comprehensive sex education programs to prevent early sexual activity and unplanned pregnancies.

We also need to reframe the question of adolescents' motivation. Too frequently, researchers and practitioners assume that adolescent sexual activity is a problem behavior whose origins are the same as those for drug use and delinquency. The association of adolescent sexual activity with pathology needs to be replaced by an acknowledgment that becoming sexually active is a normal aspect of human development as adolescents make the transition into adulthood. In our present society, however, early sexual activity and early pregnancy greatly diminish the possibility of positive developmental outcomes for adolescents. We need to learn more about how to motivate adolescents to delay sexual activity and to avoid unplanned pregnancy.

In addition to sex education programs, adolescents need programs that indirectly help to reduce the risk of unplanned pregnancy by focusing on educational expectations, educational achievement, and career preparation. Although controversial, abortion and adoption are possible resolutions of unplanned pregnancy, and they need careful consideration, along with acknowledgment of and respect for differing values on these issues. When adolescents have children, they need to continue in school, and child-care programs are important ways of helping them do so. Prevention and intervention programs should target males as well as females. Finally, separate strategies are needed for younger and for older adolescents.

Claire Brindis offers some excellent practical information on preventing unplanned

pregnancy among adolescents — drawing on and evaluating the efforts of a number of communities.[28] Although some general guidelines apply broadly, local communities will need to develop prevention plans that are suited to the particular issues and problems they face.

COMPREHENSIVE SEX EDUCATION

The sex education that adolescents receive may be too little, too late. In a study of African American adolescent females, Sherry Turner and I found that the majority had had sex education programs in school.[29] The majority also said that they had discussed sexual topics with their parents. But our analyses indicated that one-half to two-thirds of the adolescents became sexually active *before* they had had a sex education program. And many young adolescents in our study who were not sexually active had not yet had a sex education program. In addition, one-half of the adolescents found the information typically provided them to be inadequate. So, although most adolescents receive some form of sex education, the *quality* and *timing* of their programs and discussions of sexuality are crucial.

However, objections to sex education programs in the schools continue. Only 17 states and the District of Columbia include sex education as a mandated part of the school curriculum.[30] Moreover, many sex education programs promote abstinence without also providing information about contraception. U.S. policy regarding sex education stands in sharp contrast to that of other Western democracies, where sex education is far more extensive. Indeed, the only federal program for adolescent pregnancy prevention, the Adolescent Family Life Act, will not support programs that focus on contraception unless they are targeted toward the prevention of second pregnancies among adolescents who have experienced first pregnancies. The thinking represented in this federal legislation is that it is acceptable to talk about contraception with teens who have already had one baby but not acceptable to talk about contraception with teens who have yet to become pregnant!

Despite current sex education policies, some adolescents do use contraceptives. This is evidenced by the fact that adolescent pregnancies have not increased at the same rate as adolescent sexual activity has increased.[31]

In some communities, sex education is seen as the cause of adolescent pregnancy.

Many people believe that giving teens accurate information about sex and contraception will increase the numbers who are sexually active and become pregnant. There is no research to support this idea. In one small town in a rural area of California where only 25 girls were in the graduating class, more than half were pregnant or had

---

Adolescents who have high expectations for their own attainment are less likely to become sexually active.

---

already had a baby at the time of graduation. The response of the community and school was to ban sex education programs in the school.

In many instances, sex education is a small part of a health course and is not given sufficient attention. But comprehensive sex education programs that give adolescents accurate information about reproduction and contraception are needed, and they are needed before adolescents become sexually active.

Technical information about sexuality should be augmented with discussions of the close personal relationships in which the responsible expression of sexuality occurs. The current trend in our society is toward delayed marriage. And we don't have clear age norms for the appropriate time for the initiation of sexual activity. Moreover, some early sexual encounters may occur in the context of sexual harassment. Thus attention to the *relationship* in which sexual expression occurs is critical in sex education programs.

Most adolescents who attend sex education programs do so in schools. In our research, Turner and I found that very few adolescents had sex education programs in community centers or churches. The resources of these organizations could be used in a comprehensive sex education program and might be very important to adolescents' understanding of community values related to sexuality, pregnancy, and the relationships in which pregnancy occurs.

EDUCATION AND CAREER PROGRAMS

Comprehensive sex education programs are necessary but not sufficient to prevent unplanned pregnancies. In addition to programs that focus directly on sexuality and

pregnancy prevention, we need programs that focus on educational expectations and educational achievement. These programs reduce the risk of unplanned pregnancy indirectly by giving adolescents a positive focus for their lives. Anne White and I found that adolescents who have high expectations for their own educational attainment are less likely than others to become sexually active and more likely to use contra-

ceptives when they do become sexually active. Adolescents who see formal education as a viable route to adult success have a *reason* to delay sexual activity and childbearing.[32] As the Children's Defense Fund puts it, "The best contraceptive is a real future." Programs for adolescents need to emphasize the good things they can do with their lives and not just the negative possibilities that we want to prevent. If pregnancy pre-

The association of adolescent sexual activity with pathology needs to be replaced by an acknowledgment that becoming sexually active is a normal aspect of human development as adolescents make the transition into adulthood.

Photo by Kathy Sloane

vention programs focusing on abstinence can be characterized by the slogan "Just say no," then the programs I am advocating here could be characterized by the slogan "Just say yes." Adolescents need to be shown positive options that they can embrace.

Many adolescent childbearers were not performing well in school prior to their pregnancy.[33] The developmental trajectory that leads to poor outcomes for adolescent childbearers appears to be set in motion before the pregnancy and includes low achievement, low engagement in school, and even dropping out of school. Thus having a child usually does not deflect an adolescent from a positive developmental trajectory; many adolescents who bear children were already moving in a negative direction.

Therefore, we must consider the meaning and value of schools for adolescents. Schools today may not be educating and socializing adolescents appropriately for the transition to adulthood. At a time in their lives when they need more guidance from caring adults, adolescents may get less attention from them. For many adolescents, school becomes less and less meaningful. Few high school students, especially those who are not college-bound, believe that they will use the material they are expected to learn in school. Some are already working part-time jobs similar to the kinds of jobs that await them upon graduation. From their own experience, they may know that what they are expected to learn in school is not related to the employment available to them.

An apprenticeship system for adolescents, similar to that in Germany, has been proposed for the U.S.[34] In programs of this type, adolescents would be socialized to perform well not only on academic tasks but also in a real job setting.

Some current efforts to make high schools more meaningful for adolescents include a Public Service Academy, located in a high school in a very poor area of Washington, D.C. This program orients students toward careers in government — the largest employer in their community — and provides them appropriate internships and part-time government jobs. Public schools, private companies and foundations, and universities collaborated to create the Pubic Service Academy. A second example is Houston's High School for Health Professions, which has been operated as a partnership of the public school district and a Houston medical school since 1972. The majority of students in these high school programs will go on to college. However, similar programs could provide an avenue toward employment for those who do not attend college.

Overall, the educational attainment of adolescent childbearers has increased from the 1950s, and the educational attainment of African American adolescent childbearers has increased more than that of whites. Dawn Upchurch and James McCarthy investigated educational attainment among three cohorts of women who were 21 to 29 years of age in 1958, in 1975, and in 1986. Although women who delayed childbearing were more likely to have graduated from high school than adolescent childbearers, adolescent mothers in 1986 were more likely to have graduated than their 1975 or 1958 counterparts. For black adolescents who were 17 years of age or younger when their first child was born, only 16.6% had graduated in 1958, compared to 60.6% in 1986. The corresponding rates for their

---

Child rearing places enormous demands on adolescents, who must also complete their schooling and enter the workplace.

---

white counterparts were 19.6% in 1958 and 53.7% in 1986.[35]

African American adolescent mothers appear to fare better educationally than both their white and their Hispanic counterparts. The National Longitudinal Survey of Youth revealed that, among adolescent mothers whose children were in elementary school, African American mothers had achieved higher educational levels than whites or Hispanics.[36] In addition, in a study of the birth records of one midwestern state, African American childbearers deviated less from expected educational attainment than did Hispanic or white childbearers.[37]

ABORTION: A CONTROVERSIAL OPTION

Perhaps no issue involved in adolescent childbearing is more controversial than abortion. Adolescents' minor status means that their right to obtain abortions is more restricted than that of adult females.

More than 30 states have laws that require the involvement of a parent or a third party in a minor's decision regarding abortion. The "third party" requirement exists so that adolescents have the option of attempting to convince a third party — typically a judge — that they are competent to make the decision independently or that the abortion is in the adolescent's best interest. This "third party" mechanism is a way of bypassing the parental consent requirement for adolescent abortion. Data from actual court hearings indicate that adolescent minors' requests to bypass parental consent are almost always granted. Judges may find the determination of maturity or best interest difficult and may therefore grant all requests. Anita Pliner and Suzanne Yates question whether the consent legislation meets the goals of encouraging communication between parents and adolescents and protecting the rights of minor adolescents.[38] They found that health professionals working with adolescents before and after passage of the legislation indicated that psychological and medical counseling were needed more than pro forma legal procedures. Time spent on the legal proceedings might have been better spent on psychological and medical counseling.

Pliner and Yates recommend that states follow the example of Maryland, where a physician or mental health provider, instead of a judge, makes the determination of maturity and best interest. A second option they suggest is to include mandatory counseling in the legislation, as is done in Maine and Connecticut. Finally, Pliner and Yates recommend that the parental notification and consent laws be limited to adolescents 15 years of age and younger.

Although legal constraints may prevent some adolescents from seeking an abortion, many adolescents do not choose abortion in any case. We might wonder why more adolescents do not seek abortion. Laurie Zabin and Sarah Hayward found that attitudes toward abortion were not different between adolescents who chose abortion and those who carried their babies to term. The difference was that those who chose abortion were very unhappy — unequivocally so — about the pregnancy. Although other adolescents did not indicate that they had wanted or planned to become pregnant, many were ambivalent rather than completely negative about having a child. Zabin and Hayward concluded that, unless there is an "overriding reason to avoid childbearing" — a bright future that will be damaged by early childbearing — the adolescent will have the child rather than choose abortion.[39]

Despite strong feelings on all sides of the abortion controversy, little research exists to help determine the effect on an adoles-

Affordable, high-quality care for children younger than school age is not widely available. A number of high schools across the country have responded by providing child-care programs in the school building.

Photo by Kathy Sloane

cent of having an abortion compared to completing a pregnancy. More research and monitoring of outcomes of legislation should lead to appropriate policy in this area. More research is also needed on adolescents' capabilities to make various decisions about health care.[40] It may not be possible to reach consensus on the issue of abortion, but those who work to create pregnancy prevention programs must find ways to acknowledge differing values and beliefs in this area.

ADOPTION: AN INFREQUENTLY USED OPTION

When adolescents have babies, they very rarely place them for adoption.[41] The overwhelming majority — approximately 97% — of all adolescent childbearers keep their babies. Because of private adoptions and confidential records, however, statistics on adoption may not be entirely accurate. White adolescents are more likely to give their babies up for adoption than are ethnic minority adolescents. But over the past two decades the adoption rate for white adolescent parents has declined sharply, from 19% to 3%, whereas the adoption rate for African American adolescents has re-

mained relatively constant at 1%. It has been suggested that, for African American adolescent parents, an informal type of adoption may occur, with members of the extended family helping to care for the baby.

Research on factors that contribute to adolescents' decision not to place their babies for adoption suggests that adolescents feel emotionally attached to their babies and are thus unable to give them to someone outside their families. In addition, the mothers, peers, and partners of pregnant adolescents may not encourage adoption. Finally, the current organization of adoption procedures may mean that a pregnant adolescent is not given accurate information about adoption as an alternative, may feel pressured into adoption, or may be frightened by the requirement of a complete severing of ties with the baby. Together, these factors may lead adolescent parents to equate adoption with abandonment of the child.

Research on adoption outcomes is sparse. The small number of studies on mothers' responses following adoption often use clinical samples and inadequate research design. However, these studies suggest that mothers experience a long-term sense of loss following adoption and have no accept-

able outlets for expressing their emotions. Michael Sobol and Kerry Daly recommend increasing the involvement of birth parents in the adoption plan as a means of alleviating adolescent parents' belief that placing a baby for adoption is irresponsible.[42] Programs encouraging pregnant adolescents to choose adoption are funded by the federal Adolescent Family Life Act.

CHILD-CARE PROGRAMS

Although child rearing places enormous demands on adolescents, who must also complete their schooling and find a place in the work world, some adolescents are able to manage these developmental tasks. Continued education becomes a key factor in the resilience of adolescent parents. Sherry Turner and I studied three groups of African American women aged 20-24, 25-34, and 35-44 who were part of the National Survey of Family Growth. We found that women who had their first birth during adolescence generally completed fewer years of school and earned lower incomes than women who delayed childbearing.[43] Some of those who had been adolescent mothers, however, had stayed in school longer, and, when we controlled for educational attainment, we found that adolescent childbearing was not a significant predictor of adult income. The number of years of education completed was a stronger predictor of women's income than was the experience of adolescent childbearing.

Social and material support from the family, the community, and the school are essential if the adolescent mother is to remain in school. Adequate child care is especially important for adolescent parents who are enrolled in school. Affordable, high-quality care for children younger than school age is not widely available. But the provision of child care may allow adolescent mothers to resume their schooling more quickly and more easily than would otherwise be possible.

A number of high schools across the country have responded to this situation by providing child-care programs in the school building. We are in the process of studying child-care programs for the children of adolescent mothers as part of our research at the National Center on Families, Communities, Schools, and Children's Learning.

One of our study sites is Orr Community Academy, a public high school in Chicago that maintains an impressive child-care facility. Before the child-care facility was opened, the high school had already established a rich array of programs linking the school to the community and to families. The child-care center was planned in the context of an active umbrella program that connected the high school with surrounding elementary schools and with the community. In June 1989 this urban high school, 13 elementary feeder schools in the area, and a local bank initiated the Orr School Network. This network connects the schools to one another and to the city's educational, cultural, and social service resources. Network principals meet each month to plan and implement programs revolving around three major initiatives: intervening in early childhood, enriching the school years and removing academic deficits, and increasing family and community support for children. One component of the early childhood initiative is the child-care center in the high school.

The high school also contains a comprehensive health clinic for students and a prekindergarten program. The health clinic provides a broad range of health services, including contraception, to adolescents whose parents give written consent. The prekindergarten program operates four days a week in two half-day shifts; 20 children are enrolled in each shift. The high school is also a site for the Women, Infants,

> # Sexual restraint and pregnancy prevention should be presented as necessary prerequisites for a bright future.

and Children program, a federally funded supplemental program that provides food packages and nutritional counseling to eligible mothers. Another special program that operates out of the high school building is Enrichment for Latinas Leading to Advancement, a comprehensive career program for Latina students that emphasizes nontraditional areas of work for females, such as real estate, banking, medicine, and engineering.

The Orr Infant and Family Development Center, which is operated by Jane Addams Hull House, a Chicago social service agency, is licensed to serve 24 adolescent parents and their children from 6 weeks to 3 years of age. The center has an exemplary physical layout for the care and education of young children. It has its own separate entrance and an outdoor playground separated by a wall from the rest of the school grounds. A bus provides transportation exclusively for the adolescent parents and their children.

To use the center, the adolescent parent must be enrolled in school, must work in the child-care facility for one hour a day, and must take a parenting class. Adolescent parents and *their* parents must sign a contract agreeing that the adolescent will attend and pass all classes. Adolescent parents also complete a plan detailing goals that they wish to accomplish with their children. The Orr Infant and Family Development Center provides much-needed assistance to adolescent parents, but it also encourages responsibility and achievement on the part of the young parents.

PROGRAMS FOR YOUNG FATHERS

Most programs focus on adolescent females. Because the majority of fathers of babies born to adolescent mothers are young adult males, programs that seek to reach young fathers may be more effective if they are based in the community rather than in the school. One example of such a community-based program is the Responsible Fathers Program, run by the Philadelphia Children's Network. This program, which in 1992 served 57 young unwed fathers between the ages of 16 and 25, focuses on

parenting skills and encourages the men to be actively involved in their children's lives. The young men are also linked to educational resources, employment opportunities, and social services. The program promotes communication and cooperation between fathers and mothers as they raise their children. Claire Brindis provides some examples of other programs for males.[44]

SEPARATE STRATEGIES FOR DIFFERENT AGE GROUPS

The developmental needs of early adolescence, which involves the transition from late childhood, are very different from the developmental needs of late adolescence, which involves the transition to adulthood. Thus programs for older adolescents need to address such matters as completing formal schooling, entering the labor force, and maintaining responsible relationships.

Young adolescents, on the other hand, need sex education programs that begin before they become sexually active. Open discussions with parents, teachers, and counselors are also important. In these discussions, the adults should listen to adolescents, in addition to conveying adult beliefs and values. Young adolescents need accurate information about sexuality and contraception, and they need the opportunity to discuss with adults the close personal relationships in which responsible sexual expression occurs. Sexual restraint and pregnancy prevention should not be presented in negative terms but as necessary prerequisites for a bright future that would be tarnished by an unplanned pregnancy.

When young adolescents do become pregnant, they are more likely than older adolescents to face medical risks that need attention. In addition, the number of years of school remaining for young adolescent parents affects program strategies. For example, in school-based child-care programs for adolescent parents, the children served are usually under age 3. This age range is appropriate for the needs of older adolescents and would allow them to have child care until they completed high school. Children born to younger adolescents, however, would be older than 3 before the adolescent parent completed high school and would need care through a different program.

 N SPITE of the difficulties adolescents face as they grow into adulthood, we must remain optimistic. Adolescents encounter many problems as they become adults in the imperfect world we have created. Gary Melton has written about the importance of recognizing adolescents as *persons*.[45] We must respect them as such in the programs we plan for them. They are not children, even though we do not yet recognize them as adults. Adolescents' views need to be incorporated into the design and evaluation of pregnancy prevention programs. Through the dreams and aspirations of our adolescents and through the opportunities we provide them to grow into productive adults, we might truly change our society.

1. Issues of the newsletter of the National Coalition on Television Violence, June-August 1991.

2. Phyllis B. Eveleth, "Timing of Menarche: Secular Trends and Population Differences," in Jane B. Lancaster and Beatrix A. Hamburg, eds., *School-Age Pregnancy and Parenthood* (New York: Aldine, 1986), pp. 39-52.

3. Linda H. Holt, "Medical Perspectives on Pregnancy and Birth: Biological Risks and Technological Advances," in Gerald Y. Michaels and Wendy A. Goldberg, eds., *The Transition to Parenthood: Current Theory and Research* (New York: Cambridge University Press, 1988), pp. 157-75.

4. Wendy H. Baldwin, *Adolescent Pregnancy and Childbearing — Rates, Trends, and Research Findings from the Center for Population Research* (Washington, D.C.: National Institute of Child Health and Human Development, 1984); and Tom Luster and Mary Mittelstaedt, "Adolescent Mothers," in Tom Luster and Lynn Okagaki, eds., *Parenting: An Ecological Perspective* (Hillsdale, N.J.: Erlbaum, 1993), pp. 69-100.

5. *Fertility of American Women: June 1992* (Washington, D.C.: U.S. Bureau of the Census, Current Population Reports, Series P-20, No. 470, 1993).

6. "Sexual Risk Behaviors of STD Clinic Patients Before and After Earvin 'Magic' Johnson's HIV-Infection Announcement — Maryland, 1991-1992," *Morbidity and Mortality Weekly Report*, Centers for Disease Control, 29 January 1993, pp. 45-48.

7. Ibid.

8. Laurie S. Zabin and Sarah C. Hayward, *Adolescent Sexual Behavior and Childbearing* (Newbury Park, Calif.: Sage, 1993).

9. Stanley Henshaw et al., *Teenage Pregnancy in the United States: The Scope of the Problem and State Responses* (New York: Alan Guttmacher Institute, 1989); and Select Committee on Children, Youth, and Families, U.S. House of Representatives, *Teen Pregnancy: What Is Being Done?* (Washington, D.C.: U.S. Government Printing Office, 1986).

10. Henshaw et al., op. cit.

11. Ibid.

12. Luster and Mittelstaedt, p. 69.

13. Claire D. Brindis et al., *Adolescent Pregnancy Prevention: A Guidebook for Communities* (Palo Alto, Calif.: Stanford Center for Research in Disease Prevention, 1991).

14. Elise Jones et al., *Teenage Pregnancy in Industrialized Countries* (New Haven, Conn.: Yale University Press, 1986).

15. Charles F. Westoff, "Unintended Pregnancy in America and Abroad," *Family Planning Perspectives*, vol. 20, 1988, pp. 254-61.

16. Henshaw et al., op. cit.

17. Jones et al., op. cit.

18. Frank Furstenberg, Judith Levine, and Jeanne Brooks-Gunn, "The Daughters of Teenage Mothers: Patterns of Early Childbearing in Two Generations," *Family Planning Perspectives*, vol. 22, 1990, pp. 54-61.

19. *Hostile Hallways: Survey on Sexual Harassment in American Schools* (Washington, D.C.: American Association of University Women, 1993).

20. Leo Hendricks, *Unmarried Adolescent Fathers: Problems They Face and the Ways They Cope with Them* (Washington, D.C.: Institute for Urban Affairs and Research, 1979); Diane Scott-Jones and Anne B. White, "Correlates of Sexual Activity in Early Adolescence," *Journal of Early Adolescence*, vol. 10, 1990, pp. 221-38; and Freya Sonenstein, "Risking Paternity: Sex and Contraception Among Adolescent Males," in Arthur B. Elster and Michael E. Lamb, eds., *Adolescent Fatherhood* (Hillsdale, N.J.: Erlbaum, 1986), pp. 31-54.

21. Loretta S. Jemmott and John B. Jemmott, "Sexual Knowledge, Attitudes, and Risky Sexual Behavior Among Inner-City Black Male Adolescents," *Journal of Adolescent Research*, vol. 5, 1990, pp. 346-69; and Joseph H. Pleck, Freya L. Sonenstein, and Leighton C. Ku, "Adolescent Males' Condom Use: Relationships Between Perceived Cost-Benefits and Consistency," *Journal of Marriage and the Family*, vol. 53, 1991, pp. 733-45.

22. Hendricks, op. cit.

23. Joseph H. Pleck, Freya L. Sonenstein, and Scott O. Swain, "Adolescent Males' Sexual Behavior and Contraceptive Use: Implications for Male Responsibility," *Journal of Adolescent Research*, vol. 3, 1988, pp. 275-84; and Pleck, Sonenstein, and Ku, op. cit.

24. Scott-Jones and White, op. cit.

25. "Sexual Risk Behaviors."

26. Zabin and Hayward, op. cit.

27. Joy D. Osofsky, Howard J. Osofsky, and Martha O. Diamond, "The Transition to Parenthood: Special Tasks and Risk Factors for Adolescent Parents," in Gerald Y. Michaels and Wendy A. Goldberg, eds., *The Transition to Parenthood: Current Theory and Research* (New York: Cambridge University Press, 1988), pp. 209-34.

28. Brindis, op. cit.

29. Diane Scott-Jones and Sherry L. Turner, "Sex Education, Contraceptive and Reproductive Knowledge, and Contraceptive Use Among Black Adolescent Females," *Journal of Adolescent Research*, vol. 3, 1988, p. 171-87.

30. Brindis, op. cit.

31. Janet Gans et al., *America's Adolescents: How Healthy Are They?* (Chicago: American Medical Association, 1990); and Luster and Mittelstaedt, op. cit.

32. Scott-Jones and White, op. cit.

33. Dawn M. Upchurch and James McCarthy, "The Timing of a First Birth and High School Completion," *American Sociological Review*, vol. 25, 1990, pp. 224-34.

34. Stephen F. Hamilton, *Apprenticeship for Adulthood: Preparing Youth for the Future* (New York: Free Press, 1990).

35. Upchurch and McCarthy, op. cit.

36. Tom Luster and Eric Dubow, "Predictors for the Quality of the Home Environment That Adolescent Mothers Provide for Their School-Aged Children," *Journal of Youth and Adolescence*, vol. 19, 1990, pp. 475-94.

37. Diane Scott-Jones, "Adolescent Childbearing: Risks and Resilience," *American Journal of Education*, vol. 24, 1991, pp. 53-64.

38. Anita J. Pliner and Suzanne Yates, "Psychological and Legal Issues in Minors' Rights to Abortion," *Journal of Social Issues*, vol. 48, 1992, pp. 203-16.

39. Zabin and Hayward, p. 80.

40. *Adolescent Health — Vol. I: Summary and Policy Options* (Washington, D.C.: U.S. Congress Office of Technology Assessment, OTA-H-468, April 1991).

41. Michael P. Sobol and Kerry J. Daly, "The Adoption Alternative for Pregnant Adolescents: Decision Making, Consequences, and Policy Implications," *Journal of Social Issues*, vol. 48, 1992, pp. 143-61.

42. Ibid.

43. Diane Scott-Jones and Sherry L. Turner, "The Impact of Adolescent Childbearing on Educational Attainment and Income of Black Females," *Youth and Society*, vol. 22, 1990, pp. 35-53.

44. Brindis, op. cit.

45. Gary B. Melton, "Are Adolescents People? Problems of Liberty, Entitlement, and Responsibility," in Judith Worell and Fred Danner, eds., *The Adolescent as Decision-Maker: Applications to Development and Education* (San Diego: Academic Press, 1989), pp. 281-306.

Selected Resources

REPORTS

Adolescent Health — Vol. I: Summary and Policy Options. Washington, D.C.: U.S. Congress Office of Technology Assessment, OTA-H-468, April 1991.

Hayes, Cheryl D., ed. *Risking the Future: Adolescent Sexuality, Pregnancy, and Childbearing, Vol. I.* Washington, D.C.: National Academy Press, 1987.

Hofferth, Sandra L., and Cheryl D. Hayes, eds. *Risking the Future: Adolescent Sexuality, Pregnancy, and Childbearing, Vol. II: Working Papers and Statistical Appendices.* Washington, D.C.: National Academy Press, 1987.

Ooms, Theodora, and Lisa Henrendeen. *Teenage Pregnancy Prevention Programs: What Have We Learned?* Washington, D.C.: Family Impact Seminar, 1990.

Teenage Drug Use: Uncertain Linkages with Either Pregnancy or School Drop-Out. Gaithersburg, Md.: U.S. General Accounting Office, GAO/PEMD-91-3, January 1991.

INFORMATION RESOURCES

Brindis, Claire D., et al. *Adolescent Pregnancy Prevention: A Guidebook for Communities.* Palo Alto, Calif.: Stanford Center for Research in Disease Prevention, 1991.

Creighton-Zollar, Ann. *Adolescent Pregnancy and Parenthood: An Annotated Guide.* New York: Garland, 1990.

Data Archives on Adolescent Pregnancy and Pregnancy Prevention, Sociometrics, Los Altos, Calif.

Family Planning Perspectives (journal published by the Alan Guttmacher Institute).

"Special Issue: Adolescence in the 1990s: Risk and Opportunity." *Teachers College Record*, Spring 1993.

ORGANIZATIONS AND CLEARINGHOUSES

Alan Guttmacher Institute
2010 Massachusetts Ave. N.W.
Washington, DC 20036

Center for Population Options
1025 Vermont Ave. N.W.
Washington, DC 20005

Children's Defense Fund
122 C St. N.W.
Washington, DC 20001

Girls Clubs of America
205 Lexington Ave.
New York, NY 10016

National Urban League
500 E. 62nd St.
New York, NY 10021

Share Resource Center on Teen Pregnancy Prevention
P.O. Box 2309
Rockville, MD 20852

The Lifelong Impact of ADOPTION

In many cases, birthparents have trouble dealing with giving up their offspring; adoptees want to know more about their biological roots and genetic history; and adoptive parents are being confronted with issues concerning the raising of their adopted children that no one had warned them about.

Marlou Russell

Dr. Russell is a clinical psychologist in private practice in Santa Monica, Calif., specializing in adoption. She is an adoptee who has been reunited with her birthmother and two brothers.

IMAGINE BEING an adoptive parent who has gone through years of infertility treatment. You recently have adopted an infant and are at a party with it. Someone exclaims, "What a cute baby. Why, I didn't even know you were pregnant!" You wonder if you need to explain.

Now, try to imagine being a birthmother who relinquished a child 25 years ago. You since have married and had two more offspring. You strike up a conversation with someone you've just met. She asks, "How many children do you have?" You hesitate for a moment, then answer, "Two."

Finally, imagine that you were adopted as an infant. You have an appointment to see a new physician for the first time. When you arrive at the office, you are given a two-page form asking for your medical history. When you meet the doctor, he asks, "Does cancer run in your family?" You respond, "I don't know."

The adoption triad has three elements: the adoptive parent or parents, the birthparents, and the adoptee. All members are

necessary and all depend on each other, as in any triangle.

There have been many changes in adoption over the years. The basic premise of adoption in the past was that it was a viable solution to certain problem situations. The infertile parents wanted a child; a birthparent was pregnant and unable to raise her offspring; and the infant needed available parents. It was thought that all the triad members would get their needs met by adoption. The records were amended, sealed, and closed through legal proceedings, and the triad members were expected never to see each other again.

It was discovered, however, that there were problems with closed adoption. Some birthparents began having trouble "forgetting" that they had had a child and were finding it hard "getting on with their lives," as suggested by those around them. There were adoptees who wanted to know more about their biological roots and had questions about their genetic history. Some adoptive parents were having difficulties raising their adopted children and were being confronted with parenting issues that no one had told them about.

Clinicians and psychotherapists became involved because more and more adopted children were being brought in for psychotherapy and being seen in juvenile deten-

tion facilities, inpatient treatment centers, and special schools. Questions began to be raised about the impact and process of closed adoption.

From these questions, it became clear that there are new basic tenets in adoption. One is that adoption usually is a second choice for all the triad members. For example, most people don't imagine that they will grow up, get married, and adopt children. They expect that they will grow up, get married, and have kids of their own. Girls and/or women also don't expect to get pregnant and give their child to strangers to raise.

Coping with loss

A second basic tenet of adoption is that it involves loss for all involved. A birthparent loses a child; the adoptee loses biological connections; and infertile adoptive parents lose the hope for biological children. Those indirectly involved in adoption also experience loss. The birthparents' parents lose a grandchild, while the siblings of the birthparent lose a niece or nephew.

Since loss is such a major part of adoption, grieving is a necessary and important process. The five stages of normal grief and mourning, as set forth by psychologist

Elisabeth Kübler-Ross, are denial—feeling shocked, numbed, and detached; anger—maintaining that the situation is unfair; bargaining—wanting to make a deal or trade-off; depression—feeling helpless and hopeless; and acceptance—integrating and resolving the loss enough to function.

For triad members, grief holds a special significance. They may not even be aware that they are grieving or mourning their loss. Adoption can create a situation where grieving is delayed or denied. Because adoption has been seen as such a positive solution, it may be difficult for a triad member to feel that it is okay to grieve when everything is "working out for the best."

There are no rituals or ceremonies for the loss of adoption. In the case of death, society provides the rituals of funerals and the gathering of people to support the person who is mourning. If the adoption process is secret, as was the case in many adoptions of the past, there is even less opportunity for mourning. In addition, with adoption, much attention is given to the next step of raising the child or getting on with one's life.

Some triad members resolve their grief by trying to find the person they are grieving for. Search and reunion offers the opportunity to address the basic and natural curiosity that all people have in their inheritance and roots. The missing pieces can be put in the puzzle, and lifelong questions can be answered. In addition, there is an empowering aspect to search and reunion and an internal sense of timing that brings with it a feeling of being in control and trusting one's own judgment. For most people who search, knowing—even if they find uncomfortable information—is better than not knowing.

Whether someone actively searches or not, there usually is some part of the person that is searching internally. A common experience among adoptees and birthparents is scanning crowds, looking for someone who could be their parent or their child. Even triad members who say they aren't interested in seeking will express curiosity and react to the idea of search and reunion.

What holds many triad members back from searching or admitting they are doing so is the fear of causing pain to one of the other triad members. Adoptees may worry about hurting their adoptive parents' feelings and appearing to be ungrateful, while birthparents may be concerned that their child wasn't told of the adoption or that he or she will reject them.

Reunion between triad members is the beginning of a previous relationship. It is where fantasy meets reality. Reunions impact all triad members and those close to them. As with other relationships, there has to be nurturing, attention, and a respect for people's boundaries and needs. Reunions and the interactions within them show that adoption was not just a simple solution, but a process that has lifelong impact.

Finding a Balance:
Maintaining Relationships

- Marriage and Other Committed Relationships (Articles 20–25)
- Relationships between Parents and Children (Articles 26–31)
- Siblings: Another Lifelong Relationship (Articles 32 and 33)

And they lived happily ever after . . ." The romantic image conjured up by this well-known final line from fairy tales is not reflective of the reality of family life and relationship maintenance. The belief that somehow love alone should carry us through is pervasive. In reality, relationship maintenance takes dedication, hard work, and commitment.

We come into relationships, regardless of their nature, with fantasies about how things "ought" to be. Spouses, parents, children, siblings, and others—all family members have at least some unrealistic expectations about each other. It is through the negotiation of their lives together that they come to work through these expectations and replace them with other, hopefully more realistic, ones. By recognizing and acting on their own contribution to the family, members can set and attain realistic family goals. Tolerance and acceptance of differences can facilitate this process, as can competent communication skills. Along the way, family members need to learn new skills and develop new habits of relating to each other. This will not be easy, and, try as they may, not everything will be controllable. Factors both inside and outside the family may impede their progress.

From the start, the expectations both partners have of their relationship have an impact, and the need to negotiate differences is a constant factor. Adding a child to the family affects the lives of parents in ways that they could previously only imagine. Feeling under siege, many parents struggle to know the right way to rear their children. These factors can all combine to make child rearing more difficult than it might otherwise have been. Other family relationships also evolve, and in our nuclear family-focused culture, it is possible to forget that family relationships extend beyond those between spouses and parents and children.

The initial section presents a variety of aspects regarding marital and other committed, long-term relationships. The first article focuses on the multiple and often competing roles played by today's couples, who hope to fulfill individual as well as couple needs. It is a difficult balancing act to cope with the expectations and pressures of work, home, children, and relational intimacy. One possibility is a "Peer Marriage," in which couples create a truly egalitarian relationship. The reader will see that there are both positive and negative aspects to such a marriage. The basis of a marriage, assumed by many to be romantic love, is questioned in "Who Needs Love! In Japan, Many Couples Don't." Here, we learn that for many Japanese couples, it is duty and commitment that are important to the maintenance of a marriage. The next reading in this section, "For Better or Worse?" recommends marriage as a stabilizing force in relationships, for gay and lesbian couples as well as for those who are heterosexual. In "Receipts from a Marriage," Margaret Ambry addresses the shifting pattern of spending habits that couples face throughout their marriage. "Saving Relationships: The Power of the Unpredictable" presents a family systems view of the relationship process, suggesting ways in which small changes in one aspect of the family can have large impacts elsewhere.

The next section examines the parent/child relationship. In "Vanishing Dreams of America's Young Families," the author depicts their struggle and mandates our societal obligation to their children. The next two selections concern the care of children. In "A Nation (Still) at Risk?" Jay Belsky presents a cautionary exploration of the potential effects of day care on young children. His view is not encouraging. On the other hand, "The Myth of AWOL Parents" attempts to debunk the perception of parents as increasingly absent from their children's lives. The In-

ternet, often seen as dangerous to the well-being of children, can be a resource for parents, as described in "Family Affair." Two readings, "Effective Fathers: Why Are Some Dads More Successful than Others?" and "Fathers Strongly Influenced by Culture," offer a look at fathers who have been successful in their role, and the cultural influences on them as they attempt to carry out that role.

The final section expands our view beyond spousal and parent-child relationships to another family relationship—that of siblings. Both "Siblings and Development" and "The Secret World of Siblings" report on this relationship and its impact on children's development and ability to relate to others. Although raised in the same family, children do not experience identical family influence. Each child goes through a different interactive process in the family and, as a result, each can have a radically different family experience.

Looking Ahead: Challenge Questions

When you think of a marriage, what do you picture? What are your expectations of your (future) spouse? What are your expectations of yourself? What and how much are you willing to give to your marriage? Who should get married?

How is your experience of committed relationships influenced by those you saw while growing up? How do those relationships affect your own willingness to enter a committed relationship?

How should each spouse behave in a marriage? How are men's and women's roles the same or different?

What do you expect parenthood to be like? What have you learned in talking with your parents or other parents about their expectations and experiences? Why should you share parenting tasks with your spouse or partner? Why would you want or not want to have a child by yourself?

How might you use new technology, such as the Internet, to strengthen your family?

What differences have you seen in the ways in which siblings are treated in families? Why do you think this is so? What is the best way to rear children? Why should one focus on equal treatment of children?

What's Happening to

AMERICAN MARRIAGE?

Demands for intimacy, emotional support, companionship, and sexual gratification have increased, although there has been a decline in what individuals are willing to sacrifice for a relationship.

Norval D. Glenn

Dr. Glenn is Ashbel Smith Professor of Sociology and Stiles Professor in American Studies, University of Texas at Austin.

VER THE PAST three decades, there has been a period of substantial changes in the institution of marriage in the U.S. The divorce rate doubled from 1965 to 1975, increased more slowly through the late 1970s, and leveled off in the 1980s, but at such a high level that almost two-thirds of the marriages entered into in recent years are expected to end in divorce or separation. The increase in divorce, a decrease in remarriage after divorce, and a higher average age at first marriage have lowered the proportion of adults who are married. Out-of-wedlock births have increased substantially, so that one-fourth of all births now are to unmarried mothers. The proportion of married women who work outside the home has risen steadily, the increase being especially great among those with preschool-age children.

Everyone agrees that these changes are important, but different authorities and commentators disagree as to what they mean for the health and future of the institution of marriage. One point of view is that marriage is in serious trouble—that it

may disappear or lose its status as the preferred way of life for adult Americans. For example, a recent book is titled *The Retreat from Marriage,* and numerous books and articles refer to a decline or deinstitutionalization of marriage.

An opposing view, held until recently by most social scientific students of marriage, is that recent changes do not indicate decline or decay, but, rather, are adaptive and have kept the institution viable and healthy. These observers point out, for instance, that the increase in divorce has come about because people are rejecting particular marriages, rather than the institution of marriage—that most divorced persons want to remarry, and about three-fourths of them do so. Some of these commentators even view the increase in divorce positively, claiming that it reflects an increased importance people place on having good marriages and a decreased willingness to endure unsatisfactory ones. Divorce and remarriage, according to this view, are mechanisms for replacing poor relationships with better ones and keeping the overall quality of marriages high.

The evidence doesn't support consistently either the most negative or most positive views of what is happening to American marriage. For instance, the notion that it is a moribund or dying institution is inconsistent with the fact that a large percentage of Americans say that having a happy marriage is one of the most important, if not *the* most important, goal in their lives.

About two-fifths of the respondents to the 1989 Massachusetts Mutual American Family Values Study indicated this was one of their most important values, and more than 90% said it was one of the most important or very important. Approximately three-fourths of the high school seniors studied by the Monitoring the Future Project at the University of Michigan in recent years have stated they definitely will marry, and the proportion has not declined. When adults are asked what kind of lifestyle they prefer, a very large majority select one involving wedlock, and a substantial minority (more than one-third) choose a traditional marriage in which the husband is the breadwinner and the wife a homemaker.

Even when one takes into account that what people say in response to survey questions may not always reflect accurately what they think and feel, these survey data clearly demonstrate that Americans in general have not given up on matrimony. However, there is even more compelling evidence against the most extremely positive assessments of recent changes. Although having good marriages may be as important to people as ever, or may have become even more important in recent years, my research indicates that the probability of attaining them has declined to a large extent.

Those who argue that marriages in this country in general are doing quite well often cite data showing that a high and rather stable percentage of married persons give positive responses when they are asked

From *USA Today Magazine,* May 1993, pp. 26-28. © 1993 by the Society for the Advancement of Education. Reprinted by permission.

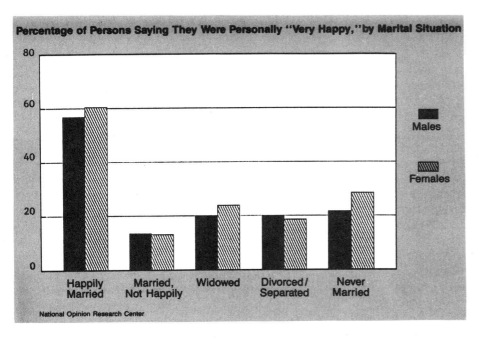

Percentage of Persons Saying They Were Personally "Very Happy," by Marital Situation

Males

Females

Happily Married | Married, Not Happily | Widowed | Divorced/ Separated | Never Married

National Opinion Research Center

about the quality of their unions. In fact, since the early 1970s, the reported quality of marriages has gone down, though not very much. Most years since 1973, the General Social Survey conducted by the National Opinion Research Center at the University of Chicago has asked people to rate their marriages as very happy, pretty happy, or not too happy. The percentage of those who cited "very happy" fell by five percentage points from 1973-76 to 1988-91, dropping from 68 to 63%.

The indicated over-all happiness quality of American marriages still would be quite high if these ratings were to be taken at their face value, but they should not be interpreted that way. Many people are reluctant to admit to an interviewer—and perhaps even to themselves—that their marriages are less than satisfactory. Therefore, an unknown, but possibly substantial, proportion of the marriages reported to be "very happy" are not of very high quality, whereas virtually all those reported to be less than very happy are seriously deficient.

What is important about the indicated trend in marital quality is not that it has been slightly downward, but that it has not been steeply upward. If, as some commentators have claimed, the increase in divorce resulted only from people becoming less willing to stay in unsatisfactory marriages, the average quality of intact marriages should have climbed in tandem with the divorce rate. The fact that it didn't means that the probability of marriages remaining satisfactory must have declined substantially.

During 1973-76, about 60% of the persons who had first married three-five years earlier were still in their first marriages and reported them to be "very happy." By 1988-91, it had declined to about 54%. For persons who first married 12-14 years earlier, the decline was greater, from 54 to 38%, while for those who married 20-24 years earlier, it dropped from 50 to 36%. There were declines of around 10 or more percentage points at most other lengths of time since the first marriage.

Those who view recent changes in American marriage positively may not find these data very alarming. To them, what is important is the kind of marriage a person eventually attains, not the success of his or her first union. From this perspective, the percentages of ever-married persons who were in marriages of any order (first, second, or subsequent) that they reported to be "very happy" are even more significant.

The changes from 1973-76 to 1988-91 show a distinct downward trend in the probability of being in a successful marriage. Among persons who have sought marital happiness by marrying at least once, a decreased proportion seem to be experiencing it. This indicates that the increase in divorce and the other changes in marriage during the past three decades have not been solely or primarily a matter of people becoming more willing and able to go from poor marriages to better ones.

Still, one might suspect that there has been one positive aspect of the changes of the past few years—namely, a decreased tendency for people to be in poor marriages. However, the proportion of ever-married persons who were in marriages they reported to be less than "very happy" increased from 1973-76 to 1988-91 at all lengths of time after the first marriage up to 20 years—the changes being in the range of three to five percentage points. Only among persons who married 20-29 years earlier was there a slight decrease in the percentage of persons in the less satisfactory unions.

Most of the decrease in the probability of being in a very happy marriage resulted from an increase in the probability of being divorced or separated. For instance, at 12-14 years after the first marriage, the percentage divorced or separated at the time of the surveys went from eight to 18%, and at 20-24 years, it rose from eight to 19%.

The most important consequences of the increase in marital failure have been on the offspring. An enormous amount of evidence, from sources varying from in-depth clinical studies to large-scale surveys, indicates moderate to severe short-term negative effects on the well-being and development of most of the children of divorce. Although the causal link is less well-established, there also apparently are some important long-term effects on a substantial minority of those whose parents divorce, including difficulty in making commitments in relationships and an increased probability of various mental health problems. Equally important is evidence for harmful effects from failed parental marriages that do not end in divorce—especially from those unions characterized by high levels of tension and conflict.

The changes in matrimony also have tended to lower the well-being of adults. Although there are exceptions, in general, those who are the happiest and most fulfilled and who function the best are those in successful marriages. On average, the happily married are the happiest, by a large margin, and the less than happily married are the least happy. In other words, to be in a good marriage is the best situation, but a poor marriage is not better than no marriage at all.

The causal relationship between marital situation and well-being is not entirely clear. Happily married individuals may do best partly because those who are the happiest and best-adjusted, for whatever reasons, are more likely than others to marry and to succeed at marriage. However, most researchers who have studied the relationship between marital situation and well-being believe that it primarily is the former that affects the latter. If so, and if the strength of the effects has not diminished markedly in recent years, the decline in the percentage of persons at various stages of adulthood who are happily married has been distinctly detrimental to their welfare.

Why the decline in marital success?

One of the most likely reasons for the decline in marital success is the well-documented increase in what persons expect of marriage. The levels of intimacy, emotional support, companionship, and sexual gratification that people believe they should get from marriage have increased, while what they are willing to give very likely has declined. In other words, the motivation for marriage has become more purely hedonistic, or more selfish. This is just one aspect of a general increase in individualism in America and throughout most of the modern world.

Another likely reason is the breakdown in the consensus of what it means to be a husband or wife. Whereas, until recently, the rights and obligations of spouses were prescribed culturally and fairly well understood by just about everyone, they have become a matter for negotiation in individual marriages. This increased flexibility in marital roles, according to its advocates, should have increased the quality of matrimony or at least the quality of the lives of married persons, and for many persons it may have done so. For others, however, it has led to discord and disappointment. The optimistic view is that we eventually will learn to deal more effectively with the new freedom and flexibility in marriage, but that remains to be seen.

Another change that was supposed to have had unambiguously positive effects, but that may not have done so, is the easing of moral, religious, and legal barriers to divorce. The reasoning of those who advocated this was that making it easier for persons to correct marital mistakes—to escape from unsatisfying, stultifying, or dehumanizing marriages—would have

positive effects on human welfare. Indeed, if one concentrates only on individual cases, as therapists and marriage counselors do, one readily can see how diminishing the guilt, social disapproval, and legal penalties of divorce has improved the quality of many lives.

However, the changes that resulted in short-term benefits to many individuals may have lessened the probability of marital success and resulted in long-term losses in the well-being of the population as a whole. One spouse's freedom—to leave the marriage, to change the terms of the marital contract—is the other spouse's insecurity. That insecurity tends to inhibit the strong commitment and investment of time, energy, and lost opportunities that are conducive to marital success. The decline in the ideal of marital permanence—one of the most well-documented value changes among Americans in recent decades—also has tended to make persons less willing and able to make the needed commitments to and investments in marriage. To the extent that a person constantly compares the existing marriage with real or imagined alternatives to it, that marriage inevitably will compare unfavorably in some respects. People are hardly aware of needs currently being well-served, but tend to be keenly attuned to them not being well-satisfied. Since attention tends to center on needs not being especially well-met in one's marriage (and there always are some), the grass will tend to look greener on the other side of the marital fence. Therefore, merely contemplating alternatives to one's marriage may engender discontent.

Those authorities who have come to recognize the negative aspects of recent changes in American marriage are dividing into two camps—those who believe that the negative changes are inevitable and irreversible and that the best we can do is to try to lessen their impact, and those who believe that at least some of the changes can be reversed. The pessimists give strong arguments for their position, pointing out, for instance, that the trend to individualism that underlies many of the changes has occurred in most parts of the modern world and may characterize an advanced stage of economic development. Furthermore, the insecurity that inhibits commitment in marriage is likely to be self-perpetuating, as it leads to marital instability, which in turn leads to further insecurity.

There are signs, however, that a reversal in some of the changes already may be occurring. In recent years, there has been a strong reaction against radical individualism among many intellectuals in this country, and attitudinal survey data indicate that a similar reaction may be beginning in the general public. Marriage is just as crucial an institution as ever, and most Americans seem to know that. What has been missing is sufficient awareness of the costs of maintaining the health of the institution. It is to be hoped that Americans will recognize that the loss of personal freedom, renunciation of pleasure seeking, and acceptance of greater responsibility necessary for good marriages will benefit themselves, their children, and the entire society.

PEER MARRIAGE

---

*What does
it take to
create a truly
egalitarian
relationship?*

PEPPER SCHWARTZ

Pepper Schwartz, Ph.D., is a professor of sociology and an author. Address: University of Washington, Seattle, Washington, 98195. Her latest book is Peer Marriage: How Love Between Equals Really Works *(Free Press, 1994).*

WHEN I TOLD PEOPLE THAT I WAS beginning a research study of couples who evenly divided parenting and housework responsibilities, the usual reaction was mock curiosity—how was I going to find the three existing egalitarian couples in the universe? Despite several decades of dissecting the sexism and inequities inherent in traditional marriage, as a society, we have yet to develop a clear picture of how more balanced marital partnerships actually work. Some critics even argue that the practice of true equality in marriage is not much more common today than it was 30 years ago. In fact, authors like Arlie Hochschild have suggested that women's liberation has made prospects for equity worse. The basic theme of her provocative book, *The Second Shift,* is that women now have two jobs—their old, traditional marital roles and their new responsibilities in the work force. A look at the spectacular divorce rates and lower marriage rate for successful women provides further fuel for the argument that equality has just brought wives more, not less, burdens.

All of this figured heavily in my own commitment to exploring the alternative possibilities for marital partnership. Ten years ago this began with *American Couples: Money, Work and Sex*, a study I did with Philip Blumstein that compared more than 6,000 couples—married, cohabitating, gay males and lesbians—looking for, among other things, what aspects of gendered behavior contributed to relationship satisfaction and durability. This study contained within it a small number of egalitarian couples, who fascinated and inspired me. We discussed them rather briefly in the book, but our editor encouraged us to make them the subject of a second study that would examine how couples manage to sustain an egalitarian partnership over time. Unfortunately, my co-author was not able to continue the project and it was not until three years ago that I began the research on what I came to call Peer Marriage. I began looking for couples who had worked out no worse than a 60-40 split on childrearing, housework and control of discretionary funds and who considered themselves to have "equal status or standing in the relationship."

I started out interviewing some of the couples originally studied for *American Couples* and then, using what sociologists call a "snowball sample," I asked those couples if they knew anyone else like

themselves that I could interview. After talking to a few couples in a given network, I then would look for a different kind of couple (different class, race, educational background, etc.) in order to extend the range of my sample. I interviewed 57 egalitarian couples, but even after the formal study was over, I kept running into couples that fit my specifications and did 10 more partial interviews.

While initially my design included only Peer Marriages, I also began to interview a lot of couples who others thought to be egalitarian, but who did not meet my criteria. Instead of throwing them out of the sample, I used them as a base of comparison, dividing them into two additional categories: "Traditionals" and "Near Peers." Traditionals were couples in which the man usually had veto power over decision-making (except with the children) and in which the wife felt that she did not have—nor did she want—equal status. The Near Peers were couples who, while they believed in equality, felt derailed from their initial goal of an egalitarian marriage because of the realities of raising children and/or the need or desire to maximize male income. As a result, the husband could not be anywhere near as participatory a father as the couple had initially envisioned. These two groups proved to be a fortuitous addition to the design. It is sometimes hard to understand what peer couples are doing that allows them to fulfill an egalitarian agenda without understanding what keeps other couples from doing the same.

Even though I consider myself to be in a Peer Marriage, I found many surprises among the Peer Couples I studied. Of course, as a researcher, one is never supposed to extrapolate from one's own experience, but it is almost impossible not to unconsciously put one's presuppositions into the hypothesis phase of the research. Clearly, people make their marital bargains for many different reasons, and face different challenges in sustaining them. Here are some of the discoveries I made that I thought might be of use to therapists.

I ASSUMED MOST COUPLES WOULD, like myself, come to egalitarianism out of the women's movement or feminist ideology. Nevertheless, while approximately 40 percent of the women and about 20 percent of the men cited feminism and a desire to be in a non-hierarchical relationship, the majority of couples mentioned other reasons. These included a desire to avoid parental models that they found oppressive in their own upbringing, the *other* partner's strong preference for an egalitarian marriage, some emotional turmoil that had led to their rethinking their relationship, or an intense desire for co-parenting. Women in particular often mentioned their own parents as a negative model. One woman said, "I want a husband who knows how to pack his own suitcase, who puts away his own clothes, who can't tell me to shut up at will . . . My mother may have been happy with this kind of marriage, but I'm still angry at my father for treating my mother like that—and angry at her for letting him." A 25-year-old husband told me, on a different theme, "My main objective in having an equal relationship was not to be the kind of father I had. I want my kids to know me before they are adults. I want them to be able to talk to me. I want them to run to me if they hurt themselves. I want our conversations to be more than me telling them they could do better on a test or that I was disappointed they didn't make the team. I want to be all the things to my kids that my dad was not. I want us to have hugged many, many times and not just on birthdays or their wedding day."

Quite a few men in Peer Marriages said they really had no strong feelings about being in either traditional or egalitarian marriages, but had merely followed their wives' lead. Typical of this group was a

high school basketball coach who said he had had a very traditional first marriage because that was the only arrangement that he and his wife could envision even when it wasn't working. But when he met his current wife, a policewoman who had been single quite a while, her demands for equality seemed perfectly reasonable to him. He just, more or less, fell into line with his future wife's ideas about the relationship. Many of these men told me they had always expected a woman to be the emotional architect of a relationship and were predisposed to let her set the rules.

Most of the couples, however, did have strong ideas about marriage and placed particular emphasis on equity and equality. Even if they didn't start out with a common agenda, most ended up sharing a high degree of conscious purpose. People's particular personal philosophies about marriage mattered less than the fact that their philosophies differentiated their family from a culture that reinforced the general belief that equality is neither possible nor even in the long-term interests of couples. Many people talked about how easy it is to slide into old and familiar roles or follow economic opportunities that started to whittle away at male participation in childrearing. It takes an intense desire to keep a couple on the nontraditional track and a clear sense of purpose to justify the economic sacrifices and daily complications it takes to co-parent. As one wife of 10 years said, "We always try to make sure that we don't start getting traditional. It's so easy to do. But we really want this extraordinary empathy and respect we have. I just know it wouldn't be there if we did this marriage any other way."

IMPORTANT AS RELATIONSHIP IDE-ology is, Peer Marriages depend at least as much on coordinating work with home and childraising responsibilities and not letting a high earner be exempt from daily participation. Previous research had shown me the connection between a husband's and wife's relative income and their likelihood of being egalitarian. So I assumed that most of the couples I interviewed would be working couples, and have relatively similar incomes. This was mostly true, although I was struck by the couples who were exceptions. Four husbands in the study had non-working wives. The men didn't want to dominate those relationships because they felt very strongly that money did not legitimately confer power. For example, one husband had inherited a great deal of money but didn't feel it was

any more his than his wife's. She stayed at home with the children, but he took over in the late afternoon and on weekends. He also was the primary cook and cleaner. In another case, a husband who earned a good deal more than his wife put all the money in a joint account and put investments in her name as well as his. Over time, she had assets equal to his. While these triumphs over income differentials were exceptions, it did make me respect the fact that truly determined couples could overcome being seduced by the power of economic advantage.

However, many Peer Marriages had a significant income differential and husbands and wives had to negotiate a lot just to make sure they didn't fall into the trap of letting the higher earner be the senior decision-maker. Even more tricky, according to many, was not letting work set the emotional and task agenda of the household. The couples needed to keep their eyes on what was the tail and what was the dog so that their relationship was not sidetracked by career opportunities or job pressures. Many Peer Couples had gone through periods in which they realized that they were beginning to have no time for each other, or that one of them was more consistently taking care of the children while the other was consumed with job demands. But what distinguished those couples from more traditional marriages was that they had a competing ideology of economic or career success that guided them when their egalitarianism began to get out of kilter.

One husband, who had an architectural practice designing and building airports, had begun to travel for longer and longer periods of time until it was clear that he was no longer a true co-parent or a full partner in the marriage. After long and painful discussions, he quit his job and opened up a home office so he could spend more time with his wife and children. Both partners realized this would cause some economic privations and, in fact, it took the husband five years to get a modestly successful practice going while the wife struggled to support the family. Without minimizing how tough this period had been, the couple felt they had done the right thing. "After all," the husband said, "we saved our marriage."

This attitude helped explain another surprise in this study. I had presumed that most of the Peer Marriages I would find would be yuppie or post-yuppie couples, mostly young or baby boom professionals who were "having it all." In fact, most of them were solidly middle class: small-business owners, social workers, schoolteachers, health professionals (but not

There was an unexpected down side for the couples who did manage to co-parent. I was unprepared for how often Peer Couples mentioned serious conflict over childrearing.

●

doctors). Apparently, people on career fast tracks were less willing to endanger their potential income and opportunities for promotion. There may be childrearing Peer Marriages out there comprised of litigators, investment bankers and brain surgeons—but I didn't find them. The closest I came to finding fast trackers in a Peer Marriage and family were high-earning women who had husbands who were extremely pleased with their partner's success and were willing to be the more primary parent in order to support her career.

When these women negotiated issues with their husbands in front of me, they seemed more sensitive about their husbands' feelings than men of comparable accomplishment with lower earning wives. For example, they did not interrupt as much as high-earning men in traditional marriages, and they seemed to quite consciously not pull rank when I asked them jointly to solve a financial problem. They told me, however, that they consciously had to work at being less controlling than they sometimes thought

they deserved to be. A very successful woman attorney, married to another, significantly-less-prominent attorney, told me that they had some problems because he wasn't used to picking up the slack when she was called away suddenly to represent a Fortune 500 company. She found herself battling her own ambitions in order to be sensitive to his desire for her to let up a bit. As she noted, "We [women] are not prepared to be the major providers and it's easy to want all the privileges and leeway that men have always gotten for the role. But our bargain to raise the kids together and be respectful of one another holds me back from being like every other lawyer who would have this powerful a job. Still, it's hard."

The other fast track exception was very successful men in their second marriages who had sacrificed their first in their climb to the top. Mostly these were men who talked about dependent ex-wives, their unhappiness at paying substantial support and their determination not to repeat the mistakes of their first marriages. One 50-year-old man, who, had traveled constantly in his first marriage raising money for pension funds, told me he was through being the high earner for the company and wanted more family time in the second part of his life. As he put it, "I consciously went looking for someone who I could spend time with, who I had a lot in common with, who would want me to stop having to be the big earner all the time. I don't want to die before I've been a real partner to somebody who can stand on her own two feet . . . and I've been a real father."

When I first realized how often the desire to co-parent led couples into an egalitarian ideology, I thought this might also lead couples to prioritize their parenting responsibilities over their husband-and-wife relationship. But these were not marriages in which husbands and wives called each other "Mom" and "Dad." For the most part, these couples avoided the rigidly territorial approach I saw in Traditional and Near Peer marriages. In both of these types of couples, I observed mothers who were much more absorbed in their children, which both partners regarded as a primarily female responsibility. As a result, women had sole control over decisions about their children's daily life and used the children as a main source of intimacy, affection and unshared secrets. They related stories about things the children told them that "they would never dare tell their father." While quite a few of the mothers talked about how "close" their husbands were with their children, they would also,

usually in the same story, tell me how much closer their children were with them. What surprised me was that while these traditional moms complained about father absence, very few really wanted to change the situation. Most often, it was explained that, while it would be great to have their husband home, they "couldn't afford it." But of course "afford" is a relative term and I sensed that the women really did not want the men interfering with their control over parenting. Or they would have liked more fatherly engagement but definitely not at the cost of loss of income. One young, working Near Peer Couple with four kids was discussing the husband's lesser parenting responsibilities with me when he said, "You know, I could come home early and get the kids by 3:30. I'd like to do that." The wife's response was to straightforwardly insist that with four kids going to private school, his energies were best used paying for their tuitions. She preferred a double shift to a shared one because her financial priorities and her vision of what most profited her children were clear.

But there was an unexpected downside for the couples who did manage to co-parent. I was unprepared for how often Peer Couples mentioned serious conflict over childrearing. Because each partner felt very strongly about the children's upbringing, differences of opinion were not easily resolved. As one peer wife said, "We are both capable of stepping up to the line and staying there screaming at each other." Another husband said, "If you only talked to us about how we deal with disagreements about the kids, you might think we were a deeply conflicted marriage. We're not. But unfortunately, we have very different ideas about discipline and we can get pretty intense with one another and it might look bad. We went to counseling about the kids and this therapist wanted to look at our whole relationship and we had to say, 'You don't get it. This really is the only thing we argue about like this.'"

Peers may, in fact, have more conflict about children than more Traditional partners because unlike Traditional Marriage, there is no territory that is automatically ceded to the other person and conflict cannot be resolved by one person claiming the greater right to have the final word. Still, while a majority of Peer Couples mentioned fights over child-related decisions, there were only a few Peer Marriages where I wondered if these arguments threatened the relationship. In the majority of them, the couples talked about how they ultimately, if not in the heat of battle, followed their usual pattern of talking until agreement was reached. What usually forced them to continue to communicate and reach a joint answer was their pledge to give the other partner equal standing in the relationship. Occasionally, a few people told me, they just couldn't reach a mutually satisfying answer and let their partner "win one" out of trust in his or her good judgement, not because they agreed on a given issue.

The couples that I felt might be in more trouble had recurring disagreements that they were never able to resolve over punishments, educational or religious choices or how much freedom to give kids. Furthermore, in each instance at least one partner said that the other partner's approach was beginning to erode the respect that made their relationship possible. Moreover, this particular kind of conflict was deeply troubling since many of them had organized their marriage around the expectation of being great co-parents. It may be that co-parenting requires that parenting philosophies be similar or grow together. Co-parents may have a particular need for good negotiating and communication skills so that they can resolve their differences without threatening the basis of their relationship.

IN CONTRAST WITH TRADITIONAL or Near Peer Couples, the partners in Peer Marriages, never complained about lack of affection or intimacy in their relationships. What they did mention, that other couples did not, was the problem of becoming so familiar with each other that they felt more like siblings than lovers. Some researchers have theorized that sexual arousal is often caused or intensified by anxiety, fear and tension. Many others have written about how sexual desire depends on "Yin" and "Yang"—mystery and difference. And quite a few women and men I talked to rather guiltily confessed that while they wanted equal partners, all their sexual socialization had been to having sex in a hierarchical relationship: Women had fantasies of being "taken" or mildly dominated; men had learned very early on that they were expected to be the orchestrators of any given sexual encounter and that masculinity required sexual directiveness. For men, sexual arousal was often connected with a strong desire to protect or control.

Peer couples complained that they often forgot to include sex in their daily lives. Unlike Traditional or Near Peers, their sexual frequency did not slow down because of unresolved issues or continuing anger, at least not in any systematic ways. These couples may start to lose interest in sex even more than the other kinds of marriages because sex is not their main way of getting close. Many Traditional and some Near Peer Couples mentioned that the only time they felt that they got through to each other was in bed. Perhaps the more emotional distance couples feel with one another, the larger the role sexuality plays in helping them feel they still have the capacity for intimacy. Being less dependent on this pathway to intimacy, partners in Peer Marriage may be more willing to tolerate a less satisfactory sexual relationship.

One husband, who worked with his wife in their own advertising firm, even talked about having developed "an incest taboo," which had led to the couple entering therapy. They were such buddies during the daytime, he had trouble treating her as anything else in the evening. The therapist this couple consulted encouraged them to assume new personas in the bedroom. For example, he told them to take turns being the dominant partner, to create scenarios where they created new characters and then behaved as they thought the person they were impersonating would behave. He gave them "homework," such as putting themselves in romantic or sexy environments and allowing themselves to imagine meeting there the first time. The wife was encouraged to dress outrageously for bed every now and then; the husband occasionally to be stereotypically directive. The therapist reminded both partners that their emotional bargain was safe: they loved and respected each other. That meant they could use sex as recreation, release and exploration. They were good pupils and felt they had really learned something for a lifetime.

In another couple, it was the wife who mentioned the problem. Her husband had been the dominant partner in his previous marriage and had enjoyed that role in bed. However, she liked more reciprocity and role-sharing in sex, so he tried to be accommodating. However, early on in the relationship he began treating her, as she put it, "too darn respectfully... it was almost as if we were having politically correct sex... I had to remember that he wasn't my brother and it was okay to be sexually far out with him."

On the other hand, Peer Couples with satisfying sexual relationships often mentioned their equality as a source of sexual strength. These couples felt their emotional security with one another allowed them to be more uninhibited and made sex more likely since both people were responsible for making it happen.

Women with unhappy sexual experiences with sexist men mentioned that for the first time in their lives they could use any sexual position without worrying about any larger meaning in the act. Being on the bottom just meant being on the bottom; it was not about surrendering in more cosmic ways. Being a sex kitten was a role for the evening—and not part of a larger submissive persona.

Many of the Peer Couples I interviewed had terrific sexual lives. The women, especially, felt they had finally met men with whom they could be vulnerable and uninhibited. As one woman said, "I used to be a real market for women's books. I wanted men who fit the stereotype of Clark Gable or Kevin Costner—few words, and when they are delivered, they are real ringers, and there is a lot of eye contact and passion, and that's about as much talking as you get. Maybe it was dating all these guys who were really like that, but even as fantasy objects, I got tired of men who didn't want to explore a feeling or who were only loving when they had a hard-on. I fell in love the first time sharing *Prince of Tides* with the guy I was dating, and fell in love with Eric [her husband] over a discussion of *Eyes on the Prize*. The sexy thing was the conversation and the quality of our mind... I can't imagine anything more boring or ultimately unsexy than a man—and I don't care if he looked like Robert Redford and earned like Donald Trump—who had nothing to say or if he did, didn't get turned on by what I was saying."

Equality brings with it the tools to have a great erotic relationship and also, at the same time, the pitfalls that can lead to sexual boredom. If couples learn that their sexual lives need not be constrained by any preconceived idea of what is "egalitarian sex" or appropriate sexual roles, there is no reason that their equality can't work for them. But couples who cannot separate their nights and days, who cannot transcend their identities in everyday life, may need guidance from a knowledgeable counselor.

WHAT ENABLES COUPLES TO SUStain a style of egalitarian relationship in a world that encourages families to link their economic destiny with the male's career and casts women in an auxiliary worker role so that they can take responsibility for everyday childcare and household chores? In Peer Couples, a sense of shared purpose helps guide the couple back to why they are putting up with all the problems that come from putting together a new model of relationship without societal or familial supports.

Peer Couples may start to lose interest in sex even more than couples in other kinds of marriages because sex is not their main way of getting close.

●

Otherwise it is all too easy for mothers to fall in love with their children and assume primary responsibility for their upbringing or for men to allow their careers to sweep them out of the home, away from their children and back into the more familiar territory they have been trained to inhabit. When this begins to happen, a couple's ideology, almost like an organization's mission statement, helps remind them what their central goal is: the marital intimacy that comes from being part of a well-matched, equally empowered, equally participatory team.

But avoiding traditional hierarchy involves a constant struggle to resist the power of money to define each partner's family roles. Peer Couples continually have to evaluate the role of work in their

lives and how much it can infringe on parenting and household responsibilities. If one partner earns or starts to earn a lot more money, and the job starts to take up more time, the couple has to face what this means for their relationship—how much it might distort what they have set out to create.

Peer Couples check in with each other an extraordinary amount to keep their relationship on track. They each have to take responsibility for making sure that they are not drifting too far away from reciprocity. Peer Couples manage to maintain equity in small ways that make sure the balance in their marriage is more than an ideology. If one person has been picking up the kids, the other is planning their summer activities and getting their clothes. Or if one partner has been responsible lately for making sure extended family members are contacted, the other person takes it over for a while. If one partner really decides he or she likes to cook, then the other partner takes on some other equally functional and time-consuming job. There's no reason that each partner can't specialize, but both are careful that one of them doesn't take over all the high-prestige, undemanding jobs while the other ends up with the classically stigmatized assignments (like cleaning bathrooms, or whatever is personally loathed by that person).

Besides monitoring jobs and sharing, couples have to monitor their attitude. Is the wife being treated as a subordinate? Does one person carry around the anger so often seen in someone who feels discounted and unappreciated? Is one person's voice considered more important than the other person's? Is the relationship getting distant and is the couple starting to lead parallel lives? Do they put in the time required to be best friends and family collaborators? Are they treating each other in the ways that would support a non-romantic relationship of freely associating friends?

There is nothing "natural" or automatic about keeping Peer Marriages going. There will be role discomfort when newly inhabiting the other gender's world. That is why some research shows that men who start being involved with a child from prenatal classes on show more easy attachment and participation in childrear-

ing activities later. While men become comfortable with mothering over time, some need a lot of help. Children will sense who is the primary parent and that will be the person to whom they run, make demands, and from whom they seek daily counsel. One direct way of helping fathers evaluate how they are doing is to help the partners measure how much the children treat them as equally viable sources of comfort and help.

Likewise, being a serious provider is a responsibility some women find absolutely crushing. Most middle-class women were raised to feel that working would be voluntary. After they have made a bargain to do their share of keeping the family economically afloat, they may regret the pressures it puts on them. The old deal of staying at home and being supported can look pretty good after a bad day at the office. But only the exceptional relationship seems to be able to make that traditional provider/mother deal for very long and still sustain a marriage where partners have equal standing in each other's eyes. Couples have to keep reminding themselves how much intimacy, respect and mutual interest they earn in exchange for learning new roles and sustaining the less enjoyable elements of new responsibilities.

Couples who live as peers often attract others like themselves and the building of a supportive community can modify the impact of the lack of support in the larger world. Like-minded others who have made similar decisions help a lot, especially when critical turning points are reached: such as re-evaluating a career track when it becomes painfully clear that it will not accommodate Peer Family life.

This study yielded no single blueprint for successful Peer Marriage. As in all couples, partners in Peer Marriages require a good measure of honesty, a dedication to fair play, flexibility, generosity and maturity. But most of all, they need to remember what they set out to do and why it was important, at least for them. If they can keep their eyes and hearts on the purpose of it all—if we help them do that—more Peer Marriages will endure and provide a model for others exploring the still-unchartered territory of egalitarian relationships.

Who Needs Love! In Japan, Many Couples Don't

Nicholas D. Kristof

OMIYA, Japan—Yuri Uemura sat on the straw tatami mat of her living room and chatted cheerfully about her 40-year marriage to a man whom, she mused, she never particularly liked.

"There was never any love between me and my husband," she said blithely, recalling how he used to beat her. "But, well, we survived."

A 72-year-old midwife, her face as weathered as an old baseball and etched with a thousand seams, Mrs. Uemura said that her husband had never told her that he liked her, never complimented her on a meal, never told her "thank you," never held her hand, never given her a present, never shown her affection in any way. He never calls her by her name, but summons her with the equivalent of a grunt or a "Hey, you."

"Even with animals, the males cooperate to bring the females some food," Mrs. Uemura said sadly, noting the contrast to her own marriage. "When I see that, it brings tears to my eyes."

In short, the Uemuras have a marriage that is as durable as it is unhappy, one couple's tribute to the Japanese sanctity of family.

The divorce rate in Japan is at a record high but still less than half that of the United States, and Japan arguably has one of the strongest family structures in the industrialized world. As the United States and Europe fret about the disintegration of the traditional family, most Japanese families remain as solid as the small red table on which Mrs. Uemura rested her tea.

A study published last year by the Population Council, an international non-profit group based in New York, suggested that the traditional two-parent household is on the wane not only in America but throughout most of the world. There was one prominent exception: Japan.

In Japan, for example, only 1.1 percent of births are to unwed mothers—virtually unchanged from 25 years ago. In the United States, the figure is 30.1 percent and rising rapidly.

Yet if one comes to a little Japanese town like Omiya to learn the secrets of the Japanese family, the people are not as happy as the statistics.

"I haven't lived for myself," Mrs. Uemura said, with a touch of melancholy, "but for my kids, and for my family, and for society."

Mrs. Uemura's marriage does not seem exceptional in Japan, whether in the big cities or here in Omiya. The people of Omiya, a community of 5,700 nestled in the rain-drenched hills of the Kii Peninsula in Mie Prefecture, nearly 200 miles southwest of Tokyo, have spoken periodically to a reporter about various aspects of their daily lives. On this visit they talked about their families.

Survival Secrets
Often, the Couples Expect Little

Osamu Torida furrowed his brow and looked perplexed when he was asked if he loved his wife of 33 years.

"Yeah, so-so, I guess," said Mr. Torida, a cattle farmer. "She's like air or water. You couldn't live without it, but most of the time, you're not conscious of its existence."

The secret to the survival of the marriage, Mr. Torida acknowledged, was not mutual passion.

"Sure, we had fights about our work," he explained as he stood beside his barn. "But we were preoccupied by work and our debts, so we had no time to fool around."

That is a common theme in Omiya. It does not seem that Japanese families survive because husbands and wives love each other more than American couples, but rather because they perhaps love each other less.

"I think love marriages are more fragile than arranged marriages," said Tomika Kusukawa, 49, who married her high-school sweetheart and now runs a car repair shop with him. "In love marriages, when something happens or if the couple falls out of love, they split up."

If there is a secret to the strength of the Japanese family it consists of three ingredients: low expectations, patience, and shame.

The advantage of marriages based on low expectations is that they have built in shock absorbers. If the couple discover that they have nothing in common, that they do not even like each other, then that is not so much a reason for divorce as it is par for the course.

Even the discovery that one's spouse is having an affair is often not as traumatic in a Japanese marriage as it is in the West. A little sexual infidelity on the part of a man (though not on the part of his wife) was traditionally tolerated, so long as he did not become so besotted as to pay his mistress more than he could afford.

Tsuzuya Fukuyama, who runs a convenience store and will mark her 50th wedding anniversary this year, toasted her hands on an electric heater in the front of the store and declared that a woman would be wrong to get angry if her husband had an affair.

"It's never just one side that's at fault," Mrs. Fukuyama said sternly. "Maybe the husband had an affair because his wife wasn't so hot herself. So she should look at her own faults."

Mrs. Fukuyama's daughter came to her a few years ago, suspecting that her husband was having an affair and asking what to do.

"I told her, 'Once you left this house, you can only come back if you divorce; if you're not prepared to get a divorce, then you'd better be patient,'" Mrs. Fukuyama recalled. "And so she was patient. And then she got pregnant and had a kid, and now they're close again."

The word that Mrs. Fukuyama used for patience is "gaman," a term that comes up whenever marriage is discussed in Japan. It means toughing it out, enduring hardship, and many Japanese regard gaman with pride as a national trait.

Many people complain that younger folks divorce because they do not have enough gaman, and the frequency with which the term is used suggests a rather bleak understanding of marriage.

"I didn't know my husband very well when we married, and afterward we used to get into bitter fights," said Yoshiko Hirowaki, 56, a store owner. "But then we had children, and I got very busy with the kids and with this shop. Time passed."

Now Mrs. Hirowaki has been married 34 years, and she complains about young people who do not stick to their vows.

"In the old days, wives had more gaman," she said. "Now kids just don't have enough gaman."

The durability of the Japanese family is particularly wondrous because couples are, by international standards, exceptionally incompatible.

One survey asked married men and their wives in 37 countries how they felt about politics, sex, religion, ethics and

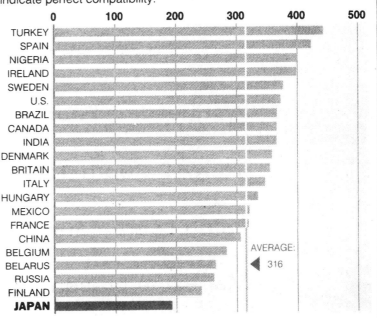

GETTING ALONG

Matchmaker, Matchmaker

How countries compare on an index of compatibility of spouses, based on answers to questions about politics, sex, social issues, religion and ethics, from a survey by the Dentsu Research Institute and Leisure Development Center in Japan. A score of 500 would indicate perfect compatibility.

TURKEY
SPAIN
NIGERIA
IRELAND
SWEDEN
U.S.
BRAZIL
CANADA
INDIA
DENMARK
BRITAIN
ITALY
HUNGARY
MEXICO
FRANCE
CHINA
BELGIUM
BELARUS
RUSSIA
FINLAND
JAPAN

AVERAGE: 316

New York Times

social issues. Japanese couples ranked dead last in compatibility of views, by a huge margin. Indeed, another survey found that if they were doing it over again, only about one-third of Japanese would marry the same person.

Incompatibility might not matter so much, however, because Japanese husbands and wives spend very little time talking to each other.

"I kind of feel there's nothing new to say to her," said Masayuki Ogita, an egg farmer, explaining his reticence.

In a small town like Omiya, couples usually have dinner together, but in Japanese cities there are many "7-11 husbands," so called because they leave at 7 A.M. and return after 11 P.M.

Masahiko Kondo now lives in Omiya, working in the chamber of commerce, but he used to be a salesman in several big cities. He would leave work each morning at 7, and about four nights a week would go out for after-work drinking or mah-jongg sessions with buddies.

"I only saw my baby on Saturdays or Sundays," said Mr. Kondo, a lanky good-natured man of 37. "But in fact, I really enjoyed that life. It didn't bother me that I never spent time with my kid on weekdays."

Mr. Kondo's wife, Keiko, had her own life, spent with her child and the wives of other workaholic husbands.

"We had birthday parties, but they were with the kids and the mothers," she remembers. "No fathers ever came."

A national survey found that 30 percent of fathers spend less than 15 minutes a day on weekdays talking with or playing with their children. Among eighth graders, 51 percent reported that they never spoke with their fathers on weekdays.

As a result, the figures in Japan for single-parent households can be deceptive. The father is often more a theoretical presence than a homework-helping reality.

3. FINDING A BALANCE: Marriage and Other Committed Relationships

Still, younger people sometimes want to see the spouses in daylight, and a result is a gradual change in focus of lives from work to family. Two decades ago, nearly half of young people said in surveys that they wanted their fathers to put priority on work rather than family. Now only one-quarter say that.

Social Pressures

Shame Is Keeping Bonds in Place

For those who find themselves desperately unhappy, one source of pressure to keep plugging is shame.

"If you divorce, you lose face in society," said Tatsumi Kinoshita, a tea farmer. "People say, 'His wife escaped.' So folks remain married because they hate to be gossiped about."

Shame is a powerful social sanction in Japan, and it is not just a matter of gossip. Traditionally, many companies were reluctant to promote employees who had divorced or who had major problems at home.

"If you divorce, it weakens your position at work," said Akihiko Kanda, 27, who works in a local government office. "Your bosses won't give you such good ratings, and it'll always be a negative factor."

The idea, Mr. Kanda noted, is that if an employee cannot manage his own life properly, he should not be entrusted with important corporate matters.

Financial sanctions are also a major disincentive for divorce. The mother gets the children in three-quarters of divorces, but most mothers in Japan do not have careers and have few financial resources. Fathers pay child support in only 15 percent of all divorces with children, partly because women often hesitate to go to court to demand payments and partly because men often fail to pay even when the court orders it.

"The main reason for lack of divorce is that women can't support themselves," said Mizuko Kanda, a 51-year-old housewife. "My friends complain about their husbands and say that they'd divorce if they could, but they can't afford to."

The result of these social and economic pressures is clear.

Even in Japan, there are about 24 divorces for every 100 marriages, but that compares with 32 in France, and 42 in England, and 55 in the United States.

The Outlook

Change Creeps In, Imperiling Family

But society is changing in Japan, and it is an open question whether these changes will undermine the traditional family as they have elsewhere around the globe.

The nuclear family has already largely replaced the extended family in Japan, and shame is eroding as a sanction. Haruko Okumura, for example, runs a kindergarten and speaks openly about her divorce.

"My Mom was uneasy about it, but I never had an inferiority complex about being divorced," said Mrs. Okumura, as dozens of children played in the next room. "And people accepted me easily."

Mrs. Okumura sees evidence of the changes in family patterns every day: fathers are playing more of a role in the kindergarten. At Christmas parties and sports contests, fathers have started to show up along with mothers. And Mrs. Okumura believes that divorce is on the upswing.

"If there's a weakening of the economic and social pressures to stay married," she said, "surely divorce rates will soar."

Already divorce rates are rising, approximately doubling over the last 25 years. But couples are very reluctant to divorce when they have children, and so single-parent households account for exactly the same proportion today as in 1965.

Shinsuke Kawaguchi, a young tea farmer, is one of the men for whom life is changing. Americans are not likely to be impressed by Mr. Kawaguchi's open-mindedness, but he is.

"I take good care of my wife," he said. "I may not say 'I love you,' but I do hold her hand. And I might say, after she makes dinner, 'This tastes good.' "

"Of course," Mr. Kawaguchi quickly added, "I wouldn't say that unless I'd just done something really bad."

Even Mrs. Uemura, the elderly woman whose husband used to beat her, said that her husband was treating her better.

"The other day, he tried to pour me a cup of tea," Mrs. Uemura recalled excitedly. "It was a big change. I told all my friends."

The case for gay (and straight) marriage.

FOR BETTER OR WORSE?

Jonathan Rauch

JONATHAN RAUCH is the author of *Demosclerosis: The Silent Killer of American Government* (Random House).

Whatever else marriage may or may not be, it is certainly falling apart. Half of today's marriages end in divorce, and, far more costly, many never begin—leaving mothers poor, children fatherless and neighborhoods chaotic. With timing worthy of Neville Chamberlain, homosexuals have chosen this moment to press for the right to marry. What's more, Hawaii's courts are moving toward letting them do so. I'll believe in gay marriage in America when I see it, but if Hawaii legalizes it, even temporarily, the uproar over this final insult to a besieged institution will be deafening.

Whether gay marriage makes sense—and whether straight marriage makes sense—depends on what marriage is actually for. Current secular thinking on this question is shockingly sketchy. Gay activists say: marriage is for love, and we love each other, therefore we should be able to marry. Traditionalists say: marriage is for children, and homosexuals do not (or should not) have children, therefore you should not be able to marry. That, unfortunately, pretty well covers the spectrum. I say "unfortunately" because both views are wrong. They misunderstand and impoverish the social meaning of marriage.

So what is marriage for? Modern marriage is, of course, based upon traditions that religion helped to codify and enforce. But religious doctrine has no special standing in the world of secular law and policy (the

"Christian nation" crowd notwithstanding). If we want to know what and whom marriage is for in modern America, we need a sensible secular doctrine.

At one point, marriage in secular society was largely a matter of business: cementing family ties, providing social status for men and economic support for women, conferring dowries, and so on. Marriages were typically arranged, and "love" in the modern sense was no prerequisite. In Japan, remnants of this system remain, and it works surprisingly well. Couples stay together because they view their marriage as a partnership: an investment in social stability for themselves and their children. Because Japanese couples don't expect as much emotional fulfillment as we do, they are less inclined to break up. They also take a somewhat more relaxed attitude toward adultery. What's a little extracurricular love provided that each partner is fulfilling his or her many other marital duties?

In the West, of course, love is a defining element. The notion of life-long love is charming, if ambitious, and certainly love is a desirable element of marriage. In society's eyes, however, it cannot be the defining element. You may or may not love your husband, but the two of you are just as married either way. You may love your mistress, but that certainly doesn't make her your spouse. Love helps make sense of marriage emotionally, but it is not terribly important in making sense of marriage from the point of view of social policy.

If love does not define the purpose of secular marriage,

what does? Neither the law nor secular thinking provides a clear answer. Today marriage is almost entirely a voluntary arrangement whose contents are up to the people making the deal. There are few if any behaviors that automatically end a marriage. If a man beats his wife, which is about the worst thing he can do to her, he may be convicted of assault, but his marriage is not automatically dissolved. Couples can be adulterous ("open") yet remain married. They can be celibate, too; consummation is not required. All in all, it is an impressive and also rather astonishing victory for modern individualism that so important an institution should be so bereft of formal social instruction as to what should go on inside of it.

Secular society tells us only a few things about marriage. First, marriage depends on the consent of the parties. Second, the parties are not children. Third, the number of parties is two. Fourth, one is a man and the other a woman. Within those rules a marriage is whatever anyone says it is.

Perhaps it is enough simply to say that marriage is as it is and should not be tampered with. This sounds like a crudely reactionary position. In fact, however, of all the arguments against reforming marriage, it is probably the most powerful.

Call it a Hayekian argument, after the great libertarian economist F.A. Hayek, who developed this line of thinking in his book *The Fatal Conceit*. In a market system, the prices generated by impersonal forces may not make sense from any one person's point of view, but they encode far more information than even the cleverest person could ever gather. In a similar fashion, human societies evolve rich and complicated webs of nonlegal rules in the form of customs, traditions and institutions. Like prices, they may seem irrational or arbitrary. But the very fact that they are the customs that have evolved implies that they embody a practical logic that may not be apparent to even a sophisticated analyst. And the web of custom cannot be torn apart and reordered at will because once its internal logic is violated it falls apart. Intellectuals, such as Marxists or feminists, who seek to deconstruct and rationally rebuild social traditions, will produce not better order but chaos.

So the Hayekian view argues strongly against gay marriage. It says that the current rules may not be best and may even be unfair. But they are all we have, and, once you say that marriage need not be male-female, soon marriage will stop being anything at all. You can't mess with the formula without causing unforeseen consequences, possibly including the implosion of the institution of marriage itself.

However, there are problems with the Hayekian position. It is untenable in its extreme form and unhelpful in its milder version. In its extreme form, it implies that no social reforms should ever be undertaken. Indeed, no laws should be passed, because they interfere with the natural evolution of social mores. How could Hayekians abolish slavery? They would probably note that slavery violates fundamental moral principles. But in so doing they would establish a moral platform from which to judge social rules, and thus acknowledge that abstracting social debate from moral concerns is not possible.

If the ban on gay marriage were only mildly unfair, and if the costs of changing it were certain to be enormous, then the ban could stand on Hayekian grounds. But, if there is any social policy today that has a fair claim to be scaldingly inhumane, it is the ban on gay marriage. As conservatives tirelessly and rightly point out, marriage is society's most fundamental institution. To bar any class of people from marrying as they choose is an extraordinary deprivation. When not so long ago it was illegal in parts of America for blacks to marry whites, no one could claim that this was a trivial disenfranchisement. Granted, gay marriage raises issues that interracial marriage does not; but no one can argue that the deprivation is a minor one.

To outweigh such a serious claim it is not enough to say that gay marriage might lead to bad things. Bad things happened as a result of legalizing contraception, but that did not make it the wrong thing to do. Besides, it seems doubtful that extending marriage to, say, another 3 or 5 percent of the population would have anything like the effects that no-fault divorce has had, to say nothing of contraception. By now, the "traditional" understanding of marriage has been sullied in all kinds of ways. It is hard to think of a bigger affront to tradition, for instance, than allowing married women to own property independently of their husbands or allowing them to charge their husbands with rape. Surely it is unfair to say that marriage may be reformed for the sake of anyone and everyone except homosexuals, who must respect the dictates of tradition.

Faced with these problems, the milder version of the Hayekian argument says not that social traditions shouldn't be tampered with at all, but that they shouldn't be tampered with lightly. Fine. In this case, no one is talking about casual messing around; both sides have marshaled their arguments with deadly seriousness. Hayekians surely have to recognize that appeals to blind tradition and to the risks inherent in social change do not, a priori, settle anything in this instance. They merely warn against frivolous change.

So we turn to what has become the standard view of marriage's purpose. Its proponents would probably like to call it a child-centered view, but it is actually an anti-gay view, as will become clear. Whatever you call it, it is the view of marriage that is heard most often, and in the context of the debate over gay marriage it is heard almost exclusively. In its most straightforward form it goes as follows (I quote from James Q. Wilson's fine book *The Moral Sense*):

> A family is not an association of independent people; it is a human commitment designed to make possible the rearing of moral and healthy children. Governments care—or ought to care—about families for this reason, and scarcely for any other.

Wilson speaks about "family" rather than "marriage" as such, but one may, I think, read him as speaking of marriage without doing any injustice to his meaning.

Secrets of the Temple

At first glance, the recent decision by a council of Reform rabbis to endorse gay and lesbian civil marriage seemed an odd deflection of responsibility: If the government should do it, why not the rabbis themselves? In fact, this is exactly where the debate is heading. And the closer it gets, the more divisive it becomes.

In Berkeley, California, a small, Conservative-movement synagogue has a solution. Netivot Shalom's Rabbi Stuart Kelman is seeking to redraw the boundaries Jewish practice places around sex while still adhering to Jewish law. In a rabbinical *responsa*, or *teshuvah*, Rabbi Kelman proposed an alternate sphere of recognition for gay and lesbian couples. Called a "covenant of love," the soon-to-be-written ceremony would be performed for gay couples wishing to sanctify lifelong, monogamous relationships. The new sphere would be distinct from Jewish marriage, which is based on a transaction of property rather than a mutual promise (brides do not voice their assent in the traditional ritual, and goods are exchanged as part of the contract). But it would offer parallel honors, including the customary week-before joint calling to the Torah complete with a flower-and-candy pelting from well-wishers.

The balance between traditional observance and liberal values addressed by Kelman's *teshuvah* is particularly tricky for the Conservative movement. Orthodox practice allows only slow and painstaking change to biblical and rabbinic law. Reform Jews do not necessarily see the law as binding (though by no means are all ready to honor gay and lesbian relationships). But Conservative Jews try to balance Jewish law and tradition with rabbinical innovation—a perennial juggling act.

The problem begins with Leviticus. "Do not lie with a male as one lies with a woman; it is an abhorrence," the Bible states, and traditional religious denominations have interpreted the passage as a resounding rejection of gay and lesbian relationships. Like the Reform rabbis, a subcommittee of the 1,400-member Rabbinical Assembly of the Conservative Movement is studying gay and lesbian commitment ceremonies. But, for now, the assembly continues to proscribe same-sex unions and does not sanction the ordination of openly gay and lesbian rabbis. The Presbyterian, Episcopalian, Methodist and Lutheran Churches hold similar positions.

Rabbi Kelman's argument for the "covenant of love" is rooted in rabbinical precedent for adapting Jewish law in response to ethical dilemmas, social currents, changing times and technological advancements. And he adopts an alternate reading of Leviticus, questioning the meaning of the Hebrew word *toevah*, traditionally translated as "abhorrence" or "abomination." Kelman argues that, rather than forbidding gay relationships, Leviticus may simply be setting them apart, thus leaving room for a distinct covenant ceremony. "In Judaism," he argues, "boundaries are permeable, not concrete. No less an authority than Rabbi Moshe Isserles [a sixteenth-century Polish scholar known as the *Ramah*] once broke the law against performing marriages on the Sabbath because he believed the standing of the bride in the community was at stake. What that says to me is that, in this case, the principle of human dignity superseded even the strictest of commandments."

But some biblical experts say that Kelman's reading of Leviticus, while well-meaning, does not hold up. "*Toevah* is a general condemnation," says Jacob Milgrom, an emeritus biblical studies professor at the University of California at Berkeley who has written extensively on the passage. "You can't hide behind the fact that the verses are a prohibition against male intercourse for Jews. That is the plain meaning of the text."

A small group of Netivot Shalom members agree. They argue that the synagogue does not honor members who commit adultery or have premarital sex and that Rabbi Kelman's *teshuvah* far oversteps the procedure for altering traditional practice. Respect for Jewish law, not the demands of a few *teshuvah* members, should determine the synagogue's policy, they believe. "Today's social or political issue is tomorrow's trash," says Seymour Kessler, who considered leaving the synagogue over the issue. "*Halakha* [Jewish law] should not be changed unless there is a long-proven need and a carefully regulated, thoughtful procedure for doing so. Is this decision a threat to tradition and to the authority of the Conservative movement? Of course it is."

Still, the Rabbinical Assembly of the Conservative Movement has posed no objection to Kelman's *teshuvah*, unlike some church bodies that have expelled or disciplined congregations for welcoming gay and lesbian members or clergy. Rabbi Joel Meyers, executive vice president of the assembly, does not think the Conservative rabbinate will advocate gay and lesbian commitment ceremonies anytime soon. But he says the movement has room for rabbis like Kelman.

Gay and lesbian members of Netivot Shalom are pleased with Rabbi Kelman's *teshuvah*. Substituting a covenant-based ritual for marriage does not trouble those who believe the traditional liturgy needs to change in any case. "I don't see this as a gay ceremony. I see it as an alternative ceremony that a straight couple might also choose to use," says Deborah, a lesbian congregant who didn't want her full name revealed.

Most important to her, Deborah says, is knowing that her family will stand on equal footing in the congregation. "I was especially concerned about how a *brit milah* [naming ceremony] for our baby might be handled," she says. "I didn't want to be at a synagogue if my family could not feel fully included. Now I feel like we belong here."

Whether or not Kelman's *teshuvah* will gain acceptance in either the Reform or the Conservative movements is an open question. A scattering of rabbis now use the traditional Jewish wedding ceremony to unite gay couples, and some gays and lesbians have formed their own separate congregations.

But at Netivot Shalom most members see Rabbi Kelman's compromise as preferable to either segregated congregations, identical marriage ceremonies or stasis. Jewish tradition holds that rabbis should only make changes their congregants are prepared to follow, and, despite the grumbling of some, many at Netivot seem proud that their synagogue is proving the Jewish tradition's ability to adapt. "I know this is a divisive issue because staying within tradition has historically been the best way to keep the Jewish community together," says Rena Dorph, a Berkeley doctoral student who observes traditional Jewish law. "But the most important thing about these couples is that they are two Jews committed to being part of the Jewish community. We've got to find a way to make room for them."

EMILY BAZELON

EMILY BAZELON is a reporter for the Alameda Newspaper Group in Northern California.

3. FINDING A BALANCE: Marriage and Other Committed Relationships

The resulting proposition—government ought to care about marriage almost entirely because of children—seems reasonable. But there are problems. The first, obviously, is that gay couples may have children, whether through adoption, prior marriage or (for lesbians) artificial insemination. Leaving aside the thorny issue of gay adoption, the point is that if the mere presence of children is the test, then homosexual relationships can certainly pass it.

You might note, correctly, that heterosexual marriages are more likely to produce children than homosexual ones. When granting marriage licenses to heterosexuals, however, we do not ask how likely the couple is to have children. We assume that they are entitled to get married whether or not they end up with children. Understanding this, conservatives often make an interesting move. In seeking to justify the state's interest in marriage, they shift from the actual presence of children to the anatomical possibility of making them. Hadley Arkes, a political science professor and prominent opponent of homosexual marriage, makes the case this way:

> The traditional understanding of marriage is grounded in the "natural teleology of the body"—in the inescapable fact that only a man and a woman, and only two people, not three, can generate a child. Once marriage is detached from that natural teleology of the body, what ground of principle would thereafter confine marriage to two people rather than some larger grouping? That is, on what ground of principle would the law reject the claim of a gay couple that their love is not confined to a coupling of two, but that they are woven into a larger ensemble with yet another person or two?

What he seems to be saying is that, where the possibility of natural children is nil, the meaning of marriage is nil. If marriage is allowed between members of the same sex, then the concept of marriage has been emptied of content except to ask whether the parties love each other. Then anything goes, including polygamy. This reasoning presumably is what those opposed to gay marriage have in mind when they claim that, once gay marriage is legal, marriage to pets will follow close behind.

But Arkes and his sympathizers make two mistakes. To see them, break down the claim into two components: (1) Two-person marriage derives its special status from the anatomical possibility that the partners can create natural children; and (2) Apart from (1), two-person marriage has no purpose sufficiently strong to justify its special status. That is, absent justification (1), anything goes.

The first proposition is wholly at odds with the way society actually views marriage. Leave aside the insistence that natural, as opposed to adopted, children define the importance of marriage. The deeper problem, apparent right away, is the issue of sterile heterosexual couples. Here the "anatomical possibility" crowd has a problem, for a homosexual union is, anatomically speaking, nothing but one variety of sterile union and no different even in principle: a woman without a

uterus has no more potential for giving birth than a man without a vagina.

It may sound like carping to stress the case of barren heterosexual marriage: the vast majority of newlywed heterosexual couples, after all, can have children and probably will. But the point here is fundamental. There are far more sterile heterosexual unions in America than homosexual ones. The "anatomical possibility" crowd cannot have it both ways. If the possibility of children is what gives meaning to marriage, then a post-menopausal woman who applies for a marriage license should be turned away at the courthouse door. What's more, she should be hooted at and condemned for stretching the meaning of marriage beyond its natural basis and so reducing the institution to frivolity. People at the Family Research Council or Concerned Women for America should point at her and say, "If she can marry, why not polygamy?"

Obviously, the "anatomical" conservatives do not say this, because they are sane. They instead flail around, saying that sterile men and women were at least born with the right-shaped parts for making children, and so on. Their position is really a nonposition. It says that the "natural children" rationale defines marriage when homosexuals are involved but not when heterosexuals are involved. When the parties to union are sterile heterosexuals, the justification for marriage must be something else. But what?

Now arises the oddest part of the "anatomical" argument. Look at proposition (2) above. It says that, absent the anatomical justification for marriage, anything goes. In other words, it dismisses the idea that there might be other good reasons for society to sanctify marriage above other kinds of relationships. Why would anybody make this move? I'll hazard a guess: to exclude homosexuals. Any rationale that justifies sterile heterosexual marriages can also apply to homosexual ones. For instance, marriage makes women more financially secure. Very nice, say the conservatives. But that rationale could be applied to lesbians, so it's definitely out.

The end result of this stratagem is perverse to the point of being funny. The attempt to ground marriage in children (or the anatomical possibility thereof) falls flat. But, having lost that reason for marriage, the anti-gay people can offer no other. In their fixation on excluding homosexuals, they leave themselves no consistent justification for the privileged status of *heterosexual* marriage. They thus tear away any coherent foundation that secular marriage might have, which is precisely the opposite of what they claim they want to do. If they have to undercut marriage to save it from homosexuals, so be it!

For the record, I would be the last to deny that children are one central reason for the privileged status of marriage. When men and women get together, children are a likely outcome; and, as we are learning in ever more unpleasant ways, when children grow up without two parents, trouble ensues. Children are not a trivial

104

reason for marriage; they just cannot be the only reason.

What are the others? It seems to me that the two strongest candidates are these: domesticating men and providing reliable caregivers. Both purposes are critical to the functioning of a humane and stable society, and both are much better served by marriage—that is, by one-to-one lifelong commitment—than by any other institution.

Civilizing young males is one of any society's biggest problems. Wherever unattached males gather in packs, you see no end of trouble: wildings in Central Park, gangs in Los Angeles, soccer hooligans in Britain, skinheads in Germany, fraternity hazings in universities, grope-lines in the military and, in a different but ultimately no less tragic way, the bathhouses and wanton sex of gay San Francisco or New York in the 1970s.

For taming men, marriage is unmatched. "Of all the institutions through which men may pass—schools, factories, the military—marriage has the largest effect," Wilson writes in *The Moral Sense*. (A token of the casualness of current thinking about marriage is that the man who wrote those words could, later in the very same book, say that government should care about fostering families for "scarcely any other" reason than children.) If marriage—that is, the binding of men into couples—did nothing else, its power to settle men, to keep them at home and out of trouble, would be ample justification for its special status.

Of course, women and older men don't generally travel in marauding or orgiastic packs. But in their case the second rationale comes into play. A second enormous problem for society is what to do when someone is beset by some sort of burdensome contingency. It could be cancer, a broken back, unemployment or depression; it could be exhaustion from work or stress under pressure. If marriage has any meaning at all, it is that, when you collapse from a stroke, there will be at least one other person whose "job" is to drop everything and come to your aid; or that when you come home after being fired by the postal service there will be someone to persuade you not to kill the supervisor.

Obviously, both rationales—the need to settle males and the need to have people looked after—apply to sterile people as well as fertile ones, and apply to childless couples as well as to ones with children. The first explains why everybody feels relieved when the town delinquent gets married, and the second explains why everybody feels happy when an aging widow takes a second husband. From a social point of view, it seems to me, both rationales are far more compelling as justifications of marriage's special status than, say, love. And both of them apply to homosexuals as well as to heterosexuals.

Take the matter of settling men. It is probably true that women and children, more than just the fact of marriage, help civilize men. But that hardly means that the settling effect of marriage on homosexual men is negligible. To the contrary, being tied to a committed relationship plainly helps stabilize gay men. Even with-

out marriage, coupled gay men have steady sex partners and relationships that they value and therefore tend to be less wanton. Add marriage, and you bring a further array of stabilizing influences. One of the main benefits of publicly recognized marriage is that it binds couples together not only in their own eyes but also in the eyes of society at large. Around the partners is woven a web of expectations that they will spend nights together, go to parties together, take out mortgages together, buy furniture at Ikea together, and so on—all of which helps tie them together and keep them off the streets and at home. Surely that is a very good thing, especially as compared to the closet-gay culture of furtive sex with innumerable partners in parks and bathhouses.

The other benefit of marriage—caretaking—clearly applies to homosexuals. One of the first things many people worry about when coming to terms with their homosexuality is: Who will take care of me when I'm ailing or old? Society· needs to care about this, too, as the AIDS crisis has made horribly clear. If that crisis has shown anything, it is that homosexuals can and will take care of each other, sometimes with breathtaking devotion—and that no institution can begin to match the care of a devoted partner. Legally speaking, marriage creates kin. Surely society's interest in kin-creation is strongest of all for people who are unlikely to be supported by children in old age and who may well be rejected by their own parents in youth.

Gay marriage, then, is far from being a mere exercise in political point-making or rights-mongering. On the contrary, it serves two of the three social purposes that make marriage so indispensable and irreplaceable for heterosexuals. Two out of three may not be the whole ball of wax, but it is more than enough to give society a compelling interest in marrying off homosexuals.

There is no substitute. Marriage is the *only* institution that adequately serves these purposes. The power of marriage is not just legal but social. It seals its promise with the smiles and tears of family, friends and neighbors. It shrewdly exploits ceremony (big, public weddings) and money (expensive gifts, dowries) to deter casual commitment and to make bailing out embarrassing. Stag parties and bridal showers signal that what is beginning is not just a legal arrangement but a whole new stage of life. "Domestic partner" laws do none of these things.

I'll go further: far from being a substitute for the real thing, marriage-lite may undermine it. Marriage is a deal between a couple and society, not just between two people: society recognizes the sanctity and autonomy of the pair-bond, and in exchange each spouse commits to being the other's nurse, social worker and policeman of first resort. Each marriage is its own little society within society. Any step that weakens the deal by granting the legal benefits of marriage without also requiring the public commitment is begging for trouble.

So gay marriage makes sense for several of the same reasons that straight marriage makes sense. That would seem a natural place to stop. But the logic of the argument compels one to go a twist further. If it is good for society to have people attached, then it is not enough just to make marriage available. Marriage should also be *expected*. This, too, is just as true for homosexuals as for heterosexuals. So, if homosexuals are justified in expecting access to marriage, society is equally justified in expecting them to use it. I'm not saying that out-of-wedlock sex should be scandalous or that people should be coerced into marrying. The mechanisms of expectation are more subtle. When grandma cluck-clucks over a still-unmarried young man, or when mom says she wishes her little girl would settle down, she is expressing a strong and well-justified preference: one that is quietly echoed in a thousand ways throughout society and that produces subtle but important pressure to form and sustain unions. This is a good and necessary thing, and it will be as necessary for homosexuals as heterosexuals. If gay marriage is recognized, single gay people over a certain age should not be surprised when they are disapproved of or pitied. That is a vital part of what makes marriage work.

It's stigma as social policy.

If marriage is to work it cannot be merely a "lifestyle option." It must be privileged. That is, it must be understood to be better, on average, than other ways of living. Not mandatory, not good where everything else is bad, but better: a general norm, rather than a personal taste. The biggest worry about gay marriage, I think, is that homosexuals might get it but then mostly not use it. Gay neglect of marriage wouldn't greatly erode the bonding power of heterosexual marriage (remember, homosexuals are only a tiny fraction of the population)—but it would certainly not help. And heterosexual society would rightly feel betrayed if, after legalization, homosexuals treated marriage as a minority taste rather than as a core institution of life. It is not enough, I think, for gay people to say we want the right to marry. If we do not use it, shame on us.

Receipts from

A Marriage

SUMMARY   Married-couple families are America's largest and most powerful consumer segment. These traditional households experience life as a roller coaster of child-rearing and spending. As married couples advance through various lifestages—from childless couples to new parents, prime-time families, mature families, and empty nesters—their spending waxes, wanes, and shifts in important ways.

Margaret K. Ambry

Margaret K. Ambry is director of consulting services at New Strategist Publications & Consulting in Ithaca, New York.

While single parents and alternative lifestyles get a lot of media attention, business's best customers are still "traditional" families. Married-couple families account for 55 percent of all U.S. households, and seven in ten Americans live in them. Married-couple families also account for 70 percent of total consumer spending. The biggest spenders—married couples with children under 18—comprise just 27 percent of all households, but the number of such households is projected to grow 12 percent during the 1990s.

Blame it on the baby boomlet. There is nothing like a child to change a couple's spending priorities, and baby-boomer par-

ents have been making a lot of changes since the mid-1980s. Having a child doesn't mean getting an automatic raise, however. When the average young married couple makes the transition from childless couple to new parents (oldest child under age 6), their total expenditures increase less than 1 percent. Yet their spending patterns shift considerably: they spend more than their childless counterparts on health care, clothing, housing, and food, and much less on alcohol, education, and transportation. They also spend more on cigarettes and less on personal care and entertainment.

As parents and children get older, income and spending increase in nearly every category of household products and services. Married couples who make the transition to prime-time families (oldest child aged 6 to 17) spend 11 percent more overall than new parents. They spend more on virtually all products and services, although they spend less on alcohol and housing.

Mature families are couples with children aged 18 or older at home. They spend 9 percent more than prime-time families, and they generally have the highest incomes. But when children finally leave home, household spending falls by almost 30 percent. Empty-nester couples spend less than mature families on everything except health care and cash contributions.

Our analysis of the 1989-90 Consumer Expenditure Survey (CEX) shows how the birth, growth, and departure of children affect a married couple's spending. It shows that a couple's lifestage is at least as important as their ages in determining consumer behavior.

CHILDLESS COUPLES

Childless couples with a householder aged 25 to 34 have an average annual before-tax income of nearly $46,000. Each year, they spend an average of $34,000, 22 percent more than the average for all American households. The biggest chunk of a childless young couple's budget (32 percent) is devoted to housing. One-fifth of their spending (20 percent) goes directly into dwellings, and another 5 percent is spent on furnishings; both are higher-than-average shares. Yet childless couples spend very little on household operations. With fewer people to care for, their average annual tab for housekeeping supplies—about $400—is less than their liquor bill.

Like other households, childless couples devote the second-largest share of their spending to transportation. Although they spend an average amount on used cars, they spend 72 percent more than the average household on new cars. Spending on new cars drops off once there are young children in the household, then bounces back. It peaks among mature families and young empty nesters.

> **When children finally leave home, household spending falls by almost 30 percent.**

Just 13 percent of a childless couple's spending goes to food, but more than half of those dollars are given to restaurants and carry-out places. In all other lifestages, couples spend the majority of their food dollars on groceries. Childless couples spend an average of $440 a year on alcohol, more than 1 percent of their average annual budget.

Payments to personal insurance, pensions, and Social Security account for nearly 12 percent of a young childless couple's budget, about $4,000 a year. Because most are two-earner households, childless couples spend 70 percent more than average on pensions and Social Security.

Childless couples devote 5 percent of their spending to clothing, a smaller share than other couples. Another 5 percent goes to entertainment, with equal shares devoted to tickets for movies, theater, sports, and other events; TV, radio, and sound equipment; and other entertainment products and services such as sports equipment and boats. Although

they have no children, childless couples also spend more than average on pets and toys.

They're young and don't have children to take to the doctor, so childless couples spend 34 percent less than the average household on out-of-pocket health-care expenses. Health care accounts for only about 3 percent of their budgets. They also spend less than average on tobacco

Doling Out

	ALL HOUSEHOLDS	CHILDLESS COUPLES	
		25 to 34	25 to
NUMBER OF HOUSEHOLDS (in thousands)	96,393	3,020	4,0
AVERAGE INCOME BEFORE TAXES	$31,600	$45,835	$37,8
AVERAGE HOUSEHOLD SIZE	2.6	2.0	3
AVERAGE TOTAL EXPENDITURES	$28,090	$34,323	$32,79
FOOD	4,224	4,533	4,49
At home	2,438	2,126	2,8
Away from home	1,787	2,407	1,6
ALCOHOLIC BEVERAGES	289	441	2
HOUSING	8,748	11,119	11,5
Shelter	4,934	7,024	6,2
Owned dwellings	2,902	4,132	4,05
Rented dwellings	1,517	2,390	1,93
Utilities, fuels, public services	1,863	1,746	1,96
Household operations	453	178	1,43
Housekeeping supplies	400	407	49
Household furnishings	1,099	1,763	1,42
APPAREL AND SERVICES	1,600	1,725	1,78
Men and boys	395	449	43
Women and girls	665	658	50
Children younger than age 2	71	38	38
Footwear	207	170	2
Other apparel products and services	262	409	24
TRANSPORTATION	5,154	6,989	6,25
Vehicle purchases	2,209	3,095	2,98
Cars and trucks, new	1,188	2,046	1,43
Cars and trucks, used	999	998	1,53
Gas and motor oil	1,016	1,216	1,14
Other vehicle expenses	1,636	2,286	1,93
Public transportation	293	392	18
HEALTH CARE	1,444	970	1,45
ENTERTAINMENT	1,423	1,867	1,59
Fees and admissions	374	485	29
TV, radios, sound equipment	441	525	48
Pets, toys, playground	263	312	39
Other products and services	345	545	42
PERSONAL-CARE PRODUCTS AND SERVICES	365	427	39
READING	155	189	15
EDUCATION	386	284	19
TOBACCO PRODUCTS	68	226	22
CASH CONTRIBUTIONS	858	791	47
PERSONAL INSURANCE, PENSIONS, SOCIAL SECURITY	2,532	4,026	3,343
MISCELLANEOUS	644	737	56

* Cash contributions include alimony, child support, cash gifts to nonhousehold members, and charitable contributions.

products, education, and cash contributions (perhaps because the latter category includes alimony and child support). They spend less than 1 percent of their money on reading materials, although the $190 spent is 22 percent more than average. Young childless couples' trips to the hairdresser, cosmetics, shampoo, and other personal-care products and services take up another 1 percent of their household spending. This share doesn't vary much from lifestage to lifestage.

NEW PARENTS

New parents are couples whose oldest

Dollars

Older families with children have the highest incomes among married couples, but new parents and mature families spend the most.

(average total income before taxes, average household size, and average annual expenditures by expenditure category and by married-couple lifestage and age of householder)

NTS to 54	PRIME-TIME FAMILIES			MATURE FAMILIES			EMPTY NESTERS		
	25 to 34	35 to 44	45 to 54	35 to 44	45 to 54	55 to 64	45 to 54	55 to 64	65 and older
4,466	3,952	7,334	2,011	1,857	3,455	1,819	2,796	4,718	7,601
3,270	$35,251	$47,845	$49,374	$49,214	$51,948	$55,216	$52,736	$38,701	$24,477
3.5	4.3	4.2	3.9	4.5	3.9	3.5	2.0	2.0	2.0
4,839	$31,500	$41,144	$41,816	$43,149	$45,163	$40,730	$40,778	$31,534	$24,136
5,424	4,993	6,403	6,820	6,634	7,015	6,508	5,252	4,685	3,809
3,350	3,175	3,742	3,724	3,993	3,854	3,830	2,674	2,668	2,399
2,074	1,818	2,661	3,096	2,640	3,160	2,677	2,579	2,017	1,411
371	250	295	271	248	343	407	348	291	192
6,539	9,861	12,518	11,986	11,244	12,052	10,264	12,263	9,034	7,407
9,005	5,397	6,946	6,829	6,176	6,584	5,079	7,179	4,496	3,524
7,003	3,296	5,423	4,604	4,803	4,763	3,848	4,939	3,250	2,335
1,029	1,716	858	1,067	728	683	582	881	390	562
2,366	2,075	2,428	2,513	2,703	2,832	2,674	2,242	2,180	1,959
2,357	760	699	638	322	345	334	301	419	512
637	463	593	596	623	574	687	579	508	482
2,174	1,166	1,852	1,411	1,419	1,717	1,490	1,962	1,432	930
2,490	1,726	2,515	2,815	2,844	2,385	2,119	2,300	1,808	1,108
600	447	704	845	846	721	517	561	457	266
882	679	1,041	1,142	1,202	966	852	1,028	887	511
385	123	53	37	41	65	64	57	39	24
225	240	343	397	315	253	293	215	205	171
399	236	373	393	440	380	393	439	220	137
6,737	6,362	7,366	7,469	9,598	9,655	8,251	7,789	5,585	4,188
2,694	3,104	3,516	3,107	4,300	4,261	3,614	3,518	2,151	1,718
1,441	1,512	1,968	1,790	2,099	2,358	2,089	1,802	1,347	1,078
1,253	1,576	1,504	1,283	2,166	1,868	1,443	1,700	788	640
1,249	1,378	1,414	1,503	1,965	1,886	1,615	1,424	1,194	883
2,387	1,769	2,127	2,468	3,070	3,035	2,607	2,424	1,808	1,307
407	111	309	391	263	473	416	423	432	330
1,862	1,262	1,699	1,794	1,518	1,736	2,123	1,705	2,154	2,824
2,478	1,741	2,486	2,216	2,923	2,358	1,974	2,059	1,765	1,069
541	363	745	621	566	588	566	449	437	428
674	610	680	746	675	644	464	534	402	306
550	401	454	425	360	306	367	407	253	199
713	368	607	424	1,322	820	578	668	673	136
453	372	521	583	562	606	592	462	410	374
281	154	209	208	174	209	216	222	198	180
298	314	633	812	1,125	1,437	1,022	573	99	35
253	353	306	300	401	404	384	321	327	163
921	458	880	1,372	1,197	1,509	1,397	1,721	1,265	1,421
5,734	2,961	4,407	4,333	3,877	4,523	4,472	4,877	3,328	882
997	692	908	837	806	931	1,001	887	585	483

Source: 1989-90 Consumer Expenditure Survey

Parents' Progress

As married couples move through life, their spending patterns change. New parents spend less on alcoholic beverages than young childless couples. As children age, couples spend more on education. When children leave, couples reduce their spending on almost everything.

(percent change in average annual expenditures of married couples by lifestage change and expenditure category)

	childless couples to new parents	new parents to prime-time families	prime-time families to mature families	mature families to empty nesters
TOTAL EXPENDITURES	0.3%	11.0%	8.8%	-29.0%
Food	2.4	29.8	8.6	-33.5
Alcoholic beverages	-33.8	-6.2	17.5	-21.8
Housing	9.5	-5.0	-6.2	-18.8
Apparel and services	10.8	20.4	-0.2	-32.7
Transportation	-10.1	12.6	24.7	-40.1
Health care	49.3	9.2	18.9	28.1
Entertainment	-5.6	25.2	1.8	-34.6
Personal-care products	-7.3	21.7	16.6	-28.6
Reading	-7.4	9.7	4.7	-3.8
Education	-28.9	178.7	101.1	-86.4
Tobacco products	12.4	26.0	25.3	-39.3
Cash contributions*	-32.1	62.8	54.6	5.7
Personal insurance, pensions, Social Security ...	-8.3	6.2	4.3	-41.7
Miscellaneous	-13.3	29.7	5.9	-32.9

Cash contributions include alimony, child support, cash gifts to nonhousehold members, and charitable contributions.

Note: A prime-time family may have both preschool and school-aged children, while a mature family may have both adult children and children aged 0 to 17.

Source: Author's calculations based on 1989-90 Consumer Expenditure Survey data

child is under the age of 6. They break down into two groups—younger parents (householders aged 25 to 34) and older new parents (householders aged 35 to 54). Although both types of households average 3.5 people, the older group's average income is just over $15,000 higher. Consequently, older new parents spend more on all major categories of products and services. They also allocate their funds differently than younger new parents do.

Both younger and older new parents devote a larger-than-average share of spending to housing—35 percent and 37 percent, respectively. Younger parents' housing expenditures are boosted by the 4 percent share that goes to household opera-

tions, mostly child care. But older parents of preschoolers outspend all other households on child care, mortgage payments, home maintenance, and other household

The average childless couple spends more than 1 percent of their entire budget on alcoholic beverages.

services such as housekeeping, lawn-and-garden work, and household furnishings.

Older new parents also spend more than younger new parents on transportation, although getting around consumes a smaller share of their total spending (15 percent versus 19 percent). Younger new parents outspend their older counterparts on cars, trucks, and other vehicles, while older new parents spend more on operating costs and public transportation.

Because of their higher incomes, older new parents are free to spend more on food and alcohol, although they allocate a smaller share of income to those categories. Food accounts for nearly 14 percent of young new parents' budgets, compared with 12 percent for older new parents. But older parents channel a larger share of funds to personal insurance, pensions, Social Security, entertainment, and cash contributions.

Older new parents outspend younger ones on all other major products and service categories, but the share they spend is similar. For example, both kinds of couples devote about 0.5 percent of their spending to reading materials. But younger couples spend an average amount, while older couples spend 81 percent more than the average household.

PRIME-TIME FAMILIES

Once the oldest child reaches school age, a family's lifestyles and spending patterns shift again. Like Ozzie and Harriet's family, the average household in the prime-time lifestage has two parents and two children, the oldest of whom is aged 6 to 17. Yet householders in this stage range in age from 25 to 54, and their average before-tax household income ranges from $35,000 for households with a head aged 25 to 34 to just over $49,000 for households with a head aged 45 to 54. Their total spending ranges from 12 percent above average for prime-time families headed by 25-to-34-year-olds to 49 percent above average for those headed by 45-to-54-year-olds.

Housing accounts for a smaller share of spending for prime-time families than for childless couples or new parents. Prime-time households headed by 45-to-54-year-olds spend just 29 percent of their budget on housing, compared with the 35 to 37 percent allocated by younger householders. With larger households and older children, however, prime-timers devote 16 percent of their budgets to food. They don't allocate more than half of their food budget to restaurants and carry-out food as childless couples do, but they tend to outspend new parents on food away from home.

Transportation claims 18 to 20 percent of a prime-time family's spending. This group outspends new parents on new vehicles, and they drive a lot more. Their tab for gas and oil is 36 percent more than the average household's.

Prime-time families have a lot to protect. That's why they spend 74 percent more than the average household on personal insurance and pensions, allocating 9 to 11 percent of their budgets to this

---

CINCINNATI, OHIO

DEMOGRAM

Tom Parker

Giving birth to twins in America isn't a big deal—it happens about 1,600 times a week. Quadruplet births, on the other hand, only happen four times a week. Quads make the evening news. But what about the 40 mothers a week who give birth to triplets? They get big guts, but what about the glory?

Janet Davis, 25, didn't even think she was pregnant. She went to the doctor for a routine exam. Later, when she gained weight faster than expected, her doctors thought her due date was wrong. So they scheduled a sonogram. "There's a very good reason you're getting so big," said the sonogram technician. "You have three babies in there." Janet, already the mother of two kids, ages 8 and 6, just sat in shock. Her mother said, "Oh, my God! I'm leaving town!" Her husband Pat got the news while at his job moving office furniture. He said he would have fainted if he hadn't been wedged into a phone booth.

That's where the fireworks ended. Janet didn't even discuss the triplets with her doctor until her next appointment a week later. Luckily, she stopped at a garage sale to look at a carseat. When she mentioned needing two more seats, the lady at the sale told her about a woman who lived just up the street with three newborn baby boys. Janet stopped and left a note on the woman's door. That's how she found The Triplet Connection.

The Triplet Connection is a nonprofit information clearinghouse and network for multiple-birth families based in Stockton, California. It was founded by Janet Bleyl, mother of ten, after a particularly difficult triplet pregnancy in 1982. According to Bleyl, the organization now has the largest database of multiple-birth information in the world. "We are in contact with more than 7,000 families of triplets and larger multiple births," she says. "And we currently work with over 1,250 expectant mothers per year."

Bleyl says that because triplets are not very common, most doctors have little experience in the special problems of large multiple pregnancies. And she adds that many doctors lack the nutritional training that is critical for these births. "We've found that the most important factor in large multiple pregnancies is keeping close track of nutrition and weight gain," says Bleyl. "As a rule, a mother hoping to walk out of the hospital with healthy triplets should plan on walking in with a weight gain of 50 to 70 pounds."

"We are also very concerned with the insidious nature of early contractions and preterm labor. In large multiple pregnancies, the uterus becomes so distended that it doesn't behave normally. Unless you take some extraordinary measures, it is often quite difficult to know if you are in premature labor. I had six kids before my triplets, but I didn't know!"

Bleyl's organization relies on two sources: a panel of medical advisors, and what she calls the "fabulous networking abilities of mothers" to help expectant parents and inexperienced physicians.

The Triplet Connection sent Janet Davis a packet of information, a medical questionnaire, an audiotape, and a quarterly newsletter. She says the material helped her check the quality of her doctor's advice. Janet's pregnancy was far from easy. Twice, she went to the hospital with premature contractions. Her doctors sent her home hooked to a Terbutaline pump to help prevent early labor. They kept track of Janet's progress with a fetal monitor hooked to a modem. The identical boys, Andrew, Adam, and Anthony, were delivered at 31 weeks—6 weeks early—by emergency C-section. Pat spent the last hour waiting at the hospital while Janet and her dad sat stuck in Cincinnati traffic.

I met the triplets at age 10 weeks. All three seemed healthy and as hard to tell apart as matching spoons. "Thanks to the good medical care, the boys were in the hospital for less than three weeks," Janet says. "The bill came to $90,000. Luckily, Pat's insurance paid most of it. Since then, Andrew and Anthony have had bouts with viral meningitis, we've moved to a different house, our car died, and our plumbing went out.

"Other than that, my biggest problem is simply getting the babies from one place to the next. Just to get into the doctor's office, I have to call ahead and ask the nurse to watch the parking lot for my arrival. Believe it or not, some mothers have figured out how to nurse triplets. Nursing is one thing, but lifting three babies is a different story. When your babies outnumber your arms, you've got problems."

If life's changes didn't throw us for a few loops, they wouldn't be changes at all. At first, most people respond with their own versions of, "Oh my God! I'm leaving town." But few of us ever really leave. We just gather our wits and do the best we can. And that's what Janet Davis is doing. She's got three bedrooms, one bath, two arms—and she's doing her best to hold seven people together. For more information: The Triplet Connection, P.O. Box 99571, Stockton, CA 95209; telephone (209) 474-0885.

3. FINDING A BALANCE: Marriage and Other Committed Relationships

> **Mature families have consistently above-average spending levels for food, transportation, entertainment, personal-care products and services, and education.**

spending category. Clothing and entertainment account for another 5 to 7 percent of their total spending. The amount spent on clothing is highest among prime-timers with householders aged 45 to 54. Households headed by 35-to-44-year-olds spend more on entertainment than others in this lifestage. Prime-time families are also among the biggest spenders on pets and toys.

MATURE FAMILIES

Mature families are couples whose oldest child at home is aged 18 or older. They have consistently above-average spending levels for food, transportation, entertainment, personal-care products and services, and education. Parents in mature families tend to be in their peak earning years, and many adult children also contribute to the family income. Average incomes in this lifestage range from a high of $55,000 for households headed by someone aged 55 to 64 to a low of $49,000 for those headed by someone aged 35 to 44. Mature families also shrink as householders age, from an average of 4.5 persons in families headed by 35-to-44-year-olds to 3.5 persons among those headed by 55-to-64-year-olds.

Compared with families in other lifestages, mature families allocate the smallest share of their budgets (25 to 27 percent) to housing, although they spend more than average on everything except rent, personal services, clothing for children younger than age 2, and household operations. What they save on housing prob-

ably goes to automobiles. Mature families spend 64 to 95 percent more than the average household on vehicles. They also spend above-average amounts on related items such as fuel and maintenance.

Because mature families support ravenous college-age youths, they spend more than other households on food and education. Their expenditures on food are at least 54 percent greater than average, and they allocate 15 to 16 percent of their budgets to food. Education eats up about 3 percent of the average mature family's spending dollar, triple the average amount.

EMPTY NESTERS

Couples' spending doesn't necessarily drop off as soon as the children leave the nest, especially if both spouses are still working. The average before-tax income of empty-nest households headed by people aged 45 to 54 is 67 percent greater than average, and their spending is 45 percent higher than average.

Income and spending do fall off among older couples. But the average income for empty nesters aged 55 to 64 is still 22 percent above the average for all households, and their spending is 12 percent above average. Among empty nesters aged 65 and older, both income and spending are below average (by 23 percent and 14 percent, respectively).

Not surprisingly, empty nesters spend more than younger couples on health care. Young empty nesters spend 18 percent more than average on health care, and their counterparts aged 65 or older spend almost twice as much as the average U.S. household. The share of spending devoted to health care by empty nesters climbs from 4 percent for pre-retirees to 12 percent among the elderly. As empty nesters age and their incomes decline, they also spend higher shares of income on food, personal-care products and services, reading, and cash contributions.

> **Children born to baby boomers will determine household spending for the rest of the decade.**

Young empty nesters spend nearly 60 percent more than the average household on vehicles, while the oldest empty nesters spend 22 percent less than average. Aging empty nesters also spend increasingly smaller budget shares on clothing, education, personal insurance, pensions, and Social Security.

Spending patterns change as children arrive and grow up. Children born to baby boomers during the 1980s and early 1990s will determine the lion's share of household spending for the rest of the decade. As they grow, their family's budget will almost certainly expand. For businesses that have struggled through the recession, this is something to look forward to.

Behind the Numbers This analysis is derived from the Bureau of Labor Statistics' annual Consumer Expenditure Survey (CEX). The unit of analysis in the CEX is a consumer unit, referred to in this article as a household. The analysis is based on a cross-tabulation of age of consumer unit head by composition of consumer unit. In order to obtain a large enough sample, data for the survey years 1989 and 1990 were combined. Because of low frequency counts, spending data could not be tabulated for all types of consumer units for all age groups. The lifestage called childless couples, for example, includes only those headed by someone aged 25 to 34 because there are so few couples headed by a person under age 25. Likewise, most couples aged 35 to 44 have children; the small number who do not are also excluded from the analysis. For more information about the CEX, contact the Bureau of Labor Statistics at (202) 272-5060. Margaret Ambry is co-author of *The Official Guide to American Incomes* and *The Official Guide to Household Spending*, to be published by New Strategist in spring 1993. Some of the data in this article come from these books.

SAVING RELATIONSHIPS:
THE POWER OF THE UNPREDICTABLE

When one partner silently switches the "rules," both partners can benefit. Welcome to the surprising world systems thinking.

Barry L. Duncan, Psy.D.,
and Joseph W. Rock, Psy.D.

Sharon, 30, and Jeff, 35, have been married for nine years. Since the recent birth of their first child, Sharon has become increasingly aware of Jeff's propensity for giving instructions and pointing out imperfections in her methods of doing things. She knows that he is usually just trying to help.

The first thing Sharon does to address the problem is mention it to Jeff. She explains that when they were first married she needed and appreciated his knowledge and experience but now sometimes feels he is treating her like a child. She asks him to please hold his comments and advice until she asks for them. Jeff agrees to make every effort to treat her like the mature, independent woman she has become.

But before long, Jeff resumes sharing his observations of the way Sharon does things and making suggestions about better ways of doing them. When Sharon points this out to him, he becomes defensive and accuses her of overreacting and not being able to accept constructive criticism.

Sharon continues to make Jeff aware of his now "critical, paternalistic, and sexist nature." She takes every opportunity to point out his need to dominate and keep her in her place. Jeff responds by defensively backing off and withdrawing from conversation in general. When conversa-

tion does occur, he seems more apt to criticize Sharon about her "crazy, feminist" ideas as well as her way of doing almost everything. Their latest interactions seem to be best characterized by an unspoken tension.

Sharon decides to try a different approach. She goes "on strike," discontinuing to do anything Jeff criticizes. When he comments that the spaghetti sauce needs more garlic, she announces she's no longer cooking. When he criticizes how the grass is cut, she blows up in anger, and both Sharon and he say many things that they later regret. Jeff decides not only to stop commenting and suggesting but to stop talking altogether. Now an unspoken hostility hovers over their relationship.

Sharon and Jeff illustrate three ways in which people get stuck in their relationships and sabotage their own attempts to improve them. First Sharon believes she is trying different strategies to improve her relationship when in reality she is trying only slight variations on a single theme: "I will make my dissatisfaction apparent to him, and he will respond with less criticism." People get stuck by trying the same basic approach over and over, even though it might not be obvious to them that they are doing so.

Further, when her first method makes things worse, she tries more of the same. A well-intentioned attempt to resolve a

small difficulty ends up turning it into a serious conflict despite good intentions. Sharon wound up with increased criticism and an overly sensitive, defensive, withdrawn husband.

Third, Sharon recognized the problem but did not succeed in getting Jeff to help solve it. Almost always, one partner notices a joint problem first. That person mentions it to the other and then proceeds to try to solve the problem, while assuming the other person is motivated and cooperative. This can be a faulty assumption even if both people agree on how serious it is or how to solve it.

A widely shared belief is that in order for a relationship to change, both partners have to actively participate in changing it. As family therapists, we disagree. We subscribe to a "systems" approach with couples. In a relationship system, a noticeable change in one person can set in motion a change in the whole system, that is, the couple.

Early in relationships, rules begin to form that grow out of patterns of ways people to relate to each other. Rules can be simple and straightforward—one partner initiates sex, one partner does the dishes; or they can be more subtle—when both partners are angry they don't yell. Sometimes the rules are talked about openly, but typically they are assumed rather than discussed, and those involved

From *Psychology Today*, January/February 1993, pp. 46-51, 86, 95. Adapted from *Overcoming Relationship Impasses* by Barry L. Duncan and Joseph W. Rock, published by Plenum Publishing Corporation. © 1991 by Barry L. Duncan and Joseph W. Rock. Reprinted by permission.

may not even be consciously aware of the assumed rules. This non-awareness causes the most difficulty when problems arise.

Rules have their uses; in recurring situations, we don't have to figure out what to do from scratch. But because rules are based on previous experience, they also maintain the status quo. The very qualities that make rules useful day-to-day can render them harmful when a relationship problem needs to be resolved. Rules simplify life by limiting options to an acceptable few. But when we get stuck in solving a problem, we need *more* options, not fewer. The assumed rules we carry into a situation prevent us from exploring potentially helpful options and limit our flexibility. They discourage change—even helpful, necessary change.

Beyond Blame: Systems Thinking

Most theories of human behavior are couched in linear cause-effect terms and offer either historical (unhappy childhood) or physical (bad nerves) explanations for behavior. Both the medical and Freudian perspectives on problem behaviors or emotional stress consider only the individual, apart from his or her relationships.

Systems theory is evolving to explain the complexities of relationships and to help resolve the problems and distress inherent in relationships. It offers a refreshing, illness-free lens through which to observe human behavior—the focus of study shifts from what goes on inside a person to what takes place between people.

In a relationship, you are not acting completely of your own free will. You are constantly influenced by your partner, and vice versa.

When two individuals come together in a relationship, something is created that is different from, larger, and more complex than those two individuals apart—a system. The most important feature of such a relationship is communication. Relationships are established, maintained, and changed by communicative interaction among members.

As relationships endure, communication sequences form patterns over time, and it is the patterning over time that is the essence of a couple system. Sometimes the enduring patterns begin to create difficulties for couples, and new patterns are need-

ed. With Jeff and Sharon, the pattern concerning the giving and receiving of advice was at the heart of their relationship problems.

In a system, all elements are mutually dependent. What one person does depends on what the other person does. In the context of a relationship, you are not acting completely of your own free will. You are constantly being influenced by your partner, and vice versa. When Sharon attempted to get less criticism, Jeff responded by criticizing more and pulling away. Each person's actions helped determine what the other did, and each person's actions affected the relationship as a whole.

A marriage, then, is not a static and fixed relationship. No matter how entrenched one's behavior or how strong one's personality, each individual is influenced by the other on an ongoing basis. *Once you recognize your partner's dependence upon your pattern of behavior, you can consciously plan and change your own behavior, thereby influencing your partner and the relationship in a constructive manner.*

Virtually every couple we see in therapy is interested in what, or who, caused their problems; they look for guilt, blame, or responsibility. But influence among people in relationships is reciprocal and mutually dependent, causality is circular. Choosing the point at which the causal chain begins is pointless and arbitrary.

One implication is that the circle can be broken or interrupted at any point, regardless of how the problem started or how long it has existed. If one person in a couple changes behavior noticeably and consistently, the other person's reactions will change, which will change the first person's reactions. In this way, one person can positively impact a troubled relationship; the partner's cooperation is not required.

Does Sharon have a problem with constructive criticism, or does Jeff have a problem with control and sexism? One partner, either partner, can interrupt the causal circle and move the relationship in another direction.

In much the same way that a stone thrown into a pond affects the surface well beyond the small point at which it enters, a small change in a specific area can lead to a positive ripple effect on the entire relationship. When there are many problems in a relationship, people assume that a major overhaul is required. Many times, however, a small adjustment, strategically employed, is all that is needed.

Communication: The Sound of Silence

Communication theory is crucial in systems thinking. Gestures, tone of voice, and facial expressions are important in understanding what someone is saying. Much has been written about body language, addressing what people "say" by their posture. What gets lost is that *all behavior is communicative.* Even silence conveys some message. There is no such thing as *not* communicating.

A spouse who routinely comes home late for dinner without calling may be saying, "Your inconvenience is unimportant compared to what happens at work" or "Your feelings are not a priority to me." The spouse who prepares dinner may not comment to the late spouse. Yet the silence may be a worse indictment than a verbal scolding.

Viewing behavior itself as a powerful means of communication significantly increases your options when verbal com-

What gets lost is that all behavior is communicative. Even silence conveys some message. There is no such thing as *not* communicating.

munication is not working. If, like Sharon, you have tried to fix your relationship problems by talking ad nauseam, then behavioral options may provide a more powerful way.

Communication occurs at different levels, even though most of us focus our attention on only one—the content, or the literal meaning of the words. Most important, but less obvious, is the relationship level. It indicates how the sender of the message is attempting to influence the receiver. It conveys a command or directive concerning the sender's needs and is an implicit attempt to influence the receiver. "My back itches" may mean "Scratch my back." "I had a rough day" may mean "Leave me alone," "I need your support," or "Fix me a drink." Even "I love you" can be an implicit command, depending upon the circumstances. It may mean "Tell me that you love me."

Influence is unavoidable in communication; it is inherent in how we interact. Just as one cannot *not* communicate, one cannot *not* influence when communicating. Implicit directives also define the nature of the relationship. The statement, "The garbage can is overflowing," not only conveys the obvious, but may also contain

Relationship Myths

Myth #1: What people say is very important and has a big impact on what they do.

Words often fall short of accurately depicting someone's intentions and we can't really guess at times what someone else really means. In the long term, behavior is what gives evidence of our true intentions.

Myth #2: People can and should understand and explain their own and others' motives.

Behavior is the result of a tremendous number of interacting influences: biological, psychological, interpersonal, situational. We never get answers to "why," only plausible-sounding guesses. Knowing "why" seldom produces a solution. *Understanding* a behavior pattern and *changing* it are often completely different. Consider *what* is happening now between you and your partner and *how* that pattern can be changed.

Myth #3: In close relationships being completely open and honest is critical if the relationship is to work.

If the person with whom you are communicating is unable or unwilling to respond honestly and openly, honesty and openness may well be a bad idea at times. Being open with someone who will use the information to manipulate you or gain power over you is like playing poker and showing your cards before you bet. An open and honest expression must be interpreted as such by the receiver of the message for it to be truly open and honest. Openness is not the only way, and, in some situations, not the best way.

Myth #4: A good relationship is one in which both people give unselfishly.

Unselfish giving is not a prerequisite for a good relationship. In fact, attempts to do so usually create more problems than they solve. Giving is an important part of any relationship. However, all of us expect something back; it helps to let the other person know what that is. Balance is also important. Rather than expecting to meet all of each other's needs, stay in practice at meeting some of your own. It adds stability to a relationship and reduces the risk of resentment. Complete selfishness certainly does not lend itself to healthy relationships, but it turns out that neither does utter unselfishness.

Myth #5: In any situation there is only one reality or one truth.

Reality is entirely dependent upon who is observing and describing it, especially in complex situations such as interactions in relationships. When two people have very different stories to tell about the same situation, it does not mean that one is lying, although each partner usually believes that about the other. Rather, each is describing reality from his or her frame of reference. A lot of time usually is wasted trying to convince your partner that you are right. This time could be better spent trying to understand the others' point of view and using that understanding to change your own behavior in a way that will help the relationship.

---

the implicit directive, "Take the garbage out." The statement defines the relationship as one in which the sender has the right to comment on the state of garbage and expect the receiver to follow the (implicit) directive.

Implicit commands are largely automatic and occur outside of awareness. As a result, we often address the most important parts of our lives, our relationships, in an extremely haphazard fashion. By becoming aware of the implicit influence in communication we can deliberately use it in improving relationships.

When we think about communication, we usually think of a speaker actively conveying a message and a listener passively receiving it. This, however, is a very inaccurate perception. Listening is an active process. We have to make sense of the speaker's words; we compare their ideas to beliefs and attitudes we hold and to perceptions about the speakers we've already formed. We consider gestures, tone of voice, and facial expressions, and the circumstances. In addition, our needs influence what we hear.

The conclusion is inescapable—the listener helps create meaning. Much of this process tends to be automatic and outside

awareness. We're seldom aware of how our beliefs and attitudes affect how we hear, or the ways we interpret nonverbal communication, much less how our own needs affect our perceptions. By paying attention to these factors, however, we can make them conscious, then control them.

The upshot is, we can choose how to interpret a given communication. Words

> **Words that hurt us before no longer have to have power. We can choose to interpret a message differently from the way the sender intended.**

or behaviors that have hurt us before no longer have to have this power. Further, we can choose to interpret a message differently from the way the sender intended. Just because people intend to hurt or manipulate us doesn't mean we have to cooperate by giving their messages the meanings they want us to get.

Often, the listener's understanding of a message is *already* different from the sender's. If a woman believes her husband is stressed out and needs time away, she

might suggest he go away for a week. If he interprets this as "She's trying to get rid of me," the whole point of her message is twisted, and caring is perceived as rejection. This may be the most common problem seen in couples: The message sent is not the message received. Finding ways to understand and express your partner's view of a situation can reduce defensiveness and change old, conflictual patterns in a relationship.

Guidelines for Change

The ideas that one person can produce meaningful change in a relationship, and that a small change can and will lead to a ripple of other changes, are not part of conventional wisdom. Nor are the implications that change can occur quickly and that it can happen without the knowledge or cooperation of one member of the couple. But strategies developed from systems concepts do work, even when both partners aren't equally motivated to change. Here, then, are some very practical guidelines for creating change in a troubled relationship where the partners are stuck at an impasse:

Create confusion. Change the rules by which you've been playing. Be unpredictable. That encourages your partner to find new ways to react.

• Do not be completely honest and open at all times. If your partner tends to manipulate or use power plays, openness just tips your hand and makes you more vulnerable.

• "Give up" power, or "lose" by telling your partner that you agree that he or she is "right," but continue to do whatever you think is best. Allow yourself to give up power verbally, to gain control behaviorally.

• Recognize that words and behaviors are not consistent. People often say one thing but do another. Believe what your partner does, not what he or she says.

• Do things that are truly different, not just variations on a theme. Allow yourself to change 180 degrees in how you approach a problem. That alteration can loosen things up and produce real change in your partner's response.

• Stay off the defensive. If you spend all your time justifying what you are doing, you become reactive and lose track of what you are trying to accomplish. Most people are too busy trying to defend themselves to see other ways of approaching a problem. Relationships are very complex and much creativity is needed.

• If your partner openly resists change, don't push. Finding a different, less confrontational path to the change can be much more effective—and less frustrating.

• Go with the flow whenever possible and recognize the disadvantages of change. Things are rarely black and white; consider the advantages of maintaining the problem. This form of creative interpretation directly addresses the ambivalence people have about changing their behavior and aligns with that part of the individual that may be reluctant to change. It helps clarify the feared consequences of change in the hope of motivating the person toward action regarding the problem.

• Start a small, positive ripple of change and let it grow by itself.

• Look at what is going well, instead of what is going wrong with your relationship. It's much easier to build on what is already there than to tear something down and start all over.

Power Disparities in Romantic Relationships

By far, the most common source of problems in a relationship involves the distribution of power. In a good relationship, ideally there is a balance of power. Unfortunately, this ideal is not always real-

ized, and neither party is happy with the unequal power. The powerless, disenfran-

The ideas that one person can produce meaningful change in a relationship, and that a small change will lead to a ripple of other changes, are not part of conventional wisdom.

chised partner feels cheated and resentful, and, whether aware of it or not, usually seeks ways to even the score. The powerful partner gets resentful because he or she has too much responsibility and carries a disproportionate share of the load.

In a relationship with a power disparity, no one wins. Yet the struggle for power underlies virtually every relationship quarrel. There are two common relationship patterns in which power is the key issue.

One involves the dependent partner who needs his partner to do things, but tries to regain the power lost to dependency by criticizing the way those things are done.

IN DEALING WITH A DEPENDENT PARTNER WHO IS RELENTLESSLY CRITICAL:
• Agree in words, but not in action, with criticism.
• Don't explain or defend yourself.
• Interpret your partner's critical message to mean you can stop doing whatever was criticized: "You're right, I am a terrible cook. I'll let you eat prepared frozen food more." Your partner will either stop in his tracks or—even better—refute the criticism himself.

The second power problem is the most common problem we see in troubled relationships. It involves one partner having control in multiple areas—money, decision-making, social life, conversation topics—such that the relationship begins to resemble that of a parent and child, with the powerful partner treating the other like a child. Even when the person in the powerful role, such as a parent, can be very kind and nurturing, the powerless partner can easily feel inferior, helpless, trapped—as well as resentful. Any attempts to speak out against the arrangement will usually sound like the helpless protestations of a child.

IN DEALING WITH A DOMINEERING PARTNER WHO PLAYS A PARENTAL ROLE:
• Do what you want to do—act independently of your partner's expectations.

If criticized, agree you were "wrong" or "misguided," but continue to do what you believe is best.

• Use "constructive payback," in which criticism from your partner is met with your "inadvertent" mistakes and "forgetfulness" (being late, stupid, inefficient) that bother your partner and make your partner's life more difficult. This indirectly expresses your anger and resentment and lets your partner know that he or she can't get away with being abusive.

Communication Problems

Three common communication patterns often make individuals unhappy. The first is lack of communication, in which one partner feels distress concerning the other's unwillingness or inability to talk about things. Unlike most other problems, the roles in this pattern consistently divide along gender lines; most often, the male partner is seen as relatively silent and the female partner distressed about it.

IN DEALING WITH AN UNCOMMUNICATIVE PARTNER:
• Do something that's a noticeable change from your previous strategies. Become less available for conversation and do not try hard to initiate or maintain discussion. Cut it short when it does start. This not only removes but reverses all pressure on the male partner. And it gives the female partner more control. The entire pattern is changing, and the power shifts.
• Interpret silence in a positive way: "We are so close we don't always have to be talking." "I feel good when you're quiet because I know that means everything is all right between us." This negates any power your partner may be expressing through silence.
• Focus less on the relationship and more on satisfying yourself. When you do things for yourself, you need less from others in the way of attention and assurance.

A second common communication problem involves a pattern in which one partner is consistently sad or negative—and verbalizes it—and the other is distressed by the complaints and frustrated in his or her attempts to help. Ordinarily, the complaint has at least some basis in fact—a life circumstance has given the person cause to feel depressed or pessimistic. Unfortunately, most people faced with a chronic complainer become cheerleaders; they assume that encouragement and information of a positive nature will help. But the complainer interprets the cheerleading as lack of understanding. Another losing strategy is ignoring the complaining so that the gates of negativism are never opened. Both strategies wind up intensifying the problem.

IN DEALING WITH A
CHRONIC COMPLAINER:

•Accept, agree, and encourage the complainer's position.

•Encourage complaining rather than trying to avoid it.

•Honestly express any negative opinions you have on the topic being complained about. (Do not express any positive opinions.) Initiate topics of complaint at every opportunity. This gives the complainer the freedom of choice to discuss other issues and positive feelings.

A third communication problem is an accuser-denyer pattern that frequently evolves when one partner accuses the other of lying. Lying may—or may not—actually be involved.

IN DEALING WITH AN ACCUSER:

•Don't explain or defend. This extremely simple solution is effective because the situation doesn't escalate—it's hard to argue with someone who doesn't argue back—and you do not appear guilty by reason of protesting too much. Accusations are often made to get an argument started; if one partner does not go for the bait, the accusation strategy stops working and is eventually dropped.

•Go one step further and reflect the insecurity of the accuser. "You're afraid that I'm having an affair." "You're concerned that you're not attractive to me anymore." "You're feeling insecure about my love for you."

Sex and Jealousy

Key aspects of couples' sex lives have little to do with what happens in bed. Jealousy and trust issues in a relationship are a prime example. Both involve one partner' suspecting that the other isn't be-

ing completely loyal or truthful. And in both, the partner who is the object of the jealous feelings or mistrust cannot remove the problem. Many different real or imagined actions can destroy trust, and jealousy certainly isn't the always the result of a real indiscretion. But sometimes it is.

An affair is a very difficult occurrence for a relationship to survive. It is much like surviving the death of a loved one; the relationship as it was before is forever lost. As in coming to grips with a death, the partner who must accept the "loss" needs to grieve, experience, and express the entire range of emotions associated with the affair.

Unfortunately, the partner who had the affair rarely facilitates this grieving process, Rather he or she tries to handle the situation with minimization, avoidance, and indignation, believing that the subject will die if ignored. "It was only sex, not love." "It's over, let's get on with our lives." "It meant nothing to me."

This strategy usually backfires because the other partner, already feeling hurt and angry at the betrayal, now feels dismissed and misunderstood—and brings up the affair even more. Already feeling defensive through guilt, the partner who had the affair gets more defensive ("How long do I have to go on like this?") The mistaken belief that the issue of the affair should be resolved quickly allows this partner to feel wronged, leading greater distance between partners.

IN DEALING WITH A JEALOUS PARTNER:

• Encourage the partner who feels betrayed to express jealous feelings, and listen nondefensively. This allows the affair to be treated as significant; the betrayed partner has no need to emphasize how important and painful an issue it is. And by encouraging discussion of the affair, the agenda of the person who feels betrayed is given priority. This restores some of the

lost power and control without necessitating a prolonged power struggle.

•Initiate at every opportunity discussion of actions or situation that provoke jealousy.

•Keep an exceptionally detailed diary of all your daily activities and recite it at length to your partner every day—in a matter-of-fact fashion. This breaks the questioning-defensiveness cycle. The information overload makes it less likely that accusations of giving partial or incomplete data will be made.

Of all the issues that are related to what happens in the bedroom, sexual frequency is the one about which we hear the most complaints. Usually, one partner decides that there is a problem—usually the partner who wants more sex. He or she begins by stating the problem and directly requesting more frequent sex. The verbal response from the partner is usually encouraging ("Okay, let's try to get together more often"), but the behavior frequently remains the same. At this point, the partner who feels deprived pulls out all the stops—adult movies, sexy clothing, candlelight dinners. The partner being pursued feels pressured and backs away further. The pursuer feels unloved and rejected, and may accuse his or her partner of being involved with someone else.

IN DEALING WITH A SEXUALLY
DISINTERESTED PARTNER:

•Remove all pressure to have sex, but increase nonsexual affection.

•Increase the time spent together in mutually enjoyable, nonsexual activities. This helps put sex back in a healthy perspective by focusing on the enjoyable parts of a relationship.

•Become less available for sex, rather than always being ready and eager. This reduces perceived pressure and frees your partner to accept the role of pursuer.

Vanishing Dreams of America's Young Families

The future of today's young parents and their small children is now in great jeopardy. Congress and the President must take immediate steps to ensure that every child has a fair start, a healthy start, and a head start.

MARIAN WRIGHT EDELMAN

Marian Wright Edelman is President of the Children's Defense Fund. This article draws upon her speech of April 14, 1992 delivered to the National Press Club in Washington D.C., and the report, issued jointly by the Children's Defense Fund and Northeastern University's Center for Labor Market Studies, entitled, Vanishing Dreams: The Economic Plight of America's Young Families. *This article and the report on which it is based is under copyright by the Children's Defense Fund, 25 E Street NW, Washington, DC.*

Americans from all walks of life are profoundly anxious—troubled by what they see around them today and even more by what they see ahead. This anxiety, not only about their own futures but also about the nation's future, is manifested in countless ways: in paralyzing economic insecurity; in an emerging politics of rejection, frustration, and rage; in a growing polarization of our society by race and by class; and in an erosion of the sense of responsibility to help the weakest and poorest among us.

But this anxiety about the future is *most* vivid when we watch our own children grow up and try to venture out on their own—struggling to get established as adults in a new job, a new marriage, a new home or a new family.

It's true that young families always have faced an uphill struggle starting out in life. But today's young families have been so battered by economic and social changes over the past two decades that the struggle has taken on a more desperate and often futile quality.

And as parents of my generation watch many of their adult children founder—failing to find steady, decent-paying jobs, unable to support families, shut out of the housing market and often forced to move back home—they know that something has gone terribly wrong. Often they don't know precisely what has happened or why. But they do understand that these young adults and their children may never enjoy the same opportunities or achieve the same standard of living or security that our generation found a couple of decades ago.

Two generations in trouble

Young families with children—those headed by persons under the age of thirty—have been devastated since 1973 by a cycle of falling incomes, increasing family disintegration, and rising poverty. In the process, the foundations for America's young families have been so thoroughly undermined that two complete generations of Americans—today's young parents and their small children—are now in great jeopardy. Figure 1 captures the poverty rates of those two jeopardized generations:

Young families are the crucible for America's future and America's dream. Most children spend at least part of their lives—their youngest and most developmentally vulnerable months and years—in young families. How we treat these families therefore goes a long way toward defining what our nation as a whole will be like twenty, fifty, or even seventy-five years from now.

What has happened to America's young families with children is unprecedented and almost unimaginable.

 From *Challenge*, May/June 1992, pp. 13-19. © 1992 by M. E. Sharpe, Inc., Armonk, NY 10504. Reprinted by permission.

Figure 1   **Poverty Rates of Families With Children,
By Age of Family Head, 1973, 1979, 1982, 1990**

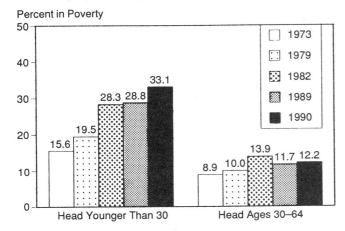

Adjusted for inflation, the median income of young families with children plunged by one-third between 1973 and 1990 (Table 1). This median income includes income from all sources, and the drop occurred despite the fact that many families sent a second earner into the workforce. As a result, poverty among these young families more than doubled, and by 1990 a shocking 40 percent or four in ten children in young families were poor .

The past two decades have been difficult for many other Americans as well. But older families with children have lost only a little economic ground since 1973, and families without children have enjoyed substantial income gains. By far the greatest share of the nation's economic pain has been focused on the weakest and most vulnerable among us—young families with children.

This is *not* a story about the current recession, although the recession surely is having a crushing impact on young families. Even comparing 1973 to 1989—two good economic years at the end of sustained periods of growth—the median income of young families with children dropped by one-fourth. Then just the first few months of the recession in 1990 sent young families' incomes plummeting to new depths.

This also is not a story about teenagers. While America's teen pregnancy problem remains tragic and demands an urgent response, only 3 percent of the young families with children we are discussing are headed by teenagers. More than 70 percent are headed by someone aged twenty-five to twenty-nine. The plight of America's young families is overwhelmingly the plight of young adults who are both old enough and eager to assume the responsibilities of parenthood and adulthood, but for whom the road is blocked.

Finally and most importantly, this is *not* simply a story about someone else's children, about minority children or children in single-parent families or children whose parents dropped out of high school.

All young families affected

Huge income losses have affected virtually every group of young families with children: white, black and Latino; married-couple and single-parent; and those headed by high school graduates as well as dropouts. Only young families with children headed by college graduates experienced slight income gains between 1973 and 1990.

In other words, the tragedy facing young families with children has now reached virtually *all* of our young families. One in four *white* children in young families is now poor. One in five children in young *married-couple* families is now poor. And one in three children in families headed by a young *high school graduate* is now poor. Nearly three-fourths of the increase in poverty among young families since 1973 has occurred outside the nation's central cities. And poverty has grown most rapidly among young families with only one child (Figure 2).

There is no refuge from the economic and social shifts that have battered young families with children. We can pretend that they won't reach our children and our grandchildren. We can pretend that those who play by the rules will be O.K.

Table 1   **Median Incomes of Families With Children By Age of Family Head, 1973–1990**
(in 1990 dollars)*

	1973	1979	1982	1989	1990	Change 1973-1990
All families with children	36,882	36,180	31,819	35,425	34,400	- 6.7%
Family head younger than 30	27,765	25,204	20,378	20,665	18,844	-32.1%
Family head age 30–64	41,068	39,978	35,293	39,525	38,451	- 6.4%
Young families' median income as a share of older families' income	68%	63%	58%	52%	49%	

Note: The money incomes of families for all years prior to 1990 were converted into 1990 dollars via use of the Consumer Price Index for All Urban Consumers (CPI-U). The U.S. Bureau of Labor Statistics has generated an alternative price index for the years preceding 1983 that conforms to the current method of measuring changes in housing costs. This index is known as the CPI-UX1. Use of this price index would reduce the estimated 1973 real income by about 7 percent, thus lowering the estimated decline in the median income of young families between 1973 and 1990 from 32 percent to approximately 25 percent. None of the comparisons of median income between various groups of families are affected by these changes.

3. FINDING A BALANCE: Relationships Between Parents and Children

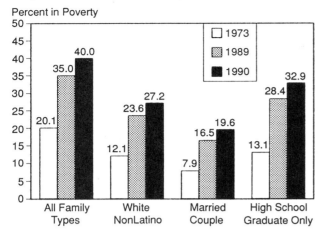

Figure 2

**Poverty Rates
of Children in Young Families,
By Characteristics of the Family Head, 1973, 1989, 1990**

We can pretend, but that will not change the reality—the reality that young families have lost a third of their median income, that two in five American children in young families live in poverty, and that these facts have devastating consequences.

Those consequences include more hunger, more homelessness, more low birthweight births, more infant deaths and more child disability. They also mean more substance abuse, more crime, more violence, more school failure, more teen pregnancy, more racial tension, more envy, more despair and more cynicism—a long-term economic and social disaster for young families and for the country. In virtually every critical area of child development and healthy maturation, family poverty creates huge roadblocks to individual accomplishment, future economic self-sufficiency, and national progress.

Plummeting incomes and soaring poverty and growing gaps based on age and education and race mean more of all these problems, yet many of our leaders seem not to understand why they are occurring. But there is not really a puzzle, when we recognize that the nation has marginalized and pauperized much of two generations of Americans—young parents and young children.

Young families not only lost income in huge amounts, but as the permanence and quality of their jobs deteriorated, they lost fringe benefits like health insurance as well. In the decade of the 1980s the proportion of *employed* heads of young families with children whose employers made health insurance available by paying all or part of the cost dropped by one-fifth. And employers cut back on coverage for dependent spouses and children even more than for workers.

Fewer and fewer young pregnant women have been getting adequate prenatal care because they are poorer and less likely to have adequate insurance or any insur-

ance. And our falling vaccination rates and renewed epidemics of measles and other wholly preventable diseases among preschoolers are being driven by plunging incomes in young families, eroding health insurance coverage, and unraveling government programs.

Falling incomes also have devastated young families in an increasingly expensive housing market. One-third fewer young families with children were homeowners in 1991 than in 1980. Young renter families increasingly are paying astronomical shares of their meager incomes for rent. More and more are doubling up or becoming homeless—in some surveys three-fourths of the homeless parents in this country are under age thirty.

Young families are not only suffering from the hunger, housing, health and other problems that their plummeting incomes have caused. They are suffering as well because they are falling further and further behind the rest of the society—imperiling their attachment to the core work force and to mainstream values and threatening their potential to reacquire the American dream in the decades to come.

In 1973 the income of older families with children was not quite one-and-a-half times that of young families with children. By 1990 it was more than double that of the young families.

Combination of causes

There is no single cause of young families' plight. Instead, they have been pummelled by a combination of profound changes in the American economy; the government's inadequate response to families in trouble; and changes in the composition of young families themselves.

Much of the increase in their poverty is due to economic shifts and to changing government policies that have made it more difficult for young families to obtain adequate incomes. These changes have hurt all young families with children, regardless of their family structure, race or ethnicity, or educational attainment.

Unlike members of earlier generations, young workers today no longer can be confident of finding stable jobs with decent wages, even if they get a high school diploma or spend a couple of years in college. Since 1973, slower growth in U.S. productivity and declines in blue collar employment made some drop in inflation-adjusted median earnings for young workers inevitable. By last year the average wages of *all* nonsupervisory workers (of all ages) in the private sector fell to their lowest level since the Eisenhower Administration.

But the losses have been focused disproportionately on young workers. The median annual earnings of heads of young families with children fell a staggering 44 percent from 1973 to 1990. In other words, in the span of less than a generation this nation nearly *halved* the earnings of young household heads with children (Table 2):

These dramatic earnings losses occurred across-the-board. For example, young white families with children were hit as hard as young Latino families: the median earnings of both groups fell by two-fifths. College graduates as well as high school graduates and dropouts lost big chunks of income. But the drop in median earnings for high school dropouts and for young black family heads has been particularly devastating—in each case more than two-thirds.

Table 2	**Median Annual Earnings of Heads of Young Families With Children, 1973 and 1990** (in 1990 dollars)		
	1973	1990	% Change 1973-1990
All heads of young families with children	22,981	12,832	-44
Married couple	25,907	17,500	-33
Male-headed	18,547	14,000	-25
Female-headed	2,073	1,878	- 9
White, non-Latino	25,024	15,000	-40
Black, non-Latino	13,860	4,030	-71
Latino	15,924	9,000	-44
Other, non-Latino	17,664	12,000	-32
High school dropout	15,014	4,500	-70
High school graduate	23,817	14,000	-41
Some college	26,496	18,000	-32
College graduate	31,795	25,721	-19

The erosion in pay levels (due in part to the declining value of the minimum wage) combined with the growth of temporary or part-time and part-year jobs to put a triple whammy on young workers: far lower annual earnings; less secure employment; and less access to health insurance and other employer-provided benefits.

The huge drop in earnings among America's young workers has not received much attention. In part it has been obscured by the almost Herculean work effort of young parents. Many young married-couple families have tried to compensate for lower wages by sending a second worker into the work force. These second earners have softened (but not eliminated) the economic blow. But the growing number of young parents working longer hours or coping with two jobs has placed young families with children under tremendous stress and generated new offsetting costs, especially for child care. Many families, moreover, have two jobs that together provide less security and less support and less access to health care than one good job did a generation ago. This two-earner strategy is totally unavailable, moreover, to the growing number of single-parent families.

Economic shifts and family changes

Today's young families with children look considerably different from those in the early 1970s. They are more likely to be minority families or single parent families. Both groups are more likely to be paid low wages and to be poor than other families. So poverty among young families and children as a whole also rises.

The growth in young female-headed families with children is in part a reflection of changing values. But the economic hardships associated with falling earnings and persistent joblessness among young adults have contributed significantly to falling marriage rates and the increasing rates of out-of-wedlock childbearing. And the fastest growth in out-of-wedlock childbearing has occurred among women in their twenties, not among teenagers, a growth driven in significant part by the earnings free-fall for young adults.

The capacity to support a family has a powerful impact on the marriage decisions of young people. More than two centuries ago Benjamin Franklin wrote: "The number of marriages. . .is greater in proportion to the ease and convenience of supporting a family. When families can be easily supported, more persons marry, and earlier in life."

Increases in poverty among young families with children are *not* the result of young Americans having more children. Indeed, young adults have responded to a tightening economic vise by postponing childbearing and choosing to have fewer children. But these attempts to adapt their behavior have been overwhelmed by the far more rapid pace of economic decline and social disintegration they have encountered.

As a result of these economic and social changes, in 1990 a child in a family headed by a parent under age 30 was:

• twice as likely to be poor as a comparable child in 1973;

• if living with both parents, two and a half times as likely to be poor as in 1973;

• nearly three times more likely to have been born out-of-wedlock than his counterpart two decades ago;

• one-third less likely to be living in a home owned by her family than just a decade ago; and

• three times more likely to see his family pay more than one-half its income for rent.

But despite the devastating suffering these numbers

suggest, children in young families have been given less and less government help over the last two decades. They were getting less to begin with—government programs are particularly stingy when it comes to helping younger adults and young children. And in the 1970s and especially the 1980s young families saw programs that might help them cut rather than strengthened and reconfigured to adapt to new realities. As a result, government programs were less than half as effective in pulling young families out of poverty in 1990 as in 1979.

Hard hit minority families

The changes of the last two decades have had a very profound impact on minority young families, especially those that are black. As Table 2 shows, the median earnings of the heads of young black families with children fell *71 percent* from 1973 to 1990 (from $13,860 to $4,030 in 1990 dollars). Their total family incomes from all sources fell 48 percent. The *median* income of these young black families is now below the federal poverty line for a family of three. In 1973 it was nearly double that poverty line. *Two out of three* children in young black families now are poor.

This crisis for young black families is contributing mightily to the tearing apart of the black community. This society cannot year after year increase the poverty and isolation and hopelessness of black mothers and fathers and children—it can't keep turning the screws tighter and tighter—without appalling consequences. We see those consequences in the emergency rooms and unemployment lines and prisons and homeless shelters and neonatal intensive care wards and morgues of our cities and our suburbs and rural towns. We see it in the omnipresent violence that destroys so many black lives and leaves blacks and whites alike so fearful. More blacks die from firearms each year in this country than died in the century's worth of despicable lynchings that followed the Civil War. More black men die from firearms every six weeks in Detroit than died in the 1967 Detroit ''riot.'' More black and Hispanic men die from firearms in Los Angeles every two weeks than died in the 1965 Watts ''riot.'' [*Editor's note*: This speech was given two weeks before the most recent outbreak of violence in Los Angeles.]

Frankly, though, I would be skeptical that this nation would attack this cataclysm for young black families were it not for the fact that young *white* families are only a step or two behind in the scope of their economic depression and family disintegration. Perhaps the most important story told in this report is the impact of two decades of this Depression for the young on three types of families we often assume are insulated from hard times:

• From 1973 to 1990 the poverty rate for children living in young *white* families more than doubled to *27 percent*.

• From 1973 to 1990 the poverty rate for children in young *married-couple* families went up two-and-a-half times—to *20 percent*.

• And the child poverty rate in young families headed by *high school graduates* went up even faster, to *33 percent*.

In other words, a generation ago white or married-couple young families or those headed by high school graduates were fairly well insulated from poverty. The damage of the last two decades has cut so broadly and deeply that now one in four white children in young families, one in five children in married-couple young families, and one in three children in families headed by young high school graduates is poor.

Private and public response

What response do we see to these problems from private and public leadership? Precious little.

Too much of the business community is wholly untroubled by stripping away from millions of Americans the minimum family-supporting wages, fringe benefits, and job security that could help make our families strong again. The Administration has no higher domestic priority than cutting capital gains taxes for the rich. The Congress and the Administration together persist in keeping defense spending above the levels of the average year in the Cold War—impoverishing our society and the world by arming ourselves not only against real external threats but against weapons-justifying fantasies, while letting the internal enemies of poverty, disintegration, violence, and hopelessness rage unabated. The Congress can't mount the political will to get Head Start—a program universally conceded to be effective and cost-effective—to more than one in three eligible children or to pass the refundable children's tax credit that experts from all parts of the political spectrum think is a minimum first step to tax equity and family economic security.

Finally, far too many of the nation's Governors and state and national legislators have responded to budget crunches and political turmoil by scapegoating the poor—trying to bolster their political fortunes by pummeling the welfare recipients whose assistance gobbles up a grand total of 2 to 3 percent of state budgets.

In hard times in the past our society usually has had escape valves—an inherent balance that gave to the powerless help from one institution when others turned their backs—from the federal government when the states were at their worst, from the courts when Congress and the executive were unresponsive. Now we seem to be in an awful time when every institution is competing to pander to the powerful and further penalize the poor.

A *fair start*

In response to the economic plight of America's young families, Congress and the President must take three immediate steps in 1992 to ensure that every child has a *fair* start, a *healthy* start, and a *head* start.

A *fair start* means renewed and sustained economic growth and enough jobs at decent wages to restore the pact our nation used to have with young families—that personal sacrifice and hard work will be rewarded with family suppporting jobs. A fair start also means enactment of a refundable children's tax credit to bolster the incomes of families with children, as proposed in recent months in various forms and amounts by the National Commission on Children and key members of Congress from both parties. Such a credit would reduce federal income taxes for middle- and low-income families and help the lowest income families that have no tax liability through a tax refund.

While creating no new bureaucracies, a refundable children's credit would target tax relief and economic support precisely to the group—families with children—that has been hardest hit by declining incomes and rising poverty rates since 1973. The Administration's alternative proposal—to expand the personal exemption for children—is extremely regressive. It gives $310 to a family with two children if their income exceeds about $100,000; $280 if it is over $50,000; $150 if income is between $15,000 and $50,000; and zero if it is under about $15,000.

Finally, a fair start means creation of a child support insurance system to give all single parents the chance to lift their families out of poverty through work, ensuring that all children who are not living with both parents receive a minimally adequate child support payment from the absent parent or the government when it fails to collect from the absent parent.

What we *don't* need in this time of great crisis for young families with children is a negative approach rooted in welfare-bashing and welfare cuts that ends up hurting children. Families on welfare are the victims of the recession, not the cause of it. They are victims of budget deficits, not the cause of them. But nearly one-fourth of all young families with children are forced to rely upon Aid for Families with Dependent Children (AFDC) to meet their basic needs, and they are extremely vulnerable to misguided attacks on this essential safety net for children.

Our political leaders know these truths. Yet during an election year too many cannot resist the temptation to direct the public's frustration and anger toward the poorest of poor Americans—those families and children who rely upon welfare for basic income support.

There *are* ways we can and must improve welfare. For example, we agree with the Administration that welfare parents often don't have enough financial incentive to work because current welfare rules strip them of virtually all of their earnings when they do work. That is why we opposed the repeal of earnings incentives by President Reagan and the Congress in 1981, and why we think they should be restored now for all welfare families, not just those in a few demonstration counties.

But most of the welfare ''reforms'' now underway in states are little more than crass attempts to slash state budgets without regard to their impact on families with children. Reducing or stopping benefits to newborns when they are the second or third child in a family, as now proposed by several states, is punitive, pointless, and immoral. Only political leaders who are hopelessly out of touch with the realities of poor families' lives could think that an extra $2.50 per day in welfare benefits would cause teen parents to have a second child, or that reducing the added benefit to $1.25/day (as the Governor of Wisconsin and the President now propose for that state) constitutes any serious effort at welfare reform. All they will succeed in doing is taking desperately needed food, clothing and shelter from infants.

It's time for the President, Congress, and more of our Governors to be honest with the American people about the problems facing our economy, our poor families and our children.

The problem is *not* large numbers of welfare parents trying to ''beat the system'' by having more children or moving to another state to get higher benefits. The problem is a set of short-sighted, budget-driven welfare rules that make it virtually impossible for parents to work their way gradually off the welfare rolls and a dearth of stable, family-supporting jobs that would allow them to make it on their own.

In many ways, the welfare problem is the same problem facing all young families with children—the result of sharply falling wages, too few job opportunities for those with little education or training, and too little investment in the skills and supports poor parents need to make it in today's economy. And serious solutions begin with a fair start, a healthy start, and a head start for our young families.

A healthy start, a head start

A *healthy start* means a national health plan to assure insurance coverage for all Americans. Children and pregnant women need basic health care *now,* however. As an immediate step, the president and Congress must extend Medicaid coverage to every low-income child and pregnant woman. And to ensure that this insurance provides real access to essential health services, not merely theoretical coverage, children need universal access to vaccines and increased funding for community health centers, and other public health activities.

A *head start* means full funding of Head Start. A first step in bolstering the productivity of our next generation of workers lies in adequate investments in quality child care and early childhood development. Every dollar invested in good early childhood development programs saves $5.97 in later special education, welfare, crime, and other costs. Yet Head Start still reaches only one in three eligible preschool children.

As recommended by prominent business groups, educators, and a broad range of study commissions that have examined the educational problems of disadvantaged children and youths, the president and Congress should ensure every child a Head Start by 1995 by enacting immediately S. 911, the School Readiness Act, and accelerating the funding increases it provides.

A head start also means passing family preservation legislation that will strengthen and preserve families in crisis so that they can better protect, nurture and support their own children. So many of these young parents want to be better parents, and with intensive family preservation services they can get the help they need.

These are essential first steps. To reach them and go beyond them, we're going to have to make the President and Congress come to recognize that child and family poverty and insecurity are a national disaster that requires our addressing them with a pittance of the zeal and shared commitment we now apply to digging out after a devastating hurricane or earthquake or confronting a crisis abroad.

A Nation (Still) At Risk?

Today, more than ever before in the United States, children are spending more time, at younger ages, in a variety of nonmaternal child care arrangements (hereafter referred to as "day care"). The most direct cause of this dramatic change in the early rearing experiences of America's children involves the timing of mothers' return to the work force after the birth of a child, which has itself been affected by economic changes in the nation and cultural changes in America's views about women.

Jay Belsky

Several decades ago re-entry into the labor force after childbirth typically was delayed in middle- and even working-class families until a child entered kindergarten; even by the 1970s the return did not occur until children were two or three years old. Today at least one of every two women aged eighteen to forty-four returns to work in the child's first year. Among college educated women, the figure is 68 percent.

Who cares for such young children when their mothers are working? Only about 15 percent of the time is it those highly visible centers that most citizens equate with the term "day care." National survey data indicate that in 1990 only 20 percent of children under three whose mothers worked were cared for in such settings, rising to 43 percent in the case of children aged three and four. Thus, especially among the nation's youngest citizens, day care typically is provided in private homes, either by a neighborhood woman caring for her own and several other children (family day care), or by a relative or nonrelative caring for the child in his or her own home (nanny, babysitter).

"Bad News" about Day Care

The dramatic changes that have taken place over the past fifteen years in the care that many infants and toddlers receive have raised questions about how such rearing influences children's development. It would not be an understatement to say that experts are not of one mind with regard to this issue. In contrast to the inclinations of many of my colleagues, I have earned the dubious honor of drawing attention to the "bad news" about day care in America. This role derives from the fact that I am no longer willing — as I once was and think many still are — to explain away and discount every disconcerting research finding to emerge in the empirical literature. At the same time, however, my reading of the evidence does not lead me to conclude that day care, even when provided to our youngest citizens, is inherently bad. Too much evidence indicates just the opposite, *when children experience good-quality care.* Day care works when children receive care from individuals who will remain with them for a relatively long period of time (low staff turnover), who are knowledgeable about child development, and who provide care that is sensitive and responsive to their individualized needs.

Sadly, such growth-promoting care is the exception rather than the rule. The abysmal salaries that child care workers earn have much to do with the high staff turnover, large group sizes, less than ideal child-to-staff ratios, and consequent limited quality of care that too many children experience. To understand the developmental effects of day care in America, we need to remember that we remain a society that is ambivalent about whether persons other than mothers should care for babies and young children and that fails to provide parents with extensive leaves to spend time with their infants (especially while receiving pay, as in many European nations). Nor do we enable parents to shift from full-time employment to part-time work (with benefits preserved) and then return to full-time employment after their child's first year or two of life. Only in the context of this "ecology of day care" can any effects of day care be fully understood.

Upon publishing in 1978 what was then the authoritative analysis of research on effects of day care, Larry Steinberg and I concluded that most of the concerns raised about the deleterious effects of day care remained empirically unsubstantiated. We noted, however, that most work at that time was on children cared for in high-quality, university-affiliated programs, designed to determine whether day care inevitably affected children in an adverse way. In consequence, we knew little about community-based child care arrangements, as well as about how age of entry into care and hours per week in care affected children.

By 1986 I had seen enough disconcerting data addressing these issues that I pointed out that there was a slow, steady trickle of evidence indicating that children whose routine, nonmaternal care began in the first year of life on a full- or near full-time basis were more likely to develop insecure attachment bonds to their parents by the end of their first year of life. They also evinced higher levels of aggression (toward agemates) and disobedience (toward adults) between the ages of three and eight years of age than other children.

In the years since then, the slow, steady trickle has, if anything, increased and, in so doing, led me to modify my viewpoint. As I read the evidence today, children with *early, extensive, and continuous* day care experience (that is, children whose care begins in the first year or so of life, on a full- or near full-time basis — more than twenty to thirty hours per week — that continues through their entry into public school) are the ones who seem most susceptible to these and other related effects. All too noteworthy is that this profile of care usage seems to characterize the experiences of increasing numbers of America's children.

Implications of the "Bad News"

What implications do I draw from such findings? Certainly not that only mothers can care for babies or that day care is inherently bad. Rather, I draw the same conclusion that the authors of the report *A Nation at Risk* drew about schooling in America in the early 1980s: something is broken and needs to be fixed. Eliminating day care is not the answer, nor is it even viable in a society that has liberated women from traditional roles and come to depend upon their contribution to our increasingly service-oriented economy. What must be done is to increase the choices available to families and the quality of care that is used by those who

choose to — or must — rely upon day care to rear their offspring.

Thus, conservative as well as liberal solutions to the day care challenge make sense. Not only must tax provisions be amended to provide more economic support for families rearing children (to increase their childrearing options), but also quality-care standards must be implemented to ensure that children's earliest years are as positive to their well-being as is the water we drink and (we hope) the schools children attend. The nation's future is at risk, now that more children, at younger ages, are spending more time in day care.

Jay Belsky, a professor of human development at the Pennsylvania State University, is recognized nationally and internationally as an expert on child maltreatment, the transition to parenthood, the development of infant-parent attachment relationships, as well as on the effects of day care on child development. He is the recipient of the prestigious Research Scientist Development Award from the National Institute of Mental Health (1984-1989) and the Penn State Faculty Scholar Medal for Outstanding Achievement in the Social and Behavioral Sciences (1992).

The myth of AWOL parents

Most interesting thing about article

interrupted

A tale of why many came to believe parents no longer spend much time caring for their kids

It started, as modern-day myths often do, with a press alert. In January 1991, *Policy Review,* a journal published by the conservative Heritage Foundation, notified select reporters that its upcoming issue would reveal the existence of a new parental time famine. "The biggest problem facing American children today is a lack of time with and attention from their parents," the story declared.

The numbers in author William Mattox's article were eye-popping. He said parents today spend "40 percent less time with their children than did parents in 1965, according to data collected from personal time diaries by sociologist John Robinson of the University of Maryland. In 1965, parents on average spent approximately 30 hours a week with their kids. By 1985, parent-child interaction had dropped to just 17 hours a week."

Mattox's numbers quickly became conventional wisdom, cited by officials in the Bush and Clinton administrations. They were picked up more than 50 times in articles and opinion pieces in places like *U.S. News, Time,* the *New York Times,* the *Los Angeles Times* and *USA Today.* They were embraced in congressional hearings, think-tank reports and books about the plight of America's children and are sure to be part of the backdrop of this week's conference led by Vice President Al Gore on how businesses can be helpful to families.

The only problem is that the numbers were wrong: There is no compelling evidence that kids today receive less attention from their parents than kids did in 1965. In fact, the incomplete evidence that does exist suggests that mothers now devote slightly *more* time to each of their kids than they did in 1965 or even in the 1920s. "We have very bad news for the sky-is-falling crowd," says Robinson.

"Rumors of the disappearance of the family are greatly exaggerated."

Twisted trail. The tale of the parental time famine is built on mistakes and misunderstandings. The story starts with Robinson, the director of the University of Maryland's Survey Research Center and one of the deans of time diary studies. In such studies, participants typically keep a record of what they did hour by hour during a given day. The data are deemed more reliable than opinion surveys, in which people often exaggerate their involvement in socially desirable activities.

In 1989, Robinson began an article for *American Demographics* magazine summarizing his findings with the sentence: "Today's mothers spend nine hours a week taking care of their children, just as much time as mothers spent in previous decades." Robinson noted that the nine hours figure referred only to primary child-care activities, such as dressing a child or helping with homework. But the diary sheets also included information on time parents spent both in the company of their children and in "secondary" child care—which occurred when a parent was engaged in other activities while caring for a child, like watching TV or doing housework.

Robinson had yet to calculate how much time parents devoted to these indirect child-care activities in 1985. But he had a full breakdown of parents' child-care time in 1965. To avoid giving the misimpression that mothers spent only nine hours a week in toto with their children, he recapped the earlier figures but did not note that they were from 1965.

Robinson then inadvertently compounded that omission. Instead of writing that parents spent about 20 additional hours a week in the company of their kids, he said they spent only eight

more hours. The lower figure—which Robinson also misread from a bar graph from his 1977 book—was supposed to represent the amount of additional time the *average individual* was in the presence of kids, so it included many folks who weren't parents.

Taking off. The parental time famine myth started taking root when Mattox took an interest in Robinson's work. Mattox was a policy analyst for the conservative Family Research Council, which declared one of its missions to be "to promote and defend traditional family values in print." When Robinson referred him to the *American Demographics* article, Mattox was dissatisfied with its conclusion that the amount of time mothers spent in primary child care had edged up. "I said, 'I don't doubt that what he's reporting here is accurate,'" Mattox recalls. "But I would not say that all we should be concerned about is primary care with children. That's the whole quality-time myth."

In Mattox's view, parents did many activities, such as taking kids to a ballgame or visiting Grandma, that were character forming but might not be recorded as primary child care. He thought the total amount of time parents spent with kids was more important than the time parents spent tending solely to children's needs.

After speaking with Robinson about how he defined categories of child care, Mattox assumed that the 1965 figures in Robinson's *American Demographics* piece were 1985 figures, tallied the flawed numbers and concluded that parents spent a total of 17 hours a week with their kids in 1985. He then compared that incorrect 17-hour figure with the correct 30-hour figure for 1965 from Robinson's book, and *voilà!*—the parental time famine myth was born.

Once the finding entered the computerized trail of news stories, it was used by many advocates to make ideological points. Liberals such as Democratic Sen. Joseph Biden of Delaware blamed the purported time famine on working parents' economic plight. Conservatives like then Health and Human Services Secretary Louis Sullivan thought they discerned immaturity and the pursuit of self-gratification as causes of the parenting deficit. An editorial writer for the *Rocky Mountain News* opined that parents were sacrificing family time "to pay their taxes." And economist Lester Thurow bemoaned in the *New York Times* that "children exist but no one takes care of them."

At *U.S. News*'s request, Robinson reran his computer tape to see how much time parents spent in nonprimary care activities for 1985. But the tape had too many buts to produce the total figure. He did find that parents spent slightly more time doing secondary child care in 1985 (3.5 hours per week) than in 1965 (3.2 hours per week). Mattox says that still leaves unresolved his big question: What happened to total contact time? "The primary and secondary time together constitute less than half of parents' total contact with children," he says. "We really aren't able to completely solve the puzzle."

Making sense. One reason the 40 percent decline figure took on "such a life of its own was because it made sense," says Mattox. As millions of women joined the work force, and as millions more children were raised by single parents, how could parental time with kids increase? Robinson's time diaries do confirm that full-time working moms spend less time tending to their children than do stay-at-home moms and that single parents spend less time on primary child care than two-parent families.

There are, however, two countervailing trends that have ensured that kids on average receive as much of their parents' undivided attention today as in the past. First, many kids still enjoy the benefit of Mom's care while they are young and not in school most of the day. In 1995, 46 percent of mothers with children age 3 and under either were not in the labor force or were unemployed, and an additional 19 percent worked only part time. Working mothers of young children often arrange their hours to free up time with their kids—roughly 40 percent of preschoolers with working moms have mothers who don't work during the day. Robinson also says his data suggest that parents across-the-board tend to spend somewhat more time tending to kids now than their 1965 counterparts did.

The second, more consequential change since 1965 is that families are smaller. As Robinson noted in his *Ameri-*

THEIR 'FAMILY FRIENDLY' IDEAS

CLINTON

- Backs $500-per-child tax credit for families earning up to $75,000.
- Signed expanded earned-income tax credit for low-income working families.
- Signed Family and Medical Leave Act requiring employers to give workers unpaid leave for childbirth or family emergencies.
- Backs guarantees of child care for mothers leaving welfare for work; vetoed welfare reform bill in part for failure to fund child care.

BILL CLINTON AND CHELSEA

DOLE

BOB DOLE, DAUGHTER ROBIN

- Has backed $500-per-child tax credit for families earning up to $110,000.
- Supports earned-income tax credit especially targeted toward families with young children.
- Backs $5,000-per-child tax credit for adopting families and tax break for parents who get adoption aid from employers. Clinton backs this, too.
- Supports tax credits to employers who provide child-care facilities for their workers' kids.

can Demographics article, smaller families allow each child to "receive more individual attention than children did two decades ago." The impact of smaller families on parental time is so profound that even when today's families are compared with those of the 1920s—when nearly all moms stayed home—today's child is still likely to receive more direct care than kids did then, according to a summary of time-diary studies by W. Keith Bryant of Cornell University and Cathleen Zick of the University of Utah in a forthcoming article in *Family and Economic Issues*. Their figures show the number of hours of primary care by white married mothers almost doubled, from .56 hours per day per child in 1924–31 to one hour per day per child in 1981.

Mattox argues that such per capita figures are misleading. He cites a hypothetical 1965 family in which Mom spent six hours a day caring for three kids versus a 1985 family in which Mom spent two hours a day caring for one child. All those children would enjoy an average of two hours a day of care, but those in 1965 would have much more contact with their

mom. "That's the cheaper-by-the-dozen theory," replies Robinson. "If, in fact, the 1965 mother with three kids is spending six hours a day with three kids, the 1985 [version of that] mother with one kid would be spending more like four to five hours a day with her only child."

Smaller families also happen to confer some advantages, compared with families of four or more kids. Children from smaller families tend to have higher IQs and are more likely to graduate from high school and to read books and newspapers. Why? Probably because their parents have more time for activities like reading when the kids are young and more resources to pay for travel and music lessons.

No one, including Robinson, questions the fact that millions of parents today feel genuinely overburdened and are disheartened by the lack of time they have with their children. But worries about a time crunch are not wholly unprecedented. As Benjamin Franklin put it two centuries ago, "What we call time enough always proves little enough."

BY DAVID WHITMAN

FAMILY AFFAIR

THE NET ALLOWS PARENTS AROUND THE WORLD TO SHARE CHILD-REARING EXPERIENCE AND ADVICE.

SOPHIE LITTLEFIELD

"*b*razelton, Ferber, Spock" a friend recited, ticking off the names of popular child-development experts on her fingers. "I read them all. I tried everything—and nothing was working. I wasn't getting more than a couple of hours of sleep a night. I was turning into psychomommy!"

Convinced that she had the only four-month-old baby on the planet who didn't understand that he was supposed to sleep at night, my friend finally posted a plea for help on **misc.kids,** one of the most popular and active Usenet newsgroups on the Internet. Immediately her e-mail in-box began to fill up with advice, stories, and encouragement. Some of the suggestions were things she'd already tried, but many were new—and a few of them actually worked. "Maybe he just decided on his own to get with the program," she admits, "but I'll be forever grateful to **misc.kids.**"

Newsgroups, mailing lists, Web sites—there are few corners of the Net that haven't been discovered by people around the world who, joined by their common interest in raising and educating children, make up the Internet parenting community. Besides infant sleeping problems, there are discussion groups for a wide range of topics—such as autism, deafness, Down syndrome, twins, fatherhood, adoption, the family bed, and home education. (Pointers to parenting newsgroups, Web sites, and mailing lists, see box "Some

Prominent Parents' Pointers." A longer list of mailing lists is on iWorld at **http://www. iworld.com/iw/extra/.**)

In looking at the Internet parent population it's nearly impossible to generalize about a group that numbers in the hundreds of thousands, if not millions—a group that represents scores of different cultures and backgrounds. And yet, in places like **misc.kids,** even a casual observer notices that things are perhaps a little different than elsewhere on the Internet.

"Net parents, compared to the general population, are upper-middle class, gender-balanced, and sincerely concerned about their kids' schooling," says Andy Carvin, an Education and Information Technology Fellow at the Corporation for Public Broadcasting (CPB) in Washington, D.C., and the developer of the CPB's EdWeb project. The demographics remain, as in most Net haunts, skewed to the privileged echelons of society, and Carvin voices concern that the community's growth will be hobbled by economic limitations to access. "The Internet parent culture is strong, but it is limited, and it will remain limited until Internet access expands into the homes of rural, poor, and inner-city parents." Carvin and many others are pursuing the lofty goal of bringing resources to the masses.

Meanwhile, the existing Internet parenting community has many traits to appreciate. They're community-minded, for one thing. Dozens of private Internauts

put their own time into building home pages full of children's resources, and Net parents also donate time to help schools launch Web initiatives. On the newsgroups and mailing lists, people gladly dispense whatever expertise they possess.

"On **misc.kids** we have great representation from all walks of life," says Lorinda Brandon, a documentation project leader and mother of two boys who is an active presence on the newsgroup. "We have doctors and researchers who can answer the truly technical questions, experienced parents who can provide advice and suggestions, parents of disabled children, parents who have lost children, and even non-parents who just like to think about how we raise our kids in this society."

Net parents also are good Net citizens who practice what they preach, even if they come off a bit, well, *preachy* in the process. The **misc.kids** welcome statement, for example, includes a generous dose of netiquette advice, reminders to write thank you notes for responses to queries, and it concludes with this brusque direction: "Please refrain from name-calling, tantrums, or other hysterics—we get enough of that from our children :-)." What's remarkable is that the community heeds this well-intentioned advice. "I think we're pretty good at apologizing and getting on with it, and maybe better at negotiating peace than other groups because, after all, we're all trying to teach these skills to our kids," says Brandon.

3. FINDING A BALANCE: Relationships between Parents and Children

Even newbies and those who commit breaches of netiquette are treated with an extra measure of good manners. Pleasant greetings along with suggestions on where to find FAQs are far more common than the scathing diatribes many a startled Net newcomer faces upon unintentionally breaking a group's rules. "When I made the mistake of posting a commercial advertisement to **misc.kids**, my mailbox was filled with flames," reports Eric Steffensen, a student at the University of Utah who has developed a children's product that he plans to market on the Web. "The surprising thing is that only one person posted his flame in the newsgroup. In other newsgroups I've been in, most flames stay in the newsgroup and don't go to e-mail."

WHOLE LOT OF PARENTS

No matter what else is said about the Internet parenting community, no one can deny there are just a heck of a lot of parents out there. With an endless tide of newcomers from commercial providers, the numbers are growing every day.

Not all of the results of growth are positive. "There are way too many posts to keep track of now, which forces groups to split into less useful groups," says Brandon. "Many people can't get the subgroups or don't have time to read them all, and the sense of community is diminished a bit."

In addition, even the kindest self-appointed welcoming committee member gets frustrated with newcomers still wet behind the ears, unversed in protocol yet eager to get their feet wet. Brandon is not alone in voicing frustration over newbie breaches. The surge in newcomers "has lowered the quality of the conversations on the Net," she says. "Many people are not taking the time to learn the accepted netiquette and they are not responding in the accepted manner." On the other hand, most people seem resigned to the extra work of separating the wheat from the chaff.

In the face of this incredible growth, how does the Internet parenting community keep any sort of control over burgeoning resources, links, and data? The answer is that they're as organized as they are wholesome. Few newsgroups can claim a well-maintained FAQ system, for example, but **misc.kids** boasts a whopping collection of more than 80 meticulously maintained FAQs. And mailing list owners work hard to stay on topic.

Newcomers to Web development also take the task of educating themselves seriously. "My first attempts were very feeble because HTML really threw me for a loop," says Dale Beasley, a Washington state science and technology teacher who works with children in the first through 8th grades. After looking over other people's efforts, though, he has developed several Web resources. "Now I can't figure out why it seemed so difficult," he said.

Not surprisingly, a community as large and active as this eventually starts reaching out of the virtual world into flesh and blood interactions. A desire to match faces with people's names prompted a number of **misc.kids** readers to put together an annual photo album, now in its second year. Volunteers collect photos and biographies and produce and distribute the hefty volume. Misc.kidders also meet for picnics in towns across the country, and smaller groups meet informally after discovering they share a geographical location as well as a passion for parenting and the Net.

CREEPING INTO THE SCHOOLS
An unexpected benefit for many online

SOME PROMINENT

MAILING LISTS
To subscribe to any of these mailing lists, send e-mail to the address indicated with a blank subject and **subscribe** *listname Your* **Name** *(i.e.,* **subscribe adoption John Smith**) *in the body of your message.*

LISTNAME address

adoption   listserv@listerv.law. cornell.edu
All about adoption.

ddline   listserv@uicvm.uic.edu
Information for parents of children with disabilities.

down-syn   listserv@vm1.nodak.edu
Information about children with Down's Syndrome.

home-ed   listserv@world.std.com
For parents interested in home schooling.

kidcafe   listserv@vm1.nodak.edu
A mailing list for kids to communicate.

parent-l   listserv@uts.edu.au
About attachment parenting and extended breastfeeding.

parenting-l   listserv@postoffice. cso.uiuc.edu
About parenting children from birth to adolescence.

y-rights   listserv@sjuvm.stjohns.edu
Young people's rights discussion group.

WORLD-WIDE WEB
CHILDREN'S LITERATURE WEB GUIDE
http://www.ucalgary.ca/~dkbrown/ index.html *Detailed information about children's books, including award winners, press releases, and information about authors.*

CHILDREN NOW
http://www.dnai.com/~children/
A nonpartisan policy and advocacy organization for children.

CUTE KIDS PAGE
http://www.prgone.com/cutekids/
Stories about cute kids. Submit your own.

CYBERSPACE MIDDLE SCHOOL
http://www.scri.fsu.edu/~dennisl/ cms.html *A resource for children in the sixth through ninth grades.*

D.O.S.A. PARENTING PAGE
http://www.linnet.ca/~ahawkins/
Question and answer forums, discussion groups, and helpful archives of information on books, parenting strategies, and support for caregivers.

EDWEB
http://edweb.cnidr.org *The Corporation for Public Broadcasting's ongoing project. Includes links to educational resources around the world and information about trends in education reform.*

FAMILY PLANET
http://family.starwave.com
News, shopping, parenting tips, expert advice.

FAMILY WORLD HOME PAGE
http://family.com/resources.html
Links to resources for Net newcomers as well as educational and parenting resources.

FIRST AID ONLINE
http://symnet.net/~afoster/safety/
Tips on how to remedy common accidents as well as dealing with major maladies.

FUN KID LINKS
http://www.ucalgary.ca/~darmstro/ kid_links.html *Pointers to child-safe sites.*

GLOBAL SHOW-N-TELL
http://www.zen.org/~brendan/ kids.html *Contains links to schools and students from all over, featuring their art and stories.*

HELPING YOUR CHILD LEARN TO READ
http://www.ed.gov/pubs/ parents/Reading/ *From the U. S. Dept. of Education with activities for children from infancy through age 10.*

KATHY'S ESSENTIAL INFORMATION FOR PARENTS
http://www.mcs.net/~kathyw/ parent.html *Links to sites about parenting.*

KIDLINK
http://www.kidlink.org *The KidLink project promotes a dialog for children age 10 to 15 and currently boasts 30,000 participants from 66 countries.*

KIDSCOM
http://www.kids.com *A communication playground for children ages 8 to 12 in English, Spanish, French, and German.*

THE KIDS ON THE WEB
http://emma.manymedia.com/ show-n-tell/sites.html *Some K-12 educational information and lots of links to fun places for kids, including activities, favorite characters' "haunts," and a guide to kids' literature.*

KIDS WEB
http://www.npac.syr.edu/ textbook/kidsweb/ *Links to resources for children's learning ranging from the arts*

An unexpected benefit for many online parents is a direct line to their kids' teachers.

PARENTS' POINTERS

through the sciences and including just-for-fun links like games and sports.

MATERNAL & CHILD
HEALTH NETWORK (MCH-NET)
GOPHER SERVER
mchnet.ichp.ufl.edu *Information about systems of care for children, especially children with special health-care needs.*

MIDLINK MAGAZINE
http://longwood.cs.ucf.edu/~Midlink/
Electronic magazine for kids 10 to 15, created largely by middle-school children. Includes links to artwork and writing from kids around the world.

MISC.KIDS FAQ COLLECTION
http://www.internet-is.com/misckids/ *FAQs dealing with infancy and beyond.*

NATIONAL PARENT
INFORMATION NETWORK
http://ericps.ed.uiuc.edu/npin/npinhome.html *Provides information to parents and those who work with parents.*

NEW PARENTS NETWORK
http://www.indirect.com/www/kstorek/parents.html *Nonprofit organization offering immunization schedules, lists of recalled toys, disability information and support services, parenting tips, and more.*

PARENT-L HOME PAGE
http://www2.helix.net/~lois/parent-l.html *Breastfeeding and attachment parenting resources.*

PARENTSPLACE.COM
http://www.parentsplace.com
A host of articles on pregnancy, breastfeeding, baby, adolescence, parenting twins, step-parenting, single parenting, children's health and education, family activities, and more. Opportunities for parenting dialog and shopping.

PEDINFO
http://www.lhl.uab.edu/pedinfo/
Information for pediatricians and others interested in child health. Includes links to many organizations from Alateen to The Virtual Children's Hospital as well as parenting and kids' resources ranging from the Barney page to online parenting magazines.

RANDY'S HOMEPAGE
http://www.cei.net/~rcox/
Social worker Randy Cox's links to children's issues resources. Of particular note: the Positive Parenting tools and newsletter.

RYAN AND ALYSHA'S
LINKS FOR KIDS
http://www.webfeats.com/illusion/ *Fun and educational links for children of all ages.*

SAFE-T-CHILD ONLINE
http://yellodino.safe-t-child.com
Public-service offering by child-security product provider Safe-T-Child Inc.

SAVE-A-CHILD
http://www.simplexservices.com/mclark/saveachild.html *Service that stores vital info (color*

photo, fingerprints, medical data, etc.) on your loved ones.

UNCLE BOB'S KIDS' PAGE
http://gagme.wwa.com/~boba/kidsi.html *A plethora of links for kids.*

WWW SCHOOLS REGISTRY
http://hillside.coled.umn.edu/others.html *Links to schools with Web servers, listed by country and by level.*

YOUNG PERSON'S GUIDE
TO HOT WEB SPOTS
http://www.osc.on.ca/kids.html
Links to pages which appeal to kids of all ages, including hip (Lollapalooza, Rolling Stones) sites for older kids.

NEWSGROUPS
Misc.kids and its split-off groups make an excellent place for fledgling cyber-parents to begin their exploration.

**alt.adoption
alt.child-support
alt.kids-talk
alt.parenting.solutions
alt.parents-teens
alt.support.breastfeeding
alt.support.single-parents
alt.support.step-parents
k12.chat.elementary
k12.chat.junior
k12.chat.senior
misc.education
misc.kids
misc.kids.computer
misc.kids.consumers
misc.kids.health
misc.kids.info
misc.kids.pregnancy
rec.arts.books.childrens**

parents is a direct line to the educators who play a key role in their kids' lives. A quick glance at a mailing list directory or Usenet newsgroup list confirms that teachers and administrators in kindergarten through high school are developing a strong Internet presence.

In many cases, the Net provides a natural ground for collaboration, offering a way for parents to find out what's new in schooling, in incorporating technology into the curriculum, and in the ongoing effort to make the Net a safe place for kids. And it's also a good place for parents to communicate their own ideas and to promote their educational agendas. "Much of the K-12 Net community is made up of concerned parents," says Carvin, and in fact he is working on a site to help parents learn about millions of dollars of grant money available so they can approach school boards armed with well-thought-out recommendations.

While parents may be startled at first to see the fruit of their children's creative processes turning up on home pages rather than taped to a refrigerator, teachers are quick to point out the benefits of a cyber setting. "The project becomes more important when the audience is real," says Caroline McCullen, a teacher at Discovery Middle School in Orlando, Fla., who along with her students publishes *MidLink Magazine*, a collaborative Web e-zine for middle school children. McCullen's students perform research and publish on the Web, as well as collaborate with students and teachers around the world to produce their 'zine.

The Baby Boomer's parenting years are coinciding with the explosion of the Internet. As more people gain Internet access and the Net matures, the parenting community should only get larger and the resources better.

Sophie Littlefield (Soph@nwu.edu) is an Internet Trainer at Northwestern University in Illinois.

what is wrong with this.

EFFECTIVE FATHERS

WHY ARE SOME DADS MORE SUCCESSFUL THAN OTHERS?

Ken R. Canfield

Ken R. Canfield is the author of The Seven Secrets of Effective Fathers and Beside Every Great Dad. His articles have appeared in Psychological Reports, Educational and Psychological Measurement, Parents, and other publications. He is the founder of the National Center for Fathering in Shawnee Mission, Kansas, which seeks to inspire and train men to be responsible fathers.

Fathers win when they actively father. There is a deep sense of satisfaction that pervades a father's life when he becomes an involved dad. Vice President Al Gore spoke to this point recently when he said, "There is nothing more noble than to see a father succeed." Bravo! I couldn't agree more. As a researcher over the past seven years, I have tapped into the experiences of some seven thousand fathers across the nation. These dads come from a range of experiences: fathers in prison, fathers in the military, stepfathers, divorced dads, inner-city fathers, suburban fathers, and fathers from different ethnic backgrounds. Each group faces some unique challanges.

AN EFFECTIVE FATHER CAN REMAIN LEVELHEADED BOTH IN A CRISIS LIKE AN AUTO ACCIDENT AND IN THE MIDST OF MEDIA MESSAGES THAT ARE HOSTILE TO TRAINING RESPONSIBLE CHILDREN.

Still, in order to systematize and understand the role of fathers as such, a survey inventory was developed, and the different dads I have just mentioned were surveyed on their practices as fathers. A national Gallup poll was conducted. The sample used for this poll differed from the national average, however, in that only 7 percent of the men who were surveyed were noncustodial fathers—all the rest were living with their families. Thus, our sample was above the national average in terms of commitment to fatherhood.

Then, in the course of this research, my colleagues and I identified a group of effective fathers within the larger group. These "effective fathers" had raised at least one child to adulthood and were nominated by peers and/or professionals who knew them. Then, in combing through the survey responses, I found seven aspects of fathering that these fathers demonstrated to a significantly greater degree than did other fathers. Here is the essence of the study.

The seven aspects of effective fathering identified are:
- Commitment
- Awareness
- Consistency

- Protecting and providing
- Loving the children's mother
- Active listening
- Spiritual equipping

1. COMMITMENT

Commitment is being both eager to be with your children and willing to be with them when you are not so eager.

The strong fathers identified by their peers scored 77 percent on the commitment scale on the questionnaire, compared with 59 percent for other fathers. The difference—18 percentage points—was greatest in this area of the survey.

How does a father strengthen commitment? One way is by verbalizing to his children that he is committed to them and available for them. Giving his school-age children his work phone number is one way of emphasizing the point.

Telling others about your commitment to your children is another way of holding yourself accountable. Don't be embarrassed to tell an office mate that you are taking an afternoon off because of a son's ball game. What you're demonstrating is that you are committed to that child.

Symbols can help, too. When the president of the United States looks up from his desk, he can see the seal of his authority. When you look around you, what have you placed within your view that reminds you "I'm a dad!"?

2. AWARENESS

Effective fathers answered that it was "somewhat true" that they knew their children. Other fathers were "undecided" or "unsure" on questions measuring awareness.

Awareness has a couple of aspects. One is knowing your child's specific moods, temperament, abilities, situation at school, friends, dreams, and so on. The other is knowing the general developmental phases in a child's life.

Another secret within the secret of being aware of your children is being aware of the ways that their mom is in tune with them and paying attention to what she notices.

Knowing your children and their situation requires that you heavily invest yourself in digesting what your children tell you. Once I was trying to understand why my son was having trouble with his teacher. By listening hard and forcing myself to pay attention over a period of time, it suddenly clicked. This teacher didn't like my son because he reminded her of someone else. That problem didn't need a father's lecture or discipline—it called for a change in schools.

3. CONSISTENCY

Ahhh, consistency. Remember the often-misquoted phrase: "*Foolish* consistency is the hobgoblin of little minds." We need consistency that isn't stifling, or boring but that communicates love to our children.

When assessed on their stability in such things as their treatment of their children, their emotions, and even their schedule for coming home, effective fathers scored 80 percent, while the others got 68 percent.

Consistency is, first of all, being there. Far too many fathers live apart from their children. But don't let that definition of fatherlessness mislead you. Fathers can be emotionally absent as well. In the movie *Hook*, the successful Wall Street lawyer (played by Robin Williams), says to his son: "When we get back, I'll go to all

the rest of your games. I promise. My word is my bond." His son, the victim of numerous broken promises, replies, "Oh, yeah. Junk bonds."

At the same time, let me offer hope to those dads who aren't living with their children: Consistency still makes a difference. Consistency in regular communication, being predictable down to the day and even the minute, speaks volumes. Consistency in financial support is crucial. And what you do during the time you spend with your children makes an enormous difference in your children's lives.

4. PROTECTING AND PROVIDING

One of the most accepted attributes of fatherhood is providing for and protecting children. That could be why the two groups of fathers we surveyed were closest in this area. Effective fathers rated 93 percent, while the others got 82 percent. These high scores are, of course, importantly a result of our sample being disproportionately made up of at-home dads.

An effective father can remain levelheaded both in a crisis like an auto accident and in the midst of media messages that are hostile to training responsible children.

I view the first formal talk I had with my son about sex as a form of protecting him. He was only seven years old, and this was not a full-blown "birds and bees" talk; it was simply a discussion about human anatomy that I undertook because my wife had noticed our son's curiosity about his older sisters. I wanted to protect my son from learning about anatomical differences in a locker-room-type situation. I wanted him to hear about these things firsthand from his dad, so that he would have a family-dom-

THE FATHERHOOD MOVEMENT

One definition of a movement includes the following three parts: A movement has (1) a group of people who identify themselves as members of the movement, (2) literature that advances their cause, and (3) opposition from other forces.

Defined this way, the "fatherhood movement" is embryonic. By and large, public advocates of responsible fatherhood do not see themselves as a coherent group but as lone prophets shouting in a wilderness of neglect. And opposition to responsible fatherhood is difficult to find.

Still, there are some developments that have the feel of a movement:

The National Fatherhood Initiative has been formed to raise public awareness of the need for responsible fatherhood. The National Fatherhood Initiative is led by Don Eberly (president), who once served as a key aide to Jack Kemp; Wade Horn (director), commissioner of Children, Youth, and Families under President Bush; and David Blankenhorn (chairman), who was a civil-rights activist and community organizer before becoming involved in research on the need for fathers to be present and involved with their families. The group hosted a National Fatherhood Summit in October 1994 to educate civic leaders. After a tour this spring and summer featuring talks by David Blankenhorn, it will be aiming to spearhead an Ad Council campaign on the need for responsible fathers.

Another effort is that of Vice President Al Gore under the name "Father-to-Father." Through meetings of researchers and social-work practitioners (which have been deliberately low-key to ensure that this cause is not seen as partisan), the group is working to develop a private-sector mentoring program matching experienced fathers with newer dads. Gore personally signs on to Father-Net, a computer bulletin board sponsored by the Children, Youth, and Family Consortium of the University of Minnesota. Gore has brought together pioneers in the area of fathering such as Jim Levine and Ed Pitt of the Fatherhood Project and Ralph Smith of the Philadelphia Children's Network.

Levine's Fatherhood Project is sponsored by the Family and Work Institute in New York City. He champions "father-friendly" policies in the workplace and has developed practical materials on how to get men involved in early childhood development programs such as Head Start.

During his years as founder and president of the Philadelphia Children's Network, Ralph Smith promoted "father reengagement," refusing to accept the assumption of many social-welfare bureaucrats that fathers are unwilling or unable to support their children. Smith, now of the Annie E. Casey Foundation, recently helped found the National Center on Fathers and Families at the Graduate School of Education at the University of Pennsylvania. This center aims at closing the research gap in the social sciences on knowledge about fathers.

Meanwhile, a grass-roots group that makes no effort at changing public opinion, Promise Keepers, has motivated a stratum of men from the churches to take up the cause of fatherhood. The Christian group, headquartered in Denver, Colorado, is impressive through raw numbers: It attracted a total of more than 280,000 men for seven day-long events in stadiums across the nation last year and aims to conduct thirteen similar events this year.

While their speakers are a cross-section of evangelical Christians, the message is consistent: Men need to be servant-leaders of their families, get together with a few other men to encourage and support one another, and cross ethnic barriers to reach toward racial harmony. This group attracted some incidental opposition, as homosexual and feminist activists rallied outside one site last year, attacking and misinterpreting the group's motives.

Other developments, spontaneous and unconnected but portending bigger changes, include the following:

• Community colleges offering parent-education classes are starting to aim not just at mother-oriented preschool classes but at classes for fathers as well. Susanne Spandau, an instructor at Pasadena City College in California, went so far as to offer a fathers-only class,

"Being A Father and Loving It." Her class was well attended.

• Corporations are beginning to see resolving work-family tensions in a new light. IDS in Minneapolis recently hosted a fathering seminar taught by professional trainers that drew an overflow crowd, exceeding management's expectations. *Personnel Journal* reported in October 1994 that currently 60 percent of *Fortune* 500 companies offer parenting education programs. Those programs do not consistently take the fathers' needs and desires into account, but they may start to.

• A quasi-corporate municipal agency has gone one better than simply offering parenting education. The Los Angeles Department of Water and Power has an actual "Fathering Program" as part of its Work and Family Life Services office. The program coordinator arranges "Daddy-n-Me" recreation outings once a quarter for employees, lends beepers to dads with expectant wives, and sponsors noontime "information groups" for dads who get together monthly to talk and share ideas.

There may be a place for this kind of "affirmative action" for dads. Work and Family Life coordinator Ray Castro puts it this way, "Every time we hung out a sign 'Family Life Workshop' moms came, so the idea was to target men." No doubt part of the appeal of their offerings is that other men identify with Castro, who told me, "As a 22-year-old with all my degrees nobody had prepared me for the toughest job I would ever have: fatherhood."

• Programs to encourage unwed urban dads to form families are springing up as well. Charles Ballard's work in Cleveland, Ohio, has been so successful that he has been funded to replicate his program in five other cities. His program, the National Institute for Responsible Fatherhood, helps unwed young men acknowledge paternity, get regular jobs so they can support their kids, and develop stable relationships with their child's mother. Many formerly unwed couples have married as a result of participating in the program. Uncovering a man's paternal instinct is actually the first step in Ballard's program—and a much-neglected one.

• Fathers' Education Network in downtown Detroit, with Don Burwell, is taking fifty-two men through weekly gatherings aimed at instilling purpose in their lives and commitment to their children.

• MAD DADS in Omaha, Nebraska, was an "emergency response" when Eddie Staton and two other fathers founded it some five years ago. Dads were needed to take responsibility not just for their own children but for those wandering the streets at night. The group, which has thirty-two chapters nationally, has as its main focus patrolling the streets and talking with young people, especially those who are out after ten at night. The group confronts drug pushers with the consequences of their actions and brings together warring gangs simply to talk. MAD DADS is now taking the step of equipping both young and old fathers so that they may be more effective in rearing their children.

—*K.R.C.*

MORE INFORMATION

NATIONAL FATHERHOOD INITIATIVE:
800-790-DADS.

FATHERNET:
612-625-7251
email address:
cyfcec@maroon.tc.umn.edu

THE FATHERHOOD PROJECT:
212-465-2044

NATIONAL CENTER ON FATHERS AND FAMILIES:
215-686-3910

PROMISE KEEPERS:
800-888-PK95.

LOS ANGELES DEPARTMENT OF Water and Power,
WORK AND FAMILY LIFE SERVICES:
213-367-3546.

NATIONAL INSTITUTE FOR RESPONSIBLE FATHERHOOD:
216-791-8336

FATHERS' EDUCATION NETWORK:
313-831-5838

MAD DADS:
402-451-3500.

—K.R.C.

inated environment within which to assimilate them.

5. LOVING YOUR WIFE

The National Center for Fathering has sponsored essay contests for children about their dads. One fourth-grader, Tasha, wrote: "He treats my mom very nicely, which makes me feel wanted." That is saying that her father's love for her mother indirectly supplies that love to her, too.

Effective fathers on the average reported their marriages were "good," while the average for typical fathers was "fair."

Fathers who are aware of the interplay between their lives and their children's lives know they need to consciously work on loving their wives. It's easy in the aftermath of birth and young children to let your own relationship slide. In fact, our research found that satisfaction with marriage typically drops off as the children grow up and then climbs back up when they leave the nest.

6. ACTIVE LISTENING

Fathering satisfaction goes down when children hit adolescence. But one trait that distinguishes the fathers who are more satisfied during those years from those who aren't is active listening.

Fathers who engage their children verbally are the most satisfied. Effective fathers scored 82 percent on items such as allowing children to disagree, creating an atmosphere of caring

and acceptance that encourages children to share their ideas, and listening closely to their concerns. Other fathers averaged 68 percent.

Active listening is part skill and part motivation. Listening skills include·

• Eye contact. Getting on the same level with your child helps the two of you have a heart-to-heart talk.

• Asking questions or paraphrasing back your child's words. This provides you with a check to make sure that you understand what he or she is saying.

• Nodding or signaling that you are listening helps, too.

Staying relaxed and stopping any "mental overtime" from your job or other interests is largely a question of motivation. So is turning off the television or other distractions.

But, ohhh, the rewards of active listening! Ron Levant and John Kelly give a wonderful example in their book *Between Father and Child*:

Twice in the course of a ten-minute soliloquy on Batman, five-year-old Harry McCann interrupted himself to ask his father, "Dad, how far away is the movie you and Mom are going to tonight?" Harry's question didn't have much to do with Batman; it had a great deal to do with his hidden message, which was "Dad, I'm anxious about the new baby-sitter who's coming tonight."

His dad was able to draw him out on the subject of his worries about the new baby-sitter and reassure him. That's active listening.

7. SPIRITUAL EQUIPPING

Here I am talking about both serving as a moral guide for your family and introducing your children to the transcendent. Children have questions—will we as dads serve as their guides and help them discover answers?

Although this is one area that has been frozen out of much public discussion (and is sometimes ignored when our research is reported in the press), it is significant that this area revealed the second-largest difference between effective dads and the others: Effective fathers averaged 72 percent here, while others averaged 56 percent.

Responding to the Gallup poll we commissioned, only 48.5 percent of Americans agreed that "fathers feel comfortable discussing spiritual matters with their children." Spiritual equipping comes as much by an exemplary life lived as by the conscious education of our families in scriptures or habits of prayer.

David Blankenhorn of the Institute for American Values addresses the issue of living exemplary lives when summing up discussions he has had with groups of dads in his book *Fatherless America*:

All the pieces of the puzzle fit together, adding up to one man: the good father. Their ideals are public as well as private. For this reason a good father is not simply a man who performs certain tasks for his children. He is a man who lives a certain kind of life.

Fathers strongly influenced by culture

Fathers have a different and often unrecognized way of empathizing with their children.

Tori DeAngelis

Monitor staff

When scores of men descended on Washington, D.C., last October for the "Million Man March," one message they heard from Nation of Islam leader Louis Farrakhan concerned their roles as fathers. Men should be responsible for their children and families, he exhorted, and resume their rightful places as heads of the household.

But what are their rightful places as fathers? Psychological research conducted in the past two decades paints a varied answer to that question. While some politicians trumpet the notion that fathers are necessary to families for their unique masculine qualities, research shows that parenting styles are often influenced by culture. And while fathers are indeed important to families, it's not necessarily because they have qualities different from those that make some women good parents.

"Most of what parents provide that has important consequences for children does not come in gender-differentiated categories," says Joseph Pleck, PhD, a social and developmental psychologist at the University of Illinois at Urbana-Champaign, who has conducted numerous studies on parenting. "But there are common elements that make up good parenting, no matter what gender you are, such as respon-

Research shows that fathering styles vary from culture to culture. But some core parenting qualities, such as the ability to connect to one's children, may be universal skills, psychologists say.

siveness, sensitivity, empathy and good judgment."

Men's empathetic reactions

But men and women learn different roles that can squelch men's expression of empathy and connection early on, psychologists say. While all children start out as emotionally responsive, by age 6 boys have learned to actively suppress their emotions, according to research by University of Connecticut psychologist Buck Park, PhD.

A study conducted in the 1980s bears that finding out in adults: psychologist Fran Grossman, PhD, found that men and women have the same empathic reactions to hearing their newborn babies cry, though their responses appear totally different. The women rush in to quell the infants' distress, while the men sit by impassively.

But when men's stress levels were tested by measuring their galvanic skin responses, they "were off the charts physiologically," showing much higher rates of agitation than the women, said psychologist William Pollack, PhD, director of the Center for

Men at McClean Hospital, Harvard Medical School's teaching hospital.

A related study by Lamb found that men and women are both equally clumsy as parents when a baby is born. A year later, though, mothers appear much more competent than fathers. But that's entirely because they've spent more time with the babies than the men, he said.

The way tests are constructed can also make men and women appear to have different parenting styles, Pollack said. A study he ran, for instance, found that men tested lower on empathy than women.

But on closer inspection, the measures for empathy turned out to be female-based, examining such factors as how often parents talked to or held their babies. Since men characteristically show caring by taking action to fix distressing situations, their version of empathy wasn't tapped by the scale. Pollack is now conducting long-term field research on fathers to examine directly how they show caring and involvement with their children.

Testing the theory

An intriguing way to test the theory of innate gender-based parenting modes is to examine child-rearing practices in different cultures, and among nonhuman primates. Male monkeys and apes show tremendous variability in fathering behavior, said Louise Silverstein, PhD, of Yeshiva University. In a species of marmosets, for instance, the father is involved in everything but breastfeeding. Because marmosets always have twins and the babies are proportionately large compared to the parents, delivering babies can leave the mother exhausted.

"The father has to be the full-time nurturer—he really is responsible for the infant care," she said.

But chimpanzees are minimally involved in fathering their young, she said.

Research also shows that male monkeys can learn to parent, Silverstein said. She cites a study conducted by psychologist Steven Suomi, PhD, of the University of Wisconsin, which found that when male and female adolescent rhesus monkeys were put in a cage with a baby monkey, the female acted as the infant's mother, feeding and caring for it. But when the female was removed from the cage, the male took over the nurturing behavior.

Even the issue of "rough-and-tumble play"—playful rough-housing with youngsters often cited as more characteristic of men—is an open question. Traditionalists in the men's movement argue that such play demonstrates fathers' more physical style.

But when social scientists began to explore the issue cross-culturally in humans, they found that fathers in Sweden and in hunter-gatherer societies rarely engage in rough play, said Silverstein. Anthropologist Barry Hewlett, PhD, looked for the style among African aborigines, and found that *aunts* were the ones to engage in such play with young children.

"The purpose of rough-and-tumble play seems to be reignite an adult's attachment to a child—a notion partly borne out by anecdotes about working moms who engage in such play with their children when they return from business trips," she said.

Equal but different?

The qualities of affiliation and autonomy are often cited as examples of how men and women parent differently. Women are supposed to help the family connect, while fathers encourage their children's autonomy. Pollack's research challenges that more traditional view, he writes in his book "In a Time of Fallen Heroes: The Re-Creation of Masculinity" (Guilford Press, 1993), co-authored with R. William Belcher, PhD, MD.

Both genders had qualities of autonomy and affiliation, he found. But men and women differed in how they *perceived* the two qualities: Men said they affiliated with their children by playing with or teaching them, while women did so through hugging and holding.

"We need to recognize that there is a *his* autonomy and a *her* autonomy, a *his* intimacy and a *her* intimacy, to read between the lines when each seems to be speaking the same language," Pollack and Belcher write.

Not all psychologists think men and women are alike as parents. Psychologist Wade Horn, PhD, believes that men and women have different biologies, different instincts.

"Using androgyny as a goal is very disturbing for the family and the well-being of children," says Horn, a former commissioner for Children, Youth and Family Services under President Bush and director of the National Fatherhood Initiative, a Lancaster, Pa.-based organization set up to foster a responsible fatherhood agenda. "It's a very uninspiring message for men" because it does not emphasize their special contributions, he said.

While the notion of a unique fathering style is questionable empirically, it may help some men participate more fully in fatherhood, Pleck said. And the more fathers are involved positively and nonabusively with their children, he said, the better off their kids are—no matter what their style.

Siblings and Development

Judy Dunn

Judy Dunn is Professor of Human Development at the Pennsylvania State University. Address correspondence to Judy Dunn, Center for the Study of Child and Adolescent Development, College of Health and Human Development, Pennsylvania State University, University Park, PA 16802.

The great majority of children—around 80% in the United States and Europe—grow up with siblings. Yet the developmental impact of the experience of growing up in close—often uncomfortably close—contact with another child within the family has until recently been little studied. The attention of investigators concerned with early developmental influences has been focused instead chiefly on parents (usually mothers) or family, often characterized in terms of structure (e.g., single-parent versus two-parent) or background variables (e.g., socioeconomic status), or in broad descriptive terms, such as "enmeshed" or "disorganized."

In the last few years, however, studies of siblings within their families have greatly increased in number,[1] and have challenged our assumptions concerning two quite different issues in developmental science. First, such studies have raised serious questions about how families influence individual development—and suggested some intriguing answers. Second, they have also shed light on the development of social understanding in young children. Here, research on siblings observed at home shows that formal assessments of very young children's abilities in experimental settings may have seriously underestimated the nature of young children's social understanding.

As an introduction to the new perspectives on these two developmental issues, consider the following incident, drawn from an observation of a 30-month-old child with his mother and his 14-month-old sister. Andy was a rather timid and sensitive child, cautious, unconfident, and compliant. His younger sister, Susie, was a striking contrast—assertive, determined, and a handful for her mother, who was nevertheless delighted by her boisterous daughter. In the course of an observation of Andy and his sister, Susie persistently attempted to grab a forbidden object on a high kitchen counter, despite her mother's repeated prohibitions. Finally, she succeeded, and Andy overheard his mother make a warm, affectionate comment on Susie's action: "Susie, you *are* a determined little devil!"

Andy, sadly, commented to his mother, "*I'm* not a determined little devil!" His mother replied, laughing, "No! What are you? A poor old boy!"

A NEW PERSPECTIVE ON THE DEVELOPMENT OF INDIVIDUAL DIFFERENCES

This brief incident serves to illustrate some of the key issues emerging from a series of systematic studies of siblings and parents in the United States and Britain,[2] which highlight why we need to study within-family processes to explain the development of individual differences. Three features of these processes, evident in the exchange between Andy and his mother, are important here: the difference between siblings in personality, the difference in their relationships with their parents, and their responses to exchanges between their siblings and parents.

Differences Between Siblings

The striking differences between siblings growing up within the same family—differences in personality, adjustment, and psychopathology—have now been documented in a very wide range of studies,[3,4] and these differences present a major challenge to investigators studying family influence. Why should two children who share 50% of their segregating genes and the same family background turn out to be so different? After all, the family factors assumed to be key in development (e.g., parental mental health, marital quality, social class background) are apparently shared by siblings.

This question of why siblings are so different is not just a matter of interest to fond parents puzzled by their children's differences. It turns out to be key to understanding the development of individual differences more generally. Extensive studies by behavior geneticists have now shown that the sources of environmental influence that make individuals different from one another work *within* rather than *between* families.[3] To understand the salient environmental influences on individual development, we have to be able to explain what makes two children within the same family different from one an-

From *Current Directions in Psychological Science,* Vol. 1, No. 1, February 1992, pp. 6-9. © 1992 by the American Psychological Society. Reprinted by permission of Cambridge University Press.

other. The message from this research is not that family influence is unimportant, but that we need to document those experiences that are specific to each child within a family, and therefore we need to study more than one child per family, with a new perspective on what are the salient influences within the family.

What could the significant processes within the family be—differences in parent-child relationships, differences within the sibling relationship itself, differences in peer relationships outside the family, or chance experiences that affect one sibling and not another? In a series of studies, the relation of each of these to children's developmental outcomes is being explored. A number of different samples have been studied in the United States and in England, including nationally representative samples, and major longitudinal studies have included adoptive and biological samples (enabling us to explore where genetic similarities and differences enter the picture). A wide variety of methods has been employed, including naturalistic observations of the families and interviews with all family members. The results of this body of research are discussed in a recent book;[2] here some illustrative points will be summarized briefly.

Differences Between Siblings' Relationships With Their Parents

It is clear that there are major differences in the affection, attention, and discipline that many siblings experience with their parents—whether the information on these differences comes from parents, children, or observers. The differences in warmth and pride that were evident in the behavior of Andy's mother toward her two children are very common. The extent of such differences and the domains in which they are most marked have now been documented in a range of differing samples of families, as have the variables related to the degree of parental differentiation (e.g., the developmental stages of the children and the mother's personality, educational background, and IQ). An important lesson from both the observational work and the experimental studies is that children are extremely sensitive to such differences.

Sensitivity of Children to Their Siblings' Interaction With Their Parents

From a remarkably early age, children monitor and react to their parents' interaction with their siblings. The example of Andy and Susie is typical: Andy monitors and responds to his mother's exchange with his sister, promptly, and with a self-comparison. A recent study showed that 20% of the conversational turns by secondborn children in one sample were attempts to join the conversation between other people.[5] The salient verbal environment for children is not solely the speech addressed to them, but includes conversations between parents and sibling.

Two lines of evidence from recent developmental work confirm the salience for young children of emotional exchanges between other people: laboratory studies of children witnessing exchanges between others and naturalistic studies of children in their families. A wealth of studies have now documented that children from the end of their first year are interested in the behavior of other family members, and especially in their emotional exchanges. In a series of studies, Zahn-Waxler and her colleagues have documented the development of children's responses to emotional displays between others, and the effects of witnessing such exchanges on play and aggressive behavior.[6,7] Naturalistic observations of siblings at home have shown that children rarely ignore disputes between others, but act promptly to support or punish one of the antagonists, and that the behavior of both firstborn and secondborn children is profoundly affected by their mothers' interactions with the other sibling.[8]

How important are these experiences of differential treatment, developmentally? The first investigations show differential experiences are linked to a range of outcome measures: In terms of adjustment, for example, children who receive less maternal affection and attention than their siblings are likely to be more worried, anxious, or depressed than other children in general. And there is now an accumulation of evidence that differential parental behavior is linked to the quality of the relationship between siblings, with more hostility and conflict found in families with greater differential parental treatment, an association found for preschool children, for siblings in middle childhood, for children with disabled siblings, and for children following divorce.[1]

Other Sources of Differential Experience

Among the other possible sources of differential experience, there is growing evidence that differences in children's experiences within the sibling relationship itself can also be related to adjustment. If instead of focusing on siblings as a dyad, we ask how similarly or differently the two siblings behave toward each other, we find there can be marked differences between the two in the affection or control they show. Whether the information comes from maternal interview, children's own accounts, or observations, the emerging picture is that in only one third of sibling pairs do the two children show very similar degrees of affection toward one another. For hostile behavior there is more reciprocity, but within a pair, the relative differences in negative behavior are correlated with later perceived self-competence, and with conduct problems and anxious or depressed behavior. For example, one study found that the more negative a younger sibling is toward the older, relative to the older's negative behavior, the higher the self-esteem of the younger 3 years later.[2] Of course, these initial findings must be treated with caution until they are replicated, and no causal inferences can be made from such correlational data.

In summary, the focus on siblings and their differential experiences within the family has changed and clarified our picture of what are the salient family influences on individual development. In an important sense children are, it appears, *family members* from early in their second year; they are interested in, responsive to, and influenced by the relationships between their siblings and parents—and this insight brings us to the second developmental arena in which sibling studies have provided illumination, the development of social understanding.

A NEW PERSPECTIVE ON THE DEVELOPMENT OF SOCIAL UNDERSTANDING

Recall the comments made by Andy in the incident with his sister and mother. Andy, in the emotional circumstances of the family exchange, made a self-evaluative comment following his mother's warm remark praising his sister. Yet he was *only* two *and a half*. This is startlingly early for a child to be evaluating himself. At this age, according to the received view of the development of self-reflective powers, based on experimental studies, he should not be able to evaluate himself in this way, or be sensitive to social comparison. Could we be misrepresenting children's sociocognitive abilities by studying them only outside the family? Here, observational studies of siblings at home have proved most illuminating.[8]

A focus on children's disputes, jokes, and cooperative play with their siblings has shown that from 18 months on children understand how to hurt, comfort, and exacerbate their siblings' pain; they understand what is allowed or disapproved in their family world; they differentiate between transgressions of different sorts, and anticipate the response of adults to their own and to other people's misdeeds; they comment on and ask about the causes of others' actions and feelings. Analyses of this growing understanding of emotions, of others' goals, and of social rules have shown that the foundations for the moral virtues of caring, consideration, and kindness are well laid by 3 years, but so too children have by this age a sophisticated grasp of how to use social rules for their own ends. The drive to understand others and the social world is, I have argued,[8] closely linked to the nature of a child's relationships within the family over this period: the emotional power of attachment to parents, of rivalry between siblings, and of the conflict between growing independence and socialization pressure. For a young child whose own goals and interests are often at odds with—and frustrated by—others in the family, it is clearly adaptive to begin to understand those other family members and the social rules of the shared family world. The study of siblings has highlighted why it is important that

social understanding should be high on the developmental agenda.

The subtlety of social understanding that children show in the family context—in contrast to their limited capabilities when faced with more abstract or formal tasks—has considerably changed our view of children's abilities, and why they change. And in addition to delineating the pattern of normative growth of social understanding, sibling studies are beginning to clarify in detail the causes of individual differences in social understanding. These differences are striking: Children vary greatly in their ability to understand the causes and consequences of emotions and to understand what other people are thinking and how this influences their behavior. In the recent burst of productive experimental research on children's understanding of "other minds," there has been little consideration of individual differences: How far such differences are related to verbal intelligence, to the quality of children's relationships, or to other family experiences has not been examined empirically. The study of children with their siblings has enabled us to test predictions concerning the significance of family relationships, parental expressiveness, and children's cognitive ability in accounting for differences in social understanding.[9]

The results highlight the importance—and the independent contribution to the variance—of a number of factors. For example, diffences in family discourse about the social world are important: Children who grew up in families in which feelings and causality were discussed performed better than other children on assessments of social understanding 14 months later. But the quality of children's relationships with their siblings is also key: Children who had experienced frequent cooperative exchanges with their siblings, for example, were more successful than other children on tasks assessing their grasp of the connections between another person's belief and subsequent behavior. Also—most notably—differences in children's social understanding are related to the quality of the relationships between their siblings and their mothers. Children who grew up in families in which they witnessed their mothers being highly attentive, responsive, or controlling to their siblings scored particularly high on social cognition assessments 1 year later.

Thus, the work on social understanding links with the first theme—the processes involved in family influence on individual differences. Examining within-family differential experiences of siblings will enlarge our understanding of the salient processes of family influences on personality and adjustment. Similarly, it is clear that studying children in the complex network of sibling and parental relationships within the family can greatly enhance our knowledge about their understanding of the social world. It is within the daily drama of family life that children's social intelligence is revealed and fostered, and siblings play a central role in that drama.

3. FINDING A BALANCE: Siblings

NOTES

1. F. Boer and J. Dunn, *Sibling Relationships: Developmental and Clinical Issues* (Erlbaum, Hillsdale, NJ, 1992).

2. J. Dunn and R. Plomin, *Separate Lives: Why Siblings Are So Different* (Basic Books, New York, 1990).

3. R. Plomin and D. Daniels, Why are children in the same family so different from each other? *The Behavioral and Brain Sciences, 10,* 1–16 (1987).

4. S. Scarr and S. Grajek, Similarities and differences among siblings, in *Sibling Relationships: Their Nature and Significance Across the Lifespan,* M. E. Lamb and B. Sutton-Smith, Eds. (Erlbaum, Hillsdale, NJ, 1982), pp. 357–386.

5. J. Dunn and M. Shatz, Becoming a conversationalist despite (or because of) having an older sibling, *Child Development, 60,* 399–410 (1989).

6. C. Zahn-Waxler and M. Radke-Yarrow, The development of altruism: Alternative research strategies, in *The Development of Prosocial Behavior,* N. Eisenberg-Berg, Ed. (Academic Press, New York, 1982), pp. 109–137.

7. E. M. Cummings, Coping with background anger, *Child Development, 58,* 976–984 (1987).

8. J. Dunn, *The Beginnings of Social Understanding* (Harvard University Press, Cambridge, MA, 1988).

9. J. Dunn, J. Brown, C. Slomkowski, C. Tesla, and L. Youngblade, Young children's understanding of other people's feelings and beliefs: Individual differences and their antecedents, *Child Development, 62,* 1352–1366 (1991).

The
Secret World
of Siblings

Emotional ambivalence often marks the most enduring relationship in life

They have not been together like this for years, the three of them standing on the close-cropped grass, New England lawns and steeples spread out below the golf course. He is glad to see his older brothers, has always been glad to have "someone to look up to, to do things with." Yet he also knows the silences between them, the places he dares not step, even though they are all grown men now. They move across the greens, trading small talk, joking. But at the 13th hole, he swings at the ball, duffs it and his brothers begin to needle him. "I should be better than this," he thinks. Impatiently, he swings again, misses, then angrily grabs the club and breaks it in half across his knee. Recalling this outburst later, he explains, simply: "They were beating me again."

As an old man, Leo Tolstoy once opined that the simplest relationships in life are those between brother and sister. He must have been delirious at the time. Even lesser mortals, lacking Tolstoy's acute eye and literary skill, recognize the power of the word *sibling* to reduce normally competent, rational human beings to raw bundles of anger, love, hurt, longing and disappointment—often in a matter of minutes. Perhaps they have heard two elderly sisters dig at each other's sore spots with astounding accuracy, much as they did in junior high. Or have seen a woman corner her older brother at a family reunion, finally venting 30 years of pent-up resentment. Or watched remorse and yearning play across a man's face as he speaks of the older brother whose friendship was chased away long ago, amid dinner table taunts of "Porky Pig, Porky Pig, oink, oink, oink!"

Sibling relationships—and 80 percent of Americans have at least one—outlast marriages, survive the death of parents, resurface after quarrels that would sink any friendship. They flourish in a thousand incarnations of closeness and distance, warmth, loyalty and distrust. Asked to describe them, more than a few people stammer and hesitate, tripped up by memory and sudden bursts of unexpected emotion.

Traditionally, experts have viewed siblings as "very minor actors on the stage of human development," says Stephen Bank, Wesleyan University psychologist and co-author of *The Sibling Bond*. But a rapidly expanding body of research is showing that what goes on in the playroom or in the kitchen while dinner is being cooked exerts a profound influence on how children grow, a contribution that approaches, if it may not quite equal, that of parenting. Sibling relationships shape how people feel about themselves, how they understand and feel about others, even how much they achieve. And more often than not, such ties represent the lingering thumbprint of childhood upon adult life, affecting the way people interact with those closest to them, with friends and coworkers, neighbors and spouses—a topic explored by an increasing number of popular books, including *Mom Loved You Best*, the most recent offering by Dr. William and Mada Hapworth and Joan Heilman.

Shifting landscape. In a 1990s world of shifting social realities, of working couples, disintegrating marriages, "blended" households, disappearing grandparents and families spread across a continent, this belated validation of the importance of sibling influences probably comes none too soon. More and more children are stepping in to change diapers, cook meals and help with younger siblings' homework in the hours when parents are still at the office. Baby boomers, edging into middle age, find themselves squaring off once again with brothers and sisters over the care of dying parents or the division of inheritance. And in a generation where late marriages and fewer children are the norm, old age may become for many a time when siblings—not devoted sons and daughters—sit by the bedside.

It is something that happened so long ago, so silly and unimportant now that she is 26 and a researcher at a large, downtown office and her younger brother is her best friend, really, so close that she talks to him at least once a week. Yet as she begins to speak she is suddenly a 5-year-old again on

Christmas morning, running into the living room in her red flannel pajamas, her straight blond hair in a ponytail. He hasn't even wrapped it, the little, yellow-flowered plastic purse. Racing to the tree, he brings it to her, thrusts it at her—"Here's your present, Jenny!"—smiling that stupid, adoring, little brother smile. She takes the purse and hurls it across the room. "I don't want your stupid present," she yells. A small crime, long ago forgiven. Yet she says: "I still feel tremendously guilty about it."

Sigmund Freud, perhaps guided by his own childhood feelings of rivalry, conceived of siblingship as a story of unremitting jealousy and competition. Yet, observational studies of young children, many of them the ground-breaking work of Pennsylvania State University psychologist Judy Dunn and her colleagues, suggest that while rivalry between brothers and sisters is common, to see only hostility in sibling relations is to miss the main show. The arrival of a younger sibling may cause distress to an older child accustomed to parents' exclusive attention, but it also stirs enormous interest, presenting both children with the opportunity to learn crucial social and cognitive skills: how to comfort and empathize with another person, how to make jokes, resolve arguments, even how to irritate.

The lessons in this life tutorial take as many forms as there are children and parents. In some families, a natural attachment seems to form early between older and younger children. Toddlers as young as 14 months miss older siblings when they are absent, and babies separated briefly from their mothers will often accept comfort from an older sibling and go back to playing happily. As the younger child grows, becoming a potential playmate, confidant and sparring partner, older children begin to pay more attention. But even young children monitor their siblings' behavior closely, showing a surprisingly sophisticated grasp of their actions and emotional states.

Parental signals. To some extent, parents set the emotional tone of early sibling interactions. Dunn's work indicates, for example, that children whose mothers encourage them to view a newborn brother or sister as a human being, with needs, wants and feelings, are friendlier to the new arrival over the next year, an affection that is later reciprocated by the younger child. The quality of parents' established relationships with older siblings can also influence how a new younger brother or sister is received. In another of Dunn's studies, first-born daughters who enjoyed a playful, intense relationship with their mothers treated newborn siblings with more hostility, and a year later the younger children were more hostile in return. In contrast, older daughters with more contentious relationships with their mothers greeted the newcomer enthusiastically—perhaps relieved to have an ally. Fourteen months later, these older sisters were more likely to imitate and play with their younger siblings and less apt to hit them or steal their toys.

In troubled homes, where a parent is seriously ill, depressed or emotionally unavailable, siblings often grow closer than they might in a happier environment, offering each other solace and protection. This is not always the case, however. When parents are on the brink of separation or have already divorced and remarried, says University of Virginia psychologist E. Mavis Hetherington, rivalry between brothers and sisters frequently increases, as they struggle to hold on to their parents' affection in the face of the breakup. If anything, it is sisters who are likely to draw together in a divorcing family, while brothers resist forming tighter bonds. Says Hetherington: "Males tend to go it alone and not to use support very well."

Pretend play is never wasted. Toddlers who engage regularly in make-believe activity with older siblings later show a precocious grasp of others' behavior.

Much of what transpires between brothers and sisters, of course, takes place when parents are not around. "Very often the parent doesn't see the subtlety or the full cycle of siblings' interactions," says University of Hartford psychologist Michael Kahn. Left to their own devices, children tease, wrestle and play make-believe. They are the ones eager to help pilot the pirate ship or play storekeeper to their sibling's impatient customer. And none of this pretend play, researchers find, is wasted. Toddlers who engage regularly in make-believe with older siblings later show a precocious grasp of others' behavior. Says Dunn: "They turn out to be the real stars at understanding people."

Obviously, some degree of rivalry and squabbling between siblings is natural. Yet in extreme cases, verbal or physical abuse at the hands of an older brother or sister can leave scars that last well into adulthood. Experts like Wesleyan University's Bank distinguish between hostility that takes the form of humiliation or betrayal and more benign forms of conflict. From the child's perspective, the impact of even normal sibling antagonism may depend in part on who's coming out ahead. In one study, for example, children showed higher self-esteem when they "delivered" more teasing, insults and other negative behaviors to their siblings than they received. Nor is even intense rivalry necessarily destructive. Says University of Texas psychologist Duane Buhrmester: "You may not be happy about a brother or sister who is kind of pushing you along, but you may also get somewhere in life."

They are two sides of an equation written 30 years ago: Michèle, with her raven-black hair, precisely made-up lips, restrained smile; Arin, two years older, her easy laugh filling the restaurant, the sleeves of her gray turtleneck pulled over her hands.

This is what Arin thinks about Michèle: "I have always resented her, and she has always looked up to me. When we were younger, she used to copy me, which would drive me crazy. We have nothing in common except our family history—isn't that terrible? I like her spirit of generosity, her direction and ambition. I dislike her vapid conversation and her idiotic friends. But the reality is that we are very close, and we always will be."

This is what Michèle sees: "Arin was my ideal. I wanted to be like her, to look like her. I think I drove her crazy. Once, I gave her a necklace I thought was very beautiful. I never saw her wear it. I think it wasn't good enough, precious enough. We are so different—I wish that we could be more like friends. But as we get older, we accept each other more."

It is something every brother or sister eventually marvels at, a conundrum that novelists have played upon in a thousand different ways: There are two children. They grow up in the same house, share the same parents, experience many of the same events. Yet they are stubbornly, astonishingly different.

A growing number of studies in the relatively new field of behavioral genetics are finding confirmation for this popular observation. Children raised in the same family, such studies find, are only very slightly more similar to each other on a variety of personality dimensions than they are, say, to Bill Clinton or to the neighbor's son. In cognitive abilities, too, siblings appear more different than alike. And the extent to which siblings *do* resemble one another in these traits is largely the result of the genes they share—a conclusion drawn from twin studies, comparisons of biological siblings raised apart and biological children and adopted siblings raised together.

Contrasts. Heredity also contributes to the *differences* between siblings. About 30 percent of the dissimilarity between brothers and sisters on many personality dimensions can be accounted for by differing genetic endowments from parents. But that still leaves 70 percent that *cannot* be attributed to genetic causes, and it is this unexplained portion of contrasting traits that scientists find so intriguing. If two children who grow up in the same family are vastly different, and genetics accounts for only a minor part of these differences, what else is going on?

The answer may be that brothers and sisters don't really share the same family at all. Rather, each child grows up in a unique family, one shaped by the way he perceives other people and events, by the chance happenings he alone experiences, and by how other people—parents, siblings and teachers—perceive and act toward him. And while for decades experts in child development have focused on the things that children in the same family share—social class, child-rearing attitudes and parents' marital satisfaction, for example—what really seem to matter are those things that are not shared. As Judy Dunn and Pennsylvania State behavioral geneticist Robert Plomin write in *Separate Lives: Why Siblings Are So Different*, "Environmental factors important to develop-

ment are those that two children in the same family experience differently."

Asked to account for children's disparate experiences, most people invoke the age-old logic of birth order. "I'm the middle child, so I'm cooler headed," they will say, or "Firstborns are high achievers." Scientists, too, beginning with Sir Francis Galton in the 19th century, have sought in birth order a way to characterize how children diverge in personality, IQ or life success. But in recent years, many researchers have backed away from this notion, asserting that when family size, number of siblings and social class are taken into account, the explanatory power of birth ranking becomes negligible. Says one psychologist: "You wouldn't want to make a decision about your child based on it."

At least one researcher, however, argues that birth order does exert a strong influence on development, particularly on attitudes toward authority. Massachusetts Institute of Technology historian Frank Sulloway, who has just completed a 20-year analysis of 4,000 scientists from Copernicus through the 20th century, finds that those with older siblings were significantly more likely to have contributed to or supported radical scientific revolutions, such as Darwin's theory of evolution. Firstborn scientists, in contrast, were more apt to champion conservative scientific ideas. "Later-borns are consistently more open-minded, more intellectually flexible and therefore more radical," says Sulloway, adding that later-borns also tend to be more agreeable and less competitive.

Hearthside inequities. Perhaps most compelling for scientists who study sibling relationships are the ways in which parents treat their children differently and the inequalities children perceive in their parents' behavior. Research suggests that disparate treatment by parents can have a lasting effect, even into adulthood. Children who receive more affection from fathers than their siblings do, for example, appear to aim their sights higher in terms of education and professional goals, according to a study by University of Southern California psychologist Laura Baker. Seven year-olds treated by their mothers in a less affectionate, more controlling way than their brothers or sisters are apt to be more anxious and depressed. And adolescents who say their parents favor a sibling over themselves are more likely to report angry and depressed feelings.

Parental favoritism spills into sibling relationships, too, sometimes breeding the hostility made famous by the Smothers Brothers in their classic 1960s routine, "Mom always loved you best." In families where parents are more punitive and restrictive toward one child, for instance that child is more likely to act in an aggressive, rivalrous and unfriendly manner toward a brother or sister, according to work by Hetherington. Surprisingly, it may not matter who is favored. Children in one study were more antagonistic toward siblings even when *they* were the ones receiving preferential treatment.

Many parents, of course, go to great lengths to distribute their love and attention equally. Yet even the most consciously egalitarian parenting may be seen as unequal by children of different ages. A mother may treat her 4-year-old boy with the same care and attention she lavished on her older son when he was 4. But from the 7-year-old's perspective, it may look like his younger brother is getting a better deal. Nor is there much agreement among family members on how evenhandedly love is apportioned: Adolescents report favoritism when their mothers and fathers insist that none exists. Some parents express surprise that their children feel unequally treated, while at the same time they describe how one child is more demanding, another needs more discipline. And siblings almost never agree in their assessments of who, exactly, Mom loves best.

Nature vs. nurture. Further complicating the equation is the contribution of heredity to temperament, each child presenting a different challenge from the moment of birth. Plomin, part of a research team led by George Washington University psychiatrist David Reiss that is studying sibling pairs in 700 families nationwide, views the differences between siblings as emerging from a complex interaction of nature and nurture. In this scheme, a more aggressive and active child, for example, might engage in more conflict with parents and later become a problem child at school. A quieter, more timid child might receive gentler parenting and later be deemed an easy student.

In China, long ago, it was just the two of them, making dolls out of straw together in the internment camp, putting on their Sunday clothes to go to church with their mother. She mostly ignored her younger sister, or goaded her relentlessly for being so quiet. By the time they were separated—her sister sailing alone at 13 for the United States—there was already a wall between them, a prelude to the stiff Christmas cards they exchange, the rebuffed phone calls, the impersonal gifts that arrive in the mail.

Now, when the phone rings, she is wishing hard for a guardian angel, for someone to take away the pain that throbs beneath the surgical bandage on her chest, keeping her curled under the blue and white cotton coverlet. She picks up the receiver, recognizes her sister's voice instantly, is surprised, grateful, cautious all at once. How could it be otherwise after so many years? It is the longest they have spoken in 50 years. And across the telephone wire, something is shifting, melting in the small talk about children, the wishes for speedy recovery. "I think we both realized that life can be very short," she says. Her pain, too, is dulling now, moving away as she listens to her sister's voice. She begins to say a small prayer of thanks.

For a period that seems to stretch forever in the timelessness of childhood, there is only the family, only the others who are unchosen partners, their affection, confidences, attacks and betrayals defining the circumference of a limited world. But eventually, the boundaries expand, friends and schoolmates taking the place of brothers and sisters, highways and airports leading to other lives, to office parties and neighborhood meetings, to other, newer families.

Adult bonds. Rivalry between siblings wanes after adolescence, or at least adults are less apt to admit competitive feelings. Strong friendships also become less intense, diluted by geography, by marriage, by the concerns of raising children and pursuing independent careers. In national polls, 65 percent of Americans say they would like to see their siblings more often than the typical "two or three times a year." And University of Indianapolis psychologist Victoria Bedford finds, in her work, that men and women of child-rearing age often show longing toward siblings, especially those close in age and of the same sex. Yet for some people, the detachment of adulthood brings relief, an escape from bonds that are largely unwanted but never entirely go away. Says one woman about her brothers and sisters: "Our values are different, our politics diametrically opposed. I don't feel very connected, but there's still a pressure to keep up the tie, a kind of guilt that I don't have a deeper sense of kinship."

How closely sibling ties are maintained and nurtured varies with cultural and ethnic expectations. In one survey, for example, 54 percent of low-income blacks reported receiving help from a brother or sister, in comparison with 44 percent of low-income Hispanics and 36 percent of low-income whites. Siblings in large families are also more likely to give and receive support, as are those who live in close geographical proximity to one another. Sex differences are also substantial. In middle and later life, sisters are much more likely than brothers to keep up close relationships.

So important, in fact, is the role that sisters play in cementing family ties that some families all but fall apart without them. They are the ones who often play the major role in caring for aging parents and who make sure family members stay in touch after parents die. And in later life, says Purdue University psychologist Victor Cicirelli, sisters can provide a crucial source of reassurance and emotional security for their male counterparts. In one study, elderly men with sisters reported greater feelings of happiness and less worry about their life circumstances.

Warmth or tolerance? Given the mixed emotions many adults express about sibling ties, it is striking that in national surveys the vast majority—more than 80 percent—deem their relationships with siblings to be "warm and affectionate." Yet this statistic may simply reflect the fact that ambivalence is tolerated more easily at a distance, warmth and affection less difficult to muster for a few days a year than on a daily basis. Nor are drastic breaches between siblings—months or years of silence, with no attempt at rapprochement—unheard of. One man, asked by a researcher about his brother, shouted, "Don't mention that son of a bitch to me!" and slammed the door in the psychologist's face.

Sibling feuds often echo much earlier squabbles and are sparked by similar collisions over shared responsibility or resources—who is doing more for an ailing

ONLY CHILDREN
Cracking the myth of the pampered, lonely misfit

Child-rearing experts may have neglected the psychology of sibling ties, but they have never been hesitant to warn parents about the perils of siring a single child. Children unlucky enough to grow up without brothers or sisters, the professional wisdom held, were bound to be self-centered, unhappy, anxious, demanding, pampered and generally maladjusted to the larger social world. "Being an only child is a disease in itself," psychologist G. Stanley Hall concluded at the turn of the century.

Recent research paints a kinder picture of the only child—a welcome revision at a time when single-child families are increasing. The absence of siblings, psychologists find, does not doom children to a life of neurosis or social handicap. Day care, preschool and other modern child-care solutions go far in combatting an only child's isolation and in mitigating the willfulness and self-absorption that might come from being the sole focus of parental attention. And while only children may miss out on some positive aspects of growing up around brothers and sisters, they also escape potentially negative experiences, such as unequal parenting or severe aggression by an older sibling. Says University of Texas at Austin social psychologist Toni Falbo: "The view of only children as selfish and lonely is a gross exaggeration of reality."

Indeed, Falbo goes so far as to argue that only children are often better off—at least in some respects—than those with brothers and sisters. Reviewing over 200 studies conducted since 1925, she and her colleague Denise Polit conclude that only children equal firstborns in intelligence and achievement, and score higher than both firstborns and later-borns with siblings on measures of maturity and leadership. Other researchers dispute these findings, however. Comparing only children with firstborns over their life span, for example, University of California at Berkeley psychologist B. G. Rosenberg found that only children—particularly females—scored lower on intelligence tests than did firstborns with a sibling.

Rosenberg distinguishes between three types of only children. "Normal, well-adjusted" onlies, he says, are assertive, poised and gregarious. "Impulsive, acting out" only children adhere more to the old stereotype, their scores on personality tests indicating they are thin-skinned, self-indulgent and self-dramatizing. The third group resembles the firstborn children of larger families, scoring as dependable, productive and fastidious.

Perhaps the only real disadvantage to being an only child comes not in childhood but much later in life. Faced with the emotional and financial burdens of caring for aging parents, those without siblings have no one to help out. But as Falbo points out, even in large families such burdens are rarely distributed equally.

parent, how inheritance should be divided. Few are long lasting, and those that are probably reflect more severe emotional disturbance. Yet harmonious or antagonistic patterns established in childhood make themselves felt in many adults' lives. Says psychologist Kahn: "This is not just kid stuff that people outgrow." One woman, for example, competes bitterly with a slightly older co-worker, just as she did with an older brother growing up. Another suspects that her sister married a particular man in part to impress her. A scientist realizes that he argues with his wife in exactly the same way he used to spar with an older brother.

For most people, a time comes when it makes sense to rework and reshape such "frozen images" of childhood—to borrow psychologist Bank's term—into designs more accommodating to adult reality, letting go of ancient injuries, repairing damaged fences. In a world of increasingly tenuous family connections, such renegotiation may be well worth the effort. Says author Judith Viorst, who has written of sibling ties: "There is no one else on Earth with whom you share so much personal history."

ERICA E. GOODE

Crises—Challenges and Opportunities

- Family Violence and Chaos (Articles 34–37)
- Sexual Issues and Infidelity (Articles 38 and 39)
- Work/Family Stress (Articles 40 and 41)
- Divorce and Remarriage (Articles 42–45)
- Caring and Caregiving (Articles 46 and 47)

Stress is life and life is stress." Sometimes stress in families gives new meaning to this statement. When a crisis occurs in families, many processes occur simultaneously as families and their members cope with the stressor and its effects. The experience of a crisis often leads to conflict and reduces the family members' ability to act as resources for each other. Indeed, a stressor can overwhelm the family system, and family members may be among the least effective people in coping with each other's responses to a crisis.

Family crisis comes in many forms; it can be drawn out or the crisis event can be clearly defined. The source of stress can be outside or inside the family, or it can be a combination of both. It can directly involve all family members or as few as one, but the effects will ripple through the family, affecting all of its members to one degree or another.

In this unit, we consider a wide variety of crises. Family violence and chaos are the initial focus. "After He Hits Her" addresses the spousal crisis of domestic violence. It explores the relationship dynamics that can be at the core of a continuing cycle of trauma and pain, or can help to begin the slow process of change. Following this is "Behind Closed Doors," a powerful description of the descent of a family into chaos and filth, overwhelmed by the alcoholism of the parents. The remainder of this section specifically focuses on children. "Helping Children Cope with Violence" shows how children growing up in violent surroundings can come away scarred for life, while "Resilience in Development" documents characteristics of children who show amazing ability to recover and adjust, even in highly dysfunctional families.

The next section deals with problems in sexuality and sexual relationships, with infidelity as the focus. In "Be-

yond Betrayal: Life after Infidelity," Frank Pittman recounts the emotional and practical wreckage that results from extramarital sex. In the next essay, Tamar Lewin reports on research suggesting that infidelity and other sexual stressors are less common in American marriages than has been assumed.

The next section looks at the work/family connection, with interesting results. "The Myth of the Miserable Working Woman" confronts many of the myths regarding women's balancing work and home. Many of the assumptions we have about the overwhelming nature of this balancing act are found to be untrue. The fact that some men may be overwhelmed by the struggle to balance home and work is the topic of "Look Who's Talking about Work and Family."

Divorce and remarriage are the subjects of the next section. Programs that have been developed to reduce the negative impacts of divorce or to reduce the likelihood of divorce are reviewed in "Should This Marriage Be Saved?" The article that follows, "The Politics of Divorce," explores political efforts to lower the rate of divorce and to reduce negative effects on children. Not surprisingly, the personal views of politicians heavily influence what they see as appropriate steps to be taken. The other two articles take an optimistic look at stepfamilies. In both, the reader has an opportunity to examine the way our culture has set stepmothers and stepfamilies in an impossible evil/angelic dichotomy. These essays show that stepfamilies, although more complex than traditional families, are not doomed to failure and unresolved conflict.

The nature of stress resulting from caring for others in the family is the subject of the final section. Two articles address issues of providing care for a family member with a debilitating, ultimately fatal condition, first from a schol-

UNIT 4

arly perspective and second from a personal perspective. When these are read together, they present a picture of challenging, sometimes frustrating, work that also contains some reward.

Looking Ahead: Challenge Questions

How does an abusive relationship develop? What can be done to prevent it? How can we help someone caught in such a relationship? If you found that someone you knew was obsessively in love with another person, what would you do? What would you do if someone you knew was a victim of abuse in a relationship?

How would you react if you learned that your spouse or partner had been unfaithful? Under what circumstances would you consider extrarelational sex?

What is the best way to work out the competing demands of work and family? Assuming there is an option, discuss whether or not both partners should work outside the home if there are small children in the home.

Discuss how divorce affects the people involved. Should the rate of divorce be reduced? If so, how? If not, why not? How has divorce affected someone you know? If the person has children, how have the children been affected?

Is your family, or that of a friend, a remarried or blended family? If so, how have you, or your friend, been affected?

What is your responsibility to the members of your family? What is their responsibility to you? What would you give up to care for your parents? What would you expect your children to give up for you? How about your spouse or partner?

After He Hits Her

This study examines the interactional dynamics following woman battering, and specifically addresses the question of whether, as time goes on, male batterers are less likely to offer accounts or aligning actions (i.e., apologies, excuses, justifications, and dismissals) for acts of violence, and whether female victims are less likely to honor the men's accounts. Based on in-depth interviews with 50 white women who had come to a battered women's shelter, the study finds that abusers generally are not likely to stop accounting for their violent behavior but that shelter victims are progressively less likely to honor the accounts. It also is found that, as time goes on, men are more likely to blame their victims for the battering. Similarities and differences between these findings and the research results used to support Walker's (1979, 1984) cycle theory of violence are discussed. Implications for practitioners working with batterers and victims are outlined.

Jane H. Wolf-Smith and Ralph LaRossa

Jane H. Wolf-Smith is an Associate Professor in the Department of Social Sciences, Gainesville College, Gainesville, GA 30503. Ralph LaRossa is a Professor in the Department of Sociology, Georgia State University, Atlanta, GA 30303.

For some time now, researchers and activists in the battered women's movement have realized that "acts of violence" are not discrete acts of physical aggression but are patterns of oppression, occurring over time and including events leading up to as well as following the use of force, itself. Thus, for example, in what may be the most widely cited theory of the pattern or cycle of violence, there is said to be at least three phases—the tension building phase, the acute battering phase, and the loving contrition phase—which ensnare women in a web of punishment and deceit (see Walker, 1979, 1984).

While much has been written about the structural and situational factors which precipitate violence toward women and, as more victims come forward, an all-too-vivid picture of both the range and severity of force in intimate relationships is being acquired, little still is known about what happens immediately after the incident—that is, "after he hits her."

Drawing on in-depth interviews with 50 white women who had been abused by their husbands or male companions, and who had come to a battered women's shelter for refuge, this study examines the interactional dynamics following acts of abuse, giving special attention to both the "acts of contrition" (and other verbal strategies) that men use and the kinds of responses that women give to these strategies. The research combines a theoretically informed approach to the concept of contrition with a methodological focus on the sequence of abuse. That is, from the beginning, the intent was to place "acts of contrition" within the class of theoretical concepts variously referred to as "techniques of neutralization" (Sykes & Matza, 1957), "remedial interchanges" (Goffman, 1971), "accounts" (Scott & Lyman, 1968), or "aligning actions" (Stokes & Hewitt, 1976); and, from the beginning, the goal was to examine whether the verbal strategies that batterers used the first time were different from the verbal strategies used later on.

The interest in whether men "repented" in different ways as time went on was sparked by the finding, reported in several previous studies, that men are likely to repent after the first incident of abuse but *increasingly less likely* to repent after subsequent incidents (see Dobash & Dobash, 1984; Ferraro & Johnson, 1983; Walker, 1984). What this means in terms of the cycle theory of violence is that, after a while, men choose to "delete" the third phase.

If, indeed, abusive men are less contrite as time goes on, this would indicate a shift in their perception of their violent acts. The fact that they would repent for their behavior the first time would indicate some acknowledgment on their part that what they did would be met with disapproval. Their lesser tendency to repent after the 2nd, 10th, or 50th time would indicate that they had begun to "normalize" their violent behavior (i.e., see their violence within the bounds of social acceptability).

The logic here is that deviance and repentance go hand in hand. If individuals feel that they have done something wrong, they often will repent for their apparent misconduct. If, on the other hand, they feel that they are acting correctly, they will not repent. Students, for example, often will talk about why they were late for class, but rarely, if ever, talk about why they were on time (Goffman, 1971; Scott & Lyman, 1968; Stokes & Hewitt, 1976; Sykes & Matza, 1957).

Stopping violence requires an all-out effort to cancel the hitting license. If what happens in abusive relationships is that the license is not only not cancelled but actually renewed and possibly upgraded (i.e., defined as more "normal" than before), battered women and their advocates need to know this. Understanding the part that "acts of contrition" play in the cycle of abuse thus will go a long way toward helping victims of abuse.

The authors wish to thank the women who participated in the study for their willingness to share their experiences; the staff of the battered women's shelter for their cooperation in arranging the interviews; and Phillip W. Davis and Paula L. Dressel for their comments on earlier versions of this article.

Key Words: cycle theory of violence, family violence, victimization of women.

From *Family Relations*, Vol. 41, No. 3, July 1992, pp. 324-329. © 1992 by the National Council of Family Relations, 3989 Central Avenue, NE, Suite 550, Minneapolis, MN 55421. Reprinted by permission.

Theoretical Rationale

A Typology of Aligning Actions

From a symbolic interactionist point of view, an act of contrition is *one* example of an *aligning action,* offered in the hope of mending, if only temporarily, a break between socially established norms and misconduct (Stokes & Hewitt, 1976). By offering aligning actions, social actors give neutral or positive meanings to behaviors that are "out of line." If, in turn, the aligning actions are "honored" by the offended party or parties (i.e., if others give the impression that they attach the same neutral or positive meanings to the apparent misconduct), then the aligning actions have the effect of "containing" or "minimizing" what otherwise might have been viewed as a relationship-threatening set of events.

When aligning actions are offered after deviant behavior, they are referred to as *accounts* (Scott & Lyman, 1968). When they are offered before a misdeed—or in the anticipation of a misdeed—they are referred to as *disclaimers* (Hewitt & Stokes, 1975). Given the interest here on what happens "afterward," the focus is on how men account rather than disclaim abusive behavior.

According to Hunter (1984), ex post facto aligning actions generally fall into four categories. Applied to woman battering, what differentiates the four categories is whether or not the batterer (a) makes the case that the violence in question deserves to be viewed as a negative act, and/or (b) says that he is responsible for the violence.

The first category is an apology. An *apology* signifies the batterer's acceptance of both the negative evaluation of the act and responsibility for the act, itself. Regret is also evident in this aligning action: "I know I shouldn't have slapped you. I'm sorry." Apologies are apparently what Walker (1979, 1984) was referring to when she talked about a "loving contrition phase" in her cycle theory of violence.

In [the loving contrition] phase, the batterer constantly behaves in a charming and loving manner. He is usually sorry for his actions in the previous phases, and he conveys contriteness to the battered woman. He begs her forgiveness and promises her that he will never do it again. (Walker, 1979, p. 65)

The batterer may apologize profusely, try to assist his victim, show kindness and remorse, and shower her with gifts and promises. (Walker, 1984, p. 96)

Being contrite or apologizing, however, is not the only account available to abusers. Other "third phase" strategies include the dismissal, the excuse, and the justification.

The *dismissal* is the opposite of an apology. Its intent is to invalidate both responsibility for the act and the negative evaluation of the act, but: "You pushed me to the limit—besides, you need to know who's boss around here."

Then there is the excuse. When using an *excuse,* the batterer accepts the negative evaluation of the act, but denies responsibility for the act: "That was a lousy thing to do—but I've been under a lot of pressure from my boss."

Finally, there is the justification. With the *justification,* the batterer accepts responsibility for the act but denies its negative evaluation: "I felt I had to do something to keep you from making a stupid decision."

A number of researchers have recognized that efforts on the part of both abusers and victims to account for abusive incidents can include more than apologies or acts of contrition. In one of the earliest studies of violence in the home, Gelles (1974) identified a variety of meanings that abusers gave to their violent acts to "explain" why they were violent—from "She asked for it" (an excuse) to "I tried to knock her to her senses" (a justification). Similarly, Ferraro and Johnson (1983), focusing not on the abusers but on the victims, described how women "rationalized" being abused, saying things like "I asked for it" (an excuse), "He's sick" (also an excuse), and "He didn't injure me" (a justification). Ferraro and Johnson (1983) also demonstrate how these accounts prevented the women from seeking help. Along the same lines, Mills (1985) described the "techniques of neutralization" that battered women use "to help them tolerate violent marriages." Mills (1985) found that one way that women "managed the violence" directed toward them was they used "justifications" (e.g., "compared to others, it seems my problems are small") to "minimiz[e] the significance of their victimization" (p. 109). Finally, Ptacek (1988), in a study of abusive men, discovered that he could classify the bulk of the men's accounts into either excuses or justifications. He also found that the men were more likely to excuse than to justify their behavior.

Drawing on Hunter's (1984) typology and following in the footsteps of Gelles (1974), Ferraro and Johnson (1983), Mills (1985), and Ptacek (1988), this study set out to determine not only whether abusers apologized for hitting their wives but also whether they dismissed,

excused, and justified their violent behavior. Because of the interest, too, in whether men stopped using aligning actions as time went on (and with repeated incidents of abuse), the study also was designed to plot the chronological sequence of accounts.

A Typology of Honoring Stances

One might suppose that a victim has only two choices when her abuser offers to apologize for, or explain, his behavior: she can reject the aligning action or she can honor it. During the preinterview stage of the study, however, it was deduced that there are at least four honoring stances that a victim may take in response to an aligning action (or set of aligning actions). The four stances are: reject, pseudohonor, ambivalently honor, and wholeheartedly honor.

When the victim *rejects* the aligning action, she makes it clear by her verbal and nonverbal behavior that the aligning action is not acceptable, and consequently not effective in smoothing the disruption caused by the abuse.

With *pseudohonor,* the victim pretends to honor the account, with both verbal and nonverbal behavior indicating acceptance, but in self-interaction and in subsequent interaction with others she does not accept the aligning action as legitimate.

When the victim *ambivalently honors* the aligning action, there is some degree of hesitation before she acknowledges its legitimacy. Her honoring stance is characterized by uncertainty, in which she is tempted to honor the account but also doubts its legitimacy.

Finally, a *wholehearted honoring* of the aligning action occurs when the victim, without hesitation, gives it legitimacy. She readily accepts whatever account is issued and fully believes its validity.

The question of whether accounts are rejected has also been the subject of several inquiries. Ferraro and Johnson (1983), for example, talked about the shifts in events and perceptions that lead women to begin to reject their abusers' rationalizations; and Giles-Sims (1983) noted how the women in her study seemed to be willing to "forgive and forget" the first abusive incident but not the most recent. As far as it is known, however, no one has developed a typology of honoring stances like the one described above and applied it to abusive situations. In order to have a clear sense of the interactional dynamics in relationships, it is important to recognize the variety of accounts that men employ *and* the variety of honoring stances that women use in response.

To summarize, the object of this study was to examine the verbal strategies that abusive men use to neutralize or negate their violent actions and the honoring stances that women take to parry these accounts. A central concern of the project from the beginning was whether aligning actions and honoring stances change over time.

Methodology

Sample

The 50 women in the sample were all residents of a battered women's shelter located approximately 50 miles from a major urban area. Hypothesizing that communication patterns after abusive behavior might vary across racial lines, and feeling that an adequate analysis of racial variation would require a much larger sample, the decision was made (due to restrictions on time and other resources) to limit the interviewees to white victims.

The average age of the women in the study was 28 years. While the variation in educational levels was from less than 8 years of education to college graduate, the average number of years completed was 11.5. About one fourth of the women were employed outside the home. Seventy-eight percent were married to their abusers, 20% were cohabiting, and 2% were dating the abuser. The average length of the relationship was 6.5 years. Ninety-eight percent of the sample had children, the average number being 2.4. The average family income for this sample was $17,585.

As reported by the women, the average age of the abusers was 30 years. The average number of years of education completed was 10.7. The majority of the abusers were employed in blue-collar jobs involving manual labor.

Interviews

The interviews were conducted by the first author over a 2-year period, beginning in the fall of 1986 and ending in the fall of 1988. The interviews lasted from 1 to 2 hours, with the average interview lasting an hour and a half. In all but one case the women were interviewed during their stay in the shelter. With the women's consent, the interviews were tape-recorded, and eventually transcribed. The 50 interviews resulted in 1,500 pages of transcripts.

In order to gain an interpretive understanding of the women's point of view, the women were encouraged to talk at length and in-depth about what they thought and how they felt about the abuse in their relationships. All were asked to report on three separate incidents of abuse—the first, the most recent, and a middle incident. For the middle incident, the victims were asked to select an abusive incident that occurred about halfway between the first and the most recent—one that "stood out" to them for some reason. The women were especially encouraged to talk about what happened *after* an abusive incident, particularly what the batterers did or said. However, the women were not specifically asked whether the batterers apologized, excused, justified, or dismissed their behavior, nor were they specifically asked whether they honored any accounts offered. When the women happened to mention an aligning action, they were asked to repeat, to the best of their recollection, what the batterer said and what they had said and felt in response. Thus, every effort was made *not to solicit* aligning actions or honoring stances.

Analysis

To classify the women's comments into one category or another, the constant comparative method of qualitative analysis was used (Glaser & Strauss, 1967). As the transcripts were read and reviewed, notations were made in the margins about categories suggested by particular sections of the transcript. Often a single passage was coded in two or more categories. Once the entire transcript was reviewed, selected passages were cut from the transcript and placed in the appropriate files. As additional transcripts were reviewed, incidents that were similar to previously noted ones were filed with them. During this time the files themselves were reviewed. Incidents were compared with other incidents within the same category, and common properties were noted. Gradually, particular categories with their own properties began to emerge. It was then possible to compare newly discovered incidents with the properties of the category, rather than with just similar incidents (see also Lofland & Lofland, 1984; Strauss & Corbin, 1990).

Changes in the nature of aligning actions and in the nature honoring stances were examined both cross-sectionally and developmentally. The cross-sectional analysis involved an examination of distributions across the three time periods, looking at the sample as a whole (N = 50). The developmental analysis involved (a) an examination of the patterns of change in aligning actions as reported by 31 (of the 50) women who provided information on aligning actions on at least two of three incidents; and (b) an examination of patterns of change in honoring stances as reported by 23 (of the 50) women who provided information

on honoring stances on at least two of three incidents. The developmental analysis, in other words, is an analysis of change within specific relationships. Sometimes, the women were not specific about when a particular aligning action or honoring stance was used. When this was the case, the women's descriptions of events were classified under a "general" category.

Limitations

There are several limitations to the study which should be considered when interpreting the results. First, the sample was limited to 50 white shelter residents. The experience of white women may be unlike that of other groups, and battered women who come to shelters may be different from other battered women in important ways. A second limitation is that female victims, rather than male batterers, were asked about the batterers' accounts. Essentially, then, the women provided "second-hand" information about the accounts employed. Third, the women were asked about interactions surrounding abusive incidents that had occurred, for most, years earlier. Ability to recall these early incidents of abuse varied from one respondent to the next, with some clearly recalling the first incident and others remembering little about it. Additionally, subsequent events may have altered the victims' perception and interpretation of these earlier incidents. Fourth, the interviewing strategy employed may have resulted in the women's failure to report both aligning actions and honoring stances surrounding abusive incidents. In an attempt to let the victims "tell their story," the women were not specifically asked whether abusers offered accounts for their behavior or, if offered, whether they were honored. Therefore, it is possible that accounts and honoring stances were employed but not reported by the women because the women were not asked about them.

Aligning Actions Following Woman Battering

Altogether, 139 aligning actions were discussed by the 50 victims. Table 1 presents the cross-sectional analysis of these accounts. As can be seen, 68% of all aligning actions issued after the first incident involved an apology only, while 67% after the middle incident and 42% after the last incident involved an apology only.

Here, for example, is how one victim, a 38-year-old mother of two, described how her husband apologized for his abuse:

Yeah, once I kind of calmed down

Table 1.
Aligning Actions Offered by Batterers After the First, Middle, and Last Incidents of Abuse: Cross-Sectional Analysis (N = 139)

	First		Middle		Last		General		Total	
	Percent	Number	Percent	Number	Percent	Number	Percent	Number	Percent	Number
Apology	68	21	67	14	42	13	30	17	47	65
With excuse	26	8	14	3	29	9	5	3	17	23
Excuse	6	2	14	3	16	5	50	28	27	38
Justification	0	0	5	1	3	1	13	7	6	9
With apology	0	0	0	0	6	2	0	0	1	2
With excuse	0	0	0	0	3	1	2	1	1	2
Dismissal	0	0	0	0	0	0	0	0	0	0
Total	100	31	100	21	100	31	100	56	100	139

Note. Percentages may not add up to 100% due to rounding.

and kind of regrouped. I went back in and when I did he was sitting on the chair, sort of mopey looking. And I walked in and I just stood there and he just jumps up and runs over and starts apologizing and hugging and crying and said he never meant to hit me and he'd never do it again.

Noteworthy is the fact that the percentages for the use of the apology (and only the apology) are very similar to the percentages that Walker (1984) reported. In Walker's (1984) study, apologies dropped from 69% after the first incident to 63% after the middle incident and to 42% after the last incident. At first glance, it thus seems that the results of this study are in accord with Walker's. However, when the categories that include the use of an apology (Apology Only, Apology with Excuse, Justification with Apology) are *combined,* a pattern different from the pattern Walker reported is uncovered. Used alone or in combination with other types of aligning actions, apologies were said to have been offered 94% of the time after the first incident, 81% of the time after the middle incident, and 77% of the time after the last incident.

A similar finding emerges in the developmental analysis. Only 32% of the women (i.e., 10 of the 31 women for whom there was enough information to carry out a developmental analysis) reported that their mates continued to use an apology (and only an apology) across the three incidents. However, when the categories that involve the continued use of the apology, (Apology Only, From Apology to Apology with Excuse, From Apology with Excuse to Apology, From Apology to Apology with Justification, From Apology with Excuse to Apology with Justification) are *combined,* it is found that 74% of individual abusers continued to use apologies with repeated incidents of abuse.

Quite often, in other words, men would offer a *mixture* of aligning actions, blending their apologies with other, more "self-preservative" accounts. One woman, for example, a 30-year-old mother of two

reported how her husband used an apology with an excuse:

There was never an "I'm sorry" for what happened. I mean he hugged and kissed me the next day and told me he was sorry but it wasn't like "I'm sorry, sorry," it was just, "Well you shouldn't have asked for that can opener. You shouldn't have been over there talking to those men." And I'm saying, "Well, all I did was ask for a can opener. I wasn't carrying on a conversation with them."

Another victim, a 21-year-old mother of one, echoed a similar theme of mixed accounts:

I had got [the baby] asleep while he was gone and he come in and laid in my lap and said, "Baby, I'm sorry." He said, "I don't believe I did that." He said, "I am sorry." And then in the next breath he said, "But you shouldn't have been up there [at your mother's house]." And then he turned and said, "I'm sorry, but they shouldn't have said that." He'd say he was sorry and then he'd say, "But ..."

Interestingly enough, none of the aligning actions described by the women could be classified as a dismissal. Possibly, batterers will resort to a dismissal rarely and only when they feel that an excuse or justification will not be honored.

Walker's (1984) findings led her to conclude that "over time in a battering relationship ... loving contrite behavior declines" (p. 97). Assuming that by "loving contrite behavior" Walker meant apologetic acts, this study failed to replicate Walker's results; according to the women interviewed for this project, while the singular use of the apology declined over time, the apology in conjunction with other aligning actions continued throughout the battering relationship.

Noteworthy, too, is what the interviews reveal about the use of the excuse. An excuse, again, is an account whereby the batterer admits that the abuse is bad

but denies responsibility. For example, a 2l-year-old mother of three reported:

He'll say things like, "If you wouldn't run your smart mouth, I wouldn't do this." And he'll say stuff like, "I don't want to do it, you make me do it." Sometimes you could just say something wrong and not even think you had bothered anybody and he'd just fuss you out or cuss you out, but he just says, "You don't know when to shut your mouth, you just go on and on." He always blames it on me, it's never his fault.

And a 25-year-old mother of four stated:

Like I'd say, "Why do you hit me all the time?" [He'd say] "Shut up, you don't need to ask. If you'd done what I asked in the first place, you never would have gotten it." So it was always like my fault. I asked him to hit me. In a sense, that's what he was saying. She deliberately did this, you know, so that's why she got it.

In Table 1, it can be seen that 6% of all aligning actions used after the first abusive incident involved the excuse alone, while 14% and 16% after the middle and last incident respectively, involved the excuse alone. Not much of a difference. However, when the categories are *combined,* a clearer picture of change emerges. Collapsing all categories that involve the excuse, either used alone or in combination with other aligning actions (Excuses Only, Apology with Excuse, and Justification with Excuse), it is found that 32% of all aligning actions after the first incident involved the use of an excuse, while 28% and 48% involved the use of an excuse after the middle and last incident, respectively. In other words, excuses, although they may be used in combination with other aligning actions, are most likely to be used after the last incident of abuse.

A somewhat similar pattern regarding the use of the excuse emerged in the developmental analysis. Although apologies were the most common account to be used across the three incidents (see

Table 2.
Honoring Stances Taken by Victims After the First, Middle, and Last Incidents of Abuse: Cross-Sectional Analysis (N = 100)

	First		Middle		Last		General		Total	
	Percent	Number	Percent	Number	Percent	Number	Percent	Number	Percent	Number
Rejection	0	0	0	0	50	13	7	2	15	15
Pseudo	3	1	6	1	42	11	29	8	21	21
Ambivalent	27	8	29	5	4	1	25	7	21	21
Wholehearted	69	20	65	11	4	1	39	11	43	43
Total	100	29	100	17	100	26	100	28	100	100

Note. Percentages may not add up to 100% due to rounding.

Table 1), in 13% of the cases (i.e., 4 of 31), batterers were said to move from an apology to an excuse; and in 23% of the cases (i.e., 7 of 31), batterers were said to move from an apology to an apology with an excuse.

The Honoring of Aligning Actions

Changes in honoring stances were analyzed in the same two ways that changes in the use of aligning actions were analyzed (i.e., cross-sectionally and developmentally). The typology of honoring stances developed prior to the interviews and described earlier (i.e., reject, pseudohonor, ambivalently honor, and wholeheartedly honor) was the coding scheme employed.

Examining the first column in Table 2, it can be seen that 20 of the 29 women who provided information on honoring stances after the first incident wholeheartedly honored the aligning actions offered. A 21-year-old mother of one, for example, said that she genuinely thought her husband's accounts were valid:

I believe he was sorry he did it. He just can't control himself. I believe he does it before he realizes it and sometimes he doesn't even remember doing it the next morning. He'll look at me and say, "I did it again, didn't I?" And I'd say, "Yeah." And he didn't remember doing it. It's just out of his memory. I think in his heart he's really sorry for doing it. He just can't help it.

Eight of the 29 women, however, were unsure, or ambivalent, about what their response should be. A 25-year-old mother of one, for example, talked of the difficulty she had trying to decide whether to honor her husband's accounts:

It was very easy for him. Crying, bawling, and I can't stand to see a man cry and he knows it, too. "I swear I'll never do it again. Things are going to be different, I promise. I won't touch you." Just a bunch of lies. Just totally convincing me and knowing better. Me sitting there telling myself "I know this isn't right."

My second wind [*sic*] was I know this isn't right, but there was something else that won over what I thought was right. My heart would say, "Okay, I'll give him another chance. It might just be true this time." And then there was this other thing inside me saying, "You idiot." I always had like two things fighting inside of me. There was one that knew better and then there was the one that let itself be guided by strings.

These findings, which show that women are likely to wholeheartedly or ambivalently honor their mates' accounts after the first incident of abuse, are consistent with the results of prior research. Giles-Sims (1983), who interviewed 31 battered women who had sought help from a battered women's shelter, asked the women whether they had been willing to "forgive and forget" the first abusive incident. The vast majority—93%—said yes. Most of the women also said that they perceived the first abusive incident as an isolated one, and they did not expect it to happen again.

Looking at the second column in Table 2, it can be seen that 17 incidents of honoring were described after the middle incident of abuse. Of these, 65% were wholehearted honoring, 29% were ambivalent honoring, and 6% were pseudohonoring. There were no rejections. These percentages are similar to those found after the first abusive incident, and illustrate that as the battering progressed, the women were *still* likely to honor the aligning actions.

The real shift in honoring stances occurred after the last incident of abuse. Only a small fraction wholeheartedly or ambivalently honored the aligning actions then. However, 42% of the women who provided information pseudohonored their mate's accounts, and 50% flat out rejected them. Thus, if the categories of pseudohonoring and rejection are *combined*, it can be said that 92% of the women did not honor the account offered, whether or not they conveyed this to the batterer. Here is how one victim, for example, a 24-year-old mother of three, described her use of the pseudohonoring stance:

When he would first apologize to me, I would try to act like I was forgiving him, or he would get mad again. He would like come up and hug me, and I would try to act like I believed him, but I would be thinking, "I just hate you, and I'm leaving you, just wait 'til I can get out of here."

And here is how another, a 35-year-old mother of two, described how she moved to flat out reject her husband's accounts:

He came to the door and he was weeping. I don't mean crying just a little bit, I mean weeping, saying, "Please don't take my kids away, they're the only persons I've got, and I've missed you'all," and all that kind of stuff. And I felt so sorry for him, I just, you know. [He said] "Let me kiss you and hug you … I am so sorry. It just got out of hand." But I just can't take that anymore. I've heard it too much, I guess.

The developmental analysis again supported the cross-sectional analysis. Eighty-seven percent of the women (i.e., 20 of the 23 for whom there was enough information to carry out a developmental analysis) shifted from honoring stances which more or less accepted the accounts issued by the abusers (wholehearted or ambivalent honoring) to honoring stances which questioned the accounts (pseudohonor or rejection).

These findings, which show that women who come to a shelter are likely to question their mates' accounts, are also consistent with other studies. Giles-Sims (1983) found that only 18% of her sample were willing to "forgive and forget" the last incident of abuse; and Ferraro and Johnson (1983) found that battered women who decide to go to a shelter generally do so only after they have rejected the rationalizations for abuse.

Implications

For counselors, therapists, and social workers who are working with abusive men and/or abused women, this study—like other recent studies on the "phenomenology" of abuse (e.g., Andrews &

Brewin, 1990; Herbert, Silver, & Ellard, 1991)—helps clarify how batterers and victims "give meaning to" and (from their point of view) "cope with" domestic violence.

If one focuses exclusively on the apology, as Walker (1984) did, the findings from this study are very similar to hers. However, if one looks at the full range of accounts that abusers use, the findings differ. According to the women interviewed in this study, the third phase in the cycle of violence is not bypassed with repeated abuse, as Walker (1984) suggested; rather the third phase is *modified* to include other types of accounts. In other words, the "content" of the stage may change, but its "form" (the offering of accounts) remains essentially the same.

This shift in the type of aligning actions is significant because of the message it conveys. In an apology, the abuser accepts responsibility and implies that what he did was wrong. When the abuser moves to the use of the excuse either alone or in combination with other accounts, he is attempting to deny responsibility for his behavior. Something else—stress, financial problems, alcohol or drug abuse, or the victim's behavior—is "causing" the abuse. Not only the batterer but also the victim may be distracted by these excuses, believing that the abuse will stop if the avowed "causes" could be eliminated (e.g., "If I/he would stop drinking, the violence would stop"). Ultimately, however, these accounts serve to perpetuate the abuse because they prevent the abuser from coming to grips with the fact that *he* is responsible for his violent behavior. Ultimately, they enable the abuser to continue *both* his violent behavior *and* his relationship with his victim.

Counselors, therapists, and social workers can help abusers and victims understand how accounts perpetuate domestic violence. Exposing the accounts for what they are—verbal strategies designed to minimize the violence—is the first step in eliminating their use and their power. It is important also for professional helpers to reject the accounts that abusers offer. Honoring apologies, excuses, and justifications leads the batterer to believe that his abusive behavior is acceptable "in some situations" and "under certain conditions." The hitting license must be *cancelled,* not qualified. The repudiation of the battering must be foremost in the practitioner's mind.

All the battered women in this study left their abusive relationships, at least temporarily. The process of getting out of an abusive relationship is a complex one, both emotionally and physically. Many women leave these relationships and return to them, often more than once (Pagelow, 1984). The honoring stance that a woman adopts can help counselors, therapists, and social workers determine whether a woman is emotionally ready to leave. The women in this study sought help from a shelter after the "last" abusive incident, an incident in which 92% (of those reporting a honoring stance) rejected or pseudohonored an account offered by the batterer. These women clearly did not believe that the abuser was sorry, that something or someone else was to blame, or that it would not happen again. Victims who honor accounts, much like the women in Ferraro and Johnson's (1983) study who offered rationalizations for the abuse which they suffered, may still believe that the abuser is sorry, that it will not happen again, and that he will change. Accounts offered by abusers and honored by victims thus serve the same purpose as victim rationalizations—that is, they prevent women from seeking aid.

Finally, it is important to emphasize that while counselors, therapists, and social workers have an obligation to help victims gain insight into their abuse, they also have an obligation to be nonjudgmental of whatever decision a woman makes about her abusive relationship. A number of women in this study talked about the loss of support they experienced from significant others when they made decisions to stay with or return to their abusers. Victims of male battering face difficult choices—choices about what to say to their abusers, choices about whether to stay. Respecting the choices that women make is an integral part of the counseling/therapeutic process. Victims must always know that there are people ready and willing to listen to them and assist them.

REFERENCES

Andrews, B., & Brewin, C. R. (1990). Attributions of blame for marital violence: A study of antecedents and consequences. *Journal of Marriage and the Family, 52,* 757-767.
Dobash, R. E., & Dobash, R. P. (1984). The nature and antecedent of violent events. *British Journal of Criminology, 24,* 269-288.
Ferraro, K. J., & Johnson, J. M. (1983). How women experience battering: The process of victimization. *Social Problems, 30,* 325-339.
Gelles, R. J. (1974). *The violent home: A study of physical aggression between husbands and wives.* Beverly Hills, CA: Sage.
Giles-Sims, J. (1983). *Wife battering: A systems theory approach.* New York: Guilford.
Glaser, B. G., & Strauss, A. (1967). *The discovery of grounded theory.* Chicago: Aldine.
Goffman, E. (1971). *Relations in public: Microstudies of the public order.* New York: Basic Books.
Herbert, T. B., Silver, R. C., & Ellard, J. H. (1991). Coping with an abusive relationship: I. How and why do women stay? *Journal of Marriage and the Family, 53,* 311-325.
Hewitt, J. P., & Stokes, R. (1975). Disclaimers. *American Sociological Review, 40,* 1-11.
Hunter, C. H. (1984). Aligning actions: Types and distributions. *Symbolic Interaction, 7,* 155-174.
Lofland, J., & Lofland, L. H. (1984). *Analyzing social settings: A guide to qualitative research and analysis.* Belmont, CA: Wadsworth.
Mills, T. (1985). The assault on the self: Stages in coping with battering husbands. *Qualitative Sociology, 8,* 103-123.
Pagelow, M. D. (1984). *Family violence.* New York: Praeger.
Ptacek, J. (1988). Why do men batter their wives? In K. Yllo & M. Bograd (Eds.), *Feminist perspectives on wife abuse* (pp. 133-157). Newbury Park, CA: Sage.
Scott, M. B., & Lyman, S. M. (1968). Accounts. *American Sociological Review, 41,* 46-62.
Stokes, R., & Hewitt, J. P. (1976). Aligning actions. *American Sociological Review, 41,* 838-849.
Strauss, A., & Corbin, J. (1990). *Basics of qualitative research: Grounded theory procedures and techniques.* Newbury Park, CA: Sage.
Sykes, G. M., & Matza, D. (1957). Techniques of neutralization: A theory of delinquency. *American Sociological Review, 22,* 667-670.
Walker, L. E. (1979). *The battered woman.* New York: Harper & Row.
Walker, L. E. (1984). *The battered woman syndrome.* New York: Springer.

BEHIND CLOSED DOORS

A Schaumburg family rebuilds after a shattering descent into chaos

Bonita Brodt

Bonita Brodt is a Tribune *staff writer.*

At 4:30 that morning, Kelly Mahnke sat alone in her living room, cross-legged and all hunched over. Her face was puffy after hours of hysterical tears. She was calmer, now. Talking on the phone.

Listening, mostly.

Then her head snapped up. She couldn't believe it. Someone was at the door.

"Who could that be?" she whispered into the receiver.

"Oh, Kelly. It's probably the police. I was so worried I called 911."

Still a little drunk, Kelly regarded the door dumbly.

"My God," she mumbled when it finally hit her. "You did *what?*"

Slowly Kelly put the phone down. At that moment, words seemed of little use. It would have been impossible to explain the inevitability of what was about to happen, for even her best friend did not know how they were living.

No one did.

The doorbell kept ringing. Heart racing, Kelly got to her feet. She wasn't wearing much, just a cream-colored underthing, but that wasn't on her mind just then. She stepped carefully and when she got to the door, she opened it just enough to slide her slender body through. Kelly had often wondered if the nightmare had an ending. She was scared.

Yes, she told the officer, she had argued with her husband and, yes, she had swallowed pills. But she said she was feeling better and her friend had overreacted and her husband and three children were upstairs sleeping.

"*Hey! Wait a minute. No! You can't go in there. No. No! It's a mess!*"

"She started grabbing at me," recalled Gerard Thommes, a patrolman for the Village of Schaumburg. "She was telling me I couldn't go in there and I said I had to. I had to make sure everyone was all right."

Kelly lunged and tried to block him. But by that time, paramedics were coming up the sidewalk, and faces appeared in neighbors' windows, watching curiously as she was moved out of the way. With all his might, Thommes pushed, but it felt as if the door was hitting something. His first thought was that the husband might be lying behind it, dead.

Eventually he was able to force the opening wide enough. But for the longest time, he just stood there, eyes following the beam of his flashlight as it danced over a mighty sea of garbage and debris.

He distinctly heard flies.

He was wondering about rats when he heard a voice. It was his and he was muttering: "What the hell?"

Until that moment, there was no "before" or "after" for the Mahnke family. Their lives were divided into two incongruous worlds.

In one, visible from the outside, the couple owned a modest townhome in a comfortable white-bread suburb. The father went to work; the mother stayed home. They did things like take their three kids fishing. Went to church sometimes. But kept to themselves, mostly.

In the other world, known only on the inside, life had totally broken down.

Fragments of toys jutted up from a thick carpeting of trash that buried the floor two-feet-under. Whole pieces of furniture had been camouflaged with debris. There were mountains of soiled clothing. Decaying leftovers still on plates. Piles of beer cans and liquor bottles in every room.

Though they didn't know it then, Roger and Kelly Mahnke were alcoholics. They drank to have fun, to avoid, to escape, to medicate.

Then drinking took from them without asking. Or maybe they just let go.

It hadn't always been like this. Custom portraits of the children—Meghan, 10, Matt, 8, and Brendan, 3—were displayed proudly on walls covered with grass cloth. A carved wooden heart that said, "Mom's kitchen" hung from a nail. But as life disintegrated, pages of family photo albums got ripped out, stepped on and matted with last night's fast food. It was a bewildering paradox even to the people who lived here. One day Kelly remembers looking around the living room and asking Roger: "What would we do if Ed McMahon came to our house with the check for a million dollars? We couldn't open the door."

Life does not afford any of us the luxury of knowing what waits around the corner. Nor do we know how we will deal with circumstance when it arrives. We may not see it coming, and we may not understand as it is happening.

We don't really know what we are capable of until we are there.

On May 5, 1995, the Mahnkes lost everything that mattered. Their self-respect. Their privacy. Their kids.

But they have surprised a lot of people in the 16 months since. A needlepoint plaque that says, "Nobody's perfect" is displayed in their living room window, facing out. They have thought a lot about what might have happened if not for the defining episode that blew up their lives.

Roger: "I would have been the same, probably."

Kelly: "I would have been dead."

Roger and Kelly married young, but they did not have a wedding. They drove to Wisconsin one day in 1982 and made it official in front of a judge. Both grew up in the same working-class neighborhood on the Northwest Side of Chicago. They dated for three months and became inseparable, feeling stronger together than they did apart.

Kelly was 18, a high school senior and working a waitress job that she hated so she could afford the $25 a week rent to live in a friend's basement. Roger was seven years older, a neighborhood longhair who played bass guitar in a garage band. He had gone from community college to steady work as a skilled laborer in heating and cooling repairs. On her key ring, Kelly still keeps the plastic-handled key from their first night in a motel.

Their first grocery receipt as a married couple is tucked inside a worn red wallet in which Kelly keeps sentimental things. She also saved a folded-up piece of lined notebook paper On one side is a heart that says, "Kelly L's Roger." On the other side, she wrote, "Mr & Mrs. Mahnke," then twice practiced a note she imagined someday writing to a teacher. It asked that her daughter be excused from having missed school on Tuesday because she had a sore throat.

Those were elements of normal life Kelly hoped for but that she and Roger never quite managed. Their picture had problems with its composition, cluttered with props that didn't belong or detracted or just plain overwhelmed.

By the time she met Roger, Kelly already had taken the initiative to distance herself from a troubled relationship with her father. Her childhood memories include punishments for not cleaning the house well enough. Though her father acknowledges Kelly could be difficult and was disciplined, he denies any of the physical abuse she says she remembers, such as being pulled down a flight of stairs by her hair. Her parents were divorced and both remarried, her mother to a man she met while both were patients in a psychiatric hospital. Kelly was close to her mother, who died at 31 from head injuries that were never fully explained. That was the year Kelly got drunk for the first time. She was 9.

Roger's upbringing was nothing out of the ordinary. His father drove buses and taxis and sometimes worked two and three jobs, while his mother was mostly at home. When he was 13, Roger took his first drink—to be different from his friends. He remembers sneaking the bottle out of a cabinet and deliberately drinking himself incoherent. Soon, he was part of the hangout at the forest preserve.

They had a lot of fun together. Roger was laid-back, Kelly feisty. Drinking was the most reliable ritual of their married lives.

This is what Roger says, his simple mantra: "We messed up."

By the time their first child was born in 1985, the Mahnkes had moved to the suburbs. A repair job had taken Roger to Schaumburg, and he found himself driving around, liking how it felt. Children bicycled freely. Playgrounds were close.

"Financially it was a real jump for us," Roger said of the two-bedroom townhouse they bought in a modest subdivision. It also meant a change in lifestyle, the move isolating them some what. Kelly does not drive; life in the car-dependent suburb isolated her, too.

Roger liked being the one to earn the money, and Kelly, though not exactly the domestic type, enjoyed the freedom of staying home. The first two children were born 17 months apart; the third in 1992.

Eventually though, they found themselves living in a world that felt as if it had been tailored to somebody else's measurements. It didn't always fit.

Life changed insidiously. Roger fell into a habit of staying out to have a couple of drinks because he felt he deserved that after a day's work. Kelly began waking up to wine coolers, unhappy at home.

"At some point, we started to drift apart," said Kelly. "I'd be at home all day angry because Roger wouldn't come home until late, and feeling like I should have gotten my high school diploma. Then I'd feel worse, because I knew I couldn't get a job anyhow because I drank all the time."

"We really didn't talk," Roger said.

The house was a barometer of what was happening.

When things were on an even keel between them, clothes made it to hangers and objects had a place of importance. There were periods when it was cleaned up enough to have a birthday party or to welcome family and friends.

But there were also darker swatches of time when the blinds were always closed, the inside carefully hidden. Whole parts of 1994 were like that.

Debbie Pyers dialed 911 the morning the house was discovered. She is a mother of two, and had met Kelly almost 10 years earlier in a Lamaze class. They were instantly drawn to each other, their eyes meeting with mutual amusement as others obediently panted through imaginary pain.

"I was brought up so differently from Kelly," said Pyers, who lives in a more affluent part of the village. The two talk on the phone every day, sometimes two and three times.

"There would be times when she would tell me something and I'd try to understand it. Their family structure was different," said Pyers. "My kids went to bed at 8:30, and it would be late, after 10:30, and we'd be on the phone talking and I'd say, 'Aren't you going to put them to bed?'"

Pyers knew Roger and Kelly drank. The friendship was clearly defined by things they couldn't do, like go out as couples to the movies because theaters didn't serve beer. But Pyers had never seen either out of control. She also noticed their children seemed cared for and happy. She was not a judgmental friend.

What she also knew was that Kelly wasn't just drinking. She was also using alcohol to dull the terror of panic attacks she battled as an adult.

"It got to the point where I was afraid to go to sleep, because I was afraid to wake up, because I would get an attack," said Kelly "I'd drink to deal with it. I know now that alcohol probably made [the attacks] worse."

Going back about six years, Pyers can recall Kelly's talking about how the house was a mess and Roger's complaining because she wouldn't clean. But Kelly was skillful keeping her at arm's length when necessary, confining their friendship to the phone for sometimes months at a time.

"One day" Pyers remembered, "I was driving and I had to go to the bathroom real bad. I was not far from Kelly's house, so I called her from the car. But she would not let me come by. She said it was just really, really a mess, and I said, 'Well, Kelly, how bad can it be?'"

It was like this:

There were flies. Dead ones. Live ones. A Polaroid tacked to the wall was so thickly covered with fly-specks the image was marred.

The inside of the refrigerator was splotched with mold, the shelves stocked with rotting food.

It had been a long time since anyone cooked a meal.

The kitchen sink was useless, without knobs or a faucet. The oven door was broken, the stove a greasy shelf where unwashed pots and bowls had come to rest. A man's suit jacket dangled from a hanger at one end of the counter. When the eggs were gone, the empty carton didn't make it to the garbage. Nothing did.

Just about every dish the family owned was dirty and lying out, not always in the kitchen. Utensils were washed on an as-needed basis, except at some point, that stopped, too. Food, then, was eaten with plastic and served on paper plates that became encrusted reminders of where meals took place. One plate was on the stairway. Another rested on the bare mattress where the whole family slept.

The family lost track of seven telephones under something. They bought clothing or appliances to replace what disappeared.

In the upstairs bathroom, plastic boxes crammed the toilet and beer cans swam in the sink.

Walking required careful detours around and over things like overturned chairs and broken fans. Underfoot, the terrain was sometimes soggy and the accompanying sound was a crunching of things being compacted or the clanging together of bottles of Zima, wine coolers and cans of Miller Lite.

The floor was not always visible, buried by piles of things that normally would have been dropped into a hamper or folded up in a drawer.

Or dumped in a bag and set outside for the garbage truck. The house smelled from a mélange of cigarette smoke, soiled clothing, decaying leftovers still in the foam carton from the drive-through window, spilled beer and human waste. The only working toilet was the one in the room behind the kitchen. But it was not stocked with toilet paper. Feces had been wiped across two walls and no one bothered to scrub it off.

This is what authorities found.

Family life went on a crash dive about 18 weeks before that, just after Christmas. But the mess had been accumulating for months. Roger and Kelly had been sliding for a year, and now they were scared—mostly about what they had become.

Roger found himself not calling home and staying out later to avoid what was waiting. It bothered him to do this, but he did it anyway. Sometimes he ignored his beeper even when he knew it was Kelly. Each time that happened, she got mad all over about the time she beeped to let him know their youngest had said "Da-da" for the first time. Roger, out drinking, did not bother to call.

When Roger finally got home at night, Kelly would sometimes stay just long enough for a good argument before taking her turn at the bars. As often as not, Roger would drink more at home, watching TV and smoking, eventually passing out in his chair.

Kelly was sick. A doctor diagnosed a problem with her liver and politely suggested she was allergic to alcohol. But even as she watched her face puff up, her skin turn pasty and her body grow lethargic, she drank.

"At first, I thought it was just a depression, but then it became physical," said Kelly. "I lost a lot of weight. At one point, I couldn't get out of bed and threw up if I did. I had Brendan on a schedule so he'd sleep until afternoon, and I remember lying there watching reruns, holding his hand as it stuck through the slats of the crib beside the bed. I couldn't remember things, not even someone's name from the TV. My hands got numb."

As the holidays approached, Roger gave the family an ultimatum: He said he would not buy a Christmas tree unless everyone helped clean.

"I wanted the kids to help me," said Roger. "I'd say 'Come on, guys. If we just get going here, we'll get it cleaned.' But they weren't used to picking up."

Nobody helped, so Roger relented. He didn't want to rob the children of a holiday and thought a good one might do everyone some good. So he cleaned alone, as best he could, and family snapshots tell the story of a happy, bountiful Christmas. But it was one that sent the family on a quick spiral down.

"We managed to get the tree and the wrapping paper out of the house, but that's about where it stopped," Kelly said. "We were getting madder and madder at each other. Some of our arguments were just like this: 'You clean it up.' 'No, you clean up.' 'No! You clean it up.' "

After Christmas, neither did.

Life, then, adjusted to the shrinking contours defined by warring parents in a house filling up with garbage. Ultimately there were no clear spots even for children to play. It was a confusing time in par-

ticular for Meghan, and Matt. Every morning, they left for a tidy suburban school with orderly classrooms, but came home to a world where they walked on trash and had to reach down into piles for pieces of clothing or shoes. Most evenings, when the yelling started, they were ordered upstairs and along with their younger brother, they'd huddle on top of the bare mattress to watch TV.

"I was kind of sad," Meghan remembered. "I could not have friends over. They were always kind of suspicious because I didn't have sleepovers, and they were always like, 'Well, why can't we come to your house?' I would say, 'Because my mom and dad don't like me to have friends over,' but I was thinking, 'I hope they don't find out.' "

Family life was a free-for-all. No bedtimes. No chores. No rules except for the one about opening the front door to visitors. If the family chose to answer, it would be "just a minute," then someone would sneak out the patio door and walk around.

"We really didn't deal with things like homework," said Kelly. "I do remember them asking for help and it depended on my mood whether I would help them or not."

For their 13th wedding anniversary in February 1995, the Mahnkes renewed their vows with the church wedding they had never had, and hosted a small reception in a private hall. Kelly addressed formal invitations sitting near a pedestal ashtray spilling over with days' worth of Roger's cigarette butts. Their theme was "Dreams Do Come True."

"It did renew us to some degree," said Roger. After the festivities, they drove to Jollet and spent the weekend on a gambling boat, where they sat in a whirlpool and drank in the room.

"It was like coming out of a dream," said Kelly of coming home. "Everything just went back to the way it was."

Worse, actually. The whole affair cost them close to $3,000, and they hadn't yet paid for Christmas.

There was a comical aspect to some of their drunken bouts. Roger would come home late and stomp heavily in his big work shoes, kicking things in all directions. He'd smoke in silence, calculating where he figured Kelly would walk next and that's where he'd toss his beer cans.

Kelly, who had been flinging hers all day, simply changed targets. Once she got so angry she hurled a can at Roger, spraying beer everywhere. She missed, however, and broke the blinds. Roger did nothing, which he knew would infuriate her. He just said "great!"

Savagely, in their lowest moments, they betrayed and turned on each other. They fought, sometimes leaving red marks and bruises. Roger remembers twisting Kelly's arm hard, trying to keep her from going out without him. Kelly remembers attacking Roger in full view of the neighbors when he got home late.

The night everything fell apart, they decided, as they did sometimes, to go out together and leave Meghan at home and in charge of her two brothers with Roger's beeper number programmed into the phone.

They spent a couple of hours at a neighborhood bar but the night ended quickly when Roger accused her of flirting. They yelled all the way home.

"I remember telling Kelly something like 'That's it. I'm out of here,' like I was going to leave her," said Roger. He stumbled upstairs, but Kelly grabbed a bottle of pills prescribed for a female problem and dumped six into her palm.

"I just tried to kill myself," she told Pyers, hysterical on the phone.

This had happened once before, a year earlier, but Pyers did not call police that time, then second-guessed herself through a sleepless night.

"She does this when she gets real upset," Pyers said of Kelly's pill-swallowing. "I don't know if it's a cry for help or if she's trying to punish the one who upset her or punish herself."

Whatever it was, Meghan was at her mother's side through much of it.

"I didn't want her to die," Meghan said.

The last thing Roger remembered was passing out on the mattress.

"Next thing I knew, there were six people standing around the bed, all in uniform. It was just like a scene out of 'Cops.' "

As he sat in an interview room at the police station, his mind cobwebbed and his face unshaven, he could hear police officers talking about him. "I'd like to kill that son-of-a-bitch," one said.

Police had taken protective custody of the children. Kelly was admitted to a hospital psychiatric ward and both she and Roger were named on misdemeanor charges of child endangerment and neglect.

He needed $100 to make bail.

"Roger looked like someone who just had the life kicked out of him," said Pyers, who drove to the police station with the money, then drove Roger home.

In the few hours he was gone, the village had found the home unfit for humans and police roped the front entry off with yellow tape that said "Crime Scene Do Not Enter" Roger ripped down the tape, then wrestled with the front door, which had been taken off the hinges and heaved by the walkway. Then he just sat down.

"I must have sat in the same spot for hours," Roger remembered. "I was stunned. Humiliated. I had lost everything. I had the phone down there with me, I had to call my mom, my work.

"Then I turned on the television and all of a sudden, it was showing exactly the spot where I was sitting. Our living room was all over the 4:30 news. I remember thinking, 'Oh, my God! The whole world can see me!' And to have the whole world see you at your most devastating moment, well, that's when I looked around that room, really for the first time, and asked myself, 'How did you let it get like this?' "

What Mary Passaglia remembered first was that she couldn't just walk in: She had to take a big step up. Passaglia, the village's environmental health supervisor, had been called out to inspect houses filled with trash, but never anything like the Mahnke house.

"It was just so unbelievable that a family could have lived in that environment. Walking through that house, I was trying to figure out where life would take place. I was able to touch the master bedroom ceiling because the piles reached the top of the mattress, and I am 5-foot-5."

She wrote this in a report:

"The odors were strong. Their sources included human feces and a variety of decaying food waste. I also found gross amounts of both live and dead flies, in addition to large amounts of fly fecal matter on the walls, ceiling, counter tops."

Passaglia also found that she liked Roger. The more she talked with him, the more she felt he was a genuinely nice man who loved his family. She was struck by a feeling that under the same set of circumstances, another man's instinct might be to bolt.

"I figured something just tragic had happened in this family," said Passaglia. "I wanted them to get their lives together and live a normal life."

Roger did not ask anyone for help.

But help arrived anyway. A nephew. Debbie Pyers. His half-brother. The wife of a guy at work. Kelly's father. As soon as Roger had cleared paths, he allowed his mother inside.

"When he opened the door, I noticed my hand had gone over my heart and I was saying, 'My God. My God. My God,' " recalled Ruth Mahnke. "I remember I turned to him and I said, 'I would have helped you.' And he said, 'Mom, it just started to get so bad and I was ashamed.' "

Roger's boss gave him vacation time for the cleanup, a job that required two 20-foot industrialized dumpsters and scores of black garbage bags.

"I had to tell myself, 'Just keep going. Just keep going,'" said Roger.

He threw just about everything out.

"The cleaning was kind of creepy" said Pyers. "It was like a hush-hush organization was doing it. We kept the blinds shut and stayed inside. I was really mad about the way those children had been living. But I loved Kelly. I loved Roger. I did not walk away."

The phone rang with crank calls and hang-ups. Passing cars slowed; the people gawked. One night, an eager gossip befriended Roger and his mother as they walked, unaware of who they were.

"Didja hear about that family that lives around here?" the young boy asked anxiously. "They all pooped in a bucket and wiped it on the walls!" Roger's mother was speechless. "You know," Roger said evenly, "I'll just bet it wasn't that bad."

The school called, and Roger stopped by to pick up envelopes for Meghan and Matt. Classmates at Collins Elementary sent notes:

Dear Matt: You are very nice to everyone. Your desk has been very clean and you have been getting good grades. I feel sorry for you and your family. You didn't do anything wrong.

Dear Meghan: We hope you come back to school. We understand that you think we will tease you, but we won't.

New kitchen tile was donated by a father at the grade school. A resident called the village to arrange to give the family a sofa. A relative bought sacks of building materials but refused Roger's money. Fresh new coatings of donated paint slathered the walls.

After hurling yet another bag into the dumpster one day, Roger walked to the townhomes' common mailbox and found himself standing next to a neighbor he did not know. She smiled, studying his face and extended a friendly hand.

"Are you sure you want to touch 'the squalor guy'?" Roger asked in all seriousness.

She hugged him. And Roger cried.

The first lawyer Roger and Kelly talked to suggested they refinance their house to pay for his services.

The second one looked at them squarely and said: "I don't know if I want *you.*" Mike Ruzicka was unnerving. He was big and when he talked, which he did a lot, his voice sounded as though it could move furniture. Mostly though, he seemed to understand where they had been and where they wanted to go.

They hired him. They wanted their kids.

Ruzicka, who specializes in juvenile matters, was once a part of the state's child welfare agency, the

Department of Children and Family Services. Originally he was an investigator on the front lines, recommending if children should be removed from a home.

"You run into a lot of dirty houses," said Ruzicka, who remembers one in particular that was so far gone he walked in, ran out, and vomited at the doorstep. Typically he would find substance abuse, alcohol, low intelligence or mental illness—underlying problems that tended to explain, not excuse.

By the time Ruzicka got involved, Roger and Kelly had chosen to accept full responsibility. They pleaded guilty to misdemeanor charges of child neglect and endangerment in a separate Circuit Court proceeding. Their punishment: a suspended six-month jail term and probation for 18 months. The day after, their doorbell rang and a deliveryman handed them a large bouquet of flowers, sent by a stranger. "I decided to be one of the people to encourage you," the card read.

Already, they had come a long way.

After Kelly spent six days in psychiatric care she came home on antidepressants. After a month of intensive out-patient therapy, she was handed her marble, a symbolic gift to remind her that if she took a drink, she could lose hers all over again.

Roger and Kelly worked with a certain resolve about doing what was necessary to mend their lives. Roger was able to adjust his work schedule so he could drive them to individual and group therapy sessions as well as parenting classes and family counseling. They also attended frequent meetings to follow a 12-step program to live without alcohol.

The night before his first Juvenile Court appearance on their behalf, Ruzicka visited the house to get to know Roger and Kelly better. They asked him to help remove an overhead light so they could wipe out the bugs.

"I guess I was kind of surprised the way the house looked—new floor, new carpet, the kitchen pretty much spotless," said Ruzicka. "The kids' rooms were looking good. It hit me that these people had taken a look at the problem and recognized what the problem was: them."

Ruzicka's goal was to reunite the family as quickly as possible.

The system, however, moved with deliberate caution. The children were not returned for 4½ months.

The Mahnkes were among 77,082 reports of neglect or abuse investigated by DCFS in fiscal 1995. Theirs was among the 40 percent found to be credible complaints. And their situation, no matter what its particulars, would be ultimately evaluated alongside some stark examples of how the state had failed to protect kids.

Having the state take custody of the Mahnke children ran counter to the judgment of Richard Zemon, a veteran DCFS investigator of 10½ years. To this day Zemon believes the state overreacted in assuming custody and did so for the wrong reasons, putting fear of bad publicity ahead of other concerns.

Zemon began assembling facts. There was no history of contact with the police, but the family had come to DCFS attention four years earlier when a neighbor complained the children had been left home alone. Zemon noted that DCFS did not intervene.

Interviewing first Roger, then the children and Kelly, he came away with a picture of a caring, though colossally dysfunctional, family. From Roger, for example, he learned that even at their worst, he and Kelly did a load of wash most nights so the children would have clean clothes.

Of particular significance was his conversation with Joel Karr, a school social worker, who told him that generally Meghan and Matt came to school clean and did not stand out except there had been a recent concern that Matt was disheveled. Karr said he talked with the Mahnkes and Kelly reacted badly when he suggested that Matt might be "neglected." But the boy's appearance immediately improved.

"All this told me something," said Zemon, "that these were not bad people, but that they let a situation get out of control. To me, unless there is an urgent risk, try to work out something without taking the kids. In removing kids, you traumatize someone. Custody is necessary when there's a real risk and when you don't have a responsible relative to help out."

Zemon drew up a plan that a copy of his official log shows was agreed to by his supervisor. He would not take formal custody, but would instead go to court for a protective order that would ensure Roger's and Kelly's cooperation while the children lived with Kelly's cousin, a Chicago police officer, who volunteered to keep them while Roger and Kelly put their lives back on track. At any point, DCFS could go to court for custody if the Mahnkes did not comply.

However, Zemon's log notes that three hours later he got a call from a higher-up saying the media wanted details. He said he was told to scrap his plan and put the children back under protective custody He was overruled.

"I had never *had* a phone call like that," said Zemon. "I was furious. I was flat-out told that because the press was asking questions, the department's position would have to be to take custody of these kids.

"I think we hung this family out to dry," said Zemon, who retired three months later from DCFS.

But DCFS noted there isn't always agreement about what is the right thing to do when protecting the best interests of children, and pointed to a history replete with examples of why caution was the most appropriate route. DCFS was already under a blistering attack from many directions for being too overburdened to effectively safeguard children. The Mahnke case triggered the memory of the house on Keystone Avenue in Chicago where police went on a drug raid in February of 1994 and discovered 19 children living amid rat droppings and garbage, most of their mothers on welfare, some on drugs.

There also was the haunting memory of 3-year-old Joseph Wallace. Though DCFS intervened, his mother, a woman with a history of mental problems, won her custody dispute, then in 1993, she hanged her son. This was a red flag in view of Kelly's emotional history. In the midst of the case, a psychologist suggested she be evaluated as manic-depressive. Kelly already noticed she was doing peculiar things, such as waking up at 3 a.m. to scrub the toilet bowl. It was determined, however, that her medication created these symptoms, which disappeared when her prescription changed.

Meghan, Matt and Brendan spent five of their first days in state custody as patients in a hospital, where they were evaluated by therapists and social workers. Then they were placed in the Chicago home of Kelly's father, James Scriven, and his wife, Carol, who themselves were parenting two young children. Scriven said it was difficult to care for three more, but felt it was his responsibility as the grandfather.

About two months into the placement, Ruzicka filed court papers alleging that the antagonistic relationship between Kelly and her father was having a negative effect on the children. Ruzicka said he had seen the children show up dirty at the DCFS office for a visit. He also alleged the Scrivens allowed the children to be baby-sat by Carol's son, who she acknowledged was an ex-convict who served time on a weapons charge. Carol Scriven said he was sometimes in the house, but denied that the Mahnke children were ever left in his care.

During the placement, the Scrivens' household, too, would come under the scrutiny of DCFS. Carol Scriven blamed Kelly for this and said it included an incident that happened while the Mahnke children were there, when Carol disciplined one of her boys for using foul language by rubbing hot pepper on his lips.

At various points, professionals who evaluated the Mahnke children found them to be wrestling with the kind of emotional problems one might expect from living in a house filled with garbage and with parents who made sure they had food and clean clothes yet left them to fend largely for themselves. All the children, Meghan in particular, were also described as having problems stemming from the separation from their parents.

"This case did not belong in Juvenile Court," said Ruzicka, who took his own kids to the Mahnke house one day and cooked steak fajitas for everyone. "Everyone panicked. Court holds a bat over your head, but these people reacted when they were slapped. Yes, they were drunks. Yes, the house was a pigsty. Yes, the kids lived like animals. But look at what they've done."

Roger and Kelly used their time without the children to learn how to walk without "crutches." They got to know each other, this time sober. They weren't exactly sure if they'd like each other but they were pleasantly surprised. They went out to dinner. Went to movies. Joined a sober bowling league. To their relief, they discovered they shared the same wicked wit as when they drank.

When the new oven arrived, the deliveryman kept peering over for a good look at the living room. He recognized the outside of the house from television, and they all talked about how bad the garbage must have been.

"You'd never know this was the same place," he said, thinking they were new owners who rehabbed. "You guys really did a great job. Those people, man, what was their name?"

Kelly and Roger looked at one another sidelong, answering together:

"Us!"

It has been a year now since Meghan, Matt and Brendan were allowed to return to their parents. The Mahnkes live as a family, two adults and now four children. Connor, the youngest, was born in July. They share the house with a parakeet, a mouse, a rabbit, a large tortoise and three hamsters.

There are rules.

No shoes on the carpet. No food anywhere except the kitchen. No playing outside until rooms are clean, and that means everything picked up off the floor.

No alcohol. Neither Roger nor Kelly has taken a drink since the moment they lost everything. They are sober, now, for a year and four months. And no excuses. Though Roger and Kelly debate end-

lessly about whether alcoholism is something the will can conquer or if it is a disease that can fell even the strongest of people, this is their explanation:

"We were wrong. It's that simple," said Roger.

"We blame ourselves," Kelly said.

Today, the Mahnkes raise their children in a house that is almost obsessive in its cleanliness.

"We both get kind of edgy when anything is out of place," said Kelly. "I'm starting to sound like my grandmother, and that scares me. The kids were eating popcorn in the kitchen the other day and I was telling them not to make a mess on 'my floor.'"

The home has been painstakingly reassembled with things of particular meaning, such as a crucifix in the living room and a kitchen plaque that says, "Home Sweet Home." Family snapshots are displayed on a sideboard and Kelly, like a museum curator, divides them into three distinct periods of Mahnke history: "Before it got bad"; "When the kids were gone"; "After we got the kids back."

Upstairs, the two bedrooms were reinvented, much to the delight of the children. Meghan has one. Matt shares the other with Brendan. Kelly and Roger sleep on the fold-out couch in the living room with Connor in a portable crib alongside. Kelly looks at him, thankful that she had the presence of mind to drink less when she was pregnant with the other three.

The house is close quarters. When Kelly was overdue with the baby, she sent the children to their rooms to play more often than usual, admitting she needed space. One day she grabbed the phone and dialed Pyers to conspire about how she might convince the doctor to help the baby along.

"It's got to come out," Kelly said. "I'm going to tell him I'm depressed."

"But he expects you to be depressed," Pyers said. "You're pregnant."

"OK," said Kelly, thinking a moment. "Then how about if I tell him I don't feel like cleaning my house?"

This kind of humor has endured through misery. It's survival instinct, Roger thinks. When he spotted his van in the parking lot after a family shopping trip recently, his favorite sentence from a newspaper story chronicling the cleanup popped into his head.

"And the maroon van sagged with the weight of garbage bags," Roger announced, voice booming. It is a family joke and Meghan and Matt giggle even though they've heard it many times.

They still get embarrassed when they go to the grocery store or order a pizza and wonder if someone recognizes them or their address. Some neighbors still look at them funny. One in particular has a habit of peering around her grill to check on their activities. When the telephone rings, no one answers before first checking the number displayed on Caller ID.

Theirs was a costly mess.

"We're completely wiped," Roger says. He estimates close to $20,000 was spent on two lawyers, counseling, building materials and all of the possessions to start over. Roger's mother gave them money and the Mahnkes cashed about $12,000 in savings bonds, some of which had not yet matured. An insurance policy had to be cashed in, too.

One night recently Roger and Kelly were sitting with Brendan at the kitchen table when he looked up and asked: "When you went away, why didn't you take me with you?"

"He thought we abandoned him," Kelly said. They explained as best they could in language a 4-year-old could understand, just as they have talked openly with both Matt, now 10, and Meghan, almost 12, about how, if alcoholism can truly be inherited, they too, could be at risk.

The family tends to cling to one another. They pile on top of each other on the sofa. Hold hands when they walk. Roger now 38, and Kelly 32, like to say they live one day at a time, never claiming to be "cured" of anything but

stronger because of what they have learned. The children go with them to family counseling. They find themselves watching Matt and Meghan, wondering how they have digested things they do not always talk about.

"At dinner the other night, I set out a bottle of sparkling grape juice," said Roger. "Matt's eyes went straight to the label and he started reading it. I told him there was no alcohol, but it got me to wondering if he trusts us. I hope he does."

For Sweetest Day, Roger went out shopping and came home with a symbolic gift that made Kelly laugh out loud when he offered it: a ceramic figurine of two happy, hugging pigs. Meghan studied it thoughtfully and then disappeared upstairs to her room.

When she came back down, she was holding a miniature bottle from her Barbie doll collection and placed it carefully between the two pigs.

"I didn't really know drinking was bad at the time," said Meghan, a slight girl who used to lie awake sometimes until after 2 in the morning, her stomach churning to the sound of angry voices. "My parents are different now. They are always working hard to make things right.

"I just think we're really lucky," said Meghan. "We're so happy now. It's like that was somebody else's house."

Helping Children Cope With Violence

Lorraine B. Wallach

Lorraine B. Wallach, M.A., is one of the founders of the Erikson Institute in Chicago and is presently a faculty member there. Her recent work includes staff training around issues of children and violence.

Children who grow up in violent communities are at risk for pathological development because growing up in a constant state of apprehension makes it difficult to establish trust, autonomy, and social competence.

Violence is epidemic in the United States today. The murder rate in this country is the fifth highest in the world. It is 10 times higher than England's and 25 times that of Spain. For many inner-city children, violence has become a way of life. In a study of more than 1,000 children in Chicago, 74% of them had witnessed a murder, shooting, stabbing, or robbery (Kotulak, 1990; Bell, 1991). Almost half (47%) of these incidents involved friends, family members, classmates, or neighbors. Forty-six percent of the children interviewed reported that they had personally experienced at least one violent crime. These figures are similar to those found in other U.S. urban areas, such as Baltimore (Zinsmeister, 1990), Los Angeles County (Pynoos & Eth, 1985), and New Orleans (Osofsky, Wewers, Hann, Fick, & Richters, 1991).

Children are exposed to several kinds of violence, including child abuse and domestic violence. And there are communities where violence is endemic, where gang bangers, drug dealers, petty crimi-

nals, and not-so-petty criminals rule the streets. For children living in these conditions, feelings of being safe and secure do not exist.

Children who are not designated victims of assault can be unintended victims. Shoot-outs between gangs and drive-by shootings result in the wounding, and often killing, of innocent bystanders. In addition, the psychological toll of living under these conditions is immeasurable. The children in these neighborhoods see violence and hear it discussed. They are surrounded by danger and brutality.

Child abuse, other domestic violence, and neighborhood violence can harm development

The effects of this kind of violence on children are widespread and can permeate all areas of development, beginning in infancy and continuing through childhood. The first task a baby faces is the development of trust—trust

in the caregiving environment and eventually in himself. Achieving a sense of trust is compromised by growing up in a violent community. Many families find it difficult to provide infants with support, love, and affection in a consistent and predictable manner when they live in a constant state of apprehension—not knowing when they are going to be victims of violence. Toddlers have difficulty developing a sense of autonomy when their families cannot help them explore their environments because their surroundings are filled with danger. Preschoolers, too, are inhibited from going out into the world. Just at the age when they should be expanding their social contacts and finding out about people beyond the family, they are restricted by the dangers lurking outside. Many children living in high-rise housing projects and other dangerous neighborhoods are cooped up inside all day because it is unsafe to go out-of-doors. The situation is even more tragic when children

From *Young Children*, May 1993, pp. 4-11. © 1993 by the National Association for the Education of Young Children. Reprinted by permission.

experience violence within the family. Where can a child find protection when she is victimized within her own home? Although domestic violence occurs in *every* kind of neighborhood, the effects may be even more damaging when compounded by the harmful effects of growing up in *violent* neighborhoods.

Children who grow up under conditions that do not allow them to develop trust in people and in themselves or learn to handle day-to-day problems in socially acceptable ways are at risk for pathological development; they are at risk for resorting to violent behaviors themselves. The anger that is instilled in children when they are mistreated or when they see their mothers or siblings mistreated is likely to be incorporated into their personality structures. Children learn by identifying with the people they love. They also identify with the people who have power and control. When children see and experience abuse and violence as a way of life, when the people who are responsible for them behave without restraint, the children often learn to behave in the same manner.

Another serious problem for children living in chaotic communities is that the protectors and the dangerous people may be one and the same. The police, who are supposed to be protectors, are often seen as dangerous by community members. In his book *There Are No Children Here,* Alex Kotlowitz (1991) describes how a young man who is idolized by his housing project community be-

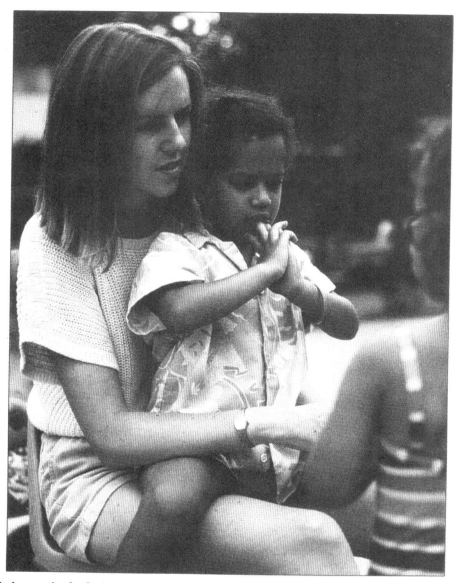

It is particularly important for children who come from chaotic environments to have firm but appropriate limits, even though children who feel powerless may try to provoke adults into a battle of wills in an effort to make themselves feel important.

The young child's protectors and the dangerous people in her life may be one and the same.

cause he is successful, has graduated from high school, is not caught up in gangs, and is still his own person is mistakenly killed by the police. What do children think when their idol is gunned down by the people who are supposed to protect them?

Children are confused when they cannot tell the good guys from the bad guys. Their teachers and the media tell them that drug dealers are bad and are the cause of the problems in the community, but the children may know

that cousins or friends or even older brothers are dealing. Some people have likened the inner city, especially housing projects, to war zones; but in a war the enemy is more often than not on the outside, and usually everyone knows who he is.

Children growing up with violence face risks other than becoming violent themselves. Children who live with danger develop defenses against their fears, and these defenses can interfere with their development. When children have to defend themselves constantly from outside or inside dangers, their energies are not available for other, less immediately urgent tasks, such as learning to read and write and do arithmetic and learning about geography and history and science. In addition to not having enough energy to devote to schoolwork, there is evidence that specific cognitive functions such as memory and a sense of time can be affected by experiencing trauma (Terr, 1981).

Boys and girls who are victims of abuse and who see abusive behavior in their families can grow up feeling as if they are responsible for what is happening. Young children cannot always differentiate between what is real and what is part of their inner lives. The literature on divorce has made clear that many children believe that they have caused the breakup of the family, even though it had nothing to do with them (Wallerstein & Kelly, 1980; Hetherton, Cox, & Cox, 1982). Children who feel guilty about the violence in their families often perceive themselves as being bad and worthless. Feelings of worthlessness can lead children to the idea that they

When children have to defend themselves constantly from inside and outside dangers, there is little energy for schoolwork. There is also evidence that specific cognitive functions such as memory and a sense of time can be affected.

are not capable of learning, which leads, in turn, to a lack of motivation to achieve in school.

Children who experience trauma may have difficulty seeing themselves in future roles that are meaningful. Lenore Terr (1983), in her study of the schoolchildren of Chowchilla who were kidnapped in their school bus, found that the views of their future lives were limited and often filled with anticipation of disaster. Children who cannot see a decent future for themselves cannot give their all to the present task of learning and becoming socialized.

Living in unpredictably frightening situations makes children feel as if they have no control over their lives. We know that young children need to feel as if they can direct some parts of their lives,

but children who are victims of violence learn that they have no say in what happens to them. This sense of helplessness interferes with the development of autonomy.

It is difficult for children to keep on growing and maturing when they have been traumatized because an almost universal reaction of children to traumatic occurrences is regression. Children slip back to stages at which they felt more secure. This is particularly true when they have only a tenuous hold on their current status.

What makes some children more resilient than others, and what can we do?

As depressing as all this sounds, however, it does not mean that all children who experience violence are doomed. It is known that some children are more resilient and withstand trauma and stress better than others. If a child has an easy temperament and makes a good fit with his primary caregiver, he or she is more likely to be off to a good start. Some lucky children are born to strong parents who can withstand the ravages of poverty and community violence and still provide some security and hope for their children. Children are shaped not only by their parents' behavior but also by their parents' hopes, expectations, motivations, and view of the future—including their children's future.

It is important to remember that children are malleable, that what happens in the early years is im-

A kindergarten teacher in a Chicago public school was discussing her dilemma concerning two boys in her classroom. All of the children were at their tables, engaged in drawing, when the teacher noticed these boys crawling under the tables, pretending to have guns. When one of the boys saw the teacher watching them, he reassured her, "Don't worry, we're just playing breaking into an apartment." The teacher questioned whether she should let the play continue or offer a more socially acceptable view of behavior. How should she react? A Head Start teacher in the group said that the boy who was taking the lead in this game had been in her class the year before, and that his family's apartment had been burglarized. The boy had been very frightened and, after that experience, had changed from a confident, outgoing youngster to a quiet and withdrawn child. Here it was a year later, and he was just beginning to play out his experience. He was becoming the aggressor in the play instead of the helpless victim. And he was regaining some of his old confidence.

portant, but that many children can overcome the hurts and fears of earlier times. Many can make use of positive experiences that occur both inside and outside their families. Child care centers, recreation programs, and schools can be resources for children and offer them alternative perceptions of themselves, as well as teaching them skills. One of the things that help determine the resiliency of children is the ability to make relationships and to make use of the people in their environments, people who provide to children what they do not get in their families or who supplement what their families cannot offer.

Child care professionals can help offset the negative effects of violence in the lives of young children by providing that supplement. Although teachers, social workers, and human service personnel cannot cure all of the hurts experienced by children today, they can make a difference.

1. **The first thing they need to do is to make sure that their programs provide opportunities for children to develop meaningful relationships with caring and knowledgeable adults.** Teachers and other staff members can offer each child a chance to form an important relationship with one of them, a relationship within which the child can learn that there are people in the world who can be of help. The best thing to offer children at risk is caring people, people who are available both physically and emotionally.

Some years ago the famous Chicago analyst Franz Alexander (1948) coined the term *corrective emotional experience* to explain the curative power of therapy, and that term best describes what child care professionals can do for children at risk. A corrective emotional experience means having a relationship with another person that touches one's deepest core—not a relationship that

is superficial or intellectual, but one that engages the emotions. It means having a relationship within which a person can redo old patterns and ties. It means feeling safe enough within a relationship to risk making basic changes in one's psychic structure. Children cannot be forced into these kinds of relationships; they can only be offered the opportunities with the hope that they take advantage of them.

Some children attach easily, and it does not take much effort on the part of the adults for these children to form attachments; these are usually the children who have had a good relationship in their past. Other children have not been lucky enough to have had the kind of relationship that makes them want to seek out others and repeat this satisfying experience; these children need more help in forming ties and trusting alliances.

What can adults do to stimulate relationships with children who do not come easily to this task? They can look into themselves and see if they are ready

for this kind of relationship—a relationship that makes demands on their emotions, their energies, and their time. Relationships with children who have inordinate needs and who do not have past experiences in give-and-take partnerships are not 50–50 propositions; adults must meet these children more than halfway.

2. **Child care professionals can organize their schedules and their time with the children so that they provide as much consistency as possible.** Attachment can be encouraged by reducing the number of people a child encounters during the day and by maximizing the amount of meaningful time and activity the child has with one adult. In this way each child is allowed to form an attachment to one person. There are several models—including therapeutic centers, child-life programs, and primary-care nursing—that use relationship as the principal tool in their interventions. Establishing significant relationships with the children who

A nine-year-old boy in a shelter for battered women told a story about his recurring dream. This is what he said: "I dreamed of someone taking me away. He was dressed like a lady, but he had a moustache. I went inside the house. It was dark. The lights were out, and there were people inside having a party. It was ugly. They were eating worms and they asked me to try one. I took one and threw it away. Then I opened the door, and the light came on in there, and I saw there were no more ghosts, and I saw I was sleeping. When I dream like that, I become afraid."

It was obvious that the boy was expressing his fears, but the exact meaning of the details was not evident—not until one of the child care workers who knew the mother reported that the abusive father was bisexual and brought his male sexual partners to the family's apartment. It then became clear that in addition to struggling with feelings about an abusive father, the boy was also frightened and confused about the meaning of his father's behavior and probably about his own sexual identification. In this case the child was able to tell about a disturbing dream through the telling of a story, and the adults were able to understand it with additional information about his family.

have suffered from trauma is the most important thing that can be done, and it is the basis for all of the work that follows. What is this other work?

3. **Child care professionals must provide structure and very clear expectations and limits.** All children, especially young children, need to know where they stand, but it is particularly important for children who come from chaotic environments to have firm but appropriate limits. It should be noted that they do not take to this kind of structure easily. It is not something they have experienced before, and the newness of it may cause anxiety and tension, just as any new situation does.

Some children see the structure of a new setting as an opportunity to assert themselves and force the adults into power struggles. Children who feel powerless may try to provoke adults into a battle of wills in an effort to make themselves feel important. But even though some of the neediest children may rebel against structure, no matter how benign, it is important to provide it so that the boundaries are clear.

4. **Early childhood professionals should offer children many opportunities to express themselves** within the confines of a comfortable and consistent schedule, with clear expectations about behavior. Children need to air their emotions; they need to tell their stories. They can do this in several activities that can be a part of any good program for children.

Except for life-sustaining activities, play is, of course, the most universal activity of children

Through play, children learn about the physical and social world. As they play, children develop a map of the world, a map that helps them make sense of the

Josephine, the child of an abused mother, told a story about a girl with red eyes who bit and scratched her mother because she was angry at her and the devil got into her body. The child care worker listened and accepted her story, thereby accepting the child's feelings. In subsequent sessions, after establishing a more trusting relationship with the child, the worker told her a story about the same little girl who told the devil not to bother her and who talked to her mother about how she was going to try harder to be nicer. By using the same characters and theme, she offered the little girl another way of relating to her mother. At the same time, the mother's worker helped her understand her own anger and supported her in trying to alter her behavior toward her daughter.

complexities that define the world today. Play, in the context of a corrective experience, offers children who live with chaos and violence a chance to redraw their world map.

Play provides an avenue for children to express their feelings. Children who are angry or hurt can take their anger out on toys, dolls, and stuffed animals. Children who feel isolated or lonely can find solace in pretending to live in a world with lots of friends. Children who are frightened can seek safety within a game by pretending to be big and strong. In other words, children can play out their own scenarios, changing their real life situations to their own design. They can invent happy endings. They can reverse roles and become the big—instead of the small—people. They can become the aggressors rather than the victims.

Play also allows children to repeat some of the bad things in their lives. Some people think that children want to forget the frightening or horrible things that they have experienced and try to put these events out of their minds. Some people think that children's play reflects only happy experiences; and many times it does. But some children gain strength from repeating situations that were overwhelming to them, as a way of trying to come to terms with the experiences.

Traumatic events have a way of staying with us. Sometimes they are repeated in dreams. Adults may review these events by talking about them with their friends and even with strangers. Adults, through discussion—and children, through play—gain control over trauma by repeating it again and again. Repetition allows the trauma victim to absorb the experience little by little, come to grips with what happened, and learn to accept it or live with it.

Expressive art is very therapeutic

In addition to being given many opportunities for dramatic play, children can benefit from a chance to paint and draw. Just as some children make sad or frightening events into happy occasions in their play, others may draw pictures of happy times, even when they are living in far-from-happy circumstances. They draw pictures of nice houses with flowers and trees and sunshine. Others draw pictures that are, or that represent, disturbing things in their lives. They draw angry or violent pictures and find solace in expressing their feelings through art and conquering their fears by putting them on paper.

Storytelling can bridge to valuable conversation

Storytelling is another way in which children can handle difficult situations and express their inner thoughts. Sharing the telling of stories can be an excellent way to open up communication between adults and children. It can establish rapport between the two and lay the basis for further discussions of a child's difficulties. It is easier for the adult to understand stories than to interpret drawings or play, and the adult is able to engage a child in a conversation about her or his story.

This does not mean that the stories children tell can be accepted verbatim. Just as play and drawing allow children to express themselves symbolically, so do stories offer them a chance to communicate an idea or feeling without acknowledging its closeness to reality. Adults often cannot understand a child's story without having some outside information about the child's life.

If we understand what children are telling us through their stories, we can help them by participating with them in storytelling. Gardner (1971) used this method in his therapy with children. After the child told a story, Gardner told the same story but with a different, healthier ending. Although teachers are not therapists, they can engage children in joint storytelling sessions and offer alternative endings to the stories told by the children.

Collaboration with families is critically important

Direct work with children is invaluable, but if it can be combined with help for parents, its effectiveness can be increased. Young children are best understood in the context of their families and communities. Professionals need to know the facts about a child's life situation, and that information can be gained from the adults who know the child well.

In addition to obtaining information from parents, the most effective help for a child is in collaboration with help for the family. Because the child is entwined with his family for many years, it is important to make changes in his familial relationships, if possible; even small changes can be important.

It is not possible for teachers and other child specialists to also be social workers and parent therapists. The person who makes contact with a child, however, is often in a good position to establish a working alliance with the child's parents. This alliance can then be used to refer parents to community agencies, clinics, churches, or self-help groups for the support, guidance, or therapy that they need. Making a good referral takes skill and patience. It cannot be done quickly, which means that teachers and child care workers must have the time to talk to parents and to make home visits if necessary. They must have time to establish contact with families as an essential part of their work with children who suffer the consequences of violence.

The problems spelled out here are formidable. They will not be easy to solve, but professionals who see children on a daily basis can be an important part of the solution. They cannot cure all of the ills and solve all of the problems that confront children today, but they can offer these children a chance to face and accept their feelings and to see alternative ways of relating to others. If child care professionals can help some—not all, but some—children find alternatives to destructive behavior, be it toward themselves or others, they have helped break the cycle of violence.

References

Alexander, F. (1948). *Fundamentals of psychoanalysis.* New York: W.W. Norton.

Bell, C. (1991). Traumatic stress and children in danger. *Journal of Health Care for the Poor and Underserved, 2*(1), 175–188.

Gardner, R. (1971). *Therapeutic communication with children: The mutual storytelling technique.* New York: Science House.

Hetherton, E.M., Cox, M., & Cox, R. (1982). Effects of divorce on parents and children. In M. Lamb (Ed.), *Non-traditional families.* Hillsdale, NJ: Lawrence Erlbaum.

Kotlowitz, A. (1991). *There are no children here.* New York: Doubleday.

Kotulak, R. (1990, September 28). Study finds inner-city kids live with violence. *Chicago Tribune,* pp. 1, 16.

Osofsky, J., Wewers, S., Hann, D., Fick, A., & Richters, J. (1991). *Chronic community violence: What is happening to our children?* Manuscript submitted for publication.

Pynoos, R., & Eth, S. (1985). Children traumatized by witnessing personal violence: Homicide, rape or suicide behavior. In S. Eth & R. Pynoos (Eds.), *Posttraumatic stress disorder in children* (pp. 19–43). Washington, DC: American Psychiatric Press.

Terr, L. (1981). Forbidden games: Posttraumatic child's play. *Journal of American Academy of Child Psychiatry, 20,* 741–760.

Terr, L. (1983). Chowchilla revisited: The effects of psychic trauma four years after a schoolbus kidnapping. *American Journal of Psychiatry, 140,* 1543–1550.

Wallerstein, J.S., & Kelley, J.B. (1980). *Surviving the breakup: How children and parents cope with divorce.* New York: Basic Books.

Zinsmeister, K. (1990, June). Growing up scared. *The Atlantic Monthly,* pp. 49–66.

Resilience in Development

Emmy E. Werner

Emmy E. Werner is Professor of Human Development at the University of California, Davis. Address correspondence to Emmy E. Werner, Department of Applied Behavioral Sciences, University of California, Davis, 2321 Hart Hall, Davis, CA 95616.

During the past decade, a number of investigators from different disciplines—child development, psychology, psychiatry, and sociology—have focused on the study of children and youths who overcame great odds. These researchers have used the term resilience to describe three kinds of phenomena: good developmental outcomes despite high-risk status, sustained competence under stress, and recovery from trauma. Under each of these conditions, behavioral scientists have focused their attention on protective factors, or mechanisms that moderate (ameliorate) a person's reaction to a stressful situation or chronic adversity so that his or her adaptation is more successful than would be the case if the protective factors were not present.[1]

So far, only a relatively small number of studies have focused on children who were exposed to biological insults. More numerous in the current research literature are studies of resilient children who grew up in chronic poverty, were exposed to parental psychopathology, or experienced the breakup of their family or serious caregiving deficits. There has also been a growing body of literature on resilience in children who have endured the horrors of contemporary wars.

Despite the heterogeneity of all these studies, one can begin to discern a common core of individual dispositions and sources of support that contribute to resilience in development. These protective buffers appear to transcend ethnic, social-class, and geographic boundaries. They also appear to make a more profound impact on the life course of individuals who grow up in adversity than do specific risk factors or stressful life events.

Most studies of individual resilience and protective factors in children have been short-term, focusing on middle childhood and adolescence. An exception is the Kauai Longitudinal Study, with which I have been associated during the past three decades.[2] This study has involved a team of pediatricians, psychologists, and public-health and social workers who have monitored the impact of a variety of biological and psychosocial risk factors, stressful life events, and protective factors on the development of a multiethnic cohort of 698 children born in 1955 on the "Garden Island" in the Hawaiian chain. These individuals were followed, with relatively little attrition, from the prenatal period through birth to ages 1, 2, 10, 18, and 32.

Some 30% of the survivors in this study population were considered high-risk children because they were born in chronic poverty, had experienced perinatal stress, and lived in family environments troubled by chronic discord, divorce, or parental psychopathology. Two thirds of the children who had experienced four or more such risk factors by age 2 developed serious learning or behavior problems by age 10 or had delinquency records, mental health problems, or pregnancies by age 18. But one third of the children who had experienced four or more such risk factors developed instead into competent, confident, and caring adults.

PROTECTIVE FACTORS WITHIN THE INDIVIDUAL

Infancy and Early Childhood

Our findings with these resilient children are consistent with the results of several other longitudinal studies which have reported that young children with good coping abilities under adverse conditions have temperamental characteristics that elicit positive responses from a wide range of caregivers. The resilient boys and girls in the Kauai study were consistently characterized by their mothers as active, affectionate, cuddly, good-natured, and easy to deal with. Egeland and his associates observed similar dispositions among securely attached infants of abusing mothers in the Minnesota Mother-Child Interaction Project,[3] and Moriarty found the same qualities among infants with congenital defects at the Menninger Foundation.[4] Such infants were alert, easy to soothe, and able to elicit support from a nurturant family member. An "easy" temperament and the ability to actively recruit competent adult caregivers were also observed by Elder and his associates[5] in the resourceful children of the Great Depression.

By the time they reach preschool

age, resilient children appear to have developed a coping pattern that combines autonomy with an ability to ask for help when needed. These characteristics are also predictive of resilience in later years.

Middle Childhood and Adolescence

When the resilient children in the Kauai Longitudinal Study were in elementary school, their teachers were favorably impressed by their communication and problem-solving skills. Although these children were not particularly gifted, they used whatever talents they had effectively. Usually they had a special interest or a hobby they could share with a friend, and that gave them a sense of pride. These interests and activities were not narrowly sex typed. Both the boys and the girls grew into adolescents who were outgoing and autonomous, but also nurturant and emotionally sensitive.

Similar findings have been reported by Anthony, who studied the resilient offspring of mentally ill parents in St. Louis;[6] by Felsman and Vaillant, who followed successful boys from a high-crime neighborhood in Boston into adulthood;[7] and by Rutter and Quinton, who studied the lives of British girls who had been institutionalized in childhood, but managed to become well-functioning adults and caring mothers.[8]

Most studies of resilient children and youths report that intelligence and scholastic competence are positively associated with the ability to overcome great odds. It stands to reason that youngsters who are better able to appraise stressful life events correctly are also better able to figure out strategies for coping with adversity, either through their own efforts or by actively reaching out to other people for help. This finding has been replicated in studies of Asian-American, Caucasian, and African-American children.[2,9,10]

Other salient protective factors that operated in the lives of the resilient youths on Kauai were a belief in their own effectiveness (an internal locus of control) and a positive self-concept. Such characteristics were also found by Farrington among successful and law-abiding British youngsters who grew up in high-crime neighborhoods in London,[11] and by Wallerstein and her associates among American children who coped effectively with the breakup of their parents' marriages.[12]

PROTECTIVE FACTORS WITHIN THE FAMILY

Despite the burden of chronic poverty, family discord, or parental psychopathology, a child identified as resilient usually has had the opportunity to establish a close bond with at least one competent and emotionally stable person who is attuned to his or her needs. The stress-resistant children in the Kauai Longitudinal Study, the well-functioning offspring of child abusers in the Minnesota Mother-Child Interaction Project, the resilient children of psychotic parents studied by Anthony in St. Louis, and the youngsters who coped effectively with the breakup of their parents' marriages in Wallerstein's studies of divorce all had received enough good nurturing to establish a basic sense of trust.[2,3,6,12]

Much of this nurturing came from substitute caregivers within the extended family, such as grandparents and older siblings. Resilient children seem to be especially adept at recruiting such surrogate parents. In turn, they themselves are often called upon to take care of younger siblings and to practice acts of "required helpfulness" for members of their family who are ill or incapacitated.[2]

Both the Kauai Longitudinal

Study and Block and Gjerde's studies of ego-resilient children[9] found characteristic child-rearing orientations that appear to promote resiliency differentially in boys and girls. Resilient boys tend to come from households with structure and rules, where a male serves as a model of identification (father, grandfather, or older brother), and where there is some encouragement of emotional expressiveness. Resilient girls, in contrast, tend to come from households that combine an emphasis on risk taking and independence with reliable support from a female caregiver, whether mother, grandmother, or older sister. The example of a mother who is gainfully and steadily employed appears to be an especially powerful model of identification for resilient girls.[2] A number of studies of resilient children from a wide variety of socioeconomic and ethnic backgrounds have also noted that the families of these children held religious beliefs that provided stability and meaning in times of hardship and adversity.[2,6,10]

PROTECTIVE FACTORS IN THE COMMUNITY

The Kauai Longitudinal Study and a number of other prospective studies in the United States have shown that resilient youngsters tend to rely on peers and elders in the community as sources of emotional support and seek them out for counsel and comfort in times of crisis.[2,6]

Favorite teachers are often positive role models. All of the resilient high-risk children in the Kauai study could point to at least one teacher who was an important source of support. These teachers listened to the children, challenged them, and rooted for them—whether in grade school, high school, or community college. Similar findings have been reported by Wallerstein and her associates from their long-term observations of youngsters who coped effectively with their parents' divorces[12] and by Rutter and his associates from their studies of inner-city schools in London.[13]

Finally, in the Kauai study, we found that the opening of opportunities at major life transitions enabled the majority of the high-risk children who had a troubled adolescence to rebound in their 20s and early 30s. Among the most potent second chances for such youths were adult education programs in community colleges, voluntary military service, active participation in a church community, and a supportive friend or marital partner. These protective buffers were also observed by Elder in the adult lives of the children of the Great Depression,[14] by Furstenberg and his associates in the later lives of black teenage mothers,[15] and by Farrington[11] and Felsman and Vaillant[7] in the adult lives of young men who had grown up in high-crime neighborhoods in London and Boston.

PROTECTIVE FACTORS: A SUMMARY

Several clusters of protective factors have emerged as recurrent themes in the lives of children who overcome great odds. Some protective factors are characteristics of the individual: Resilient children are engaging to other people, adults and peers alike; they have good communication and problem-solving skills, including the ability to recruit substitute caregivers; they have a talent or hobby that is valued by their elders or peers; and they have faith that their own actions can make a positive difference in their lives.

Another factor that enhances resilience in development is having affectional ties that encourage trust, autonomy, and initiative. These ties are often provided by members of the extended family. There are also support systems in the community

that reinforce and reward the competencies of resilient children and provide them with positive role models: caring neighbors, teachers, elder mentors, youth workers, and peers.

LINKS BETWEEN PROTECTIVE FACTORS AND SUCCESSFUL ADAPTATION IN HIGH-RISK CHILDREN AND YOUTHS

In the Kauai study, when we examined the links between protective factors within the individual and outside sources of support, we noted a certain continuity in the life course of the high-risk individuals who successfully overcame a variety of childhood adversities. Their individual dispositions led them to select or construct environments that, in turn, reinforced and sustained their active approach to life and rewarded their special competencies.

Although the sources of support available to the individuals in their childhood homes were modestly linked to the quality of the individuals' adaptation as adults, their competencies, temperament, and self-esteem had a greater impact. Many resilient high-risk youths on Kauai left the adverse conditions of their childhood homes after high school and sought environments they found more compatible. In short, they picked their own niches.

Our findings lend some empirical support to Scarr and McCartney's theory[16] about how people make their own environment. Scarr and McCartney proposed three types of effects of people's genes on their environment: passive, evocative, and active. Because parents provide both children's genes and their rearing environments, children's genes are necessarily correlated with their own environments. This is the passive type of genotype-environment effect. The evocative type refers to the fact that a person's partially heritable characteristics, such as intelligence, personality, and physical

attractiveness, evoke certain responses from other people. Finally, a person's interests, talents, and personality (genetically variable traits) may lead him or her to select or create particular environments; this is called an active genotype-environment effect. In line with this theory, there was a shift from passive to active effects as the youths and young adults in the Kauai study left stressful home environments and sought extrafamilial environments (at school, at work, in the military) that they found more compatible and stimulating. Genotype-environment effects of the evocative sort tended to persist throughout the different life stages we studied, as individuals' physical characteristics, temperament, and intelligence elicited differential responses from other people (parents, teachers, peers).

IMPLICATIONS

So far, most studies of resilience have focused on children and youths who have "pulled themselves up by their bootstraps," with informal support by kith and kin, not on recipients of intervention services. Yet there are some lessons such children can teach society about effective intervention: If we want to help vulnerable youngsters become more resilient, we need to decrease their exposure to potent risk factors and increase their competencies and self-esteem, as well as the sources of support they can draw upon.

In *Within Our Reach*, Schorr has isolated a set of common characteristics of social programs that have successfully prevented poor outcomes for children who grew up in high-risk families.[17] Such programs typically offer a broad spectrum of health, education, and family support services, cross professional boundaries, and view the child in the context of the family, and the family in the context of the community. They provide children with sustained access to competent and caring adults, both professionals and volunteers, who teach them problem-solving skills, enhance their communication skills and self-esteem, and provide positive role models for them.

There is an urgent need for more systematic evaluations of such programs to illuminate the process by which we can forge a chain of protective factors that enables vulnerable children to become competent, confident, and caring individuals, despite the odds of chronic poverty or a medical or social disability. Future research on risk and resiliency needs to acquire a cross-cultural perspective as well. We need to know more about individual dispositions and sources of support that transcend cultural boundaries and operate effectively in a variety of high-risk contexts.

Notes

1. A.S. Masten, K.M. Best, and N. Garmezy, Resilience and development: Contributions from the study of children who overcame adversity, *Devel-opment and Psychopathology, 2*, 425–444 (1991).

2. All results from this study that are discussed in this review were reported in E.E. Werner, Risk resilience, and recovery: Perspectives from the Kauai Longitudinal Study, *Development and Psychopathology, 5*, 503–515 (1993).

3. B. Egeland, D. Jacobvitz, and L.A. Sroufe, Breaking the cycle of child abuse, *Child Development, 59*, 1080–1088 (1988).

4. A. Moriarty, John, a boy who acquired resilience, in *The Invulnerable Child*, E.J. Anthony and B.J. Cohler, Eds. (Guilford Press, New York, 1987).

5. G.H. Elder, K. Liker, and C.E. Cross, Parent-child behavior in the Great Depression, in *Life Span Development and Behavior*, Vol. 6, T.B. Baltes and O.G. Brim, Jr., Eds. (Academic Press, New York, 1984).

6. E.J. Anthony, Children at risk for psychosis growing up successfully, in *The Invulnerable Child*, E.J. Anthony and B.J. Cohler, Eds. (Guilford Press, New York, 1987).

7. J.K. Felsman and G.E. Vaillant, Resilient children as adults: A 40 year study, in *The Invulnerable Child*, E.J. Anthony and B.J. Cohler, Eds. (Guilford Press, New York, 1987).

8. M. Rutter and D. Quinton, Long term follow-up of women institutionalized in childhood: Factors promoting good functioning in adult life, *British Journal of Developmental Psychology, 18*, 225–234 (1984).

9. J. Block and P.F. Gjerde, Early antecedents of ego resiliency in late adolescence, paper presented at the annual meeting of the American Psychological Association, Washington, DC (August 1986).

10. R.M. Clark, *Family Life and School Achievement: Why Poor Black Children Succeed or Fail* (University of Chicago Press, Chicago, 1983).

11. D.P. Farrington, *Protective Factors in the Development of Juvenile Delinquency and Adult Crime* (Institute of Criminology, Cambridge University, Cambridge, England, 1993).

12. J.S. Wallerstein and S. Blakeslee, *Second Chances: Men, Women and Children a Decade After Divorce* (Ticknor and Fields, New York, 1989).

13. M. Rutter, B. Maughan, P. Mortimore, and J. Ousten, *Fifteen Thousand Hours: Secondary Schools and Their Effects on Children* (Harvard University Press, Cambridge, MA, 1979).

14. G.H. Elder, Military times and turning points in men's lives, *Developmental Psychology, 22*, 233–245 (1986).

15. F.F. Furstenberg, J. Brooks-Gunn, and S.P. Morgan, *Adolescent Mothers in Later Life* (Cambridge University Press, New York, 1987).

16. S. Scarr and K. McCartney, How people make their own environments: A theory of genotype → environment effects, *Child Development, 54*, 424–435 (1983).

17. L. Schorr, *Within Our Reach: Breaking the Cycle of Disadvantage* (Anchor Press, New York, 1988).

Recommended Reading

Haggerty, R., Garmezy, N., Rutter, M., and Sherrod. L., Eds. (1994). *Stress, Risk, and Resilience in Childhood and Adolescence* (Cambridge University Press, New York).

Luthar, S., and Zigler, E. (1991). Vulnerability and competence: A review of research on resilience in childhood. *American Journal of Orthopsychiatry, 61*, 6–22.

Werner, E.E., and Smith, R.S. (1992). *Overcoming the Odds: High Risk Children From Birth to Adulthood* (Cornell University Press, Ithaca, NY).

Beyond Betrayal: Life After

INFIDELITY

Frank Pittman III, M.D.

Hour after hour, day after day in my office I see men and women who have been screwing around. They lead secret lives, as they hide themselves from their marriages. They go through wrenching divorces, inflicting pain on their children and their children's children. Or they make desperate, tearful, sweaty efforts at holding on to the shreds of a life they've betrayed. They tell me they have gone through all of this for a quick thrill or a furtive moment of romance. Sometimes they tell me they don't remember making the decision that tore apart their life: "It just happened." Sometimes they don't even know they are being unfaithful. (I tell them: "If you don't know whether what you are doing is an infidelity or not, ask your spouse.") From the outside looking in, it is insane. How could anyone risk everything in life on the turn of a screw? Infidelity was not something people did much in my family, so I always found it strange and noteworthy when people did it in my practice. After almost 30 years of cleaning up the mess after other people's affairs, I wrote a book describing everything about infidelity I'd seen in my practice. The book was *Private Lies: Infidelity and the Betrayal of Intimacy* (Norton). I thought it might help. Even if the tragedy of AIDS and the humiliation of prominent politicians hadn't stopped it, surely people could not continue screwing around after reading about the absurd destructiveness of it. As you know, people have *not* stopped having affairs. But many of them feel the need

to write or call or drop by and talk to me about it. When I wrote *Private Lies,* I thought I knew everything there was to know about infidelity. But I know now that there is even more.

ACCIDENTAL INFIDELITY

All affairs are not alike. The thousands of affairs I've seen seem to fall into four broad categories. Most first affairs are cases of *accidental infidelity,* unintended and uncharacteristic acts of carelessness that really did "just happen." Someone will get drunk, will get caught up in the moment, will just be having a bad day. It can happen to anyone, though some people are more accident prone than others, and some situations are accident zones.

Many a young man has started his career as a philanderer quite accidentally when he is traveling out of town on a new job with a philandering boss who chooses one of a pair of women and expects the young fellow to entertain the other. The most startling dynamic behind accidental infidelity is misplaced politeness, the feeling that it would be rude to turn down a needy friend's sexual advances. In the debonair gallantry of the moment, the brazen discourtesy to the marriage partner is overlooked altogether.

Both men and women can slip up and have accidental affairs, though the most accident-prone are those who drink, those who travel, those who don't get asked much, those who don't feel very tightly married, those whose running buddies

screw around, and those who are afraid to run from a challenge. Most are men.

After an accidental infidelity, there is clearly the sense that one's life and marriage have changed. The choices are:

1. To decide that infidelity was a stupid thing to do, to confess it or not to do so, but to resolve to take better precautions in the future;

2. To decide you wouldn't have done such a thing unless your husband or wife had let you down, put the blame on your mate, and go home and pick your marriage to death;

3. To notice that lightning did not strike you dead, decide this would be a safe and inexpensive hobby to take up, and do it some more;

4. To decide that you would not have done such a thing if you were married to the right person, determine that this was "meant to be," and declare yourself in love with the stranger in the bed.

ROMANTIC INFIDELITY

Surely the craziest and most destructive form of infidelity is the temporary insanity of *falling in love.* You do this, not when you meet somebody wonderful (wonderful people don't screw around with married people) but when you are going through a crisis in your own life, can't continuing living your life, and aren't quite ready for suicide yet. An affair with someone grossly inappropriate—someone decades younger or older, someone dependent or dominating, someone with problems even bigger than your own—is so crazily stimulating that it's like a drug that can lift you out of your depression and enable you to feel things again. Of course, between moments of ecstasy, you are more depressed, increasingly alone and alienated in your life, and increasingly hooked on the affair partner. Ideal romance partners are damsels or "dumsels" in distress, people without a life but with a lot of problems, people with bad reality testing and little concern with understanding reality better.

Romantic affairs lead to a great many divorces, suicides, homicides, heart attacks, and strokes, but not to very many successful remarriages. No matter how many sacrifices you make to keep the love alive, no matter how many sacrifices your family and children make for this crazy relationship, it will gradually burn itself out when there is nothing more to sacrifice to it. Then you must face not only the wreckage of several lives, but the original depression from which the affair was an insane flight into escape.

People are most likely to get into these romantic affairs at the turning points of life: when their parents die or their children grow up; when they suffer health crises or are under pressure to give up an addiction; when they achieve an unexpected level of job success or job failure; or when their first child is born—any situation in which they must face a lot of reality and grow up. The better the marriage, the saner and more sensible the spouse, the more alienated the romantic is likely to feel. Romantic affairs happen in good marriages even more often than in bad ones.

MYTHS OF INFIDELITY

The people who are running from bed to bed creating disasters for themselves and everyone else don't seem to know what they are doing. They just don't get it. But why should they? There is a mythology about infidelity that shows up in the popular press and even in the mental health literature that is guaranteed to mislead people and make dangerous situations even worse. Some of these myths are:

1. Everybody is unfaithful; it is normal, expectable behavior. Mozart, in his comic opera *Cosi Fan Tutti,* insisted that women all do it, but a far more common belief is that men all do it: "Higgamous, hoggamous, woman's monogamous; hoggamous, higgamous, man is polygamous." In Nora Ephron's movie, *Heartburn,* Meryl Streep's husband has left her for another woman. She turns to her father for solace, but he dismisses her complaint as the way of all male flesh: "If you want monogamy, marry a swan."

We don't know how many people are unfaithful; if people will lie to their own husband or wife, they surely aren't going to be honest with poll takers. We can guess that one-half of married men and one-third of married women have dropped their drawers away from home at least once. That's a lot of infidelity.

Still, most people are faithful most of the time. Without the expectation of fidelity, intimacy becomes awkward and marriage adversarial. People who expect their partner to betray them are likely to beat them to the draw, and to make both of them miserable in the meantime.

Most species of birds and animals in which the male serves some useful function other than sperm donation are inherently monogamous. Humans, like other nest builders, are monogamous by nature, but imperfectly so. We can be trained out of it, though even in polygamous and promiscuous cultures people show their true colors when they fall blindly and crazily in love. And we have an escape clause: nature mercifully permits us to survive our mates and mate again. But if we slip up and take a new mate while the old mate is still alive, it is likely to destroy the pair bonding with our previous mate and create great instinctual disorientation—which is part of the tragedy of infidelity.

2. Affairs are good for you; an affair may even revive a dull marriage. Back at the height of the sexual revolution, the *Playboy* philosophy and its *Cosmopolitan* counterpart urged infidelity as a way to keep men manly, women womanly, and marriage vital. Lately, in such books as Annette Lawson's *Adultery* and Dalma Heyn's *The Erotic Silence of the American Wife,* women have been encouraged to act out their sexual fantasies as a blow for equal rights.

It is true that if an affair is blatant enough and if all hell breaks loose, the crisis of infidelity can shake up the most petrified marriage. Of course, any crisis can serve the same detonation function, and burning the house down might be a safer, cheaper, and more readily forgivable attention-getter.

However utopian the theories, the reality is that infidelity, whether it is furtive or blatant, will blow hell out of a marriage. In 30 odd years of practice, I have encountered only a handful of established first marriages that ended in divorce without someone being unfaithful, often with the infidelity kept secret throughout the divorce process and even for years afterwards. Infidelity is the *sine qua non* of divorce.

3. People have affairs because they aren't in love with their marriage partner. People tell me this, and they even remember it this way. But on closer examination it routinely turns out that the marriage was fine before the affair happened, and the decision that they were not in love with their marriage partner was an effort to explain and justify the affair.

Being in love does not protect people from lust. Screwing around on your loved one is not a very loving thing to do, and it may be downright hostile. Every marriage is a thick stew of emotions ranging from lust to disgust, desperate love to homicidal rage. It would be idiotic to reduce such a wonderfully rich emotional diet to a question ("love me?" or "love me not?") so simplistic that it is best asked of the petals of daisies. Nonetheless, people do ask themselves such questions, and they answer them.

Falling out of love is no reason to betray your mate. If people are experiencing a deficiency in their ability to love their partner, it is not clear how something so hateful as betraying him or her would restore it.

4. People have affairs because they are oversexed. Affairs are about secrets. The infidelity is not necessarily in the sex, but in the dishonesty.

Swingers have sex openly, without dishonesty and therefore without betrayal (though with a lot of scary bugs.) More cautious infidels might have chaste but furtive lunches and secret telephone calls with ex-spouses or former affair partners—nothing to sate the sexual tension, but just enough to prevent a marital reconciliation or intimacy in the marriage.

Affairs generally involve sex, at least enough to create a secret that seals the conspiratorial alliance of the affair, and makes the relationship tense, dangerous, and thus exciting. Most affairs consist of a little bad sex and hours on the telephone. I once saw a case in which the couple had attempted sex once 30 years before and had limited the intimacy in their respective marriages while they maintained their sad, secret love with quiet lunches, pondering the crucial question of whether or not he had gotten it all the way in on that immortal autumn evening in 1958.

Both genders seem equally capable of falling into the temporary insanity of romantic affairs, though women are more likely to reframe anything they do as having been done for love. Women in love are far more aware of what they are doing and what the dangers might be. Men in love can be extraordinarily incautious and willing to give up everything. Men in love lose their heads—at least for a while.

MARITAL ARRANGEMENTS

All marriages are imperfect, and probably a disappointment in one way or another, which is a piece of reality, not a license to mess around with the neighbors. There are some marriages that fail to provide a modicum of warmth, sex, sanity, companionship, money. There are awful marriages people can't get all the way into and can't get all the way out of, divorces people won't call off and can't go through, marriages that won't die and won't recover. Often people in such marriages make a *marital arrangement* by calling in marital aides to keep them company while they avoid living their life. Such practical affairs help them keep the marriage steady but distant. They thus encapsulate the marital deficiency, so the infidel can neither establish a life without the problems nor solve them. Affairs can wreck a good marriage, but can help stabilize a bad one.

People who get into marital arrangements are not necessarily the innocent victims of defective relationships. Some set out to keep their marriages defective and distant. I have seen men who have kept the same mistress through several marriages, arranging their marriages to serve some practical purpose while keeping their ro-

---

In general, monogamous couples have a lot more sex than the people who are screwing around.

5. Affairs are ultimately the fault of the cuckold. Patriarchal custom assumes that when a man screws around it must be because of his wife's aesthetic, sexual, or emotional deficiencies. She failed him in some way. And feminist theory has assured us that if a wife screws around it must be because men are such assholes. Many people believe that screwing around is a normal response to an imperfect marriage and is, by definition, the marriage partner's fault. Friends and relatives, bartenders, therapists, and hairdressers, often reveal their own gender prejudices and distrust of marriage, monogamy, intimacy, and honesty, when they encourage the infidel to put the blame on the cuckold rather than on him- or herself.

One trick for avoiding personal blame and responsibility is to blame the marriage itself (too early, too late, too soon after some event) or some unchangeable characteristic of the partner (too old, too tall, too ethnic, too smart, too experienced, too inexperienced.) This is both a cop-out and a dead end.

One marriage partner can make the other miserable, but can't make the other unfaithful. (The cuckold is usually not even there when the affair is taking place). Civilization and marriage require that people behave appropriately however they feel, and that they take full responsibility for their actions. "My wife drove me to it with her nagging"; "I can't help what I do because of what my father did to me"; "She came on to me and her skirt was very short"; "I must be a sex addict"; et cetera. Baloney! If people really can't control their sexual behavior, they should not be permitted to run around loose.

There is no point in holding the cuckold responsible for the infidel's sexual behavior unless the cuckold has total control over the sexual equipment that has run off the road. Only the driver is responsible.

6. It is best to pretend not to know. There are people who avoid unpleasantness and would rather watch the house burn down than bother anyone by yelling "Fire!" Silence fuels the affair, which can thrive only in secrecy. Adulterous marriages begin their repair only when the secret is out in the open, and the infidel does not need to hide any longer. Of course, it also helps to end the affair.

A corollary is the belief that infidels must deny their affairs interminably and do all that is possible to drive cuckolds to such disorientation that they will doubt their own sanity rather than doubt their partner's fidelity. In actuality, the continued lying and denial is usually the most unforgivable aspect of the infidelity.

One man was in the habit of jogging each evening, but his wife noticed that his running clothes had stopped stinking. Suspicious, she followed him—to his secretary's apartment. She burst in and confronted her husband who was standing naked in the secretary's closet. She demanded: "What are you doing here?" He responded: "You do not see me here. You have gone crazy and are imagining this." She almost believed him, and remains to this day angry about *that* than about the affair itself. Once an affair is known or even suspected, there is no safety in denial, but there is hope in admission.

I recently treated a woman whose physician husband divorced her 20 years ago after a few years of marriage, telling her that she had an odor that was making him sick, and he had developed an allergy to her. She felt so bad about herself she never remarried.

I suspected there was more to the story, and sent her back to ask him whether he had been unfaithful to her. He confessed that he had been, but had tried to shield her from hurt by convincing her that he had been faithful and true but that she was repulsive. She feels much worse about him now, but much better about herself. She now feels free to date.

7. After an affair, divorce is inevitable. Essentially all first-time divorces occur in the wake of an affair. With therapy though, most adulterous marriages can be saved, and may even be stronger and more intimate than they were before the crisis. I have rarely seen a cuckold go all the way through with a divorce after a first affair that is now over. Of course, each subsequent affair lowers the odds drastically.

It doesn't happen the way it does in the movies. The indignant cuckold does scream and yell and carry on and threaten all manner of awful things—which should not be surprising since his or her life has just been torn asunder. But he or she quickly calms down and begins the effort to salvage the marriage, to pull the errant infidel from the arms of the dreaded affairee.

When a divorce occurs, it is because the infidel can not escape the affair in time or cannot face going back into a marriage in which he or she is now known and understood and can no longer pose as the chaste virgin or white knight spotless and beyond criticism. A recent *New Yorker* cartoon showed a forlorn man at a bar complaining: "My wife understands me."

Appropriate guilt is always helpful, though it must come from inside rather than from a raging, nasty spouse; anger is a lousy seduction technique for anyone except terminal weirdos. Guilt is good for you. Shame, however, makes people run away and hide.

The prognosis after an affair is not grim, and those who have strayed have not lost all their value. The sadder but wiser infidel may be both more careful and more grateful in the future.

mance safely encapsulated elsewhere. The men considered it a victory over marriage; the exploited wives were outraged.

I encountered one woman who had long been involved with a married man. She got tired of waiting for him to get a divorce and married someone else. She didn't tell her husband about her affair, and she didn't tell her affairee about her marriage. She somehow thought they would never find out about one another. After a few exhausting and confusing weeks, the men met and confronted her. She cheerfully told them she loved them both and the arrangement seemed the sensible way to have her cake and eat it too. She couldn't understand why both the men felt cheated and deprived by her efforts to sacrifice their lives to satisfy her skittishness about total commitment.

Some of these arrangements can get quite complicated. One woman supported her house-husband and their kids by living as the mistress of an older married man, who spent his afternoons and weekend days with her and his evenings at home with his own children and his sexually boring wife. People averse to conflict might prefer such arrangements to therapy, or any other effort to actually solve the problems of the marriage.

Unhappily married people of either gender can establish marital arrangements to help them through the night. But men are more likely to focus on the practicality of the arrangement and diminish awareness of any threat to the stability of the marriage, while women are more likely to romanticize the arrangement and convince themselves it is leading toward an eventual union with the romantic partner. Networks of couples may spend their lives halfway through someone's divorce, usually with a guilt-ridden man reluctant to completely leave a marriage he has betrayed and even deserted, and a woman, no matter how hard she protests to the contrary, eternally hopeful for a wedding in the future.

Philandering

Philandering is a predominantly male activity. Philanderers take up infidelity as a hobby. Philanderers are likely to have a rigid and concrete concept of gender; they worship masculinity, and while they may be greatly attracted to women, they are mostly interested in having the woman affirm their masculinity. They don't really like women, and they certainly don't want an equal, intimate relationship with a

Every marriage is a thick stew of emotions ranging from lust to disgust.

member of the gender they insist is inferior, but far too powerful. They see women as dangerous, since women have the ability to assess a man's worth, to measure him and find him wanting, to determine whether he is man enough.

These men may or may not like sex, but they use it compulsively to affirm their masculinity and overcome both their homophobia and their fear of women. They can be cruel, abusive, and even violent to women who try to get control of them and stop the philandering they consider crucial to their masculinity. Their life is centered around displays of masculinity, however they define it, trying to impress women with their physical strength, competitive victories, seductive skills, mastery of all situations, power, wealth, and, if necessary, violence. Some of them are quite charming and have no trouble finding women eager to be abused by them.

Gay men can philander too, and the dynamics are the same for gay philanderers as for straight ones: the obvious avoidance of female sexual control, but also the preoccupation with masculinity and the use of rampant sexuality for both reassurance and the measurement of manhood. When men have paid such an enormous social and interpersonal price for their preferred sexuality, they are likely to wrap an enormous amount of their identity around their sexuality and express that sexuality extensively.

Philanderers may be the sons of philanderers, or they may have learned their ideas about marriage and gender from their ethnic group or inadvertently from their religion. Somewhere they have gotten the idea that their masculinity is their most valuable attribute and it requires them to protect themselves from coming under female control. These guys may consider themselves quite principled and honorable, and they may follow the rules to the letter in their dealings with other men. But in their world women have no rights.

To men they may seem normal, but

women experience them as narcissistic or even sociopathic. They think they are normal, that they are doing what every other real man would do if he weren't such a wimp. The notions of marital fidelity, of gender equality, of honesty and intimacy between husbands and wives seem quite foreign from what they learned growing up. The gender equality of monogamy may not feel compatible to men steeped in patriarchal beliefs in men being gods and women being ribs. Monogamous sexuality is difficult for men who worship Madonnas for their sexlessness and berate Eves for their seductiveness.

Philanderers' sexuality is fueled by anger and fear, and while they may be considered "sex addicts" they are really "gender compulsives," desperately doing whatever they think will make them look and feel most masculine. They put notches on their belts in hopes it will make their penises grow bigger. If they can get a woman to die for them, like opera composer Giacomo Puccini did in real life and in most of his operas, they feel like a real man.

Female Philanderers

There are female philanderers too, and they too are usually the daughters or ex-wives of philanderers. They are angry at men, because they believe all men screw around as their father or ex-husband did. A female philanderer is not likely to stay married for very long, since that would require her to make peace with a man, and as a woman to carry more than her share of the burden of marriage. Marriage grounds people in reality rather than transporting them into fantasy, so marriage is too loving, too demanding, too realistic, and not romantic enough for them.

I hear stories of female philanderers, such as Maria Riva's description of her mother, Marlene Dietrich. They appear to have insatiable sexual appetites but, on closer examination, they don't like sex much, they do like power over men, and underneath the philandering anger, they are plaintively seeking love.

Straying wives are rarely philanderers, but single women who mess around with married men are quite likely to be. Female philanderers prefer to raid other people's marriages, breaking up relationships, doing as much damage as possible, and then dancing off reaffirmed. Like male philanderers, female philanderers put their victims through all of this just to give themselves a sense of gender power.

Spider Woman

There are women who, by nature romantics, don't quite want to escape their own life and die for love. Instead they'd rather have some guy wreck his life for them. These women have been so recently betrayed by unfaithful men that the wound is still raw and they are out for revenge. A woman who angrily pursues married men is a "spider woman"—she requires human sacrifice to restore her sense of power.

When she is sucking the blood from other people's marriages, she feels some relief from the pain of having her own marriage betrayed. She simply requires that a man love her enough to sacrifice his life for her. She may be particularly attracted to happy marriages, clearly envious of the woman whose husband is faithful and loving to her. Sometimes it isn't clear whether she wants to replace the happy wife or just make her miserable.

The women who are least squeamish and most likely to wreak havoc on other people's marriages are victims of some sort of abuse, so angry that they don't feel bound by the usual rules or obligations, so desperate that they cling to any source of security, and so miserable that they don't bother to think a bit of the end of it.

Josephine Hart's novel *Damage,* and the recent Louis Malle film version of it, describe such a woman. She seduces her fiancee's depressed father, and after the fiancee discovers the affair and kills himself, she waltzes off from the wreckage of all the lives. She explains that her father disappeared long ago, her mother had been married four or five times, and her brother committed suicide when she left his bed and began to date other boys. She described herself as damaged, and says, "Damaged people are dangerous. They know they can survive."

Bette was a spider woman. She came to see me only once, with her married affair partner Alvin, a man I had been seeing with his wife Agnes. But I kept up with her through the many people whose lives she touched. Bette's father had run off and left her and her mother when she was just a child, and her stepfather had exposed himself to her. Most recently Bette's man-

All marriages are imperfect, a disappointment in one way or another.

ic husband Burt had run off with a stripper, Claudia, and had briefly married her before he crashed and went into a psychiatric hospital.

While Burt was with Claudia, the enraged Bette promptly latched on to Alvin, a laid-back philanderer who had been married to Agnes for decades and had been screwing around casually most of that time. Bette was determined that Alvin was going to divorce Agnes and marry her, desert his children, and raise her now-fatherless kids. The normally cheerful Alvin, who had done a good job for a lifetime of pleasing every woman he met and avoiding getting trapped by any of them, couldn't seem to escape Bette, but he certainly had no desire to leave Agnes. He grew increasingly depressed and suicidal. He felt better after he told the long-suffering Agnes, but he still couldn't move in any direction. Over the next couple of years, Bette and Alvin took turns threatening suicide, while Agnes tended her garden, raised her children, ran her business, and waited for the increasingly disoriented and pathetic Alvin to come to his senses.

Agnes finally became sufficiently alarmed about her husband's deterioration that she decided the only way she could save his life was to divorce him. She did, and Alvin promptly dumped Bette. He could not forgive her for what she had made him do to dear, sweet Agnes. He lost no time in taking up with Darlene, with whom he had been flirting for some time, but who wouldn't go out with a married man. Agnes felt relief, and the comfort of a good settlement, but Bette was once again abandoned and desperate.

She called Alvin hourly, alternately threatening suicide, reciting erotic poetry, and offering to fix him dinner. She phoned bomb threats to Darlene's office. Bette called me to tell me what a sociopathic jerk

Alvin was to betray her with another woman after all she had done in helping him through his divorce. She wrote sisterly notes to Agnes, offering the comfort of friendship to help one another through the awful experience of being betrayed by this terrible man. At no point did Bette consider that she had done anything wrong. She was now, as she had been all her life, a victim of men, who not only use and abuse women, but won't lay down their lives to rescue them on cue.

Emotionally Retarded Men in Love

About the only people more dangerous than philandering men going through life with an open fly and romantic damsels going through life in perennial distress, are emotionally retarded men in love. When such men go through a difficult transition in life, they hunker down and ignore all emotions. Their brain chemistry gets depressed, but they don't know how to feel it as depression. Their loved ones try to keep from bothering them, try to keep things calm and serene—and isolate them further.

An emotionally retarded man may go for a time without feeling pleasure, pain, or anything else, until a strange woman jerks him back into awareness of something intense enough for him to feel it—perhaps sexual fireworks, or the boyish heroics of rescuing her, or perhaps just fascination with her constantly changing moods and never-ending emotional crises.

With her, he can pull out of his depression briefly, but he sinks back even deeper into it when he is not with her. He is getting addicted to her, but he doesn't know that. He only feels the absence of joy and love and life with his serenely cautious wife

Once an affair is known or even suspected, there's no safety in denial but there is hope in admission.

and kids, and the awareness of life with this new woman. It doesn't work for him to leave home to be with her, as she too would grow stale and irritating if she were around full time.

What he needs is not a crazier woman to sacrifice his life for, but treatment for his depression. However, since the best home remedies for depression are sex, exercise, joy, and triumph, the dangerous damsel may be providing one or more of them in a big enough dose to make him feel a lot better. He may feel pretty good until he gets the bill, and sees how much of his life and the lives of his loved ones this treatment is costing. Marriages that start this way, stepping over the bodies of loved ones as the giddy couple walks down the aisle, are not likely to last long.

Howard had been faithful to Harriett for 16 years. He had been happy with her. She made him feel loved, which no one else had ever tried to do. Howard devoted himself to doing the right thing. He always did what he was supposed to do and he never complained. In fact he said very little at all.

Howard worked at Harriett's father's store, a stylish and expensive men's clothiers. He had worked there in high school and returned after college. He'd never had another job. He had felt like a son to his father-in-law. But when the old man retired, he bypassed the stalwart, loyal Howard and made his own wastrel son manager.

Howard also took care of his own elderly parents who lived next door. His father died, and left a nice little estate to his mother, who then gave much of it to his younger brother, who had gotten into trouble with gambling and extravagance.

Howard felt betrayed, and sank into a depression. He talked of quitting his job and moving away. Harriett pointed out the impracticality of that for the kids. She reminded him of all the good qualities of his mother and her father.

Howard didn't bring it up again. Instead, he began to talk to Maxine, one of the tailors at the store, a tired middle-aged woman who shared Howard's disillusionment with the world. One day, Maxine called frightened because she smelled gas in her trailer and her third ex-husband had threatened to hurt her. She needed for Howard to come out and see if he could smell anything dangerous. He did, and somehow ended up in bed with Maxine. He felt in love. He knew it was crazy but he couldn't get along without her. He bailed her out of the frequent disasters in her life. They began to plot their getaway, which consumed his attention for months.

Harriett noticed the change in Howard, but thought he was just mourning his father's death. They continued to get along well, sex was as good as ever, and they enjoyed the same things they had always enjoyed. It was a shock to her when he told her he was moving out, that he didn't love her anymore, and that it had nothing whatever to do with Maxine, who would be leaving with him.

Harriett went into a rage and hit him. The children went berserk. The younger daughter cried inconsolably, the older one

Most affairs consist of a little bad sex and a lot of telephoning.

became bulimic, the son quit school and refused to leave his room. I saw the family a few times, but Howard would not turn back. He left with Maxine, and would not return my phone calls. The kids were carrying on so on the telephone, Howard stopped calling them for a few months, not wanting to upset them. Meanwhile he and Maxine, who had left her kids behind as well, borrowed some money from his mother and moved to the coast where they bought into a marina—the only thing they had in common was the pleasure of fishing.

A year later, Harriett and the kids were still in therapy but they were getting along pretty well without him. Harriett was running the clothing store. Howard decided he missed his children and invited them to go fishing with him and Maxine. It surprised him when they still refused to speak to him. He called me and complained to me that his depression was a great deal worse. The marina was doing badly. He and Maxine weren't getting along very well. He missed his children and cried a lot, and she told him his preoccupation with his children was a betrayal of her. He blamed Harriett for fussing at him when she found out about Maxine. He believed she turned the children against him. He couldn't understand why anyone would be mad with him; he couldn't help who he loves and who he doesn't love.

MEN AND WOMEN WHO CHEAT

Howard's failure to understand the complex emotional consequences of his affair is typically male, just as Bette's insistence that her affair partner live up to her romantic fantasies is typically female. Any gender-based generalization is both irritating and inaccurate, but some behaviors are typical. Men tend to attach too little significance to affairs, ignoring their horrifying power to disorient and disrupt lives, while women tend to attach too much significance, assuming that the emotions are so powerful they must be "real" and therefore concrete, permanent, and stable enough to risk a life for.

A man, especially a philandering man, may feel comfortable having sex with a woman if it is clear that he is not in love with her. Even when a man understands that a rule has been broken and he expects consequences of some sort, he routinely underestimates the extent and range and duration of the reactions to his betrayal. Men may agree that the sex is wrong, but may believe that the lying is a noble effort to protect the family. A man may reason that outside sex is wrong because there is a rule against it, without understanding that his lying establishes an adversarial relationship with his mate and is the greater offense. Men are often surprised at the intensity of their betrayed mate's anger, and then even more surprised when she is willing to take him back. Men rarely appreciate the devastating long-range impact of their infidelities, or even their divorces, on their children.

Routinely, a man will tell me that he assured himself that he loved his wife before he hopped into a strange bed, that the women there with him means nothing, that it is just a meaningless roll in the hay. A woman is more likely to tell me that at the sound of the zipper she quickly ascertained that she was not as much in love with her husband as she should have been, and the man there in bed with her was the true love of her life.

A woman seems likely to be less concerned with the letter of the law than with the emotional coherence of her life. It may be okay to screw a man if she "loves" him, whatever the status of his or her marriage, and it is certainly appropriate to lie to a man who believes he has a claim on you, but whom you don't love.

Women may be more concerned with the impact of their affairs on their children than they are with the effect on their mate, whom they have already devalued and discounted in anticipation of the affair. Of course, a woman is likely to feel the children would be in support of her affair, and thus may involve them in relaying her messages, keeping her secrets, and telling her lies. This can be mind-blowingly seductive and confusing to the kids. Sharing the secret of one parent's affair, and hiding it from the other parent, has essentially the same emotional impact as incest.

Some conventional wisdom about gender differences in infidelity is true.

More men than women do have affairs, but it seemed to me that before the AIDS epidemic, the rate for men was dropping (philandering has not been considered cute since the Kennedy's went out of power) and the rate for women was rising (women who assumed that all men were screwing around saw their own screwing around as a blow for equal rights.) In recent years, promiscuity seems suicidal so only the suicidal—that is, the romantics—are on the streets after dark.

Men are able to approach sex more casually than women, a factor not only of the patriarchal double standard but also of the difference between having genitals on the outside and having them on the inside. Getting laid for all the wrong reasons is a lot less dangerous than falling in love with all the wrong people.

Men who get caught screwing around are more likely to be honest about the sex than women. Men will confess the full sexual details, even if they are vague about the emotions. Women on the other hand will confess to total consuming love and suicidal desire to die with some man, while insisting no sex ever took place. I would believe that if I'd ever

seen a man describe the affair as so consumingly intense from the waist up and so chaste from the waist down. I assume these women are lying to me about what they know they did or did not do, while I assume that the men really are honest about the genital ups and downs—and honestly confused about the emotional ones.

Women are more likely to discuss their love affairs with their women friends. Philandering men may turn their sex lives into a spectator sport but romantic men tend to keep their love life private from their men friends, and often just withdraw from their friends during the romance.

On the other hand, women are not more romantic than men. Men in love are every bit as foolish and a lot more naive than women in love. They go crazier and risk more. They are far more likely to sacrifice or abandon their children to prove their love to some recent affairee. They are more likely to isolate themselves from everyone except their affair partner, and turn their thinking and feeling over to her, applying her romantic ways of thinking (or not thinking) to the dilemmas of his increasingly chaotic life.

Men are just as forgiving as women of their mates' affairs. They might claim ahead of time that they would never tolerate it, but when push comes to shove, cuckolded men are every bit as likely as cuckolded women to fight like tigers to hold on to a marriage that has been betrayed. Cuckolded men may react violently at first, though cuckolded women do so as well, and I've seen more cases of women who shot and wounded or killed errant

husbands. (The shootings occur not when the affair is stopped and confessed, but when it is continued and denied.)

Betrayed men, like betrayed women, hunker down and do whatever they have to do to hold their marriage together. A few men and women go into a rage and refuse to turn back, and then spend a lifetime nursing the narcissistic injury, but that unusual occurrence is no more common for men than for women. Marriage can survive either a husband's infidelity or a wife's, if it is stopped, brought into the open, and dealt with.

I have cleaned up from more affairs than a squad of motel chambermaids. Infidelity is a very messy hobby. It is not an effective way to find a new mate or a new life.

It is not a safe treatment for depression, boredom, imperfect marriage, or inadequate gender splendor. And it certainly does not impress the rest of us. It does not work for women any better than it does for men. It does excite the senses and the imaginations of those who merely hear the tales of lives and deaths for love, who melt at the sound of liebestods or country songs of love gone wrong.

I think I've gotten more from infidelity as an observer than all the participants I've seen. Infidelity is a spectator sport like shark feeding or bull fighting—that is, great for those innocent bystanders who are careful not to get their feet, or whatever, wet. For the greatest enjoyment of infidelity, I recommend you observe from a safe physical and emotional distance and avoid any suicidal impulse to become a participant.

Sex in America: Faithfulness in Marriage Is Overwhelming

Tamar Lewin

While several previous studies of sex in America have created a popular image of extramarital affairs, casual sex and rampant experimentation, an authoritative new study of American sexual practices—widely described as the most definitive ever—paints a much more subdued picture of marital fidelity, few partners and less exotic sexual practices.

In the new study, based on surveys of 3,432 men and women 18 to 59 years of age, 85 percent of married women and more than 75 percent of married men said they are faithful to their spouses. And married people have more sex than their single counterparts: 41 percent of all married couples have sex twice a week or more, compared with 23 percent of the singles.

But cohabiting singles have the most sex of all, with 56 percent reporting that they had sex twice a week or more.

"We have had the myth that everybody was out there having lots of sex of all kinds," said John H. Gagnon, a co-author of the study. "That's had two consequences. It has enraged the conservatives. And it has created anxiety and unhappiness among those who weren't having it, who thought, 'If I'm not getting any, I must be a defective person.'"

"Good sense should have told us that most people don't have the time and energy to manage an affair, a job, a family and the Long Island Rail Road," said Mr. Gagnon, a sociology professor at the State University of New York at Stony Brook.

The study is considered important because it is one of the first to rely on a randomly selected nationally representative sample. Most previous sex studies—from the Kinsey reports in the 1940's and the Masters and Johnson study in the 1960's to more recent popularized studies—by, for example, Playboy magazine, the researcher Shere Hite and Redbook magazine—relied on information from volunteers, a method that may seriously skew the results, experts say, because those who are interested in sex and are most sexually active tend to participate.

"A lot of the people we approached initially said, 'Oh, you don't want to talk to me, I haven't had a partner in three years,' and those people wouldn't have taken part in previous studies, where self-selection decided who would fill out the questionnaires," said Edward O. Laumann, a sociology professor at the University of Chicago who is one of the coauthors of the study.

For an American man, the median number of sexual partners over a lifetime is six; for a woman, the me-dian is two. But the range in the number of lifetime sexual partners varied enormously, with 26 percent reporting only one lifetime partner, while one man in the study reported 1,016 partners and one woman reported 1,009.

To one of the most politicized questions in human sexuality—how common is homosexuality—the study offers a fuzzy answer: It depends.

A subdued picture of few partners and less exotic sexual practices.

For many years, the conventional wisdom was that 1 in 10 Americans was homosexual, a number that came from a 1948 Kinsey report that 10 percent of the men surveyed had had exclusively homosexual relations for at least three years between the ages of 16 and 55. Many recent studies have debunked that figure, including a study last year finding that only 1 percent of the male population was homosexual.

In the new study, 2.8 percent of the men and 1.4 percent of the women identified themselves as homosexual or bisexual. But when the question is asked differently the numbers change.

About 9 percent of the men and 5 percent of the women reported having had at least one homosexual experience since puberty. Forty percent of the men who had a homosexual experience sometime in their life did so before they were 18, and not since. Most women, though, were 18 or older when they had their first homosexual experience.

And when asked whether having sex with someone of the same sex seemed appealing, 5.5 percent of the women said the idea was somewhat or very appealing. About 6 percent of the men said they were attracted to other men.

The survey also found that homosexuals cluster in large cities. More than 9 percent of the men in the 12 largest cities identified themselves as homosexual, compared with less than 4 percent of the men in the suburbs of those cities and only about 1 percent of the men in rural areas. Lesbians also tend to cluster in cities, but not to the same extent as gay men.

The study asked about many different sexual practices, but found that only three were appealing to more than a small fraction of heterosexual Americans.

The vast majority of heterosexual Americans said they included vaginal intercourse in almost every sexual encounter. Many people said that oral sex and watching a partner undress were also appealing, but men were substantially more likely to enjoy both practices than women.

Most men and women said they did not find such practices as anal intercourse, group sex or sex with strangers very appealing, but again, the men were more interested than the women.

Among the other findings were these:

• More than half the men said they thought about sex every day, or several times a day, compared with only 19 percent of the women.

• More than four in five Americans had only one sexual partner, or no partner, in the past year. Generally, blacks reported the most sexual partners, Asians the least.

• Three-quarters of the married women said they usually or always had an orgasm during sexual intercourse, compared with 62 percent of the single women. Among men, 95 percent said they usually or always had an orgasm, married or single.

• Less than 8 percent of the participants reported having sex more than four times a week. About two-thirds said they have sex "a few times a month" or less, and about 3 in 10 have sex a few times a year or less.

• Both men and women who, as children, had been sexually touched by an adult were more likely, as adults, to have more than 10 sex partners, to engage in group sex, to report a homosexual or bisexual identification and to be unhappy.

• About one man in four and one woman in 10 masturbates at least once a week, and masturbation is less common among those 18 to 24 years of age than among those who are 24 to 34.

• Among marriage partners, 93 percent are of the same race, 82 percent are of similar educational level, 78 percent are within five years of each other's age and 72 percent are the same religion.

To gather data for the study, conducted by the National Opinion Research Center at the University of Chicago, 220 researchers spent several months in 1992 conducting face-to-face interviews. Those who agreed to participate—almost four out of five of those contacted—were also given written forms to place in a sealed envelope, so that the oral answers to some of the most intrusive, potentially embarrassing questions could be checked against what they wrote privately.

"There were some differences, but it never amounted to much, percentage-wise," Professor Laumann said. "Of course, you can't be sure that everyone told the truth all the time, but most of the time our interviewers had the sense that people were being extremely candid."

The sex survey grew out of a 1987 attempt by the Federal Government to develop data on sexual practices that would help in the fight against AIDS. The authors got money from the Government to develop a methodology for such a survey, but Senator Jesse Helms, a North Carolina Republican, persuaded the Senate in 1991 to block the financing to carry out the survey. The authors then got money to continue their work from several private foundations.

Among the survey's important implications was the finding that more than a third of the younger women said that peer pressure had made them have sex for the first time, compared with only 13 percent of those from previous generations. The authors suggest, therefore, that one important part of preventing teen-age pregnancy is helping young women learn to resist peer pressure.

The survey results are being published in two forms, one a paperback book, "The Social Organization of Sexuality" (University of Chicago Press), written by Mr. Gagnon, Mr. Laumann, Robert T. Michael, dean of the graduate school of public policy studies at the University of Chicago, and Stuart Michaels, a researcher at the University of Chicago.

The other version is a general-interest hard cover book, "Sex in America: A Definitive Survey" (Little, Brown and Company), by Mr. Gagnon, Mr. Laumann, Mr. Michael and Gina Kolata, a science reporter for The New York Times.

The Myth of the Miserable Working Woman

She's Tired, She's Stressed Out, She's Unhealthy, She Can't Go Full Speed at Work or Home. Right? Wrong.

Rosalind C. Barnett and Caryl Rivers

Rosalind C. Barnett is a psychologist and a senior research associate at the Wellesley College Center for Research on Women. Caryl Rivers is a professor of journalism at Boston University and the author of More Joy Than Rage: Crossing Generations With the New Feminism.

"You Can't Do Everything," announced a 1989 USA Today *headline on a story suggesting that a slower career track for women might be a good idea. "Mommy Career Track Sets Off a Furor," declaimed the* New York Times *on March 8, 1989, reporting that women cost companies more than men. "Pressed for Success, Women Careerists Are Cheating Themselves," sighed a 1989 headline in the* Washington Post, *going on to cite a book about the "unhappy personal lives" of women graduates of the Harvard Business School. "Women Discovering They're at Risk for Heart Attacks," Gannett News Service reported with alarm in 1991. "Can Your Career Hurt Your Kids? Yes, Say Many Experts," blared a* Fortune *cover just last May, adding in a chirpy yet soothing fashion, "But smart parents—and flexible companies—won't let it happen."*

If you believe what you read, working women are in big trouble—stressed out, depressed, sick, risking an early death from heart attacks, and so overcome with problems at home that they make inefficient employees at work.

In fact, just the opposite is true. As a research psychologist whose career has focused on women and a journalist-critic who has studied the behavior of the media, we have extensively surveyed the latest data and research and concluded that the public is being engulfed by a tidal wave of disinformation that has serious consequences for the life and health of every American woman. Since large numbers of women began moving into the work force in the 1970s, scores of studies on their emotional and physical health have painted a very clear picture: Paid employment provides substantial health *benefits* for women. These benefits cut across income and class lines; even women who are working because they have to—not because they want to—share in them.

There is a curious gap, however, between what these studies say and what is generally reported on television, radio, and in newspapers and magazines. The more the research shows work is good for women, the bleaker the media reports seem to become. Whether this bizarre state of affairs is the result of a backlash against women, as *Wall Street Journal* reporter Susan Faludi contends in her new book, *Backlash: The Undeclared War Against American Women,* or of well-meaning ignorance, the effect is the same: Both the shape of national policy and the lives of women are at risk.

Too often, legislation is written and policies are drafted not on the basis of the facts but on the basis of what those in power believe to be the facts. Even the much discussed *Workforce 2000* report, issued by the Department of Labor under the Reagan administration—hardly a hotbed of feminism—admitted that "most current policies were designed for a society in which men worked and women stayed home." If policies are skewed toward solutions that are aimed at reducing women's commitment to work, they will do more than harm women—they will damage companies, managers and the productivity of the American economy.

THE CORONARY THAT WASN'T

One reason the "bad news" about working women jumps to page one is that we're all too willing to believe it. Many adults today grew up at a time when soldiers were returning home from World War II and a way had to be found to get the women who replaced them in industry back into the kitchen. The result was a barrage of propaganda that turned at-home moms into saints and backyard barbecues and station wagons into cultural icons. Many of us still have that outdated postwar map inside our heads, and it leaves us more willing to believe the horror stories than the good news that paid employment is an emotional and medical plus.

In the 19th century it was accepted medical dogma that women should not be educated because the brain and the ovaries could not develop at the same time. Today it's PMS, the wrong math genes or rampaging hormones. Hardly anyone points out the dire predictions that didn't come true.

You may remember the prediction that career women would start having more heart attacks, just like men. But the Framingham Heart Study—a federally funded cardiac project that has been studying 10,000 men and women since 1948—reveals that working women are not having more heart attacks. They're not dying any earlier, either. Not only are women not losing their health advantages; the lifespan gap is actually widening. Only one group of working women suffers more heart attacks than other women: those in low-paying clerical jobs with many demands on them and little control over their work pace, who also have several children and little or no support at home.

As for the recent publicity about women having more problems with heart disease, much of it skims over the important underlying reasons for the increase: namely, that by the time they have a heart attack, women tend to be a good deal older (an average of 67, six years older than the average age for men), and thus frailer, than males who have one. Also, statistics from the National Institutes of Health show that coronary symptoms are treated less aggressively in women—fewer coronary bypasses, for example. In addition, most heart research is done on men, so doctors do not know as much about the causes—and treatment—of heart disease in women. None of these factors have anything to do with work.

But doesn't working put women at greater risk for stress-related illnesses? No. Paid work is actually associated with *reduced* anxiety and depression. In the early 1980s we reported in our book, *Lifeprints* (based on a National Science Foundation–funded study of 300 women), that working women were significantly higher in psychological well-being than those not employed. Working gave them a sense of mastery and control that homemaking didn't provide. More recent studies echo our findings. For example:

• A 1989 report by psychologist Ingrid Waldron and sociologist Jerry Jacobs of Temple University on nationwide surveys of 2,392 white and 892 black women,

conducted from 1977 to 1982, found that women who held both work and family roles reported better physical and mental health than homemakers.

• According to sociologists Elaine Wethington of Cornell University and Ronald Kessler of the University of Michigan, data from three years (1985 to 1988) of a continuing federally funded study of 745 married women in Detroit "clearly suggests that employment benefits women emotionally." Women who increase their participation in the labor force report lower levels of psychological distress; those who lessen their commitment to work suffer from higher distress.

• A University of California at Berkeley study published in 1990 followed 140 women for 22 years. At age 43, those who were homemakers had more chronic conditions than the working women and seemed more disillusioned and frustrated. The working mothers were in good health and seemed to be juggling their roles with success.

In sum, paid work offers women heightened self-esteem and enhanced mental and physical health. It's unemployment that's a major risk factor for depression in women.

DOING IT ALL—AND DOING FINE

This isn't true only for affluent women in good jobs; working-class women share the benefits of work, according to psychologists Sandra Scarr and Deborah Phillips of the University of Virginia and Kathleen McCartney of the University of New Hampshire. In reviewing 80 studies on this subject, they reported that working-class women with children say they would not leave work even if they didn't need the money. Work offers not only income but adult companionship, social contact and a connection with the wider world that they cannot get at home.

Doing it all may be tough, but it doesn't wipe out the health benefits of working.

Looking at survey data from around the world, Scarr and Phillips wrote that the lives of mothers who work are not more stressful than the lives of those who are at home. So what about the second shift we've heard so much about? It certainly exists: In industrialized countries, researchers found, fathers work an average of 50 hours a week on the job and doing household chores; mothers work an average of 80 hours. Wethington and Kessler found that in daily "stress diaries" kept by husbands and wives, the women report more stress than the men do. But they also handle it better. In short, doing it all may be tough, but it doesn't wipe out the health benefits of working.

THE ADVANTAGES FOR FAMILIES

What about the kids? Many working parents feel they want more time with their kids, and they say so. But does maternal employment harm children? In 1989 University of Michigan psychologist Lois Hoffman reviewed 50 years of research and found that the expected negative effects never materialized. Most often, children of employed and unemployed mothers didn't differ on measures of child development. But children of both sexes with working mothers have a less sex-stereotyped view of the world because fathers in two-income families tend to do more child care.

However, when mothers work, the quality of non-parental child care is a legitimate worry. Scarr, Phillips and McCartney say there is "near consensus among developmental psychologists and early-childhood experts that child care per se does not constitute a risk factor in children's lives." What causes problems, they report, is poor-quality care and a troubled family life. The need for good child care in this country has been obvious for some time.

What's more, children in two-job families generally don't lose out on one-to-one time with their parents. New studies, such as S. L. Nock and P. W. Kingston's *Time with Children: The Impact of Couples' Work-Time Commitments,* show that when both parents of pre-schoolers are working, they spend as much time in direct interaction with their children as families in which only the fathers work. The difference is that working parents spend more time with their kids on weekends. When only the husband works, parents spend more leisure time with each other. There is a cost to two-income families—the couples lose personal time—but the kids don't seem to pay it.

One question we never used to ask is whether having a working mother could be *good* for children. Hoffman, reflecting on the finding that employed women—both blue-collar and professional—register higher life-satisfaction scores than housewives, thinks it can be. She cites studies involving infants and older children, showing that a mother's satisfaction with her employment status relates positively both to "the quality of the mother-child interaction and to various indexes of the child's adjustment and abilities." For example, psychologists J. Guidubaldi and B. K. Nastasi of Kent State University reported in a 1987 paper that a mother's satisfaction with her job was a good predictor of her child's positive adjustment in school.

Again, this isn't true only for women in high-status jobs. In a 1982 study of sources of stress for children in low-income families, psychologists Cynthia Longfellow and Deborah Belle of the Harvard University School of Education found that employed women were generally less depressed than unemployed women. What's more, their children had fewer behavioral problems.

But the real point about working women and children is that work *isn't* the point at all. There are good mothers and not-so-good mothers, and some work and some don't. When a National Academy of Sciences panel reviewed the previous 50 years of research and dozens of studies in 1982, it found no consistent effects on children from a mother's working. Work is only one of many variables, the panel concluded in *Families That Work,* and not the definitive one.

What is the effect of women's working on their marriages? Having a working wife can increase psychological stress for men, especially older men, who grew up in a world where it was not normal for a wife to work. But men's expectations that they will—and must—be the only provider may be changing. Wethington and Kessler found that a wife's employment could be a significant buffer *against* depression for men born after 1945. Still, the picture of men's psychological well-being is very mixed, and class and expectations clearly play a role. Faludi cites polls showing that young blue-collar men are especially angry at women for invading what they see as their turf as breadwinners, even though a woman with such a job could help protect her husband from economic hardship. But in highly educated, dual-career couples, both partners say the wife's career has enhanced the marriage.

THE FIRST SHIFT: WOMEN AT WORK

While women's own health and the well-being of their families aren't harmed by their working, what effect does this dual role have on their job performance? It's assumed that men can compartmentalize work and home lives but women will bring their home worries with them to work, making them distracted and inefficient employees.

Perhaps the most dangerous myth is that the solution is for women to drop back—or drop out.

The only spillover went in the other direction: The women brought their good feelings about their work home with them and left a bad day at home behind when they came to work. In fact, Wethington and Kessler found that it was the *men* who brought the family stresses with them to work. "Women are able to avoid bringing the contagion of home stress into the workplace," the researchers write, "whereas the inability of men to prevent this kind of contagion is pervasive." The researchers speculate that perhaps women get the message early on that they can handle the home front, while men are taking on chores they aren't trained for and didn't expect.

THE PERILS OF PART-TIME

Perhaps the most dangerous myth is that the solution to most problems women suffer is for them to drop back—or drop out. What studies actually show is a significant connection between a reduced commitment to work and increased psychological stress. In their Detroit study, Wethington and Kessler noted that women who went from being full-time employees to full-time housewives reported increased symptoms of distress, such as depression and anxiety attacks; the longer a woman worked and the more committed she was to the job, the greater her risk for psychological distress when she stopped.

What about part-time work, that oft-touted solution for weary women? Women who work fewer than 20 hours per week, it turns out, do not get the mental-health work benefit, probably because they "operate under the fiction that they can retain full responsibility for child care and home maintenance," wrote Wethington and Kessler. The result: Some part-timers wind up more stressed-out than women working full-time. Part-time employment also provides less money, fewer or no benefits and, often, less interesting work and a more arduous road to promotion.

That doesn't mean that a woman shouldn't cut down on her work hours or arrange a more flexible schedule. But it does mean she should be careful about jumping on a poorly designed mommy track that may make her a second-class citizen at work.

Many women think that when they have a baby, the best thing for their mental health would be to stay home. Wrong once more. According to Wethington and Kessler, having a baby does not increase psychological distress for working women—*unless* the birth results in their dropping out of the labor force. This doesn't mean that any woman who stays home to care for a child is going to be a wreck. But leaving the work force means opting out of the benefits of being in it, and women should be aware of that.

As soon as a woman has any kind of difficulty—emotional, family, medical—the knee-jerk reaction is to get her off the job. No such solution is offered to men, despite the very real correlation for men between job stress and heart attacks.

What the myth of the miserable working woman obscures is the need to focus on how the *quality* of a woman's job affects her health. Media stories warn of the alleged dangers of fast-track jobs. But our *Lifeprints* study found that married women in high-prestige jobs were highest in mental well-being; another study of life stress in women reported that married career women with children suffered the least from stress. Meanwhile, few media tears are shed for the women most at risk: those in the word-processing room who have no control at work, low pay and little support at home.

Women don't need help getting out of the work force; they need help staying in it. As long as much of the media continues to capitalize on national ignorance, that help will have to come from somewhere else. (Not that an occasional letter to the editor isn't useful.) Men need to recognize that they are not just occasional helpers but vital to the success of the family unit. The corporate culture has to be reshaped so that it doesn't run totally according to patterns set by the white male workaholic. This will be good for men *and* women. The government can guarantee parental leave and affordable, available child care. (It did so in the '40s, when women were needed in the factories.) Given that Congress couldn't even get a bill guaranteeing *unpaid* family leave passed last year, this may take some doing. But hey, this is an election year.

Look Who's Talking About Work and Family

Rosalind Barnett and Caryl Rivers

Rosalind Barnett is a clinical psychologist. Caryl Rivers is a journalist based in Los Angeles.

We feminists have been saying for a long time that "women's issues" in the workplace are really people issues. Flextime, family leave, child care, the ability to work at home are not just for women, nor are they policies that only women want. But no matter how often we beg to differ, the idea still exists in corporations, in the media, and in our public agencies that families are women's responsibility. Part of the problem is that men have yet to speak up to demand benefits for themselves and their children. The other part is that the powers that be don't seem to believe that men care about this stuff. So it's time to hear from the men. A new study provides insight into that age-old question: What do men really want? Rosalind Barnett, of the Murray Research Center at Radcliffe College, and journalist Caryl Rivers present interesting news about modern men in this excerpt from their book based on Barnett's research: men define themselves more through their families and children than through their jobs and, just like women, men often find it difficult to balance work and family. Studies like this may be an important step in bringing women and men together to fight for greater flexibility at work.

—The Editors

The ghosts of old images still shape society's ideas about manhood. People believe that men are what they do. After all, the male quest is literature's great story. And the quintessential image of American manhood is the lone cowboy with little connection to women or children. No wonder the idea of work as a primary influence in men's lives holds sway. That view even dominates public policy on men's health. You will find volumes on the impact of work on men's health, but many of the most often-cited studies never even mention men's home lives.

Yet when researchers ask the right questions, the results are intriguing. Joseph Pleck, a University of Illinois psychologist, has conducted several studies on men and masculinity. In one, a representative study of U.S. men published in 1993, Pleck concluded that "men in contemporary industrial culture seek their primary emotional, personal, and spiritual gratification in the family setting." Another study showed that what happens to a man at midlife is influenced mainly by what's happening in his family. Pleck says that his research indicates that men experience their family life as far more psychologically significant than their jobs. Finally, our own study shows that as far as men's health is concerned, work and family play equally powerful roles.

But U.S. corporations still operate as if a job were more important to a man than his family. Companies run seminars on the dangers of Type A behavior, techniques to reduce stress at work, and time management. Barely a whisper is aimed at men about juggling home and work problems. Yet these issues have a huge impact on today's working man. In a Dupont company study conducted between 1985 and 1989, the percentage of men reporting difficulties managing work and family increased dramatically. A 1987 study of 1,200 employees in a Minneapolis company showed that a higher percentage of fathers than mothers reported both difficulties with child care and dual-career problems. And a study of two companies in the Northeast showed that 36 percent of fathers and 37 percent of mothers reported "a lot of stress" in balancing their work and family lives. For men, missing work when child care arrangements break down is more strongly associated with stress, poor health, and diminished well-being than it is for women.

In our study, the surprising finding—given the conventional wisdom—was that work turned out to be just as important to women as to men, and family life had as much impact on men's health as it did on women's—sometimes even more so. The study

five years earlier. The Dupont survey found that 56 percent of the company's male employees favored flexible schedules allowing more family time, and 40 percent would consider working for another employer who offered more flexibility. And a 1992 Canadian study

and State University looked at a number of variables in the lives of dual-earner couples—number of children, work hours, problems with kids and spouses, coping strategies—and found that, for men, the flexibility of their work schedules had the strongest impact on their lives. Having enough time to deal with family issues was linked to less distress on the job and in their marriages. Another study found that flexibility at work had more impact on men's stress levels than it did on women's.

Men's family life is far more psychologically significant for them than their jobs.

threw cold water on a number of accepted ideas:
• Work is the most critical factor in a man's health and happiness.
• Women bring the home problems with them to work; men tune everything else out while on the job.
• Problems with children have a greater impact on women than on men.

One of our most surprising findings was that problems in a man's relationship with his child have a significant impact on his physical health—while problems at his job do not. The men in our study who had the fewest worries about their relationships with their children also had the fewest health problems. Those who had the most troubled relationships with their children had the most health problems.

Men worried about their children's choice of friends, safety, and performance in school; they worried about whether they were being good fathers. The more of these worries that men had, the more they experienced such physical symptoms as insomnia, chest pain, lower back pain, indigestion, and rashes. Once we factored the quality of their relationships with their children into their health picture, job stress had no significant impact on men's health.

Because of the assumption that women are the ones worrying about home and hearth, flexibility has been ghettoized as a women's issue. But recent studies help debunk that notion. As reported by the *Wall Street Journal*, a 1993 study by the Families and Work Institute showed that one third of U.S. men under 40 would consider giving up raises and advancement for a better home life—twice the number who felt that way

of 20,000 male and female employees found that three quarters wanted more flexibility.

A 1991 study conducted by researchers at Virginia Polytechnic Institute

Still, many men equate being a father with bringing home the bacon—as do their bosses. Colin Harrison, an editor at *Harper's* magazine, wrote in the New York *Times*: "Even though parental leave is now law, I doubt that the nation's bosses have changed their opinions much since a 1986 survey cited by the Washington *Post*. When chief executives

first person

A READER AND HER JOB

BEFORE WE HAD OUR DAUGHTER, Erin who's four, and our son, Tory, who's almost three, my husband and I agreed that one of us would always stay home with the kids. For the first two years he did the child care, and now I've been doing it for two years. We don't have much money, but we're not into material things. People used to say, "Has Rick found a job yet?" Now they say to me, "Are you doing anything?"—as if I were watching TV and eating bonbons all alone.

When I went back to teaching after my first child, I missed holding my daughter. It's a little like an amputation: you've lost something, but still feel like it's there. But I didn't make the decision to stay home because it was hard to leave the baby. It was because I believe that only a parent can give a young child the best care. I'm following my mother's example; she raised six kids and that was the most important thing in her life. Of course, I had a choice, which she didn't have. I don't know if that makes it easier or harder.

I've often felt like the only feminist staying home with the kids. People assume that if you do this you're a traditional, conservative person. I just recently found the Feminist Mothers at Home site on the Internet. It turns out, there are so many of us, the site has a waiting list!

The hardest part about being at home is the constancy of it. I'm with the kids all the time. There's no chance for a break with other adults. Consulting is so much easier, it's almost like free time. Luckily, my husband knows he has it easier than I do and takes over when he comes home. When the kids start school, I'll spend more time consulting. If we have a third child, it will be Rick's turn to stay home.

As a feminist, I always find little pleasures in my day. Once, I told my daughter that the plumber was coming and she said, "When is she going to get here?" Another time, my son showed his toy screwdriver to Rick and said, "Look, I have tools just like Mommy."

and human resources directors at 1,500 of the nation's largest companies were asked what a reasonable length of time would be for paternity leave, 63 percent of those who responded said 'none.'"

Harrison describes his own "parental leave": "Although I work in a reasonably progressive office, as the birth of our first child neared, no one came to me and said, 'We hope you'll feel comfortable taking a few weeks off.' I asked about a paternal leave policy; there was none. So I arranged to take two weeks of vacation."

Which is exactly, research shows, what men do. They take sick time, vacation time—anything to deal with family needs or emergencies and not admit they're doing it. Joseph Pleck found that 87 percent of the fathers he studied reported taking days off when a child was born. Seventy-five percent of a sample of 1,395 fathers of newborns in Minnesota, Oregon, Rhode Island, and Wisconsin took leave from work. But fathers don't think of such arrangements as paternity leave. Why do they sneak around, avoiding formal paternity leave? Because the culture still doesn't think men ought to leave work to deal with kids.

Another reason that men adopt this informal leave is that they get paid days off, and most paternity leave is unpaid.

"Taking a formal parental leave almost always leads to loss of pay," notes Pleck, "a particularly important factor if the mother is also taking unpaid leave or leaving her job." Parental leave also requires getting formal approval, while the informal system can be managed by the employee on his own.

Our research shows that we must make it possible for working men and women to have the flexibility to see to the needs of children. Rigid policies in many workplaces make it nearly impossible for parents to respond to family emergencies or arrange to be with children at important times.

Should This Marriage Be Saved?

Many Americans are trying to make marriages more permanent—and divorce more difficult

ELIZABETH GLEICK

O N A CHILLY MONDAY NIGHT, Laura Richards and Mark Geyman are sitting in a living room in Jeffersonville, Indiana, their hands clasped tightly together in Laura's lap. This attractive, clean-cut couple met last May through a mutual friend and got engaged in November, and they are happy to tell John and Patti Thompson, their mentors in the St. Augustine Catholic Church's marriage-preparation program, all about their wedding plans. It will be a big June affair, Laura says, with eight bridesmaids and eight groomsmen, two flower girls, a ring bearer and two priests. Patti Thompson cuts through the chatter. "How much time have you put into your marriage?" she asks, adding pointedly, "Your wedding is just one day. Your marriage is the rest of your life."

The conversation grinds to a brief, awkward halt, then takes a turn into the wilderness—into the thicket of this young couple's most intimate concerns and darkest fears. Patti tells Laura, a 29-year-old department store salesclerk, that in her opinion it is O.K. to take birth-control pills on the advice of her doctor to help with PMS. Then John, coordinator of family ministry at St. Augustine, says, "Is either one of you jealous?"

"Yeah," admits Mark, who works in international customer service for United Parcel Service. He laughs and adds, "She gets jealous of some of the girls in the office," then explains how Laura once visited him at his previous job and became uncomfortable after she overheard him repeatedly compliment a female co-worker on her job performance. Laura smiles nervously, fidgets with a pen and says nothing.

Patti urges Laura and Mark to continue discussing Laura's jealousy when they are alone together. Soon the Thompsons hit upon other prickly topics: Mark's compulsive neatness and Laura's worry that her future mother-in-law has reservations about the pending nuptials.

After Mark and Laura leave, the first of four 90-minute sessions completed, the Thompsons—who have been married 31 years and have raised four children—offer an assessment of this couple's chances at marital harmony. It is based not just on gut impressions but also on a computer printout of the pair's "premarital inventory"— more than 100 questions about everything from the number of children they want to whether they are comfortable being naked in front of each other. Mark and Laura, who scored 72 out of 100 on this compatibility test, should do just fine, says Patti, but "there are just some things that smack you in the face that say they've got some work to do."

Working on a relationship, of course, is an activity that everyone—save for perhaps the most wildly romantic and misguided among us—has come to regard as a sometimes thrilling, sometimes infuriating, but always necessary exercise. But Mark and Laura, well meaning, full of love and hope, with their lives ahead of them and their family values just taking shape, are actually on the cutting edge—even if it is an old blade. Although the Catholic Church has always required engaged couples to undergo pre-Cana counseling—usually just one day of talks from a priest and a married couple about finances, communication and family planning—a more intensive form of preparation is coming into practice not only among Catholics but also among churchgoers of all denominations across America. Last November clergy in the Louisville, Kentucky, area became the 26th religious coalition in the U.S. to adopt standard premarital procedures that, in the words of the Kentuckiana

Marriage Task Force, express "the seriousness with which we view marriage and the preparation we are convinced is vital." Says Michael McManus, author of the 1993 *Marriage Savers* and a national leader of this particular bandwagon: "We're preventing bad marriages. If it is the job of a church to bond couples for life, it has to provide more help before and after."

If this new marital *gravitas* were simply a church-based phenomenon, it would not be a phenomenon at all; the clergy has traditionally attempted to shore up the moral foundations of people's private lives. But a growing recognition that marriages are not to be entered into—or dissolved— lightly because of the enormous social and economic costs is dawning in some unlikely places and crossing political lines. Conservatives who espouse "family values" have long lamented the trend toward throwaway marriage and quickie divorce. But in President Clinton's recent State of the Union speech he too took time out to introduce the Revs. John and Diana Cherry, whose ministry convinces couples "to come back together to save their marriages and to raise their kids." Meanwhile, there is a new sensitivity among divorce lawyers that breakups can have a devastating effect on everyone involved—and so comes a nudge toward reconciliation or mediation, lost revenues be damned! An increasing number of marital therapists believe it is their job to save the relationship rather than simply help each party pursue his or her chosen path.

Several people have gone so far as to suggest imposing a waiting period for marriage licenses, modeled after gun laws. "Both kinds of licenses," explains historian Glenda Riley, author of *Divorce: An American Tradition*, "create a volatile situation." And just last week, a group of mostly female state lawmakers in Washington introduced a bill that would require marriage licenses to come with warnings about spousal abuse. "I would say, simply, 'Beware. Stop, look, listen and be cautious,' " said state senator Margarita Prentice, a co-sponsor of the bill, which is expected to pass the Democratic Senate but run into trouble in the Republican House. "Marriage is serious business."

In 1993, 2.3 million couples—in living rooms and city halls, in churches and synagogues and backyards, on mountaintops and while scuba diving—performed that most optimistic of human rituals and got married. That same year, 1.2 million couples agreed, officially, that their marriages could not be saved. Again in 1993, the Bureau of the Census projected that four out of 10 first marriages would end in divorce. Indeed, the number of divorces began soaring in the mid-60s and has declined only slightly since peaking at a little over 1.2 million in 1981. Thus, despite sporadic cheers about falling divorce rates, couples have not gotten much better at staying together—not yet anyway. Divorce, Glenda Riley claims, reflects the true American spirit; after the country achieved independence, she says, people wrote divorce petitions that read something like: "My husband is tyrannical. If the U.S. can get rid of King George, I can get rid of him."

THE INSTITUTION OF MARRIAGE underwent a particularly rebellious and dramatic shift when women entered the work force. "People don't have to stay married because of economic forces now," explains Frank Furstenberg Jr., co-author of the 1991 Divided Families and a sociology professor at the University of Pennsylvania who has been studying divorce for 20 years. "We're in the midst of trying to renegotiate what the marriage contract is—what men and women are supposed to do as partners." But the chips in these negotiations are often young children, emotionally fragile, economically vulnerable—for despite their work outside the home, most women still suffer a severe income drop after divorce. The by-product of what remains the world's highest divorce rate is millions of children thrown into poverty, millions more scarred by bifurcated lives and loyalties.

Almost no one disputes there are many valid reasons for divorce—among them, domestic violence, child abuse and substance abuse. Mere incompatibility seems reason enough, when no children are involved. But the breakup of families is increasingly seen not only as a personal tragedy but also as a social crisis. Which may be why, suddenly, there seems to be so much attention being paid to preventing divorce. "We're seeing a trend in the past couple of years toward cou-

ples doing more work to preserve and strengthen relationships," says Froma Walsh, co-director of the Center for Family Health at the University of Chicago.

Certainly marital therapy has become big business in the past decade or so, though few hard figures are available. Some 4.6 million couples a year visit 50,000 licensed family therapists, up from 1.2 million in 1980. Thousands of couples swear by such programs as PAIRS (Practical Application of Intimate Relationship Skills), the semester-long relationship class offered by the PAIRS Foundation in 50 U.S. cities (as well as 16 other countries), or Retrouvaille, a church-sponsored program in which couples who have weathered their own marital difficulties run weekend seminars for other couples in trouble.

"People are poorly trained for marriage today," says Joyce Clark, a coordinator for Retrouvaille in Youngstown, Ohio. From her 34-year marriage she recognizes all the stages of matrimony: romance, casual irritation, (he doesn't put the toilet seat down; she stays on the phone too long), then total disillusionment. "This is when many couples decide to bail out. They don't realize that they can still work back to romance," says Clark, who suffered through five years of misery after discovering her husband Pat had had an affair. Then she and Pat attended a Retrouvaille weekend and learned how to forgive, how to get over it—and how to fight. "Everyone I knew who had the same problem was divorced," says Joyce of the crisis in her marriage. "I wanted to find one person who survived and was in good shape. Now we work in the movement because somebody out there is waiting to see us."

Perhaps the newest, and most unlikely, recruits in the battle against divorce are lawyers. Last fall Lynne Gold-Bikin, a divorce attorney in Norristown, Pennsylvania, who chairs the family law division of the American Bar Association, founded the Preserving Marriages Project. "Divorce lawyers as individuals have no vested interest in saving marriages," Gold-Bikin says. "It's not our business. But we know the problems more than anyone else. Every day we see kids being yanked back and forth. Enough. I'm sick of people not recognizing what they're doing."

Last October, Gold-Bikin took her project—to which some 3200 lawyers have contributed time and money—to more than 50 high-school classrooms nationwide. During five sessions, juniors and seniors do role-playing exercises and homework designed to give an overview of family law and show how difficult it can be to maintain a serious relationship. "We're trying to teach these things to kids because many are not learning them at home," Gold-Bikin says. In March, Gold-Bikin will conduct a weekend seminar for couples who have been married one year; after that, she hopes to create a marriage-

Taking Stock

PREPARE (Premarital Personal and Relationship Evaluation), a set of 125 questions developed by University of Minnesota family social science professor David Olson to assess a couple's compatibility, has been administered to some 500,000 couples worldwide. The results are computer scored, and, claims Olson, can determine with 80% to 85% accuracy which couples will divorce. "Ten percent [of those who take the inventory] are so shocked by their poor scores, they break their engagement," contends Michael McManus, author of Marriage Savers. *"That can be painful, but much less painful than a divorce with two kids." Individuals are asked if they · "Agree Strongly," "Agree," are "Undecided," "Disagree," or "Disagree Strongly" with statements such as the following:*

▶ I believe most disagreements we currently have will decrease after marriage.

▶ I expect that some romantic love will fade after marriage.

▶ I am concerned about my partner's drinking/smoking.

▶ I wish my partner was more careful in spending money.

▶ I am satisfied with the amount of affection I receive from my partner.

▶ My partner and I sometimes disagree regarding our interest in sex.

▶ I have some concerns about how my partner will be as a parent.

▶ We disagree on whether the husband's occupation should be a top priority in deciding where we live.

▶ I can easily share my positive and negative feelings with my partner.

▶ My partner is less interested in talking about our relationship than I am.

▶ We have some important disagreements that never seem to get resolved.

▶ I enjoy spending some time alone without my partner.

▶ At times I feel pressure to participate in activities my partner enjoys.

▶ My partner and I agree on how much we will share the household chores.

▶ We sometimes disagree on how to practice our religious beliefs.

preservation program for corporations, which she claims suffer tremendous productivity losses because of divorce.

All such efforts are applauded by Judith Wallerstein, the California clinical psychologist who first raised public consciousness about the lasting damage of divorce. After studying 131 children of divorce over a span of 15 years, she found them to be at higher risk for depression, poor grades, substance abuse and intimacy problems. "We started to report this," she says, "and people got angry. They said, 'Impossible! If it's good for the parents, it's good for the children.' They wanted to believe that divorce and women's lib would take care of everything."

Though Wallerstein's results are debatable, they have definitely seeped into the zeitgeist and affected not only efforts to stay married but also how people approach divorce. More and more often, couples are seeking to avoid ugly fights over custody, property and money. A St. Louis, Missouri, couple who do not want their names used are dissolving their marriage after 17 years, two daughters, couples therapy and individual counseling. They have chosen to use a mediator and work out the details at the kitchen table. "It's a much healthier environment for [the children]," says the wife, a Presbyterian minister. "They see that we still treat each other with respect." The six- to eight-month process will cost $2,500 and produce a divorce decree, a property agreement and a parenting plan to be submitted for court approval.

On the state level too, there is a growing belief that if divorcing couples cannot reconcile, they should at least be taught how to split in a reasonable fashion. Bucking the trend to make divorce ever easier and quicker, Utah and Connecticut have mandatory education programs for all parents of minor children entering the family court. Six states are considering such regulations in a current session of their legislature. "This is the latest trend in family courts," says Michael Pitts, who until recently was executive director of the Children's Rights Council in Washington, "and it is a lasting one."

In many other states, including Maryland, Virginia, New Jersey and Florida, divorce-education classes are required in some counties, or at the discretion of some family court judges. Some family judges have even taken it upon themselves to involve the children directly. As of last November, divorcing parents in Dade County, Florida, attend one mandatory course, while children attend another, called Kids in Divorce Succeeding (KIDS). Sherri Thrower, a 30-year-old mother of five, says the parenting classes have really helped her. "There were a lot of cobwebs in my mind," she says. "A lot of confusion." She and her husband tried several times to reconcile for the sake of the children, but the attempts ultimately failed. Now her main concern is for her kids. "I don't want to teach them anything bad about their father," she says. "My son has been missing him more and more. He doesn't know how to deal with it." Thrower's children have attended the KIDS program, which uses a curriculum called Sandcastles.

IN SANDCASTLES THE CHILDREN ARE divided into small groups by age, and each group is run by a therapist and a teacher. Older children may write poems, do role-playing or create their own talk shows, while the younger kids draw pictures of their families and talk about them, or write letters to their parents and read them aloud. "When you come home from court, I want you to have a happy face, not a sad one," reads Edward, 10, during the Saturday morning session. "Mom, I love you. Dad, I miss you," says Dave. Another child reads, "If you were divorced, you wouldn't fight. I wish you were divorced." Explains psychotherapist Gary Neuman, who developed Sandcastles: "When kids see there are all these other kids experiencing the same type of things, it immediately alleviates the intense feelings of isolation children of divorce experience."

Though the Federal Government has no jurisdiction over marriage and divorce, indirectly the impact of federal programs is enormous. Current welfare policy, for example, pays AFDC benefits only when there is no man in the house, thus fueling divorce and abandonment. And in a broader sense says University of California, Berkeley, sociology professor Arlie Hochschild, author of the landmark study about two-career marriages, *The Second Shift*, "we do not have a family-friendly society." Better day care, plentiful jobs at decent wages, flex-time and job sharing would all help to reduce the stresses on American households, which are overtaxed, overburdened and overwhelmed. And while entering into marriage with the utmost care and deepest consideration can only be to the good, it may be marriage itself—along with the most basic institutions like the workplace—that continues to need refining. "I would say we're in a stalled revolution," says Hochschild, "Women have gone into the labor force, but not much else has changed to adapt to that new situation. We have not rewired the notion of manhood so that it makes sense to men to participate at home. Marriage then becomes the shock absorber of those strains."

Mark Geyman and Laura Richards are convinced that they are increasingly prepared to handle those strains. Since they began meeting with Patti and John Thompson, says Mark, "we have done a lot of talking, more than we were." They have had conversations about whose family they will see during holidays and how they will handle their finances. And they have tried to grapple with the problem of Laura's jealousy. "It's been helpful," says Mark. "I think she's beginning to open up a little more. She's being more trusting." The fact that one of Laura's sisters is going through a divorce makes the idea of building a secure marriage from the outset feel all the more urgent to this young couple. And in spite of the problems that have begun to crop up during a time when they wish only to focus on the excitement of planning a wedding, Laura insists she is looking into her future with, well, a somewhat tempered confidence. As she puts it, "I'm still sure we want to get married, and everything."

—Reported by
Ann Blackman/Washington, Gideon Gil/Jeffersonville,
Jenifer Mattos/New York, Elizabeth B. Mullen/San
Francisco, Sophfronia Scott Gregory/Miami, and
Leslie Whitaker/Chicago

THE POLITICS
OF
DIVORCE

That broken marriages create a societal cost is now a matter of

consensus. How to reduce it is a subject of ferocious dispute.

ROB GURWITT

Rob Gurwitt can be reached by e-mail at robbg@well.com.

Not long ago, *Consumer Reports* decided to ask its readers how they felt about lawyers. The magazine had them rate the help they'd received for everything from preparing their wills to writing prenuptial agreements. Some 30,000 people responded, and on most fronts at least a slight majority—in a somewhat surprising turn of events—pronounced themselves happy. Only one legal arena, in fact, prompted more than half of the people responding to say they were dissatisfied. They were the ones who had been involved in di-

vorce and child custody cases.

Yet if the people who've been through a divorce feel cheapened by the legal rigmarole, you should hear the people who deal with divorce—or with its results— professionally. Take Barry Schneider, the presiding domestic relations judge in Maricopa County Superior Court, in Phoenix. "We encourage people to go out and put together their diaries of every petty offense they can think of," he says, with an edge to his voice. "I mean, I hear trials on diaper counts: Who changes more diapers, who get up for midnight feedings. We make them catalogue these inadequacies and then keep poking and keep poking. We fuel their anger and animosity. Sometimes I want to bang them on the head and say,

'What, are you nuts? Look what you're doing to each other and your kids!' "

Or Jessie Dalman, a Republican state representative in Michigan, who, first as a county commissioner and now as a state legislator, has found herself working with social service professionals trying to deal with the aftermath of divorce and with the courts on how to improve the divorce process. "After I came to the legislature," she says, "there were some hearings on reforming the friend-of-the-court system. I went to one, and sat through six hours of testimony. You listen to all of that, and you think, 'There's 169 people here that testified, and I've never heard such misery in my life! There's *got* to be a better way to resolve conflict in couples.' "

There has always been a great deal of anger and frustration surrounding the whole subject of divorce. There always will be. But at the moment, there is something more—a mounting crusade to do something about it. Talk radio, network television, and op-ed pages of the *New York Times*—all are filled with conversation about the effects of divorce and the conviction that they need to be addressed. "There is an increasing belief that the divorce revolution has failed," says David Blankenhorn, president of the Institute for American Values and a leading voice among those pressing for a renewed focus on keeping families intact. "There's just a weariness with the whole thing."

And so, pushed in no small part by people like Schneider and Dalman, divorce is elbowing its way onto the legislative agenda. Over the past two years, the number of marriage- and divorce-related bills in state legislatures has skyrocketed, jumping from an inconsiderable number in 1994 to some 500 measures last year and again to 750 this year, although that figure includes some bills that were carried over from last year's session. "I've been covering this issue since 1991," says Jeanne Mejeur, a program principal at the National Conference of State Legislatures who analyzes family-related legislation, "and it's never been like this."

To be sure, some legislatures are doing little more than tinkering, stiffening the penalties for failing to pay child support, for instance, or changing the procedures for determining alimony. But there are more ambitious undertakings afoot as well. Dalman, along with Republican Governor Terry E. Branstad of Iowa, is at the fore of a movement to make divorces harder to get. Schneider is taking part in a widespread effort to change the laws to force divorcing parents to pay more attention to the needs—and future prospects—of their children. Some states are considering lengthening the waiting period before a couple can get a divorce or requiring couples who file for divorce to get counseling, and in a handful, legislators are taking on the even more ambitious task of trying to head off divorce by inducing couples to think before they marry: They are drawing up bills to encourage, or even require, premarital counseling.

In essence, state legislatures have emerged as the battleground for a fundamental reassessment of the place of divorce in a healthy society. In the welter of bills that lawmakers have crammed into the hopper, a debate is taking shape between those who argue that divorce, in and of itself, has been harmful to families and communities and needs to be curtailed, and those who believe that changing the *process* can remedy, or at least lessen, its more damaging effects. It is an argument that pits those who believe society must again begin thinking of divorce in moral terms against those who argue that the real issue is the way divorce is conducted.

There was a time, not very long ago, when a genuine consensus on this subject seemed to exist in America: The sole task for legislators was to make divorce easier. "Many books and papers and academic speeches were devoted to putting forward ideas about why this was good," says David Blankenhorn. "Among the reasons were that it would improve marriage by helping people get out of bad relationships and find a better one; it would help reduce the incidence of domestic violence; it would free us from these rigid institutional constraints and allow people to find happiness in a mate; children would be better off because, although there might be initial dislocation, in the long run they would be happier because their parents would be happier. Well, you know, each one of those promises has proven to be empty."

Yet if public disillusionment with divorce focused only on its impact on adults' lives—if, in other words, the only people a divorcing couple affected were themselves—it's doubtful that divorce would be drawing the kind of attention it has enjoyed of late. The fact is, though, slightly more than half of the couples going through a divorce every year have children, which translates into a little over 1 million children each year who are involved in divorces, according to the National Center for Health Statistics. So even though the divorce rate has declined some 10 percent from its peak in 1980, the number of children who have been affected by a divorce mounts considerably with every passing year.

And it is now pretty much beyond argument that divorce exacts a social cost in its impact on children. That notion first came to widespread notice through the pioneering work of Judith Wallerstein, a California psychologist who studied 131 children of divorcing couples over a 15-year period. She found them, on the whole, to be at greater risk than children in two-parent families for a range of problems, from depression to poor grades to substance abuse. Further studies have shown a correlation with crime, out-of-wedlock births and a general difficulty as adults in forming stable relationships, either with other adults or with the community as a whole. "The children of divorce have not been served by this process," says Blankenhorn. "They've been damaged. The evidence is overwhelming that this has maimed an entire generation of children."

The legal system is largely powerless to stand in the way of couples who cannot get along; the focus ought to be on making sure they don't hurt their children.

It is such sentiments that have fueled the efforts of Dalman and Branstad, who have garnered much attention for their efforts to repeal no-fault divorce. In truth, Dalman has introduced a package of bills that looks much like the state of the art on divorce policy these days: a requirement that couples applying for a marriage license either receive pre-marital counseling or pay more for their license; mandatory attendance at a divorce education program in cases where children are involved; a requirement that divorcing parents file a plan showing how they intend to carry out their responsibilities as parents after the divorce.

It is Dalman's main bill, though, that has occasioned most of the controversy. Her measure in Michigan—which forms the basis for the move to repeal no-fault divorce in Iowa, and has spurred similar efforts in Georgia, Kentucky, Illinois, Washington and several other states—declares that where one partner in a couple does not want a divorce, the person seeking to end the marriage has to demonstrate grounds: whether adultery, substance abuse, the imprisonment of his or her spouse, long-term physical or mental abuse, or desertion. "The focus," she says, "is to do two things: to support the institution of marriage and the marriage contract; and to support the party who doesn't want the divorce—that was the party that was most harmed by the no-fault reforms that went through in the '70s."

This attention to no-fault comes in large part because critics such as Dalman trace today's uncomfortably high divorce rate—the U.S. Census Bureau estimates that four of every 10 first-time marriages end in divorce—to the start of the so-called "no-fault revolution" in 1969, the year that the governor of California, Ronald Reagan, signed the first such bill into law. Over the next few years, every other state followed suit. In a *New York Times* op-ed article late last year, former White House domestic policy adviser William A. Galston brought the matter to the national stage by lamenting the adverse impact of divorce on children and calling for a return to tougher legal standards for obtaining a divorce. "In the end," he wrote, "it comes down to a moral question. Is our society willing to put the well-being of children first, even when it may conflict with adult desires and restrain our passion for autonomy?"

Standing in the way of such arguments is a loose collection of family law attorneys and feminist thinkers who worry that bills like Dalman's will make it harder for women trapped in marriages they don't like to escape them. "The reason no-fault swept across the country," says Michael Robbins, the former chair of the Michigan bar's family law section and a leading opponent of Dalman's no-fault measure, "was a recognition on the part of individuals and legislators that no law had the power to force people to stay together when they didn't want to. Before 1969, under the fault system, people were saying and doing almost anything to get around the law."

Yet Robbins also recognizes that Dalman's and similar measures are less about the legal advisability of assigning fault in divorce cases than they are about putting barriers in the way of divorce. And that, he argues, is pointless. "You can't legislate morality, you can't legislate friendliness and you can't legislate people getting along," he says. "The problem isn't divorce; divorce is the result of other problems, and if you want to reduce the divorce rate, you need to identify them. Simply saying, 'You can't get a divorce!' isn't going to eliminate the problems that resulted in those people wanting to get a divorce in the first place."

I t is this sense, that the legal system is largely powerless to stand in the way of couples who cannot get along, that drives those who believe the conduct of divorce cases, rather than the institution itself, needs changing. These critics argue that since we can't—or shouldn't—keep people from divorcing, our focus ought to be on making sure they don't hurt their children.

There are plenty of critics who believe that the legal process of divorce itself plays a role in harming children.

The notion that this might be possible also finds its foundation in recent social science scholarship. Just as Wallerstein's work paints a grim picture of the emotional wreckage left behind by divorce, there is also a respectable body of research that suggests that divorce need not be an

unmitigated calamity for children.

"When we look at young adults whose parents divorce, there's no question that they're at higher risk of mental health problems and other difficulties," says Andrew Cherlin, a Johns Hopkins University sociologist who studies the issue. "Even so, most of them don't actually show those difficulties. So while it's a mistake to say that divorce doesn't hurt kids, the data also contradict the belief that divorce is inevitably a disaster for most children." The work of Cherlin and others suggests that the roots of many children's problems may lie with family conflict, economic instability or other difficulties that were present before their parents got divorced.

Moreover, there are plenty of critics who believe that the legal process of divorce, with its high drama, incitement of conflict and emotional hostage-taking, itself plays a role in harming children. "My reading of the research, and my own research, tells me it's not so much the divorce itself as certain mediating factors that determine whether divorce will have highly negative effects," says Edward Kruk, an associate professor of social work at the University of British Columbia. "If you want to ameliorate the impact of divorce, the key factors are reducing conflict between parents, maintaining parenting roles and responsibilities and meaningful relations between parents and children, and providing children support through the transition."

This is where people such as Barry Schneider come in. "Adjudication as a system of dispute resolution doesn't really fit family disputes," he says. "A family situation needs to address questions of the future. Instead, what we have are custody fights, and merely by defining it in those terms, we've lost. The only way we can make it better is by getting through to parents that it's not a proprietary issue of who's entitled to these kids, but that they've got to become better citizens and better parents. They've got to grow up." And so he is backing efforts in Arizona to require that divorcing parents take a class on the effects of divorce on children.

"Divorce education" is, in fact, becoming increasingly common. Utah and Connecticut both require it; Indiana, Mississippi, North Carolina, Texas and a slew of other states are considering it; and counties in many states—a dozen new ones each month, at the current rate—are going ahead on their own and adding either voluntary or mandated programs for divorcing parents. Typically, these last anywhere from two to six hours and look at how children react to divorce, the best ways to manage conflict, and the long-term psychological benefits of an amicable process.

"It is not group therapy," says Rob Chestnut, a federal prosecutor in Alexandria, Virginia, who was one of the moving forces behind his state's legislation giving judges the ability to require such classes. "The seminar presumes you're getting a divorce. It tries to get parents to focus on what's happening from a kid's perspective." Even so, says Bob Marshall, a Republican member of the Virginia House of Delegates who sponsored the measure, the seminars sometimes wind up damping the urge to separate. "What we wanted to do was let parents know they've got to go the extra mile and pay attention to their children," he says, "to tell them that the obligation to nurture doesn't cease with the signing of the divorce decree. But sometimes, when parents see what divorce does to kids, they rethink their separation. At least, it's happened enough to make mention of it."

There is a somewhat related effort that is also gathering steam around the country. It focuses on requiring parents to develop so-called "parenting plans" before the divorce can be granted. These bills, which have surfaced in New Jersey, Maryland, Florida and Maine, among other states, are modeled on legislation that went into effect in Washington State in 1988. They are a genuine effort to get at a particularly difficult problem: the fact that some 50 percent of the divorced parents who are not granted custody—mostly men—simply drop out of their children's lives. "The worst thing that can happen to a child post-divorce is that one of the parents disappears," says Wade Horn, director of the National Fatherhood Initiative, an organization based in Lancaster, Pennsylvania, aimed at combating fatherlessness. "Children seem to do best following divorce if both parents make real the statement that most parents say to them: 'We're divorcing each other, not you.'"

Horn points to the pioneering work of Charles Ballard, the Cleveland social worker whose Institute for Responsible Fatherhood has achieved great success in getting unmarried fathers to pay child support by focusing on connecting them emotionally with their children. "What most child-support agencies do is they establish paternity, then get a child support award in place, then get the father to start paying, and *then* worry about things like getting the father involved," says Horn. "Courts do the same thing in divorce cases. They say, 'The first thing we'll do is get child support arrangements in place, then we'll make sure you're paying, and then, if we have any energy left over, we'll worry about whether you're getting enough visitation.' Well, they should take a lesson from Charles Ballard, and say, 'The first thing we're going to do is decide how we're going to keep both of you involved in your child's life.'"

The question, of course, is how much of an impact parenting plans and divorce education will have on children's well-being in the long run. Robert Levy, a professor at the University of Minnesota Law School who teaches family law, argues that they may work for many couples, but that it would be a mistake for society to pin its hopes on them. "There are a sufficient number of fathers who aren't sufficiently interested in their kids and of mothers who are either abused or hate their former husbands,"

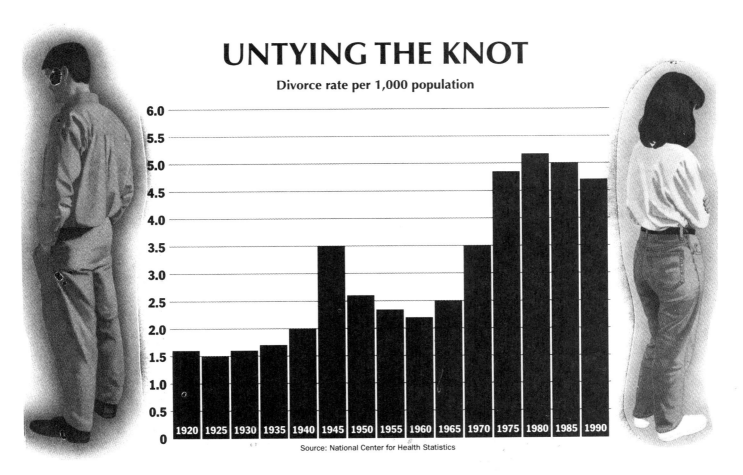

UNTYING THE KNOT

Divorce rate per 1,000 population

| 1920 | 1925 | 1930 | 1935 | 1940 | 1945 | 1950 | 1955 | 1960 | 1965 | 1970 | 1975 | 1980 | 1985 | 1990 |

Source: National Center for Health Statistics

4. **CRISES: Divorce and Remarriage**

he says, "that the likelihood of transforming the entire divorced population into one in which both parents share time and share parenting responsibilities is living in a fairy tale."

Indeed, in the rush to legislate new divorce arrangements, not many people seem to be asking just how effective legislation to change the divorce laws can be in the first place. It is an issue that both conservatives and liberals might ponder, albeit for different reasons.

Frank Furstenberg, a University of Pennsylvania sociologist who has been studying the impact of divorce for some 20 years, argues that if the goal of legislators is to tilt society in favor of healthy family life, divorce is probably the wrong target. "There's nothing I know of to suggest that these kinds of legal practices can create the condition of stable, well-functioning families," he says. "The kinds of things that we know create dissension, conflict and stress in a family require a different sort of medicine. But it's not a medicine that most legislators are very sympathetic to prescribing: child care support, income support, more generous parental leave, reducing conflict between work and family. All of those things are clearly ways of our society demonstrating its commitment to helping families support their children, and we seem to be retreating from them."

Horn, by contrast, believes that such steps as parenting plans, divorce education and repealing no-fault can all help, but that the final answers lie in society at large, in changing a culture that has come to accept divorce as a legitimate option in too many circumstances. "The fact that some kids do OK with divorce," he says, "should not be our guide; just because some kids grow up OK in Bosnia doesn't mean that growing up in Bosnia is to be recommended. We need to decide that divorce is a bad thing, and that it has bad consequences for children. We need to restigmatize it."

In the meantime, it may not be a bad thing that no clear answers to the divorce dilemma seem to have asserted themselves. Some states over the next few years may well repeal no-fault. Others will leave it intact but try to ensure that divorces do as little harm as possible. Taken together, in other words, the states will be serving their purpose as laboratories of social change. A few years down the road, we should be able to compare the results.

lessons from stepfamilies

Yes, they are more complicated. But they're also richer. Stepfamilies turn out to be living laboratories for what it takes to create successful relationships. They have surprising things to tell us all about marriage, gender relations, parenting, and the intricacies of family life.

Virginia Rutter

Virginia Rutter is a freelance writer living in Seattle who reports on family, marital, and sex research, among other things. She has worked as public affairs director at the Johns Hopkins School of Public Health and the American Association for Marriage and Family Therapy. She is currently coordinating a project on collaborative, psychosocial health care.

Here we are, three decades into the divorce revolution, and we still don't quite know what to make of stepfamilies. We loved the Brady Bunch, but that was before we discovered how unreal they were. Now that stepfamilies embrace one of three children and, one way or another, impact the vast majority of Americans, we can't seem to get past seeing them as the spawn of failure, the shadow side of our overidealized traditional family. When we think of them at all, we see only what they are not—hence their designation as "nontraditional" families, heaped with unwed moms, gay parents, and other permutations that make up the majority of families today. By the year 2000, stepfamilies will outnumber all other family types.

Despite their ambiguous standing, stepfamilies are getting first-class attention from social scientists. Much of what they are discovering is eye-opening. Although, for example, it is widely known that second marriages are less stable than first ones—with a break-up rate of 60 percent, versus 50 percent for first marriages—that statistic paints stepfamilies with too broad a brush; it conceals their very real success. A far more useful, more important fact is that stepfamilies do indeed face instability, but that shakiness occurs early in the re-

marriage—and may ultimately be traced to lack of support from the culture. In denying them the status of "real family," we may be doing much to undermine their chances of success. Nevertheless, once remarriage families make it over the early hurdle, they are even stronger than traditional families.

Let this turnabout truth serve as a metaphor for what is now coming to light about stepfamilies. They are certainly more complex than first-marriage families—but they are also richer. New information about what really goes on, and what goes wrong, in stepfamilies will definitely change the way you think about them. It also promises to change the way you think about *all* families. Among the new findings:

• Contrary to myth, stepfamilies have a high rate of success in raising healthy children. Eighty percent of the kids come out fine.

• These stepkids are resilient, and a movement to study their resilience—not just their problems—promises to help more kids succeed in any kind of family, traditional or otherwise.

• What trips stepkids up has little to do with stepfamilies per se. The biggest source of problems for kids in stepfamilies is parental conflict leftover from the first marriage.

•A detailed understanding of the specific problems stepfamilies encounter now exists, courtesy of longitudinal research—not studies that tap just the first six months of stepfamily adjustment.

•Stepfamilies turn out to be a gender trap—expectations about women's roles and responsibilities are at the root of many problems that develop in stepfamilies.

•After five years, stepfamilies are more stable than first-marriage families, because second marriages are happier than first marriages. Stepfamilies experience most of their troubles in the first two years.

•Stepfamilies are not just make-do households limping along after loss. All members experience real gains, notably the opportunity to thrive under a happier relationship.

•The needs of people in stepfamilies are the needs of people in all families—to be accepted, loved, and cared about; to maintain attachments; to belong to a group and not be a stranger; and to feel some control by maintaining order in their lives. It's just that these needs are made acutely visible—and unavoidable—in stepfamilies.

THE MYTHS AND THE RESEARCH

Despite the prevalence of stepfamilies, myths about them abound. You probably know some of them: There's an Evil Stepmother, mean, manipulative, and jealous. The stepfather is a molester, a sexual suspect—Woody Allen. The ex-wife is victimized, vindictive, interfering—a She-Devil. The ex-husband is withdrawn, inept, the contemporary Absentee Father. And the kids are nuisances intent on ruining their parents' lives; like Maisie in Henry James' story of 19th century post-divorce life, they play the parents and stepparents like billiard balls.

The familiarity of these myths can't be blamed solely on Dan Quayle, nor on nostalgia for the 1950s. Stepfamilies are a challenge. There are attachments that must be maintained through a web of conflicting emotions. There are ambiguities of identity, especially in the first years. Adults entering stepfamilies rightly feel anxious about their performance in multiple roles (spouse, instant parent) and about their acceptance by the kids and by the ex-spouse, who must remain a caring parent to the children. When an ex-spouse's children become someone else's stepchildren and spend time in a "stranger's" home, he or she worries about the children's comfort, their role models—and their loyalty.

Out of this worry are born the mythic stereotypes—and the fear of reliving a bad fairy tale. A stepmother, for example, forced to take on the role of disciplinarian because the children's biological father may lack a clear understanding of his own responsibilities—is set up to be cast as evil.

> ## 'Stepfamilies turn out to be a gender trap—expectations about women's roles are at the root of many problems that develop in stepfamilies.'

Still, there is a growing recognition among researchers that for every real pitfall a myth is built on, stepfamilies offer a positive opportunity in return. Researchers and stepfamilies are asking questions about resilience and health, not just pathology. In "The Family In Transition," a special issue of the *Journal of Family Psychology* in June 1993, editors and stepfamily researchers Mavis Hetherington, Ph.D., and James Bray, Ph.D., explained it this way: "Although divorce and remarriage may confront families with stresses and adaptive challenges, they also offer opportunities for personal growth and more harmonious, fulfilling family and personal relationships. Contemporary research is focusing on the diversity of responses to divorce, life in a single-parent household, and remarriage."

It is now clear from detailed research that the adaptation to stepfamily relation-ships depends on the timing of the transition in the children's lives, the individuals involved, and the unique changes and stresses presented to the group.

THE 80 PERCENT WHO SUCCEED

Take Hetherington's research, considered the definitive, longitudinal study of post-divorce families, conducted at the University of Virginia. She found that children in post-divorce and remarriage families may experience depression, conduct disorders, lower academic performance, and delinquency. Such problems are the result of reductions in parental attention that may immediately follow divorce or remarriage. There are the distractions of starting a new marriage. Such lapses may also be the outgrowth of parental conflict. They may reflect a noncustodial parent's withdrawal from the scene altogether. There's the stress of reductions in resources—typically, the lowered income of divorced mothers—and the disruption of routines, so highly valued by children, when two residences are established.

Hetherington, however, is quick to point to her finding that 80 percent of children of divorce and remarriage do *not* have behavior problems, despite the expectations and challenges, compared to 90 percent of children of first marriage families. Kids whose parents divorce and remarry are not doomed.

This high success rate, Hetherington and others recognize, is a testament to the resilience of children. Further study, she believes, can teach us more about the strengths summoned up in stepfamilies—and how to support them. But that would also contradict the gloom-and-doom scenarios that, though they do not actually describe most stepfamilies, often get trotted out on state occasions.

Needless to say, scientifically researching strength and resilience in stepfamilies, complete with a control group, poses great challenges. Building a scientific model of stepfamilies isn't simply trying to pin down a moving target, it's like trying to pin down many moving targets—up to four sets of kids from previous marriages in as many residences at different times—with none of them on the same radar screen at once.

From the standpoint of the kids, yes, they feel loss going into a stepfamily—it certifies that their original family exists no more. And it takes time to adjust to a new set of people in family roles. But the new arrangement is not just a problem appearing in their lives by default. Elizabeth Carter, M.S.W., director of the Westches-ter Family Institute, points to specific opportunities a stepfamily affords. Children acquire multiple role models, they get a chance to see their parents happier with other people than they were with each other. They learn how to be flexible.

Because they come into the world with no relationship ties but must forge their own, stepfamilies provide a living laboratory for studying what makes all families successful, insists psychologist Emily Visher, Ph.D., who cofounded the Stepfamily Association of America in 1979 with her husband, psychiatrist John Visher, M.D., after finding herself in a stepfamily and no rules to go by. For their pioneering efforts, the Vishers jointly received a Lifetime Contribution Award from the American Association for Marriage and Family Therapy at its annual meeting last fall.

Addressing an audience packed to the rafters in a mammoth sports arena, Visher

> ## 'Stepfamilies provide lessons for all families, because their emotions and problems are common—but they are exposed by an open structure.'

emphasized that "stepfamilies provide lessons for all families, because their emotions and problems are common to all people—but they are exposed by the open structure of stepfamilies." The process of bonding and belonging is made entirely, sometimes painfully, visible.

THE COPARENTING FACTOR

It turns out that it's the parents, not the stepfamily, that make the most difference in the success of stepfamilies.

"Remember, divorce isn't ending the family. It is restructuring it," explains Carter. "Parents and children don't get divorced. Parents and children aren't an optional relationship. One of the biggest issues for stepfamilies is: How can we stay in touch?" The steady, regular involvement of both biological parents in their children's lives come what may is known in the family biz as coparenting.

Today's most familiar stepfamily setup is a mother and her biological children living with a man who is not their birth father, and a noncustodial father in another residence—although the dilemmas of maintaining parenting responsibilities are much more complicated than who lives with whom. The U.S. Bureau of the Census reports that 14 percent of children in stepfamilies live with their biological father, 86 percent live with their biological mother and their stepfather. Whatever the situation, the parents' job is to find a way to stay in touch with each other so that both can remain completely in touch with their children.

Study after study shows that divorce and remarriage do not harm children—parental conflict does. That was the conclusion of research psychologists Robert Emery, Ph.D., of the University of Virginia, and Rex Forehand, Ph.D., of the University of Georgia, in a 1993 review of the divorce research. Sociologist Andrew Cherlin, Ph.D., author of the classic *Divided Families,* reported in *Science* magazine that children with difficulty after divorce started having problems long before divorce took place, as a result of parental conflict.

While divorce forces temporary disruption and a period of adjustment to loss and to new routines, marital conflict produces long-term disturbances. Depression and anger, often acted out in behavior problems, substance abuse, and delinquency, are all especially common among children in families where conflict rages. Following divorce, adversarial coparenting or the withdrawal of one of the parents from his or her (but usually his) role undermines children's healthy development.

The solution, of course, is cooperation of the parents in coparenting following divorce and remarriage. Desirable as it is, cooperative parenting between divorced spouses is rare, attained only in a minority of cases, Hetherington and Bray note.

WHY IS COPARENTING SO DIFFICULT?

Most marriages don't end mutually with friendship—so jealousy and animosity are easily aroused—and ex-spouses aren't two folks practiced at getting along anyway. Yet the ability of exes to get along is a key to the success of a new stepfamily.

Remarriage of one or both ex-spouses only enlarges the challenge of getting along

—while possibly increasing tension between the ex-spouses responsible for coparenting. A stepparent who becomes a part of the kids' lives usually has no relationship to the child's other biological parent; if anything there is hostility.

The ideal, says John Visher, is creation of a "parenting coalition" among the parents and stepparents in both households. "From the beginning, the new couple needs to work together in making family decisions." One of the most important is how, and by whom, the children will be disciplined, and on that score the evidence is clear: only a birth parent has the authority to discipline his or her children.

Betty Carter is quick to warn, however, that stepparents cannot interfere with their spouse in parenting. Involved but not interfering? A parenting coalition requires the parents include their new spouses in family decisions. The new spouses, for their part, must support the parenting duties and the coparenting bond between the ex-spouses.

IT TAKES RESPECT

The glue that makes it all happen is respect, the Vishers report. Both parents must require kids and stepparents to treat one another with respect. Only then can bonds between them develop. Despite feelings of jealousy and animosity, first and second spouses must also accord one another respect to accomplish the coparenting tasks the children need to do well.

For their part, the kids also need each of the coparents to refer to the other parent with respect. Children are quick to pick up hints of hostility on either side. For them, hostility becomes an invitation to play the grown-ups off each other, and to imitate unkind behavior.

'Children are quick to pick up hints of hostility on either side. For them, it becomes an open invitation to play the grown-ups off each other.'

When the parents are adversarial, their hostility inhibits children from freely spending time with both parents, and the kids suffer. They lack the one-on-one attention that breeds a sense of self-value. And they are torn in half. All in all, it's a recipe for disappointment and anger.

ANY HELP?

"If you can help parents and stepparents early on to deal with issues of child-rearing appropriately, they have a lot of potential for giving stability to children and exposing them to appropriately happy relationships," says Australian research psychologist Jan Lawton. Lawton is spokesperson for The Stepfamily Project at the University of Queensland, a major government study of behavioral interventions for stepfamilies with troubled children.

What kind of help do stepfamilies need? Information and support. Stepfamily support groups exist across the United States, many of them organized by the Stepfamily Association. The organization responds to about 400 information requests each week from stepfamilies—while 7,000 new stepfamilies are forming weekly.

Stepfamily functioning improves dramatically when participants know which problems are normal, which are temporary, and that it takes time for people to integrate themselves and feel comfortable in a stepfamily. Lawton's study has demonstrated the benefits of practical guidance, and she has found that even a little help goes a long way. "The positive part of this study is that we can help stepfamilies with a very minimal amount of therapy and self-help, aimed at the right areas." The components of the Queensland program are a map of stepfamily problem areas.

•Child-Management Training, for parents and stepparents, to help them focus their attention on the children at a time when there's a tendency to slip a little on monitoring and disciplining the kids. The adults often get overly absorbed in their new romance.

•Partner-Support Training for newly remarried couples, since they don't automatically work together as a team during the first two years, when they are also at high risk for divorce. Such support helps them while their relationship is undergoing trial by fire in the new stepfamily.

•Communication and Problem-Solving Training for the entire new stepfamily helps everyone learn to talk together, understand each other, and learn how to solve problems and reach consensus.

Lawton reports as much as a 60 percent reduction in behavior problems and about 50 percent improvement in child adjustment, self-esteem, and parent/stepparent conflict. While therapy had a slight margin over self-help, persons in both groups outperformed by far the control group that received no help during the study. Those with the most troubled children do best with formal therapy; the rest do fine with self-help. Indeed, programs families could apply at home are especially useful, since stepfamilies involve people already weighed down by multiple demands, and coordinating a formal appointment can be formidable.

The key, Lawton says, is to reach stepfamilies at the beginning when they need basic information about what to expect. Lawton's next project is a prevention study, seeking the most effective ways to help all stepfamilies—not just ones where the children have behavior problems.

MORE HELP: A HAPPY MARRIAGE

If coparenting can be accomplished, children benefit in at least two ways. They feel loved by both biological parents; no child can thrive without affectionate connections. And they gain from being exposed to remarried adults in a successful intimate relationship. Especially when remarriage occurs before the children are teenagers, there is great potential for easy adaptation and smooth development.

A remarriage at adolescence, however, poses added challenges to adjustment and success of the stepfamily, Bray and Hetherington report. It's a critical time of identity formation. Daughters are particularly apt to get into fights with stepmothers. Sexual tension may develop between stepfather and a budding adolescent stepdaughter, manifest in aloofness and what every parent knows as snottiness. Even if the divorce occurred many years before, a parent's remarriage during a child's teen years can revive adjustment difficulties that may have cropped up during the divorce.

Generally, though, a successful second marriage helps to reduce—if not eliminate—kids' problems. Divorced people are generally more compatible with their second partner than their first—even though there is a higher divorce rate among second marriages.

Clinical psychology lore has it that the high divorce rate is because the spouses are making the same mistake again. Divorcing spouses have problems with intimate relationships, not with a particular partner, the thinking goes, and they are more apt to bail out a second time.

But this view is totally contradicted by those who have closely scrutinized many stepfamilies. The Vishers are among them. So is University of Southern California sociologist Constance Ahrons, Ph.D. They point out that a lot of second divorces are the result not of conventional marital deterioration but of problems in integrating into a household children and adults who are not related to each other.

"The divorce rate among remarried families is high in the first two years—then it slows down," says Lawton. "By about the five-year period, second relationships are more stable than first relationships. I see these couples at very high risk during the first few years, but thereafter offering great benefits to the children."

LOOKING AT THE PROBLEMS

While stepfamilies are doing a lot better than they're generally given credit for, a not insubstantial 20 percent of them—or twice the number of first-marriage families—do have problems with the kids. The research illuminating the specific problems in stepfamilies points to the basic requirements of stepfamilies as the major stumbling blocks. Cooperative coparenting. Equal involvement of both parents after the divorce. Noninterference by stepparents.

‘Sexual tension may develop between stepfather and adolescent stepdaughter, and manifest in aloofness and snottiness.’

Support for the coparenting relationship.

Bray's longitudinal study of stepfamilies has tracked mothers, stepfathers, and children, who were around six years old at the time of remarriage, over the next seven years. During the early months of remarriage, behavior problems rise steeply among the children. This is a time when stepfamilies are not yet cohesive—they are not likely to think of themselves as a unit.

Gradually, behavior problems subside over the next two years. By then stepfamilies are just as likely as first-marriage families to have developed useful ways of communicating, rules of behavior, and discipline. They may not consider themselves as cohesive, but objective evaluation finds few practical differences.

In Bray's study, trouble with the children developed when there was a reduction in time and attention from one or both parents, and reduced resources. These parental lapses, Bray notes, arise most often from problems of coparenting, and difficulties of stepparents in supporting the coparenting role.

But even the reduced parental attention does not doom the children. Hetherington observes that the reduced parental attention can also be seen as an opportunity for the children to take on responsibility. The end result is that some children—almost always daughters—wind up more capable and competent.

Others, however, particularly at adolescence, respond to the lapse of parental attention by going off and experimenting with sex or drugs. Younger children may display more conduct problems and depression. Both younger and older kids are at risk for lower academic achievement.

While few distinctions turn up between the ways daughters and sons react to being in a stepfamily, Bray did find increased conflict between stepfathers and stepdaughters at puberty. Hetherington also found difficulties with teenage daughters, and warns that remarriage when a daughter is entering adolescence promises to produce tremendous tension and resentment on the part of the daughter.

Daughters, who have grown close to their mothers and increasingly identify with them at the onset of puberty, will have difficulty with the addition of either a mother's new spouse, who is competition for her, or a father's new spouse—who is competition for her mother. What the girls are feeling is divided loyalty.

DIVIDED LOYALTIES

Stepfamilies are littered with possibilities for loyalty conflicts, say the Vishers. A particularly common one revolves around entry of new stepparent. A mom feels hostile toward her ex-husband's new partner; kids understand that their mom wants them to feel the same way. The same kids are also being asked by their dad to love the new wife, whom he loves. The kids feel torn because their parents are pulling them in opposite ways.

It is an axiom of psychology that when kids feel torn, they erupt in symptoms—like bad behavior or depression. It may be a desperate attempt to draw attention away from the unresolvable conflict between the parents. Whatever the source of divided loyalties, once kids feel them, they develop problems—if not behavior problems or depression, then the symptoms of anxiety. The solution? Back to coparenting. It is up to the adults to rise above jealousy or romanticism and work together for the good of the kids.

The respect they use to make the system operate must include appreciation for the inevitability of ambivalent feelings in the kids. And that, says Emily Visher, is one of the most important lessons from stepfamilies for all families. "The ability of adults to share with children ambivalence over loss and change determines how well they will do in the future. It paves the way for sharing other thoughts. It leads to a sense of mastery of whatever life presents."

‘Lesson #1: The ability of adults to share with kids ambivalence over loss and change determines how well they will do in the future.’

One of the sizable traps in remarriage is the temptation a new spouse may feel to interfere with the coparenting process, observes William Doherty, Ph.D., family social scientist at the University of Minnesota. The new spouse may feel insecure or jealous of the coparent's continuing attachment to the former spouse. Still, that only succeeds in dividing the loyalty of the biological parent. A weekly conversation with an ex-spouse about the kids might trouble an anxious new spouse—but the communication is essential and the stepparent has the obligation to adjust, just as the parents do, for the good of the kids.

On the other hand, no stepparent should be expected to love, or even like, a partner's kids, nor must demands be placed on kids to love the stepparent. Loyalty just can't be forced. A strong couple relationship is necessary to the success of the stepfamily, but it cannot hinge on whether the stepparent likes the kids, marital therapists agree. After all, a stepfamily essentially brings together strangers.

THE BASIC NEED: ACCEPTANCE

Stepfamilies can't push members into close relationships; still, they may feel the pain of absence of intimacy. Stepfamily life throws into bold relief very fundamental human needs—above all, says John Visher, the need to be a part of something. Entry into a stepfamily puts members in a position of assessing whether they are an insider or an outsider. A new wife belongs to her new husband, and he to her, but she is not a natural part of the husband's children's life. Feeling like an outsider to their relationship may be upsetting to her.

There's no fast solution for the inside/outside dilemma; stepfamilies come with a big catch in their very structure. The relationship between the parents and children predates the new marital relationship. It may even seem to outweigh it. A parent's love for a child must always be unconditional; couple love is not.

Joan Giacomini, a remarried parent and university administrator in Seattle, warns that it is hard for stepmothers to adjust to the fact that they are not number one to their new spouse. "There may be a handful of number ones, but you aren't the only number one," she says.

That gives rise to an all-too-common scenario: a remarried stepparent—often the stepmother—asks, "who is it going to be, me or your kids?" It's a false question—it leads to what Carter calls a "fake fight"—because it erroneously equates parent–child relationships and marital relationships, apples and oranges. Children are dependents; parental obligations to them are always unconditional.

Because the loyalty challenge rests on a mistaken assumption, Carter says, the proper solution is acceptance that relationships between parent and child are qualitatively different from those between spouses. Still, such conflicts can recur from time to time, as life continually presents new situations that assault the loyalties, resources, and time of kids and spouses.

THE ULTIMATE TRAP

Name a stepfamily dilemma and women—biomothers, stepmothers, even stepdaughters—are at the center of the problem. Psychologists know that women are always more likely to express distress wherever troubles exist. But stepfamilies are the ultimate gender trap. Ever-sensitive to interpersonal problems, women sense problems all over the place in stepfamilies.

Traditional male and female roles are troublesome enough, for the marriage and the children, in first-marriage families. But they wreak havoc on stepfamilies, Carter explains; they don't work at all. Indeed, researchers report that there's more equality in the marriage and in the distribution of domestic tasks in stepfamilies. But they still have a lot to learn—or unlearn—about gender roles and domestic life.

"No matter what we say or how feminist you are, everybody knows that women take care of children and men bring in most of the money. This sucks the stepmother into a quagmire of traditional domestic roles; it's not only that somebody makes her do it, she also does it to herself," explains Carter, coauthor of *The Invisible Web: Gender Patterns in Family Relationships*.

"We are raised to believe that we are responsible for everybody. A stepmother sees the children as unhappy and the husband as ineffectual, and she moves in to be helpful. Mavis Hetherington's research shows the consequence of this: a lot of fighting between teenage stepdaughters and stepmothers." Nevertheless, women move toward a problem to work on it—whether it's theirs to work on or not.

Trouble is, explains Carter, "in stepfamilies, everybody has to be in charge of their own children. A biological father has to understand that it is his responsibility to take charge. The stepmother has to back off, let the father do the monitoring and caretaking of the kids—even let him do it wrong. This is very hard to do; it flies in the face of all our gender training."

What's more, a large body of research on depression and marriage demonstrates that women's self-esteem becomes contingent upon relationships going smoothly; it holds in stepfamilies, as well. Women get depressed when stepfamily life goes badly, and they blame themselves.

For all its difficulty, the way parents in stepfamilies devise to take care of their own children contains another lesson for all families. "Stepfamilies demonstrate the importance of one-on-one relationships," says Emily Visher. "Parent–child alone time maintains the security of relationships. It requires conscious planning in all families. The health of all families resides in the quality of the relationships between members."

4. CRISES: Divorce and Remarriage

THE MYTH OF THE HAPPY FAMILY

If stepfamilies make it out of the gender trap, there's one more to avoid—the myth of the nuclear family. Successful stepfamilies let go of their fantasy of a traditional family life, reports James Bray. They become more realistic, less romantic, and more flexible about family. They can cope with what life deals.

But remarriage often sets up conditions pulling the other way. "There's often a sense of defensiveness," explains Betty Carter. "There's a feeling of 'let's not rock the boat this time. Let's be a happy family immediately so we can prove that this complicated thing—the divorce, the new marriage—was the right move.' People try to achieve an instant family, they don't allow for disgruntlement, fear, anxiety. Now we know it takes about five years for a stepfamily to become fully integrated."

Carter advises stepfamilies to "kiss the nuclear family good-bye. Stepfamilies simply cannot draw a tight circle around the household in the same way that nuclear families do. That always excludes somebody." The stepfamily's task is to keep permeable boundaries around the household, to facilitate coparenting, and to allow children access to the noncustodial parent.

It's a lot like tightrope-walking. "At the very time a stepfamily is trying to achieve its own integration, it has to keep the doors wide open and stay in touch with another household. You are not the lord of all you survey, as in the traditional family myth. You are on the phone regularly with someone about whom you feel, at best, ambivalent."

WHAT TO CALL IT?

Perhaps the most concrete evidence that old-fashioned family ideas don't work for stepfamilies is in the labels stepfamilies prefer for themselves.

Some people reject the label "stepfamily" altogether. Joan Giacomini is one. She is divorced from her grown children's father; he is remarried and has a toddler boy. Joan's husband has grown children from his first marriage, too, but she doesn't want to be referred to as a stepmother, nor does she like the idea of someone being referred to as the "stepmother" of her children.

"In our cases, we don't do any mothering. No one else is mother to my children, and my husband's children have their own mother," she explains. "One of my main goals is to respect their first family, so that they can have their relationships without worry about me." Despite dropping the "step" terminology, Giacomini's various families comprise a successful stepfamily that has respect, shared responsibility, even shared holidays.

Many stepfamilies who start off using step terminology eventually drop it all, reports James Bray. It may be the surest sign of integration. The terms "stepmother" and "stepfather" help clarify roles and remind everybody who belongs to whom, and under what terms, in the transition. Later, though, they don't bother with such names. "Labels connote a struggle for identity that doesn't exist anymore for these groups," says Bray.

For other stepfamilies, such as Ned and Joanna Fox—my mother and her husband—in Charlotte, North Carolina, there is little thought of stepfamily integration.

Nobody considers it a stepfamily, nor is anyone a stepsibling or stepparent. The kids were grown when the divorces and remarriages occurred, and none of the kids seem particularly interested in getting involved with the others. While Joanna's children treat Ned like an uncle, and value his love for Joanna, Ned's children don't warm up to the situation.

The moral of the story: Every stepfamily is different.

Some reject not merely the "stepfamily" label but stepfamily roles as well. In fact, the best way for a new spouse to move into stepparent life, suggests Barry Dym, Ph.D., a family psychologist (and remarried father) in Cambridge, Massachusetts, may be to find a different role than that of stepparent. The term itself may force the relationships into an unrealistic, and even intrusive, parental mold.

Dym suggests that stepmothers might do better modeling themselves after a favorite aunt—involved, but not the mother. My favorite aunt provides acceptance, guidance, honesty, but the obligation on either side is voluntary. If I become a stepmother, I think I'll be an aunt.

The naming issue underscores what stepfamilies have that original families don't always get: there is no monolithic view of what a stepfamily is supposed to be, or even be called. To catalog stepfamily experiences would be to catalog all relationships—there is endless variety, and unlimited routes to success or failure. Unlike traditional families, stepfamilies allow much more room for diversity. And equality. Count that as the ultimate lesson from stepfamilies.

THE MYTHS AND MISCONCEPTIONS OF THE STEPMOTHER IDENTITY

DESCRIPTIONS AND PRESCRIPTIONS FOR IDENTITY MANAGEMENT*

There are two cross-cultural and trans-historical myths associated with stepmotherhood: the evil stepmother myth and the myth of instant love. The tenacity of these myths has served to stigmatize stepmothers. This paper describes the myths associated with stepmothers, details how these myths affect stepmother life, reveals dilemmas in identity management for stepmothers, and indicates identity management strategies stepmothers might utilize.

Marianne Dainton

Marianne Dainton is a doctoral student at Ohio State University, Department of Communication, 319 Neil Hall, Columbus, OH 43210.

In America there are a multitude of family forms, one of which is the stepfamily. Statistics indicate that currently 16% of all married couples in this country have at least one stepchild (Moorman & Hernandez, 1989). Moreover, current predictions are that 35% to 40% of children born in the 1980s will spend time in a stepparent family before they are young adults (Coleman & Ganong, 1990a).

Although researchers are increasingly turning their attention to the stepfamily form, there are many areas of stepfamily life that have not received adequate attention (Coleman & Ganong, 1990a). One such area is the effect of myths about stepfamily relations on stepfamily members. A focus upon myths is salient to the study of stepfamilies in general, and stepmothers in particular, because of the prevalence of myths concerning step-relations. For example, at least three of the Brothers Grimm's fairy tales—"Hansel and Gretel," "Cinderella," and "Snow White"—revolve

*The author would like to thank Patrick McKenry and Dirk Scheerhorn for editorial comments, and three anonymous reviewers for their valuable suggestions.

Key Words: identity management, myths, stepmothers, stigma.

around the actions of an evil stepmother. These stories may appear innocuous enough, unless of course you happen to be a stepmother or a stepchild. "Fairies do not exist, and witches do not exist, but stepmothers do exist, and therefore certain fairy tales are harmful rather than helpful to large segments of the population" (Visher & Visher, 1979, p. 6).

The myths associated with stepmotherhood may constrain stepmothers' identity management. Identity management refers to efforts on the part of stepmothers to foster preferred perceptions about themselves. Accordingly, this article examines some of the impediments to the identity management strategies enacted by stepmothers. Specifically, throughout the course of this article the myths and misconceptions of stepmotherhood will be identified, the implications of these myths for stepmothers will be discussed, issues of identity will be elaborated, and, finally, some initial steps toward identity management strategies for stepmothers will be detailed.

STEPMOTHER MYTHS

The term *myth* is popularly conceived to be analogous to "falsehood." Indeed, myths often contain false and/or negative information. Scholars, however, define myth as a recurring theme or character type that incorporates infor-

mation about cultural standards (Birenbaum, 1988). Thus, myths represent a way of viewing the world that embodies a culture's beliefs, regardless of whether these beliefs are accurate.

According to Bruner (1960), myths can be characterized by two components. The first component is an externalization, which Bruner describes as a "corpus of images and identities" (p. 280). This externalization provides a cultural explanation of the way the world works. The second component is an internalization. Bruner argues that a myth can only exist to the extent that cultural members internalize personal identities based upon the externalized corpus of ideas propagated by the myth.

Regarding stepmotherhood, there are two generic myths that are simultaneously cross-cultural and transhistorical (Schulman, 1972). The first of the myths is that of the *evil stepmother,* a myth propagated through fiction of all forms. The second myth is that of *instant love,* wherein a stepmother is expected to immediately assimilate into a family and to love the children as if they were her own. Each will be discussed in turn.

Myth #1: The Evil Stepmother

The myth of the evil stepmother has a strong and inveterate legacy; the negative connotations of the term *step* were firmly in place as early as 1400 (Wald,

1981). Moreover, scholars have identified the existence of evil stepmother folktales in virtually every part of the world. In fact, Smith (1953) identifies 345 versions of the "Cinderella" story alone, revealing the evil stepmother myth as a global phenomenon.

Although evil stepmothers appear in all genres of fiction, the evil stepmother is particularly prevalent in fairy tales (Wald, 1981). In an analysis of fairy tales, one researcher found that the most frequent representations of evil included bears, wolves, giants and ogres, witches, and stepmothers (Sutton-Smith, 1971, cited in Wald, 1981). Thus, fairy tales suggest that stepmothers are the equivalent of wild animals and supernatural beings—entities that children have very little chance of facing in real life—in their wicked treatment of children.

Myth #2: Instant Love

The second myth is instant love (Schulman, 1972; Visher & Visher, 1988; Wald, 1981). This myth is based upon cultural standards about mothering (Visher & Visher, 1988), and the resulting societal expectations about stepmothers' assimilation into the family. Specifically, the myth maintains that remarriage in and of itself creates an instant family, that stepmothers should (and will) automatically love their stepchildren, and that stepchildren will automatically love their stepmother. Further, because of this love, mothering is assumed to come naturally and easily.

In reality, none of the above necessarily happens. Counselors working with stepmothers suggest that many women are surprised and dismayed when they don't feel immediate love for their stepchildren (Lofas & Sova, 1985). Moreover, stepchildren are often afraid, unsure, and uncomfortable with the changes in the family, and may express these feelings by being surly and resentful. As a result, many stepmothers experience a great deal of ambivalence regarding their stepchildren (Ambert, 1986).

The Prevalence of These Myths Today

Despite the increasing number of stepfamilies in America today, the myths identified above show no signs of losing strength. In a series of research efforts, one group of researchers found that the role of stepmother elicited more negative connotations than any other family position (Bryan, Coleman, Ganong, & Bryan, 1986; Ganong & Coleman, 1983). Specifically, stepmothers were perceived as less affectionate, good, fair, kind, loving, happy, and likable, and

more cruel, hateful, unfair, and unloving. More recently, researchers have determined that these negative perceptions still stand, although there is little difference in the perceptions of stepmothers and stepfathers (Fluitt & Paradise, 1991; Ganong, Coleman, & Kennedy, 1990). Similarly, clinicians assert that the myth of instant love has yet to be replaced by more realistic expectations (Visher & Visher, 1988).

Individually, these myths negatively affect the experiences of stepmothers. For example, both clinical and empirical evidence reveals that stepmothers identify the wicked stepmother myth as directly contributing to the stress they experience in adapting to the stepmother role (Duberman, 1973; Hughes, 1991; Visher & Visher, 1979). Further, counselors have identified the unrealistic expectations associated with the myth of instant love as a possible cause of stress for stepmothers in general, and have suggested that such expectations may actively interfere with the family integration that the myth promises (Visher & Visher, 1988).

Ironically, these myths provide external images of the stepmother that are at polar extremes; one myth depicts stepmothers as unrealistically evil, the other as unrealistically loving and competent. Together, these contradictory images may contribute to identity management difficulties, as stepmothers must struggle with internalizing two conflicting sets of ultimately unrealistic expectations. Clearly, taking on the mantle of stepmother includes not only taking on the responsibility of a family, but taking on a host of potential identity management challenges (Hughes, 1991; Visher & Visher, 1979, 1988).

THE CONCEPT OF IDENTITY

Before discussing the identity issues associated with stepmotherhood, some fundamental issues surrounding the concept of identity itself must be addressed. In so doing, some critical distinctions between key terms need to be made. Finally, a framework for understanding identity management must be constructed.

First, *identity* can be defined as an individual's self-concept (McCall & Simmons, 1978). Thus, an individual's identity involves beliefs about whom he or she is, and how he or she should be perceived and treated in social life (Schlenker, 1980). Although our identities are frequently manifested in the roles that we enact, the notion of identity is broader than that of roles. Definitionally, *roles* are expectations held

about the occupant of a social status or a position in a social system, while *identity* is a constellation of all of the roles an individual performs (McCall & Simmons, 1978).

The same distinction can be made between role performance and identity management. A *role performance* (also known as *role enactment*) is the individual's day-to-day behavior associated with a given role (McCall & Simmons, 1978). *Identity management,* on the other hand, is a broader concept; it is an individual's efforts to foster perceptions (usually positive) relevant to his or her self-concept. Similar terms include *self-presentation* (Goffman, 1959) and *impression management* (Schlenker, 1980).

The definitions above imply that an identity is chosen. This is not always the case. McCall and Simmons (1978) assert that individuals do not entirely have discretion in the roles they will enact, and hence in the perceptions others will have of them. For example, most stepmothers do not choose the stepmother persona; it is thrust upon them when they choose to marry a man with children. Identity management for stepmothers, then, is not simply the process of maintaining preferred perceptions, but of preventing unwanted perceptions associated with preconceived evaluations of a given social role.

To clarify, McCall and Simmons argue that each role identity has two elements: the *conventional* and the *idiosyncratic.* The conventional aspect of a role identity consists of social stereotypes. These stereotypes might be captured in myths such as the myths associated with stepmotherhood. The idiosyncratic elements of a role identity, on the other hand, are those characteristics an individual modifies and elaborates within the given role.

IDENTITY DILEMMAS

Generally, identities are inferred by appearance and actions (McCall & Simmons, 1978). In the case of stepmothers, however, the perceptions associated with stepmotherhood are not conveyed by appearance or actions, but are label-bound. Accordingly, stepmothers fulfill the requirements of being a stigmatized group. *Stigmas* are products of definitional processes in which a defining attribute (such as being a stepmother) eclipses other aspects of the stigmatized person, including individual personalities and abilities (Ainlay, Coleman, & Becker, 1986; Stafford & Scott, 1986). Thus stigmas are categorizations that often involve negative affect (Jones et al., 1984).

Goffman (1963) posits that stigmatization is the result of the relationship between a particular attribute and a stereotype about that attribute. "Society establishes the means of categorizing persons and the complement of attributes felt to be ordinary and natural for members of each of these categories" (Goffman, 1963, p. 2). Ironically, the "ordinary and natural" attributes that society has established for stepmothers (through myths) are that they are inherently wicked, yet capable of providing instant love. It is the very fact that stepmothers are characterized in such an extraordinary manner that causes their stigmatization.

Further, Goffman (1963) argues that there are two primary types of stigmas: the *discredited* and the *discreditable*. Discredited individuals are those in which the stigma is immediately apparent (e.g., those with physical deformities). Discreditable individuals are those whose stigma is not known or immediately perceivable. The fact that stepmothers' stigma is not visually apparent would lead one to believe that they have a discreditable stigma. That is, despite fairy tales' depiction of stepmothers as evil hags, real stepmothers look just like real mothers. Their stigma is not immediately apparent.

However, with different audiences stepmothers are sometimes discredited and sometimes discreditable. For example, members of the stepfamily are aware of a woman's stepmother status, so in their eyes she is discredited. In the general public, however, a stepmother remains merely discreditable. This contradiction brings up one of the major problems stepmothers have with identity management; part of the dilemma of managing a stepmother identity is the public/private dichotomy. Stepmothers believe that they are judged based on stepmother myths in both the public and private arenas of social life (Hughes, 1991). Because of this, stepmothers may find themselves with the paradox of having inconsistent identity management strategies become necessary to manage the same identity.

Goffman (1963) has identified two broad classes of identity management strategies. *Corrective practices* are what people do after their preferred identity is threatened. According to Goffman, it is likely that discredited individuals will be forced to engage in corrective strategies. *Preventative strategies,* on the other hand, are behaviors an individual uses to avoid negative perceptions. In general, the discreditable will rely on preventative strategies.

In order to determine which class of strategies to enact, a stepmother must consider a contextual matrix. That is, stepmothers must consider where they are and who their audience is in order to select the appropriate identity management techniques (McCall & Simmons, 1978). This matrix might look like the one in Figure 1.

As the matrix shows, stepmothers face competing concerns when selecting identity strategies: *who* and *where*. Within each of these superordinate categories is a dichotomy. For example, when considering who, a stepmother might be in the company of her family or she may be in the company of some generalized others. When considering *where,* she might be in private (e.g., at home) or in public (e.g., a restaurant).

Taking each quadrant of the grid in turn, the following issues are stressed. First, the upper left quadrant is one in which there is little inconsistency. Here, stepmothers are with their family in private. Given that they are already discredited in this forum (i.e., their stigma is known), it is likely that they will utilize corrective identity management strategies in this case. Such strategies might include assertive techniques described by Jones and Pittman (1980) like *exemplification* (projecting integrity), *self-promotion* (showing competence in mothering), or *ingratiation* (being helpful and positive).

Similarly, there is probably little quandary about strategy selection when in the others/public quadrant; here, the stepmother is discreditable (her stigma is not known). Accordingly, it is likely a stepmother would select what Goffman (1963) describes as preventative strategies, such as *passing* (behaving in a way consistent with a nonstigmatized identity without specifically claiming to be nonstigmatized) or using *disidentifiers* (behaviors deliberately used to indicate a nonstigmatized identity, e.g., saying "my son" instead of "my stepson").

The two remaining quadrants might cause psychological tension between competing identity management options, however. For example, in the family/public quadrant, an initial reaction might be to use preventative strategies. After all, other patrons of a restaurant have little need to know that the normal family seated next to them might in fact be a stepfamily. However, if a stepmother selects such strategies she is neither accomplishing her goal of overcoming negative perceptions within the family, nor is she safe from intentional or unintentional unmasking. The last quadrant, others/private, is liable to involve a very different sort of tension. An example of such a situation is holding a professional gathering at home. Given that the interaction is at home, her stigma is already known among family members who may be present. Therefore, corrective strategies might seem appropriate. However, because she is also with nonintimate others, preventative strategies might be preferred. Here, the tension reflects a pull towards actively managing existing negative stereotypes within the family, and at the same time preventing others from learning of the stigma.

Confounding contextual constraints are the ways in which expectations based upon stepmother myths affect our identity management. That is, people might interpret a stepmother's behavior as negative (even if by objective measures it is not) simply because stepmothers' behaviors are expected to be negative (Coleman & Ganong, 1987a; for a discussion about how this process might work, see Darley & Gross, 1983). A dilemma that stepmothers face, then, is whether they should use corrective strategies at all, since any efforts to actively repair others' perceptions might be interpreted unfavorably. She is stuck in a "damned if you do, damned if you don't" situation.

A final identity management dilemma stepmothers face is related to the

Figure 1. *Matrix for Stepmothers' Identity Management Strategies*

		Who	
		Family	Others
Where	Private	Corrective	???
	Public	???	Preventative

extent to which they play an active parenting role. That is, in attempting to fulfill the stepparent role, stepmothers are in a double bind. On one hand, they are expected to love the child as if he or she were their own, but on the other hand, they are often sanctioned against adopting a bona fide parental role (Visher & Visher, 1979). Thus, becoming a stepmother requires a careful balancing act, wherein a woman must regulate perceptions of involvement without being perceived as overinvolved or uncaring.

The dilemma described above is complicated by the ambiguity associated with the stepmother role. According to Cherlin (1978), remarriage represents an "incomplete institution" because there are few norms or rules to define expected behavior in stepfamily life. Cherlin posits that this ambiguity causes stress on family members. There is recent evidence for this hypothesis; in a review of the literature, Fine and Schwebel (1991) identified role ambiguity as the core difficulty in stepfamilies.

Role ambiguity involves four types of uncertainty: (a) uncertainty about the scope of one's responsibilities; (b) uncertainty about the particular behaviors needed to fulfill one's responsibilities; (c) uncertainty about whose expectations for role behavior must be met; and (d) uncertainty about the effects of one's actions on the well-being of oneself and others (King & King, 1990). This uncertainty is a function of the difference between stepfamily roles and biological family roles, and the difference between effective stepfamily functioning and effective biological family functioning (Coleman & Ganong, 1987b). There are two primary differences: (a) the degree of clarity about which behavior is appropriate for a given role, and (b) the degree to which the role is either ascribed or achieved (Walker & Messinger, 1979).

IDENTITY MANAGEMENT STRATEGIES

Given the dilemmas of identity management outlined above, the selection of specific strategies may be complex, if not overwhelming, to a stepmother. However, research has provided some preliminary answers as to which strategies stepmothers are likely to use, whether such strategies are likely to work, and which strategies are not often used but might be beneficial given the specific identity problems stepmothers face.

First, because the nature of the stigma of being a stepmother is not immediately apparent to those who don't know a woman's stepmother status, an identity strategy frequently selected for the general public is one of concealment (e.g., Duberman, 1975; Jones et al., 1984).

> For many women who have chosen to become stepmothers, the realization that they are part of a minority group comes as a bit of a shock. But by masquerading as a natural mother, altering her true identity in order to fit into a society and to be accepted as part of a "normal" family, a stepmother acts like any member of a minority group who is striving to conform. (Morrison, Thompson-Guppy, & Bell, 1986, p. 17)

Concealment is an example of a preventative strategy (Goffman, 1963). Despite the frequency of use of this strategy, however, some counselors have suggested that concealment is ineffective as a long-term solution (Morrison et al., 1986).

A more proactive strategy for public identity management is what Jones et al. (1984) call *confrontation and breaking through*. This strategy involves acknowledging one's stepmother status and working to frame the identity in a constructive and commendable context. Recall McCall and Simmon's (1978) distinction between the conventional and idiosyncratic elements of identity. Based on this distinction, one way to accomplish confrontation and breaking through might be to foster the idiosyncratic elements of the stepmother identity, while simultaneously diminishing the conventional elements. However, due to the strength of the myths of stepmotherhood, such efforts might be construed negatively. As Coleman and Ganong (1987a) noted, people's expectations of negative behavior might lead them to perceive even idiosyncratic elements negatively.

Moving from individual identity management efforts to societal efforts to change the stigma of stepmotherhood, one controversial public strategy that has been suggested is to change the label. If the term *stepfamily* engenders negative reactions, some authors contend we should just change the name to one without such negative connotations (see Coleman & Ganong, 1987a, for a summary of the debate). This can be classified as a corrective strategy. Alternatives to stepfamily include *blended* or *reconstituted family*. What the associated changes in the name of *stepmother* would be is unclear. Other scholars believe that changing the terminology would be confusing (Wald, 1981) or insulting (Lofas & Sova, 1985), or would only add to the mystification (Hughes, 1991).

There have also been some specific strategies identified to overcome the myths within the stepfamily itself. Based on empirical evidence, Cissna, Cox, and Bochner (1990) assert that an effective way to overcome myths about stepmotherhood involves two steps. First, they claim, the remarried partners must establish the solidarity of the marriage in children's minds. Then, they say, the partners should use this solidarity to establish the credibility of the stepparent as a valid parental authority. Such efforts are clearly corrective in nature, and take into account overly negative expectations due to the evil stepmother myth as well as overly positive expectations due to the myth of instant love.

Taking quite a different approach, Salwen (1990) proposes that stepmothers might remove themselves from the parenting role altogether by insisting that the biological father take on all parenting responsibilities. This does not mean that stepmothers cannot be supportive or nurturing to their stepchildren. However, Salwen argues that by avoiding the parental role, stepmothers simultaneously avoid the negative expectations associated with the role. They are therefore free to work on positive, nonparental relationships with their stepchildren that are not weighted down by preconceived, unfavorable perceptions. Again, such a strategy is an effort to achieve a middle ground between the two myths.

A similar, but perhaps less radical, approach to identity dilemmas within the stepfamily is to focus on alternative role enactment. Furstenberg and Spanier (1984) posit that the stepparent role is ambiguous, as there is no single prescribed role for stepparents (see the section on role ambiguity above). Thus, they should feel free to try on various roles until they find one that fits (see also Walker & Messinger, 1979). Alternative roles a stepmother can don to ease her interactions with stepchildren include *primary mother* (which works only if the biological mother is physically and/or psychologically dead to the child), *other mother,* and *friend* (Draughon, 1975).

Related to alternative roles in managing identity, simply finding a name that a child is comfortable calling the stepmother might assist in the individualization of a stepmother's identity (Visher & Visher, 1988). Very often, a child avoids finding a name for his or her stepmother, referring to her simply as "you" or "she." By insisting on a name, the stepmother moves out of the realm of the group of all stepmothers (a stigmatized group) to personhood (Maglin & Schniedewind, 1989). Possible names include the stepmother's own first name, a mutually agreed upon nickname, or a variation of mother not used for the biological mother (Wald, 1981).

Finally, while not directly related to the problems of stepmothers, Crocker and Lutsky (1986) have identified three strategies for changing cognitions about stigmas. First is the *sociocultural* approach, which emphasizes a change in socialization practices. In the case of stepmothers in particular, this might involve replacing evil stepmother fairy tales with stories with more positive messages. Second is the *motivational* approach. This involves redefining group boundaries to allow the stigmatized persons to become part of the normal population. For example, the category of *mothers* might be expanded to include stepmothers. Lastly, Crocker and Lutsky identify *cognitive* approaches to changing stigmas. This involves proving the stereotype wrong. In global terms this might mean a public relations campaign of sorts for stepmothers. More specifically, however, it might involve allowing a stepmother's positive actions within the stepfamily to prove the myth wrong (i.e., replacing conventional elements of identity with idiosyncratic elements).

IMPLICATIONS FOR RESEARCH

There are several directions for future research. First, Goffman's theoretical differentiation between corrective and preventative identity management strategies needs to be operationalized. Specific research questions might be "What communicative behaviors serve corrective functions?" and "What communicative behaviors serve preventative functions?"

Second, because our knowledge of the identity management strategies stepmothers actually use is quite limited, it would be of interest to identify the specific identity management strategies stepmothers select, when they select them, and why. In addition, future research should strive to fill in the empty squares of the identity matrix detailed by Figure 1. That is, research should focus upon what identity management strategies women select when in a private setting with nonfamily members, and, perhaps more interestingly, what they do when they are with family members in a public situation. Moreover, researchers should ascertain whether the theoretical predictions of strategies that have been identified are correct.

More important than merely identifying what women do, however, is to identify what actually works. A repertoire of strategies is useless unless they actually assist a stepmother in overcoming the negative perceptions associated with stepmotherhood. Thus, critical research questions include: "What specific identity management strategies work to overcome negative public perceptions?" and "What strategies work to overcome negative perceptions within the family?"

IMPLICATIONS FOR PRACTICE

The issues raised here also have several implications for educators and counselors working with stepfamilies. Most importantly, practitioners can enact two global strategies to ameliorate the identity management difficulties stepmothers face. The first strategy is to assist individual stepmothers in overcoming some of the myths and misconceptions associated with this family role. Ideally, this assistance would take place before the formation of the stepfamily. By presenting future stepmothers—and all stepfamily members—with the reality of stepmother life before the remarriage, the frustrations associated with the myths of the evil stepmother and of instant love might be avoided. A first step in such counseling might be the completion of the Personal Reflections Program (Kaplan & Hennon, 1992).

More realistically, however, this assistance will likely be sought after the identity management difficulties have been encountered. In this case, practitioners might offer some of the strategies described in the previous section on identity management. In addition, referral to organizations proffering support to stepmothers and stepfamilies might be warranted. Finally, preliminary evidence suggests that the use of fiction can assist stepfamilies and stepfamily members in counseling (Coleman & Ganong, 1990b).

The second strategy is to actively work to diffuse these myths and misconceptions on a societal level. This paper points to the need for greater attention to the messages we are sending children about stepmothers. Family life educators and primary school educators might be especially important in normalizing the stepfamily experience (Crosbie-Burnett & Skyles, 1989). Family life educators can assist in debunking the myths by informing the public about the realities of stepmothers and stepfamily life. Similarly, primary school educators might be recruited to assist in this information campaign. Through programs such as the Classroom Guidance Program discussed by Crosbie-Burnett and Pulvino (1990), by selecting texts and children's literature that include normal stepfamilies, and by incorporating stepfamily roles in everyday classroom discussions, grade school teachers might make great strides in overcoming the evil stepmother myth.

CONCLUSION

The stepmother role is a stressful one that is particularly challenging in terms of identity management. Stepmothers must combat the firmly entrenched myths of the wicked stepmother and of instant love. Despite the fact that the stepfamily form is becoming increasingly more common, empirical and clinical evidence suggests that stepmother myths show little sign of changing (Bryan et al., 1986; Ganong & Coleman, 1983; Fluitt & Paradise, 1991). Thus, identity issues will remain salient for stepmothers for some time to come. Accordingly, researchers and practitioners must incorporate the concept of identity when considering the experiences of stepmothers.

REFERENCES

Ainlay, S. C., Coleman, L. M., & Becker, G. (1986). Stigma reconsidered. In S. C. Ainlay, G. Becker, & L. M. Coleman (Eds.), *The dilemma of difference: A multidisciplinary view of stigma* (pp. 1-13). New York: Plenum Press.

Ambert, A. (1986). Being a stepparent: Live-in and visiting stepchildren. *Journal of Marriage and the Family, 48,* 795-804.

Birenbaum, H. (1988). *Myth and mind.* Lanham, MD: University Press.

Bruner, J. S. (1960). Myth and identity. In H. A. Murray (Ed.), *Myth and mythmaking* (pp. 276-287). Boston: Beacon Press.

Bryan, H., Coleman, M., Ganong, L., & Bryan, L. (1986). Person perception: Family structure as a cue for stereotyping. *Journal of Marriage and the Family, 48,* 169-174.

Cherlin, A. (1978). Remarriage as an incomplete institution. *American Journal of Sociology, 86,* 634-650.

Cissna, K. N., Cox, D. E., & Bochner, A. P. (1990). The dialectic of marital and parental relationships within the stepfamily. *Communication Monographs, 57,* 44-61.

Coleman, M., & Ganong, L. (1987a). The cultural stereotyping of stepfamilies. In K. Pasley & M. Ihinger-Tallman (Eds.), *Remarriage and stepparenting: Current research and theory* (pp. 19-41). New York: Guilford.

Coleman, M., & Ganong, L. (1987b). Marital conflict in stepfamilies: Effects on children. *Youth and Society, 19,* 151-172.

Coleman, M., & Ganong, L. H. (1990a). Remarriage and stepfamily research in the 1980s: Increased interest in an old family form. *Journal of Marriage and the Family, 52,* 925-940.

Coleman, M., & Ganong, L. H. (1990b). The uses of juvenile fiction and self-help books with stepfamilies. *Journal of Counseling and Development, 68,* 327-331.

Crocker, J., & Lutsky, N. (1986). Stigma and the dynamics of social cognition. In S. C. Ainlay, G. Becker, & L. M. Coleman (Eds.), *The dilemma of difference: A multidisciplinary view of stigma* (pp. 95-122). New York: Plenum Press.

Crosbie-Burnett, M., & Pulvino, C. J. (1990). Children in nontraditional families: A classroom guidance program. *School Counselor, 37,* 286-293.

Crosbie-Burnett, M., & Skyles, A. (1989). Stepchildren in schools and colleges: Recommendations for educational policy changes. *Family Relations, 38,* 59-64.

Darley, J., & Gross, P. H. (1983). A hypothesis confirming bias in labeling effects. *Journal of Personality and Social Psychology, 44,* 20-33.

Draughon, M. (1975). Stepmother's model of identification in relation to mourning in the child. *Psychological Reports, 36,* 183-189.

Duberman, L. (1973). Step-kin relationships. *Journal of Marriage and the Family, 35,* 283-292.

Duberman, L. (1975). *The reconstituted family: A study of remarried couples and their children.* Chicago, IL: Nelson-Hall.

Fine, M. A., & Schwebel, A. I. (1991). Stepparent stress: A cognitive perspective. *Journal of Divorce and Remarriage, 17,* 1-15.

Fluitt, M. S., & Paradise, L. V. (1991). The relationship of current family structures to young adults' perceptions of stepparents. *Journal of Divorce and Remarriage, 15,* 159-174.

Furstenberg, F. F., Jr., & Spanier, G. (1984). *Recycling the*

4. CRISES: Divorce and Remarriage

family: Remarriage after divorce. Beverly Hills, CA: Sage.

Ganong, L., & Coleman, M. (1983). Stepparent: A pejorative term? *Psychological Reports,* **52,** 919-922.

Ganong, L., Coleman, M., & Kennedy, G. (1990). The effects of using alternate labels in denoting stepparent or stepfamily status. *Journal of Social Behavior and Personality,* **5,** 453-463.

Goffman, E. (1959). *The presentation of self in everyday life.* New York: Doubleday Anchor.

Goffman, E. (1963). *Stigma: Notes on the management of spoiled identity.* New York: Simon & Schuster.

Hughes, C. (1991). *Stepparents: Wicked or wonderful?* Brookfield, VT: Gower Publishing Co.

Jones, E. E., Farina, A., Hastorf, A. H., Markus, H., Miller, D. T., & Scott, R. A. (1984). *Social stigma: The psychology of of marked relationships.* New York: W. H. Freeman.

Jones, E. E., & Pittman, T. S. (1980). Toward a general theory of strategic self-presentation. In H. Suls (Ed.), *Psychological perspectives on the self.* Hillsdale, NJ: Lawrence Erlbaum Associates.

Kaplan, L., & Hennon, C. B. (1992). Remarriage education: The Personal Reflections Program. *Family Relations,* **41,** 127-134.

King, L. A., & King, D. W. (1990). Role conflict and role ambiguity: A critical assessment of construct validity. *Psychological Bulletin,* **107,** 48-64.

Lofas, J., & Sova, D. B. (1985). *Stepparenting.* New York: Zebra Books.

Maglin, N. B., & Schniedewind, N. (1989). Women and stepfamilies. Philadelphia: Temple University Press.

McCall, G. J., & Simmons, J. L. (1978). *Identities and interactions* (rev. ed.). New York: The Free Press.

Moorman, J. E., & Hernandez, D. J. (1989). Married-couple families with step, adopted, and biological children. *Demography,* **26,** 267-277.

Morrison, K., Thompson-Guppy, A., & Bell, P. (1986). *Stepmothers: Exploring the myth.* Ottawa, Canada: Canadian Council on Social Development.

Salwen, L. V. (1990). The myth of the wicked stepmother. *Women and Therapy,* **10,** 117-125.

Schlenker, B. R. (1980). *Impression management: The self-concept, social identity, and interpersonal relations.* Monterey, CA: Brooks/Cole.

Schulman, G. L. (1972). Myths that intrude on the adaptation of the stepfamily. *Social Casework,* **53,** 131-139.

Smith, W. C. (1953). *The stepchild.* Chicago, IL: University of Chicago Press.

Stafford, M. C., & Scott, R. R. (1986). Stigma, deviance, and social control: Some conceptual issues. In S. C. Ainlay, G. Becker, & L. M. Coleman (Eds.), *The dilemma of difference: A multidisciplinary view of stigma* (pp. 77-91). New York: Plenum Press.

Visher, E. B., & Visher, J. S. (1979). *Stepfamilies: Myths and realities.* Secaucus, NJ: Citadel.

Visher, E. B., & Visher, J. S. (1988). *Old loyalties, new ties: Therapeutic strategies with stepfamilies.* New York: Brunner/Mazel.

Wald, E. (1981). *The remarried family: Challenge and promise.* New York: Family Services Association of America.

Walker, K. N., & Messinger, L. (1979). Remarriage after divorce: Dissolution and reconstruction of family boundaries. *Family Process,* **18,** 185-192.

CONTINUITIES AND DISCONTINUITIES IN FAMILY MEMBERS' RELATIONSHIPS WITH ALZHEIMER'S PATIENTS*

Thirty families who cared for a family member with Alzheimer's Disease were asked to provide narratives of daily care over one and one-half years. A key finding of the hermeneutic analysis of their narratives was that different family members experience their relationship with the AD patient to be continuous, continuous but transformed, or radically discontinuous with their relationship prior to the disease. Responsiveness to these qualities of family relations by professionals may ease family members' caregiving efforts.

Catherine Chesla, Ida Martinson,
and Marilou Muwaswes

Catherine Chesla is an Assistant Professor and Ida Martinson is a Professor in the Department of Family Health Care Nursing, University of California, San Francisco, California, 94143. Marilou Muwaswes is an Associate Clinical Professor, Physiological Nursing, University of California, San Francisco.

The central concern in research on families and Alzheimer's Disease (AD) in the past ten years has been to identify factors that place family members at risk for negative outcomes because of their involvement in AD care (Bowers, 1987; Colerick & George, 1986; Liptzin, Grob, & Eisen, 1988; Ory et al., 1985; Quayhagen & Quayhagen, 1988). This research has identified AD family caregivers to be at risk for poor physical health, mental health, and quality of life, when compared with family members who are not caregivers (Kuhlman, Wilson, Hutchinson, & Wallhagen, 1991). Family burden, resources (including social support), and AD patient characteristics and symptoms im-

*This research was conducted as part of a larger study "Impact of Alzheimer's Disease on the Family and Caregiver," by Ida Martinson, P.I., Catherine Gilliss, Glen Doyle and Marilou Muwaswes, Co-Investigators. The project was funded by Biomedical Research Support Grant, School of Nursing, University of California, San Francisco; Academic Senate Grant, UCSF; NRSA Post-Doctoral Fellowship Grant #1F31 NR06020, National Center for Nursing Research, NIH; Alzheimer's Disease and Related Disorders Association Paine-Knickerbocker Graduate Research Award.

Key Words: Alzheimer's disease, dementia, family caregiving, family relationships, intergenerational relationships.

(Family Relations, 1994, 43, 3-9.)

pact negative family outcomes, although factors that place family members most at risk remain to be specified (Baumgarten, 1989). In all of this research, however, AD patients are assumed to be a demand or a drain on family members.

Persons with AD are frequently described as experiencing a loss of self as the disease unfolds (Cohen & Eisdorfer, 1986). Progressive loss of memory, along with personality and behavior changes common to the disease, are thought to overwhelm those with the disease. AD patients are characterized as suffering from a biomedical disorder that severs them from their history and severely restricts their potential in life. The biomedicalization of dementia (Lyman, 1989) has restricted the scope of research to disease progression and biologic processes that give rise to the disease. Research about those who care for demented elders has similarly been restricted by the pervasiveness of the biomedical perspective to the questions about how the disease, in its various stages of progression, impacts family members. Largely unasked, and therefore unanswered, are questions about the lived experience of AD for the person with the disease, the family member's experience of living with and caring for the person with AD, and how qualities of the caregiving environment might influence disease progression (Lyman, 1989).

Research on caregivers of AD patients often progresses from the implicit assumption of particular relations between the ill family member and others in the family. One member in the relationship is assumed to be the passive recipient of care, holding less interpersonal power yet imposing demands and burdens. In a parallel way, the caregiving member is assumed to be an active provider, possessing relatively greater interpersonal power, but at risk of negative outcomes because of the burdens and risks experienced. Recent caregiver research suggests that the quality of relations between ill and other family members is complex, and that factors such as centrality of the relationship, personal qualities of both members, and the degree of reciprocity in the relationship may impact outcomes for both the ill and non-ill family members (Walker, Pratt, & Oppy, 1992; Wright, Clipp, & George, 1993).

One aim of this investigation was to question the assumption of a fixed relation between the family and the person with AD and additionally to specify the range of relations that were apparent in the day-to-day lives of family members living with a person with AD. As part of a larger study aimed at understanding the *experiences* of family members who cared for a person with AD over time, we critically examined family members' self-initiated discussion of relations with the person with AD, as well as the content and nature of those relations. Working directly from family members' narratives, we attempted to understand these relations in ways that formal theories, such as exchange or friendship theory, may have missed. We were interested in the whole of the family's experience; what was salient and meaningful for the family members themselves, the difficulties or demands they encountered (Martinson, Chesla, & Muwaswes, 1993) and the skills and practices they developed in living with a person with AD. Through family members' narratives over an 18-month time span, it was evident that relationship issues were paramount to family members in their everyday lives and that qualitatively distinct forms of relations between ill members and other family members were evident.

Relationships Between Caregivers and Family Members with AD

Although little attention has been paid to the positive or sustaining aspects of caring for a family member with AD, detailed studies of the relationship between the AD patient and the family show that: (a) relationships change over time and intimacy declines with time for some but not for all family members (Blieszner & Shifflett, 1990); (b) care of a family member with AD brings both suffering and rewards; and (c) reciprocity in the relationship with a family member with dementia seems to be a key aspect reported by families, but can take many forms (Farran, Keane-Hagarty, Salloway, Kupferer, & Wilken, 1991; Hirschfeld, 1983; Orona, 1990).

Blieszner and Shifflett (1990) produced a sensitive analysis of caregivers' responses to the first 18 months of care after AD had been diagnosed. They found that intimacy between AD patients and family caregivers diminished over the first 18 months of care and that a host of emotional responses was elicited for family caregivers at each point in time. At diagnosis, there was relief at having an understanding of what was happening, but also anger, sadness, and grief. Six months into the disorder, family members focused on the loss of the previously established relationship with the AD patient. One year and six months after diagnosis, caregivers were found to be coping with a dramatically changed but continuing relationship. Coping strategies that predominated were redefining the relationship, working on closure in the relationship, and working on expanding caregiver role responsibilities. These investigators found that, although caregivers on average felt less intimate with the person with AD, some caregivers reported increased intimacy

as the disease progressed (Blieszner & Shifflett, 1989).

Hirschfeld (1983) developed in her grounded theory study a concept of "mutuality" in caregiver, care receiver relations. Mutuality was defined as the caregiver's capacity to find: (a) gratification in the relationship with the impaired person; (b) positive meaning from the caregiving situation; and (c) a sense of reciprocity, even in situations where the elder had severe dementia. The sample of 30 caregivers included both spouses and children of elders with senile brain disease. Most striking was Hirschfeld's finding that the higher the mutuality in the relationship, the less likely the caregiver was to consider institutionalization of the elder.

In a small grounded theory study of family members who cared for a member with AD, Orona (1990) focused on identity loss of the AD patient and its impact on the dyadic relationship over time. Using a social constructionist framework, Orona noted temporality as an important subjective aspect of the caregiving experience. Facets of temporal experience were: (a) the use of memories to maintain the identity of the AD person, (b) the re-enactment of meaningful social interactions with the AD person, and (c) the use of memories as a basis for constructing new images for the future. Caregivers were found to engage in "identity maintenance" via everyday activities with the AD family member, and when reciprocity was lost, these relatives "worked both sides of the relationship," or took on both the caregiver's and the AD patient's social roles, in order to continue some part of the past relating.

In summary, detailed studies that have examined a family member's experience with a relative with dementia over time undermine any standard depiction of the process. Rather, they demonstrate complex variability in issues of intimacy, reciprocity, and management of life tasks given the unbalanced capabilities of well and ill members. Questions remain about the basic nature of these relations and how they evolve over time.

METHOD

This study was designed within a tradition known as hermeneutic phenomenology (Benner & Wrubel, 1989; Packer & Addison, 1989; Van Manen, 1990). The aim of the method is to explain particular and distinct patterns of meaning and action in the lives of those studied, taking into account the context in which they live, their history, and their particular concerns. Rather than trying to characterize a modal or group response, research within this method

provides detailed explanations of varied patterns of human understanding and action. The method is: (a) systematic in its use of practiced modes of questioning the informant about experiences; (b) explicit in its attempt to articulate, through careful interpretation of a text, the meanings embedded in human experience; (c) self-critical and self-corrective in its continual examination of interpretations made on a text; and (d) a shared interpretation that is consensually agreed upon by multiple readers (Van Manen, 1990).

This phenomenological study was part of a multifaceted, longitudinal study of the impact of Alzheimer's Disease on the family and caregiver (Martinson, Gilliss, Doyle, & Muwaswes, 1983). Only the phenomenologic interview data are reported here. Fifteen spouses and fifteen adult-child family members were recruited from support groups and clinics serving AD patients. Semistructured, intensive interviews were conducted at intake and every six months for 18 months. In each interview, family members were asked to reflect on their experiences in the previous 6 months and on changes in the AD patient, family members' feelings, and care arrangements. They were asked to provide narratives of salient, difficult, or memorable episodes of care that had arisen in the past 6 months. Full narratives of the episodes, preceding events, caregivers' emotions, thoughts, and actions throughout the episodes and outcomes were elicited. The interviews, which lasted approximately one hour, were audiotaped and transcribed verbatim.

Hermeneutic interpretation (Packer & Addison, 1989; Van Manen, 1990) of texts from the interviews comprise this paper. The first author, educated in Heideggerian philosophy and hermeneutics, directed the interpretive process and interpreted all texts with the third author. The second author was familiar with all interview texts and provided consensus on summary interpretations.

Interpretation was comprised of two interwoven processes: thematic interpretation and interpretation of exemplars. Three levels of thematic interpretation were used to uncover and isolate themes in a text: (a) the holistic approach, (b) the selective approach, and (c) the detailed or line-by-line approach. In the holistic approach, the whole text was read through and described as a piece in an attempt to capture the fundamental meaning of the text as a whole. In the selective approach, aspects of the text that stood out as essential or revealing of the phenomenon under study were the focus. A line-by-line detailed reading was then completed in which the text was examined for what it revealed about the experience. After completing all three steps, the text was examined in its entirety, in its particular salience, and for fine-grained nuances.

Interpretation of exemplars occurred simultaneously with the search for general themes. Exemplars are narratives of whole incidents of family care elicited from participants in the interviews. All relevant aspects of each exemplar were coded together, including the family member's recollection of what preceded the episode, how the episode unfolded, emotions at the start and throughout the episode, actions considered and taken, direct and indirect clues to what was at stake for the family, and the family member's retrospective reworking of the situation. These episodes, in their complete form, served as examples of particular patterns of action that included a rich description of the situation and responses that evidenced family member's understandings, concerns, and practical involvements with the AD patient.

FINDINGS

Description of Informants

Eighteen of the family members interviewed were female (7 wives and 11 daughters), and twelve were male (8 husbands and 4 sons). The mean age of family members was 57 years. Family members were predominantly Caucasian and from middle socioeconomic strata.

Eight male and 22 female persons with AD entered the study. Their mean age was 74 years (range 59-86) and the mean duration of the illness was 4 years (range 1-11 years). Twenty persons with AD at the start of the study resided in the home of a family member, seven were institutionalized in a nursing or board and care home, and three lived alone. Residence status changed with each data collection period, and at six months 17 AD patients lived in their caregiver's home, 11 lived in institutions, 1 lived alone, and 1 person with AD died. By 18 months, 8 were living in the caregiver's home, 8 were institutionalized, 1 was still living alone, 8 persons with AD had died, and 5 family members had withdrawn from the study.

Severity of the AD patients' illness, as measured by the Mini-Mental Status Exam (Folstein, Folstein, & McHugh, 1975) indicated moderate to severe cognitive dysfunction. Mean scores for AD patients were 9.4 (*SD* = 6.7) at induction and 6.4 (*SD* = 8.06) six months later on a 30-point scale, where a score below 24 indicates some cognitive impairment. On a second measure of illness severity, the Older Adults Multifunctional Assessment Questionnaire (Fillenbaum & Smyer, 1981), the AD patients scored significantly lower (*p* < .001) on mea-

sures of physical health and activities of daily living than a comparison group of institutionalized elderly.

Interpretive Findings

Continuity and discontinuity in the relationship between the family member and the person with AD were salient issues in two paradigm cases in an early reading of the narratives. A paradigm case is an outstanding instance of a pattern of narratives that seem to go together, the coherence of which is visible only through the whole reading of a particular case. Continuity and discontinuity in these two cases seemed to set up the kind of care that the family member had with the AD patient. The finding challenged our assumption of what AD relations might be, which most closely resembled a third pattern we eventually observed and labeled *continuous but transformed*. After recognition and identification of three dominant forms of relating through paradigm cases, the texts from the remaining informants were identified as being strongly similar to the aspects of relating evident in these three predominant forms.

One aspect of the experience of living with and caring for a family member with AD is presented in this article: the existential relation that family members had with their spouse or parent with AD as evidenced by their narratives of providing day-to-day care. Three forms of relationship will be presented: (a) a relationship that is maintained as continuous with the relationship between caregiver and AD patient prior to the disease, (b) a relationship that is continuous but is transformed by the disease, and (c) a relationship in which there is radical discontinuity between the present and prior relationship.

Relationship as Continuous

Some family members found possibilities in their relationships to continue to be a wife, daughter, husband or son to the person with AD. Despite the changes in the person with AD, family members continued to define themselves "in relation to" the patient in ways that paralleled their relations prior to the disease. These family members interpreted small gestures or statements made by the AD patient as continuous with past behavior and found remnants of the AD patient's intentions, wishes, likes and dislikes in present behavior. Dramatic losses and changes in the relationship were not denied and there was particular sensitivity in this group to patients' functional and memory losses. Despite realistic assessment and grieving, these family members felt a sense of connection to and continuity with the patient. They watched for, held pre-

cious, and felt comforted by, familiar responses and behaviors by the patient.

One woman exemplifies continuous relating with an AD spouse. She is a 75-year-old woman who had been married to her husband for more than 54 years. The husband had shown signs of AD for the past 10 years and during the course of the study declined from almost complete dementia to death.

This woman's narratives provide evidence that her relationship to her husband is almost unaltered from the life they shared prior to the illness. Despite the AD, she finds access to his person, his intelligence, and his capacity to comfort her. She is distressed that her husband, who never used profanity, now curses her in anger and tries to hit her if he is confused. However, the man with whom she built a life and a family, the person that comprised her world prior to the illness, continues to define her world and focus her daily concerns. She finds comfort that they can share a bed together and feels his presence very strongly in her life. In the first two interviews, when they lived together in their retirement apartment, she noted repeated instances where her husband seemed present and interacted with her in familiar ways:

> Wife: The other morning, for instance, he woke up early and I was just barely awake, and he reached over and held my hand. So you know that is a lot really. He's here. He always has been a very gentle, caring sort of person.

She noted incidents where he commented on her clothes, "I always liked you in that," or tried to comfort her when she became tearful. From an outsider's perspective, his behavior could have been interpreted as random or meaningless, but the woman interprets it as meaningful, coherent, and indicative of his past and present personhood.

This woman's respect for her husband's continuity of person appears in the way she approaches his physical care. She values his lifelong habits and practices and continues them for him now that he cannot carry them out.

> Wife: My son said 'Well you don't have to shave Dad everyday.' I said, 'I know he doesn't have much of a beard but he likes being shaved.' He sometimes sings when I'm shaving him. I remember he always used to clean his finger nails every morning when he was getting ready to go. So why not do that?

In a similar way, this woman relied on past relationship patterns with her husband to comfort *her*. She told of two stressful incidents in which her husband wandered away from her. In both incidents, her husband was found within minutes, but she experienced extreme anxiety and distress, fearing he might be harmed or permanently lost. Both times, she calmed her husband and comforted herself by sitting and talking with him.

> Wife: Well, I talk to him. I just say, 'you know, you really scared me, and you worry me when you wander away like that. I can't keep track of you all the time.' I just talk like you would in general.
>
> Interviewer: And that helps you?
>
> Wife: Yea.
>
> Interviewer: Do you think that sinks in?
>
> Wife: No. It's helpful for me to talk to him. We always talked a lot.

Conversing with her husband re-enacted a 54-year-old ritual in which they sat together and had a glass of wine each night when her husband returned from work. This ritual was time-honored and practiced no matter what was happening with their household of seven children.

One year into the study, the husband had a stroke and had to be placed in a nursing home. While this dramatically changed the nature of her care responsibilities, her relationship with her husband continued largely unchanged. She went to the nursing home for many hours each day to monitor his care and bring him foods he liked. In the final interview, after her husband died, she recounted her sense of continuity with her husband.

> Interviewer: So the Alzheimer's disease didn't take that away from you, that happy feeling of being married to Ron and that relationship you felt with him?
>
> Wife: No, it never did. Never. I would have been happy to bring him home again. . . . I mean, I would have gone on indefinitely. One of the books I read said they usually have Alzheimer's for about 15 years. So I figured that I had about another 7 years to go. He'd come home from the hospital before, so I thought he'd be coming home again, I really did.
>
> Interviewer: So you really felt you had an ongoing relationship with him?
>
> Wife: Yes.

This case demonstrates several aspects of a continuous relationship with an AD family member: (a) the interpretation that the AD patient is still present despite the disease, (b) the interpretation that the person with AD reciprocates in positive ways, and (c) the AD patient continues to define the spouse's or child's world in stable and relatively unchanging ways.

In a similar way, adult children maintained the parent in a place of respect and esteem despite the advance of the disease. Although the parent could not provide advice or support, he or she was still respected and honored by the child as his or her parent. Adult children in this group expressed concern that they "try to maintain her dignity" and "not strip everything away from her."

One daughter's capacity to see her mother in small aspects of the mother's behavior remained present, as in the prior case, throughout the 18-month study. During that time, the mother's physical and mental health declined, she suffered numerous strokes, and the AD progressed to the extent that the mother required placement in a board and care home and eventually a nursing home. Still, the daughter felt an attachment to what she saw in her mother's behavior and appearance that still represented "mother." The daughter continued practices that her mother had maintained throughout her lifetime: coloring her hair red and manicuring her nails. Until the end of the study, the daughter claimed that her relationship with her mother was alive and vibrant.

> Interviewer: So you still very much have that bond with her?
>
> Daughter: Oh yes. I will sit there with her in the evenings. I'll sit on the bed and she's in the wheelchair, and I'll put my arm around her and cuddle with her.
>
> Interviewer: She still likes affection from you?
>
> Daughter: Oh yes. She responds to that. Awhile back when I told her I loved her, I was very richly rewarded because she told me, 'I love you.' That just leveled me. I try to hang on to what's still left of her. She still knows me; she still knows chocolate; she still remembers hymns; she's not gone yet. There's still Mama there.

Relationship is Continuous but Transformed

Another group of family members described the AD patient as fairly lost to them because of AD. These spouses and children saw minimal, residual, and fleeting signs of the AD person's personality and either had doubts about their accessibility or saw them as totally inaccessible. What remained, however, was a strong commitment to the relationship, to maintaining contact with the person that the patient had *become* in the disease. Because of the changes in the AD patient, past relations were mourned, and current relations were on a new footing.

> Interviewer: Is she still the same person to you?
>
> Daughter: No. Oh no! She's a totally different person. She's not Helen anymore. She's not my mom. No. She's just there in body.

These family members found ways to relate to the patient as the symptoms progressed, and continued to adapt their ways of relating as the AD person's capacities became more constricted. For example, one man reported in the first three interviews that his greatest fear was that his wife would no longer recognize him. In the abstract, he feared that her lack of recognition would break the thin continuity that he felt with her. Additionally, he said he was most sustained by his wife's contentment and recognition. Then in the last interview, his wife increasingly did not recognize him. He then found a new way to stay connected to her in her current capacities. He no longer worried that she recognize him but found it essential that she appreciate him and accept his care. Her willingness to eat what he prepared and her cooperation with the caregivers he hired were taken as signs of her acceptance of his care.

Family members who experienced their relationships as transformed lived more in synchrony with the actual decline in the AD patient's functioning than did those family members who experienced continuity in relations with the AD member. Their relationship with the patient evolved and changed with the changes in the disease. They saw their possibilities for relating to the person with AD as being more firmly bounded by the actual symptomatic changes in the person than did those family members who experienced a continuous relationship with the family member with AD.

In the continuous but transformed relationship, reciprocity between the patient and family members was seen as minimally possible and always in doubt. The patient's fleeting smiles or signs of pleasure were noted by family members and brought them satisfaction. What distinguished these family members from those in the continuous relationship category is the fact that small gestures by the AD patient were not interpreted as indications that the patient was still "there" in the same way that those who had continuous relationships interpreted these signs.

> Daughter: I just feel like I've already lost her. She's here but she isn't here. It's probably the most difficult thing.

Spouses found living in this ambiguous relationship difficult because they could no longer relate to their partner as an intimate friend or sexual partner and at the same time they remained married and deeply committed to the spouse. Children also experienced the ambiguity in relations as a dilemma, although the day-to-day impact on their lives was less than for spouses. The children never talked of finding a replacement relationship for that which they had lost, but many of the spouses wished this were possible.

In families where the relationship was transformed, the primary relationship concerns were to provide sensitive care that maintained the dignity of the person and to sustain the AD patient's functional abilities. One spouse, who exemplifies these concerns, demonstrated that to be a good husband to his wife meant providing good care. To this end, he gave up his job in international business and turned his energies entirely to the care of his wife. In his interviews he was exclusively focused on his wife's care requirements and how to sensitively meet them in a way that maintained her current functioning and dignity. He was deeply committed to taking good care of his wife, deeply grieved when there was any evidence that he was not doing a good job, and satisfied when he was successful.

Relationship is Radically Discontinuous

In the third form of relating to a family member with AD, the relationship with the spouse or parent was radically discontinuous with the relationship that existed prior to the illness. These family members found no continuity in the AD patient's personhood and instead found that the AD rendered the patient unrecognizable. They found the behaviors and symptoms of AD to be an affront to the person he or she had been prior to the disease. The relationship these family members experienced was less emotional, less personal and more clinical than that of the first two groups. In their interpretation, the spouse or parent was lost in the disease, and therefore the family member could not continue a truly personal relationship. The concern of these family members for the patient was more objective, abstract, and less tailored to the particular needs of their AD family member.

The coping narratives of these family members focused on caregiving arrangements and problems. When the AD patient gave signs of recognition or pleasure, these family members, like others, were pleased and touched. They did not, however, attempt to elicit such signs and did not interpret such signs as evidence of purposeful, personalized behavior. They diminished the importance of instances of recognition. Instead, there was more of a clinical distancing

and evaluation of the person's disease process.

Emotional distancing was evident in a daughter whose mother had contracted the disease eight years earlier. The daughter described a recent incident where her mother said something that actually seemed to make sense. The daughter was about to take her mother off the commode and the mother said "no" because she needed to stay longer. This moment of possible lucidity in a woman who had not been lucid for 2 years surprised the daughter. But when the interviewer probed about how the incident affected her, she replied:

Daughter: I don't think it made a difference. I found it interesting that she said 'no' definitely. I thought to myself, how does the correlation go there?

The mother's statement raised for the daughter a clinical question, rather than a relational response. The daughter wondered about how the disease worked, rather than how her mother experienced the disease. Witnessing her mother make sense, and thus have some possibility of making meaningful contact with current reality, made the daughter feel neither closer to nor more distant from her mother. In this daughter's understanding of the situation, the possibility of connecting with her mother simply was not present.

One husband provides some insight about how this emotional break in his relationship with his wife occurred. He recounted that prior to the AD they were "best friends," "did everything together" and in many ways she defined his life. When facing up to her illness, he recognized the only way that he could stay in a relationship with his wife was if he were to "die" himself.

Husband: I think somehow I'm hardened. If I can say it like that. I've become hardened to a lot of it. It may be by design. Because I had to decide, when I talked about that turning point, whether I was going to live, or whether I was going to sit here and curl up and die because she's got that disease. I don't know if the word's martyr or. . . . Anyway I'm not going to sit around here and let it kill me. I think that's what it was doing.

The dissolution of the relationship with his wife is also evident in this man's hopes and fears for the future. The best possible life he hoped for was: "I would feel good if she died, the sooner the better." He also felt that the worst life for him would be if his wife were to continue to live, and hold him in this "limbo" of being "married, but not married."

Family members who realized radical discontinuities in their relationships

with the AD patient may have had a wide variety of predisposing factors. Perhaps they as a group had more conflicted relations with the person with AD prior to the disease, and thus the disease introduced unsurmountable distance. Perhaps they had difficulty coping with the pervasive losses that one must face as a loved one progresses through AD and distancing was one way of warding off the pain of these losses. We lack the data to thoroughly understand *how* family members came to a discontinuous relationship with the AD patient. What was evident was that these family members found few, if any, possibilities for relating to the person with AD that paralleled their relationship prior to the disease.

Despite the emotional distance that typified the discontinuous relationship, providing good care was a central and focusing concern for family members who experienced this relationship. Proper diet, supervision, safety, and comfort of the AD patient were all raised as issues in the family members' narratives. Providing or arranging care demanded extensive daily effort and time and some of these family members were the primary or sole providers of care. What distinguished the care concerns of this group of families was their relative lack of concern that the care be tailored to the present or past personal needs of the AD patient.

DISCUSSION

In this intensive study of the relationships between family members and AD patients over time, we discovered qualitatively distinct ways that family members interpreted the AD patient's accessibility, capacity to reciprocate affection and concern, and capacity to *relate* as parent or spouse to the family member. For some family members of persons with AD, the loss of self and transformation of the person with AD by the disease were not complete. For these family members, the life and capacities of the person with AD were still a part of their ongoing relationship either fully or in a diminished and transformed way. For other family members, however, the disease covered over the person, overrode their relational possibilities, and care became much more strategic or objectified.

All three forms of relating (continuous, transformed, or discontinuous) presented here were evident in both the children's and spouses' relations with the person with AD. With the exception of continuous relating, both male and female caregivers experienced each form of relating. In our group of informants, there were no male caregivers who demonstrated the continuous form of relating, and wives of persons with AD were the most predominant in this group of caregivers. We acknowledge that the forms of relating that we present may not represent all of the possibilities for how relations between family and the person with AD might evolve. For example, we interviewed only persons who maintained some kind of relationship with the person with AD, whether that relationship was personal or merely organizational. Thus, we have no information on the ways in which family members may sever their relationship with the person with AD.

The severity of illness in the person with AD did not seem to determine the form of relationship that was described by the family member. Moderate to severe Alzheimer's disease was evident in all three forms of relationships when data from both family member ratings and interviewer ratings were considered. The disease itself, and the progression of the disease, was not a clear determinant of what the relationship might be.

Our findings support and further articulate detailed qualitative studies of AD family relationships reported to date. Like Blieszner and Shifflett (1990), we found that closeness between the person with AD and the family members diminished for some but remained strong for others over time, despite sometimes dramatic progression of the dementia and, thus, a decrease in the AD person's "objective" capacities to relate. Orona (1990) reported interactions similar to those we observed in the first two groups of our sample: the reenactment of familiar rituals and the searching for and success at finding familiar behaviors and expressions in the AD patient. She similarly reported the phenomena we observed in the continuous relationships of "working both sides" of the relationship, filling in additional meanings for vague or difficult to interpret behaviors by the person with AD.

Hirschfeld (1983) combined three dimensions of mutuality in a single concept. Considering Hirschfeld's concept of mutuality in light of our own findings, we believe that her three aspects of mutuality might offer greater explanatory power in terms of caregivers' involvements if they are examined independently. In this study, we found that: (a) the caregiver's capacity to find gratification in the *relationship* with the impaired person, (b) *positive* meaning of caregiving, and (c) a sense of *reciprocity* with the care recipient, all aspects of mutuality, did not combine in meaningful ways in our groups of family members who provided care. For example, family members in the continuous group seemed to experience all three dimensions of mutuality in a consistent, coherent fashion. Family members in the con-

tinuous but transformed group also experienced positive meanings from the care situation, questionable reciprocity, and some gratification from the relationship, but here it was a relation acknowledged to be changed by the disease. Finally, family members in the discontinuous group experienced substantial positive meanings from giving care, but found no sense of reciprocity in the caregiving relationship and made almost no mention of relationship gratifications with the AD patient. We believe that Hirschfeld identified important explanatory dimensions in the relationship of family and persons with AD and argue for further refinement of the "mutuality" concept so that each dimension be examined as qualitatively distinct.

Our findings are not in conflict with, but are distinct from, the prevailing themes in the literature on family factors and AD care. This literature has largely ignored the quality of the relationship between the person with AD and the family member who provides care, assuming instead that the former is a passive, uninvolved recipient of care and the latter is burdened by the responsibility for this passive object/person. We wish to argue that the qualitative aspects of the relationship between the AD person and the family members described in this research deserve a more prominent place in research on family processes in relation to AD care. Alongside continuing efforts to identify factors that place the family at risk for negative outcomes, conceptualizations and investigations of family care processes must begin to include an awareness of relationships that may be sustaining and meaningful. As Hirschfeld's research demonstrated a decade ago, the relational qualities may have powerful explanatory power in how families function over time.

CLINICAL IMPLICATIONS

Recognizing that family members who care for a person with AD have distinct relations with that person is vital to their sensitive care and support. Relying on standardized responses to the family situation, or relying on the pervasive literature that emphasizes the losses, burdens, and difficulties in AD care, may lead professionals to overlook the family members' possibilities for hope, satisfaction, and continuity in their relations with and care of the AD patient.

Care for family members who experience their relationship as continuous might explicitly legitimatize their experience of the person as present and encourage their efforts to continue the AD patient's habits and practices. The biomedicalization of dementia (Lyman,

1989) may be so complete that family members feel criticized or isolated because they continue to relate to the person with AD. In recognizing the two-way nature of the family relations, health professionals should give credence to the AD patient as a person with a history and recognize further the AD patient's capacity to carry on in a meaningful way in relationships despite the debilitations of the dementia. Rather than emphasizing the negative changes wrought by the disease, health professionals might learn from family members how the disease makes possible continued exercise of lifelong marital or parental relations. Family members additionally might inform practitioners about authentic commitments to the care of beloved family members that are neither self-sacrificing nor "loving too much." For some, care of the person with AD is the genuine working out and fulfillment of a lifelong relationship; therefore, it is not experienced as burdensome but sustaining and meaningful.

The group of family members who experience a continuous relationship with the person with AD might have the most difficulty, however, with recognizing the true limitations that occur over time in the AD person's abilities. Although all caregivers we observed provided safe and protective environments, some had their choices for care restricted because they believed that the person with AD was capable of doing things that seemed unlikely. Respectful solicitation of what family members perceive as the capabilities of the AD person, and feedback by the professional regarding these perceptions are warranted.

Family members who experienced their relationship with the AD patient as continuous but transformed might similarly benefit from interventions that respect their efforts at continued close relations with the person with AD. These family members, who are more in synchrony with the changes of the disease, are particularly apt to observe firsthand a decline in the AD patient's abilities. Care of these family members may involve helping them find ways to maintain their commitment to closeness, while at the same time being respectful of the AD patient's new restrictions. Providing examples of how other family members have coped with this dilemma, like the spouse who no longer needed his wife's recognition, but merely needed her acceptance of his care, might make these transitions easier.

Work with family members who experience their relationship with the person with AD as discontinuous could focus on helping them find some continuities in the person despite the AD, assisting them with appropriate care arrangements, and showing appreciation for their existential experience of distance from their prior relations with the person with AD. These family members may need help in recognizing that AD dementia does not immediately and totally transform a person, and that she or he may actively contribute to and participate in the life of the family. These family members may also benefit from a frank discussion about how we live in a culture where caring for others is seldom valued, and how the person providing care may be misunderstood as "addicted" to or dependent upon his or her need to care for others (Dreyfus & Rubin, in press). Offering a positive connotation for care of a family member who has AD may make closer relations possible for these families. Both of these interventions, however, must be tempered by attention to the family member's current possibilities in relation to the AD patient. Some family members, because of their background with the AD patient or because of their current social context, cannot tolerate closer emotional proximity to the AD patient, and thus their distance must be honored.

REFERENCES

Baumgarten, M. (1989). The health of persons giving care to the demented elderly: A critical review of the literature. *Journal of Clinical Epidemiology*, 42, 1137-1148.

Benner, P., & Wrubel, J. (1989). *The primacy of caring, stress and coping in health and illness.* Menlo Park, CA: Sage.

Blieszner, R., & Shifflett, P. A. (1989). Affection, communication and commitment in adult-child caregiving for parents with Alzheimer's disease. In J. A. Mancini (Ed.), *Aging parents and adult children* (pp. 231-242). Lexington, MA: Lexington Books.

Blieszner, R., & Shifflett, P. A. (1990). The effects of Alzheimer's disease on close relationships between patients and caregivers. *Family Relations*, 39, 57-62.

Bowers, B. J. (1987). Intergenerational caregiving: Adult caregivers and their aging parents. *Advances in Nursing Science*, 9(2), 20-31.

Cohen, D., & Eisdorfer, C. (1986). *The loss of self.* New York: Norton.

Colerick, E. J., & George, L. K. (1986). Predictors of institutionalization among caregivers of patients with Alzheimer's Disease. *Journal of the American Geriatrics Society*, 34, 493-498.

Dreyfus, H., & Rubin, J. (in press). Kierkegaard on the nihilism of the present age: The case of commitment as addiction. *Synthese*.

Farran, C. J., Keane-Hagerty, E., Salloway, S., Kupferer, S., & Wilken, C.S. (1991). Finding meaning: An alternative paradigm for Alzheimer's Disease family caregivers. *The Gerontologist*, 31, 483-489.

Fillenbaum, G. G., & Smyer, M. A. (1981). The development, validity and reliability of the OARS Multidimensional Functional Assessment Questionnaire. *Journal of Gerontology*, 36, 428-434.

Folstein, M., Folstein, S., & McHugh, P. (1975). Mini-mental state: A practical method for grading the cognitive state of patients for the clinician. *Journal of Psychiatric Research*, 12, 189-198.

Hirschfeld, M. (1983). Homecare versus institutionalization: Family caregiving and senile brain disease. *International Journal of Nursing Studies*, 20, 23-32.

Kuhlman, G. J., Wilson, H. S., Hutchinson, S. A., & Wallhagen, M. (1991). Alzheimer's disease and family caregiving: Critical synthesis of the literature and research agenda. *Nursing Research*, 40, 331-337.

Liptzin, R., Grob, M., & Eisen, S. (1988). Family burden of demented and depressed elderly psychiatric inpatients. *The Gerontologist*, 28, 397-401.

Lyman, K. A. (1989). Bring the social back in: A critique of the biomedicalization of dementia. *The Gerontologist*, 29, 597-605.

Martinson, I. M., Chesla, C., & Muwaswes, M. (1993). Caregiving demands of patients with Alzheimer's Disease. *Journal of Community Health Nursing*, 10, 225-232.

Martinson, I., Gilliss, C. L., Doyle, G., & Muwaswes, M. (1983). *The impact of Alzheimer's Disease on the family and caregiver.* San Francisco: University of California.

Orona, C. J. (1990). Temporality and identity loss due to Alzheimer's Disease. *Social Science in Medicine*, 30, 1247-1256.

Ory, M. G., Williams, T. F., Emr, M., Lebowitz, B., Rabins, P., Salloway, J., Sluss-Radbaugh, T., Wolff, E., & Zarit, S. (1985). Families, informal supports and Alzheimer's Disease. *Research on Aging*, 7, 623-644.

Packer, M. J., & Addison, R. B. (1989). *Entering the circle: Hermeneutic investigation in psychology.* Albany: SUNY Press.

Quayhagen, M. P., & Quayhagen, M. (1988). Alzheimer's stress: Coping with the caregiving role. *The Gerontologist*, 28, 391-396.

Van Manen, M. (1990). *Researching lived experience.* London, Ontario: Althouse.

Walker, A. J., Pratt, C. C., & Oppy, N. C. (1992). Perceived reciprocity in family caregiving. *Family Relations*, 41, 82-85.

Wright, L. K., Clipp, E. C., & George, L. K. (1993). State of the art review: Health consequences of caregiver stress. *Medicine, Exercise, Nutrition & Health*, 2, 181-195.

EMBRACING OUR MORTALITY
❖ ❖ ❖ ❖ ❖ ❖

HARD LESSONS

Learning to let go of the uncontrollable

ELLEN PULLEYBLANK

Ellen Pulleyblank, Ph.D., is a psychologist in private practice. Address: 230 California Avenue, Suite 200, Palo Alto, CA 94301.

HANGING ON THE WALL OF OUR LIV-ing room in Palo Alto was a photograph of my 3-year-old daughter, Sarah, hands on her hips, her name emblazoned on her sweat-shirt. She was formidable even at that age, taking on her six-foot father, never flinch-ing as he towered above her, challenging her typical response of "No." She would build a fort in her room and decide who could enter and who would be barred. No easy child to live with, but how I admired her will. When she was a teenager, Sarah looked at that photograph on the wall, and then at her father, inert in his wheelchair, hooked up to a ventilator. The now 14-year-old Sarah asked me where I thought that feisty little girl had gone. I imagined that, like me, she had been slammed so hard by circumstance that she had simply disap-peared.

In the summer of 1985, during a sabbati-cal year in Europe, my husband, Ron, be-gan having trouble tying knots. Then came difficulty with riding a bicycle and undoing buttons. In October, at a hospital in the Netherlands, he was diagnosed with Amyo-trophic Lateral Sclerosis, or Lou Gehrig's Dis-ease. By the end of the year, he could not dress himself and fell frequently. Just be-fore Christmas, a year later, he could no longer breathe on his own and was put on

a ventilator. He came home from the hospi-tal–via ambulance–to round-the-clock nursing care. He could not feed himself, and it be-came progressively harder for him to swal-low and speak. His body, below the neck, became utterly still. And that is how we lived–Ron and I and our daughters Caitlin and Sarah–for seven years.

During those years, part of me van-ished. I am embarrassed when I re-member how strong and certain I used to be. Until Ron was diagnosed, I be-lieved unquestioningly in personal re-sponsibility and free will. I had faith in human beings' capacity for change, and I took that faith forward into my life, into my work as a therapist, and into my relationships.

Such beliefs had shaped my life since the time in my early twenties when I was hospitalized with what was then called a nervous breakdown. Ron and I were newly married, and he was in graduate school, studying electrical en-gineering. I had no idea what I was go-ing to do with my life and I couldn't stop crying. One day a young woman, also a patient at the hospital, jumped off the roof. At that moment, I realized that I was the only one who could keep myself safe and alive.

I went to graduate school, began to work as a family therapist, got my Ph.D., and took care of my growing family. In the 1970s and early 1980s, when we lived in Stockton, California, I

was part of a group of women who raised $1 million dollars to start a mul-ti-service womens' center. I was often admired for my guts, my energy and my willingness to help—qualities that I took for granted, without even noticing the personal and societal supports that held me up and made it possible for me to be so confident.

That is the part of me that vanished after Ron got sick. At first, I tried to take charge, make do, run the show, but I couldn't keep it up. I began to see the world as a place containing tragic forces beyond our understanding, beyond our ability to adapt. I was hum-bled by how little I knew about myself, others and the universe.

Now, after Ron's illness and death, my psychology practice is less about reliev-ing suffering or changing experience or cir-cumstances and more about learning how to bear suffering and stay alive. Before, I believed that right thinking, feeling and acting led to relief, and that I could help show the way. But tragedy showed me that sometimes there can be no relief, at least not at first. There was nothing I could do that even touched the depth of my family's pain and difficulties.

Watching Ron become more and more disabled and ultimately choose to die changed what I now pay attention to and how I respond. My work with my clients now is built on what I learned:

To bear pain by paying attention to it;

I remember sitting on the deck one afternoon with Ron. He was cold. I massaged his arms and hands, got him more warm clothing, and moved his chair into the sun. He was still cold and he was crying. I realized that all I could do was sit next to him and bear the pain with him. It was so little, but it was all I could do and I couldn't do it for long.

To witness the suffering of others by staying present and doing only what is possible;

To stop expecting rational explanations for the unexplainable;

To ask the community for help;

To let go of control of the uncontrollable; and

To focus less on our responsibility to ourselves, and more on what we have to offer each other.

FOR MONTHS AFTER RON CAME home from the hospital and was on the ventilator, I would sometimes sit bolt upright in the middle of the night, thinking that something horrible was about to happen, and then realize that it already had. I would try to figure out what to do, try to distract myself, and then give up and lie awake. One night, in desperation, I went toward my fear instead of moving away from it—I gave it all my attention, feeling the physical sensation in the pit of my stomach, and watching: I didn't fight my sensations; I let go of control. I stopped trying to protect myself from the stark terror of the unknown. I was swept up and knocked out by my fear.

By then, Ron was sleeping alone in a hospital bed, his ventilator beeping regularly through the night. For months I could not decide where to sleep. Sometimes I spent the night on the living room couch or in a spare upstairs bedroom. Wherever I lay, I began to follow the nightly ritual of going toward my pain. When I couldn't stand it, I would count backwards for relief, follow my breath, and then go toward my fear

again. One night, I had the unmistakable feeling that I was being held in loving arms. This feeling came back from time to time, giving me comfort and a sense of well-being. After a while, I learned how to summon it at will, by breathing, staying with my pain and remembering and thinking of loving arms.

SIMON, A SHORT, PUDGY, BEARDED man, wearing a yarmulke, his clothes in disarray, asked for a session alone. Usually I see him with his wife or with other family members. He tells me that he has brought a list of reasons why he's having such a hard time looking for a job.

"I am too old. I am too fat," he reads. "The market is very bad right now. If I move to where the children are, they might move away and then where would I be? I am depressed and have little enthusiasm."

I fidget, wondering if I remembered to turn off the oven. I ask questions designed to show him how he is giving up his power and refusing to take responsibility for himself. He goes along with me for a while and then says, with surprising clarity, "You just don't get what is happening to me."

Three years earlier, his father, aged 86, had died suddenly. Simon had called on Sunday, as he usually did, and his mother had told him his father was out for a walk. Later that night, Simon's father had a heart attack, but his mother didn't let Simon know, because she didn't want to upset him. The following Thursday, his father was dead.

Simon dissolves into tears. "I miss my father," he wails.

"I am sorry," I say, "and I am sorry I didn't understand what a hard time you are having and how hard it must have been to write that list. Please read it to me again."

"I am too old. I am too fat. The market is very bad right now. If I move to where the children are, they might move away and then where would I be? I am depressed."

I listen intently, my own tears flowing as he focuses on his losses, finally offering him the attention he needs to stay with the pain.

I remember sitting on the deck one afternoon with Ron, trying to help him. He was having a bad day. He was cold. I massaged his arms and hands, got him more warm clothing, and moved his chair into the sun. He was still cold and he was crying. I realized that all I could

do was sit next to him and bear the pain with him. It was so little, but it was all I could do and I couldn't do it for long. My pain welled up, threatening to overwhelm me. I got up and went inside, leaving Ron on the deck, retreating from his suffering into my own.

Sometimes, now, I can bear incredible pain, and sometimes I can help my clients bear it too. Sometimes all we can do for one another is witness suffering by staying present.

SUSAN, WHOSE FATHER HAS COMmitted suicide, complains of confusion, exhaustion and feelings of anxiety when she is with her mother. She tells me all she is doing to try and help, while her mother stays mired in grief.

I suggest we sit together and just watch our breathing. It is a miracle: we don't have to do anything, the breath just comes. I ask her to imagine her mind as a sky and let thoughts, feelings and images fly by, in and out, not minding what flies through. Then I ask her to direct her attention to her body and suggest she locate where the strongest sensations are. I tell her to focus her attention on these sensations, to go toward them rather than move away from them.

Susan says it is unbearable knowing how sad her mother feels. She desperately wants to help. Obviously, we could work on boundary issues (and no doubt we will in other family sessions) but now I find myself working with Susan's desire to help. I ask her if she is willing to learn to witness her mother's pain and not try to change it. She struggles with this idea for a while and then I ask her to close her eyes again and practice watching her mother in pain. Silently she weeps as she watches her mother grieve, but her own breathing slows and deepens. She leaves the session later with a sense of relief.

◆ ◆ ◆ ◆

Before Ron was diagnosed, I thought that I could make sense of almost anything. I had lived in other cultures and worked with families from different ethnic backgrounds. I knew how to step aside and hear and appreciate different versions of reality and other experiences of suffering. Ron and I had always tried to understand each other and to communicate, and by and large we'd succeeded. Nothing, I felt, was insurmountable. But that began to change on the day in the Netherlands that I went to Ron's hospital room and met the doctor in the corridor. He was grave. Without looking me in the eye, he told me that

Ron would die within the year. He said it would be better if I did not tell him.

I immediately went into Ron's room and told him what the doctor had said. I was determined that whatever happened, we would face it together and talk about it. He looked at me without saying very much, and then we cried. We cried, along with our two daughters, for about two weeks.

Afterward, Ron decided he would go on with his life, as much as he could, as though nothing had changed. He continued his sabbatical, and when the year was over, he went back to work as an electrical engineer at Hewlett Packard in Palo Alto. I helped him dress in the mornings, and his colleagues gave him rides to work and carried his lunch tray for him. In December, after he woke up unable to breathe, the doctor in the emergency room told me that if we didn't put him on a ventilator, he would die. We didn't understand then that if you choose to turn a ventilator on, you will someday have to choose to turn it off.

Ron came home and worked half-time, using a special computer. He focused on staying alive, on keeping things the same. He continued to enjoy life and to value every day. Although his determination to go on was inspiring, he found it hard to understand why the children and I were grieving and why we felt so overwhelmed. His unspoken demand to us was that everything be as normal as possible, and that we not be too sad. As he struggled to stay alive, his world narrowed and he became oblivious to us. He stopped thinking about money and didn't notice when things were broken in the house. His most significant relationships were often with the nurses who cared for him 24-hours-a-day and who saw his illness from his perspective.

We lived parallel lives. I needed Ron to understand my fear and grief. He needed me to be unemotional and accept him as he was. He was angry with me for grieving, for trying to separate, although we never gave up the effort to understand each other. I was appalled at my inability to accept our circumstances. Nothing made sense.

Only in the last months of his life could Ron acknowledge the effects his illness had on him and on us. Just before Ron died, when even I could barely understand his labored speech, we talked about what had happened to us. It was beyond understanding. Only at the end could we look at each other with kindness and forgiveness, realizing

that we both had tried our best, but for the most part, we had failed. Things sometimes just don't make sense, and no amount of understanding and empathy or talk will explain them.

GABRIELLE, AGED 12, CAME IN with her father, George, and her new stepmother, Joan. Her parents divorced three years ago, after her mother fell in love with a neighbor and asked her father to leave. Her father has since remarried, and Joan has two children of her own. For months, Gabrielle has been raging and throwing tantrums, both at her own mother's house and with Joan.

She has decided not to speak to Joan either in my office or at home. Her rage has turned into a silent protest. Her father cares for her deeply and is worried about her. Joan is angry and disappointed because no matter what she does, Gabrielle does not like her and will not cooperate.

Gabrielle's father patiently describes his daughter's feelings to me. He tries to coax her to talk. She won't. I become interested in her silence and wonder out loud if, with her silence, Gabrielle has found a way to express her anger without hurting herself or others. I ask George and Joan to talk about what it will take to allow her silence, to respect it and to admire her honesty. Gabrielle looks out from behind the pillows she is hiding under. I ask them if we might sit together in silence and acknowledge with Gabrielle how difficult things have been, and how, from her point of view, none of it makes any sense. At the end of the session, Gabrielle cautiously begins to speak.

◆ ◆ ◆ ◆

About two years after Ron went on the ventilator, we started to run out of money. I couldn't think straight and I wasn't sleeping. One day I had lunch with my friends from the Stockton women's center. I had always been seen as the strong one, and they still saw me that way. They marveled at how I could do it.

Finally, I looked at them and said, "Help me. I can't do it. I can't." I felt such shame. How often I had offered to help others, feeling so magnanimous, blithely unaware of how hard it is to turn to others, to say you cannot manage your life on your own.

Of course they helped me. A community formed around us. People raised money—about $300,000 over the next

few years. Others visited or gave me respite time or helped us take Ron on extravagant outings to the symphony and even on vacations to a cabin near the sea. Near the end of Ron's life, a group of friends began meditating at our house weekly.

I had never thought of myself as the kind of person who would need help. Without the help that I asked for and received, we would have become destitute in every way.

NAOMI CAME TO SEE ME WITH HER parents, deeply confused about the source of her sadness. She is 14, very depressed, and refuses to go to school. She says she feels like an outsider and is treated like one. She tells me she lives in a community where everyone looks and tries to act the same. Her father, whose parents were Holocaust survivors, remembers going through much the same thing when he was younger. Her mother thinks Naomi has always been very sensitive, and mentions her own family's history of depression.

But when I meet with Naomi alone, she tells me more about the tangled communal and familial roots of her sorrow. Once, she tells me, her father came to her school and talked about what had happened to his parents in Auschwitz, and the kids snickered. None of their families had known similar experience. Since then, she has told other kids very little about her background. How is she to feel part of her community when her experience is so different, and she has shared so little of it? As she talks, I am reminded of how I felt walking around the streets of Palo Alto when Ron was disabled, looking at all the perfect houses and wondering what I was doing there with my disheveled life.

In family sessions, Naomi's father talks more about his own feelings of isolation when he was growing up. He tells Naomi how identifying with his history and with other Holocaust survivors had helped him. He realizes he hadn't told her this before because he hoped that she could be unaffected by the tragedy, but now he helps her become part of a community stretching through space and time.

The more Naomi acknowledges, to herself and to others, how the Holocaust has influenced her, the easier her life becomes. She makes a new friend at Wednesday-night school at Temple. At school, she begins to build community not by trying to fit in, but by identifying with her history and asking her friends to listen to her experiences. She is surprised to find out that most of the time, they are interested and friendly.

IN THE SPRING OF 1993, RON wrote a letter to our families, telling them that he had begun to think about dying. It had become almost impossible for him to use the computer. He was losing all speech. When I asked him whether we should sell the house, he finally realized that we were $150,000 in debt. I was exhausted; both of our daughters had stayed close to home, their lives on hold. For eight years, he had been determined to stay alive and keep things the same, and now he began to let go. Month by month, conversation by conversation, Ron got clearer and clearer. One day he decided to die, just as he decided so many other things in his life. He would think and think, and suddenly he would know.

Once he made the decision, he began to say goodbye in one halting conversation after another. By then, very few of us could understand him. I could do so only by focusing all my attention on each word. If I got a word wrong, even if it was close in meaning, Ron would ignore my attempt and repeat his word again and again, until I got it right. He said all of his goodbyes in his own way.

Then it was time. We sat in the living room—Ron, our daughters, Caitlin and Sarah, me, the doctor and a woman friend. The doctor gave Ron a small dose of morphine so he could relax.

Therapy is more than helping clients to take appropriate and responsible action to achieve their goals. I meet regularly with a group of therapists and physicians to explore what might be called "the work of the soul"–learning how to face the broad questions of human existence and to tolerate the realization that much of life is beyond our control.

Ron wanted to die naturally, without tubes or drugs. The doctor first removed the gastrostomy tube and then the ventilator. As soon as the tubes were gone, Ron's face changed. The strained, frozen look on his face melted, and my handsome husband returned. I found myself breathing more deeply, letting go deeper and deeper, as if my life depended on it. It was as if I was birthing Ron's death. My daughters, our friend and I held onto each other. Ron's body did not move as he died, and yet we all felt him leap out of that chair. Sarah later said she had literally held us down, because the energy was so strong that she was afraid

it would lift us all away. She had held onto me especially, because she thought I might want to leave with him, and she was right.

It is only recently that I feel glad that I am still here and not with Ron. Death seems so close. Life paled in the face of death. Only time, tears and loving arms made it possible for me to return to what I think of as "normal."

What I learned in all this is that birth and death are somehow the same, but each has its time and place. Ron's choice to go on the ventilator extended his life until the time when he was ready, after exploring all the possibilities he could see, to die.

In my work with clients, I find that quite often they, too, are talking about either their fear of death or their fear of life. I find myself asking them more about their views of life and death, and more about their spiritual beliefs and the practice of prayer. Over the past year, I have contemplated suicide, not knowing how to reattach myself to the earth. I wanted to die, partly out of curiosity, partly to follow Ron. Mostly I was caught in a flood of pain that did not let me see anything beyond my own suffering. But I chose to live: my suicide would have disrupted my possibilities here on earth. I once heard Carl Whitaker speak about all the forms of suicide he had considered, and how he ultimately chose life as the best form, since it, too, leads to death. I see the choices that Ron and I made in that same light: Though they may both sound like acts of will—choosing life, choosing death—I see them both as a letting go of control, as reentering a stream that is hurtling us to who knows where.

Families, Now and into the Future

What is the future of the family? Does the family even have a future? These questions and others like them are being asked. Many people fear for the future of the family. As previous units of this volume have shown, the family is a continually evolving institution that will continue to change throughout time. Still, certain elements of family appear to be constant. The family is and will remain a powerful influence in the lives of its members. This is because we all begin life in some type of family, and this early exposure carries a great deal of weight in forming our social selves, who we are and how we relate to others. From our families, we take our basic genetic makeup, while we also learn and are reinforced in health behaviors. In families, we are given our first exposure to values, and it is through families that we most actively influence others. Our sense of commitment and obligation begins within the family as well as our sense of what we can expect of others.

Much writing about families has been less than hopeful and has focused on ways of avoiding or correcting errors. The four articles in this unit take a positive view of family and its influences on its members. The emphasis is on health rather than dysfunction.

Increasing evidence of genetic factors in physical as well as mental health serves to promote the need for awareness of our family's health history. "Trace Your Family Tree" considers how charting your relatives' medical history can save your life. Ruth Papazian provides a useful technique for mapping out your family health history so that you can anticipate, plan, and possibly change your health behaviors. The next article, "Happy Families: Who Says They All Have to Be Alike?" provides glimpses of an assortment of happy, healthy families.

Geoffrey Cowley and Karen Springen's "Rewriting Life Stories" describes narrative therapy, a new and promising approach in family therapy that sees life as a series of stories that can be rewritten to find one's own strengths rather than weaknesses. Concluding this volume, "Rituals for Our Times," by family therapists Evan Imber-Black and Janine Roberts, describes the ways in which rites and ceremonies are used to strengthen families. Through examples, readers see how they might use ritual in their own families.

Looking Ahead: Challenge Questions

What type of future do you see for yourself after having charted your family's health history? What changes do you see yourself making in your life?

What decision have you made about long-term commitments—marriage or some other relationship? How about children?

How would rewriting your life story, or aspects of it, benefit you?

What is the state of rituals in your family? What rituals might you build in your family? Why bother?

TRACE YOUR FAMILY TREE

Charting your relatives' medical history can save your life

RUTH PAPAZIAN

Ruth Papazian, a New York City-based writer specializing in health and medicine, is constructing a family tree for herself and her niece and nephew.

When it comes to health, the apple doesn't fall far fom the family tree: Research suggests that an astonishing number of diseases—from rare to common—have some sort of hereditary link.

That is why constructing a family health tree can offer life-saving glimpses into your future. If you're at risk of inheriting a serious disease, you can get regular checkups to spot early symptoms and increase the chances for a cure. You may also want genetic counseling, to learn the risk of passing a disease on to your children.

Aside from health problems caused by accident or infectious disease, you can assume that most every disease in your family's background has some sort of genetic basis. These can be divided into two classes: *susceptibility diseases,* in which genes don't cause the problem but influence your risk of becoming ill; and *purely genetic diseases,* which people almost invariably develop if they inherit the requisite genes.

Susceptibility diseases typically occur later in life and include major ailments such as heart disease, diabetes (especially the non-insulin-dependent type) and several types of cancer, including breast, lung, colorectal (colon and rectal), prostate, ovarian and skin. The inherited tendency to develop a disease probably results from complex interactions among several genes. Also on the list of disorders with a genetic component: rheumatoid arthritis, allergies, asthma, glaucoma, Alzheimer's disease, osteoporosis, glaucoma and behavioral and emotional problems including schizophrenia, alcoholism and depression. ("Hereditary Risk" lists for several diseases the increased risk faced by someone with an afflicted parent.)

Although genes set the stage for these disorders, the actual illness is usually caused in part by some environmental factor—cigarette smoke in the case of lung cancer, for example, or high-fat diets in heart disease and non-insulin-dependent diabetes, as well as prostate, colorectal and perhaps ovarian cancer. Luckily, people who know that a susceptibility disease lurks in their family tree may be able to control those nongenetic risk factors, or at least be on the alert for early symptoms.

For example, if your mother or sister developed breast cancer before menopause, your lifetime risk would be as

From *American Health,* May 1994, pp. 80-84. © 1994 by Ruth Papazian. Reprinted by permission.

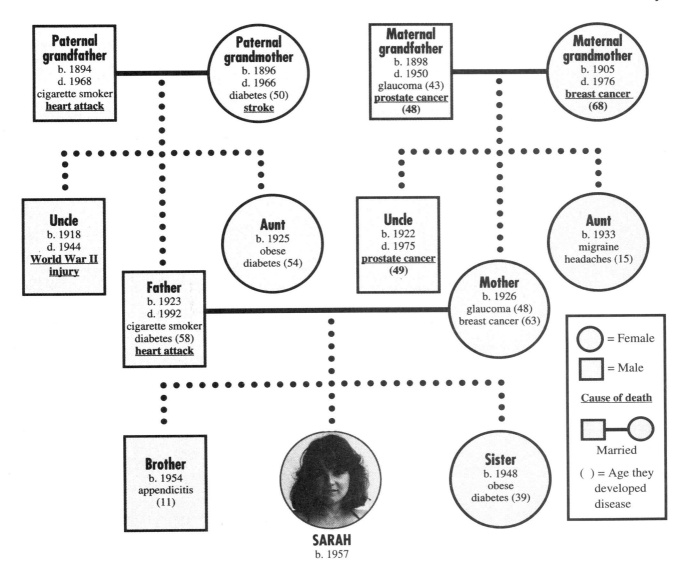

Paternal grandfather
b. 1894
d. 1968
cigarette smoker
heart attack

Paternal grandmother
b. 1896
d. 1966
diabetes (50)
stroke

Maternal grandfather
b. 1898
d. 1950
glaucoma (43)
prostate cancer
(48)

Maternal grandmother
b. 1905
d. 1976
breast cancer
(68)

Uncle
b. 1918
d. 1944
World War II injury

Aunt
b. 1925
obese
diabetes (54)

Uncle
b. 1922
d. 1975
prostate cancer
(49)

Aunt
b. 1933
migraine
headaches (15)

Father
b. 1923
d. 1992
cigarette smoker
diabetes (58)
heart attack

Mother
b. 1926
glaucoma (48)
breast cancer (63)

Brother
b. 1954
appendicitis
(11)

SARAH
b. 1957

Sister
b. 1948
obese
diabetes (39)

○ = Female
□ = Male
Cause of death
□—○
Married
( ) = Age they developed disease

SARAH'S FAMILY MEDICAL HISTORY

Sarah risks inheriting non-insulin-dependent diabetes from her father's side of the family and breast cancer and glaucoma from her mother's side. But the two fatal heart attacks on her father's side shouldn't cause concern; both occurred relatively late in life and probably stemmed from major risk factors—smoking (her grandfather) and both smoking and diabetes (her father).

Diabetes: Sarah's sister already has it. Sarah and her brother should have their blood sugar monitored regularly; they can help ward off the disease by exercising and adopting a prudent diet.

Glaucoma: Sarah and her two siblings should have yearly eye exams to detect glaucoma at its early stages.

Breast cancer: Sarah and her sister face a higher than normal risk, since their mother and maternal grandmother developed it. Both sisters should have a baseline mammogram between the ages of 30 and 35, and yearly mammograms after 35; her sister should lose weight, since obesity adds to her risk.

Finally, Sarah should alert her brother to the fact that he's at increased risk for *prostate cancer.* His maternal grandfather and uncle both developed it early in life. He needs regular screening: each year, a digital rectal exam, plus a PSA (prostate-specific antigen) test.

great as one in three, vs. one in nine for other women. (Early onset of any disease increases the probability that heredity played a role.) A family history of breast cancer means you should get annual mammograms beginning at age 35, plus frequent professional exams.

s for purely genetic diseases, there are more than 4,000—most of them rare—that result from defects in single genes. If you have such a disorder in your family tree, your chance of inheriting it depends on the nature of the gene responsible.

For instance, if one of your parents died of a heart attack before age 60, there's a one-in-five chance that he or she had familial hypercholesterolemia (an inherited extremely high cholesterol level); if so, there's a 50-50 chance you have it too. The gene responsible for familial hypercholesterolemia is "dominant": Inherit a defective version from one parent and you'll get the disease, even if your other parent gave you a normal copy.

Familial hypercholesterolemia, which affects one in every 500 people, can clog arteries and lead to a heart attack at an early age. If you have a family history of heart disease, be sure to get your cholesterol level measured. Once detected, an abnormally high cholesterol level can often be controlled with a lowfat diet and cholesterol-lowering drugs.

Familial adenomatous polyposis, another inherited disorder, afflicts one in 8,000 people and almost always results in intestinal cancer. ("Surviving a Family Curse," below, describes a family coping with this dominant-gene problem.) Other dominant diseases include Huntington's disease (the degenerative nervous-system disorder that killed singer Woody Guthrie), adult polycystic renal disease (a kidney disorder) and Marfan's syndrome (characterized by abnormally long limbs and heart problems). Diseases controlled by a dominant gene rarely skip a generation, so you've probably been spared if neither of your parents had the disease, even if a grandparent did.

Fortunately, most purely hereditary diseases are "recessive": that is, they afflict only those unlucky enough to inherit two copies of a defective gene—one from each parent. The most common of these recessive diseases seem to target certain ethnic groups.

For example, about one in 25 white Americans carries the gene for cystic fibrosis (CF), one of the most common lethal hereditary diseases (for those of northern European descent the risk is somewhat higher). The gene defect in CF results in a thick, sticky mucus in the lungs; the mucus encourages severe respiratory infections that usually prove fatal by age 30.

A CF carrier—with one abnormal and one normal gene—will be healthy. But if someone with the gene marries another carrier, their offspring will have a one-in-four chance of inheriting two defective copies of the gene and being born with CF. Following the discovery in 1989 of the gene that causes CF, a blood test became available that can tell whether a person is a carrier and whether a couple's fetus will develop the disease. ("Family Roots" lists several ethnic groups, the diseases to which they're susceptible, and how common those diseases are.)

Purely hereditary diseases (or disorders) that usually affect only men are called X-linked recessive diseases. The best known are hemophilia, color blindness and Duchenne muscular dystrophy. An X-linked disorder is transmitted from mother to son by a gene on one of her two X chromosomes. Each son has a 50-50 chance of getting the disease, from inheriting just a single copy of the recessive gene.

Mom may be a healthy carrier, since her other X chromosome carries a normal copy of the gene, which masks the defective one. But her son, with his X chromosome paired with a Y from his father, isn't as lucky. A woman should suspect she may be a carrier of an X-linked disorder if the disease has shown up in a male relative.

Virtually every month, researchers identify a gene linked to yet another hereditary disease; these findings are leading to increasing numbers of blood tests to identify people who carry these genes or who are destined to develop the diseases. ("Testing for Risk" lists some of these diseases.) To take advantage of these advances, you must first learn whether you or other family members are at risk.

Surviving a Family Curse

Larry Howard* had considered his family's medical history a curse, but knowing about it probably saved his life.

Larry's mother, three brothers and a sister all had been diagnosed with familial adenomatous polyposis, a disease in which thousands of polyps—tiny wartlike growths—sprout from the lining of the large intestine (colon). People with this condition (about one in 8,000) almost always develop colon cancer from polyps that turn malignant.

Larry's mother and his four affected siblings had to have their colons removed to prevent cancer from taking hold—the treatment reserved for severe cases. But Larry and his other sister, Mary, thought they had been spared.

Since early adolescence, when the polyps generally arise, Larry and Mary had taken part in the Johns Hopkins

University familial polyposis study, undergoing annual sigmoidoscopies (visual examination of the lower third of the colon) and receiving clean bills of health. Ten years ago, when Larry was 32, he was told he didn't need any more checkups, since his risk of having inherited the disease seemed minimal.

Then last year he and Mary were given a new blood test, developed at Johns Hopkins, that identifies the gene that causes familial polyposis. The test determined that Mary did not carry the defective gene, but Larry did. Sure enough, a subsequent exam revealed sprouting polyps.

Larry plans to have his colon removed later this year. His three children have taken the blood test too: One of the three has tested positive.

*Not his real name.

Gathering information about illnesses that run in your family is not as daunting as it may seem—especially if you ask relatives for help. Here is a guide for constructing your medical family tree:

1. Make a list of your first-degree relatives (parents, siblings and children) and second-degree relatives (grandparents, aunts and uncles). Adding more peripheral branches to your tree usually isn't worthwhile: The more distant the relative, the less relevant his medical fate is to you (you and your second cousin, for example, inherit only about 3% of the same genes). A possible exception: when you need more evidence to confirm a pattern involving a serious health problem such as cancer or heart disease.

2. Construct your family tree, using the sample on p. 225 as a guide. Your name and the names of your siblings go on the bottom row. On the row above, put the names of your parents, along with the names of their brothers and sisters. The names of all four grandparents go on the top line. It's customary to put male relatives in squares and female ones in circles and to indicate marriages by connecting relatives with horizontal lines.

3. Record the following information for each relative:
● *Date of birth, date of death and cause of death.* If necessary, you can usually obtain this information from the death certificate. To get a copy, contact the department of vital records in the state where the relative lived. (Be sure to check the family Bible first—birth and death certificates are often tucked inside the covers.)
● *All known illnesses and major surgeries, including the age when they occurred.* This information could be more relevant than the cause of death—if an uncle had a heart attack at age 40 but died 20 years later from an automobile accident, for example. Medical records are the most reliable sources for this information.

Ask relatives who are still living either to give you copies of their medical records or to sign a consent form allowing their doctors to give you this information. To obtain a deceased relative's records, contact the doctor or hospital that treated him; those names should be on the death certificate. You may have to provide a letter of consent from your relative's next of kin, as well as a copy of the death certificate.
● *Lifestyle factors that may have contributed to illness.* For instance, heart disease would be less of a genetic threat if you found that the uncle who suffered the heart attack at age 40 was a chain smoker. Most every family has a self-appointed "historian" who is the repository of family lore. You may be able to learn about relatives' lifestyles by talking to that person.
● *Occupation (optional).* This information may be important if there were job-related factors (such as exposure to toxic chemicals) that may have contributed to illness, miscarriage or birth defects.
● *Unusual physical characteristics.* Prominent features or chronic skin rashes could hint at certain medical conditions or birth defects (but you'll want to corroborate your hunches with medical records or other documents). Again, the family historian may be a good source. Family photo albums can also be revealing: A grandmother's "dowager's hump," for example, probably indicates that she had osteoporosis.

As you research your family medical tree, be prepared for difficulties. Information may be unavailable (some family

TESTING FOR RISK

The genes responsible for more than 300 diseases, most of them rare, can now be identified through blood tests. In some cases, these tests detect the gene itself; in others, they identify DNA "markers" that suggest the gene is present.
● **Cystic fibrosis**
● **Familial hypercholesterolemia**
● **Duchenne muscular dystrophy**
● **Fragile-X syndrome** (the most common inherited form of mental retardation)
● **Huntington's disease**
● **Neurofibromatosis** (a nerve disease characterized by dozens of skin tumors all over the body)
● **Retinoblastoma** (an eye tumor that usually occurs in childhood)
● **Sickle-cell anemia**
● **Tay-Sachs disease**
● **Thalassemia** (a blood disorder that occurs most often in people of Mediterranean descent)
● **Wilms' tumor** (a malignant kidney tumor that usually occurs in childhood)
Source: *Heredity and Your Family's Health,* by Aubrey Milunsky, M.D. (Johns Hopkins University Press, 1992)

FOR MORE HELP

Free pamphlets
● **"Genetic Counseling,"** GC Pamphlet, March of Dimes, 1275 Mamaroneck Ave., White Plains, NY 10605.
● **"Genetic Counseling: Valuable Information for You and Your Family,"** the National Society of Genetic Counselors, 233 Canterbury Dr., Wallingford, PA 19086-6617.
● **"Where to Write for Vital Records,"** Superintendent of Documents, U.S. Government Printing Office, Washington, DC 20402.

Books
● **Heredity and Your Family's Health** by Aubrey Milunsky, M.D. (Johns Hopkins University Press, 1992).
● **How Healthy Is Your Family Tree? A Complete Guide to Creating a Medical and Behavioral Family Tree** by Carol Krause (Collier Books).

Organizations
● **The Hereditary Cancer Institute,** Creighton University School of Medicine, 2500 California Plaza, Omaha, NE 68178.
● **Gilda Radner Familial Ovarian Cancer Registry,** Roswell Park Cancer Institute, Elm and Carlton streets, Buffalo, NY 14263.
● **University of Utah Cardiovascular Genetics Research Clinic,** 410 Chipeta Way, Room 161, Research Park, Salt Lake City, UT 84108.
● **The Hereditary Disease Foundation,** 1427 Seventh St., Suite 2, Santa Monica, CA 90401.

Family Roots

Risk of certain genetic diseases in specific races or ethnic groups.

Racial or ethnic background	Diseases	Carriers	Afflicted
Italian or Greek	Thalassemia	1 in 10	1 in 400
African	Sickle-cell anemia	1 in 12	1 in 650
Caucasian	Cystic fibrosis	1 in 25	1 in 2,500
Eastern or Central European Jewish (Ashkenazic), Cajun American or French Canadian	Tay-Sachs disease*	1 in 30	1 in 3,600
Mediterranean Jewish (Sephardic) or Armenian	Familial Mediterranean fever**	1 in 45	1 in 8,000

*Neurological disorder invariably fatal within the first five years of life. **Repeated bouts of fever and abdominal pain.
Adapted from *Choices, Not Chances: An Essential Guide to Heredity and Health,* ©1977 by Aubrey Milunsky, M.D.
By permission of Little, Brown and Company.

Hereditary Risk

Estimated risk for some common disorders that are influenced by inherited genes but not directly caused by them. Risks are for people with one parent who had the disease. The risk would be greater if a second parent or a sibling also had the disease.

Disease	General population	One parent with condition
		Lifetime risk
Alcoholism	5%	10% to 20%
Alzheimer's disease	2% to 5%	19%
Asthma	4%	26%
Cancer, breast	11%	22%*
Cancer, colon	4%	10%
Cancer, ovarian	1%	5%
Cancer, uterine	3%	9%
Diabetes (non-insulin-dependent)	2%	5% to 10%
Duodenal ulcer	10%	30%
Glaucoma	2%	4% to 16%
Manic depression	1%	25%
Migraine	5% to 10%	45%
Schizophrenia	1%	8% to 18%

*The risk may be three times as great as in the general population if the mother was premenopausal when her cancer was diagnosed.
©1992 by Consumers Union. Reprinted by permission from *Consumer Reports on Health.*

members may not cooperate, for example), or it may not exist (as when a child died and no diagnosis was ever made) or it may not be accurate (family legend, for example, may attribute an aunt's pregnancy loss to a miscarriage when in fact she had an abortion).

A little tact goes a long way. Family members may not want to talk about sad events or what they consider to be the family's dirty laundry. A good approach: "My doctor is in-terested in Cousin Bobby's condition because it could affect the children I may have. Can you tell me about his problem so that we can calculate the risks?" Offer to share your completed tree with relatives, along with the opinions of medical or genetic experts you consult.

Now that you've constructed your family tree, here are some tips on interpreting it:
● Your tree's two most important "branches" are your mother and father: Each gave you half your genetic inheritance, so their diseases will be most relevant to you and your siblings.
● The earlier a disease develops, the more likely that heredity played a role in it (except for ailments with obvious non-genetic causes such as infections).
● A disease that strikes two or more relatives at the same age is likely to be strongly influenced by heredity.
● A clustering of cases of the same disease on one side of the tree is more likely to suggest that genes play a strong role in causing it than a similar number of cases scattered on both sides. On the other hand, your risk of inheriting a purely hereditary disease like cystic fibrosis would actually be greater when it's present on both your mother's and father's side.

If you have questions about your family tree, you should show it to your doctor. If the doctor suspects a genetic problem, you will probably be referred to a genetic counselor, who can assess your risk of developing the diseases you're worried about, and of passing them on to a child. A counselor can also tell prospective parents if a fetus can be tested for conditions of concern.

Genetic counselors typically have a master of science degree in genetics and are certified by the American Board of Medical Genetics. Your family doctor, obstetrician or pediatrician can probably refer you to one, or you can contact a major hospital or medical school in your area or your local chapter of the March of Dimes for referrals (for further information, see "For More Help").

Your medical family tree should be a living, growing document. As you and your brothers and sisters get married and have children, keep adding to it: It can contribute to your health today and to the health of future generations.

Happy Families

WHO SAYS THEY ALL HAVE TO BE ALIKE?

Susan Chollar

Susan Chollar writes about science and health for a number of national magazines.

It's Thursday evening in Watsonville, a small agricultural town on California's central coast. Cathy Chavez-Miller is fixing dinner for her "blended" family: her husband, Mike, her stepson, Cliff, and her son from her first marriage, Patrick, who spends half his time with his father. "At times it's been a real challenge," she says, "but we really enjoy each other and wouldn't change the way things are." On the opposite coast, it's nighttime in suburban Washington, and mental health therapist Shelly Costello tucks her five-year-old twins Chelsea and Carly into bed. Worn out after 10 hours in day care followed by a rowdy evening at home with Mom, the kids are soon fast asleep. But Shelly, a single parent, must tackle a sinkful of dirty dishes and a couple of loads of laundry before she can call it a day. Her philosophy concerning our oldest social institution: "I don't believe in the rule that a family has to have two parents living together, but I do believe that people have to be happy. As long as a family is happy, it will be a good place for children to grow up."

American families are not what they were 40 years ago when Father Knew Best and every household was presumed to live *The Life of Riley*. Ozzie and Harriet and the Cleavers have long since given way to Murphy Brown and the *Full House* gang, and the traditional two-parent family sometimes seems like an endangered species.

We all know the statistics: Half of all marriages in the U.S. end in divorce, and nearly a third of our children are born out of wedlock. As a result, four out of 10 kids don't live with both of their biological parents; one in four lives in a single-parent home; and almost one in six families includes at least one step-child.

Critics such as former Vice President Dan Quayle have blamed these demographic changes for everything from the Los Angeles riots and the growing wave of violence among teenage boys to declining scholastic performance. But while social scientists don't deny that American children and parents face greater chal-

THE STRONGEST PREDICTOR OF SUCCESS IS THE LEVEL OF CONFLICT BETWEEN A MOTHER AND HER CHILD: LESS IS BEST.

lenges than ever before, they increasingly question the assumption that broken homes and single-parent families per se are threatening children. Several recent sophisticated studies suggest that growing up under the same roof with both biological parents is less crucial to a child's psychological health than growing up in a stable home.

"The quality of the individuals and relationships in the household matters more than who the particular actors are," says Dr. Frank Mott, a senior research scientist at the Center for Human Resource Research at Ohio State University in Columbus. "If you have a happy home, you'll probably have well-adjusted children." In other words, the atmosphere of the home counts for more than the type of family who inhabits it—even when it comes to "broken" homes.

In 1980 Dr. Paul Amato, an associate professor of sociology at the University of Nebraska in Lincoln, began charting the progress of 2,000 marriages; over the course of his study, 15% ended in divorce. In 1992 he contacted 500 adult children from those failed marriages and measured their psychological and social adjustment. The offspring of the failed unions tended to fall into two distinct groups: Those from marriages in which there had been little external conflict before the divorce were likelier to have personal problems as young adults than those from overtly troubled marriages.

Amato believes that children from seemingly harmonious homes that break up bear the greater scars because, to them, "the divorce means the loss of a stable home. Although the parents were unhappy with the

From *American Health*, July/August 1993, pp. 52-57. © 1993 by Susan Chollar. Reprinted by permission.

marriage, from the child's perspective it wasn't really that bad."

For children who had lived in homes where there were arguments and perhaps physical violence, however, divorce often meant an end to discord. Therefore, the adult children from such homes tended to have better psychological health—and even stronger social relationships and marriages—than those from homes in which there had been little external conflict before divorce. "To the children," Amato concludes, "the consequences of divorce depend on the quality of the marriage prior to it." He adds: "It might be better for children to be in a well-functioning divorced single-parent family than a nuclear family marked by high levels of conflict."

Research on families headed by single women also suggests that the quality of a home is more important than its cast of characters. Sociologist David Demo, an associate professor of human development and family studies at the University of Missouri in Columbia, examined the emotional health and academic performance of 742 teens from the four most prevalent types of households: intact two-parent, never married single-parent, divorced single-parent and stepfamily.

When Dr. Demo analyzed all his data, he found that the type of family a child belonged to was a surprisingly weak predictor of the child's well-being and achievement. Although teens who resided with both biological parents tended to do better academically and behaviorally, they did only slightly better than those from never-married single-parent families. The most powerful predictor of the young people's adjustment and academic performance was the level of conflict between mother and child: Less is best.

"Dan Quayle argues that families headed by never-married mothers are inherently harmful to children," says Demo, "but the data don't show that. In fact, the never-married [single-parent] family offers a type of continuity that can parallel that of intact two-parent families." He summarizes his research this way: "Families are diverse by race, class, structure and well-being. Some are in trouble, some are doing very well. And some are somewhere in-between."

If some divorces—but not all—cause problems, so do some stepfamilies. Dr. Louise Silverstein, a family therapist and an assistant professor of psychology at Yeshiva University in New York City, observes that research shows relationships are often more difficult in stepfamilies, particularly for girls who find themselves living under the same roof with their mother's new husband. Boys who accompany their mother to a new household seem to fare better, presumably because there is less sexual tension in their relationship with a same-sex stepparent.

Children who deal with strife that continues between parents *after* divorce also often suffer. Silverstein illustrates with a case history: The parents of three-year-old Sean separated in a tangle of bitterness and anger when his mother, Mary Ann, was six months into a second pregnancy her husband, Tom, opposed. When Tom reacted by embarking on an affair with Mary Ann's closest friend, their conflict escalated into screaming matches and even physical violence that showed no sign of abating months after their marriage dissolved. "They were completely out of control," says Silverstein. Unfortunately Sean was his parents' real victim: Over eight months, his once normal behavior deteriorated into frequent tantrums and a severe case of separation anxiety.

Researchers who found that children from broken homes generally don't do as well as those whose parents stayed together may have misinterpreted the causes. Nearly half of single-parent families live in poverty, for example, compared with only 8% of married families. Almost 12 million households are headed by women, whose economic status is slashed by at least a third following divorce; never-married mothers are among the poorest members of our society. In many single-parent homes, low income—not divorce—causes children to live in high-crime neighborhoods and to have more health and academic problems.

Sociologist Nicholas Zill is vice president of the Westat research corporation in Rockville, Md., which explores social issues for the federal government, among other clients. "If you are the classic Murphy Brown type with all the advantages, and you decide to have a child out of marriage," he says, "your child is not nec-

essarily at risk. But if you're a teenager with little education or money, that can be a recipe for disaster."

Assessing the effects of growing up in a household headed by a single woman is clearly not a simple matter. Ohio State's Mott analyzed data about 1,714 youngsters aged five to eight from various socioeconomic backgrounds, to see if a father's absence from the home caused academic and/or behavioral problems. He discovered that those from fatherless homes indeed scored lower on math and reading achievement tests. But additional probing revealed that the children's mothers scored lower on aptitude tests than the married mothers; they also tended to be poorer and were more likely to have dropped out of school. When he compared children in the sample from similar socioeconomic backgrounds, he found that they performed equally well, regardless of a father's presence.

When it came to behavior, the absence of a father didn't correlate with any particular problems among black children. But fatherless white children had significantly more behavioral difficulties than peers who had fathers, even when income and education levels were similar. White girls and white boys from fatherless homes were less sociable and less independent than white children from homes with fathers. In addition, white boys from fatherless homes were also more prone to hyperactivity, peer conflict, anxiety and depression.

Mott offers several suggestions for these race- and gender-based differences. Girls may be less vulnerable than boys in the absence of a father, he says, because they're closer to their mothers. And black children are part of a culture in which single parenting is not only more prevalent but also more accepted. While nearly half of the fatherless black households in Mott's study had never had a paternal presence, 94% of similar white homes had; many more white children had "lost" their fathers due to divorce or other family disruption. "From a child's perspective," says Mott, "never having had a father in the home may be better, at least in a psychological sense, than having had one who left." Along with more accepting attitudes toward families without fathers, many

The '50s: Not So Happy Days

The 1950s are often portrayed as a simple time when fresh-faced children flourished in nuclear families, men ruled their castles with wisdom and benevolence, and women relished their roles as ever-nurturing wives and mothers. Not so, says Stephanie Coontz, a family historian at The Evergreen State College in Olympia, Wash. "The reality of these families was far more painful and complex than the situation-comedy reruns or the expurgated memories of the nostalgic would suggest," she writes in *The Way We Never Were: American Families and the Nostalgia Trap* (Basic Books, 1992, $27). "Contrary to popular opinion, *Leave It to Beaver* was not a documentary." A quarter of Americans, a third of U.S. children and nearly two-thirds of the elderly were desperately poor, making do without food stamps or housing programs. Half of two-parent black families lived in poverty, and 40% of black women with small children had to work outside the home.

Even for families who came closer to the Cleaver mold, life was often not as simple or happy as it appeared. A quarter to a third of '50s marriages eventually ended in divorce. Many who described their unions as "happy" in national polls nonetheless admitted many dissatisfactions with their mates and day-to-day lives. Child and spouse abuse was common, though largely unacknowledged.

For women in particular, the '50s were not what they seemed to be on *Ozzie and Harriet*. (In his new book, *The Fifties*, author David Halberstam argues that the real-life Nelsons—dominated by autocratic, workaholic Ozzie, who stole "the childhood of both his sons and used it for commercial purposes"—were in fact a dysfunctional family.) "It was a period where women felt tremendously trapped,"

says Coontz. "There were not many permissible alternatives to baking brownies, experimenting with new canned soups and getting rid of stains around the collar." In some states, husbands had legal control over family finances. In 1954, an article in *Esquire* magazine labeled working wives a "menace." Feminist values and lack of interest in childbearing were considered abnormal, if not pathological. Some women unwilling or unable to fulfill their expected domestic roles were subjected to electroshock or confinement to psychiatric institutions. Throughout the '50s, the press reported a growing wave of frustration and resentment among full-time homemakers, whose use of tranquilizers and alcohol skyrocketed.

To those who point to the '50s as an era of conservative sexual values, look again, says Coontz. Birth rates among teenagers reached numbers since unequaled. The percentage of pregnant white brides more than doubled, and the number of babies born out of wedlock and put up for adoption rose 80% between 1944 and 1955. "What we now think of as 1950s sexual morality," writes Coontz, "depended not so much on stricter sexual control as on intensification of the sexual double standard."

Although Coontz's research shines light on the weaknesses of American families from earlier historical periods as well, she denies that family bashing is her goal. "To say that no easy answers are to be found in the past is not to close off further discussion of family problems, but to open it up," she says. "Only when we have a realistic idea of how families have and have not worked in the past can we make informed decisions about how to support families in the present or improve their future prospects."

with boys and girls raised by gay parents also tends to refute the conventional wisdom. After reviewing studies of the children of lesbian mothers, Dr. Charlotte Patterson, an associate professor of psychology at the University of Virginia in Charlottesville, concluded in the October 1992 issue of *Child Development* that there was no evidence that these children's development had been compromised in any significant respect. "Children don't need a father to develop normally," says Silverstein, "and future research on children raised by gay fathers will probably show that they don't need a mother either. What children need are affectionate, nurturing adults—regardless of their gender or biological relationship—who love them."

Considering the very real challenges of growing up in a nontraditional home, family researchers are quick to acknowledge the advantages that the *right kind* of traditional family can confer. If the worst scenario is a family marked by hostility and conflict, "the best situation," says Nebraska's Amato, "is to grow up in a family where there are two adults who get along well and love the child. Two parents can supervise a child better, provide more practical help, discipline and guidance, and serve as effective role models."

What is most promising about the new research, says Missouri's Demo, "is the suggestion that a lot of these changes in traditional family structure are not harmful to children. But what is disturbing is that the studies point out that negative and disruptive events in children's lives do have important effects on their well-being. Those are the real problems—and those are the patterns that are increasing in our society."

One point on which family experts agree is that we should spend our energy on securing a happy future for our children rather than waxing nostalgic about the past. "It is important to look at the realities of how families are actually functioning," says Westat's Zill, "rather than labeling some as inevitably bad and others as inevitably good." Adds Amato: "All of these types of families are here to stay. And by and large, all of them can work quite well. We need to concern ourselves with making sure that each of them works as well as it can."

black communities offer single parents more extended-family support.

This extra help can make the difference between success and failure in families of any color, says Yeshiva's Silverstein, offering another case history as an example: Alice, now a well-adjusted, young white adult, was raised in a household consisting of her mother, grandmother and aunt; the mother was the breadwinner, while

the grandmother created a warm, nurturing atmosphere. "The additional adults also acted as an emotional safety net for Alice," Silverstein says. "If she had a fight with her mother, there was always her grandmother or aunt to comfort her. And their presence meant she didn't have to experience her mother's anger or disappointment so intensely."

The newest research conducted

Rewriting Life Stories

Mind: Instead of looking for flaws in people's psyches, 'narrative therapy' works at nurturing their forgotten strengths

Geoffrey Cowley and Karen Springen

Last August, Lorraine Grieves fell into a familiar pattern: "The rule in my head was, I couldn't have any food, and if I did, I had to purge." Fearing for her life, the 21-year-old Vancouver woman's doctor sent her to a psychiatric ward where, for three weeks, she sat surrounded by fellow sufferers with feeding tubes dangling from her nose. Under the house rules, anyone who left a meal unfinished was fed liquid calories or plugged into a feeding machine. And if a patient resisted that drill, she was eligible for a straitjacket. Hospital staffers monitored the ward closely, but the women found ways to evade them. Though Grieves weighed just 103 pounds, she did sit-ups in bed and ran in the shower. When hooked up to a feeding machine, she would wait until no one was looking and then disconnect the tubes. "we'd all sit there sometimes with our tube dripping into the garbage," she recalls. "After all, they were giving you the thing you're most afraid of."

Narrative therapy recognizes that one's psyche is not a fixed, objective entity but a fluid social construct that can be "re-authored" to correct mental problems.

Today, Grieves carries a healthy 125 pounds on her 5-foot, 5-inch frame, and she's no longer dominated by the craving to be thinner. What finally kept her from starving herself was not the prison-style discipline of the hospital, she says, but the perspective she gained through her conversations with a local psychotherapist named Stephen Madigan. Unlike the professionals she'd consulted in the past, Madigan didn't reinforce her sense that there was something wrong with her. Instead, he worked at driving a wedge between her and her problem. He got her to think about the rare moments when anorexia and bulimia *didn't* control her life. He coaxed her to focus on what that experience felt like. And as she began to think of anorexia as a hostile oppressor, not the whole of her own being, he inspired her to fight back. If a person told you to deprive yourself of food and water, he asked, wouldn't you revolt? Yes, she realized, she would revolt. And with the support of other sufferers, she did.

Like Madigan, a small but growing number of psychotherapists are shedding ideas that have dominated their field for a century. Loosely united by what they call a "narrative" approach, they're forging a new conception of mental suffering and devising new strategies for easing it. The psyche, from their perspective, is not a fixed, objective entity but a fluid social construct—a story that is subject to revision. And the therapist's job is to help people "re-author" stories that aren't doing them justice. The new approach is still far from orthodox, but its adherents—mainly family therapists in Australia, New Zealand and North America—are applying it to everything from marital conflict to psychosis. And as Lorraine Grieves's experience suggests, their efforts are changing people lives. Narrative therapy is "more than a new set of techniques," Omaha therapist Bill O'Hanlon wrote recently in The Family Therapy Networker. "It represents a fundamentally new direction in the therapeutic world."

At the heart of the new approach is the postmodernist idea that we don't so much perceive the world as interpret it. The buzz of sensory experience would overwhelm us without some frame of reference, says Michael White, an Australian therapist who helped launch the narrative movement in the late 1980s. So we collapse our experience into narrative structures, or stories, to make it intelligible. As we forge identities, we inevitably give some patterns of experience more weight than others, and cultural pressures help determine which patterns define us. If our "dominant stories" happen to center on problems, they can become spiritual prisons, As the Berkeley, Calif.-based therapists Jennifer Freeman and Dean Lobovits have written, a "problem-saturated" dominant story tends to "filter problem-free experiences from a person's memories and perceptions," so that "threads of hope, resourcefulness and capability are excluded from a person's description of self."

That's where therapy comes in. Conventional Freudian psychotherapy tends to assume that people's problems stem from internal pathologies that need to be identified, scrutinized and corrected. Narrative therapy, as conceived by White and his colleague David Epston of Auckland, New Zealand, takes a different tack. Instead of looking for flaws in people's psyches, the therapist helps people spot omissions in their stories. "No problem or diagnosis ever captures the whole of a person's experience," says Epston. "The person has other ways of acting and thinking, but they get neglected because they lie in the shadows of the dominant story." Practitioners have different tricks for helping people recover forgotten strengths, but the process follows a predictable arc.

Small discoveries can have big effects. One small discovery can be when a person seeking help feels, even for an instant, that they are not dominated by their problem.

Danny's story: The first step is to initiate what's known in the trade as an externalizing conversation. "People come in thinking, 'I'm depressed. This diagnosis defines me. I'm a failure'," says Freeman, the Berkeley therapist. "There's usually very little distance between the person and the problem. That feeling of being defective can immobilize people." To counter that feeling, the therapist typically invites the client to personify the problem—to give it a name and talk about how it's affecting his life. As you see from a videotaped conversation between White and a 5-year-old named Danny, the effect can be transformative. Danny has already seen many counselors when his mom brings him to White's office at the Dulwich Centre in Adelaide, Australia. No one has been able to toilet-train the bubbly, sweet-natured kindergartner; he won't bother with a trip to the bathroom, no matter how awful the consequences. But White engages Danny in a conversation about two characters named Sneaky Poo and Sneaky Wee, and within minutes the child is talking about how they take advantage of him.

How does Sneaky Poo make you feel?
I start to have tears. It just sneaks out.
So it makes you feel sad. How else does it make you feel?
It makes me feel angry.
Anything else?
Yes, it stinks and it sticks to me. It hurts and its hard to get off.
Does Sneaky Poo cause trouble in your friendships with other kids?
Sometimes they just want to go away.
I can see that Sneaky Poo is causing a lot of trouble in your life. What would you like instead?
I'd be happy if it didn't come out any time except in the toilet!

Danny is soon scheming to put Sneaky Poo in his place, and doing timed laps around the office to show that he's a faster runner than his newfound adversary. Throughout the exchange, White proposes nothing directly. He simply asks questions that create an opening for the boy to act on the problem without acting against himself. "[The other] therapists had succeeded in making him think of himself as the problem," White says. "No one had invited him to recount the problem's effects on his own life." Danny returned for several visits, but within six weeks Messrs. Poo and Wee had been vanquished.

Sparkling moments: To "externalize" a problem is not necessarily to solve it. The next step in the therapeutic process is to identify "unique outcomes"—those sparkling moments when the person seeking help has *not* been dominated by the problem. Those small discoveries can have big effects. Consider what happened last year when Epston had an hourlong conversation with Jermaine, a black 17-year-old from Ann Arbor, Mich. Jermaine has always suffered from life-threatening asthma, and as a teenager he'd grown so indifferent about treating and monitoring it that he was rarely out of the hospital for more than three days at a stretch. Despairing over his irresponsibility (he had also started committing petty juvenile offenses), his mother had recently placed him in a state institution.

In chatting with Epston, Jermaine quickly establishes that asthma has been messing up his life, and that he'd like to assert some control over it. Then Epston asks a pivotal question: "Tell me, has there ever been a time when asthma tried to pull the wool over your eyes and somehow you didn't keel over?" It turns out that he had staved off a trip to the hospital just that morning, by testing himself and taking his medication. Epston bears down enthusiastically on the meaning of the event, and Jermaine is soon proclaiming himself "asthma smart" and predicting a winning streak. A year later, the streak is all but unbroken.

New identities: There's more to changing a life than noticing a "unique outcome." The value of those moments is that they illuminate the resources a person can use to succeed on a larger scale. "we're not just telling people, 'You can do it!'" says therapist Jill Freedman of the Evanston Family Therapy Center, outside Chicago. "we're asking questions, in the hope that they'll help people see things about themselves that they weren't seeing before."

Liz Gray, a 52-year-old, self-employed accountant, used to think of herself as a servant. That was the assigned role of girls in her Irish Catholic household. and she continued to play the role as an adult. She laughs when she remembers teaching a course for tax preparers at an H&R Block office—and voluntarily cleaning the bathroom while she was there. When she started suffering panic attacks a few years ago, the therapists she consulted declared her "codependent" and told her she'd been psychologically damaged as a toddler. But the conversation changed when she started seeing Gene Combs at the Evanston Family Therapy Center.

Combs wanted to know how Gray, 20 years divorced, had managed to run a household, raise two children, look after her aging mother and run her own business. What did it say about her that she was able to do all that? Was she a victim, or was she a survivor? What resources had she drawn on? "As the patient identifies the exceptions to the dominant story of pathology," says New York psychiatrist Christian Beels, "the plot becomes thick and many-stranded." After two years of monthly sessions with Combs, Gray still suffers occasional panic attacks, which she treats with a tranquilizer. But she says she doesn't feel "broken" anymore. "I'm rewriting a story that someone told me a long time ago about what happens to women in this world," she says. "The idea of a queen keeping track of a house is a very different story from a victim saying, 'Oh my god, I'm overwhelmed'."

Going public: Unlike most other approaches, narrative therapy isn't a secretive transaction between the therapist and the client. Since the stories that define us are "negoti-ated and distributed within communities," White observes it's only reasonable to "engage communities in the renegotiation of identity." In Vancouver, Lorraine Grieves and others have organized an "anti-anorexia/anti-bulimia league" to fight the social pressures that encourage women to starve themselves. In Berkeley, Jennifer Freeman encourages the children she sees to chronicle their struggles for anthologies like "The Temper Tamer's Handbook" and "The Fear Facer's Handbook." And narrative therapists everywhere are incorporating audiences into the therapeutic process.

It's not an entirely new idea.

With the client's consent, a family therapist will often have other therapists observe a session from behind a screen. Normally, the observers share their impressions only with the therapist who recruited them. But narrative practitioners often invite their clients to watch the "reflecting team" deliberate. The Moore family had that experience last fall, when they spent an hourlong session with Michael White at the Evanston Family Therapy Center. Jane Moore and her second husband, Clint, an Episcopal priest, had been married for several years when Jane's 16-year-old daughter, Jennifer, left her father to live with them. They felt they needed help in becoming a family, but as they listened to the reflecting team, they realized they had already started to function as one. "It was a wonderful surprise to find out that other people perceived you as having the qualities you thought you were looking for," says Jane.

Narrative therapy doesn't have all the answers people need, but it incites them to ask different questions that may well lead to positive life choices.

There are of course limits to what any of these exercises can accomplish. No form of talk therapy is likely to eliminate a biologically based depression or psychosis. And traumatic experiences, such as childhood abuse, don't just go away when people focus on their strengths. "There is such a thing as true mental illness," says San Diego psychiatrist Harold Bloomfield, "Some people just need drugs." Many proponents of narrative therapy would agree, but they would add that there's more than one way of living with an illness. "The question is how you want to face the experiences you're stuck with," says

Beels. """What kind of relationship are you going to have with depression? What have you found effective? It's not an either-or situation, where you're cured or defeated. It's a lifetime battle."

Some experts worry that narrative enthusiasts, in their reluctance to "pathologize" people, will give their problems short shrift. They fear that by focusing solely on the problem at hand—anorexia, pants-soiling or panic attacks—a therapist may ignore larger issues that need to be confronted. But to narrative purists, such questions simply reflect a particular view of the world. "In traditional therapy, the audience is the therapist," say Beels. "What

does the therapist expect? He expects that we have not gotten to the bottom of this problem yet. He expects that things are not better than we thought, but worse." In fact, he says, the sources of people's suffering—traumatic memories, low self-esteem, whatever—are not that mysterious. Any line of inquiry will draw them out, and they need to be acknowledged. But they don't need monuments built to them. As Epston puts it, "Every time we ask a question, we're generating a possible version of a life." Narrative therapy doesn't have all the answers people need. Its beauty is that it incites them to ask different questions.

Rituals
FOR OUR TIMES

**Evan Imber-Black
and Janine Roberts**

Evan Imber-Black is the director of the Family and Group Studies program of the Department of Psychiatry at Albert Einstein College of Medicine. Janine Roberts is the director of the Family Therapy program of the School of Education at the University of Massachusetts.

EVERY FOURTH OF JULY, PAUL and Linda Hoffman pack their three children and their dog into the station wagon and drive 250 miles to Paul's sister's home, where all of the Hoffmans gather. The event is fairly unpleasant. The women spend the day cooking, which Linda resents, while the men watch sports, an activity Paul doesn't care for. The young cousins spend most of the day fighting with one another. In the evening, Grandpa Hoffman sets off fireworks, but no one really pays attention. On the fifth of July, Paul and Linda drive home, wearily vowing that this is the last year they will spend their holiday this way.

The following June, however, when Paul and Linda dare mention that they are thinking about doing something different for Independence Day, Paul's sister calls and tells them how upset their parents will be if the couple and their children don't come this year. Alternate plans fall by the wayside, and on the Fourth of July into the car they go.

Does this story sound at all familiar to you? Because of experiences like the Hoffmans', in which celebrations are static and meaningless, many of us have minimized the practice of rituals in our lives. One

• • • • • • • • •

How today's families are developing innovative rites and ceremonies to ease difficult transitions, heal relationships, and celebrate life.

• • • • • • • • •

woman we know who grew up in a family whose rituals were particularly confining put it this way: "I don't want any rituals in my life. Rituals are like being in prison!"

Yet in these times of rapid and dramatic change in the family—with more children being raised by single parents, more mothers working outside the home, fewer extended families living in close proximity—rituals can provide us with a crucial sense of personal identity as well as family connection. Despite the changing status

of the family, membership within a family group is still the primary way that most people identify themselves. Rituals that both borrow from the past and are reshaped by relationship needs of the present highlight for us continuity as well as change. A family in which ritual is minimized may have little sense of itself through time. Everything simply blends into everything else.

As family therapists who have been working with and teaching the use of rituals since the late '70s, we have encountered an increasing number of people who are longing to revitalize the rituals in their lives. They just don't know how. Rituals surround us and offer opportunities to make meaning from the familiar and the mysterious at the same time. Built around common symbols and symbolic actions such as birthday cakes and blowing out candles, or exchanging rings and wedding vows, many parts of rituals are well known to us.

A ritual can be as simple as the one that sixty-two-year-old Eveline Miller practices when she needs to sort things through. She goes to her grandmother's rocking chair, sits, and rocks. When she was a child and needed comfort, this was where she used to go to lay her head upon her grandmother's lap. Her grandmother would stroke her hair and say, "This too will pass." Now, as Eveline rocks and thinks, she repeats those words to help calm herself and provide perspective.

Rituals also can be more elaborate and creative, such as one that Jed and his wife, Isabel, a couple in their early twenties, designed for Jed's brother. Several months after Jed married Isabel, his mother died suddenly, leaving Jed's nineteen-year-old

From *New Age Journal*, September/October 1992, pp. 70-73, 140. Excerpt from *Rituals for Our Times: Celebrating, Healing, and Changing Our Lives and Relationships* by Evan Imber-Black and Janine Roberts. © 1993 by Evan Imber-Black and Janine Roberts. Reprinted by permission of HarperCollins Publishers, Inc.

brother, Brian, orphaned. Brian came to live with Jed and Isabel. The young couple thus found themselves not only newlyweds but also new "parents." One day Brian told them, "You know, I feel like I don't have a security blanket. My friends at school, other people in my classes—most of them have at least one parent still alive. Their parents can help them if they're having trouble in school, or if they need a place to stay, or can't find a job. And I don't have that security blanket because both of my parents are dead."

What Brian had said seemed so important to him that Jed and Isabel talked about it between themselves and eventually came up with an idea: They would make Brian a quilt—a security blanket. Jed's sister had an old nurse's uniform of their mother's that they could use for material. An older brother had a Marine camouflage shirt of their father's. They found some other old fabric among their mother's things. Then, as they began to cut the material into squares, they realized that they would need help sewing them together into a quilt. Jed thought of his maternal grandmother, who had sewn a number of quilts for other family members.

The siblings and the grandmother began gathering in secret to sew the quilt and share memories of Brian's parents and their earlier life. And when the family gathered to celebrate the grandmother's eightieth birthday, Brian was given the quilt—a blanket that symbolized both the ability of Jed and Isabel to "parent" in creative ways and the new network of contact that had been built between the siblings and their grandmother. Together, these family members had proved to be Brian's "security blanket."

The symbols and symbolic actions of rituals embrace meaning that cannot always be easily expressed in words. Eveline Miller's rocking chair, for example, was much more than a place to sit; it evoked safety, reassurance, and the memory of her grandmother. Brian's quilt was not just a cover; it represented the interconnected people in his life—from the past and the present—whom he could carry with him into the future. The textures, smells, and sounds of ritual symbols—an heirloom rocking chair, a family-made quilt—can be powerful activators of sensory memory. Family members may recall scenes and stories of previous times when similar rituals were enacted or some of the same people were together. Rituals connect us with our past, define our present life, and show us a path to our future.

FAMILY RITUALS TAKE A VARIETY OF FORMS. There are daily practices, such as the reading of a child's bedtime story or the sharing of a mealtime. There are holiday traditions, some celebrated with the community at large (seasonal events such as the solstice, religious events such as Passover, national events such as the Fourth of July) and others exclusive to a particular family (birthdays, anniversaries, reunions). Then there are life-cycle rituals, which mark the major transitions of life.

All human beings throughout the world and throughout time are born, and all die. All of us experience emerging sexuality. And most create sustained adult relationships to form new family units and new generations. Such changes are enormously complicated, involving both beginnings and endings; holding and expressing both pain and joy. They may shape and give voice to profoundly conflicting beliefs about our personal existence and our relationships. It's little wonder that every culture in the world has created rituals to celebrate and guide our way through these life-cycle passages.

The truly magical quality of rituals is embedded in their capacity not only to announce a change but to actually create the change. Given that volumes have been written advising people how to change, and that people spend countless hours in therapy, often agonizing over their inability to make needed changes, it is easy to see why rituals exist in all cultures, to ease our passage from one stage of life to another. Using familiar symbols, actions, and words, rituals make change manageable and safe. Simply knowing which rituals lie ahead during a day, a year, or a lifetime stills our anxiety. Change is *enacted* through rituals and not simply talked about—couples don't change from being single to being married by talking about marriage, but rather by participating in a wedding ceremony. Teens don't graduate from high school when a teacher says "you're finished now"; they attend proms, picnics, and the graduation ceremony itself.

As families have changed, life-cycle events have changed too, and there are many crucial transitions for which there are no familiar and accepted rituals in our culture. Changes that often go unmarked include divorce, the end of a nonmarried relationship, adoption, forming a committed homosexual relationship, leaving home, pregnancy loss, and menopause. Since life-cycle rituals enable us to begin to rework our sense of self and our rela-

tionships as required by life's changes, the lack of such rituals can make change more difficult.

Rituals tend to put us in touch with the profound circle of life and death, so it is not surprising that healing moments emerge spontaneously during these cele-

● ● ● ● ● ● ● ● ●

A family in which ritual is minimized may have little sense of itself through time.

● ● ● ● ● ● ● ● ●

brations. If you keep that in mind when changes are occurring in your life or in the lives of those close to you, you can plan a ritual to specifically generate healing.

Healing a Broken Relationship
The crisis of shattered trust and broken promises can lead to genuine atonement, forgiveness, reconciliation, and relationship renewal or, alternatively, to chronic resentment, bitterness, parting, and isolation. Since rituals are able to hold and express powerful contradictory feelings, such as love and hate, anger and connectedness, they enhance the possibility of relationship healing.

For Sondra and Alex Cutter, ritual provided a way to bury that past. The Cutters had spent seven of their twelve years of marriage in bitter arguments about a brief affair Alex had had just before their fifth anniversary. Sondra didn't want to leave her marriage, but she felt unable to let go of the past. Alex, in turn, had become extremely defensive about his behavior and was unable to genuinely show Sondra that he was sorry. In couple's therapy, Sondra and Alex were asked to bring two sets of symbols of the affair. The first set of symbols was to represent what the affair meant to each of them at the time it occurred. The second set was to symbolize what the affair had come to mean in their current life together. As a symbol of her feelings at the time of the affair, Sondra brought a torn wedding photograph to show that the affair meant a break in their vows. Sondra was surprised by Alex's symbol: an old picture of his father, who had had many affairs. "I thought this was just what husbands did," said Alex. "I thought this was what made you a man, but I found out quickly that this didn't work for me and for what I wanted my marriage to be. Then we couldn't get past it." Sondra had never heard Alex speak about the affair in this way. Her belief that the affair meant he didn't love her and that he loved another woman began to shift for the first time in seven years.

As a symbol of what the affair meant currently, Alex brought the wheel of a hamster cage, remarking, "We just go round and round and round and get nowhere." Sondra brought a bottle of bitters, and said, "This is what I've turned into!" After a long conversation engendered by their symbols, Sondra said quietly, "This is the first time in seven years that we've talked about this without yelling and screaming." When the therapist asked if they were ready to let go of the past, both agreed that they were. They decided to revisit a favorite spot from early in their relationship and to bury these symbols there. During the ceremony, Alex cried and for the first time asked Sondra to forgive him, which she readily did. They followed this with a celebration of their anniversary, which they had stopped celebrating seven years earlier.

This healing ritual was created as part of couple's therapy, but you don't need the help of a therapist to create rituals to effect healing. Common to all healing rituals is a dimension of time—time for holding on and time for letting go. Selecting symbols to express painful issues generally allows for a new kind of conversa-

tion to emerge. Taking some joint action together, such as symbolically burying the past, can impart a new possibility of collaboration. Creating a ritual together can help you to rediscover the playful parts of your relationship, such as the couple who "put an affair on ice," placing symbols in their deep freezer and agreeing that they could only fight about the affair after they had thawed these symbols out!

A Ceremony for Grieving

There is no life that is lived without loss. We all experience the death of people we love and care for deeply. When healing rituals have not occurred, or have been insufficient to complete the grief process, a person can remain stuck in the past or unable to move forward in meaningful ways. Even the unhealed losses of previous generations may emerge as debilitating symptoms in the present. When this happens, new rituals can be created to address the need for healing.

Joanie and Jeralynn Thompson were identical twins who had a close and loving

Rituals shape our relationships and give us a basis for a healthy society. Simply having a family meal together helps establish a stronger sense of self.
(UN photo/John Isaac)

relationship. They went away to the same college and planned to graduate together. During their junior year, however, Jeralynn developed leukemia. She died within the year. Before her death, Jeralynn talked with Joanie about how important it was that Joanie continue college and graduate. Joanie did go back to school after her sister's funeral, but she found it impossible to study. At the urging of friends, she took a year off in order to be with her family and begin to deal with the terrible loss of her sister. But a year turned into two years, two years into three. Finally, her family insisted that she go back to college. Joanie returned to school and finished all of her courses, but remained unable to do her senior thesis. She didn't graduate that June. "I don't know how I can graduate without Jeralynn," she told her mother. "It'll mean that she's really gone." Once her mother began to understand what was stopping Joanie from finishing, she talked with her daughter about how they might honor Jeralynn's life while still celebrating Joanie's entering adulthood with her college graduation. After developing a plan with her mother, Joanie finished her thesis in time to graduate the following December.

Joanie and her mother planned a special ceremony to be held two nights before graduation. They invited extended family and close friends, asking them to bring symbols of Jeralynn and to speak about her openly. During a very moving ceremony, many people spoke about what they thought Jeralynn would have wished for Joanie. One aunt made a video that showed places the two sisters had both loved, and after showing it told Joanie, "These places still belong to you." Joanie's father brought photographs of several pets the twins had raised, carefully pointing out the individual contributions each twin had made to these animals. Then, in a five-minute talk, he highlighted the strengths and gifts of each young woman and gave Joanie permission to be her own person. People grieved the loss of Jeralynn openly and then embraced Joanie for finishing school and going on in life.

Several months later, settled in a new job as a teacher, Joanie talked about this ceremony and her graduation: "They all helped me to graduate. If we hadn't had our memorial first, I know all I would have been wondering about on graduation day was what my family was feeling about Jeralynn's death. Instead, all of it was out in the open. We could be sad together and then we could be happy together on my graduation day. They call graduation a

Rituals connect us with our past, define our present life, and show us a path to our future.

commencement, an ending that's really a beginning, and that's what mine was. I miss my sister terribly—I'll always miss her—but my family and friends helped me take the next step in my life, and Jeralynn's spirit was right there with me."

Celebrating Recovery from Illness
Sometimes very important changes take place but remain unacknowledged. This may be because the changes are difficult to talk about, because they bring up the pain of how things used to be, or because no one had thought about how to mark the change. In our experience, recovery from medical or psychiatric illness is an aspect of change that is seldom marked by a ritual. Families, relationships, and the individual's own identity remain stuck with the illness label, and behavior among family members and friends remains as it was when the person was ill.

Adolescents who have recovered from cancer or adults who are now healthy after heart surgery often maintain an "illness identity," and others treat them accordingly. A ritual can declare in action that a person has moved from illness to health. Such a ritual might include a ceremony of throwing away no-longer-needed medicines or medical equipment, burning or burying symbols of a long hospital stay, or writing a document declaring new life and health.

After recovering from breast cancer,

Gerry Sims had a T-shirt made that read HEALTHY WOMAN! She wore this T-shirt to a family dinner and announced to everyone that they were to stop treating her as a patient, and that, in particular, she wanted people to argue with her as they had before she became ill. Then she handed out T-shirts to her husband and children that read HUSBAND OF A HEALTHY WOMAN, CHILD OF A HEALTHY WOMAN, and TEEN-AGER OF A HEALTHY WOMAN. Everyone put on his or her T-shirt and for the first time spontaneously began to talk about what they had been through together during Gerry's year-long illness. They cried out loud to each other. Following this, Gerry's teen-age daughter picked a fight with her, just as Gerry had hoped!

A Rite of Passage
Like many life-cycle passages, a child leaving home is an event that carries deeply mixed feelings, including a sense of joy and accomplishment, fear regarding what lies ahead, sadness over the loss of relationships in their present form, and curious anticipation about what life will look like next. This life-cycle passage of leaving home may be even more difficult when the leaving is unanticipated or when the child has grown up with a handicap. Creating a leaving-home ritual whose symbols and symbolic actions speak to the many contradictory issues can ease this passage for everyone in the family.

Jennifer Cooper-Smith was born with some severe disabilities that affected her capacity to read, write, and speak. During her childhood she took the handicap in stride despite the cruel teasing of other children and despite coming from a family where high academic achievement was the norm. Through it all she taught her family a lot about perseverance in the face of enormous struggles and about building on strengths rather than focusing on weaknesses.

When Jennifer reached nineteen, since her disabilities would preclude her going to college, it was clear that high school graduation was to be her rite of passage. The family wanted to create a ritual that would both honor all that she had accomplished and send her forth into the adult world with confidence.

Jennifer wanted a party at a Chinese restaurant with her favorite festive food. Her mother and stepfather invited people who were important to Jennifer—extended family who lived far away, friends who had supported her, special teachers and co-workers from her part-time job. The invitation included a secret request for special items—poems, letters, photos, stories, drawings, and so on—to help make a "becoming an adult woman" album for Jenni. During the weeks before the party, her mom worked secretly to construct the album, which began at the time Jennifer joined the family as an adopted infant and included sections that marked significant stages of her development. Although the handicaps had sometimes made it difficult for both Jennifer and those around her to notice her growth and changes, this album recorded them for all to see.

When Jennifer arrived at the party, the album was waiting for her as a special symbol of her development. What she still didn't know, though, was that the album was open-ended, and a new section, "Becoming an Adult Woman," was about to be added during the party. After dinner, when people were invited to give their presentations to Jennifer, a moving and unexpected ceremony unfolded. Person after person spoke about how they experienced Jenni and what she meant to them,

and they gave her their own special brand of advice about living.

Her grandma Dena gave Jenni a photograph of Dena's late husband—Jenni's grandfather—down on his knees proposing marriage. She spoke about enduring love and her wish that Jenni would have this in her life. Her aunt Meryle Sue read an original poem, "Portrait of Jenni," and then spoke through tears about what this day would have meant to Jenni's grandfather and how proud he would have been of her. Her cousin Stacey wrote a poem that captured who Jenni was to her and offered words about Jenni's future. Advice about men and what to beware of was given by Jenni's step-grandfather and received with much laughter. Photographs of strong women in history were presented.

Person after person spoke with grace and love and special stories about Jennifer's strengths. Her mother watched as Jennifer took in all that she was to people and the sometimes unknown impact that her own courage had had on family and friends. And then all who gathered wit-

nessed the emergence of Jennifer, the adult woman, as she rose from her seat and spoke unhaltingly and with no trace of her usual shyness, thanking each person in turn for what they had given her in life, and talking about the loss of her grandfather and her wish that he could be with her today. She ended with all that she anticipated next in her life.

The weeks and months following this ritual were perhaps even more remarkable than the ceremony itself. Her family experienced a changed Jennifer, a Jennifer who moved from adolescence to young womanhood—starting a full-time job, auditing a community college course, traveling by herself, making new friends, and relating on a previously unseen level.

As all of these examples illustrate, rituals ease our passage through life. They shape our relationships, help to heal our losses, express our deepest beliefs, and celebrate our existence. They announce change and create change. The power of rituals belongs to all of us.

Index

Credits/Acknowledgments

Cover design by Charles Vitelli

1. Varied Perspectives on the Family
Facing overview—Courtesy of Pamela Carley.

2. Exploring and Establishing Relationships
Facing overview—Courtesy of Cheryl Greenleaf. 78—Photo by Kathy Sloane.

3. Finding a Balance
Facing overview—United Nations photo by L. Barns. 128—Photos by Darryl Heikes/USNWR.

4. Crises—Challenges and Opportunities
Facing overview—Dushkin/McGraw·Hill Companies. 196, 197—Illustrations by Kim Barnes.

5. Families, Now and Into the Future
Facing overview—Courtesy of Louis Raucci Jr.

ANNUAL EDITIONS ARTICLE REVIEW FORM

■ NAME: _____ DATE: _____

■ TITLE AND NUMBER OF ARTICLE: _____

■ BRIEFLY STATE THE MAIN IDEA OF THIS ARTICLE: _____

_____

■ LIST THREE IMPORTANT FACTS THAT THE AUTHOR USES TO SUPPORT THE MAIN IDEA:

_____

_____

_____

_____

■ WHAT INFORMATION OR IDEAS DISCUSSED IN THIS ARTICLE ARE ALSO DISCUSSED IN YOUR TEXTBOOK OR OTHER READINGS THAT YOU HAVE DONE? LIST THE TEXTBOOK CHAPTERS AND PAGE NUMBERS:

_____

_____

_____

_____

■ LIST ANY EXAMPLES OF BIAS OR FAULTY REASONING THAT YOU FOUND IN THE ARTICLE:

_____

_____

_____

_____

■ LIST ANY NEW TERMS/CONCEPTS THAT WERE DISCUSSED IN THE ARTICLE, AND WRITE A SHORT DEFINITION:

_____

_____

_____

_____

*Your instructor may require you to use this ANNUAL EDITIONS Article Review Form in any number of ways: for articles that are assigned, for extra credit, as a tool to assist in developing assigned papers, or simply for your own reference. Even if it is not required, we encourage you to photocopy and use this page; you will find that reflecting on the articles will greatly enhance the information from your text.

We Want Your Advice

ANNUAL EDITIONS revisions depend on two major opinion sources: one is our Advisory Board, listed in the front of this volume, which works with us in scanning the thousands of articles published in the public press each year; the other is you—the person actually using the book. Please help us and the users of the next edition by completing the prepaid article rating form on this page and returning it to us. Thank you for your help!

ANNUAL EDITIONS: MARRIAGE AND FAMILY 97/98
Article Rating Form

Here is an opportunity for you to have direct input into the next revision of this volume. We would like you to rate each of the 51 articles listed below, using the following scale:

1. **Excellent: should definitely be retained**
2. **Above average: should probably be retained**
3. **Below average: should probably be deleted**
4. **Poor: should definitely be deleted**

Your ratings will play a vital part in the next revision. So please mail this prepaid form to us just as soon as you complete it.
Thanks for your help!

Rating	Article	Rating	Article
	1. The New Crusade for the Old Family		27. A Nation (Still) at Risk?
	2. The Family: Home Sweet Home		28. The Myth of AWOL Parents
	3. The Way We Weren't: The Myth and Reality of the "Traditional" Family		29. Family Affair
	4. The Family under Siege by Its "Friends"		30. Effective Fathers: Why Are Some Dads More Successful than Others?
	5. African American Families: A Legacy of Vulnerability and Resilience		31. Fathers Strongly Influenced by Culture
	6. Love: The Immutable Longing for Contact		32. Siblings and Development
	7. What Makes Love Last?		33. The Secret World of Siblings
	8. Why Don't We Act Like the Opposite Sex?		34. After He Hits Her
	9. Studies Put Genetic Twist on Theories about Sex and Love		35. Behind Closed Doors
	10. Choosing Mates—the American Way		36. Helping Children Cope with Violence
	11. The Mating Game		37. Resilience in Development
	12. Back Off!		38. Beyond Betrayal: Life after Infidelity
	13. Choosing a Contraceptive		39. Sex in America: Faithfulness in Marriage Is Overwhelming
	14. Men, Sex, and Parenthood in an Overpopulating World		40. The Myth of the Miserable Working Woman
	15. Staying Power: Bridging the Gender Gap in the Confusing '90s		41. Look Who's Talking about Work and Family
	16. Albanian 'Virgins' Wear the Pants in Their Families		42. Should This Marriage Be Saved?
	17. What a Baby *Really* Costs		43. The Politics of Divorce
	18. Adolescent Childbearing: Whose Problem? What Can We Do?		44. Lessons from Stepfamilies
	19. The Lifelong Impact of Adoption		45. The Myths and Misconceptions of the Stepmother Identity
	20. What's Happening to American Marriage?		46. Caregiving: Continuities and Discontinuities in Family Members' Relationships with Alzheimer's Patients
	21. Peer Marriage		47. Hard Lessons
	22. Who Needs Love! In Japan, Many Couples Don't		48. Trace Your Family Tree
	23. For Better or Worse?		49. Happy Families: Who Says They All Have to Be Alike?
	24. Receipts from a Marriage		50. Rewriting Life Stories
	25. Saving Relationships: The Power of the Unpredictable		51. Rituals for Our Times
	26. Vanishing Dreams of America's Young Families		

(Continued on next page)

ABOUT YOU

Name _____ Date _____

Are you a teacher? ❑ Or a student? ❑

Your school name _____

Department _____

Address _____

City _____ State _____ Zip _____

School telephone # _____

YOUR COMMENTS ARE IMPORTANT TO US !

Please fill in the following information:

For which course did you use this book? _____

Did you use a text with this *ANNUAL EDITION*? ❑ yes ❑ no

What was the title of the text? _____

What are your general reactions to the *Annual Editions* concept?

Have you read any particular articles recently that you think should be included in the next edition?

Are there any articles you feel should be replaced in the next edition? Why?

Are there other areas of study that you feel would utilize an *ANNUAL EDITION?*

May we contact you for editorial input?

May we quote your comments?